The Grand Strategy of Philip II

The Grand Strategy of Philip II

Geoffrey Parker

Yale University Press
New Haven and London

Set in Garamond by Best-set Typesetter Ltd, Hong Kong
Printed in Great Britain by Redwood Books, Wiltshire

Library of Congress Cataloging-in-Publication Data

Parker, Geoffrey, 1943–
The Grand Strategy of Philip II/Geoffrey Parker.
Includes bibliographical references and index.
ISBN 0–300–07540–5
1. Spain – History – Philip II, 1556–1598.   2. Philip II, King of
Spain, 1527–1598.   3. Spain – Strategic aspects.   I. Title.
DP179.P39   1998
964'.043'092 – dc21
98–07352   CIP

A catalogue record for this book is available from the British Library.

2 4 6 8 10 9 7 5 3 1

For Susie, Ed, Richard and Jamie Parker

Contents

Illustrations

Plates

Tables

Figures

Acknowledgements

Thirty years ago Helli Koenigsberger alerted me to the need to determine whether or not Philip II possessed a Grand Strategy, suggesting the sort of questions that one should ask and some of the evidence that one might find. I did not begin to give serious thought to the issue until 1987, however, in response to two invitations. First Williamson Murray asked me to contribute a chapter to a volume he proposed to edit on 'The making of strategy': my assignment would be Habsburg Spain. Later that year, following the publication of Paul Kennedy's *Rise and fall of the great powers*, Don Higginbotham asked me to critique Chapter 2, entitled 'The Habsburg bid for mastery', as part of his symposium on that important volume. I cannot believe that my name would have occurred to either Murray or Higginbotham without a recommendation from John Lynn, my colleague at the University of Illinois at Urbana-Champaign (where I had just begun to teach). My first debt of gratitude, therefore, is to all these historians who encouraged me to examine whether Philip II did indeed have a Grand Strategy, and helped me to find ways of rediscovering it.

Preliminary versions of four chapters in this book have appeared elsewhere: Chapter 4 in E. Ladewig Petersen, K. J. V. Jespersen and H. Stevensborg, eds, *Clashes of culture. Essays in honor of Niels Steensgaard* (Odense, 1992); Chapter 7 in K. Nielson and B. J. C. McKercher, eds, *Go spy the land* (New York, 1992); Chapter 8 in H. Soly and R. Vermeir, eds, *Beleid en bestuur in de oude Nederlanden. Liber Amicorum Prof. Dr Michel Baelde* (Ghent, 1993); and Chapter 9 in *The Mariner's Mirror*, LXXXII (1996). My thanks go to the editors and publishers who allowed me to reproduce here some of the work they commissioned.

I would also like to thank those who have shared their special insights with me. Apart from the assistance acknowledged in each chapter, I must single out the contributions of four scholars who made me aware of important aspects of the subject which I might otherwise have ignored. Clara García-Ayluardo and Nancy van Deusen did their best to keep Philip's American possessions in the picture; Mario Rizzo enlightened me about Spanish Italy; and Fernando Bouza shared with me his unrivalled knowledge of the intricacies and intimacies of Philip's life and reign.

This book was conceived, researched and written after multiple sclerosis transformed my life in 1987. While I hope that my health problems have not affected the quality of the end-product, they certainly complicated the process of preparation. That I managed to finish is due in large part to the kindness and sensitivity of a host of librarians and archivists who did everything they could to facilitate access to their collections; to the generous research support from the three United States universities at which I have taught over the last decade; and to the energy of the research assistants (financed by those same universities) who helped me to prepare the data – Jeffrey McKeage, Mary Sprunger and Edward Tenace at Illinois; Paul Allen, Paul Dover, Martha Hoffman-Strock and Michael Levin at Yale; and Charles Sharpe at Ohio State. I thank them all, and also Bethany Aram, Cristina Borreguero Beltrán, Richard Kagan and Catherine Lawrence, who secured various materials for me at short notice, and Paul Hibbeln for help with compiling the index.

Finally I am most grateful to those who critiqued my typescript and gave me valuable comments and suggestions: Paul Allen, Tom Arnold, Mark Choate, Eliot Cohen, Jo Guilmartin, Michael Levin, Phil Tetlock and Nancy van Deusen read the first part; Robert Baldock, Jeremy Black, Fernando Bouza, Robert Cowley, Derek Croxton, Antonio Feros, Fernando González de León, Helli Koenigsberger, Ned Lebow, Peter Pierson, María José Rodríguez-Salgado and Matthew Waxman read it all. I have recorded additional scholarly debts in the notes to each chapter.

This book is dedicated to my four children – Susie, Ed, Richard and Jamie – in gratitude for the love and happiness that they have brought into my life.

Note on Conventions

Where an established English version of a foreign place-name exists (Corunna, The Hague, Brussels, Venice, Vienna) I have used it, otherwise I have preferred the style used in the place itself today. Likewise, with personal names, I have adopted standard English versions (William of Orange, Don John of Austria and, of course, Philip II), but otherwise used the style and title used by the person concerned.

To avoid confusion and facilitate comparisons, all sums of money mentioned in this book have been given in Spanish ducats, each one roughly equivalent in the later sixteenth century to one escudo (or crown) and to two florins. About four ducats made up one pound sterling.

On 24 February 1581 Pope Gregory XIII ordered that the calendar should be advanced by ten days. Different countries adopted the 'new style' at different times, however: Spain on 4/15 October 1582, most (but not all) of the provinces of the Netherlands in rebellion against Philip II on 14/25 December 1582, the 'loyal' provinces on 11/22 February 1583, and so on. All dates in this book are given in New Style from October 1582 unless otherwise stated, and throughout I have assumed that each calendar year began on 1 January (and not on 25 March, as in the Julian-Old Style-Calendar).

Preface

Philip II began to exercise power in 1543, at the age of sixteen, when his father Charles V appointed him regent of Spain. In 1554 he became king of Naples and of England and the following year Charles made him ruler of the Netherlands. In 1556 he succeeded to his father's dominions in America and most of Europe, and in 1580 he acquired Portugal and its overseas possessions. From then until his death in 1598 Philip ruled the first global empire in history – yet no one has so far attempted to study precisely how he did so: what strategic priorities underlay his policies, what practices and prejudices influenced his decision-making, what external factors affected the achievement of his goals.

Good reasons explain this neglect. Above all, hundreds of thousands of papers written by or to the king have survived, creating a daunting mountain of data. Just as Philip proved unable to absorb in full all the relevant information concerning the multiple states of his Monarchy and the problems that faced them, so no individual historian could possibly find the time to read and review all the relevant material available for all areas over the entire reign. Nor would one necessarily be much the wiser for doing so, first because so many important papers have been lost, and second because so many important matters concerning the formation of policy can never be known. In the words of President John F. Kennedy, 'The essence of ultimate decision remains impenetrable to the observer – often indeed to the decider himself . . . There will always be dark and tangled stretches in the decision-making process – mysterious even to those who may be most intimately involved.'[1]

This book therefore approaches Philip II's Grand Strategy via a series of soundings. Part I proceeds horizontally (as it were), examining the general context of Spain's strategic culture: the king's distinctive system of government; the 'information overload' that threatened to engulf it; and the various strategic priorities and assumptions deployed to overcome the disparity between aims and means. Here the data come from all periods and from all major theatres of operations. It is impossible, however, to examine either the actual formation or the execution of Philip's Grand Strategy on the same scale – not just because of the loss of documents and the 'mysterious' nature of the decision-making process, but also because a proper consideration of the king's policies requires an examination of the strategies and aims of his allies and his enemies as well. As historians of the Cold War have clearly shown, a 'symmetrical' study based on the records of *all* the participants, one that can measure the perceptions (and misperceptions) of each state about the others against 'reality', is the only viable methodology for international relations.[2] The rest of the soundings in this book therefore proceed 'vertically', dealing in detail only with those areas in which a symmetrical approach can be applied. Part II examines the surviving documentation – from the Habsburgs, their allies and their adversaries – for the formation of strategy in just three case-studies: Philip's unsuccessful efforts to maintain his authority in the Netherlands between 1555 and 1577 (Chapter 4); his defective peacetime management of foreign relations with Scotland and England between 1558 and 1585 (Chapter 5); and the mobilization of diplomatic, economic, military and naval resources for his abortive attempt to conquer England between 1585 and 1588 (Chapter 6). Part III examines three aspects of the execution of Grand Strategy (with special reference to those chosen areas) in which it appears that fatal flaws doomed the king's policies to defeat: his inability to prevent foreign intelligence services from penetrating his designs (Chapter 7); his failure to coordinate logistics and communications at the operational level (Chapter 8); and, finally, his imperfect appreciation of changing technology and tactics in war (Chapter 9). Chapter 10 considers the lessons drawn by the king and his ministers from the Armada's failure, and the Conclusion discusses whether the outcome might have been different with other policy options, another ruler, or a different strategic culture.

The choice of these particular case-studies reflects both the pattern of documentary survival and the linguistic limitations of the author. To begin with, the loss of a ship carrying Philip's personal papers from the Netherlands to Spain in 1559 makes it virtually impossible to recreate his Grand Strategy before that date. By contrast the king's decision to make Mateo Vázquez his private secretary in 1573 introduced an administrator whose tidy habits – especially his custom of dating virtually every piece of paper that came across his desk – make it possible to recreate on a daily and sometimes hourly basis the evolution of royal policy. Tens of thousands of royal 'billetes' (memoranda) survive in reasonable order until Vázquez's death in 1591. Equally important, Philip came to confide his innermost hopes, fears and frustrations to Vázquez (who was also his chaplain), and so their correspondence often reveals the king's aims and motives as well as the process by which he reached his decisions. The need for 'symmetry' in considering Habsburg policy means, however, that I have been able to use only certain parts of this rich harvest: above all, Philip's Mediterranean strategy remains largely outside the compass of this volume because the records of his adversaries – the Ottoman sultan and his North African vassals – are written in languages that few today can read. Another account of Spain's Mediterranean strategy based exclusively on western sources makes no sense; a proper study of the subject must await a scholar with the appropriate repertory of linguistic and palaeographic skills.[3] In contrast, however, the public and private archives of two of Philip's other principal adversaries, England and the Dutch Republic, are as plentiful as those of any sixteenth-century state (and, in the case of England, far better catalogued). They not only reveal the serious misperceptions entertained by Philip and his advisers about their enemies, but also show that strategic decision-making in both countries suffered from many of the same problems. Furthermore, Philip's Grand Strategy met its nemesis at the hands of these two states. In the Mediterranean, as in the Americas, the king achieved most of his policy goals; in the Netherlands and against England he did not, thus beginning the decline of Spain as a great power. It is important to understand the reasons for that failure.

Methodologically, this volume combines three types of evidence. First the king's holograph policy statements, which survive in abundance for the 1570s and 1580s, have been cited extensively. They are complemented by the records of the various government institutions and, where they survive, of the leading ministers (for the private archives assembled by the dukes of Alba and Medina Sidonia or by Cardinal Granvelle, among others, contain many papers that would today be kept in a state repository). Second, the dispatches of the dozen or so resident ambassadors at the court of Spain have been examined. Although excessive reliance on the views of foreign diplomats has sometimes led historians into error, when rigorously compared with the actions and internal records of policy debates by the government under scrutiny, ambassadorial reports (as Leopold von Ranke demonstrated over a century ago) constitute a source of fundamental importance for the study of political history during the early modern era.[4] Finally, considerable use has been made of comparative material from other centuries. In order to evaluate the performance of Philip as the chief executive officer of a complex 'multinational' enterprise, parallels from three areas have been included. First, modern strategic studies have been exploited, on the assumption that many of the challenges facing global empires in the twentieth century probably resembled those that faced their sixteenth-century precursors. Thus Philip's decision in 1574 not to end the Dutch revolt by opening the sea-dikes and flooding the rebellious provinces is contrasted with the strikingly similar reluctance of President Lyndon Johnson almost four hundred years later not to destroy the Red River dike system of Vietnam in order to flood areas inhabited by opponents of US policy (p. 137 below). Next, current business management theory has been examined on the similar grounds that the CEOs of 'global enterprises' across the centuries also probably handled many similar problems and did so in similar ways. The work of analysts like Peter F. Drucker on what makes an 'effective executive' has been cited in order to show that some (although not all) of Philip's management techniques meet modern criteria. Some things, indeed, never change: 'People are time-consumers and most people are time-wasters' is one of Drucker's epigrams that Philip would have heartily endorsed – hence his much-criticized insistence on avoiding meetings (see p. 21 below). Finally, the conduct of other absolute rulers in other centuries has been used in order to assess the nature of Philip's problems and responses. All too often the king (like other leaders) has been judged by those with no experience of wielding power. It may be true that some of the king's administrative habits – such as creating separate, often competing, organs to deal with similar problems, or insisting that his information come from many separate sources – confused his officials and placed an excessive burden on his own shoulders; but since other statesmen, including Franklin Roosevelt and Winston Churchill, did precisely the same (pp. 31–2 below) historians should not be too quick to condemn.

These comparisons also help to avoid the common temptation to dismiss failures as inevitable and to assume that, if only the participants had been a little more 'rational', they would have tailored their plans more closely to their resources. The much-maligned George III, ruler of another empire on which the sun never set, addressed this fallacy eloquently in a letter to his chief minister, Lord North, during the American Revolutionary War:

> No inclination to get out of the present difficulties . . . can incline me to enter into what I look upon as the distruction of the empire. I have heard Lord North frequently drop that the advantages to be gained by this contest could never repay the expence. I owne that, let any war be ever so successful, if persons will set down and weigh the expences they will find . . . that it has impoverished the state, enriched individuals, and perhaps raised the name only of the conquerors. But this is only weighing such events in the scale of a tradesman behind his counter. It is necessary for those in the station it has pleased Divine Providence to place me to weigh whether expences, though very great, are not sometimes necessary to prevent what might be more ruinous to a country than the loss of money.

To understand what seemed rational to early modern statesmen and strategists, their mental universe and assumptions must enter the equation.[5]

This book seeks to engage three groups of readers. First, and most obviously, those who share the author's fascination with Philip should find something of interest here. It is now thirty-two years since I first struggled to read the king's tortuous script; yet it survives in such copious quantities that much of what he wrote has inevitably remained unread. However, I believe that enough material composed by the king and his intimate advisers has been consulted to provide a coherent picture of how they viewed the changing international situation and how they strove to turn events to their advantage. Second, the strategic analysts from whom I have learned so much may be surprised to find that the same issues and problems that they study in the modern world also confronted statesmen and officials four hundred years ago. They too may therefore find something of value in this volume. Finally, many of those with an interest in the rise and fall of great powers will be challenged by the 'non-linear' conclusions of this study, for in each of the case-studies examined small factors apparently produced relatively rapid and wholly disproportionate consequences.

The non-linear theory of historical causation has long been unfashionable. Fernand Braudel, for example, the most eminent European historian of this century, dismissed 'events' as merely 'surface disturbances, crests of foam that the tides of history carry on their strong backs'; he sought the explanation for major phenomena in the complex structures of the Past. Writing in May 1946, he issued an explicit warning that

> The historian who takes a seat in Philip II's chair and reads his papers finds himself transported into a strange one-dimensional world, a world of strong passions certainly, blind like any other living world, our own included, and unconscious of the deeper realities of history, of the running waters on which our frail barks are tossed like cockleshells. A dangerous world, but one whose spells and enchantments we shall have exorcised by making sure first to chart those underlying currents, often noiseless, whose direction can only be discerned by watching them over long periods of time. Resounding events are often only momentary outbursts, surface manifestations of these larger movements and explicable only in terms of them.[6]

'Often', however, is not the same as 'always'. I do not believe that history is always a linear process in which the explanation for every major event must be sought in developments that stretch back decades if not centuries; on the contrary, relatively minor developments have sometimes produced a disproportionate, even decisive impact without being merely 'surface manifestations' of larger movements. It seems to me that the non-linear processes found in Nature also operate in History, since a small event – sometimes called 'the tipping point' – can sometimes start a new trend; and nowhere do tiny and seemingly trivial forces produce unexpected major changes more frequently than in war. This is pre-eminently true of combat; but it also affects strategy, which involves the deployment of such huge quantities of men, money, munitions and ancillary services – logistics, communications, intelligence – that outcomes and results can seldom be predicted on any rational basis.[7]

Many of Philip II's contemporaries agreed. To the Amsterdam magistrate Cornelis Pieterszoon Hooft, writing in 1617, the defeat of Spain seemed, even in retrospect, very remarkable: 'Our origins were very small and modest,' he wrote. 'In comparison with the king of Spain we were like a mouse against an elephant.'[8] In the 1570s and 1580s, the focus of this volume, time after time Philip mobilized sufficient resources – not only military and naval but also diplomatic, economic and moral – to secure victory, only to be thwarted by something that he had failed to foresee, and for which his plans left no place. This is not to claim, of course, that structural considerations played no role in the outcome: the fact that Philip's decision-making style left no place for contingencies or fall-back strategies proved a crucial defect; so did the circumstance that the Monarchy he had to defend lacked geographical cohesion, so that several exposed parts repeatedly came under threat from one enemy or another. In the end it is a question of balance: as always, both agent and structure must be given their due; but to this author it seems, first, that relatively small factors played a disproportionate part in frustrating a Grand Strategy that, on the face of it, stood an excellent chance of success; and, second, that the character of Philip II himself offers the best explanation of how History's mice (to use Hooft's metaphor) could take on an elephant and win, thereby transforming the entire course of western history.

Chronology

	Spain, Portugal, Italy and the Mediterranean	France, Germany and the Netherlands	England, Scotland and Overseas
1548		Augsburg Transaction	
1549–50		Philip in the Netherlands	
1550–51	War with Turks in the Mediterranean begins (to 1578)	Philip in Germany; Habsburg family compact at Augsburg	
1554	Philip II leaves Spain (until 1559); war of Siena (to 1555); Charles V abdicates as king of Naples in favour of Philip		Philip marries Mary Tudor and resides in England (to 1555)
1555	Paul IV elected pope (to 1559)	Charles V abdicates in Brussels, which becomes Philip's capital (to 1559)	
1556	Charles abdicates as king of Spain in favour of Philip; Paul IV declares war on Philip and Charles (to 1557)	Truce (February) and war (July) with France	
1557	First 'decree of bankruptcy'; French invade Italy	Battle of St Quentin	Philip returns briefly to England, which declares war on France and Scotland (to 1559)
1558		Battle of Gravelines; Francis, dauphin of France, marries Mary queen of Scots; Charles abdicates as Holy Roman Emperor, his brother Ferdinand succeeds (to 1564)	Death of Mary Tudor, succeeded by Elizabeth (to 1603); Scottish Protestants begin rebellion against regency government led by Mary of Guise; Mary queen of Scots marries Francis of France
1559	Peace with France; Philip returns to Spain; 'General Visitation' for the Spanish states in Italy; Pius IV elected pope (to 1565)	Peace of Cateau-Cambrésis; Philip marries Elisabeth de Valois (to 1568); death of Henry II of France; Francis II succeeds; Philip leaves Netherlands for Spain	Peace of Cateau-Cambrésis; French reinforcements drive back Scottish Protestants until English fleet cuts them off; Philip returns to Spain; Francis II and Mary Stuart become joint rulers of Scotland and France (to 1560), with claims to England and Ireland

	Spain, Portugal, Italy and the Mediterranean	France, Germany and the Netherlands	England, Scotland and Overseas
1560	Second 'decree of bankruptcy'; Djerba expedition	Death of Francis of France, Charles IX succeeds (Catherine de Medici regent)	English army enters Scotland, secures withdrawal of French (treaty of Leith) and toleration for Protestantism
1561	Philip moves Court to Madrid		Mary Stuart returns to Scotland
1562	Council of Trent reconvenes for final session (to 1563)	First French civil war (to 1563)	
1563	Turks besiege Oran; Philip in Aragon (to 1564)	Spanish expeditionary force helps French crown against Huguenots; English trade war with Netherlands (to 1565)	Trade war between England and the Netherlands (to 1565)
1564	Peñón de Vélez expedition; last French garrisons leave Italy; Corsican revolt against Genoa (to 1569)	Granvelle leaves Netherlands; Maximilian II elected Holy Roman Emperor (to 1576)	French colonists settle in Florida
1565	Turks besiege Malta		Spanish forces attack French settlers in Florida; Miguel López de Legazpi claims Philippines for Spain
1566	Pius V elected pope (to 1572); Sultan Suleiman campaigns in Hungary but dies there; Selim II succeeds (to 1578)	Iconoclastic Fury and rebellion in the Netherlands; Philip resolves to send the duke of Alba with an army to restore order	French in Florida imprisoned or executed
1567		Second French civil war (to 1568); Alba and his army arrive in Brussels; 'Council of Troubles' created	Mary Stuart deposed and imprisoned
1568	Don Carlos arrested and dies; revolt of Moriscos begins (to 1571); death of Elisabeth de Valois	Third French civil war (to 1570); William of Orange and his brothers unsuccessfully invade Netherlands	Mary Stuart escapes and flees to England; 'Junta Magna' in Spain establishes new policies for American colonies; John Hawkins and Francis Drake defeated at San Juan de Ulúa; Philip orders the recall of English ambassador John Man; Elizabeth seizes treasure ships sailing from Spain to Flanders

1569	*Nueva Recopilación* published	Orange and his brothers fight with Huguenots in France; Spanish troops help French crown against Huguenots; trade war between Philip and England (to 1573); Alba imposes new taxes on the Netherlands	New trade war between England and Philip's possessions (to 1573); 'Northern rebellion' against Elizabeth
1570	Turks invade Venetian Cyprus; Turkish vassal takes Tunis	Charles IX begins collaboration with Huguenots (to 1572); Philip marries Anna of Austria (to 1580); Alba reforms the Netherlands legal system	Papal bull declares Elizabeth deposed and excommunicated
1571	Spain occupies Finale and signs the Holy League (with Venice and the pope); Turks complete conquest of Cyprus; battle of Lepanto	Alba decrees Alcabala for the Netherlands	'Ridolfi Plot' against Elizabeth; Legazpi captures Manila; attempt to impose Alcabala in Mexico
1572	Gregory XIII elected pope (to 1585)	William of Orange and his brothers invade Netherlands, but lasting success only in Holland and Zealand; massacre of Huguenots in Paris (St Bartholomew's Day) and other French cities; fourth French civil war (to 1573)	England and Scotland send initial assistance to Dutch rebels; Viceroy Don Pedro de Toledo begins campaign against the last Inca outposts in Peru
1573	Venice makes separate peace with Turks; Spain recaptures Tunis but surrenders Finale to imperial commissioners	Spaniards take Haarlem but fail against Alkmaar; Alba recalled, replaced by Don Luis de Requeséns (to 1576)	Drake raids Panama; partial restoration of trade between Philip and Elizabeth
1574	Turks take Tunis and La Goleta	Spaniards fail to take Leiden; Charles IX provides financial aid to Dutch but dies, succeeded by Henry III; fifth French civil war (to 1576)	Peace of Bristol between Elizabeth and Philip
1575	Third 'decree of bankruptcy'; *Relaciones topográficas* compiled in Castile	Abortive peace conference at Breda between Philip and the Dutch; Spanish treasury declares 'bankruptcy'	
1576		Spanish army in the Netherlands mutinies; most Netherlands provinces make peace with Holland and Zealand; independent States-General convened; Don John of Austria arrives to govern the Netherlands (to 1578); Rudolf II elected Holy Roman Emperor (to 1612)	

	Spain, Portugal, Italy and the Mediterranean	France, Germany and the Netherlands	England, Scotland and Overseas
1577		Don John first makes peace with States-General, then breaks it (hostilities continue until 1607); sixth French civil war	Drake's 'circumnavigation' begins (to 1581); *Relaciones topográficas* ordered for Spanish America
1578	One-year truce with the Turks (extended for a second year); death of Sultan Selim II; death of Sebastian of Portugal (Cardinal Henry succeeds)	Henry III's brother Anjou leads French aid to States-General; prince of Parma governs Netherlands for the king (to 1592)	
1579		Abortive peace conference at Cologne between Philip and the Dutch	Philip covertly sponsors Smerwick expedition
1580	One-year truce with the Turks; death of Henry I of Portugal; Philip claims succession, invades and moves to Portugal (to 1583); Dom Antonio (claimant to the Portuguese throne) seeks support in France and England	Seventh French civil war	Smerwick garrison surrenders and is executed
1581	Three-year truce with the Turks; Philip crowned king of Portugal	States-General depose Philip II and recognize Anjou as 'prince and lord of the Netherlands'; Anjou betrothed to Elizabeth of England; French troops occupy Cambrai (to 1595)	Portuguese overseas empire recognizes Philip's succession
1582	Azores campaign	French support for Dom Antonio in Azores	Edward Fenton's voyage to the Moluccas fails in Brazil
1583	Philip returns to Castile; Terceira campaign	Parma reconquers Flanders coast	Philip covertly supports plots hatched by Throckmorton and by French Catholics against Elizabeth
1584	One-year truce with the Turks (the last)	Anjou dies, leaving Henry of Navarre as heir presumptive to French crown; William of Orange assassinated; French Catholics led by Henry of Guise form a League and sign treaty of Joinville with Spain; Parma reconquers most of Flanders	Throckmorton plot discovered; Ambassador Mendoza expelled; English colony established at Roanoke (to 1585); Spanish attempt to measure longitude via simultaneous observation of a lunar eclipse in Europe, Mexico, Manila and Macao

1585	Revolt of Naples; Sixtus V elected pope (to 1590); duke of Savoy marries Infanta Catalina; Philip in Aragon (to 1586); Drake raids Galicia, the Canaries and Cape Verde Islands	Treaty of Nemours between Henry III and French Catholic League; Parma reconquers most of Brabant; Elizabeth of England signs treaty of Nonsuch with States-General	Drake attacks Philip's possessions in Spain, the Canaries, Cape Verde and (1586) the Caribbean; treaty of Nonsuch signed with the Dutch; earl of Leicester sent as governor-general of the Dutch Republic (to 1588). Hostilities with Spain last until 1603–4
1586	Preparations for Armada begin	Eighth French civil war (to 1598)	Hawkins blockades the Spanish coast; Babington plot against Elizabeth; Cavendish begins circumnavigation (to 1589)
1587	Drake's raid on Cadiz	German Protestant troops, raised by Huguenots, defeated by League and Spanish forces; Parma prepares to invade England	Drake attacks Cadiz and captures a Portuguese East Indiaman
1588	Spanish Armada; duke of Savoy annexes Saluzzo	Parma stands ready to invade England; Henry III flees Paris and the League takes control (to 1594); assassination of Henry of Guise	Bourbourg peace conference; the Spanish Armada
1589	English attack Corunna and Portugal	Henry III assassinated; Huguenot leader Henry of Navarre becomes Henry IV, but not recognized by Catholic League; Navarre defeats League at Arques; Parma suggests peace talks with the Dutch	English raid on Corunna and Portugal
1590	Urban VII (1590) and Gregory XIV elected pope (to 1591); *Millones* tax voted in Castile	Navarre defeats League at Ivry; Spanish expeditionary force lands in Brittany; Parma breaks Navarre's siege of Paris; duke of Savoy invades Provence	English fleet cruises off the Azores
1591	Innocent IX elected pope; revolt of Aragon; capture of the *Revenge* off the Azores	Dutch under Maurice of Nassau begin reconquest of North Netherlands; abortive peace conference at Cologne between Philip and the Dutch	English fleet cruises off the Azores, *Revenge* lost; English expeditionary force to Brittany (to 1595)
1592	Clement VIII elected pope (to 1605); Philip visits Old Castile and Aragon	English expeditionary force to Normandy; Parma breaks Navarre's siege of Rouen, but dies soon afterwards	English expeditionary force to Normandy (to 1593)
1593	Unrest in Portugal (Alemtejo, Beja)		

	Spain, Portugal, Italy and the Mediterranean	France, Germany and the Netherlands	England, Scotland and Overseas
1594		Henry IV gains Paris and Rouen	Outbreak of Tyrone's rebellion in Ireland (to 1603)
1595	France declares war (to 1598)	Henry IV declares war on Philip II (to 1598) and defeats Spanish expeditionary force from Milan	Drake and Hawkins lead major expedition to the Caribbean (to 1596); first Dutch fleet sails for East Indies
1596	Anglo-Dutch fleet captures and sacks Cadiz; Spain sends aid to Irish rebels; Spanish Armada sails against England but driven back; fourth 'decree of bankruptcy'	Archduke Albert becomes ruler of Spanish Netherlands (to 1621) and captures Calais from French; Spanish treasury issues 'decree of bankruptcy'	Anglo-Dutch expedition captures and sacks Cadiz; Spanish aid arrives for Irish rebels, who decide to continue their resistance (to 1603)
1597	Papacy annexes Ferrara; third Spanish Armada sails unsuccessfully to Brittany		English expedition to the Azores
1598	Peace of Vervins; death of Philip II	Edict of Nantes ends French civil war; treaty of Vervins ends war with Spain; Spaniards leave Brittany and Calais; Philip 'devolves' government of Netherlands jointly to Albert and his daughter Isabella (whom Albert marries), and dies soon afterwards; Philip III inherits the rest of his father's Monarchy	Tyrone defeats English in battle; English raid Puerto Rico; several Dutch fleets sail for East Indies
1601			Spanish expeditionary force lands at Kinsale (evacuated 1602)
1603			Irish rebellion ends; death of Elizabeth; James VI of Scotland succeeds and orders a cease-fire in war against Spain
1604			Peace of London
1607		Ceasefire in the Netherlands (Twelve Year Truce agreed 1609)	

Introduction: Did Philip II
Have a Grand Strategy?

Some scholars have flatly denied that Philip II, ruler of the first empire in history upon which the sun never set, possessed a Grand Strategy. According to Fernand Braudel in 1946, 'He was not a man of vision: he saw his task as an unending succession of small details . . . Never do we find general notions or grand strategies under his pen.' 'He never outlined a plan or programme for his reign,' wrote H. G. Koenigsberger in a penetrating study of 1971, 'nor did any of his ministers . . . [And] for this failure there can be only one reasonable explanation: they had no such plan or programme.' The assumption that the king lacked a 'blueprint for empire' underlies most writing about the general policy aims of Habsburg Spain. Paul M. Kennedy wholly accepted this premise in his chapter on 'The Habsburg bid for mastery' in *The rise and fall of the Great Powers* (1987): 'It may appear a little forced to use the title "The Habsburg bid for mastery",' he wrote, because 'despite the occasional rhetoric of some Habsburg ministers about a "world monarchy," there was no conscious plan to dominate Europe in the manner of Napoleon or Hitler.'[1]

Not every Grand Strategy is aggressive, however, nor does it merely involve war. Rather each encompasses the decisions of a given state about its overall security – the threats it perceives, the ways it confronts them, and the steps it takes to match ends and means – and each involves 'the integration of the state's overall political, economic and military aims, both in peace and war, to preserve long-term interests, including the management of ends and means, diplomacy and national morale and political culture in both the military and civilian spheres'. According to Basil Liddell Hart,

> Grand Strategy should both calculate and develop the economic resources and manpower of nations in order to sustain the fighting services. Also the moral resources – for to foster the people's willing spirit is often as important as to possess the most concrete forms of power . . . Moreover, fighting power is but one of the instruments of Grand Strategy – which should take account of and apply the power of financial pressure, of diplomatic pressure, of commercial pressure, and, not least, of ethical pressure, to weaken the opponent's will.

According to Edward Luttwak, Grand Strategies should be judged primarily according to 'the extent of their reliance on costly force as opposed to the leverage of potential force by diplomacy ("armed suasion"), by inducements (subsidies, gifts, honors), and by deception and propaganda', because the architectural dictum of Mies van de Rohe also applies here: 'Less is more' – the most effective Grand Strategies do as little as is necessary to defeat or deter challengers.[2]

Although Philip II worried periodically about cash-flow problems (see p. 199 below), he could clearly afford to use 'costly force' throughout his reign – indeed he sometimes fought on several fronts at once – thanks to the vast resources, both demographic and material, at his disposal (see Figure 1). The economy of Spain, the hub of the Monarchy, continued buoyant and productive (at least in comparison with the rest of Europe) at least until the 1580s, and other dominions (especially southern Italy and the Americas) contributed handsomely to the imperial budget. Nevertheless Philip also deployed diplomacy, inducements, deception, deterrence and (to a lesser degree) propaganda – as well as financial, commercial and ethical pressure – in pursuit of his strategic goals.[3]

The absence of a comprehensive masterplan among the papers of Philip and his ministers does not prove the absence of comprehensive ambitions: as Paul Kennedy shrewdly recognized, 'had the Habsburg rulers achieved all of their limited regional aims – even their *defensive* aims – the mastery of Europe would virtually have been theirs'.[4] The very size of Philip's possessions meant that he

Figure 1   Philip's Monarchy enjoyed peace for only six months: between February and September 1577, when hostilities ceased in both the Netherlands and the Mediterranean. Thereafter, although the king never went to war with the Turks again, conflict returned to the Netherlands (lasting until 1609) and began with England (1585–1603), involving attacks on Spain, the Atlantic Islands, the Americas and the High Seas. After 1589 Philip became increasingly involved in the French Religious Wars until the peace of Vervins in 1598. Meanwhile, overseas, the Portuguese outposts in Africa and South Asia engaged in various hostilities: first against their local enemies, above all in Ceylon, and then against the Dutch.

Philip II's wars

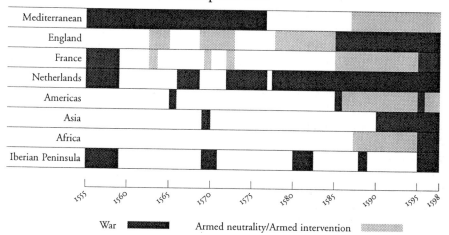

War ▬▬▬▬▬   Armed neutrality/Armed intervention ▦▦▦▦

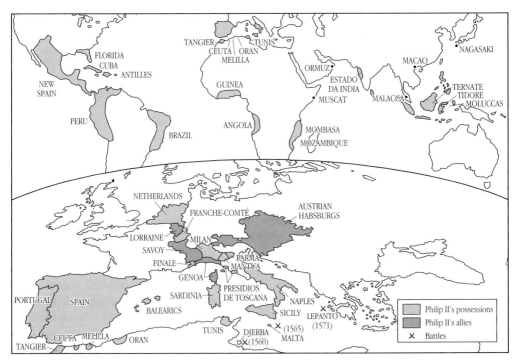

Plate 1   Philip II's empire. The annexation of Portugal and her overseas empire in 1580 made Philip II the ruler of the first empire in history on which the sun never set. Although its core – and its king – remained in Europe, issues concerning Africa, Asia and America regularly flowed across Philip's desk and required countless decisions.

could almost always plausibly argue that something or someone threatened the security of one area or another. Although he failed to succeed to Charles's Imperial title, by 1577 his Monarchy's 'banners and standards have crossed more than one third of the world, from Sicily to Cuzco and to the province of Quito, a distance which includes nine hours of difference . . . And if we measure its extent, from north to south, it covers one quarter of the earth.' By the end of his reign, with the conquest of the Philippines in full swing and Portugal and its global possessions annexed, Philip's dominions spanned all twenty-four of the world's time-zones, making it (according to one contemporary) 'the greatest empire known since the creation of the world' (Plate 1).[5] In the grudging words of William Camden, a vigorous opponent, Philip had become 'A prince whose empire extended so farre and wide, above all emperors before him, that he might truly say, *Sol mihi semper lucet*: the sunne always shineth upon me'.[6]

   Meanwhile cultural imperialism, combined with cruder forms of propaganda, extended the king's influence far beyond the bounds of the Monarchy itself. Numerous works written by the dynasty's subjects and supporters openly called upon the Habsburgs to establish a 'Universal Monarchy'. Charles V's election in 1519 as Holy Roman Emperor gave rise to polemics inviting the new ruler to imitate the achievements of his namesake Charlemagne and unite all Christendom, and his imperial coronation by the pope in 1530 occasioned a fresh torrent of prophetic pamphlets which portrayed Charles as a second Augustus.

Juan Ginés de Sepúlveda, later appointed tutor to the future Philip II, wrote one of the more extreme of these imperialist tracts and no doubt tried to pass his ideas on to his young charge.[7] Philip's journey from Spain to the Netherlands in 1548, the victory of Lepanto in 1571 and the annexation of Portugal in 1580 all provoked similar literary effusions urging the Habsburgs to acquire a 'Universal Monarchy'. A further spate of universalist literature written in the 1590s, in both Italy and Spain, culminated in the apocalyptic 'Monarchy of Spain' begun by Tommaso Campanella in 1600.[8]

The imperial theme also appeared in the works of art commissioned by Philip and his Court. The iconography of the king's ceremonial entry into Lisbon in 1581 included one triumphal arch that showed Janus surrendering the keys of his temple 'as if to the lord of the world, who holds it securely under his rule', while another bore the legend 'The world, which was divided between your great-grandfather King Ferdinand the Catholic and your grandfather King Manuel of Portugal, is now linked into one, since you are lord of everything in the East and West'.[9] A medal struck in 1583 made the same point more concisely: it showed the king with the inscription PHILIPP II HISP ET NOVI ORBIS REX (Philip II, king of Spain and the New World) on the obverse, and on the reverse, around a terrestrial globe, the uncompromising legend NON SUFFICIT ORBIS (The world is not enough) (Plate 2). This bold device quickly came into general use. When Sir Francis Drake and his men entered the Governor's Mansion in Santo Domingo in 1586 they found a 'scutchion' of the royal arms of Spain which contained a globe and a scroll 'wherein was written these words in Latin NON SVFFICIT ORBIS'. The English – understandably – found it a 'very notable marke and token of the vnsatiable ambition of the Spanishe King and his nation' (Plate 3) and Drake apparently took it away with him in disgust.[10] Another medal of 1585, in a conscious attempt to go beyond the PLUS ULTRA ('Onwards and upwards') motto of Charles V, displayed the zodiac with the phrase ULTRA ANNI SOLISQUE VIAS ('Beyond the solar circuit of the year', a slight emendation of Vergil's tribute to the unprecedented power of the Roman Emperor Augustus in the *Aeneid*) 'because God has given him [Philip] a greater inheritance; and with his great power he could be lord of Cambodia and China and of other vast provinces if he wished'.[11] All over Europe, Spanish art, drama, dress and even comedy found eager imitators.[12]

Nevertheless Philip constantly sought to reassure his neighbours that they had nothing to fear from him. At the very beginning of his reign he stated unequivocally that 'I would very much like to justify my actions to the whole world and show that I do not lay claim to other states' (although he quickly added 'I also wish it to be clearly understood that I will defend the lands which [Charles V] has given me'). In 1572, as he mobilized a vast army to suppress the Dutch Revolt and, at the same time, placed his forces elsewhere in Europe on standby, the king assured the rulers of Italy that 'I have no intention of breaking the general peace, which is the thing I myself most wish to preserve, and have urged on all of my ministers. But if ill-intentioned people should think of taking advantage of the

Plates 2 and 3 *Non suffict orbis*. After the 'union of crowns' in 1580, a new conceit boldly commemorated the creation of Philip's global empire. A medal of gilded bronze, probably cast in 1583, shows the king on one side and a globe surmounted by a horse on the other, together with the uncompromising legend NON SUFFICIT ORBIS – 'The world is not enough'. Three years later, horse, globe and legend had all been incorporated into the royal arms of Spain as the official 'logo' of the monarchy (at least in the Governor's mansion in Santo Domingo *right*).

troubles [in the Netherlands] in order to attack my estates and disturb the peace, they will be restrained when they see that I am ready.'[13] His refrain remained much the same later in the reign: 'I have no reason to be driven by ambition to acquire more kingdoms or states, or to gain reputation, because Our Lord in his goodness has given me so much of all these things that I am content,' he wrote in 1586; and in the 1590s he proclaimed: 'God is my witness that I have never made war to gain more kingdoms, but only to maintain them in the [Catholic] faith and in peace.'[14] If Spain nevertheless went to war with foreign powers the king always protested that his sole motive was self-defence – that he only fought when he was himself attacked. Thus he could truthfully assert that the Habsburgs' conflicts with France had always begun with a French ultimatum or declaration of war: in 1521, 1536, 1542, 1552 and 1556 – with another projected attack on Spain in 1572 averted only by the assassination of the chief architect of the operation, Gaspard de Coligny. Philip could likewise claim that his wars against the Ottoman Turks were primarily defensive, with Spain mobilizing her forces only after an assault upon her or upon one of her allies: after the capture of Tripoli from the Knights of St John in 1551, or after the conquest of Cyprus from the Venetians in 1570.[15]

The states of sixteenth-century Europe faced the same 'security dilemma' that affected their successors in the twentieth, however: every move made by the dominant power to preserve the status quo inevitably seemed threatening to its neighbours and therefore increased international tension.[16] The French, German and English governments all felt directly threatened by the powerful army maintained by the king nearby in the Netherlands after 1567 – and not without reason, for it intervened in France in 1569 and in the 1590s, as well as in the Rhineland in the 1580s; and it aimed to invade England in 1571, in 1576–77 and again in 1587–88. As Lord Burghley, chief minister of Elizabeth I, once observed: 'If he [Philip II] once reduce the Low Countries to absolute subjection, I know not what limits any man of judgment can set unto his greatness.' England would become a prey to Philip's 'insatiable malice, which is most terrible to be thought of, but most miserable to suffer'. Even after the failure of the Armada, Burghley continued to believe that Philip aimed 'to be lord and commander of all Christendom'.[17] Seen from Paris, the encircling arms of the Habsburgs – whose embrace extended from Navarre through northern Italy and Franche Comté to the Netherlands – seemed equally intimidating. According to the French Protestant leader Coligny, 'In sight of the wisest' Philip aimed 'to make himself monarche of Christendome, or at least to rule the same'; in 1585, his successor Henry of Navarre complained of 'the ambition of the Spaniards who, having acquired domination of so many lands and seas, believe no part of the world to be inaccessible to them'; and the following year the French envoy in Madrid warned his government that Philip 'sought to make himself the greatest [monarch] of all the princes in Christendom'. In the early seventeenth century several French pamphleteers called for a pre-emptive strike in order to break what they perceived to be Habsburg encirclement:

On the one side [of France] is Franche-Comté and on the other Naples and Milan. Seeing Spain in the forefront and Flanders to the rear, will you not yourself say *'And what security?'* Here, on the contrary is Navarre, which was once the border of France with Spain and today is that of Spain to France. *And what security?*[18]

The popes, too, felt uneasy about the temporal power of Spain, for Philip's lands surrounded the Papal States and they depended heavily upon the grain supplied by Habsburg Sicily. Moreover, no pontiff could overlook either the sack of Rome in 1527 by the troops of Charles V or the ruthless use of hunger and force against Pope Paul IV in 1556–57 by those of his son. Papal support for the 'crusades' of the Spanish Habsburgs, whether launched against infidels or heretics, therefore tended to remain muted for fear that any Habsburg success might reinforce the dynasty's European ascendancy. Ironically, Philip himself best expressed this strategic dilemma. In a splenetic outburst he told the pope in 1580: 'Most of the misfortunes that have befallen my possessions have occurred because I have tried so hard to defend the church and extirpate heresy. But the greater these [misfortunes] have become, the more Your Holiness has forgotten them!' The pope remained unimpressed, and the following year the king again let off steam on the subject, this time to a minister:

I assure you that [the pope's indifference] already has me weary and very close to losing my patience . . . I believe that, if the Netherlands belonged to someone else, the pope would have performed miracles to prevent them being lost by the church; but because they are my states, I believe he is prepared to see this happen because they will be lost by me.

'There is a lot more I would and could say in this vein,' the king concluded, 'but it is midnight and I am very tired, and these thoughts make me even wearier.'[19]

English, French and papal fears of Spain's aggressive aspirations were not entirely misplaced. Despite their protestations to the contrary, Philip and his ministers clearly believed that, at least sometimes, 'to defend it is necessary to attack', since protecting all vulnerable areas would cost far more and achieve far less than a well-aimed stroke at any declared (or even potential) enemy.[20] His government regularly received, and duly considered, papers that proposed expanding the Monarchy by force. Thus in November 1571, in the aftermath of Lepanto, an ambitious 'Discourse' arrived at Court explaining how to exploit Spain's unexpected advantage with an attack on Tunis (which was in fact assaulted and captured in 1573), and then on Bizerta, Bougie and Algiers, since these successes in the western basin of the Mediterranean would inevitably tip the balance of power in Europe in Spain's favour. The duke of Alba, Spain's foremost military commander, entirely agreed, albeit for other reasons: when asked for his advice on how to exploit the victory, he strongly recommended an operation to 'clean up' the Barbary coast –

but as the essential preliminary to an attack on Constantinople, since 'It is essential for an efficient conquest not to leave on the flanks anything that might cause a diversion. That is the "abc" of all who embark on this profession [of arms]'.[21] In 1574, upon hearing of the death of Charles IX of France, the governor of Spanish Lombardy urged Philip to seize the favourable opportunity 'which will not recur for many years' in order to seize Saluzzo, Toulon, Marseilles 'and other places in France which, because they are poorly defended and cannot be relieved, will be easy to take'. This single stroke would solve all of Philip's strategic problems, he argued, because the French

> shelter and stimulate the heresies which lead – and have always led – the Turks to [attack] Christendom . . . They are the ones who arm North Africa and support Algiers, and supply them with weapons, equipment and other things; the ones who incite and assist the prince of Orange and the rebels against Your Majesty; the ones who stir up and support the hostile intentions of the princes of the Empire.

A preventive strike against them, the governor concluded, would thus be wholly justified.[22]

Similarly combative proposals flowed in periodically from further afield. In 1583 the governor of the Philippines urged his master to sanction an expedition to conquer China; the next year an official in Macao asserted that 'With less than 5,000 Spaniards Your Majesty could conquer these lands [China] and become lord of them, or at least of the maritime areas, which are the most important in any part of the world'; and the same year the bishop of Malacca advocated pooling the resources of Spain and Portugal in order first to conquer south-east Asia, and then to annex southern China, so that 'His Majesty will be the greatest lord that ever was in the world'.[23] In 1585 one of Philip's officials in Manila called for the king 'to evict and expel the Muslims from all the Philippine islands, or at least to subject them and make them pay tribute, vanquishing those in Java, Sumatra, Acheh, Borneo, Mindanao, Solo, the Moluccas, Malacca, Siam, Patani, Pegu and other kingdoms which venerate Mohammed'. The following year a 'general assembly' of the Spanish inhabitants of the Philippines, led by the bishop and the governor, drew up a lengthy memorandum advocating the conquest of China and sent a messenger to Spain with orders to present their arguments to the king in person.[24] More imperialist schemes followed in the 1590s: Manoel de Andrada Castel Blanco, a Portuguese priest long resident in America and Africa, forwarded to the king an ambitious global strategy, arguing that the fortification of six widely separated strongpoints – Johore, St Helena, Goeree, Sierra Leone, Bahia and Santa Catalina – would guarantee Iberian commercial supremacy around the globe; and various enthusiasts in east Asia continued to harp on the ease with which China and Japan might be conquered by the Iberians.[25]

Although Philip decided not to act on any of these expansionist suggestions, a 'global' strategic vision clearly underlay other more modest initiatives undertaken by his government. In 1559, for example, having created a new council to advise him on the administration of his extensive Italian dominions, the king commissioned a simultaneous *visita*, or general inspection, for his three main peninsular possessions – Lombardy, Naples and Sicily – in order to reform and streamline their bureaucracies.[26] In 1567 he established a *visita* for the council of the Indies headed by Juan de Ovando, a minister who, according to a colleague, 'Normally dealt with all business entrusted to him by anatomizing it, creating new skeletons and proposals until he found all their heads; then he would study the heads and master them'. Ovando found almost a thousand matters that required attention, but (characteristically) isolated just two major areas in need of urgent reform: first, the councillors possessed little knowledge of the Americas and so did not understand their problems; second, neither the council nor its ministers in America showed sufficient familiarity with the legislation in force. To remedy the first, Ovando proposed the creation of a 'chronicler and cosmographer of the Indies' and commissioned a series of geographical and territorial investigations to elicit information on the New World (see pp. 61–5 below); for the second he recommended the collection and publication of all current laws (a project begun immediately although not completed until 1680). Meanwhile, in 1568, following rumours that the pope might revoke the royal rights of patronage in the New World and appoint a nuncio for the Americas, Philip created a high-powered committee to overhaul the entire administration of Spain's overseas colonies. The 'Junta Magna', as it became known, made recommendations for all areas of colonial policy: to improve religious observance it advocated appointing bishops born on the American continent and the creation of four new tribunals of the Inquisition; to ameliorate the lot of indigenous subjects it proposed reforms to the landholding system; to stimulate the economy it devised new regulations for mining, commerce and manufacture; to augment the crown's revenues, it advocated a combination of tribute levied on communities rather than on individuals, and a new sales tax (the *alcabala*).[27]

Not all of the junta's recommendations took effect immediately or in full, but some of them formed part of an even broader policy initiative. At much the same time Philip's ministers in the Low Countries began to overhaul the legal system and introduced new taxes there too. In January 1568, just before the Junta Magna began to meet, the duke of Alba, Philip's governor-general in the Netherlands, wrote that he intended to implement the king's instructions to 'place these provinces under a single [system of] law and customs', creating (as Alba put it) 'a new world'. In just over two years new legislation both unified the criminal law and standardized the procedure in criminal trials throughout the Low Countries, while over a hundred local customs were codified.[28] At the same time, at Philip's insistence, Alba proposed new taxes to the representative assemblies of the Netherlands in order to balance his budget and end his financial dependence on Spain. One was 'the Hundredth Penny', a 1 per cent tax on all capital, collected as a percentage of the yield of each investment during the year 1569–70 rather than on its declared value (thus discouraging undervaluation): it has been hailed as the 'most modern tax ever levied in early modern Europe'.[29] The duke also proposed a 10 per cent sales tax, known both as the 'Tenth Penny' and as the *alcabala*. He justified these new taxes in terms remarkably similar to those used shortly afterwards in Philip's decree of November 1571 for all of Spanish America, which ordered the 'viceroys, presidents and judges of our Audiencias, and governors of the provinces of Peru, New Spain, Chile, Popayán, New Granada and of all other parts of our Indies' to impose a sales tax:

> You are well aware that my treasury is exhausted, consumed and encumbered by the great and continuous expenses that I have incurred here for many years, sustaining large armies and navies for the defence of Christendom and of my kingdoms, and for the conservation and upkeep of my states and lordships. Neither my revenues, nor the projects and expedients attempted, nor the assistance and taxes of these kingdoms [of Castile] have sufficed.

The king therefore commanded all 'Spanish, mestizo, mulatto and free Black subjects' throughout the Americas to shoulder the cost of their own defence by paying the new sales tax.[30] An imperial government that could, with a single order and a single justification, impose a new tax on an entire continent thousands of kilometres away, and at the same time introduce innovative levies in the Low Countries, hundreds of kilometres distant in another direction, possessed both the vision and the machinery to pursue a Grand Strategy.[31]

In the military and diplomatic sphere, although some of Philip's designs failed, others spectacularly succeeded. Philip's agents conquered most of the Philippines, recovered much of the Netherlands, and acquired the entire Portuguese empire. In 1587–88 the king assembled an amphibious force, at the staggering cost of 30,000 ducats a day, that represented (according to friend and foe alike) 'the largest fleet that has ever been seen in these seas since the creation of the world' and 'the greatest and strongest combination, to my understanding, that ever was gathered in Christendom'.[32] For the last twenty-five years of his reign he maintained between 70,000 and 90,000 soldiers in the Low Countries – in what some enthusiasts called *Castra Dei* (God's encampment) – with perhaps as many men again serving in garrisons elsewhere around the globe. In 1593 even one of his inveterate enemies, William Louis of Nassau, had to admit that Philip ranked as 'the greatest monarch in the world'.[33] Why, then, did he fail to achieve so many of his major foreign policy goals?

PART I: THE CONTEXT OF STRATEGIC CULTURE

One reason the Kennedy and Johnson administrations failed to take an orderly, rational approach to the basic questions underlying Vietnam was the staggering variety and complexity of other issues we faced. Simply put, we faced a blizzard of problems, there were only twenty-four hours in a day, and we often did not have time to think straight. This predicament is not unique to the administration in which I served or to the United States. It has existed at all times and in most countries. I have never seen a thoughtful examination of the problem. It existed then, it exists today, and it ought to be recognized and planned for when organizing a government.[1]

Robert Strange McNamara, the author of this lament, has, like Philip II, generally had a very bad press. Both men failed to achieve most of their policy goals; both sacrificed lives, resources and reputation on a prodigious scale; both left their countries weaker than when they took office. Furthermore, McNamara's 'explanation' for his failure – which recurs frequently in his memoirs – overlooks the obvious fact that every Great Power must expect to confront a 'blizzard of problems', and so cannot normally concentrate on a single threat for long. To expect otherwise, as McNamara seems to have done, is unrealistic, unreasonable and unwise.

The government of Philip II naturally differed greatly from that of the United States four centuries later. Most obviously, its ruler exercised absolute power by hereditary right, coming to power by genes rather than 'grey cells' – and a somewhat restricted pool of genes at that, given the remarkable propensity of many European dynasties, led by the Habsburgs, to marry close relatives (see table 3, p. 79 below and table 7, p. 294). Perhaps because of this in-breeding, the number of outstandingly successful, intelligent and sympathetic hereditary rulers remains fairly small. Moreover, sixteenth-century communications also varied dramatically from those of today: then, messages from distant theatres of operations took weeks if not months to arrive (and decisions took just as long to send back), whereas a modern commander-in-chief can consult with his subordinates at the front in 'real time'. Finally, sixteenth-century statesmen, confronted by the religious passions unleashed by the Reformation, found their freedom to manoeuvre – and above all their ability to compromise – severely restricted by ideology. Admittedly, some leaders managed to overcome this: Henry of Navarre, leader of the French Protestants, converted to Catholicism in 1593 specifically to secure the surrender of the nation's capital, allegedly remarking as he did so that 'Paris is well worth a Mass'. Philip II and most of his contemporaries could never have done that.

Perhaps, however, these contrasts are more apparent than real. Outstandingly successful, intelligent and sympathetic statesmen are rare in any age, whatever their path to power; although slow by twentieth-century standards, Philip II's communications system worked faster and better than that of any rival state; and the ideological passions unleashed by communism have exercised a powerful influence on modern international relations. Above all, the same three considerations shaped strategic culture in the sixteenth century as in the twentieth: first, the prevailing structure of command and control – the means chosen by each government to formulate and achieve its strategic goals; second, the network of communications and intelligence created to assemble information on the prevailing threats and to overcome the obstacles posed by time and distance; and, finally, the assumptions that inform its strategic vision and influence the selection of its strategic priorities, so that despite the 'blizzard of problems' that faced them, they still had 'time to think straight'.

Towards the end of his self-serving memoirs of the 1960s, Robert McNamara once more paused to address the structural problem that he held largely responsible for the failure of his Vietnam policies:

Readers must wonder by now – if they have not been mystified long before – how presumably intelligent, hardworking, and experienced officials – both civilian and military – failed to address systematically and thoroughly questions whose answers so deeply affected the lives of our citizens and the welfare of our nation. Simply put, such an orderly, rational approach was precluded by the 'crowding out' which resulted from the fact that Vietnam was but one of a multitude of problems we confronted. Any one of the issues facing Washington during the 1960s justified the full attention of the president and his associates.[2]

The three chapters that follow examine how, four centuries earlier, Philip II and his 'presumably intelligent, hardworking, and experienced officials' addressed the 'multitude of problems' that confronted the global empire over which they ruled, and the nature – and adequacy – of the command structure, the communications system, and the assumptions that they brought to the task.

1   *'The Largest Brain in the World'*

For much of his life Philip II, like his contemporary Elizabeth Tudor, lacked a suitable successor. Had he died in 1555, at the same age as his grandfather, Philip I (28), he would never have succeeded to the throne; had he died in 1570, at the same age as his only surviving son, Philip III (43), his possessions would have passed to his four-year-old elder daughter; had he died in 1585 at the same age as his father Charles V (58), he would have left his vast Monarchy to a sickly son of seven.[3] In fact, like Elizabeth, Philip II lived longer than any previous sovereign of his dynasty, but of course no one at the time – whether friend or foe – could foresee this. Thus in 1574 a concerned minister begged 'Your Majesty, on whose life and health every present undertaking depends, to rest and recover from your labours'; while in 1580, when the duke of Alba found out that his master had fallen ill with a fever, he berated his chief ally at Court: 'It is not reasonable, sir, that when His Majesty is ill, even only slightly, I should not know about it within a matter of hours'.[4] In 1583, according to a minister in the Low Countries, the Dutch rebels 'placed all their hope in the king's death'; three years later, the French ambassador in Madrid wrote that 'Well-informed Spaniards foresee a dramatic change in the entire Monarchy should Philip die'; and shortly after that the Venetian ambassador argued that the whole Spanish Monarchy 'is held together by the authority and wisdom of the king, and if he were to die everything would fall into confusion and danger'.[5]

In the event, from the time of his father's abdication in 1555–56 until his own death in 1598 aged 71 Philip ruled absolutely. At the beginning of the reign, when he promoted a man of humble birth to be primate of all Spain, the wife of a courtier irreverently commented: 'These are the miracles that the king now wishes to perform, and they seem very like those of Christ, who made men out of clay'; by its end, however, many of his servants and subjects genuinely saw him as the incarnation of God on earth, believed he had been a saint, and attributed miracles to him.[6] Philip himself made no such claims – on one occasion he wrote 'I don't know if [people] think I'm made of iron or stone. The truth is, they need to see that I am mortal, like everyone else' – but he seldom had qualms about exercising his absolute power over life and death. On the one hand, in 1571 he

pardoned numerous prisoners in Spain and the Indies to celebrate the birth of a
son and heir, and in 1580 as he entered his new kingdom of Portugal in triumph
he freed prisoners along his route.[7] On the other hand, during the decade 1566–
76 he had over 1,200 of his Low Countries' subjects executed by a special legal
tribunal because they disagreed with his views on religion and politics. In 1580
he placed a price on the head of William of Nassau prince of Orange, his most
eminent Dutch vassal, and four years later he rewarded handsomely the family of
the prince's assassin. Foreigners who opposed him could likewise expect no mercy
if they fell into his power. In 1572, when his forces in the Netherlands captured
some of Orange's high-ranking French supporters, Philip ordered that they be
kept under strict guard but 'should any fear arise that they might be rescued, it
will be necessary to kill them'. A year later he ordered them to be secretly
murdered anyway.[8]

These, however, were extreme and unusual cases. Philip normally took great
pains to exercise his authority through established constitutional channels. On
one occasion he sent back a set of orders unsigned since 'it seems to me that there
are problems, because those for the three kingdoms of the crown of Aragon, and
especially the one for Aragon itself, will not be obeyed and are against the *fueros*
[local customs]'. All royal letters for his eastern kingdoms, the king pointed out,
should be issued by the council of Aragon and he ordered them to be redrafted.[9]
Thanks in part to this sensitivity, Philip enjoyed great popularity among most of
his subjects. When he returned to Madrid in 1583, after an absence of almost
three years in Portugal, the enthusiastic crowds that poured out of the city to
welcome him 'stretched over a mile from the palace, as much outside the city as
inside, with as many men and women at the windows and on the roofs. It was
almost incredible. I would never have thought that this city contained half of the
people whom I saw then.'[10]

Despite at least seven assassination attempts, for most of his reign Philip
travelled unarmed through crowded streets and deserted fields; he drank cups of
water proffered by ordinary people along the way; he ate the fresh catch offered by
local fishermen; when he visited a university town he attended public lectures
along with the students; and when a religious procession passed him as he walked
in the streets, he fell to his knees among the crowd in shared reverence.[11] Philip
always worked with his study door open, and ministers would sometimes panic
when they saw him 'enter the patio of this building entirely alone', unprotected
against attack. He, like Elizabeth, could proudly boast: 'Let tyrants fear: I have
always so behaved myself, that under God I have placed my chiefest strength and
safeguard in the loyal hearts and goodwill of my subjects'.[12]

On most occasions Philip dressed simply – indeed to some the king's modest
attire made him look 'just like a physician' or even 'just like the citizens'.
Although he was fastidious about personal cleanliness, he remained conservative
in taste: he had a new suit of clothes made every month, but the design and the
colour – black – remained the same, a perfect example of the 'dignity through
understatement' advocated in Castiglione's influential *Book of the Courtier*.[13] That

Plate 4   Philip II in 1587 by Alonso Sánchez Coello. Portraits of Philip II in later years normally showed him dressed simply in black, conveying his majesty not through the outward symbols of kingship but through dignity and 'serenity'. His only ornament here is the insignia of the Order of the Golden Fleece. Sánchez Coello intended this understated portrait of his master, then aged sixty, to go to Pope Sixtus V, but Grand Duke Ferdinand of Tuscany saw it and asked to have it; the painter agreed, but expressed the hope that the recipient would use his influence at the Roman Curia to obtain a benefice for his impecunious son.

is how he appears at the height of his power in the Alonso Sánchez Coello's portrait of 1587 (Plate 4). Nevertheless, Philip instilled instant respect in all who met him. When she entered his presence one day in the 1570s, Teresa of Ávila 'began to speak to him totally agitated because he fixed his penetrating gaze on me and seemed to see into my soul . . . I told him what I wanted as quickly as I could.' When Venetian ambassador Leonardo Donà had an audience, he spent hours beforehand 'reading and re-reading more than ten times' the letters and instructions that he had received in case Philip should ask him a question. One of the king's earliest biographers confirmed that 'Brave men who had withstood a

Plate 5   Philip II listens to Leonardo Donà at an audience, by Marco Vercellio. Donà became Venetian ambassador in Spain in 1570, at the age of thirty-three, and served for over three years. He eventually became doge (1606–12), which may explain why the portrait he commissioned shows him towering over Philip at one of his numerous audiences. Philip, according to custom, received the ambassador standing and appears to be listening attentively; Donà, who subsequently wrote down the king's every word, rarely received more than a non-committal sentence in reply.

thousand dangers trembled in his presence, and no one looked on him without emotion.'[14] Everyone also remarked on his remarkable self-control: the same Donà, when obliged in 1573 to tell the king in a public audience that Venice had defected without warning from its Spanish alliance and made a separate peace with the Turks, noted in amazement that he listened to the terms of the treaty impassively – except that 'his mouth made a very small, ironic movement, smiling thinly' (Plate 5). Most people likewise paid tribute to Philip's intelligence. Towards the end of his reign, even a critic admitted that 'His

Majesty's brain must be the largest in the world'; while just after his death, a court preacher (who also noted that 'with a sideways glance he sent some people to their grave') compared Philip's wisdom with that of Solomon 'so that if, in order to become king, one had to enter a competition, as for a university chair . . . ours would have won the professorship of the realm without difficulty and by a large margin'.[15]

All these examples, however, referred to Philip's official 'body' which represented his majesty and power to the world. Like all kings, Philip also possessed a mortal body of flesh and blood. As the Valencian humanist (and royal councillor) Fadrique Furió Ceriol wrote in 1559:

> Every prince is made up, as it were, of two persons: the first, the natural person, is fashioned by the hands of nature and as such is given the same essence as other human beings. The other is a gift of fortune and the favour of heaven, created to govern and protect the public good, for which reason we call it the public person . . . Each and every prince may therefore be considered in two distinct and different ways: as a man and as a sovereign.

Philip created a distinct institutional setting for each of his two 'persons'. By the 1560s, thanks to the elaborate Burgundian etiquette of the Spanish Court, almost 1,500 persons attended on the king (about 800 in his household, over 200 in the stables, more than 100 in the chapel and so on) while hundreds of other officials manned the central organs of government: over 100 in the court's special police force (the Alcaldes de Casa y Corte); 79 in the council of Finance and its various dependent bureaux, 53 in the council of Castile, 39 in the council of Aragon, 25 in the council of the Indies, and so on. Such a huge concentration of people – with their families, servants and ancillary staff, they may have totalled 4,000 – could scarcely travel around in the king's wake, and so Philip decided to establish a fixed centre for his government.[16] He tried out both Valladolid and Toledo, but in June 1561 opted for Madrid because of its central location, its excellent water supply, and its open situation which would enable both the palace and the city to expand with minimal difficulty. And expand they did: the surviving registers for six parishes of the city recorded 242 baptisms in 1560, but 410 in 1561 and 627 in 1562; by the end of the reign, Madrid had become (after Seville) the largest city in Spain. Meanwhile, major building programmes in the 1560s and 1580s more than doubled the size of the royal palace (Plate 6).[17]

As María José Rodríguez-Salgado has perceptively noted, the king's decision to establish an elaborate Court in Madrid had, as its corollary, the creation of a periphery of private retreats to which he could periodically escape and live more informally. The king alternated between these two institutional settings. In the spacious rooms on the upper floor of the Madrid palace, flanked by his magnificent collections of tapestries, paintings and other trappings of Christian kingship, and with his ministers toiling on the floor below,

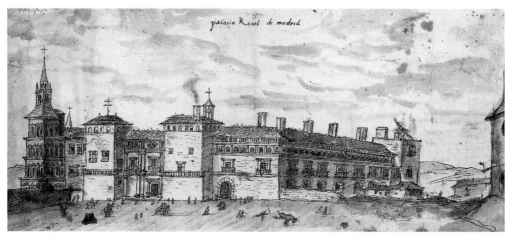

palacia Real de madrid

Plate 6   The Royal Palace, Madrid, *c.* 1569, by Anton van den Wyngaerde. Philip made Madrid his capital in 1561 and immediately began to expand the royal palace (Alcázar). Work began almost at once on the 'Torre dorada' (on the far left), with three high-windowed floors beneath a pointed slate roof in the Flemish style, and on the new galleries to the right of the two original towers of the southern façade – constructed according to plans amended by the king himself. (Van den Wyngaerde's sketch shows building still in progress on the 'Torre de la Reina' at the northeast corner of the complex.) The king enjoyed the views of the Manzanares valley from the 'Golden tower', and from the rooms along the western façade, where he worked and held audiences while his ministers toiled in their offices below.

He was easily accessible for formal and informal audiences. The king set aside part of his day to see people and receive petitions. He made sure that those without official business or regular access could approach him on his daily walks to and from church. He communicated daily with his advisers and councillors. His days were hectic, full of direct pressure, and he dealt with a great diversity and quantity of business.[18]

The truth of this emerges from an incident in 1577, while the king was in Madrid. Philip's private secretary asked if Juan Fernández de Espinosa, one of the financiers engaged in a crucial rescheduling of Spain's debts, might call on him at 2 p.m., but the king protested:

Let him come at half past three, because it is already two o'clock, and I have no time to see the queen and her children except right now. And impress upon him that he will have to leave at four, because I have a lot of audiences then – even though I have [already] held thirty today. And, in view of that, just look at the back-log of papers I shall have![19]

Naturally, such a frenetic pace could not be sustained indefinitely and the king regularly sought solace in one of his country palaces: Aranjuez, Valsaín (near Segovia), the Pardo and (above all) the Escorial. There, his life – and his style of government – took on a totally different aspect. When the same Juan Fernández de Espinosa arrived at Aranjuez bearing a special licence from the council of

Finance to discuss important business with the king, he received very different treatment:

> I do wish that Juan Fernández had arranged the audience in Madrid, because he could have had one there, even though I was busier . . . I have brought so many papers down here with me that if I start giving audiences I shall not be able to think of reading any of them . . . I need time and quiet, and with audiences believe me I shall have neither.

The note concluded briskly: 'I am replying to this now so that Juan Fernández will not be detained in the hope of an audience that I cannot give him.'[20]

Philip's desire to limit the number of meetings is easily explained. To begin with, they could last a long time. Thus in September 1588 José de Acosta, SJ, received an audience in order to present a lengthy paper on the problems faced by the Jesuit Order in Spain. The king read each point, after which Acosta offered clarification; sometimes the king asked questions (while speaking of the 'secretary of Father Borgia, the king interrupted and said "Which Father Borgia?" I said "The one who was General of our Order". "You mean Father Francis" said the king; "Yes, sire, Father Francisco de Borgia, our General"'). Acosta's blow-by-blow account of the meeting filled four closely written sides of foolscap; it can hardly have lasted less than an hour. Nevertheless at the end of it Philip took no decision but announced that a particular minister would convey his views at a later stage.[21]

Audiences for ambassadors could take just as long and proved no more conclusive – the king invariably agreed at the end only to 'think about it' – yet with up to fourteen envoys resident at the Court, each constantly seeking the chance to put the concerns of his principals to the king in person, small wonder that the king sometimes complained that ambassadors' visits had 'made me waste the day'.[22] Yet diplomatic audiences could not be entirely avoided: most of them took place because a foreign government instructed its representative to explain a particular policy, to seek clarification of Spain's intentions, or to protest against one of Philip's actions – and to do it in person. The king might procrastinate, but eventually the ambassador had to be both seen and heard. Sometimes, indeed, the occasion could be exploited in order to obtain or impart information. Thus on 31 October 1571 Ambassador Donà received a full description from Venice of the victory of Lepanto three weeks before. He hurried to see the king, who happened to be in his chapel, and told a courtier his business; Philip at once invited him to sit in the same pew. 'Straight after the incense', Donà gave him the news, to which the king listened attentively, and they then knelt side by side as the palace choir sang the *Te Deum* 'with the most beautiful harmony I ever heard'. Philip kept the ambassador with him for the rest of the day in order to make sure of every detail.[23] Another use of audiences emerged a few days later when Ambassador Fourquevaux of France came to complain about the conduct of his Spanish counterpart in Paris. Philip listened attentively, but then began to grill Fourquevaux on some recent

rumours: was it true that Jeanne d'Albret, queen of Navarre, had set out from her
Court at Pau on a journey to Paris to meet with Charles IX? Was Louis of Nassau
(Orange's brother) among her entourage? Fourquevaux had to answer both questions affirmatively, and perhaps rashly ventured that several leading Huguenots
wanted to persuade the king of France to accept Louis into his service, since he was
a German prince who held no territory in Philip's dominions. No doubt, Philip
replied, the leading Huguenots wanted Charles IX to do many foolish things, but
he reminded Fourquevaux that Louis had waged open war against him in the
Netherlands in 1568, with the clear implication that Charles should therefore
send him away.[24]

Normally, however, Philip said virtually nothing at audiences – Donà, who
wrote down every word in his subsequent reports to the Doge and Senate of
Venice, seldom recorded more than one sentence ('although, as usual, his words
were most gracious') – but this taciturnity may have stemmed from the fact that
the king sometimes had difficulty in remembering what people said to him at
formal encounters. When turning down yet another request for a personal meeting he confided one day to his secretary: 'I can remember little from audiences –
although do not tell anyone that! I mean from most of them.' Furthermore,
written requests gave him more time to consider the best response.[25] Whenever
he could, therefore, the king preferred communications from others in writing.
When a prominent nobleman asked to see him, Philip replied: 'If you were closer
to Court, it might be appropriate to hear the details from you in person, but
. . . since you can write securely [a letter] for my eyes alone, I think it would
be best if you did so'.[26] Shrewd ambassadors indulged the king's preference.
Fourquevaux, for example, sometimes ignored commands from his master to seek
an audience with Philip, especially in summer: 'I know that I would please him
more if I communicated with him by letter,' he explained, because 'he prefers
ambassadors to deal with him by letter rather than in person while he resides in
his country houses'.[27]

Not everyone proved so tactful. Philip's understandable desire to protect his
privacy equally understandably infuriated some of those who wanted to see him
but could not. It was all very well, lamented the nuncio (dean of the diplomatic
corps), for the king to insist on receiving requests for action in writing, provided
he then replied to them; but 'It is rather irritating to have the king living so close
[at the Escorial], and not occupied with anything important [!], and yet for four
months I have been unable to secure an audience and I have received an answer
to none – or very few – of the memorials I have sent him in this time.'[28] Some
Spaniards shared the frustration. Traditionally, the culture of royal courts had
been largely oral and so transacting everything in writing seemed novel: 'God did
not send Your Majesty and all the other kings to spend their time on earth so that
they could hide themselves away reading and writing, or even meditating and
praying,' thundered Don Luis Manrique, the king's almoner, and he proceeded
to criticize 'the manner of transacting business adopted by Your Majesty, being
permanently seated at your papers . . . in order to have a better reason to

escape from people'. According to another court critic, 'it seems as if Your Majesty's efforts have gradually made him totally inaccessible and built a tower without doors and windows, so that you cannot see other people and they cannot see you'.[29]

The king nevertheless remained set in his ways, certain that he could transact far more business on his own than in meetings with others. Thus in 1576, while forwarding a pile of papers from Hernando de Ávalos, a government auditor appointed to introduce double-entry book-keeping into the Castilian treasury, the king's personal secretary cautiously suggested that

> It might be of great benefit both to Your Majesty and his ministers, and to [the dispatch of] business, to start listening to some [ministers in person] . . . because in that way they could clarify anything Your Majesty doubted or did not understand; and Your Majesty could still, in order to avoid an immediate decision and to think about it more, ask them to put what they had said in writing, and later reply to them in writing with your decision.

Philip dismissed this out of hand: '[Speaking] as one who has already almost 33 years of experience in handling public affairs, it would be a lot of work to listen to them and then see them again to give a response – especially those like Ávalos who talk all the time.'[30] A few years later, a courtier suggested that the king should spend twice as long listening as he spent writing; while Cardinal Granvelle, a minister with even more experience of government than the king himself, regretted that Philip so seldom made use of the pomp of Burgundian court ceremonial, 'in order to be more respected by his subjects. But', Granvelle added wearily, 'he has already made up his mind to live in seclusion so that, after 56 years, I have little hope of seeing any change'.[31]

The criticism was unfair, however. Aranjuez, the Pardo and the Escorial may have been 'secluded', and the king may have spent increasing amounts of time there as the reign advanced, but they did not serve as vacation resorts where he idled away his time in hunting, shooting and fishing (although he regularly indulged in all three). Rather they offered him the opportunity to govern (as he said) in the way that experience had proved to be the most efficient. José de Sigüenza, who saw the king at close quarters for the last two decades of his life, claimed that he managed to transact four times as much business while he resided at the Escorial; and an ambassador noted that although the king 'spends most of his time away from the Court, in part to escape from tiring audiences and in part to take care of business matters better, he never stops reading and writing, even when he travels in his coach'.[32]

The majority of the papers that Philip dealt with came from the various councils in Madrid whose number increased in the course of the reign from eleven to fourteen (see Table 1). The councils' principal function was to discuss the incoming letters and memoranda in a given area of responsibility and to

The councils of Philip II
(with the dates of their creation)

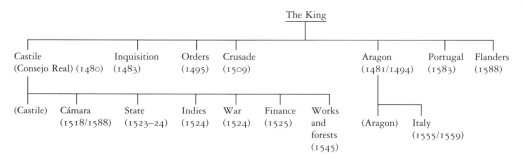

Table 1 The conciliar system of government created by Charles V and his advisers in the 1520s served Philip well. Despite the relentless expansion of the matters with which he and the central bureaucracy had to deal, he found it necessary to create only three new institutions: the council of Italy in the 1550s and the councils of Portugal and Flanders in the 1580s. Each organ, however, met for ever longer as the reign advanced, and the quantity of paperwork generated increased alarmingly.

recommend what action, if any, the king should take: they never initiated policies. Moreover, strict lines of demarcation defined their duties. Thus the council of War considered and reported on letters concerning the crown's armed forces, both naval and military, within Spain; but the council of State, which possessed exclusive responsibility for all Spain's interests in Europe, whether diplomatic, commercial or military, supervised the crown's armed forces in the Netherlands and Italy. Likewise, the council of the Indies dealt with military and naval affairs in Spanish America, while after 1583 a new council reported directly to the king concerning the defence of Portugal and its overseas possessions. Budgets for all military operations underwent review by yet another organ, the council of Finance.[33]

Government ministers throughout the Monarchy received strict orders to send their correspondence to the proper central institution. Thus at the beginning of his reign the king instructed his viceroys in Italy to direct all matters relating to 'administration, justice, the patrimony and revenues of our crown and treasury, other routine affairs and also matters concerning individuals (such as pardons, rewards, evaluations and the provision of offices)' to the newly created council of Italy, and matters of war or peace and relations with other rulers to the council of State. In fact matters soon became more complicated: ministers abroad also corresponded with the king from time to time via the councils of Finance, Aragon, Castile, Orders and Inquisition. Indeed a memorandum composed by a member of the central government in the 1570s on how to allocate incoming business between the various councils contained no fewer than 326 categories, each with its own administrative procedure. In the next decade Philip created two new councils – Portugal and Flanders – and reformed a third (the Cámara de Castilla, which handled patronage, judicial appeals and negotiations with the Cortes – or Parliament – of the realm), creating even more administrative categories until in the 1590s attempts were made to simplify the system. Ministers in America, for example, received orders to streamline their correspondence with the council of the Indies, so that 'Everything that you used to write in many letters, you will now condense into four [categories], according to their contents: administration, justice, war and finance.'[34]

The king himself rarely attended council meetings: everyone noted as exceptional his presence at the debates of the council of State in 1566 on the correct policy to follow in the Netherlands.[35] Except for the council of Castile, which by tradition attended on the king as a group once a week, Philip received the recommendations of each body in a written report (known as a 'consulta') to which he would write or dictate the appropriate response.[36] The council secretary would then draft a reply for the king's approval, and send the final version for his signature. Difficult or urgent issues considered by the council would be discussed with either its secretary or its president in individual meetings (which might last for two hours) or handled via 'billetes', the legion of memoranda that provide our principal source on the king's thoughts and decisions (Plate 7).[37]

The council secretaries possessed great power. First, they dealt directly with those who came to Court on council business – even ambassadors in the case of the council of State (when Secretary of State Antonio Pérez fell from power in 1579 the representatives of Genoa learned that no Italian political business could be resolved until the king appointed his successor).[38] Second, secretaries had orders to highlight pressing affairs and refer them to the king for immediate attention: as the king wrote to a council secretary in 1583, 'Although I am busy, if the matter is urgent and needs to be seen, send it to me here, even though it is in draft.' When time was deemed to be of the essence, Philip even allowed a final version of an order or letter to be submitted for his signature, along with the supporting consulta.[39] Finally, council secretaries not only chose which letters and papers to show to the king and which to summarize, they also determined when he would see them. In May 1574, although the war in the Netherlands occupied almost all of the king's waking hours, his private secretary still forwarded a dossier with a cover note that read: 'Although I see how occupied you are with the Low Countries, and that the crisis there leaves little time to deal with other things, I thought I should bring to Your Majesty's attention this letter from Don Diego de Mendoza . . .'[40] On occasion secretaries might also withhold letters addressed to the king. Thus in 1576 Antonio Pérez informed Don John of Austria (Philip's brother) that he had 'resolved not to show to His Majesty' a letter in which Don John 'spoke ill of the marquis of Mondéjar [viceroy of Naples], something unworthy of the person who wrote it and of the person to whom he wrote'; and three years later he informed the Spanish ambassador in Paris that 'our master is very pleased with your letters, and has seen all of them – I mean the ones that he ought to see'.[41] In 1588 Pérez's successor, Don Juan de Idiáquez, likewise intercepted and suppressed a letter addressed to the king by the duke of Medina

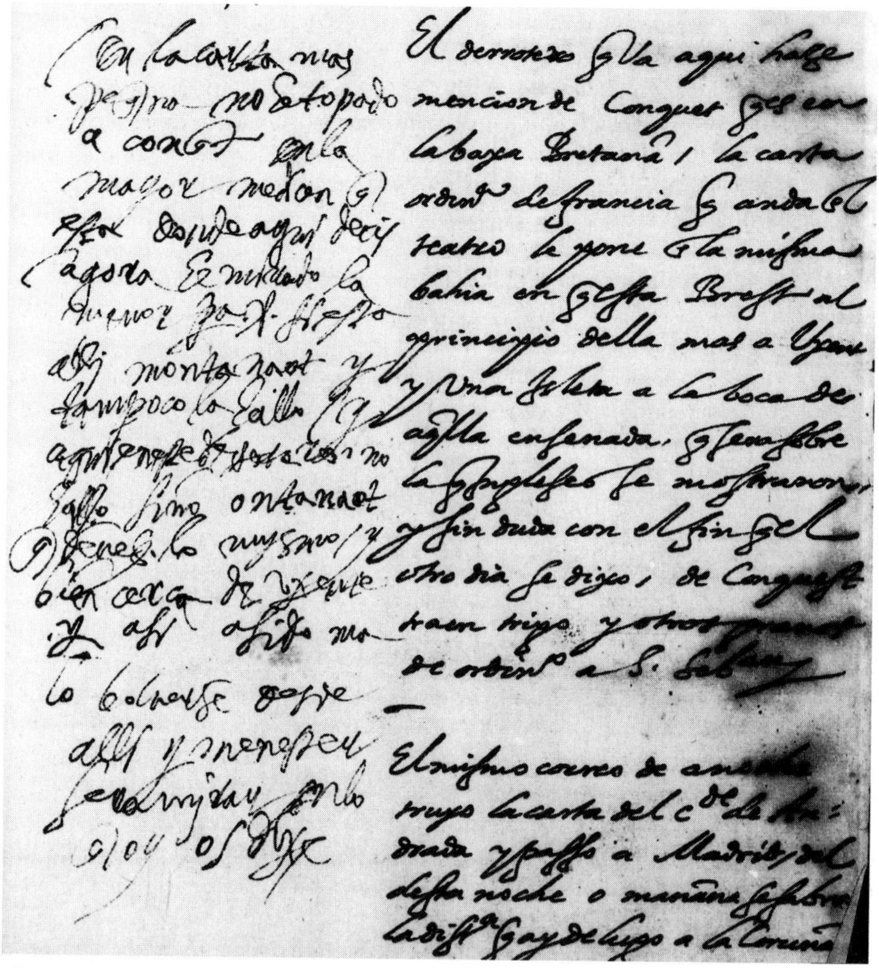

Plate 7   A 'billete'. The internal memoranda of the Spanish government (known as 'billetes') left a broad margin for the reply. This item, from spring 1588, shows the king and his secretary of state trying to identify the places mentioned in a letter reporting that an English fleet lurked off Brittany. Don Juan de Idiáquez (on the right) forwarded to the king the itinerary ('Derrotero' or *Rutter*) printed in preparation for the voyage of the Armada from Lisbon to the Channel, noting the location of 'Conquet which is in Lower Brittany', and confirming that he had also checked a map of France in the 'Teatro' (the *Theatrum orbis terrorum* of Abraham Ortelius). In the left-hand margin Philip replied that he had also checked two maps and the 'Derrotero' himself (where he found one place name misspelled).

Sidonia, declining his appointment to command the Spanish Armada and expressing serious doubts about the wisdom of the enterprise itself. 'We did not dare to show His Majesty what you have just written', Idiáquez and his colleague Don Cristóbal de Moura announced, and went on to rebuff the duke for his pusillanimity: 'Do not depress us with fears for the fate of the Armada, because in such a [just] cause God will make sure it succeeds.'[42]

Other defects marred the conciliar system. For example, some councillors used their position in order to favour or discredit other ministers, especially those serving abroad. In the 1560s two factions developed, one centred around Ruy Gómez de Silva, the king's groom of the Stole (*sumiller de corps*) whom court protocol required never to let the king out of his sight, the other around the duke of Alba, the head of the royal household.[43] Each man tried to gain the king's support for his candidates and policies at the expense of the other, causing all ministers to tread carefully. Thus in 1565 the duke of Alba refused to share his views on the correct policy to be followed in the Netherlands with Ruy Gómez, although both men served on the council of State, and the secretary of the council told the king that 'I do not know whether he will even tell me'.[44] Ten years later Don Luis de Requeséns, governor-general of the Netherlands (the most powerful overseas executive position in the Monarchy), worried about maintaining his credit at Court. To this end he began to write directly to the king so that criticisms of the policies of his predecessor, the duke of Alba, would not be seen by the council of State (on which Alba sat);[45] and he devoted considerable time to analysing whether his conduct might offend any prominent courtier, who would then criticize his policies and thus jeopardize their outcome (and his standing with the monarch).[46] A few years later, the unpopularity of Antonio Pérez became so great that one colleague, Mateo Vázquez (the king's private secretary and chaplain), left the Court and another, Gabriel de Zayas (also a cleric and Pérez's predecessor as secretary of state, subsequently demoted to secretary of the council of Italy), refused to speak with him when they met in the palace. The impasse only ended with Pérez's dismissal.[47] Even given harmonious relations between ministers, so many persons reported directly and separately to the king that confusion could easily arise. According to one adviser, in 1565:

> His Majesty makes mistakes, and will continue to make mistakes, in many matters because he handles them with different people, sometimes with one, at other times with another, concealing something from one minister but revealing other things. It is therefore small wonder that different and even contradictory orders are issued . . . It cannot fail to cause grave problems for the conduct of business and many inconveniences.[48]

In the course of his reign Philip introduced certain procedures to deal with these various defects. First, a number of key advisers served on several councils – a position on both State and War, or on Indies and Finance, was common; a seat on State, War and Finance was not unknown – so that they knew what was happening in other advisory bodies and could, at least in theory, help to coordinate affairs. For example Francisco de Erasso, who had served the Spanish Habsburgs for thirty years, had by 1559 become the secretary of no fewer than six councils and a member of two more. Such overlaps served a useful purpose because, otherwise, the councils operated almost entirely in the dark: each body dealt directly with the king, without knowing what other organs might be doing. Thus, in the felicitous formulation of a modern historian, 'The council of Finance had no idea where the money was going, nor the council of War when it was coming'.[49]

As the volume of incoming papers began to rise, however, the pressure on individuals holding many posts, like Erasso, became intolerable and so Philip introduced another administrative innovation. Between 1566 and 1572 Cardinal Diego de Espinosa, president of the council of Castile and Inquisitor-General, became an 'alter ego' – in the words of Ambassador Fourquevaux, 'another king in this Court' – and courtiers advised their friends abroad to run everything of importance past Espinosa because 'he is the man in all Spain in whom the king places most confidence and with whom he discusses most business, concerning both Spain and foreign affairs'. The cardinal did not sit on many councils, however: instead he kept abreast of business through a series of informal committees, known as 'juntas'. Thus in 1571, following the conclusion of the 'Holy League' with Venice and the Papacy against the Turks, a 'committee of two' (one of them Espinosa) reviewed all reports arriving from Italy and recommended appropriate actions in the naval campaign that culminated in the battle of Lepanto. When Espinosa died, ministers speculated on who would succeed to 'the superintendence of matters of war, state and finance, the handling of consultas and all the rest of the burden [of business] which the cardinal carried'.[50] The king, however, decided not to delegate the same degree of power to anyone else. 'I believed that it was right to entrust many matters which concerned my royal office to the cardinal', he informed Espinosa's successor as president of the council of Castile. 'And perhaps good reasons existed for it then. But experience has shown that it was not a good thing; and although it meant more leisure and less work for me, I do not think it should be allowed to continue.'[51]

Instead of an 'alter ego' or Favourite – the system that his son and grandson would later adopt – Philip chose to work after 1572 with a 'chief of staff': Espinosa's senior clerk, Mateo Vázquez, almost immediately became the king's private secretary and, for most of the period until 1585, played a leading role in deciding what matters should be handled by the juntas – for that part of Espinosa's system survived him – and who should serve on them. He also often acted as their secretary and arranged both their timetable and their agenda.[52] In addition, Vázquez handled the king's extensive 'private' correspondence. Vázquez sometimes received orders to drop everything and read important incoming papers at once – 'Look at these while I eat and take a siesta, and send them to me for when I awake, so I can see them and decide what to do about them' – because almost from the beginning of his reign Philip allowed his ministers, whether at Court or abroad, to write to him directly if they had a problem that they deemed confidential, in effect short-circuiting the entire central bureaucracy.[53] He told them: 'You may also put on the envelope "to be placed in the king's hands", because I have ordered that such letters should be brought to me sealed so that, when I have seen the contents, I can arrange what is most convenient for my service.'[54]

Inevitably some ministers abused the system but they did not do so for long. Thus in 1574 the king sharply rebuked the governor of Milan:

> I told you [when I appointed you] what you might write 'to be placed in the king's hands', and it applied only to what I said in that letter. These matters should not be confused with those to be handled by the councils, which could reply to you better, confining yourself in letters 'to be placed in the king's hands' solely to details that could better inform me, and which you can see should not be known to others.

A decade later the king lost his temper with another minister who insisted on referring too much to him directly: 'Sending letters "to be placed in the king's hands" is a terrible thing, because I often lack the time even to open them. In fact it only serves to slow business down, because I have had these two letters for days but have only been able to open them now.'[55] Nevertheless when in the following year a senior minister suggested discontinuing the practice, the king refused: it played a vital role in preventing any attempt by senior advisers to manipulate his access to information.[56]

The king was prepared to read almost anything that came across his desk, whether or not he had asked for it, and some unsolicited information and advice – often from people (especially clerics) not directly involved in government – clearly influenced his subsequent decisions. Perhaps the most spectacular example occurred in 1586, when Bernardino de Escalante, a priest and inquisitor, sent in a detailed plan (complete with map) for the overthrow of Elizabeth Tudor that later became the blueprint for the entire 'Enterprise of England' (see p. 186 and Plate 25 below).[57] The king showed special concern that his subjects in the Americas should be able to write to him whenever they chose, 'so that we can receive [their letters] and be informed of what they wish to tell us', and he repeatedly threatened that any official who attempted to withhold or divert a letter addressed to the king would be severely punished.[58] The success of Gerónimo de Mendieta, a Franciscan residing in Puebla (Mexico), in getting a dossier concerning the rights of native Americans to the king's desk in 1588 testifies to the king's sincerity in this matter. Mendieta sent his information by a special courier, who delivered it (via the commissary-general of the Order in Madrid) directly to Mateo Vázquez, because 'the archive of the council of the Indies is full of treatises and writings in favour of the poor Indians' which (Mendieta feared) the king never saw. Philip duly studied the dossier and asked to see the cleric who had brought it from Mexico. At an audience two days later the messenger, José de Acosta, provided interesting information about the Americas which the king ordered Vázquez to follow up.[59]

This and Philip's other attempts at 'open government' certainly helped to counter the fragmentation of his administrative system and to provide some independence from his administrative staff, but only at the cost of creating a torrent of papers with which he had to deal in person. In 1559, even before he returned to Spain, the French ambassador at his Court commented that Philip seemed 'well versed in his affairs and does not waste an hour, spending the whole day long on his papers'; and for the rest of his reign the king read and commented on countless incoming letters, consultas, petitions and memoranda.[60] The quantity in each category increased steadily throughout the reign. Thus the council of War, which produced scarcely two bundles of working papers a year in the 1560s, turned out over thirty a year in the 1590s – a fifteen-fold increase – while every year the council's secretaries prepared nearly 2,000 letters on military and naval business. The output of other bodies increased at a similar pace: the council of Finance, which met only twice a week in the 1550s, by 1580 transacted business every morning for three or four hours and sometimes continued into the afternoons; while the council of the Indies, instead of just meeting for three hours every morning, from 1571 began to meet three afternoons a week as well.[61] Every day piles of consultas came to Philip's desk from his various councils and he had to decide in person how to deal with each item. He also received seemingly endless petitions. In the month of March 1571, for example, over 1,250 individual petitions, an average of over 40 a day, arrived for the king's consideration; and between August 1583 and December 1584 some 16,000 petitions crossed his desk – an average of 1,000 a month, still over 30 a day.[62] In addition, the king read, and if necessary emended, the text of outgoing letters; and, at least until the 1570s, he seems to have signed in person every order, however minor, issued in his name.[63] On one occasion he informed his private secretary: 'I did not call you in today so that I could get through my paperwork – the least of which was to sign some 400 signatures'.[64] By the 1580s, according to the Venetian ambassador:

> I am reliably informed by someone who frequents his private apartments that he is never idle, for besides his desire to read himself all the incoming and outgoing correspondence of all areas, and from all the ambassadors and ministers of his vast dominions . . . , and besides the many prayers which he says, he writes every day with his own hand more than a ream of letters, between billetes, consultas and orders, which he constantly sends to his councillors, judges, secretaries and ministers in this way, and countless other secret business that he handles with other individuals. It is hardly to be believed how much time he spends in signing letters, licences, patents and other affairs of grace and justice: on some days it amounts to 2,000 [items].

By this time, the king in fact dictated many of his decisions on consultas (often to Mateo Vázquez), adding only his initials, and he used a stamp to sign routine correspondence. In 1594 he began to allow his son and heir to sign orders for him, and after 1597 he rarely put pen to paper. For most of his reign, however, in the words of an English spy, writing formed Philip's 'common occupation, and thereby he dispatcheth more than any three secretaries; and in this manner with his pen and purse governeth the world'.[65]

Governing the world with his pen took a heavy toll. 'I have 100,000 papers in front of me . . .', one frenetic note to a secretary began, while another ran: 'So far I have not been able to get free of these devils, my papers, and I still have some to deal with tonight; and I shall even take some to read in the countryside, which is where we are going right now.'[66] At times, the pressure of work drove him to despair. One night in 1578 he complained:

I have just been given this other packet of papers from you, but I have neither the time nor the strength to look at it. I will not open it until tomorrow. It is already after ten o'clock and I have not yet had dinner. My table is full of papers for tomorrow because I cannot cope with any more today.

Later that same year he lamented that so many 'matters have come up that cannot be neglected, I do not believe that any human resources would suffice to deal with them all – especially not mine, which are very weak and getting weaker every day with all the things that have to be done'.[67] A few years later he faced so many decisions that his temper got the better of him:

Some things are going to have to wait, because everything cannot be done at once. Try and do something to hold them up because I cannot take any more. Anyone who looks at how I spent today will see that just two men detained me for more than two hours and left me with more papers than I can manage in many more [hours]. So I am shattered: God give me strength and patience.

The dossiers nevertheless continued to arrive and repeatedly kept Philip from his dinner (normally served at nine o'clock):

It is ten o'clock and I have neither eaten nor lifted my head all day – as you can see by the size of the dossier addressed to Zayas [joint secretary of state]. So you should send the package from Hernando de Vega [president of the council of the Indies] back to me tomorrow . . . because [just now] my eyes and head cannot take any more.[68]

Long before the typewriter, the Xerox machine and the word-processor, Philip was drowning in a sea of paper, and as the reign advanced he tried on various life-jackets. In the 1560s he instructed his secretaries to make a précis of long letters – even from his beleaguered lieutenants in the Netherlands – because he could not find time to read them in full. By the 1570s he received as a matter of routine a summary of the main points of each letter so he could see at a glance whether he wanted to read it. Since the burden of paperwork still increased, however, the pressure on the king continued to grow: 'I have never seen so many papers mount up as now,' he complained in 1584.[69] The following year, therefore, he began to

rely upon a small permanent 'steering committee' of senior ministers to review –
and above all to condense – the dossiers that required his consideration: at first the
Junta de Noche (the 'Committee of the Night', with Vázquez as secretary), then
from 1588 the Junta de Gobierno (the 'Government Committee') and later the
Junta Grande (the 'Big Committee'). In essence, these bodies received consultas
from all the councils (except the council of State) and prepared a brief summary,
together with recommendations, so that the king could immediately see the
problem, the council's proposed solution, and his senior advisers' suggestions for
action. Those who wrote directly to the king were now urged to 'use as few words
as possible' because he no longer 'dared to look' at long papers.[70]

Philip still insisted on taking all decisions in person. According to the French
ambassador in 1588: 'The king is as assiduous and all public affairs pass through
his hands, without him trusting or delegating to anyone – as if he were still forty
years old.' He worked with two illuminated clocks 'day and night always before
his eyes' and 'he lived with such regularity and precision that his daily actions and
occupations were counted and determined by minutes'. The pressure nevertheless
remained relentless. One day in 1587 the king lamented that while he had been
working on one dossier his valets had brought in 'ten or twelve more', and in the
course of four days in 1596 the Junta Grande forwarded to the king no fewer than
fifty-five consultas, each one requiring numerous decisions.[71] Even in August
1598, the last month of his life, the king reserved some important decisions for his
personal attention and, given his utter prostration, serious delays resulted: immediately after his death, his son ordered all councils to resolve forthwith the
mountain of petitions from individuals which had gone unanswered because of the
late king's 'continuous ailments and other infirmities'.[72]

The balance of evidence nevertheless suggests that, throughout his reign,
Philip II managed to devote immediate attention to really important items. Thus
in May 1586, as he struggled to deal with the havoc wrought by Drake's raid in
the Caribbean, the king ordered Vázquez to make sure that he saw only papers
about defence issues 'rather than about individuals, unless it is something urgent'.
In June 1588, preoccupied with getting the Armada to sea against England, he
commanded the council of Finance to discuss ways of finding the necessary funds,
and 'to deal with nothing else, and to meet for no other purpose'; and he ordered
his other ministers in Madrid to 'moderate their dispatch of papers for some days'.
If this did not happen, Vázquez should delay all incoming mail 'until we have
been able to get on top of these other matters which are so important'.[73] The
'priority mail' system sometimes created its own problems: later that same year
the king's spirits sagged when he received a package of papers by express messenger. 'These urgent dispatches destroy me', he sighed, 'because they stop me
from doing the things I had planned to deal with today.' Nonetheless, he handled
the pressing issues at once, putting his other files to one side.[74]

Many of the king's servants remained unsympathetic. Scarcely had Philip come
to the throne than his cousin and principal military commander, Emmanuel
Philibert of Savoy, complained that the king tried to do too much in person; and

in 1571 Don Diego de Córdoba, a prominent member of the king's entourage, regretted that life at Court had degenerated into 'papers and more papers, and the number grows every day' because the king 'writes memoranda every hour, and even when he is getting up, eating or retiring his [valets] come in with papers . . . that, in the end, do not amount to anything'. Three years later, Don Diego commented that 'His Majesty has been working in recent days even more than usual in reading and writing papers, until they come out of his backside (may Your Lordship forgive me) . . . because on Saturday morning at 3 o'clock he had terrible diarrhoea'; and when in 1575 rumours spread that the king might lead an expedition to Algiers in person, Córdoba fervently hoped he would go, 'so that for a while he would stop working with so many papers. Certainly it is sad to see what he is doing to himself'.[75]

So why did he do it? Philip's administrative style – with its insistence on keeping the central government compartmentalized, on transacting everything in writing and on reserving so many matters for his own scrutiny – has drawn much criticism from historians as well as from contemporaries. Those with direct experience of governing might be less harsh; indeed, many other statesmen have adopted similar practices. To take two twentieth-century examples, in the 1930s President Franklin D. Roosevelt deliberately created overlapping organs of government and divided authority among them, often entrusting them to men of clashing temperaments in order to ensure both that his subordinates would always turn to him for decisions and that he got advance notice of the choices that had to be made. As in Philip's case, this created enormous pressures on the chief executive. Thus Roosevelt's decision to establish two separate agencies to handle new public works policies meant that he had to deal with all competing claims, and between 1935 and 1938 'something like a quarter of a million individual projects – ranging from suspension bridges to sewing circles – passed . . . across the President's overcrowded desk'. In 1944, when forty-seven war agencies reported directly to him, Roosevelt once exclaimed: 'The details of this job are killing me'; but he was prepared to pay that price in order to retain the power to make the decisions that mattered to him.[76] Likewise, when Winston Churchill became British prime minister and minister of defence in 1940 he introduced several administrative procedures that resembled those of Philip II. On the one hand, he transacted as much business as possible in writing and 'spent very little time interviewing people . . . [A]ll had to address him in writing, and his replies or instructions came back in writing'.[77] At an early stage Churchill informed the War Cabinet:

Let it be very clearly understood that all directions emanating from me are made in writing, or should be immediately afterwards confirmed in writing, and that I do not accept any responsibility for matters relating to national defence on which I am alleged to have given decisions unless they are recorded in writing.

These 'directions' covered far more than national defence. In the words of a close collaborator:

> The stream of messages, covering so wide a range of subjects, was like the beam of a searchlight ceaselessly swinging round and penetrating into the remote recesses of the administration so that everyone, however humble his range or function, felt that one day the beam might rest on him and light up what he was doing. In Whitehall the effect of this influence was immediate and dramatic. The machine responded at once to his leadership.

Admittedly some of Churchill's concerns seemed trivial ('Could trophies taken in the First World War be reconditioned for use? . . . What was to be done with the animals in the [London] Zoo in the event of bombardment?') and although 'nobody complained that he neglected the vital for the insignificant', as with Philip II 'there were those who lamented his preoccupation with detail in matters great as well as small'.[78]

The king's constant 'preoccupation with detail' stemmed not only from a desire to retain control over decisions, but also from a deep suspicion that his ministers would attempt either to deceive him or to withhold unwelcome information. Ambassador Donà of Venice warned his masters that 'by nature, [the king] is both very prudent and very suspicious', and in his 'Relation' to the Senate at the end of his embassy in 1573 he repeated that Philip never entirely trusted anyone: 'They say that the king suffers from the same malady as his father: that is, suspicion.' Likewise, Cristóbal Pérez de Herrera (who had known the king well) claimed shortly after the king's death that Philip 'was a great friend of secrecy'. Even the adulatory biography of Lorenzo van der Hammen – one of the first to be published in Spain – admitted that 'suspicion, disbelief and doubt formed the basis of his prudence'.[79]

Once again, many later statesmen have been praised for showing a healthy distrust of their subordinates; others have made serious blunders because they did not. An influential and well-informed study of recent occupants of the White House states that 'Presidents are always being told that they should leave details to others. It is dubious advice.' Rather,

> To help himself he must reach out as widely as he can for every scrap of fact, opinion, gossip, bearing on his interests and relationships as President. He must become his own director of his own central intelligence . . . [O]n the one hand, he can never assume that anyone or any system will supply the bits and pieces he needs most; on the other hand, he must assume that much of what he needs will not be volunteered by his official advisers.[80]

In Philip's case, suspicion and secrecy seemed to become ends in themselves. This tendency emerged with particular clarity in the king's voluminous correspondence with Mateo Vázquez: 'You and I must be like confessors,' he told Vázquez on one occasion, and the 'arch-secretary' frequently received orders to transcribe documents – even intercepted items not addressed to the king – 'so that no one knows', or to engage in a secret correspondence with one councillor about the conduct of another.[81] Philip once told Vázquez mysteriously that a matter 'should be handled with much secrecy and dissimulation, so that not only will what is under discussion not be known, but not even that anything is being discussed'.[82] 'Secrecy and dissimulation' indeed formed one of the commonest expressions in the king's vocabulary, and many people found it frustrating. According to Ambassador Fourquevaux:

> He is not a prince who says what is in his heart; rather, he is one of the greatest dissimulators in the world. I can certainly say – because his own ministers say it – that he knows how to pretend and conceal his intentions better than any king . . . up to the time and the hour at which it suits him to let them be known.[83]

Philip also suspected that his officials, if not subjected to ceaseless supervision, might either embezzle money or in other ways abuse their power. Spain already possessed two standard procedures to ensure administrative probity. On the one hand, all executive officers had to submit as a matter of routine to a period of scrutiny, known as a *residencia*, immediately after their turn of duty: during this public process, which lasted up to two months, anyone could press charges and the judge (normally the official's successor) was obliged to investigate each one. On the other hand, whenever the crown suspected malfeasance, it established a more systematic and searching review carried out in secret: the *visita*. A viceroy once compared *visitas* with 'the little dust storms that commonly blow up in the squares and the streets, with no other result than to raise the dirt, straw and other refuse there, and let it fall down again on the heads of the people', but he exaggerated: the procedure – or just the threat of one, for a *visita* could be created without warning at any time – undoubtedly helped to deter and discover corruption, inefficiency and oppression.[84] The crown exported both processes from Spain to the Americas (where over sixty *visitas generales* of various institutions in the colonies took place between 1524 and 1700), to Spanish Italy (Philip ordered a *visita general* for the administration of the duchy of Milan in 1559 and again in 1581, both lasting for several years) and to the Netherlands (where the entire Spanish administration underwent a searching scrutiny between 1594 and 1602).[85]

These techniques served to maintain relatively high standards among royal officials in the far corners of the empire. The king also made efforts to ascertain (or at least to insinuate that he had ascertained) detailed information even on his ministers at Court. According to a papal diplomat, Philip 'was so well informed and advised, not only of every detail concerning his royal household but of what goes on in his whole Court and his various dominions, that it is amazing. He even knows what every minister here eats, and how he spends his time.'[86] More

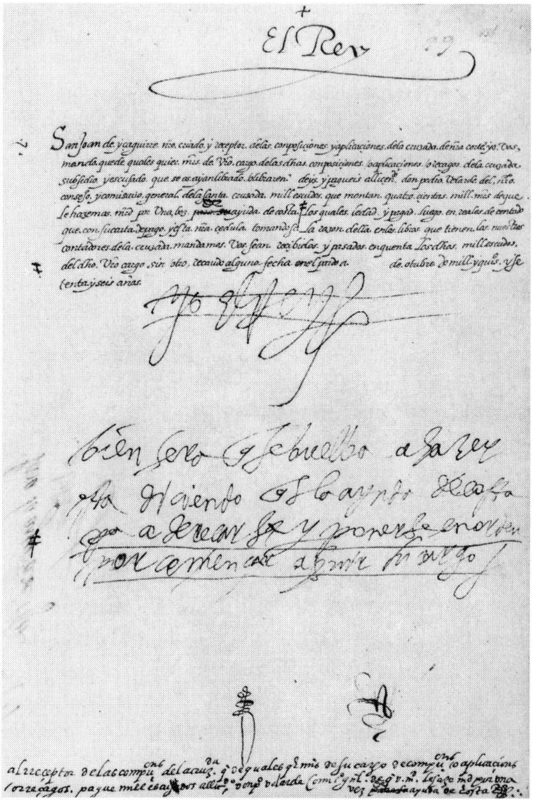

Plate 8 Philip II corrects his paperwork. In October 1576 a routine order to reimburse 1,000 escudos to an official for out-of-pocket expenses came across the king's desk. Philip affixed his 'stamp' (a new device to save him having to sign every document himself) but then noted that the reason for the payment had been omitted. He therefore crossed out his signature and wrote out the phrase to be added. Since several hundred documents like this could require the king's approbation in the course of a day; it seems remarkable that he had time to spot and correct such errors and ambiguities.

important, thanks to his insistence on reviewing everything himself, officials could never be sure what the royal eye might spot, and so no doubt they exercised caution both in carrying out the king's commands and in feathering their own nests.[87]

Philip regarded very few matters as lying beyond his own personal competence. One of them concerned the law: thus when in 1587 a secretary asked what steps should be taken to deal with the apocalyptic preaching of Miguel de Piedrola, a Madrid 'plaza prophet', the king snapped back: 'Since I am not a lawyer, I do not know what to say about such things'.[88] On other occasions he claimed that he could not make sense of either the calligraphy or the language of a document, and so could not make a decision (although he usually asked his ministers to remedy these defects so that he could handle the matter in person later on).[89] Philip intervened personally in virtually every aspect of government. He spent hours clarifying – or trying to clarify – the documents he read, both incoming and outgoing. He sometimes crossed out a neatly written order prepared for his signature because he had spotted some ambiguity or inaccuracy, with the curt, schoolmasterly phrase 'Do it again [*Buélbase a hazer*]' (Plate 8); at other times he

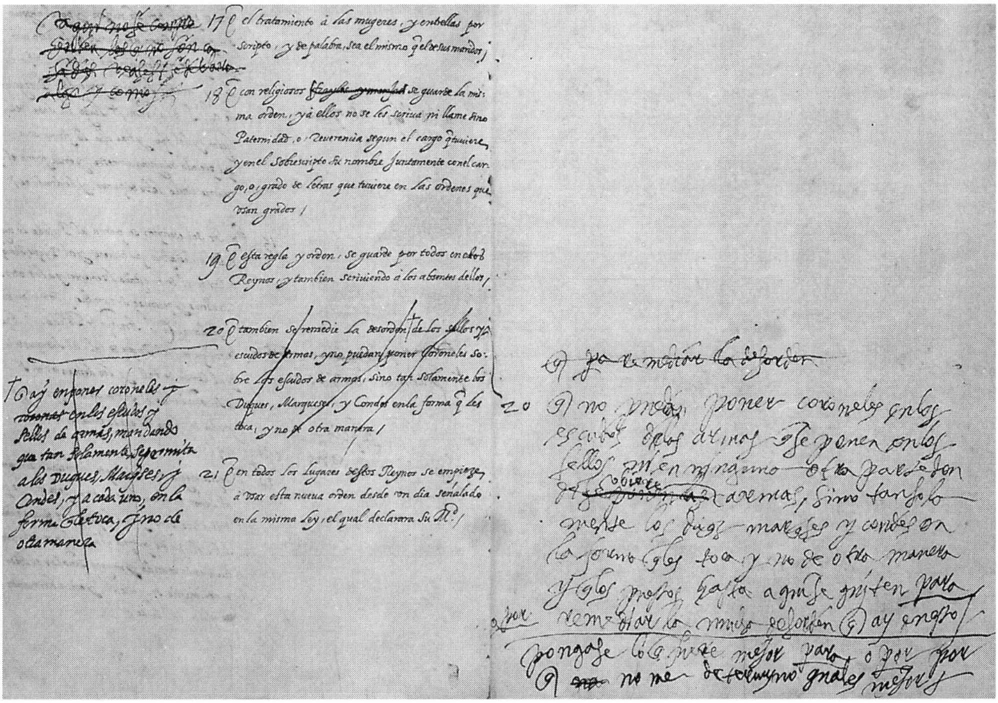

Plate 9   Philip II gives up trying to correct the 'Proclamation on etiquette'. Philip spent a great deal of time preparing the *Pragmática de las cortesias* issued in 1586, which reduced the elaborate styles of address that had arisen in Spain. This page shows one of the final drafts, but still the king remained dissatisfied. He tried to amend clause 18, on how to address members of religious Orders, but thought better of it; then he moved to clause 20, on who could put a coronet above the coat of arms on their seals. First his private secretary Mateo Vázquez added some corrections (lower left), then the king crossed out both original and emendations and entirely redrafted it (lower right) – only to stumble over the syntax.

corrected errors in the letters he received, or annotated the final version of outgoing dispatches.[90] In 1585–86 he meddled extensively with at least six drafts of the 'Proclamation on etiquette', which, among other things, reduced his own titles from 'Sacred Catholic Royal Majesty' to 'Sire', until eventually even he was at a loss for words. In the clause that determined the weighty issue of who should have the right to place coronets on their seals, a clause that he had already drafted and redrafted several times, he finally gave up on the syntax and told his secretary: 'Put whatever seems best – "para" or "por" – because I cannot decide' (Plate 9).[91] He also insisted on deciding for himself a host of other apparently inconsequential matters: the disposition of church benefices (such as those vacated by the death of Cardinal Granvelle); matters of palace etiquette (who should be allowed to enter which room; who should travel in which coach; how he should be greeted on official visits) and architecture (what each room in the various royal palaces should be used for); and who should serve in his household (even down to who should be chosen as cook for his children's kitchen, a post which could attract up to twenty applicants).[92]

Perhaps the king's obsessive concern with these specific issues of ecclesiastical patronage, court precedence, protocol, lodgings and personnel, can be explained by their intrinsic sensitivity – the 'Proclamation on etiquette', for example, provoked outrage among both courtiers and ambassadors when it was published, and the pope threatened to excommunicate the king and put his proclamation on the Index.[93] Furthermore, contemporaries still expected their kings to attend to all business of state in person, just as they had always done. Once the amount of business to transact increased ten- or fifteen-fold, however, this assumption became unrealistic. 'We write and send couriers so much that I do not know how we have time to do anything else', as one of the king's frustrated secretaries put it.[94] Admittedly this transition affected all early modern European rulers – Elizabeth's ministers also complained about their mounting workload (p. 226 below) – but Philip exacerbated the problem through his incorrigible urge to meddle. His ministers often tried to bridle their master's enthusiasm to know and do everything. 'I am sorry to fatigue Your Majesty with such trifling matters . . .', one ventured in 1562, but to no avail: 'They do not fatigue me, they delight me!' the king replied. Philip sometimes seems to have put pen to paper just for the sake of it. One day in 1565, having already written twice to one of his secretaries, he suddenly thought of something else: 'In both of the notes that I sent to you today I wanted to say something that I will tell you now, but I kept on forgetting, although I had it on the tip of my tongue [*teniéndolo en el pico de la lengua*].' And what was this urgent piece of information? That he had decided not to send a copy of the trilingual edition of the Bible to the Escorial, because the library there already had one. Two years later he laboriously encrypted a lengthy letter himself because he did not trust anyone else to do it, and on another occasion he transcribed in person parts of two letters received from an agent in England so that only the extract, not the entire document, could be forwarded to a minister.[95] Late one night, Philip began a long note to Mateo Vázquez to say that: 'I still have some things to do, and I am very tired, so I do not think I will see you tonight. But let me tell you some things now . . .' Three and a half holograph pages followed.[96] The king could spend an entire paragraph speculating whether a word might be missing from a letter of instruction; he might labour to improve the translation of a report written in French; and he once scribbled an entire page to his secretary smugly drawing attention to his alertness when he spotted a 'remarkable error' in a recent papal brief (the cover page claimed it referred to one thing but the document itself dealt with quite another).[97]

The king believed that he always knew his business better than anyone else. In July 1559, when he came under intense pressure from his Netherlands advisers to stay in Brussels, and from his Spanish councillors to return, Philip angrily rejected a new paper of advice and ordered: 'This letter will not be seen by the council: show it to nobody . . . I only want to do what I know is best for me – which is to go [back to Spain] – without going around to seek the advice of anyone.' Twenty years later, when a minister proposed that the council of State be consulted about a crucial move to end the Dutch Revolt, 'His Majesty said no, because these were matters which they [the councillors] would not understand because they had no information about the Netherlands . . . So it would be best to take the decision first and then tell the council.'[98]

The attractions of creating a system of government that resembled a 'panopticon', in which only the person at the centre can see everything, are obvious; but so are the dangers. Modern theories of corporate organization emphasize the need for the chief executive officer to possess two key qualities: a clear vision and the ability to delegate. First and foremost, all corporate leaders must define clear objectives for their enterprise, develop a plan for achieving those objectives, and then systematically monitor progress against the plan, adjusting it to circumstances as necessary. Corporate leaders must therefore ask the 'open questions' – what, when and why – and visualize how the enterprise should evolve over the next few years. In addition, however, they must choose and coach subordinates to realize these goals, and then delegate to these men and women the task of achieving them. Corporate success depends upon granting a broad measure of autonomy to the leaders chosen and trained by the CEO. Under no circumstances should he or she try to micromanage. Policy and operations must be kept entirely separate: leaders set goals and give directions while managers implement them and generally encourage efficiency. The worst form of corporate organization, according to modern theory, is the 'crisis management' model, in which the CEO attempts to do everything in a dictatorial and secretive manner, reduces employees at all levels to simple functionaries and then, overwhelmed by such a burden of responsibility, restricts the goals of the organization to the negative aim of coping with each successive challenge and trying to avoid mistakes – sometimes termed a 'zero-defects mentality'. Unfortunately for his monarchy, this became the precise style of leadership adopted by Philip II at various critical junctures during his reign.[99]

Admittedly the pattern was not uniform. The king almost always had a clear idea of the objectives for which he strove – justice, the good of his vassals, and the advancement of God's cause and his own (see Chapter 3 below) – and often sponsored impressive efforts of rationalization and planning to help achieve them. Thus in 1568 he initiated simultaneous measures to overhaul and simplify the legal system of both the Netherlands and the Americas (p. 9 above) and the following year, with his permission and support, a massive work entitled *The laws of the realm* (*Leyes del reyno,* later known as the *Nueva Recopilación*) published all the laws in force in Castile, plus some 300 royal proclamations. It remained the standard legal code in all royal courts until 1805. In 1582, just after his coronation as king of Portugal, Philip commissioned a similar codification of all the laws in force: *The Philippine Ordinances* (*Ordenações Philipinas*) went to the printers in 1593 and remained in force for half a century.

Throughout his reign, Philip also excelled in selecting capable subordinates to carry out his strategic plans. The difficulty of this part of CEO's duties is often underestimated, for someone who succeeds at one level of command may prove incompetent at another, and often the only way for a leader to discover the abilities and weaknesses of individual personnel is to try them out in new tasks. Philip normally entrusted his fleets to men who had made war their profession: Don García de Toledo, who commanded the successful relief of Malta (1565), had led galley squadrons since 1535 and held several important land commands; Pedro Menéndez de Avilés had commanded amphibious expeditions to the Netherlands, convoys sailing between Spain and the Caribbean, and the Florida expedition (1565–66), before being appointed to lead the king's Atlantic fleet in 1574; and Don Alvaro de Bazán (later marquis of Santa Cruz and, from 1584, captain-general of the Atlantic Fleet) had led a galley squadron in many Mediterranean campaigns (including Lepanto) and masterminded the naval side of the conquest of Portugal (1580) before taking charge of the victorious combined operations to the Azores (1582) and Terceira (1583). Even the duke of Medina Sidonia, the king's controversial choice to succeed Santa Cruz as commander of the Armada, had spent most of his adult life helping to prepare the dispatch of the annual Indies fleet from Andalusia, and in 1587 had responded vigorously and prudently to Drake's raid on Cadiz. (In at least one regard the king's choice proved inspired: Medina arrived in Lisbon in March 1588 to find the Armada in chaos, yet he managed to lead it to sea just two months later.)[100]

The same willingness to recognize and reward talent wherever he saw it marked Philip's military appointments. Although the duke of Alba could boast grandee status, he had been personally groomed for high command by Charles V: he was a professional soldier to his fingertips. Most of the king's other commanders likewise possessed extensive military experience, especially those trained by Alba in Italy and the Netherlands, and most of the exceptions were blood relatives whom the king evidently assumed would automatically excel in military and naval command.[101] Thus Philip's half-brother, Don John of Austria, had never seen war on either land or sea when the king appointed him captain-general of the Mediterranean fleet (1568 and 1571–76) and of the forces raised to suppress the revolt of the Alpujarras (1569–71). In 1577 Philip justified sending his nephew, Alexander Farnese prince of Parma, to assist Don John as commander-in-chief in the Netherlands despite the opposition of the council of State in Madrid on two grounds: 'because my brother insists on it so much, and because I believe he can be of service, judging by what I have heard of his person up to now'. When Don John died, the king immediately appointed Parma – who had fought at Lepanto and elsewhere – to succeed him.[102] As commanders, both men triumphantly vindicated the king's expectations (although Philip had taken care to surround them with expert advisers). Moreover Philip showed admirable fidelity towards those to whom he had entrusted his armed forces. Although he recalled Alba from the Netherlands in 1573 when he lost confidence in the duke's ability to end the Dutch Revolt, he resisted pressure to impose some punishment for the 'excesses' alleged against his regime in Brussels; and although many blamed both Parma and Medina Sidonia for the Armada's failure, the king was not amongst them (see pp. 229–32 below).[103]

Philip also spent time 'coaching' his chosen subordinates. He recognized that a command structure is not a mere piece of architecture but also a collection of relationships, and he took great care both to avoid appointing 'people on whom we cannot rely to assist us when need arises' and to 'mentor' those whom he did trust. When Parma's parents both died in 1586, for example, the king wrote a warm note of condolence, urging his nephew to 'accept it with Christian constancy' and 'to look after your own health', adding in his own hand, 'Although you have lost your parents within such a short time, I am still here to take their place'.[104] Such mentoring possessed special importance in Philip's Monarchy because, to save time, he expected his senior officials to move around from one posting to another without coming back to Court for a briefing. Admittedly the duke of Alba remained at Court for six months after his appointment as governor-general of the Netherlands in 1566, discussing with the king all aspects of the situation and the role expected of him; Viceroy Don Pedro de Toledo delayed his departure for Peru in 1568 in order to participate in the discussions of the 'Junta Magna', convened to devise solutions to the various problems of the Americas (p. 9 above); Pedro Menéndez de Avilés received personal instruction from the king before leaving to command the High Seas fleet in 1574; and Don John of Austria returned to Madrid at Christmas 1574 to discuss with the council of State the appropriate strategy and funding for the Mediterranean campaign he was to direct the following year.[105] These examples, all from the first half of the reign, proved exceptions, however. Far more typical was the experience of Don Luis de Requeséns who in 1571, after serving as Don John's deputy in the Alpujarras and at Lepanto, went directly to govern Lombardy and then on to the Netherlands two years later (being told that instructions on how to carry out his most difficult role as Alba's replacement would be waiting for him in Brussels). Likewise Requeséns's brother Don Juan de Zúñiga served as ambassador in Rome in 1568–79 and then as viceroy of Naples in 1579–82 without returning to Spain, and the count of Olivares served successively as ambassador in Rome (1582–91), viceroy of Sicily (1591–95) and Naples (1595–99) without setting foot in Spain. Even within the peninsula, the king saw no need to brief his senior commanders in person: Medina Sidonia received orders to travel directly from his home near Seville in 1588 to take command of the Armada in Lisbon; like Requeséns, he was told that he would find full Instructions at his destination.[106] Philip also normally declined to attend strategic discussions among his advisers. In 1588 Martín de Bertendona, in charge of one of the Armada's squadrons in Lisbon, exclaimed: 'How I wish Your Majesty could be present for our debates, because it would be very different to discuss matters in Your presence, where we could not fail to see the truth, than to discuss it here, where those who understand [what they are talking about] and those who do not all give their opinion, and sometimes shameful things are heard'. But Bertendona wished in vain.[107]

Indeed except for the 1550s, when he yearned to lead his armies to victory in person, Philip deliberately kept away from his troops during operations. Although he went to Andalusia during the Morisco rebellion (1570), Portugal after its annexation (1580–83), and Aragon after its revolt (1592), he visited only areas in which hostilities had entirely ceased. Admittedly in March 1588 he told Medina Sidonia that 'If I were not needed so much here, to provide what is necessary for that [enterprise] and for many other things, I would be very pleased to join [the Armada] – and I would do so with great confidence that it would go very well for me.'[108] This remarkable statement seems to have been pure hyperbole, however, intended to encourage a dispirited commander. Philip's normal feelings on the subject emerged in a letter written somewhat earlier to his daughter Catalina, duchess of Savoy, when it seemed that her husband intended to lead a military expedition in person:

> The duke must not be present nor even near [his troops]. Although I say this partly because I wish him life, and because you need him alive, I believe I am more moved by concern for his reputation, for if the enterprise succeeds, he will gain as much prestige if he is absent as if he is present (and perhaps even more if he is absent); but if he fails in what he plans (which can happen, since these things are in the hands of God, not men), then his loss of prestige will be far greater if he is present.[109]

Perhaps: but more successful warlords – including his father Charles V and his rival Henry IV in the sixteenth century, Lincoln in the nineteenth, Clemenceau and Churchill in the twentieth – have found that there is no substitute either for seeing the situation in a theatre for oneself, or for building bonds of confidence and trust with theatre commanders through regular personal meetings. Without question, in the 1560s Philip should have moved back to the Netherlands to restore the shattered authority of his government; and in 1587–88 he should have returned to Lisbon in order to ensure that everything possible was done to get the Armada to sea on time.

Naturally, no CEO can be in all places of crisis at once, but (again like other warlords) Philip should also have entrusted important instructions and policy advice to confidential aides who could convey the spirit as well as the letter of such communications to those whom he could not brief in person. That had been common practice during the 1550s, when vital messages about strategy exchanged between Philip (whether in Spain, England or the Netherlands) and his father had normally been carried by leading councillors such as Alba, Ruy Gómez and Erasso, who received extensive briefing on the matter so that they could explain any obscurity in the written message.[110] In later years, however, even critical communications – such as the final instructions to Parma and Santa Cruz, the commanders chosen to execute the Enterprise of England – were entrusted to mere couriers who knew nothing of the contents.[111]

This notable change in governmental practice, coupled with the king's reluctance to leave the comfort of his Castilian palaces, deprived him of a vital element of effective decision-making: reliable feedback. Without either seeing for himself, or hearing verbatim accounts from trusted aides, Philip became entirely dependent on what he was told by the subordinates to whom he had communicated the orders (and he did not always listen even to them: see pp. 195–7 below). He could therefore never test whether the assumptions on which his decision had been made remained valid, or whether they had become obsolete and needed to be re-examined. Time and again, ignorance of the facts on the spot caused the king to persist 'in a course of action long after it ha[d] ceased to be appropriate or even rational', producing many serious and costly errors.[112]

Perhaps Philip's greatest failure as a CEO, however, lay in his inability to understand his finances. Admittedly, he sometimes showed great foresight. Thus in 1582 and again in 1583 he ordered his treasury officials to prepare an imperial budget for the two succeeding years, in order to assure a more stable and predictable flow of money to all his undertakings, and he built up a 'strategic reserve' of coined money in both Milan and Madrid. Although the decision to overthrow Elizabeth Tudor late in 1585 undermined these prudent measures, the Enterprise of England also gave rise to much long-range planning because the king recognized at the outset that it would take two years to mobilize the necessary resources (see Chapter 6 below).[113] Normally, however, Philip complained bitterly that he could not comprehend the analyses sent to him by his financial officials: 'I have already told you on other occasions how little I understand of these matters – and in this case I certainly understood very little, almost nothing, of this paper, although I have read it more than twice.' Sometimes he sent back impenetrable memorials unread, with a curt dismissal: 'The author must understand this [paper] better than I do, because I cannot understand it at all'; or 'I read this paper by Juan Fernández [de Espinosa], but not the others, because I do not understand anything about them and would not know what to say.'[114] He recognized that financial considerations 'are so many and so important that truly I feel dismayed at not knowing what to do with them, since it is so important to succeed in making the right decision', but he often struggled in vain.[115] 'To be frank,' he complained after reading a particularly complex proposition,

> I do not understand a word of this. I do not know what I should do. Should I send it to someone else for comment, and if so, to whom? Time is slipping away: tell me what you advise. Or would it be best for me to see the author (although I fear I shall not understand him)? Perhaps if I had the papers in front of me it might not be too bad.[116]

In 1588 the shortage of funds became so acute that the king began to receive a special statement every Saturday from his treasury advisers to show how much cash they had in hand – the grand total was often less than 30,000 ducats, the cost of the Armada for just one day – and how many obligations remained outstanding. Philip II, generally reputed the richest monarch in the world, then spent several hours 'balancing his cheque book' in order to decide which of his debts he could afford to pay, and which he would have to defer (see Plate 26, p. 199).[117]

Philip's 'zero-defects mentality' and his fear of failure, reflected in his repeated statements to ministers that 'it is so important to get it right', in part stemmed from a sense of inferiority.[118] The careful education provided by Charles V for his son and heir in the art of government heightened Philip's awareness of the need for success in order to prove himself worthy of his father and his mission, and of the disgrace of failure. Shortly after Charles's abdication, a declaration of war by the French and excommunication by the pope in 1556 severely shook the young king's confidence and he pleaded with Charles 'to help and aid me, not only with his advice and counsel, which is the greatest strength that I could have, but also with the presence of his person and authority'. Philip begged his father to leave the monastery to which he had retired and resume governing, because 'when this alone becomes known to the world, I am entirely convinced that my enemies will behave differently'.[119] In the event, the spectacular defeat of the French at St Quentin and the successful blockade of Rome soon provided reassurance; but although the king's confidence in his ability to govern grew with age, deep insecurity still manifested itself in smaller, more personal matters. For example, when in 1566 (at the age of 39) he became a proud father for only the second time, he very much wanted to carry the baby to the font for baptism in person, but worried about how best to do it. A few days before the ceremony he practised carrying a doll of the right size and weight around; and yet, despite the rehearsal, apparently fear of making some mistake during the actual ceremony at the last moment made him surrender the honour to a relative.[120]

Crises, when so much more can go wrong, dramatically increase the stress level of people in power, and Philip was no exception. Thus in spring 1565, with trouble brewing in the Netherlands and a Turkish attack in the Mediterranean imminent, he confessed to one of his ministers that 'the burden of business weighs on me in such a way that I do not know what I am saying or doing'. He nevertheless continued to push himself to the limit, working on his papers until 'one o'clock [in the morning], and everyone around me is going to sleep'. A little later he lamented:

> I am so busy and so deprived of sleep, because I need to spend most of the night going over the papers that other business prevents me from seeing in the day. So I am just beginning on these papers of yours – those of today and of yesterday – now, which is after midnight, because I could not do so before.[121]

Ten years later, humiliated by defeats in both the Mediterranean and the Netherlands, and with his treasury almost empty, the king again pushed himself to exhaustion. '[I am writing] with my eyes half closed,' he began one letter; 'Although the tiredness is less than yesterday, my eyes are in a terrible state,' he noted in another.[122] When, in spite of all his efforts, his cause continued to lose ground, he assured his secretary that: 'If God does not perform miracles – which we, for our sins, do not deserve – we will be unable to maintain ourselves for [many more] months, let alone years. Nor do I have the vitality or health to withstand the worry I feel about this, and thinking about what may happen – and in my lifetime. So, fearing this, I am making haste with my Will.' A few months later, with the situation still bleak, the king felt 'in a foul mood and fit for nothing' as he read reports of discontent among the taxpayers of Castile, on whose increased contributions 'depends the remedy for everything, if a remedy is still to be found, although in truth I doubt it because everything seems about to fall apart. How I wish I could die, so as not to see what I fear.' Opening the other letters on his desk depressed him even further. 'When I saw how they started, I read no further,' he wrote, adding gloomily: 'If this is not the end of the world, I think we must be very close to it; and, please God, let it be the end of the whole world, and not just the end of Christendom.'[123] Before long Philip felt 'so exhausted' that he even gave up on his paperwork: 'Since I have not sent you anything, you can imagine what must be happening here at the moment. Certainly I do not know how I stay alive.'[124]

No aspect of the policy-making process can long remain immune to the effects of stress. According to a recent study:

> Stress can impair attention and perception: important areas of the crisis situation may escape scrutiny, conflicting values and interests at stake may be ignored, the range of perceived alternatives is likely to narrow but not necessarily to the best option, and the search for relevant options tends to be dominated by past experience.

For Philip, as for later statesmen, acute stress in times of crisis increased 'cognitive rigidity' and thus served to impair 'the ability to improvise and [to] reduce creativity, diminish receptivity to information that challenges existing beliefs, increase stereotyped thinking, and reduce tolerance for ambiguity leading to a premature termination of the search for information'. Time and again, when under stress the king first became obsessed by concern for the present and the immediate future, at the expense of longer-range considerations; then he fixed upon a single approach, continuing to use it even when its viability had become questionable; and finally he abandoned all attempts to find alternative strategies and instead resigned himself to the inevitable.[125]

At times, physical illness also prevented Philip from transacting business during a crisis. Some of his ailments were perfectly normal: arthritis ('I got up late today because I had gout in one foot'), indigestion ('I have stomach ache today') and, of course, lots of colds. 'I cannot handle any further business just now', he informed his secretary one day, 'because I have a terrible cold – which I already had last night – and I am certainly not fit to read or write.' And when more papers nevertheless arrived, the king lost his temper and scribbled on the dossier (as he sent it back) 'Look at the medicine I get to cure my cold!'[126] More frequently he complained about the tired eyes, at least until he began to wear spectacles in the 1580s. His dependence on them is illustrated by his decision one day not to take any business papers with him on a trip because 'my sight is not as good as it used to be for reading in a coach' and 'I am ashamed to wear glasses in public'. He also tried to read less and began to insist that no more work should be sent to him late at night: 'I was already in bed last night when this [package] came', he scolded his secretary, 'and, as you know, my doctors do not wish me to see any papers after I have eaten dinner'. On another occasion he complained that reading so many papers made him cough: 'I have got a terrible cough and cold, and I am convinced it comes from the papers because as soon as I pick them up I start to cough'.[127]

Here, clearly, Philip found excuses to avoid work, and it seems suspicious that upon the arrival of inconvenient or unwelcome news he sometimes took to his bed with either a physical complaint or one of the migraines he described as 'a terrible head [*ruin cabeza*]'. The king himself admitted this: in 1573 he told the duke of Alba that 'just as I think that the concern I feel for events there [in the Netherlands] is partly to blame for my fever, so I am convinced that the good news you sent recently has cured me'.[128] But, whatever the causes, the consequences of the king's illnesses could be extremely serious, especially as he grew older. Thus in February 1587 Philip (almost sixty years old) went to bed, disabled by arthritis, and there he stayed until the following July. Even though Drake's raid on Cadiz in April called for urgent measures, Philip's incapacity dramatically lengthened the delays inherent in his administration and by May the pressure of unresolved business had become acute. In the revealing phrase of the king's valet: 'God grant complete health and long life to His Majesty. His pain afflicts me, because when he gets it in his leg we feel it in our heads, and everything stops.' A few days later, the secretary of the council of War, desperately trying to organize not only the departure of the Armada but also imperial defence in the wake of Drake's raid, complained bitterly that 'a lot of time is being wasted in consultations, and His Majesty is slow to respond; so we are losing time that cannot be recovered'. He suggested that more matters be delegated to his council for decision, 'because the situation is extraordinary and it seems reasonable that the manner of transacting business should be extraordinary too'.[129] But nothing seemed to change. In June, again according to the king's valet: 'My heart melts to see His Majesty so tired and weak, and the machinery of state in suspense'; and, two weeks later, 'His Majesty's eyes are still running, his feet tender, his hand recovering; and the world is waiting.' After a few weeks of this, the king's ministers became as exhausted as their master: 'His Majesty says that, because he is so very tired he cannot return the papers that he has tonight', reported a member of the Junta de Noche, and then added: 'To tell you the truth, sir, we are all falling to pieces.'[130]

High stress occasionally induced a psychological crisis. Early in 1569, following the death of his son and heir Don Carlos and of his wife, Elisabeth de Valois, and with the Moriscos of Granada in open revolt, the king apparently longed to abdicate. In a remarkable letter to his chief minister he confided:

These things cannot fail to cause pain and exhaustion, and, believe me, I am so exhausted and pained by them, and by what happens in this world, that if it was not for the business of Granada and other things which cannot be abandoned, I do not know what I would do . . . Certainly I am no good for the world of today. I know very well that I should be in some other station in life, one less exalted than the one God has given me, which for me alone is terrible. And many criticize me for this. Please God that in heaven we shall be treated better.

The failure of his policies in the Netherlands in 1574–75 and against England in 1588 produced renewed bouts of deep depression.[131]

Surely, however, a few stress-induced 'dark nights of the soul' were inevitable in an active political life that spanned half a century. It would be remarkable – perhaps even sinister – if a statesman who ruled a global empire almost constantly at war never experienced a moment's doubt, depression, even despair. Moreover, these anguished episodes have only come to light because of the king's remarkable habit of committing his innermost thoughts to paper as they occurred to him, and the equally remarkable chance that so many of those papers have survived. The significant issue is not whether – or even how often – Philip felt unequal to the tasks of state that confronted him, but the extent to which these and his other problems compromised the ability of the 'largest brain in the world' to act as an effective chief executive: to deal with the rising tide of information that flowed over his desk, to formulate a coherent strategy for the world-wide Monarchy over which he ruled, and to delegate authority to his lieutenants so that they could implement that strategy effectively.

2 *Distance: Public Enemy Number 1?*

'From Plato to NATO', Martin van Creveld has suggested,

> the history of command in war consists essentially of an endless search for
> certainty . . . To make certain of each and every one of a vast majority of details
> . . . each and every one of which must be coordinated with all the others in
> order to achieve optimum results – that is the purpose of any command system
> . . . Certainty itself is best understood as the product of two factors: the amount
> of information available and the nature of the task to be performed.[1]

The 'amount of information available' has not, however, remained either constant
or regular over time. On the contrary, developments in information technology
have periodically transformed both its quality and quantity – silicon chips and
satellites in the late twentieth century; telegraph and telephone in the nineteenth
century; regular couriers and resident ambassadors in the sixteenth century. All of
these improvements in information technology possessed the potential to confuse
as well as to clarify, because they generated – at least for a time – more data than
the human mind could handle.

Oswald Spengler wrote (somewhat patronizingly) of the pressure of events that
he believed had precipitated World War I: 'In the Classical world, years played no
role, in the Indian world decades scarcely mattered; but here the hour, the minute,
even the second is of importance. Neither a Greek nor an Indian could have had
any idea of the tragic tension of a historic crisis like that of August, 1914, when
even moments seemed of overwhelming significance'. And within Europe, the
onset of the crisis seemed incomprehensible without the tensions created by
the latest information technology. According to Sir Edward Satow, a diplomat
writing in 1917 as the war entered its fourth terrible year:

> The moral qualities – prudence, foresight, intelligence, penetration, wisdom –
> of statesmen and nations have not kept pace with the development of the means
> of action at their disposal: armies, ships, guns, explosives, land transport, but,
> more than all that, of rapidity of communication by telegraph and telephone.

These latter leave no time for reflection or consultation, and demand an immediate and often hasty decision on matters of vital importance.[2]

In Philip II's day, of course, communications functioned far more slowly than this; indeed much has been made of the relatively slow pace at which news then normally travelled. The king himself, in his final paper of advice to his son, blamed many of the problems he had encountered on 'the distance that separates one state from another'; while Fernand Braudel later suggested that in the sixteenth century 'distance was "Public enemy number 1"' and that it explained a good part of the decisions taken by the Prudent King.[3] Nevertheless, the problem can be exaggerated. Although news travelled slowly by today's standards, it still often arrived too fast and too copiously for the good of its recipients. If one substitutes 'couriers and diplomats' for 'telegraph and telephone', Sir Edward Satow's analysis becomes as appropriate for Philip II and Elizabeth Tudor as for Theobald von Bethmann-Hollweg and Sir Edward Grey. The 'matters of vital importance' that arrived on their desks at times of crisis did not allow them, either, adequate 'time for reflection and consultation'.

Philip II could count on a postal service of unprecedented quality. The Taxis family created a direct courier link between Spain and the Netherlands through France, with 106 relay stations (each provided with at least two horses), soon after Philip of Burgundy became king of Castile in 1504. In 1516 his son Charles signed a contract with the Taxis company that established guaranteed times for various services to link him with his representatives in Germany, Italy, Spain and the Netherlands; and two years later, Charles and Francis I of France agreed to accord the service diplomatic immunity, permitting all couriers on official business free passage across their territories in time of peace, and every week scores of messages passed safely along the chain.[4] From 1560, an 'ordinary' courier left Madrid for Brussels (and vice versa) on the first day of each month (and later on the 15th also), with additional 'extraordinary' messengers dispatched as necessary, while a similar service linked Madrid with both Rome and Vienna. In 1567 the duke of Alba established a new postal chain, with two horses at each relay station, from Milan to Brussels during his march to the Netherlands along what would later be called 'the Spanish Road', providing an alternative link with Spain whenever civil war rendered passage through France unsafe. In 1572 he began to send two copies of all his letters to the king: one through France and the other down the Spanish Road to Italy and from there to Barcelona by sea.[5]

Charles Howard Carter, a noted diplomatic historian, has suggested that:

> Foreign policy is fundamentally a matter of decisions made; that the quality of those decisions (and thus of the foreign policy) is governed by the quality of the men making them and by the quality of the information on which they are based; and that the quality of the information is even more important to the quality of the decisions than that of the men.[6]

The 'superior quality' of Philip's information emerges clearly in the correspondence of envoys from other states who repeatedly found themselves at a disadvantage at the Court of Spain because Philip knew about developments before they did. On 15 October 1569, for example, Philip 'with a smile on his face' announced to Ambassador Fourquevaux of France at an audience that his master's army had won a major victory over the Protestants (at Moncontour, near Poitiers, on the 3rd): a special messenger from an agent in Lyon had just arrived with the news. Confirmation of the victory came on the 21st with an express courier sent by the Spanish ambassador in France. Fourquevaux, however, only heard the news from his own government later. A few months afterwards, wondering nervously whether his courier carrying important documents had reached the French Court, Fourquevaux learned from the Spanish secretary of state that he had: Philip's ambassador in Paris had just reported his safe arrival. In 1576 the Florentine envoy suffered acute embarrassment when news arrived in Madrid from the king's agents in Italy that two members of the ruling Medici family had, within a matter of days, accused their wives of adultery and murdered them. Unfortunately for the diplomat, both ladies belonged to the powerful Toledo dynasty (headed by the duke of Alba) and for the next four weeks he remained 'the most confused man in the world', lacking a letter from his master to confirm (let alone explain) the story, forced to hide behind pillars and curtains in the royal palace every time he sighted Alba or one of his relatives.[7]

More awkwardly – and far more compromisingly – foreign ambassadors sometimes lacked a courier of their own to carry an urgent letter, and therefore entrusted the dispatch to a messenger in Spanish service. For example, when in 1571 Charles IX reproached Fourquevaux (on grounds of cost) for using express messengers too frequently, the diplomat reported virtuously that he had, in five and a half years, sent only eighteen express couriers, plus an extra fourteen cheaper agents who had carried his letters on foot to Bayonne, where they entrusted them to the regular French postal service. Many of his other urgent letters, he asserted, had left with the Habsburgs' couriers going to Paris *en route* for Brussels or to Lyon *en route* for Vienna. He made no comment on how the practice might have compromised the security of communications with his master, although it may help to explain how the Spanish ambassador in Paris always seemed to know the contents of Fourquevaux's dispatches.[8] The experience of Ambassador Leonardo Donà of Venice (1570–73) followed much the same pattern: Philip and his ministers always seemed better informed. On 6 June 1571 a royal express messenger from Rome brought news that the representatives of Spain, Venice and the Papacy had just concluded a League dedicated to the defeat of the Ottoman Turks eighteen days earlier – a very fast journey. A papal courier arrived with confirmation on the 10th but Donà himself only received word from his principals on the 28th. Later that year, although he was the first person at Court to receive a full account of the victory of Lepanto, when he arrived to share the news with the king he discovered that Philip had got word of it half an hour before. Like Fourquevaux, Donà also regularly allowed Spanish couriers to carry his urgent dispatches (mostly unciphered); sometimes he even delivered them in advance to Secretary of State Antonio Pérez so that they would be on hand whenever the king's express messengers left for Italy. Even the mysterious disappearance of two packages sent in this way failed to shake Donà's trust: he judged that his news simply could not wait for the 'ordinary' courier and never seems to have considered the possibility that Pérez might have been secretly reading his mail.[9]

Communications between the Court and its overseas possessions normally followed the rhythm of the annual trading convoys. Carracks left Lisbon for Goa every March or April, in order to catch the westerly monsoon upon entering the Indian Ocean in July and arrive in September or October (hence the volumes of royal letters in the Goan archives are called to this day 'Monsoon Books'); ships carrying the replies would try to leave India each December or January, so as to gain the easterly monsoon back. Monsoons also dominated the sailings of the 'Manila galleon', which left Acapulco each spring and reached the Philippines about three months later, returning the following year in June or July but taking about six months (due to the prevalence of easterly winds). Fleets of up to 150 vessels left Seville for the Caribbean each summer and returned the following autumn. Even letters written in Mexico to coincide with the departure of these fleets rarely arrived in Spain in under four months; those from Lima, Peru, often took between six and nine months, and those sent from the Philippines might take up to two years.[10]

Urgent news could often be sent at other times, however. For example, Philip informed his new overseas territories of his succession to the Portuguese crown in letters signed at Badajoz on 7 November 1580: they reached Goa, the capital of Portuguese India (by overland courier to Ormuz, at the mouth of the Persian Gulf, and thence by ship), on 1 September 1581, and Malacca (by ship) on 23 November. Remarkably, by the time the letters reached Macao, in March 1582, news of Philip's succession had already arrived via Mexico and Manila. 'Advice ships' could also cross the Atlantic rapidly at any time. In 1585 a vessel carrying priority mail left Seville for Panama in April and got there and back in three months and twelve days – although a letter reporting the feat noted that 'this is the fastest speed that has been seen for many years'. Unpredictability also characterized communications with the Far East: on 31 December 1588 the bishop of Malacca sat down to reply to royal letters written in spring 1586, spring 1587 and spring 1588, which had all arrived at the same time.[11]

These aberrations make it very difficult to reconstruct with confidence the average pace of routine correspondence between the king and his ministers, but the records of the Audiencia of the viceroyalty of New Spain (Mexico) shed an unexpected beam of light because they occasionally registered full details of communications received from the king. Thus in August 1583 a courier arrived in Mexico City from Veracruz (where the annual trading fleet had just arrived) bearing four letters and forty-six orders (cédulas) from the king addressed either to the Audiencia or to the viceroy (who had just died, so the Audiencia opened his mail too: see Figure 2). The letters, dated June and July 1582 (having just missed the annual fleet of that year) and March and April 1583, answered missives sent from Mexico City between February 1580 and November 1582 – delays that stretched from nine to forty-two months. The cédulas likewise displayed strong variations in 'turn-around time': of the 46 received in August 1583, 7 had been issued the previous May (a lapse of only three months), 20 in April (a lapse of four months) and 7 earlier that same year (a lapse of between five and eight months); 7 more had been signed in the second half of 1582, and so missed the previous year's fleet which left Spain early in July. But why one cédula signed in 1581 and four signed in the first half of 1582 should only have been sent on the fleet that left in June 1583 remains a mystery. Clearly some part of the king's government had under-performed. In November 1590, the Audiencia again recorded the details concerning the arrival of royal mail – this time only two letters and five cédulas. The letters, signed the previous June and July, dealt with matters referred to the king between February 1587 and February 1590 – once more a surprisingly

Figure 2   On 27 August 1583 four letters and forty-six orders from the king arrived in Mexico City. They had come to the port of Veracruz on the annual convoy from Spain, and there a royal courier conveyed them at top speed to the capital. Nevertheless much of the information contained in the royal letters must have seemed 'stale' since they replied to letters written in Mexico between February 1580 and November 1582, a delay of between nine months and three-and-a-half years. The orders (cédulas) displayed the same variation; one of those received in August 1583 had left Philip's desk on 31 May 1583, less than three months before, but another had been signed on 5 March 1581, over two years before. Source: AGNM *CRD* II/15–36.

Communications between Philip II and Mexico in 1583

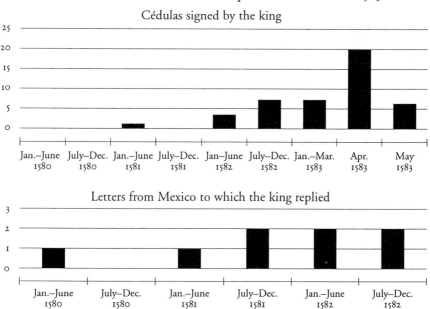

Cédulas signed by the king

Jan.–June 1580	July–Dec. 1580	Jan.–June 1581	July–Dec. 1581	Jan.–June 1582	July–Dec. 1582	Jan.–Mar. 1583	Apr. 1583	May 1583

Letters from Mexico to which the king replied

Jan.–June 1580	July–Dec. 1580	Jan.–June 1581	July–Dec. 1581	Jan.–June 1582	July–Dec. 1582

wide range; while the incoming cédulas dated from November 1587, May 1588, November 1589 and February and July 1590 – a lapse of between four months and four years.[12]

'Normal efficiency' for the communications of Philip's Monarchy in Europe is equally hard to establish. Of thirty-two letters from the Court received by the Spanish ambassador in Paris during the year 1578, the fastest took only seven days and the slowest forty-nine; sixteen letters (half of the total) took between ten and fourteen days. So far no systematic study based on government archives has been attempted, but a meticulous analysis of the time taken by some 10,000 letters to reach Venice earlier in the century offers a useful frame of reference (see Table 2). Despite the marked variation between the fastest and slowest recorded times, the data (perhaps unsurprisingly) show that the closer the location, the more letters arrived at the 'normal' (that is, the most common) time: only 12 per cent from London and Valladolid, rising to 26 per cent from Naples and 38 from Rome.[13]

These striking contrasts reveal that the principal informational problem that confronted governments in the sixteenth century was not so much that messages came late (although this could of course cause difficulties) but rather that their arrival proved totally unpredictable – a classic example of the 'friction' later described by Carl von Clausewitz (pp. 205–6 below). It confirms Philip's own observation that 'couriers either fly or sleep' and explains why on occasion he dreamed of an 'air mail' service: in 1576, when he appointed Don John of Austria (then in Naples) to take command in the Netherlands, Philip wistfully observed, 'I heartily wish that the man who carries this letter could have wings to fly – and you too, so that you could get there more rapidly'.[14] In fact, important information often did travel extremely fast: in 1566, the 'year of wonders' in the Netherlands, individual couriers managed to convey vital messages along the postal chain between Brussels and the Court of Spain in eleven, ten and, in one case, only nine days (an average speed of 150 kilometres each day).[15] News of the victory of Lepanto in 1571 covered over 3,500 kilometres in just under twenty-four days (again an average speed of over 150 kilometres a day); and the following year a galley carrying letters from Philip's fleet in Messina reached Barcelona – almost 1,500 kilometres away – in only eight days, having 'flown rather than sailed'.[16] A ship carrying news of the French attempt to capture Antwerp in 1583 reached Lisbon in eight days; another bearing information on Parma's preparations for the invasion of England) in 1588 arrived in only five.[17] But these were all exceptions, and men recorded them precisely because they occasioned surprise.

Relatively few messengers from the Netherlands took less than two weeks to reach the Court of Spain and sometimes – due to broken bridges, bad weather, bandits, sickness or the lack of horses at a postal relay station – they might take three weeks, three months, sometimes even longer. A Spanish bishop in 1557 complained that a letter from the Netherlands had taken so long to arrive that 'it could have gone to America two or three times and still got here sooner'; the king's decision in July 1573 to order a switch from a policy of 'hard war' against

News arriving at Venice between 1497 and 1522

Place of origin	Number of letters	Shortest time (in days)	Longest time (in days)	Normal time (in days)	Normal cases	
					Number	percentage
Brussels	138	9	35	10	24	17
Burgos	79	11	42	27	13	16
Constantinople	365	15	81	34	46	13
London	672	9	52	24	78	12
Naples	682	4	20	8	180	26
Paris	473	7	34	12	62	13
Rome	1,053	1.5	9	4	406	38
Valladolid	124	12	63	23	15	12
Vienna	145	8	32	13	32	22

Table 2 The 'Diaries' of Mario Sanudo, a town busybody, recorded the date on which some 10,000 letters arrived in Venice and also the date on which they were written. From this raw data Pierre Sardella calculated the longest, the shortest and the 'normal' time taken by letters from various destinations between 1497 and 1522. His findings revealed 'normal' to be a meaningless category, especially for more distant locations: thus of the 124 letters received from Valladolid, the administrative capital of Spain, only fifteen arrived after the 'normal' time lapse of 23 days – others took less than two weeks and one took over two months. Such unpredictable communications undermined government planning. Source: Braudel, *Mediterranean*, I. 362.

the Dutch to one of conciliation took six weeks to reach the Netherlands – too late to be implemented.[18] Even worse could happen. In 1568, two Spanish couriers were murdered in southern France and their letters (from ministers in Brussels and Paris) opened and destroyed. From time to time, the chronic insecurity of the roads in the south of France compelled the Spanish ambassador in Paris to entrust dispatches to ordinary travellers going on foot.[19] The same uncertainty character-ized other postal routes. In August 1570 couriers reached the Court of Spain almost simultaneously from Sicily, Rome, Florence and Venice, but their arrival followed a whole month during which no messages at all had got through from Italy; in 1582, and again in 1591, Spanish couriers were assassinated as they travelled between Naples and Rome; and on most postal routes letters were occasionally intercepted and read. Even communications over shorter distances could sometimes languish: in the Netherlands, in the crisis year of 1566, the governor of the outlying province of Friesland, trying to get help from the central government in Brussels, found that 'messengers on foot go faster'; while in Spain communications between the Court and the city of Palencia (scarcely 200 kilo-metres away) likewise went on foot – and could take two weeks! The command system of the Spanish Monarchy had literally slowed to a walk.[20]

Bad weather and natural disasters could delay communications even further, especially by sea. For example, over the winter of 1567–68 adverse weather meant that letters from Philip's ambassador in London took three months to arrive in Madrid (and the king's replies took a further two); while Spanish attempts to support rebellion in Ireland repeatedly ran into difficulties because vital messages took so long to reach their destination. Thus a courier bearing promises of assistance to the earl of Tyrone left Madrid on 19 August 1596 but only delivered them on 7 October, while the earl's reply did not reach Madrid until 26 November; and although another Irish chief wrote to Philip in May 1596, and the king signed his reply in August, it only reached Ireland in June 1597.[21] On the continent, in 1574 Spanish ministers in Brussels reckoned to receive replies to dispatches sent to Rome via the ordinary courier within six weeks but in 1575 the onset of plague in northern Italy meant that they had to wait seven and even eight weeks. In 1581 letters sent by Philip's ambassador in Prague, then the emperor's capital, to Lisbon, where the king resided, took about one month in summer but almost two in winter.[22]

Some officials deliberately exploited postal delays and irregularities in order to buy time before they implemented an unpopular command, and some have drawn attention to the maxim, common in the Habsburg Monarchy, 'I obey but I do not execute [*obedezco pero no cumplo*]'. Thus in 1569 the Audiencia of Mexico declined to carry out a direct order from the king to arrest 'one Espinola' for murder because the man's identity and forename were not given. But such controlled disobedience could only go so far: the following year the king supplied the missing data and called for immediate action, observing, 'You should not have had this scruple, since the said Espinola had committed such a [heinous] crime'. More seriously (and more effectively) the duke of Parma, faced by a royal demand in December 1585 to prepare a strategy for the conquest of England, stalled for as long as he could and when, four months later, he finally completed his assessment, he entrusted it to a personal messenger whom (he told the king) he would send 'by the most direct route': this, it turned out, involved travelling down the Spanish Road from Brussels via Besançon, Chambéry and Turin to Genoa, a sea crossing to Barcelona, and so to Madrid, arriving only after another two months, in June 1586 – by which time it was of course too late to implement the conquest that year.[23]

In fact, however, ministers rarely entrusted important communications to a single messenger: whenever delays or disruption threatened the postal service (for instance in wartime), vital letters went out in duplicate and even triplicate (attaching further copies of previous dispatches also became standard practice).[24] Moreover, news seldom travelled along only one route: data normally fanned out to numerous centres, to be relayed onwards to yet others, so that information that might move slowly by one channel might arrive relatively swiftly by another.[25] Thus in 1572, when a party of Dutch rebels captured first Brill and then Flushing, the duke of Alba (in Brussels) hoped to keep the news from the king until he had dealt with the problem: 'Affairs here are in a much worse state than I am telling His Majesty,' he confided to a relative at Court. Even before he wrote these words, however, letters from merchants and other ministers in the Netherlands containing full details of the setbacks had reached the king; and when Alba eventually brought his master up to date, he received a stern rebuke for the delay in doing so. The duke's (rather feeble) response was that 'since the merchants and other people who like to write are active in many areas, it does not surprise me that Your Majesty should have received news of what happened at the Brill and on Walcheren before I wrote about it.'[26]

The duke had a point: people in the sixteenth century thirsted for 'the latest news' and did not like waiting for it. In 1561 the viceroy of New Spain informed the magistrates of Veracruz (the port of entry for all vessels arriving from Spain) that the merchants of Mexico City had complained that 'it is customary to release [in Veracruz] the letters and orders that come from the kingdom of Castile for the said merchants and other private individuals only two or three days after the orders of His Majesty have been dispatched here, so that their addressees should not see them before the Royal Audiencia sees its own letters'. The merchants claimed that these delays prejudiced their business interests, and so the viceroy decreed that the first or second courier leaving Veracruz with the king's letters could also carry private correspondence if their mailbags had space; but, he continued, on reaching Mexico City the couriers must still 'come straight to my palace and bring me and the Royal Audiencia the letters and packages from His Majesty for me or for them first'. Any courier breaking this order would be banished from the capital for two years on the first offence, and would receive 100 lashes and perpetual banishment for the second. It would be hard to find better testimony to the value placed upon up-to-date information both by Philip's ministers and by his subjects.[27]

Thanks to the efforts of hundreds of couriers, Philip II disposed of unprecedented varieties (as well as quantities) of information on recent developments. At the summit stood the data gathered by his ambassadors. Spain maintained the largest diplomatic establishment of any state to that date with permanent embassies in Rome, Venice, France, Genoa, Vienna, the Swiss cantons and Savoy (also in Lisbon until 1580 and in London until 1584) as well as temporary missions elsewhere when occasion required. Philip's envoys, most of them younger sons of the nobility (many with university, administrative or military experience), seemed able to penetrate almost every secret: in the 1560s, embassy officials in either London or Paris managed to obtain and copy a map of the French settlements in Florida (which greatly assisted Pedro Menéndez's subsequent campaign to destroy them), and in the 1580s the papal cipher clerk, the English ambassador in Paris and the comptroller of Elizabeth's household (to name but the most prominent) all accepted money from Philip's diplomats.[28] The king received a report from each ambassador at least once a week, if not more often, and he expected to receive information on absolutely everything. When in 1563 his envoy at the council of Trent failed to mention in his letters that an issue of interest to Spain had been discussed, the king rebuked him at some length: 'I cannot refrain from telling you now that I am amazed that something of such importance should have happened without you finding out, because I believe that nothing, whether great or small, should be done in that council without you knowing all about it.' The king also expected his viceroys, generals and other commanders to keep him meticulously informed of developments. During his campaign to conquer Portugal in 1580, the duke of Alba wrote progress reports to the king almost daily (and on some days he sent two, three and even four letters, with more to the leading ministers at Court); while somewhat later the marquis of Santa Cruz (commander of the Armada in Lisbon) maintained his own spies in England, and sent their (sometimes superior) reports to the king for comparison with those received from his ambassador in Paris.[29]

Philip also expected his ministers abroad to correspond extensively with their colleagues. His instructions to a new ambassador to the Court of Savoy in 1595 stressed not only the need for regular correspondence with Madrid, but for 'continual' contact with the governors of Milan and Franche-Comté, the viceroys of Naples and Sicily, the governor-general of the Netherlands, and the Spanish ambassadors in Rome, Genoa, Venice and Vienna. Philip prepared a special letter for each of these officials, to be sent by the envoy on his arrival in Turin, enjoining them in the king's name to correspond with their new colleague. He also expected to receive copies of these exchanges himself.[30] Many ministers of the crown in fact already possessed good reason to exchange information. Some were close relatives: Thomas Perrenot de Chantonnay (Philip's ambassador in Paris and then Vienna in the 1560s) was Cardinal Granvelle's brother; despite their different surnames, Don Luis de Requeséns and Don Juan de Zúñiga were also brothers and wrote to each other several times a month (in 1573, when the king appointed the former to govern the Netherlands, Zúñiga drafted the various letters in which his brother tried to decline the poisoned chalice).[31] Others were clients: when in 1557 Zúñiga travelled to the Netherlands to serve the king for the first time, Requeséns wrote a letter asking Granvelle to look after him, since 'my brother is your great servant, and understands very well the obligation that we both have to serve you'. Aspiring courtiers later attached themselves to one or other of Philip's leading Spanish advisers, such as Ruy Gómez da Silva, the duke of Alba or Cardinal Espinosa (who kept a detailed register of promising young men, noting the names of their sponsors and the suitable jobs available).[32] Once appointed, all 'clients' made a point of keeping their patron well informed. In addition, in the 1560s Alba presided over an informal 'Academy' in Madrid which counted among its members a whole future generation of the king's servants: Idiáquez, Moura, Zúñiga, Silva and Olivares (to name just those who appear frequently in these pages) all belonged, and they seem to have maintained regular contact with each other for the rest of their lives, both in and out of ministerial office.[33] Thus the archive of Don Juan de Zúñiga, ambassador in Rome and later viceroy of Naples, contained thirty boxes of correspondence with his colleagues between 1571 and 1583; while Philip's ambassador to the Venetian Republic received over 1,000 missives from other ministers in 1587–88 alone.[34]

This extensive exchange of letters represented a massive investment, for each express courier carrying messages from the Netherlands to Spain cost 400 ducats, and each one from Sicily to Spain cost 360 (far more than the annual salary of a galley captain or a university professor). The total cost of express messengers dispatched by the central government averaged almost 3,000 ducats a month (equivalent to the wages of an entire infantry regiment) at the beginning of the reign, rising to 9,000 by the end, while maintaining just the postal chain between Brussels and Savoy cost almost 1,000 ducats a year by the 1580s. The remuneration of couriers normally constituted the largest item in the budget of every ambassador.[35]

Merchants, too, maintained their own communications network and exchanged political as well as commercial information. Simón Ruiz of Medina del Campo, for example, ran a commercial enterprise which grew tenfold in value between 1561 and his death in 1597, from 35,000 to 360,000 ducats – relatively modest by the standards of the later sixteenth century. Yet his correspondents resided in Portugal, the Netherlands, France and Italy (with a few in America and Germany) and Ruiz devoted two days of every month – the days before the 'ordinary couriers' left – to writing and dictating letters that would bring everyone up to date (often attaching to each a duplicate of the preceding dispatch, in case it had been lost, and sometimes sending up to five copies of important letters by different routes). His agents abroad reciprocated faithfully: they normally wrote at least every fortnight, with additional express messengers when something important for their master's business cropped up. They also kept in close touch with Philip II's ministers – especially after Ruiz began to lend money to the government in the 1570s, making it essential to monitor the fortunes of the Monarchy as well as the vicissitudes of the market. Their combined efforts eventually generated an archive of over 50,000 letters at Ruiz's headquarters in Medina del Campo and created a major clearing house for information on which the government could draw. The couriers of Ruiz and other merchants, as well as ordinary travellers, might also pick up and pass on extra news, much of which also reached the Court and helped to inform the king of events.[36] Finally, even though Philip condemned opening other people's letters as 'a sin again God', from time to time he sinned himself. He occasionally ordered mail to be intercepted and transcribed 'so that nobody will know, and keep a copy in case I should want it', or 'without a living soul knowing or seeing . . . even though the letters are not for me', and sometimes even 'in a script that no one will recognize'.[37] In 1590 Spanish agents secured four letters sent by the French envoy in Madrid to Henry IV; each was sent to a 'codebreaker' at Court, who forwarded his efforts to Philip.[38]

Most of these communications concerned time-sensitive material relating to an immediate problem, and some feared that they did not provide sufficient information for long-term decision-making. According to Fray Gerónimo de Mendieta, writing from New Spain in the 1560s, 'Your Majesty is like a blind man who has excellent understanding but can only see exterior objects . . . through the eyes of those who describe them to you.'[39] But this was an overstatement: although Philip had never visited the Americas (to which Mendieta specifically referred), between 1548 and 1559 he had spent a year in Germany, two years in England and almost five in the Netherlands (including an extensive tour through almost all the provinces). He had also visited Italy and crossed the Alps twice. In addition he travelled all over the Iberian peninsula, living (in all) for over three years in Aragon and for almost as long in Portugal. The king possessed a prodigious memory for what he had read and seen, on which many contemporaries commented, which assisted him greatly in keeping up with all the responsibilities of his office; and on occasion he used his personal knowledge of far-away people and places to devastating effect. When in 1574 the Inquisitor-General tried to dismiss some criticisms of the Holy Office, Philip retorted that 'in the past we all know that [abuses] have been numerous, and I can assure you that in Valencia I saw them with my own eyes'.[40]

Philip constantly sought to update and extend his personal knowledge, both about his own possessions and about those of his neighbours, 'through the eyes of those who describe them'. By way of example, in June 1588 the king signed a typical 'fact-finding' enquiry to the viceroy of Mexico. The viceroy had recently reminded the king that a special 'charity tax' levied on the native population financed the work of the friars and others who preached Christian doctrine in the countryside, but noted that 'with the diseases that have occurred among the said Indians since the year 1576 a large part of them have died, and although the tax yield has fallen and the number of those to be instructed has declined [the preachers] enjoy the same remuneration'. The viceroy therefore proposed that the stipends paid to the clergy involved 'should be reduced in proportion to the fall in the number of natives'. The king, however, demanded more information on every aspect of the case before reaching a decision. The fact that Philip and his ministers found time to launch this enquiry at a moment when they struggled to cope with the crisis caused by the Armada's unexpected return to Spain after being hit by a storm – and anxiously sought to save money wherever possible – is highly revealing. Even in 1598, with death fast approaching, the king found time to rebuke the viceroy of Portuguese India for failing to send on some letters received in Goa from the emperor of Ethiopia, because no one had been able to translate them into Portuguese. 'There is no shortage of people here who can do so,' he wrote irritably, and ordered that any similar communications in the future should be forwarded without fail.[41]

Furthermore Philip could call upon the personal knowledge of his well-travelled advisers: ministers Don Luis de Requeséns and Ruy Gómez da Silva and secretaries Gonzalo Pérez and Gabriel de Zayas had all accompanied Philip on his Grand Tour of Europe in 1548–51, and all but Requeséns had also been with him in England; the count of Olivares had been to England, fought in Italy and at St Quentin, and carried out a diplomatic mission to France before becoming ambassador in Rome, viceroy of Sicily and later Naples, and finally councillor of State; Don Juan de Idiáquez had served five years as ambassador in Italy before becoming secretary of state; the marquis of Almazán, an outspoken councillor of War, had previously represented Philip at the imperial Court and served as viceroy of Navarre; and Don Hernando de Toledo, another prominent councillor of War, had visited England and France, fought in Flanders and Italy, and served as viceroy of Catalonia. Francisco de Erasso, the duke of Alba and Cardinal Granvelle had all acquired first-hand knowledge of almost every part of western Europe: when the king sought advice in 1566 on the best way to travel from Spain to the Netherlands, Granvelle described and assessed every possible itinerary, by both land and sea, on the basis of his own personal experience.[42] The king and his councillors also possessed long institutional memories and frequently cited precedents and examples from the past – sometimes going back several decades. When in 1559 and again ten years later some suggested that France and Spain should conquer England jointly and then partition it, the duke of Alba vetoed the idea because 'recent' experience had shown that such arrangements would not work: he referred to the treaty of Granada in 1500 concerning the partition the kingdom of Naples between the two 'superpowers'.[43]

In addition, Philip set out systematically to collect new data about his possessions. In 1559 he set up simultaneously a 'General Visitation' for each of his three dominions in the Italian peninsula, partly in order to accumulate and collate information about them. Shortly afterwards he launched three related projects in his Spanish kingdoms. First, he sent out the Dutch artist Anton van den Wyngaerde to prepare a series of cityscapes: sixty-two finished views of some fifty Spanish cities, and preparatory sketches for several more, have survived, all executed from a slight elevation and in similar panoramic format (Plate 10).[44] To set beside these urban images Philip commissioned a second project: a complete map of the Iberian peninsula on an unprecedented scale. The principal

Plate 10   A view of Barcelona in 1563 by Anton van den Wyngaerde. The Flemish 'court painter' van den Wyngaerde came to Spain in 1561–62 and from then until his death in 1571 travelled around Spain and North Africa painting city-scapes. Sixty-two 'finished' topographical views of cities and towns survive, of which Barcelona (done, as the Latin inscription on the watchtower atop Montjuich states, 'from life') is one of the first. Philip intended to have them engraved and published, presumably in some sort of atlas, but they became scattered between Vienna, London and Oxford, remaining largely unknown until the nineteenth century. Fortifications dominate Barcelona: the tenth-century walls, with the famous 'Ramblas' beyond, and the fourteenth-century extension enclosing the Arrabal suburb. The impressive 'Atarazanas' (dockyards), where the royal galleys were made and maintained, lie at the city's southeastern corner.

cartographer, Pedro de Esquivel, professor of mathematics at the university of Alcalá de Henares and an expert in surveying, began work in the 1560s and, in the somewhat gushing appraisal of a contemporary,

> One could say without exaggeration that it was the most careful, diligent and accurate description ever to be undertaken for any province since the creation of the world . . . There is not an inch of ground in all of Spain that has not been seen, walked over or trodden on by [Esquivel], checking the accuracy of everything (insofar as mathematical instruments make it possible) with his own hands and eyes.

Esquivel left his work largely 'completed when he died, and His Majesty has it in his Chamber'.[45] This item today probably forms part of the remarkable atlas of twenty-one maps now in the Escorial library, the first (and most complete) of which covers the whole peninsula (Plate 11). The rest of the maps provide a series of sectional surveys, all done to the same scale, in which Portugal is the best covered and Aragon and Catalonia the worst. It is worth lingering over this achievement because, on a scale of 1:430,000 (similar to that of standard aeronau-

Plate 11   The Escorial Atlas: map of the whole peninsula. In the 1570s and '80s a team of cartographers, led first by Pedro de Esquivel and then by João Bautista de Lavanha and Juan López de Velasco, surveyed the entire Iberian peninsula – almost 500,000 square kilometres – and portrayed the results in an atlas of twenty-one sheets. The first map (shown here), although slightly skewed because the surveyors made no allowance for the curvature of the earth's surface, provided a remarkably accurate overview of the physical and urban geography of both Spain and Portugal. The rest of the atlas contained the largest European maps of their day to be based on a detailed ground survey.

tical charts today), the Escorial atlas contains by far the largest European maps of their day to be based on a detailed ground survey. No other major western state of the sixteenth century possessed anything like it, for where Apian's map of Bavaria, based on a survey carried out between 1554 and 1561, covered over 43,000 square kilometres, and Seco's map of Portugal (printed in 1560) covered almost 90,000, the Escorial atlas covered an area of no less than 497,000.[46]

The third of Philip's geographic projects for Spain consisted of a series of questionnaires, later known as the *Relaciones topográficas*, sent out to various communities in the 1570s. The idea seems to have originated with the royal chronicler, Juan Páez de Castro, who prepared a list of questions to be sent to each place in Castile requesting information about its geography, history, economy,

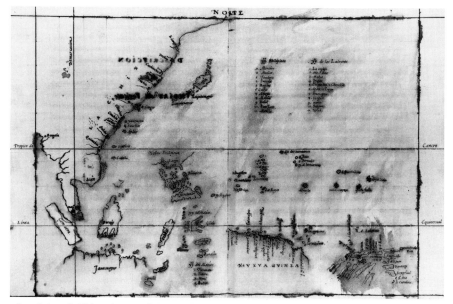

Plate 12   Juan López de Velasco's map of the Pacific. In 1574–75 Velasco, Philip's 'cosmographer and chronicler of the Indies', prepared a treatise containing all the knowledge – cartographic as well as written – on the location of the 'demarkation line' established in 1494 to separate Portuguese from Spanish overseas possessions. In the process, Velasco produced the first ever map of the western Pacific, running from Java to Japan. Although the map displays latitudes with surprising accuracy, all longitudes are remarkably favorable to Spain: thus Malacca is correctly shown just north of the Equator, but almost astride the 180° meridian (the line entitled 'demarcación'), implying that everything to the west 'belonged' to Spain. In fact Malacca lies only 103° East, so everything shown on this map actually 'belonged' to Portugal.

Plate 13   Disk recording the lunar eclipse of 17 November 1584. Velasco also played a key role in a project to establish longitude, and so 'fix' the demarkation line in the eastern hemisphere. Materials to record the lunar eclipse predicted for 17/18 November 1584 went out to various European cities and also to Mexico, Manilla and possibly Macao in the hope that a comparison of the local times at which the eclipse began and ended, and the moon's precise elevation above the horizon, would reveal the difference – and thus the distance – between them. On the night foretold, a team of astronomers in Mexico City duly recorded their observations on a series of disks drawn to the precise size requested by Velasco; unfortunately for his plan, however, the eclipse had already begun by the time the moon rose over Mexico, and in any case the clocks available were inaccurate. Fixing longitude had to wait a further two centuries, until the invention of chronometers capable of keeping accurate time at sea.

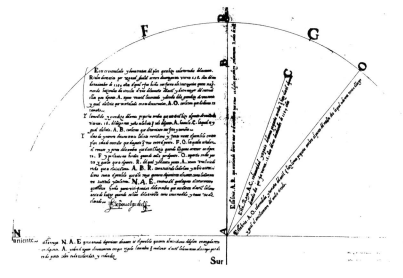

population and 'antiquities' as a prelude to writing a detailed history and description of the kingdom; but Páez died in 1570, before it could be distributed. Five years later, however, Juan de Ovando, president of the councils of Finance and the Indies and one of Philip's most energetic ministers, sent a questionnaire based on Páez's list to all communities in New Castile. Returns for some 600 villages, and for the city of Toledo, have survived in eight enormous manuscript volumes (at least five more of them once existed).[47] Ministers discussed extending the survey to Aragon and Portugal.[48]

At the same time, Ovando began to prepare similar questionnaires for the various communities of Spanish America (37 questions in 1569, 200 in 1571, 135 in 1573) and also dispatched scientists – botanists, zoologists, herbalists and cartographers (notably Francisco Domínguez) – to gather specimens, make drawings of the flora and fauna, and prepare maps of Philip's overseas possessions.[49] He also commissioned Juan López de Velasco, formerly Ovando's secretary and now 'royal cosmographer and chronicler of the Indies', to compile two works – 'A geography and general description of the Indies' and 'A demarcation and division of the Indies' – which displayed in cartographic as well as written form all data known about the western hemisphere. The two works, presented to the council of the Indies in 1574–75, contained surprisingly accurate maps of the Americas and the Caribbean, as well as the first map ever drawn of the western Pacific (Plate 12).[50]

The results of the questionnaires and of the surveys proved disappointing, however, and so in 1577 López de Velasco decided to send out a simpler list of fifty-five questions (printed this time) accompanied by a request for a map, a description of each community and – most ambitious of all – a calculation of longitude based on simultaneous observations of two predicted lunar eclipses. Once again a great deal of data flowed in, with numerous detailed descriptions, and almost 100 maps of individual communities.[51] No one, however, succeeded in calculating longitude – which the government desired both to improve cartographic precision and, even more, to establish accurately the division between the Portuguese and Spanish spheres of influence in east Asia (laid down by the treaty of Tordesillas in 1494 but only fixed for the western hemisphere) – so Philip's new 'Academy of Mathematics' organized one more attempt. Over the winter of 1582–83, experts prepared a package of materials for observing the lunar eclipse forecast for 17 November 1584 (including instructions on how to prepare recording disks of the same size: see Plate 13) and sent them in advance not only to Antwerp, Toledo and Seville, but also to Mexico City, Manila and perhaps even Macao. To assure the accuracy of the observations they also sent the noted Valencian astronomer Jaume Juan to Mexico well ahead of time in order to assemble the necessary instruments and liaise with the local experts. On 17 November 1584, right on schedule and with two clocks and a barrage of other instruments beside them, Jaume Juan and his associates recorded their observations of the eclipse on the roof of the archbishop's palace in Mexico City.[52]

Admittedly, these various ventures all failed to achieve the goals anticipated.

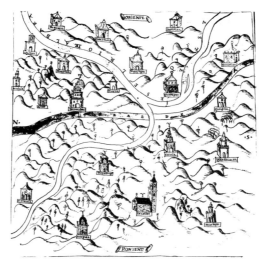

Plate 14   Map of Ixcatlan in Mexico. As 'cosmographer and chronicler of the Indies', Velasco was charged with preparing a detailed survey – economic and natural as well as geographic and historical – of Spain's American possessions. In 1577 he therefore sent out a three-page printed questionnaire asking for the same information from every community. Three of the fifty questions involved making maps: a sketch of the area showing the layout of the streets and plazas, and the main buildings, plus (for towns by the sea) a map of the coast and of the adjacent islands. Almost one hundred maps eventually came back, but only the few prepared by Europeans familiar with the same cartographic conventions as Velasco proved usable. The superb map produced by the corregidor of Santa Maria de Ixcatlan (Oaxaca province) looks just like an engraving, with 'east' clearly marked at the top and the 'Royal Road to Oaxaca' crossing the river Alvarado and snaking among mountainous communities (each one represented by a church).

Plate 15   Map of Muchtitlan in Mexico. Most of the maps prepared in response to the 1577 questionnaire were the work of native artists who used the cartographic conventions and 'picture writing' of the Aztec empire. Each of the thirteen settlements of Muchtitlan (Guerrero province) is symbolized by a conventional building, together with its name in both Spanish and image: thus at the lower left we find San Lucas Tepechocotlan, with a symbol (probably the one imposed by the Aztecs when they conquered the area and imposed their tribute) that shows a pot of fruit (*xocotli*) atop a hill (*tepetl*) – because Tepechocotlan means 'Place of the fruit hill' (-*tlan* means 'place of' in Nahuatl). No doubt Velasco failed to make any sense of this – or of the seventy or so similar cartographic representations by Nahua painters.

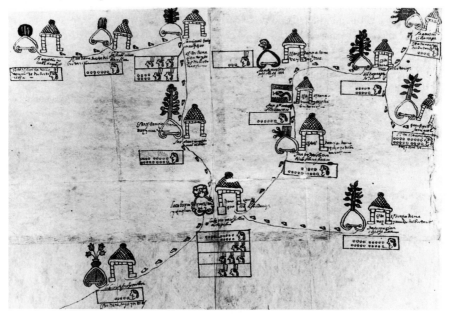

The king had been on the point of sending van den Wyngaerde's cityscapes to the Netherlands for engraving and publication when the Dutch Revolt broke out and prevented him; the 'Atlas of Spain', like the detailed history and description to be based on the *Relaciones topográficas*, remained incomplete and unpublished; in 1583 Francisco Domínguez had still not finished his maps of Mexico. In addition, much of the data actually sent from America proved unintelligible – especially the maps, most of them prepared by Indian cartographers who used unfamiliar conventions (see Plates 14 and 15) – and even Jaume Juan failed to make usable observations because, when the moon first became visible in Mexico, the eclipse had already begun and so he could only record its end (furthermore, given the inaccuracy of the clocks available, he could of course not be sure of the exact time anyway).[53] Nevertheless, despite these shortcomings, the combined impact of the various flows of information organized by Philip impressed everyone. In the awed phrase of an observer at the Court of Spain in 1566, writing to his master in the Netherlands: 'As Your Lordship knows, nothing happens there that is not immediately known here'.[54]

Why, therefore, did Philip fail to translate so much knowledge – so much more knowledge than any of his rivals possessed – into irresistible power? After all, as Michel Foucault once observed: 'Knowledge constantly induces the effects of power . . . It is not possible for power to be exercised without knowledge, it is impossible for knowledge not to engender power.' Yet Philip II's own officials made fun of his impotence, joking that 'If we have to wait for death, let us hope that it comes from Spain, for then it would never arrive', and examples of (and complaints about) the king's failure to take and communicate decisions abound in the surviving records.[55] In 1546, when Philip was barely twenty and had served as regent of Spain for only three years, some complained that 'he takes too long to deal with business', while in 1560 Philip's secretary of state reported: 'I have been ill these past few days, but that has not prevented me from attending to business punctually, since decisions are taken so slowly that even a cripple could keep up with them'. Five years later he became more specific, lamenting to a colleague that the king's 'natural condition is never to decide anything'; and indeed at precisely this time Philip deliberately refrained for six months from telling his regent in the Netherlands that he wished her to follow a tough line against heresy (actually, he scarcely wrote to her at all.[56] In 1571 Don Luis de Requeséns, then deputy commander of the Mediterranean fleet, fretted that 'the original sin of our Court – which is never completing or doing anything at the right time – has grown greatly . . . and is growing every day'. Four years later the same Requeséns, now struggling to suppress the Dutch Revolt at the head of an army of 80,000 men, claimed that he had not heard directly from the king for nine months, and protested that 'His Majesty delays so much in resolving all his affairs that he later has to do so without sufficient time or thought'.[57] Foreign observers agreed. According to the French ambassador in 1560, Philip's decision 'to be master, minister and secretary at the same time is a great virtue, but it produces such notable delays and confusion that all those who reside here to ask for something are desperate'. A decade later his successor complained that 'the decisions of the Spanish Court are so uncertain and take so long that those who think they will receive dispatches in a week will not get them within a month'. In 1577 the papal secretary of state, waiting in vain for the king to commit his resources to a descent upon Ireland, fumed that 'The sole cause of this dilatoriness is His Majesty's irresolution'.[58]

And yet Philip took scores of decisions each and every day throughout his long reign. On 31 August 1566 for example (admittedly after a protracted period of silence) a courier left Madrid carrying over 100 letters in French and Dutch from the king to various members of his administration in the Netherlands, while another courier carried additional letters in Spanish. A decade later Philip claimed to have signed 400 letters at a single sitting; in 1587 he sometimes signed over 20 letters a day just on Armada business; and in spring 1588 the daily total rose to almost 50.[59] Moreover he created or reformed no fewer than three archives expressly to conserve the documents generated and needed by his administration: while still regent of Spain for his father, he took steps to store state papers systematically in the castle of Simancas for the crown of Castile (1545) and in a purpose-built edifice in Barcelona for the crown of Aragon (1552); and in 1558 he ordered an archive to be opened in 'the church of St James of the Spaniards' in Rome to conserve all papal briefs and bulls in his favour. He also ensured that both important and routine papers got deposited in these repositories where, when need arose, his ministers could always consult or copy them.[60]

Many explanations have been offered – both by his contemporaries and by historians – for Philip's notable delays in decision-making. The commonest one advanced at the time concerned the king's insistence on trying to do everything himself. In 1584 Cardinal Granvelle, after working in Madrid for five years, often in close contact with the king, complained bitterly that

> I see in all matters these delays, so pernicious and in so many ways prejudicial to our own affairs, including the most important ones, which become lost to view with so much delay. And the reason is that His Majesty wants to do and see everything, without trusting anyone else, busying himself with so many petty details that he has no time left to resolve what matters most.

Somewhat later the papal nuncio in Spain complained that 'His Majesty wants to see and do every single thing himself, yet that would not be possible even if he had ten hands and as many heads'. The most comprehensive indictment came in 1589 from Don Juan de Silva, who had served the king for over half a century as page, soldier, ambassador and councillor:

> We have known for years that the detailed attention that His Majesty devotes to the most trifling things is a subject for regret, because when a man finds things to do in order to avoid working, it is what we call a pastime; but when

he works in order to find things to do it cannot be given the name it deserves. It is certainly true that His Majesty's brain, although it must be the largest in the world, like that of any other human being, is not capable of organizing the multitude of his affairs without making some division between those that he should deal with himself and those that he cannot avoid delegating to others. It is equally true that His Majesty does not make this distinction . . . Instead he leaves nothing entirely alone and takes from everyone the material that should be delegated (concerning individuals and details), and so does not concentrate on the general and the important because he finds them too tiring.

Warming to his theme, Don Juan continued:

Thus no one takes responsibility for the most important matters pending between His Majesty and his ministers, and everything is decided at random, casting our bread upon the waters but never getting any back. As a result we spend time and effort in avoiding the measures that are needed, in taking them when we lack time, money and opportunity, in making savings that cost three times more than is saved, in starting in haste because we are late, and in starting badly because we are in haste. Whoever does not see this must be blind.[61]

But should these critics be believed? Some of them, after all, wrote in anger and frustration: Granvelle by 1584 was an embittered old man who had been twice brutally shunted from the centre to the periphery of power – once twenty years before when Philip dismissed him as his chief minister in the Netherlands, and again when the king's return from Portugal in 1583 marginalized him; while Silva in 1589 sulked on his country estates because the king had not rewarded him as he felt he deserved.[62] The ambassadors, by definition, wrote in at least partial ignorance of how Philip really governed. All of them resented the fact that he did not concentrate on the matters of primary concern to *them*.

The king himself never denied the delays: not for nothing did he adopt as his motto *Yo con el tiempo* ('Time and I are a match for anyone') and, in secret correspondence, the codename 'Fabius' (after the Roman general who defeated Hannibal by delaying tactics). When the general of the Jeronimite Order complained in 1589 that an earlier letter to the king had not been answered, Philip immediately took full responsibility and told his secretary: 'The blame for the delay is mine, because with the pressure of business I have not been able to see it or order a reply. You had better tell the General this: that one cannot always do what one wants.' And when the king's patronage secretary likewise complained shortly afterwards that several papers sent some days before had not been returned, yet again Philip accepted the blame: 'I am very sorry that the pressure of business should be such that it does not leave me time to see to these things, or many others that I should, but I cannot manage any more. However, I shall do everything possible.'[63] But the reason for the delays, however, was not inefficiency or 'meddling' (as Granvelle and Silva claimed) but the exact reverse: his 'priority mail system' (p. 30 above). The king knew that he lacked the time to take care of everything and therefore, with the aid of his secretaries, he took care of the most important matters first. Placating a Jeronimite general and the patronage secretary did not come high on the king's list of priorities and so he put them off. Similarly, in the summer of 1588, when a grandee complained that he had received no response to an earlier petition, Philip informed his secretary firmly (albeit with characteristic prolixity):

> You can tell him that you have reminded me [about this] several times, and that I very much wanted to see it; but that getting the Armada in Portugal to sea and related business have kept me, and still keep me, so busy that I have had no time for it. In addition on some days I have been afflicted by gout (although that would not have stopped me, only what I have just said), and much time and trouble has been – and is still – necessary to amass all the money that has been spent and still needs to be spent.

A few months later, the same secretary forwarded the first consultas of the new president of the council of the Orders and begged the king to review at least some of them 'so as not to discourage him', even though he realized that this would be a considerable imposition, since so many consultas now awaited the king's attention – 'they say in Madrid that Your Majesty has 800 here'. Philip replied wearily that things were not nearly so bad, because only 300 consultas lay piled up around his desk: he would review them as soon as he had dealt with more urgent items.[64]

A glance at the administrative methods adopted by recent occupants of the White House to deal with the pressures of their office places Philip's problems and solutions in a useful perspective. According to one analyst:

> A President's own use of time, his allocation of his personal attention, is governed by the things he has to do from day to day . . . [His] priorities are set not by the relative importance of a task, but by the relative necessity for him to do it. He deals first with the things that are required of him next. Deadlines rule his personal agenda. In most days of his working week, most seasons of his year, he meets deadlines enough to drain his energy and crowd his time regardless of all else . . . What makes a deadline? The answer, very simply, is a date or an event or both combined . . . Dates make deadlines in proportion to their certainty; events make deadlines in proportion to their heat. Singly or combined, approaching dates and rising heat start fires burning underneath the White House. Trying to stop fires is what Presidents do first. It takes most of their time.[65]

Thanks to the dedication of his secretaries and his 'priority mail system', Philip II normally knew which 'fires' he had to stop. Why, then, did he sometimes fail to act swiftly to put them out?

Occasionally, especially in the first half of the reign, imperfections in the king's filing system caused delays. Thus in the summer of 1566, when Philip wished to consider a report from the council of the Indies about the voyage of Miguel López de Legazpi to the Philippines, he could not find any maps to show him where the islands were. 'Tell the councillors [of the Indies]', he commanded his secretary, Francisco de Erasso, with obvious irritation:

> That they are to make every effort to find all the papers and charts which exist on this, and to keep them safe in the council offices; indeed the originals should be put in the archives at Simancas, and authenticated copies taken to the council. I think that I have some [maps of the area] myself, and I tried to find them when I was in Madrid the other day – because if I do have them, that is where they will be. When I get back there, if I remember and if I have time (which I don't just now), I shall look again. Do you think you could find something on this, Erasso? I would like you to search, and make sure that anything you find is looked after as I have just said, with the council always in possession of the copies.[66]

A few years later the king wanted to find a copy of the holograph instructions that his father had given him in 1543, 'but I do not know if I have them, or where they might be, nor do I have time to find them or 100,000 other papers'. In 1576 having again temporarily mislaid some papers, the king confessed that

> I have been very careless today. Last night they brought me this file from Fuenmayor [a treasury official] and this morning this other one from the president of [the council of] the Orders. I put them on a desk where I had other papers, so that I could see them later, but because I had many audiences, and the rest of the files that I gave you, and lots of other papers that I signed earlier, I forgot about them – so that even though we spoke this evening about Fuenmayor's paper, I did not remember them until now, when it is already nine o'clock.

But then the king had a stroke of luck: 'having just asked for dinner [to be served], while taking a stroll, and walking near the desk, I happened to see them and read them'. He returned the dossiers, with his decision, at once. One day in 1581, however, Philip's filing system completely failed him: he could locate neither a copy of the letter he had written to his cousin Archduke Ferdinand of Tyrol ('although I must have done so, because he has written to acknowledge receiving it') nor the description of a machine to strike coins that the archduke's agent had given him ('I thought he gave it to me along with other papers, but I cannot find it'). He asked his secretary what to do next.[67] Nevertheless, just as a few dark nights of the soul do not indicate a manic depressive (p. 45 above), so a few misfiled papers and overdue letters scarcely indicate a terminally inefficient bureaucrat – and, in any case, during the second half of the reign complaints about lost papers dwindled.

A more serious cause of delay, again particularly in the first half of the reign, stemmed from Philip's deliberate decision during a crisis to do nothing for a while. In the summer of 1565, for example, he tried to delay all major decisions while he concentrated on defeating the Turkish assault on Malta; and an experienced diplomat overseas, waiting in vain for instructions, petulantly observed: 'As for our master, everything is put off until the morrow, and the main decision taken in everything is never to take a decision.' The king himself agreed. When Count Lamoral of Egmont arrived at Court in March with orders from the Brussels government to ascertain the king's intentions towards the Netherlands, just as news arrived of the westward journey of the Turkish Grand Fleet, Philip deliberately procrastinated: 'I have drafted my answer in this way', he told his secretary, 'so that Egmont will not be able to force me into a decision . . . My intention, as you will have gathered, is neither to resolve these demands of the count, nor to disillusion him about them, for then he would worry us to death and we would never be finished with him.'[68]

Although profoundly frustrating for agents in the field, some delays in committing resources during a crisis made sense, so that the king could benefit from the best available information and thereby minimize the risk of error. 'The premium on haste', as a modern analyst has observed, 'is undoubtedly the greatest piece of mischief that can be introduced onto military forces.' In the words of another: 'The fine art of executive decision consists in not deciding questions that are not now pertinent, in not deciding prematurely, [and] in not making decisions that cannot be made effective.' Throughout the summer of 1565, until news arrived that Malta had been relieved, Philip put off decisions on all other matters, even the Netherlands, because they ran a high risk of being irrelevant, premature and ineffective.[69]

As the reign advanced, however, the king seemed more willing to take risks. Complaints from his subordinates abroad centred less on frustrating neglect and increasingly on unwanted interference. Even in the early years, tensions appeared between the evident need for delegation to his agents on the spot and Philip's strong reluctance to relinquish control. Thus in 1557, having heard that Florida might be suitable for settlement, the king decided to rescind his earlier prohibition on any new expeditions of discovery in the Americas and informed the viceroy of New Spain, 'On account of the great confidence that we have in your person, we have decided to remit this matter to you, as the person on the spot, so that you can see what it would be best to do for God's service and mine, as well as for the good of the country. Do whatever seems best to you in this.' Similarly in 1569, as part of an effort to bring ministerial overspending in the New World under control, the king ordered that the amount of any payment made without a specific warrant bearing his signature would be deducted from the viceroy's personal salary; but the folly of this soon became apparent – 'Because you lack my order to do so, you might not do what our service requires' – and so the king reversed his policy two years later.[70] Late in 1576, when all the information available to him suggested that the Turkish navy would not sail west the following year, the king decided on a drastic reduction in the galley fleet. Ministers prepared detailed instructions for the Mediterranean commander on how to effect the 'reformation' but, as he signed the final version, Philip experienced a twinge of doubt and added in his own hand the crucial proviso: 'Nevertheless, if this seems inappropriate to you, and that diminishing our fleet now might call forth [that of] the enemy, you may maintain it until the end of the summer'.[71]

By the 1580s, once his information-gathering techniques had expanded, lengthy delays tended to arise from the king's insistence that he should take all major decisions himself in the light of the unequalled wealth of data at his disposal. As he strove to coordinate all the resources of his Monarchy for the Armada campaign, for example, he urged his envoys abroad to provide a constant stream of news, 'because now is the time to advise me of everything minute by minute'.[72] The unprecedented torrent of information generated by such orders, all of which he strove to review for himself, seems to have convinced Philip that he really did have all the relevant data at his fingertips and that, although a given theatre commander's understanding of local circumstances might be second to none, thanks to his unique information network he alone could appreciate the overall position. In October 1587 he informed the marquis of Santa Cruz, commander of the Armada, that 'the success and failure of an enterprise is decided by days and hours' and urged him to 'believe me as one who has complete information on the present state of affairs in all areas', so that under no circumstances could any variation from his masterplan be permitted.[73] He stressed this even more with Santa Cruz's successor, Medina Sidonia. Even in mid-August 1588, a week after the Armada had been worsted in battle and driven north into Scottish waters, Philip continued to insist that the success of the enterprise depended upon following his instructions to the letter. Only in mid-September (as the remnants of the storm-tossed fleet approached the Spanish coast) did he relent: ministers now drafted orders for Medina Sidonia to land in Scotland, ally with the local Catholics and winter there.[74] All this was of course nonsense. Philip did not – could not – have 'complete information on the present state of affairs in all areas'; and, even had he somehow managed this feat, most of the information would have been seriously out of date by the time he had communicated it to his theatre commanders.

A third and final factor that slowed the pulse of the Spanish Monarchy stemmed from Philip's 'zero defects mentality' (p. 42 above). His insistence that 'it is so important that we get everything right', combined with his desire to take all important decisions himself, left no place for error. Before finally authorizing any major action the king tried to ensure that everything was in perfect order. Thus in 1571, as he waited anxiously for Spain's Mediterranean fleet to put to sea, Venetian ambassador Leonardo Donà noted with irritated fascination the king's insistence on having absolutely everything ready before starting the campaign:

I see that, where naval warfare is concerned, every tiny detail takes up the longest time and prevents voyages, because not having oars or sails ready, or having insufficient quantities of ovens to bake biscuits, or the lack of just ten trees or masts, on many occasions holds up for months on end the progress of the fleet.

Perhaps worse still, once the last oar, sail, oven and mast had been assembled, the king expected everything to happen like clockwork. As the duke of Medina Sidonia put it in 1588, as he nervously led the Armada into the English Channel: 'The plan is that the moment I arrive [off the coast of Flanders] the duke of Parma should come out with his ships without making me wait for him for a moment. On this depends the whole success of the campaign.'[75] This assumption was, of course, wholly unreasonable given the limitations imposed by sixteenth-century information technology.

It might be argued in his defence that Philip was only an 'armchair' strategist since he had scarcely ever experienced war at first hand (not at all since 1558), and so could not appreciate the truth of the axiom expressed by Helmut von Moltke, chief of the Prussian General Staff in the mid-nineteenth century, that 'no plan survives contact with the enemy for more than twenty-four hours'. However, many of Philip's contemporaries displayed greater realism. Thus Elizabeth of England and her advisers all shared the king's practical ignorance of war, but they certainly anticipated Moltke's point. Elizabeth's Instructions to Howard of Effingham for the Armada campaign, for example, seem a model of prudence. Having surveyed the various potential threats facing her realm, she concluded on a tone very different from – and far more realistic than – Philip's orders to Medina Sidonia:

Lastly, forasmuch as ther may fall out many accidents that may moove you to take another course than by these our instructions you are directed, we therfore think it most expedient to refer you therin to your own judgement and discretion, to doo that thing you may think may best tend to the advancement of our service.

And her ministers realized – and on occasion gently reminded her – that 'you cannot thinke of all things at all times'.[76]

Like all statesmen, Philip resembled the captain of a riverboat: he could maintain steerage way only as long as his ship moved faster than the current. As the volume of information demanding assessment and the number of decisions required of him mounted, resolutions inevitably came more slowly. His insistence on acquiring ever more data, and his illusion that this enabled – entitled – him to micromanage operations throughout his global empire, paradoxically served to diminish his control. He never seems to have grasped the need to recognize his own limitations, especially during any crisis that expanded dramatically the number of urgent decisions required, despite the fact that (in the words of an eminent contemporary strategic analyst):

> There is only so much that any human can absorb, digest and act upon in a given period of time. The greater the stress, the more individuals will ignore or misrepresent data, mistake and misconstrue information, and the greater will be the prospects for confusion, disorientation and surprise . . . [Furthermore,] the spatial and, essentially, the temporal distribution of information relevant to decisions in war means that many key pieces will remain inaccessible at any given place. Those who have held senior positions in corporations or military services need only reflect on how much they did not know about what was taking place in their own organizations to appreciate the reality of information being temporally or spatially inaccessible.

In short, 'More information from more sources, made available more quickly than ever before, equals system overload . . . Processing and transmission technologies far outstrip our ability to assimilate, sort and distribute information'.[77]

And yet warnings about precisely this danger were readily to hand. Thanks to the sermons to which he listened throughout his long life, Philip must have heard more than once the lesson taught to the Hebrew leader Moses on the exodus from Egypt to Palestine by his father-in-law Jethro. Attending to everything in person, Jethro insisted, 'is not right. You will tire yourself out, and the people with you, for the work is too heavy for you. You cannot do it all alone.' True; yet in overlooking the significance of this text Philip by no means stood alone. To take a striking later example, between 27 June and 3 August 1914, the governments in St Petersburg, Berlin, Vienna, Paris and London generated between them at least 6,000 documents assessing the growing international crisis, a total of well over 1.5 million words – far too much to digest and master. Moreover the flow was not uniform: the total of incoming messages from ambassadors to each of the five foreign ministers rose from an average of four per day at the beginning of the crisis to over forty at the end, and the number of messages exchanged directly between the various heads of state increased from two per day to over twenty. The pressures thus generated overwhelmed the decision-making structures of all the European states and thus helped to plunge them into war.[78]

However, Philip II's strategic planning did not suffer simply because he, like the statesmen of 1914, accumulated more knowledge than could be assimilated, sorted and absorbed in time; the real problem lay in the fact that his system of government required all these processes to be carried out by the king in person. Like Moses, Philip believed that he alone could mediate divine grace to his people and handle all problems adequately. Although he ruled over a Monarchy composed of so many different and dispersed territories, each with its own separate identity and independent sentiments, he insisted that all the councils and juntas at the centre – like the various ministers, institutions and corporations on the periphery – should wait to receive their orders from the king in person. Inevitably, even without crises, as the business generated by each organ increased, the possibility that Philip would be able to play his designated role punctually became ever more remote.

The consequent information overload – disposing of more data than could be processed by a single brain – produced three problems for Philip's Monarchy. At the operational level, as already noted, it led to attempts at micromanagement. These were clearly doomed to failure because, as John F. Guilmartin has written, 'No amount of communications can replace a competent and responsible commander on the scene. To attempt to do so is to invite disaster.'[79] Philip failed to appreciate that 'complete information on the present state of affairs in all areas' – even had he possessed it – still could not enable him to micromanage a complex military operation from his distant headquarters. At the planning level, information overload produced two further serious consequences. First, Philip sought seclusion at least in part to increase the time available for the undistracted study of the information that poured in; yet this sheltered him from the 'real world' to a dangerous degree. Second, and far more deleterious, since no amount of time or effort sufficed to digest the entire corpus of data available, the king evolved certain strategies for selecting only those pieces of information that broadly corresponded to the plan already adopted.

The attractions of maintaining harmony between one's beliefs, actions and reactions are obvious: mutual consistency helps every individual to interpret, retain and recall information, and it confers continuity on behaviour patterns. Its dangers, however, are equally apparent: it can create 'cognitive rigidity' in favour of information consonant with decisions that have already been taken and against any data that challenges them. The very fact that information compatible with the existing plan will be used to confirm the choices already taken serves to inhibit the development of alternative beliefs. To use a classic case, the conviction that an adversary's military preparations are merely bluff will delay the realization that they are 'for real', because the two scenarios so closely resemble each other.[80] Finally, the search for consistency leads to flawed efforts to rationalize all policies in terms of the favoured option: instead of seeing that the objective can only be attained at the cost of sacrificing some other goals, all considerations are made to support the chosen decision – indeed new justifications may be added later in order to strengthen the case for the favoured policy and to make it seem the only sensible choice.[81]

Of course the evidence available to any statesman during a crisis usually permits multiple interpretations – indeed, on occasion, the bulk of the evidence may not support the correct explanation – and hunches and experience count for much. Rulers who managed to make the right decision have often been just as stubborn and biased as their less successful opponents. However, leaders in a state of high stress – like Philip in 1587–88 – seem preternaturally disposed to accept data that support their preconceived ideas and to avoid anything that contradicts them, whether by banishing Cassandras from their courts, by dismissing or

ignoring dissenting reports, or (worst of all) by distorting all incoming information so that it supports their previous assumptions.[82]

Nevertheless, all statesmen need a theoretical structure, a frame of reference of
some kind, both to know the difference between what is right and what is merely
opportune, and in order to establish (and maintain) priorities and uphold broad
policies; otherwise 'deadlines' and 'trying to stop fires' will not leave time for
anything else. Part of that frame of reference comes from practical experience –
from prolonged exposure to the details of operation and of policy. But beliefs,
values and prejudices also play their part. The imperial vision imparted by his
father and an almost unshakable conviction that he was engaged in God's work
helped Philip to interpret the unprecedented quantities of information at his
disposal, and to make his decisions. As the king once loftily observed to a
dispirited subordinate: 'You are engaged in God's service and in mine – which is
the same thing': throughout his reign, Philip believed profoundly that God would
provide whatever lay beyond human powers of prediction or execution, and he
repeatedly counted upon miracles to bridge the gap between intention and
achievement, to fill the interstices in his strategic plans.[83] Furthermore, his pas-
sionate faith encouraged the adoption of over-ambitious goals and created a sort
of 'messianic imperialism' that proved to be, at one and the same time, one of the
greatest strengths and one of the greatest weaknesses of his Grand Strategy.

3 'With God on Our Side'

Although neither Philip II nor his ministers formulated their own 'blue-print for empire', they certainly inherited one and regularly consulted it. In January 1548 Philip's father Charles V prepared a comprehensive review of the problems that faced him and sent it to his 20-year-old son, then serving as regent in Spain. The long document, sometimes known as Charles's 'Political Testament', soon became well known in government circles. At least twenty-eight manuscript copies survive and in 1600 the Spanish ambassador in Savoy reminded his sovereign of 'what His Majesty the emperor said in the instructions that he gave the late king our lord [Philip II]' and suggested that its strategic analysis still held good. Philip himself referred respectfully to the various papers of advice that his father had given him: 'I remember a lesson that His Majesty [Charles] taught me very many years ago,' he told a councillor in 1559, 'and things have gone well for me when I followed it and very badly when I did not'; and as he began to draw up instructions for his own successor in 1574, he sought to base them on those 'which the emperor wrote for me in his own hand.[1] In 1606 Prudencio de Sandoval printed the full text of Charles's comprehensive review of imperial Grand Strategy in his best-selling *History of the life and deeds of the Emperor Charles V*.[2]

Charles began his 'Political Testament' by urging the prince to 'submit all your desires and actions to the will of God' and to make the defence of the Catholic faith his primary responsibility. He then regretted the cost of 'the wars that I have been forced to fight so many times and in so many places' to defend the empire – even though, he noted with a trace of smugness, 'with God's help (for which let Him be thanked) I have conserved, defended and added other [lands] of great quality and importance'. The primary need, therefore, was to assure them a period of peace in which to recover. However,

> Avoiding war and keeping it at bay is not always in the power of those who want it . . . especially of those who rule realms as great and as numerous and as far-flung as God, in His goodness, has given me and which, if He pleases, I shall

leave to you. Rather this depends on the good or ill will of neighbours and other states.

The emperor then launched into an extended and highly perceptive survey of the prevailing international situation and of the Grand Strategy best suited to preserve Philip's inheritance intact.[3]

'Common sense and experience', Charles began,

> show that unless you watch and take the trouble to understand the actions of other states and rulers, and maintain friends and informants in all areas, it will be difficult if not impossible to live in peace, or to avoid, oppose, and remedy anything that is attempted against you and your possessions . . . especially since (as I have already noted) they are separated one from another, and the object of envy.[4]

Therefore 'your first and most secure friendship and trust' must be with Ferdinand, Charles's brother and designated successor as Holy Roman Emperor. On the one hand, his uncle Ferdinand would be a valuable councillor; on the other, as emperor, his support would prove essential for Philip's control over northern Italy and the Low Countries – both imperial fiefs – and for the maintenance of easy and secure communication between them. Philip followed this advice meticulously. His correspondence with Ferdinand reveals a combination of respect and affection, with both monarchs striving to pursue policies that, if not always identical, were at least compatible; and when his uncle died, Philip grieved.[5] More than twenty years later Philip still remembered Ferdinand affectionately: when a secretary sent him a document praising his uncle's piety and steadfastness for the faith, 'because I thought Your Majesty would like to read it', the king scribbled enthusiastically: 'I knew the Emperor Ferdinand. We spent almost a year together, in 1551, at Augsburg in Germany, in the company of the emperor my father, and I saw a lot of him because we got on very well.'[6]

The king's memory had become selective, however. The Augsburg meeting to which he referred in fact created serious discord in the house of Habsburg, for Charles used bluster and threats in order to try and compel his brother first to renounce his claim to succeed him as emperor in favour of Philip and then, when that failed, to name Philip – rather than Ferdinand's own son Maximilian – as next in line (Tables 3a and b). Ferdinand eventually crumbled; but German public opinion strongly opposed the deal and in 1555, after becoming king of England, Philip formally renounced his claim to succeed his uncle.[7] No sooner had Ferdinand gained the imperial title in 1558 than he reneged on another promise extorted at Augsburg: to recognize Philip as his 'imperial Vicar' in Italy. Instead, he now insisted that his deputy must reside in the peninsula, and although he offered to confer the title 'the moment His Highness goes to Italy', both men knew this remained an empty promise.[8] In all other respects, however, Ferdinand treated Philip 'as one of his own sons' and served as 'the guarantor of peace and

The family of Charles V

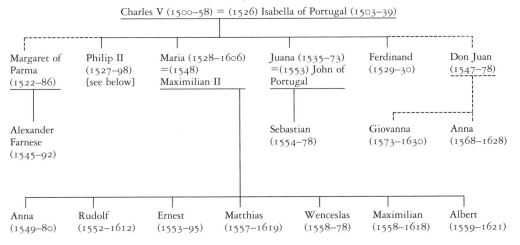

Charles V (1500–58) = (1526) Isabella of Portugal (1503–39)

Margaret of Parma (1522–86)	Philip II (1527–98) [see below]	Maria (1528–1606) =(1548) Maximilian II	Juana (1535–73) =(1553) John of Portugal	Ferdinand (1529–30)	Don Juan (1547–78)

Alexander Farnese (1545–92)

Sebastian (1554–78)

Giovanna (1573–1630)

Anna (1568–1628)

Anna (1549–80)	Rudolf (1552–1612)	Ernest (1553–95)	Matthias (1557–1619)	Wenceslas (1558–78)	Maximilian (1558–1618)	Albert (1559–1621)

The family of Philip II

Philip II (1527–98) =

(1) Maria of Portugal (m 1543–45)	(2) Mary Tudor (m 1554–58)	(3) Elisabeth de Valois (m 1560–68)	(4) Anna of Austria (m 1570–80)

Don Carlos (1545–68)

Isabella (1566–1633) =(1599) Albert of Habsburg

Catalina (1567–97) =(1585) Charles of Savoy

Ferdinand (1571–78)	Carlos Lorenzo (1573–75)	Diego (1575–82)	Philip III (1578–1621)	Maria (1580–83)

Tables 3a and 3b In the sixteenth century the Habsburgs tended to produce either huge families or none at all. Of the numerous children of Philip II's sister María and her husband Maximilian, only Anna had children; and of Charles V's other legitimate grandchildren only two, besides Anna, produced heirs: Catalina and Philip III.

unity in the family'.[9] For a time his successor Maximilian (emperor 1564–76) seems to have recognized his older cousin and brother-in-law as the senior member of the dynasty, entrusting to Philip the negotiation of marriage contracts for two of his daughters – one to Charles IX of France, the other to Philip himself – in 1569. The following year a Spanish minister wrote of 'the fraternal feelings between Your Majesty [Philip] and the emperor, obliging you to treat his affairs as if they were your own'.[10] All this changed dramatically in 1571 when Spanish troops invaded the tiny imperial fief of Finale Ligure (see p. 84 below). Maximilian, who had not been consulted, first organized a diplomatic offensive to force them out and then, far from naming Philip as his Vicar, began to maintain agents of his own in Milan in order to watch over his interests in Italy and to keep Spanish ambitions in check. Worse still, Maximilian repeatedly declined to assist Philip after civil war broke out in the Netherlands in 1572, instead publicly advising his cousin that he should make concessions to the Dutch rebels.[11] His sons proved even less cooperative: Matthias served, in open defiance of Philip, as governor-general of the rebellious Netherlands provinces for four years (1577–81), while Rudolf II (emperor 1576–1612) exploited Spain's temporary weakness in order to force Philip to negotiate with his Dutch rebels at a formal peace conference in 1579. Close political cooperation between the two branches of the family did not resume until the second decade of the seventeenth century.

The first prescription for stability in Charles's 'Political Testament' thus did not work out as planned; neither, initially, did the second. 'You already know how the present Pope, Paul III, has treated me,' the emperor complained, and expressed the hope that a change of pontiff would improve matters. He saw two areas of potential conflict – papal claims to suzerainty over Naples and Sicily, and the extensive royal rights of patronage over the church in Spain and the Americas – and advised his heir to 'behave with the submission that a good son of the church should show, and without giving the popes any just cause for offence with you. But do this without any prejudice to the pre-eminences, prosperity, and peace of the said kingdoms.'[12] In other words, Philip should give nothing away. However, not long after Philip succeeded his father in 1556 the new pope, Paul IV, excommunicated him (and Charles) and declared war. The king felt outraged, and complained loud and long to his uncle Ferdinand that the pope's actions

> lacked justification, reason and cause, as all the world has seen, because I have not only given him no cause for this, but rather His Holiness owes me favour and honour because of the way I have served and revered him and the Holy See, both in bringing England back to the Faith and in everything else I could do.

This proved to be the nadir of Philip's relations with the Papacy: in September 1557, after a campaign waged with exemplary restraint by the duke of Alba, Paul IV agreed not to make war on Philip, or to assist others who did, and to refrain from building further fortifications in the Papal States.[13] After Paul's death, the king set about forging an alliance with Rome that would benefit both parties. He began to provide substantial pensions and gifts to prominent cardinals (in 1562 Carlo Borromeo, the new pope's nephew, received Spanish benefices worth 15,000 ducats) and occasionally to the pontiff himself (in 1579 the pope allegedly received a gift of 50,000 ducats when one of Philip's leading advisers became a cardinal). By 1591, 47 of the 70 cardinals pocketed a Spanish pension. The king also supplied Rome with Sicilian grain and wine when necessary; and, at the pope's request, he provided galleys to get rid of corsairs and (on one occasion) sent troops to stifle a tax revolt.[14] On the other hand, Philip regularly attempted to prevent the election of a pope hostile to him, occasionally threatening to withhold grain shipments and once (in 1590) even moving troops and galleys to the frontier in order to influence the outcome of a conclave.[15] The Papal States had virtually become a Spanish satellite.

In return for all this the king received many favours: the proceeds of heavy taxes on the Spanish church (worth over 1 million ducats annually); approval of his nominations to all major benefices in his dominions throughout Europe and the Americas; prisoners from Roman gaols to serve on his galleys; even the creation of Spanish saints, starting with Diego de Alcalá in 1588 (fifteen of the twenty-seven saints created over the following century were born subjects of the kings of Spain). And yet, just as his father had commanded, he gave nothing away. During a dispute with the pope over jurisdiction in Naples, the king wrote firmly to his ambassador in Rome: 'In the rights that I have, and that my predecessors have handed down to me, there will be no change'. Philip may not have received the comprehensive support from Rome that he considered his due, but it was far more than his father had ever got.[16]

Charles's assessment of the secular powers of Italy in 1548 proved a model of shrewdness. The emperor began by reviewing the history of his relations with the six major independent states of the peninsula. The republic of Venice had previously opposed Spain, he noted, but a treaty in 1529 had settled all earlier differences and Charles exhorted his son to uphold its terms and 'to keep good friendship with [the Venetians], favouring them as good allies as much as possible'. In the same year, the dukes of Florence had become beholden to him when imperial forces laid siege to their rebellious capital and (the following year) restored the Medici to power; ever since, Charles noted, the dukes had been 'very solicitous for me and my affairs' and he enjoined Philip to maintain good relations with them too. Of the other major independent states, Ferrara's allegiance seemed less sure, for although the emperor had likewise intervened to uphold the integrity of the duchy, its ruler was related to the French royal family; Mantua had always been the emperor's most loyal associate in Italy; and Lucca's overriding political goal lay in preserving the general peace of Italy. The republic of Genoa, finally, constituted Spain's most important ally in Italy, both because of its economic ties with various Habsburg dominions, and because it permitted access from Naples, Sicily, Sardinia and Spain to Lombardy, Germany and the Netherlands: Philip must therefore do his utmost to preserve and strengthen the ties that bound the Genoese government to him.[17]

Philip followed his father's advice faithfully and used a wide range of instruments to preserve peace in the peninsula, to consolidate his power there, and to stifle all initiatives by others because 'The preservation, peace and grandeur of Spain depends on the affairs of Italy being well ordered'.[18] Since he lacked the resources to achieve all his goals by force alone, Philip created a sophisticated and complex 'diplomatic system' – perhaps the first of early modern times – in order to maintain Spanish dominance in Italy. A series of marriage alliances helped to retain Mantua within the Habsburg orbit: its Gonzaga dukes belonged to the small number of dynasties from which the Habsburgs regularly chose their spouses, and Philip ordered his agents in Italy to watch over Mantua's interests 'as if they were our own . . . on account of the great obligation we have to favour the affairs of the said duke like our own'.[19] Commercial, political and strategic considerations bound the patricians of Genoa equally tightly to Spain: 80 per cent of the republic's long-distance trade by sea involved Philip's territories, while Genoese merchant-bankers became deeply involved in his finances (by 1575 loans to the king of Spain absorbed perhaps 40 per cent of the total wealth of the Genoese aristocracy); and whenever the oligarchs who ran the republic encountered opposition, whether from their own citizens (during the civil unrest of 1574–76) or from foreign powers (during the Corsican insurrection from 1559 to 1569) Philip rushed to their rescue. Spain maintained a permanent ambassador in Genoa (others resided in Italy only in Rome, in Venice and, from 1570, in Turin), to oversee its interests and (whenever required) to ensure the election of a favourable Doge.[20]

Mantua and Genoa, however, were only two among almost 300 'imperial fiefs' in northern Italy. Most of them lay in the hands of sixty or so dynasties, which Philip dominated by a combination of rewards and threats.[21] On the reward side, he could offer to transfer some adjacent Spanish territory to a loyal ally (as he dangled the restitution of Piacenza before the duke of Parma and the cession of certain fortresses in Tuscany before the duke of Florence) or to arrange a marriage with a Habsburg princess (in 1585 Duke Charles Emmanuel of Savoy wed Philip's younger daughter Catalina). He could also subsidize the military endeavours of a favoured client – Savoy, described as 'the gateway and bastion of all the states that His Majesty holds in Italy', did particularly well: between 1582 and 1592 the duke received some 700,000 ducats, and 66,000 annually for the rest of the reign. Spain could even, if need arose, take a state under its formal protection.[22] The king also appointed members of Italy's ruling families to prestigious executive posts in the Monarchy: Vespasiano Gonzaga, duke of Sabbionetta, became viceroy of (successively) Navarre, Valencia and Naples; Marco Antonio Colonna, from a prominent Roman family, served a long term as viceroy of Sicily; Gian Andrea Doria, head of Genoa's dominant patrician family, commanded Spain's Mediterranean galley fleet and became a member of the council of State; Alexander Farnese, prince and later duke of Parma, served as captain-general of the Army of Flanders from 1578 to 1592.[23] Other members of Italy's ruling families (particularly heirs apparent) also resided for a time at the Court of Spain, where they received both lavish entertainment and constant encouragement to see the world through Spanish eyes – Alexander Farnese, for example, lived at Philip's Court between 1557 and 1566, in England and the Netherlands as well as in Spain. The king could also offer a wide range of other rewards: pensions, presents, land, offices and honours culminating in a knighthood of the Golden Fleece, the foremost order of chivalry in Europe, whose members Philip (grand master of the order) called 'my cousin'.[24]

All these devices aimed to preserve the 'pax hispanica' by peaceful means because, in the words of one minister, should the Italian states 'lose their respect for words, it will be hard to regain it with deeds'.[25] The king, therefore, also maintained an extensive network of agents and spies throughout the peninsula, suborned the servants of other rulers, and even resorted on occasion to assassination in order to achieve his ends.[26] In addition, he regularly volunteered his services as mediator in territorial disputes between the turbulent rulers of the peninsula – especially those of his allies who hated each other – and exhorted everyone to help preserve 'the peace of Italy, without permitting changes that might threaten its tranquillity'.[27] Thus in 1568–70, he backed Ferrara in a bitter dispute with Rome, warning the pope that 'conserving the peace that Italy enjoys today was in everyone's interests, and that [His] Majesty would not approve of anyone starting a war'; while a decade later, when the ambassador of Ferrara appeared in Madrid with '39 or 40 dossiers' and a map to seek Spanish support for a proposal to annex by force an area contested with the republic of Lucca, a royal minister bluntly repeated that Spain 'would not suffer anyone to disturb the peace of Italy' and offered binding arbitration instead.[28] When in 1588 Philip's son-in-law the duke of Savoy invaded and occupied the marquisate of Saluzzo, which by law should have reverted to Henry III of France, Philip (taken by surprise) at first ordered him to withdraw, in order to avoid jeopardizing the peace of Italy, and only gave his approval after hearing that Henry had murdered the duke of Guise, leader of the French Catholic League.[29]

Naturally, like his father before him, Philip did not place his trust in diplomacy alone. After all, many Italians longed for the return of an Italy 'where no prince could impose his will on another', and the king took seriously any sign of independence. In particular, the impressive new fortifications constructed by various peninsular rulers caused him concern because, should war break out, they might successfully resist a siege by Spanish forces. As a military engineer boasted to the duke of Mantua, 'When Your Excellency will have your city completely fortified, you will be able to reply to those who ask "Who is your friend", "[I am the] friend of God and the enemy of everyone else." '[30] Against such potential threats the Habsburgs constructed state-of-the-art fortifications in their own dominions – Sicily, Naples, Sardinia and above all Milan – and maintained a small but well-trained standing army in each, as well as squadrons of galleys in their main Mediterranean ports. Charles's 'Political Testament' urged Philip not to neglect these defences: 'Even though you will inherit large debts and exhausted countries, and will need to look for savings wherever you can, you must not for that reason avoid keeping at all times some Spanish garrisons in Italy,' he warned, because they offered the best defence against 'outbreaks of war and attempts to seize territory'. He also extolled the value of the fleets.[31] Once again his son hearkened and obeyed, although the cost did indeed plunge Naples and Milan (at least) deep into debt: the treasury of the former ran a deficit in every year of Philip's reign save one; that of the latter never broke even, despite constant subsidies from Spain, Naples and Sicily.[32] On the one hand, the king increased the number of galleys maintained by his various Mediterranean states from 55 in 1562 to 155 in 1574, rendering his naval strength so overwhelming that several Italian states (including Genoa, the Papacy and Savoy) virtually demilitarized themselves, choosing to disband their own fleet and to rely instead on Philip's galleys for their defence.[33] On the other hand, the king maintained substantial forces in the numerous fortresses of the states directly under his rule. By 1572 seventeen towns in the duchy of Milan, which he and his ministers regarded as 'the military core and boundary of all that His Majesty holds in Italy', boasted garrisons; so did a dozen outposts in friendly states beyond the frontiers of the duchy.[34] Despite its vulnerability, thanks to these powerful defences Milan served as a secure marshalling yard for Philip's resources in Europe, and its archives bristle with transit permits for troops, weapons, armour and specie going to the Mediterranean fleet, Germany and above all the Netherlands.[35]

Philip regarded his Italian garrisons as a 'rapid reaction force' to deal with any threat to his European interests. In 1567, for example, 10,000 Spanish veterans previously stationed in Sicily, Naples, Sardinia and Milan marched over the Alps to the Netherlands in order to restore order. New recruits from Spain took their place. In 1571 these troops, now seasoned and experienced themselves, boarded the galleys of both Philip and Venice and featured prominently at the victory of Lepanto against the Turks.[36] More controversially, earlier that same year Spanish units based in Lombardy also invaded and annexed the marquisate of Finale Ligure which, though small, possessed great strategic importance: it separated the territories of the republic of Genoa; it could offer a Mediterranean port to the neighbouring landlocked powers of Mantua, Savoy and Milan; and it might serve as a valuable transalpine base for France. In 1566 the subjects of Finale had rebelled against their ruler, and two years later the duke of Savoy took advantage of the turmoil to annex some disputed villages along his border. Philip allowed this to pass, but in 1571 intelligence reports indicated that France stood poised to occupy the rest. Acting on direct orders from Madrid, the governor of Milan launched a surprise attack and occupied Finale, allegedly to forestall a French descent. Lacking the title 'Imperial Vicar', however, the king had to back down: Emperor Maximilian mobilized almost all the independent states of Italy to condemn Philip's unauthorized initiative, compelling Spanish forces to with-draw.[37] The king never again used force against an imperial fief. When in 1574 one of Spain's clients pleaded for armed assistance, the new governor of Milan declined: 'However much power the king may possess,' he wrote, 'I cannot persuade myself that it is either safe or sound [for us] to take up arms in Italy for anybody'. And later that same year, when another minute independent territory south of Milan erupted in rebellion against its ruler, Philip allowed the grand duke of Tuscany to restore order, even though the Spanish governor of a nearby fortress had already intervened with his troops.[38]

Apart from these minor disturbances, no wars broke out in Italy for fifty years after the peace of Cateau-Cambrésis in 1559 – in marked contrast to the preceding and succeeding half-centuries. Part of the credit for this belongs to Philip's pacific policies, but equally it derived from the weakness of France. Even though the last French garrisons abandoned Italy in 1574, France still constituted the greatest potential threat to the Spanish system in the later sixteenth century, just as it had in 1548 when Charles wrote his 'Political Testament'. In that document, the emperor claimed that he had always tried to live in peace with the French king, and he advised his son to do the same. But, he continued (with an almost audible sigh), the French had 'made many peaces and truces with me, none of which they kept – as is well-known – except during the periods when they could not renew the war or wanted to wait for an opportunity to harm me clandestinely'. No doubt, he mused, they would continue to do so, trying to regain the territories and rights he had compelled them to renounce both in the Low Countries and in Italy.

> [But] you must insist that the said renunciations shall remain for ever in being and in force, and in no way depart from them, because I captured all of them, and you will inherit and possess them, with full rights and evident justification. And if you should show weakness in any part of this, it will open the door to bringing everything back into question . . . It will be better to hold on to everything than to let yourself be forced later to defend the rest, and run the risk of losing it. If your predecessors with the grace of God held on to Naples and Sicily, and also the Low Countries, against the French, you should trust that He will assist you to keep what you have inherited.[39]

Apart from unswerving trust in God, the emperor saw only one practical solution to the feud: for Philip to marry a French princess, and to make it a condition of the match that France should evacuate the territories of the duke of Savoy, occupied since 1536. Admittedly the available Valois princesses were all very young but the emperor felt strongly that a way should be found to restore the duke of Savoy, who had been his loyal ally, to his inheritance as part of any permanent settlement, partly because of the duchy's strategic situation linking Lombardy and Franche-Comté, and partly 'so that all will see and know that you take the requisite care of your own security and of [your allies] too'.[40]

Once again, the emperor's words proved prophetic. Although it took another decade of war, at the peace of Cateau-Cambrésis in 1559 Philip did indeed force the French to recognize all his rights and possessions in both the Low Countries and Italy; he married Elisabeth de Valois immediately afterwards; and he also secured the restoration of the duke of Savoy to his lands. Admittedly the French, too, made gains from the treaty, but only from others: Calais from England, some enclaves in Lorraine from the Holy Roman Empire, and a few fortified bases in Savoy. 'Truly', wrote Cardinal Granvelle, 'these peace negotiations have been directed by God Himself because, although we have settled things so much to our advantage, the French are delighted'.[41] Philip had admirably fulfilled his father's stern command: he had gained a lasting peace, married his enemy's daughter and secured the restoration of his ally, but he had surrendered nothing.

For most of the next forty years France fell prey to religious conflict. Although this paralysed Spain's hereditary enemy, and thus vastly improved Philip's overall strategic position, the king still felt threatened by the military power and the undisguised hostility of the French Protestants. As he put it in 1562:

> Neither the service of God, which is the most important service, nor my own and the welfare of my states, will allow me to neglect helping the Catholics [in France]. I know well that something will be risked in this, but certainly much more will be risked in allowing the heretics to prevail; for if they do, we may be certain that all their endeavours will be directed against me and my states.

Five years later he gloomily observed, 'the flames are spreading everywhere, so that if the [French] monarchy does not make haste to put them out they may be consumed by the fire', and thence they might spread to Spain. He twice sent troops to fight for his brother-in-law, Charles IX.[42] The disintegration of royal power in France during the 1570s, and the fear that the crown now lacked the will as well as the means to extirpate heresy, led Philip to subsidize the leading Catholic magnates. As a Spanish grandee noted: 'The wars in France bring peace for Spain, and peace in Spain brings war for France – thanks to our ducats.' After 1585 money flowed regularly to the French Catholic League and, after the assassination of the childless Henry III in 1589, Philip once again sent in troops. This time they stayed, and the king used their presence (albeit maladroitly) to try and persuade the Catholics to accept his daughter Isabella (Henry's eldest niece) as sovereign, in preference to the Protestant leader Henry of Navarre; but after three years of open war he had to admit defeat. As a Spanish minister at the end of his reign put it, 'if one wished to compare [the Monarchy] with a human body, then France would be its heart'. Philip had failed to exploit the advantages afforded him by four decades of civil wars: France remained as threatening in 1598 as it had been when Charles composed his political testament fifty years before.[43]

The emperor concluded his Instructions with a rapid review of other strategic concerns. He recommended that good relations should be maintained with Portugal and England, while the king of Denmark – even though his father had deposed Charles's brother-in-law and usurped his throne – should be left to rule in peace. Once more Philip obeyed: in 1554, after complicated negotiations, he married Mary Tudor and became king of England, then for a decade after her death in 1558 he protected her sister and successor Elizabeth (see Chapter 5); he also offered close support to his young Portuguese nephew, Sebastian, and after his death in 1578 secured the throne for himself and his heirs. For the first time in many centuries a single monarch ruled the entire Iberian peninsula. In the Baltic, Philip played off Poland, Denmark and Sweden in order both to safeguard an adequate supply of grain to his dominions when needed and (after 1572) to minimize support in the region for his Dutch rebels.[44] On all these counts, yet again Charles would have been proud of his son.

The emperor's 'Political Testament' perceived only three areas of special difficulty. First, Charles fretted about the manner in which the indigenous population of his American colonies had been subjugated by their conquerors: his son must strive to find a balance between 'your royal pre-eminence, and the best interests' of the various groups of inhabitants on the other continent.[45] Second, he worried even more about the lack of resources to defend his far-flung possessions: all his realms had paid heavily for his previous wars and could not be expected to continue contributing taxes at the same high levels. This problem was not new – Charles's Instructions to Philip in 1543 had warned that 'Your treasury will be in such a state [when you succeed me] that it will give you a lot of trouble' – but matters deteriorated rapidly.[46] When he abdicated, Charles left short-term debts of 7 million ducats (almost seven times the annual revenues of Castile) bearing interest payments that absorbed all available income.

Two factors later exacerbated these fiscal problems. On the one hand, Philip's realms enjoyed complete peace for only six months during his entire forty-two-year reign (in 1577), and for much of the time he fought on more than one front – against the Turks and the Dutch (1572–77); against the English and Dutch (1585–89); against the English and Dutch and in France (1589–98) (see Figure 1 above). On the other hand, the cost of fighting in all theatres constantly increased: military expenditure rose dramatically not only because the number of troops, warships and fortifications financed by Philip II grew, but also because of general price inflation. Looking back in the 1590s, a senior military administrator observed:

> If comparison were made between the present cost to His Majesty of the troops who serve in his armies and navies, and the cost of those of the Emperor Charles V, it will be found that, for an equal number of men, three times as much money is necessary today as used to be spent then.

The military budget accordingly increased prodigiously: defeating the German Protestants in 1546–47 required scarcely 1 million ducats from Spain, but the army deployed in the Netherlands against France in 1552–59 absorbed 2 million each year, and the Army of Flanders in the 1590s cost almost 3 million annually.[47] In 1557 Philip therefore took the dramatic step of suspending all payments from his treasury (a measure often called a 'decree of bankruptcy') and began to discuss rescheduling debt repayments. Three years later, upon finding that the obligations of the Castilian treasury totalled 29 million ducats, he did the same again; but government borrowing once more began to spiral until in 1574 treasury officials in Castile estimated total debts and liabilities at 81 million ducats, a sum equivalent to almost fifteen times the total annual revenue. The following year, Philip again suspended all payments and began negotiations with his bankers for a new rescheduling of his debts. In 1596 he repeated the process a fourth time.[48]

Admittedly these 'decrees of bankruptcy' affected only Castile – the treasury of Naples, for example, continued to make payments throughout the reign, even though its debts increased fourfold – but since Castile served as the financial motor of the entire Monarchy, its periodic fiscal collapses had serious repercussions on the king's Grand Strategy.[49] Thus in 1559, Philip's decision to return to Spain despite the precarious political situation in northern Europe (see pp. 150–1 below) stemmed principally from the financial crisis that threatened to engulf him: 'We must all seek the remedy,' he told his ministers, 'as I shall do to the utmost of my ability. And since it is not here [in the Netherlands] I shall go to Spain to seek it.'[50] The suspension of payments in 1575 immediately doomed the efforts of Philip's armies to crush the Dutch Revolt, for without the services of international bankers

> Even if the king found himself with ten millions in gold and wanted to send it all here, he has no way of doing so with this bankruptcy decree, because if the money were sent by sea in specie it would be lost, and it is impossible to send it by letters of exchange as hitherto because no merchant there [in Spain] can issue them, nor can anyone here [in the Low Countries] accept and pay them.

Within six months the soldiers of the Army of Flanders, starved of their pay, had indeed either mutinied or deserted; and within a year the king's representative had been forced to accept a treaty of peace with the rebels.[51] The bankruptcy of 1596 likewise undermined Spain's simultaneous attempts to defeat Henry IV of France, Elizabeth of England and the Dutch Republic.[52] Credit problems may not have forced Philip to sue for peace immediately, and indeed he occasionally boasted that he would never compromise simply because of lack of funds; nevertheless bankruptcy eventually induced him at least to open talks – in 1558–59 with the Turks and French; in 1576–77 with the Turks and Dutch; and in 1597–98 with the French, English and Dutch.[53]

A third and last problem perplexed Charles in 1548: the future of the Low Countries, his native land. Although he had completely crushed his opponents in the region by then, the extreme distaste of the provinces for foreign rule, and the evident difficulty of governing them from Spain, nevertheless caused him anxiety. He therefore contemplated making Philip's sister María and her husband, Ferdinand's son Maximilian, joint rulers of the Netherlands. The provinces would thus be linked to the Holy Roman Empire, freeing Spain of the need to defend them; but he promised Philip that he would not make a final decision 'until you can come here, and see the country for yourself'.[54]

The possibility of severing the link between Spain and the Netherlands had already been considered in 1544, when Charles promised to marry his daughter

María to Francis I's younger son, the duke of Orléans, as a means of securing a more lasting peace between Habsburg and Valois, with either Lombardy or the Low Countries serving as María's dowry. Only the sudden death of Orléans solved the dilemma.[55] The 'devolution plan' of 1548 also remained a dead letter. Admittedly, fifty years later, Philip implemented exactly the same scheme in favour of María and Maximilian's youngest son Albert, who was married to his own daughter Isabella, but by then it was too late: major rebellions had rocked the Netherlands in 1566 and again in 1572 and 1576, so that by 1598 only ten of the seventeen provinces remained under Spanish control.

The emperor's hesitation in alienating the Netherlands stemmed mainly from strategic considerations. As many of Charles's councillors had reminded him in 1544, the Low Countries 'play an essential role in keeping the king of France in check'; and, as Charles had insisted earlier in his 'Political Testament,' surrendering anything to anyone might compromise 'reputation'; he also feared that ceding one possession might well lead to unrest in others.[56] All three arguments resurfaced repeatedly during his son's reign (and after). 'I am well aware', Philip wrote in 1558, 'that it is from the Netherlands that the king of France can best be attacked and forced into peace'; in 1582 Philip's principal adviser on foreign affairs repeated that 'The surest means we have of keeping France in check is to maintain strong forces in the Netherlands'; and even after devolving power to Albert and Isabella, the Spanish council of State emphasized that the Low Countries still served as 'the bridle with which to check and restrain the power of the French, the English and the Dutch, whose forces, should that shield fail, would attack Your Majesty and his kingdoms on all sides, which would produce even greater expenses and damage'.[57]

Likewise the risk of losing 'reputation', whether through failing to make good a claim or by making concessions, worried Philip as much as his father. Thus in 1573 the king decided to continue to fight against the Turks in the Mediterranean despite the defection of his principal ally, Venice, because to sue for peace would 'lose the common esteem of the world'. Four years later his ministers advised him that negotiations with the Dutch rebels were incompatible 'with the honour and reputation of Your Majesty, which is your greatest asset': anything but war would 'strain Your Majesty's conscience and hazard your honour and prestige'.[58] Yet again in 1588–89 Spain refused to make peace with its northern adversaries in the wake of the Armada's failure: concerning England, one councillor 'welcomed the indications that His Majesty wishes to invade again, because I consider trying to recover the reputation and authority that may have been compromised by the outcome of the recent enterprise to be of great importance'; concerning the Dutch, even though 'to attempt to conquer the rebellious provinces by force is to speak of a war without end', the king's senior advisers saw no alternative because 'Christian obligation requires the preservation of one's reputation inviolate'.[59]

Charles's argument that weakness in one area would sooner or later compromise his son's hold elsewhere also resurfaced frequently in later years. In 1558, just after the death of his wife Mary Tudor, a councillor admonished the king that if he failed to retain England, 'the Low Countries, and in consequence Italy and the Americas, would stand in great danger of being lost'; shortly afterwards, with England already moving out of the Habsburg orbit, another minister repeated that if he lost the Low Countries, Philip's other possessions – in the Americas and the Mediterranean, as well as in the Iberian peninsula – would at once come under attack by land and sea.[60] In 1566, with disorder spreading throughout the Netherlands, a minister in Rome warned that 'All Italy is plainly saying that if the rebellion in the Low Countries is allowed to continue, Lombardy and Naples will follow'. The council of State in Madrid accepted the argument totally: 'If the Netherlands situation is not remedied', it warned, 'it will bring about the loss of Spain and all the rest'. Many others – by no means all of them Philip's officials – subscribed to this 'domino theory'. According to the papal secretary of state in 1567, 'If the Netherlands are lost, Spain will enjoy neither peace nor security, so that the true and perhaps the only way to secure Spain and also the other states [of His Majesty] is to make the supreme and ultimate effort to cure the Netherlands [problem] now'. 'There is a danger that Milan, Naples and Sicily will rebel, seeing such a terrible storm in the Netherlands,' echoed the French ambassador in Madrid. A few years later the governor of Milan warned: 'I greatly fear that the Netherlands will in the end be lost, and with that everywhere else will rebel'.[61] Before long even Philip's chief financial adviser argued that Spain must fight on in both the Mediterranean and the Netherlands, despite the intolerable strain on the treasury, 'in order to restrain and defeat our Muslim and Protestant enemies, because it is certain that if we do not defeat them, they are going to defeat us'; while the king himself came to fear that 'If the Low Countries are lost, the rest [of the Monarchy] will not last long'.[62]

When in 1577 Philip's councillors once more discussed whether to fight in the Netherlands or to make concessions in order to secure peace, they again warned that clemency would be taken for weakness and would 'put at risk the obedience of other vassals who, it is greatly to be feared, would take it as an example to rebel themselves'.[63] Shortly after Philip's death, the council of State advised his son and successor that 'the security of the rest of Your Majesty's kingdoms depends in large measure upon the conservation of the "obedient provinces" [in the Netherlands] and the recovery of those that have rebelled'; and that abandoning the Low Countries 'in a way that suggested to the world that we lacked the forces to keep them, would cause others to lose respect', so that the king's opponents in Italy, Portugal, Aragon and even Castile 'would reveal their evil intentions, which perhaps they refrain from showing only through fear of punishment'. Finally in 1605, according to a veteran councillor, 'the conservation of the Netherlands is so essential that, if they are lost, I greatly fear that the Monarchy of Spain will not long survive'.[64]

Philip II's Grand Strategy was not entirely predicated on the guidelines laid down in his father's reign, however. To begin with, Italy and the Netherlands ceased to form the centre of gravity. Philip's decision in 1559 to locate his headquarters in Spain reflected the fact that the financial, economic and human resources of the peninsula, and of its American colonies, had become the mainstay of his power; and as time passed his dependence on them increased. Writing only a year after the move south, a former Spanish ambassador in England complained that 'Every week it is necessary to remind people [here] that there are other kingdoms and states that depend on us, and we on them.' By 1564, however, the perspective of most courtiers had changed. Refuting those who urged the king to return to the Netherlands, Secretary of State Gonzalo Pérez compared the Spanish Monarchy to the human body and asserted: 'We must all thoroughly understand that since [Spain] is the principal member from which we must cure and restore all the others, I do not know how His Majesty could leave it.'[65] Six years later the king's speech to the Cortes of Castile reassured the assembly that 'His Majesty [knows] how necessary and convenient his presence is in these kingdoms not only for their own good and advantage, but also to act and provide for [the needs of] the other states, since these kingdoms are the centre, the heart and the principal part of all his dominions'. Nevertheless, some ministers continued to insist that the Monarchy remained a distinct political entity with priorities of its own that transcended those of the individual components. Thus in 1573, when a group of cardinals pressed Philip either to reside in Italy, to direct the campaign against the Turks, or in the Netherlands, to supervise the conduct of the war there, his ambassador in Rome (Don Juan de Zúñiga) reminded them that

> Since Your Majesty rules so many kingdoms and states, and since in their conservation and in the life and well-being of Your Majesty reposes the entire welfare of Christendom, it is not enough to believe that the journey should be of benefit to the affairs of either Italy or the Netherlands if it is not of benefit to the entire global empire which depends on Your Majesty.[66]

Zúñiga had pinpointed a source of tension that affected several early modern states formed by the union (often dynastic) of a number of previously independent components: although the strategic priorities of the most powerful state eclipsed those of other regions, it seldom effaced them. Admittedly 'sub-imperialism' never became as potent under Philip II as during the reign of his son, when powerful proconsuls initiated policies that served the interests of the region they governed rather than of Castile or of the Monarchy as a whole, but it remained a force to be reckoned with. Some powerful viceroys occasionally involved the king in a policy that could produce only local benefit (such as the Djerba expedition of 1560, earnestly desired by the viceroy of Sicily: see pp. 118 and 152 below); rather more of them managed to undermine royal initiatives that did not coincide with regional interests (thus the governor of Milan resisted Philip's explicit commands to expel all Jews from the duchy for over a year in the 1590s: see p. 277 below). The various regents in Brussels proved particularly adept at pursuing a regional strategy. Thus between 1569 and 1571 the duke of Alba disagreed fundamentally with Philip's desire to overthrow Elizabeth of England, which ran counter to the economic and political interests of the Netherlands, and deployed a remarkable array of devices to thwart the king (pp. 157–63 below).

Nevertheless, although this disharmony between the strategic interests of the major components of the Monarchy sometimes undermined effective policy-making, Philip's Grand Strategy increasingly reflected the traditional foreign policy goals of Spain. First and most obvious among these lay the absolute conviction that the interests of the Iberian peninsula must take precedence over all others. As one councillor starkly observed during the Portuguese succession crisis of 1578–80: 'In terms of the utility, the good and the strength of Spain, and of the grandeur and power of Your Majesty, uniting the crowns of Portugal and Castile matters more than the reconquest of the Netherlands'; and during these years the funds sent from Spain to the Low Countries duly plummeted.[67] In 1592, following the rebellion of Aragon, another adviser reminded Philip that 'Spain is the centre and the heart of this great Monarchy', and that any problem in the peninsula should be given top priority, 'because if Spain holds firm, the Indies and the other dominions of Your Majesty will be [automatically] preserved'.[68]

Second among Spain's traditional strategic goals came a determination to defend the Catholic church against all enemies, both inside and outside Europe. This committed Philip – who inherited the title 'king of Jerusalem' from Ferdinand of Aragon – to 'use our forces and power against the infidel', turning back the Muslim tide in the Mediterranean and protecting (if not extending) the remaining Christian outposts of the East. In 1559, although he made a favourable peace with France, Philip bungled negotiations with the Ottoman Turks for a truce, and for the next eighteen years he placed the defence of the Mediterranean above all other foreign obligations.[69] Even the outbreak of rebellion in the Netherlands failed to change this key strategic choice – although the duke of Alba and others protested loud and long that peace should be made with the Turks in order to concentrate on internal enemies. To the duke, crushing heresy seemed more important than defeating the infidel, but the king did not agree. Although his agents secured a lasting truce with the sultan in 1578, until the end of his reign Philip continued to seek ways to abase the Turks, welcoming imaginative (if fruitless) attempts to coordinate operations with other enemies of the Ottomans in the Middle East and the Balkans.[70]

Philip, like his father before him, also opposed Protestantism as strenuously and unequivocally as he opposed Islam. In 1566 he reminded the pope of 'the great and numerous obligations and burdens that I bear in the maintenance and protection of my kingdoms, in the continuous war that I wage against the infidel, and in the defence of Christendom and the public cause of the Catholic religion'.[71] On several occasions Philip declared himself ready to sacrifice all his dominions, if necessary, rather than imperil the integrity of the Catholic faith. 'Above all things I entrust matters of religion to your care,' he informed his chief minister in the Netherlands in 1560, 'because you can see how necessary it is, and how few people in this world watch out for it. And so the few of us who remain must take greater care of Christendom, and if necessary we will lose everything in order to do what we should in this'. Six years later he assured the pope that 'rather than suffer the least damage to the Catholic church and God's service I will lose all my states, and a hundred lives if I had them'. In 1585 the king's resolve remained unshaken:

[Although] I hope that Our Lord, in whose service this war [in the Nether-lands] has been waged and sustained at the cost of so much blood and money . . . , will arrange things with His divine providence, either through war or negotiation, so that the world will know, by the happy outcome, the fruit of trusting in Him, always keeping before us this firm resolve; nevertheless, should God be pleased to permit another outcome, for our sins, it would be better to spend everything in His cause and service, than for any reason to waver.

In 1590 Philip lamented that the debts he had already incurred for 'the defence of our holy faith and the conservation of my kingdoms and lordships' would increase further with 'the war with England and the events in France, which I could not – and cannot – neglect, because I have such a special obligation to God and the world to deal with them; and also because if the heretics prevail (which I hope God will not permit) it might open the door to worse damage and danger, and we shall have war at home'. A few months later, when a minister made an impassioned plea for the king to cut back on his wars in France, the Netherlands and the Atlantic, Philip reminded him that 'These are not matters that can be dropped . . . because they involve the cause of religion, which must take pre-cedence over everything.'[72]

He felt strongly that other Catholic rulers should show similar firmness. Throughout the 1560s he worried that Charles IX of France and his advisers 'are headed for the worst possible destination, which is a deal with their rebellious subjects' and constantly exhorted them to take a firm line against heresy. Philip also warned his cousin Maximilian (whose policy of religious moderation as Holy Roman Emperor he found alarming) that 'To believe that a passion as great as the one which surrounds the choice of religion . . . can be settled by gentleness and concessions, or by other means that avoid firmness and punishment, is to be greatly deceived'. According to Philip, the threat (at least) of force should always be present.[73]

Behind these uncompromising assertions that religious principle should always prevail over political calculation lay a distinctive political philosophy which might be termed 'messianic imperialism'. At its simplest level, it meant that (as the statements above make clear) Philip felt that he possessed a direct mandate to uphold the Catholic faith at almost all times and in almost all places. Many of his subjects agreed. Thus Luis Cabrera de Córdoba prefaced his *History of Philip II, king of Spain* (Madrid, 1619) with a splendid engraving of the king in armour (and garters) defending the figure of 'religion' with his sword: the motto reads

Plate 16   Frontispiece of Luis Cabrera de Córdoba, *Historia de Felipe II, rey de España*. The first part of Cabrera's study appeared in 1619, providing the best account available of Philip's life and reign written by a contemporary. The author, who (like his father before him) had attended on the king personally, portrayed him throughout as defender of the faith – starting with the image on the first page. Here Philip in armour has drawn his sword to protect the Virgin Mary, who carries a cross and chalice, with the Escorial in the background. 'Religion is the highest priority' proclaims the epigraph.

Plate 17   Spanish writers long continued to portray the king as defender of the faith. Fray Gaspar de San Agustin's *The conquest of the Philippine Islands, the secular by the arms of King Phillp II, the Prudent, and the spiritual by the friars of the Order of St Augustine*, first published in 1698, showed the king leading his conquistadors while St Augustine advances with his friars. At the centre we see not only the Philippines but also Borneo, China and Siam, which the Order also aspired to win for the Catholic church. A ray of Divine light falls upon Philip, with crown and sceptre, and the sun shines on his empire.

Plate 18   An illustration from José de Rivera Bernárdez's urban history of 1732, *Brief description of the very noble and loyal town of Zacatecas*, likewise showed the king (left) with the first settlers of the city (right). They hold a globe marked 'Philippus II', beneath the sun and moon (which never set on the Spanish empire). The Virgin Mary protects and oversees the enterprise and the motto proclaims 'Work conquers all'.

SUMA RATIO PRO RELIGIONE ('Religion is the highest priority': see Plate 16). Artists often showed Philip in direct communion with God, either at prayer (El Greco's *Dream of Philip II* and Pompeo Leoni's fine sculpture of him kneeling before the altar in the basilica at the Escorial), interceding for the dead (Titian's *Gloria* and El Greco's *Burial of the count of Orgaz*), making an ostentatious sacrifice to God (Titian's *Offering of Philip II*), or merely displaying some reminder of his piety (as with his rosary in Sophanisba Anguisciola's Prado portrait of the late 1570s).[74]

These works of art – although few people saw most of them – formed part of a powerful propaganda exercise. Whenever the king went on progress, triumphal arches and cheap prints portrayed his 'sacred majesty', while sermons and medals celebrated the achievements conferred on him by Providence (see Plate 2 above). Even a century later, published chronicles of Spanish expansion – including Fray Gaspar de San Agustín's account of the conquest of the Philippines in 1698 (Plate 17) and José de Rivera Bernárdez's history of Zacatecas in New Spain in 1732 (Plate 18) – still explicitly represented the king receiving direct divine assistance as he carried out God's purpose.[75] Philip seems to have eschewed only written polemics to advance or justify his cause, and the few efforts made on his behalf usually fell flat: thus an answer to William of Orange's blistering attack on the king's methods and morals perished almost without trace (only one copy of the anonymous *Antiapologia* has survived, as against five French, two Dutch, one English, one Latin and one German editions of Orange's *Apology* in 1581 alone). Philip authorized only one official publication about the Armada, a somewhat austere list of all the ships, stores, troops and 'celebrities' recorded in the last muster before the fleet left Lisbon, a copy of which the English later used as a scorecard to record its losses.[76]

Perhaps Philip's reticence to explain or justify his actions in prose stemmed from the conviction that it should not be necessary – that it somehow called their legitimacy into question (much as the Papacy had at first disdained to defend its position against Lutheran attack). Perhaps also, however, the king considered it superfluous because a host of Catholic writers – some but not all his subjects – did the job for him. In northern Europe, state-sponsored polemicists based in Cologne, Douai and Antwerp after 1579 presented the king's cause as God's cause. In 1588, Cardinal Allen in Rome produced literature aimed at convincing the Catholics of England that the Armada came to liberate them, while in Spain Luis de Góngora and Lope de Vega (among others) wrote poems and Pedro de Ribadeneira published a hard-hitting *Ecclesiastical history of the English schism* and a pungent *Exhortation to the soldiers and captains who are going on this campaign to England*, to justify Philip's decision to overthrow Elizabeth on political as well as religious grounds. Both tracts argued that Spain's reputation and security as well as the Catholic church would benefit from the 'crusade' which the king, heroically supported by the pope and by the Jesuit Order (to which Ribadeneira belonged), had decided to launch. God's cause, Philip's cause and Spain's cause were portrayed as one.[77]

Some Catholic writers went even further, hailing Philip as a new King David – a comparison first made in a sermon soon after he became king of England in 1554. At his coronation as king of Portugal in 1581, observers felt that 'crowned, with the sceptre in his hand, he looked like King David'; and several funeral orations later drew the same parallel.[78] Philip certainly viewed himself as 'rex et sacerdos' – king and priest – and he invested much time and effort in exercising the rights of ecclesiastical patronage vested in his office. To begin with, he selected all bishops and abbots personally – as he boasted to the pope on one occasion: 'I do not reward services by granting bishoprics, but rather I go and search in corners for the most suitable subjects for Our Lord's service' – and he showed no compunction in sending 'turbulent and scandalous' prelates into exile.[79] Throughout Spain and America, no new religious order or convent could be founded, and no papal bull proclaimed, without his express permission.[80] On one occasion the king told his ambassador in Rome to ask the pope not to promote any Spanish cardinals without asking him first (and rather pedantically added, 'Tell him that "Spaniard" refers to the whole of Spain, because over there I believe they think it means only Castile'). Another time, upon finding that his nominee for the vacant bishopric of the Canaries was illegitimate, he asked the pope to overlook the irregularity; and when the pope declined, the king simply asked again more insistently. When Philip learned that the pope wished to review in Rome certain cases judged by the Inquisition in Spain, he flatly refused to cooperate ('It is not just of His Holiness to allow this [a judicial review], and I will not permit [it]'); and upon learning that canonries at Jaca cathedral had been monopolized by a few families he virtually commanded the pope to end the practice.[81] The archive of the Spanish embassy in Rome contains hundreds of insistent letters in support of the king's nominees to the various ecclesiastical vacancies in his dominions, while in Naples Philip sent out inspectors to ensure that church patrons fulfilled their obligations and that parish priests performed their duties properly 'because these things affect our own interests'. At least one pontiff complained that 'in all the king's dominions His Majesty's ministers interfere too much in ecclesiastical jurisdiction'.[82]

On a more personal level, in the 1570s Philip strenuously opposed papal attempts to replace traditional plainsong with the more 'lively' music composed by Palestrina because he did not like it; and in the 1580s he gave notice that he would not allow 'his' bishops to adopt the shorter coloured costumes ordered by the pope because he preferred the traditional long black vestments.[83] He also requested papal dispensation for himself and his children to eat meat on 'fast days', 'since I do not wish to try changing our regimen'; and at the first Mass celebrated in the basilica of the Escorial the king sat in his pew close to the main altar and paid close attention to the order of service, 'looking at his missal throughout the Mass to see that [the celebrants] followed what it ordained, and if he noted anything that was not quite right, he immediately sent along a message to point it out'.[84]

The Escorial epitomized Philip's conception of his dual role as king and priest. At the front of the basilica he placed statues of six biblical kings of Israel, descendants of David and ancestors of Christ; at the back he erected apartments for himself and his family. He evidently modelled the whole edifice on the Temple erected by Solomon in Jerusalem: both monarchs executed an idea initiated by their fathers; both used gold, bronze and precious stones as the principal adornments; both attached a royal palace to the shrine they erected to honour God.[85] The Escorial represented far more than a pious replica of Solomon's Temple, however. Politically, it stood as a monument to the Habsburgs' defeat of their arch-enemy, since it commemorated Philip's victory over the French at St Quentin. Polemically it served as a visible bastion against the rising tide of heresy, since its liturgy, its relics and its religious iconography ceaselessly affirmed the validity of Catholic doctrine. Dynastically, it provided a magnificent complex in which the royal family could live, rule, pray and die as exemplars of Counter-Reformation piety, and also a mausoleum where the king could bury his relatives and sanctify their memory. During his life Philip specified that a daunting number of masses should be said for the souls of his departed relatives – 7,300 per year (excluding the anniversary liturgies) according to one of the Escorial's monks – and his will called for masses for his soul to be said constantly by all the priests of the Escorial for the first nine days after his death (with 30,000 more masses 'as rapidly as possible' at an Observant Franciscan monastery); after that the Escorial's monastic community was to hold for the repose of his soul a High Mass every day until Christ's Second Coming, additional anniversary masses on the dates of his birth and death, and continuous prayers around the clock before the Blessed Sacrament 'for ever and ever'.[86]

Philip's personal possessions naturally reflected his piety: the posthumous inventory of his goods mentions innumerable religious books, paintings and other artefacts. Above all, he gathered together at the Escorial no fewer than 7,422 relics, including 12 entire bodies, 144 complete heads and 306 entire limbs.[87] More significant, some authors described Philip's lifestyle as 'recogido', a significant term which implied a search for inner sanctity and religious purity; and indeed the king sometimes deliberately withdrew from government altogether in order to concentrate on his devotions.[88] In Lent, and at times of crisis, he went on retreat, and throughout his life he spent a considerable part of each day at prayer. As a matter of principle he held up all business while he communed with God – whether for an hour or so during a service, or for several days when on retreat – and he regularly used this excuse to his ministers for delaying decisions: 'I could not send you any more tonight because today we had a sermon'; 'I could not see the rest [of these papers] yesterday, nor until now today, because of the Mass'; and 'I cannot do anything more tonight, because it is late; nor do I think I can tomorrow because it is a day of vespers and matins'.[89]

No doubt these religious activities, which allowed the king to step back temporarily from political concerns and to clear his mind, renewed his strength to cope with problems of state. (They also occasionally allowed him to catch up on his sleep: in 1584, while at the Escorial during Holy Week, he confessed to his daughters that he had just 'heard two of the longest sermons of my life, although I slept through part of them'.) Perhaps his devotions also afforded an opportunity for Philip to lay out his options before God and seek guidance, something that (like other Spanish statesmen) he may have done with his confessor too.[90] More important, however, worship encouraged the king to see politics in religious terms: to justify difficult political choices on the grounds that they were necessary not only for the interests of Spain but also for the cause of God; to attribute victories to divine intervention and favour; and to rationalize defeats and failures either as a divine test of Spain's steadfastness and loyalty or as a punishment for momentary human presumption.

Some of these elements of course form the stock-in-trade of many leaders. In the twentieth century, Charles de Gaulle, Winston Churchill and, above all, Adolf Hitler all regarded themselves as in some way 'called' by Providence, and believed their actions in the service of their country to be directed by God.[91] In the early modern period, an even stronger element of 'Providentialism' underlay the strategic thinking of almost all states. Philip's Protestant enemies also regarded their victories as the result of direct divine intervention – a view epitomized by the inscription on a Dutch medal struck to celebrate the destruction of the Spanish Armada: GOD BLEW AND THEY WERE SCATTERED. They likewise saw their history

as pre-determined by Providence, and viewed wars against enemies of their faith
as a crusade – much as Philip II did. One French Protestant warrior, for example,
hailed the outcome of the Armada campaign in purely biblical terms: 'The duke
of Parma's plan has been thwarted, and seeing the chariots of Egypt overthrown
has put his nose out. God is wonderful in his works, which smash the designs of
this world just when people are ready to shout "victory".' [92] Even Philip's Muslim
nemesis, Sultan Suleiman the Magnificent (1520–66), sought to project the image
of an eschatological saviour; and as the Islamic Millennium (1591 by Christian
reckoning) approached, his successors, as well as contemporary Safavid and Mogul
rulers, saw the world in increasingly apocalyptic terms. [93] But messianic sentiments ran particularly strongly in the Iberian peninsula. In the early sixteenth
century, King Manuel of Portugal (Philip's grandfather) believed himself destined
to become emperor of the East, as did his contemporary Ferdinand of Aragon
(Philip's great-grandfather); and Charles V clearly thought that his enterprises
deserved to succeed because they sought to advance the cause of the Catholic
faith. [94] Some of Philip's subjects even argued that religion formed the glue that
held together the entire Monarchy. According to Fray Juan de Salazar, 'The
principal reason why Spain has been able to acquire the kingdoms it rules, and the
fundamental reason of state that it uses to conserve them, is religion'. More than
all other states, wrote Tommaso Campanella, the Spanish Monarchy 'is founded
upon the occult providence of God and not on either prudence or human force';
and he and many others saw its History as a heroic progression in which miracles
offset disasters – even the Moorish Conquest of 711 and, eventually, the Armada
– as Spain continued its uneven but divinely ordained advance towards world
monarchy. [95]

Philip himself saw his political mission in Providential terms from a very early
stage. In 1543 the colophon to the handsome atlas prepared by Battista Agnese as
a present from Charles to his son when he began to serve as regent of Spain showed
the figure of Providence giving the world to the young prince, then aged 16 (Plate
19). The victory of St Quentin on St Lawrence's Day, 1557, moved the king to
found his monastery and mausoleum at El Escorial, dedicated to that saint because
'he understood that such an illustrious beginning to his reign came through the
saint's favour and intercession'. In 1559, as he waited impatiently for a favourable
wind to take him back to Spain, Philip wrote: 'Everything depends on the will of
God, so we can only wait to see how best He can be served. I trust that, because
He has removed other worse obstacles, He will remove this one too and give me
the means to sustain my kingdoms, so that they will not be lost.' [96] The king's
conviction that his interests coincided with those of God grew after his return to
the peninsula. Although he seems to have equated them explicitly only once –
when he reassured his dispirited governor-general in the Netherlands, Don Luis
de Requeséns that 'You are engaged in God's service and in mine, which is the
same thing' (p. 75 above) – in many other letters he linked them implicitly. He
once urged an adviser 'to tell me in all things what you think is best for the service
of God, which is my principal aim, and therefore for my service'; and when he

Plate 19 Frontispiece of the 'Atlas' presented by Charles V to Philip II in 1543. Charles left Spain in the hands of his sixteen-year-old son when he departed from the peninsula to direct a new war with France in 1543. Apart from detailed 'instructions' on how to govern, he commissioned a sumptuous atlas of the world from the Italian cartographer Battista Agnese. The frontispiece bristled with appropriate imagery: on the right an eagle holds the Habsburg coat of arms while Neptune commands a trireme; on the left the young prince, dressed as a Roman, reaches up for the globe which Providence prepares to hand him.

heard of another minister's ill-health, he wrote: 'I trust that God will give him strength and health [to deal with] all the great troubles that afflict His service and mine'.[97] He sometimes even insisted that his own business should come before divine worship: he ordered ministers to see some financial papers immediately, even if it meant that they would miss church, because 'it will be far better for God's service to conclude these matters than to hear the weekly offices' and he opposed letting his councillors attend services more often during Lent because 'it is also important for God's service that they transact [business of state]'.[98]

The coincidence of the spectacular victory at Lepanto over the Turks and the birth of a son and heir to Philip in 1571 greatly strengthened these messianic tendencies. For example, it provoked a veritable torrent of letters from the king's chief minister, Cardinal Diego de Espinosa, drawing attention to such indubitable signs of God's special Providence towards Spain, 'which leaves us with little more to desire but much to expect from His divine mercy'. Espinosa even compared

Lepanto with the drowning of Pharaoh's army in the Red Sea. Meanwhile, in Italy, many speculated that Philip would continue, with God's grace, to reconquer the Holy Land and revive the title 'Emperor of the East' while the most famous painter of the age, Titian, prepared *The offering of Philip II* to commemorate the two events.[99] The following year, the massacre of St Bartholomew (p. 126 below) impressed even the normally sceptical duke of Alba as clear evidence of God's efforts to further both His own cause and that of Spain:

> The events in Paris and France are wonderful, and truly show that God has been pleased to change and rearrange matters in the way that He knows will favour the conservation of the true church and advance His holy service and His glory. And, besides all that, in the present situation, these events could not have come at a better time for the affairs of the king our lord, for which we cannot sufficiently thank God's goodness.[100]

Shortly afterwards the government organized a gigantic prayer-chain throughout Castile to seek divine guidance and protection for the king, as principal defender of the Catholic faith. The archbishopric of Seville (for example) was divided into 1,100 separate devotional stations, each of which had three days assigned annually – in strict rotation – for the recital of a special prayer. Meanwhile, the bishops received instructions to seek out 'persons whose prayers may prove particularly acceptable' and to beg them to ask God for the success of the campaign in the Netherlands. When, in spite of all these efforts, the situation continued to deteriorate, Mateo Vázquez tried in May 1574 to console his master with the thought that:

> God, who can do anything, is our greatest strength in these troubles, since we have seen that He always looks out for Your Majesty, and in your greatest necessities gives the greatest signs of favour: St Quentin, Lepanto, Granada . . . These indications arouse great expectations that, since Your Majesty fights for the cause of God, He will fight – as He has always done – for the interests of Your Majesty.[101]

After the loss of Tunis and La Goletta later that year, however, some of Philip's subjects began to criticize the king and his policies. In November, the faithful Vázquez reported that: 'Yesterday I heard [at Court] what I myself had greatly suspected about La Goleta, that people believe that [its loss] was due to God's anger'. The bankruptcy, the collapse of royal power in the Netherlands and the new round of taxes demanded from the Cortes in 1575–76 fanned the flames of disenchantment and even clerics at Court, such as the king's almoner Don Luis Manrique, added their voices to the refrain that God had 'repented' of His support for Philip and 'had begun to cause Your Majesty great difficulties in his kingdoms and states, and in his own family' (one young prince died in 1575; the crown prince in 1578). With rather more circumspection, Mateo Vázquez also drew his master's attention to the large number of setbacks to his plans and suggested that 'we should look very closely at the reasons why God is angry with us'.[102]

The death of King Sebastian and many of his nobles in the battle of Alcazarquivir in 1578, which left Philip as heir presumptive to the Portuguese throne, temporarily terminated this pessimism. Many ministers saw the catastrophe as the handiwork of God, 'because Divine Providence does not permit an extraordinary event, such as the one that has befallen this land, without great cause'. Later, the coincidence of a victory of Spanish forces in the Azores on St Anne's Day in 1582 and of the recapture of the island of Terceira on the same day one year later, suggested to one of Philip's secretaries that, apart from the saint, 'it must have been the late Queen Anna, our sovereign lady [who died in 1580], praying to God for victory'. The king agreed: 'I thought exactly the same thing one year ago; and although St Anne must have played a large part in these excellent events, I have always believed that the queen could not be without a share in our good fortune.' Even a hardened veteran of the campaigns, Don Lope de Figueroa, shared this outlook: Philip, he pointed out, had opposed a papal attempt to remove St Anne's name from the calendar of saints, and here was his reward.[103] Other soldiers burst into verse to celebrate Spain's new-found power. According to Hernando de Acuña:

> The glorious time, sire, either approaches
> Or has come, when the Heavens foretold
> One flock and one shepherd in the world . . .
> And announced to the earth, for its accord,
> One monarch, one empire and one sword.

The verses of Spain's other soldier-poets – such as Francisco de Aldana, Alonso de Ercilla and Fernando de Herrera, whose work circulated widely during the 1580s and 1590s – also displayed a self-intoxicating rhetoric which called for Spain to conquer the world.[104]

Such striking consistency in outlook stemmed in part from the common background shared by many of the king's servants. To begin with, over half of the men whom Philip appointed to major positions in the central government not only held law degrees, but had also attended one of Spain's six *colegios mayores* (graduate schools) where most of them continued their legal studies: 75 councillors of Castile and several of its presidents, 39 councillors of the Indies and all but one of its presidents, and so on. The crown reserved perhaps 150 senior appointments in Castile for graduates of the *colegios mayores*.[105] Furthermore, a large number of ministers were clerics, including council presidents (Cardinals Granvelle, Espinosa and Quiroga; six of Philip's eight presidents of the council of the Indies), council secretaries (Gonzalo Pérez, Mateo Vázquez and Gabriel de Zayas), ambassadors (Álvaro de la Quadra in the empire and England; Diego Guzmán de Silva in England, Genoa and Venice) and even viceroys (Granvelle in Naples; Pedro

Moya de Contreras, archbishop of Mexico, in New Spain). Many secular ministers shared the same devout outlook on politics: Don Francés de Álava, for example, who served as ambassador in France between 1564 and 1571, protested that if, in the course of his official duties, 'I am [required] to become an instrument that raises human considerations above divine ones, I hope that God removes me from this world'; and his correspondence with Secretary of State Zayas (admittedly a priest) exuded religious fervour – one letter cheerily concluded: 'Spirits up, God before us, and a fig for all the heresy in the universe.'[106]

Such uniformity of belief within the government's senior cadres, especially since it reflected the views of the king, no doubt helped to promote harmony of aims and policies. It may also, of course, have encouraged inflexibility – a dogged adherence to established policies, despite mounting evidence that they were not working – but even some of the king's Spanish critics shared the same messianic outlook and deployed a similar supernatural panoply to try and change his mind. Thus in 1566, as the Protestant tide reached its height in the Netherlands, an influential Catholic preacher warned the king:

> The holy bones of the Emperor your father are complaining and his spirit will demand God's punishment against you if you allow the loss of those provinces, without which Spain cannot live in safety. Your Majesty inherited not only your states and kingdoms from your ancestors, but also your religion, valour and virtue. I dare to say humbly to Your Majesty that you will forfeit the glory of God if God should lose his honour and his place over there [in the Netherlands] where Your Majesty is his lieutenant.

In 1580, some deduced that the plague that decimated the royal army – and even the royal family – as it entered Portugal was a warning from God to desist from the annexation, and in 1586 the nuncio claimed to have reminded the king, in an audience, of the Prophet Ezekiel's admonition to identify public sins that might offend the Deity.[107] After the failure of the Spanish Armada, Ribadeneira (who had been one of its most vocal supporters) solemnly informed the government that:

> The judgements of God are most secret, so that we cannot know for certain the purpose of His Divine Majesty in the extraordinary fate He has decreed for the king's powerful fleet. Nevertheless, seeing that the cause was so much His, and was undertaken with such a holy intent, and was so much desired and assisted by the whole Catholic church, the fact that He was not moved by the pious prayers and tears of so many and such great devotees makes us fearful that there are serious reasons why Our Lord has sent us this affliction . . . So that it is both necessary and advisable to seek and consider the causes that may have moved God to punish us in this way.

Ribadeneira went on to offer five reasons why God might be offended with Spain in general and with her king in particular.[108]

Even some Catholics in the service of other rulers shared Philip's Providential vision. In 1585 the papal nuncio in Madrid, while sympathizing with the embarrassment caused to Philip by Drake's destructive West India raid, suggested to his master that 'I expect that God will not abandon Spain's cause'; and in the spring of 1588 almost all the Italian ambassadors at the Court of Spain openly expressed their hope that the Armada would succeed since (in the words of one of them) 'we have God on our side, and it is to be believed that He will not abandon His cause, which in this case is the same as that of His Majesty'.[109]

In Philip II's world everything was felt to have a direct cause. Everyone therefore searched for the hand of Providence in human affairs and tried to discern and implement God's purpose. News of a defeat or a setback normally provoked Philip to wonder when 'God would return to support His cause', and if his fortunes received an unexpected boost he told his ministers 'God has done this'.[110] When in doubt about the correct policy to follow, Philip consulted committees of theologians noted for their apparent ability to interpret the will of God: for example, in 1565 he referred the appropriate treatment of heretics condemned by the Inquisition in the Netherlands to a Junta de Teólogos; and in 1579 he again sought the opinion of a number of theologians (some individually, others collectively) on whether or not to enforce his claim to the Portuguese throne.[111] Many of his subjects consulted prophets. In the 1580s Sor María de la Visitación (the 'nun of Lisbon'), Miguel de Piedrola (the 'soldier prophet') and Lucrecia de León – the first in Lisbon and the other two in Madrid – won widespread followings with their predictions. Their success (and that of others) prompted Juan Horozco y Covarrubias, frustrated because 'everyone' in Spain had begun to prophesy that 'in the year 1588 Spain will be lost', and that the Enterprise of England would fail, published a work entitled *Treatise of true and false prophecy* which sought to discourage the practice and discredit most of the practitioners.[112] He failed: in that very year the duke of Medina Sidonia asked the 'nun of Lisbon' to bless the Armada as he prepared to lead it down the Tagus; while Joseph Creswell, a Jesuit chosen to play a prominent part in the re-Catholicization of his native England should the Armada succeed, went to consult 'a holy man who enjoyed such contact with Our Lord that he might well have known something of His plans' before leaving Rome. (The 'holy man' discouragingly but accurately predicted that the fleet would 'go up in smoke'.)[113]

Philip and his supporters did not stand alone in their Providentialism. Throughout the early modern period rulers on both sides of the confessional divide created by the Reformation sought to identify God's purpose and to frame their public and private lives accordingly.[114] Thus Charles I, king of England, Scotland and Ireland from 1625 until his death on the scaffold in 1649, repeatedly adopted a Providential view of public affairs. In 1642, at war with important groups of his subjects in all three kingdoms, he declared that his victory would show that God had forgiven his sins, whereas defeat would prove that his punishment would continue until he had left this world: 'I have set up my rest upon the justice of my cause,' he wrote, 'being resolved that no extremity or misfortune shall make me yield; for I will either be a Glorious King or a Patient Martyr.' Three years later, after his crucial defeat at Naseby, Charles refused a suggestion that he should seek the best terms possible from his adversaries because:

> If I had any other quarrel but the defence of my religion, crown, and friends, you had full reason for your advice; for I confess that, speaking either as a mere soldier or statesman, I must say that there is no probability but of my ruin. Yet as a Christian, I must tell you that God will not suffer rebels and traitors to prosper, or this cause to be overthrown . . . A composition with them at this time is nothing else but a submission, which, by the grace of God, I am resolved against, whatever it cost me; for I know my obligation to be, both in conscience and honour, neither to abandon God's cause, injure my successors, or forsake my friends.[115]

One of the victors of Naseby, Oliver Cromwell, likewise felt total confidence in the justice of his cause, having been taught since his schooldays that 'Nothing in this world comes to pass by chance or adventure, but only and alwaies by the prescription of [God's] will'; and when, more than a decade later, one of his own enterprises (the 'Western Design') met with failure, he took it as an irrefutable sign of divine displeasure.[116]

Such total reliance on the hand of Providence could under certain circumstances produce an absence of policy – 'the forgoing of trust in fleshly reasoning and its instruments and institutions', as a critic wrote of Cromwell – but Philip and his ministers did not normally fall into this error. On the contrary, a conviction that 'Heaven helps those who help themselves' appears repeatedly in their correspondence.[117] In 1588, as he struggled to get the Armada to sea, the king hectored his council of Finance on the need to do everything possible to find the necessary funds so that 'I can say that I have fulfilled my obligations'. A few days later he again reminded a minister of 'the time and trouble' he had invested 'to find all the money that has been spent, and which still needs to be spent, so that nothing on my part remains to be done [in order to complete] what has been started'.[118]

Rather, Philip's brand of messianic imperialism led to the error of adopting unrealistic policies, doing everything humanly possible to put them into effect and then relying on divine intervention to 'bridge the gap'. Thus in 1571, when his plan to support an English Catholic rising began to collapse, Philip convinced himself that the invasion formed part of God's design both for His cause and for Spain, and so must go forward anyway.

> I am so keen to achieve the consummation of this enterprise, I am so attached to it in my heart, and I am so convinced that God our Saviour must embrace it as His own cause, that I cannot be dissuaded. Nor can I accept or believe the contrary, and this leads me to understand matters differently [from other people], and makes me play down the difficulties and problems that spring up;

so that all the things that could either divert or stop me from carrying through this business seem less threatening to me.

On this occasion, Philip recognized the dangers of such presumption, adding: 'I know that this is how this confidence in God should be interpreted, without letting ourselves be led to undertake enterprises that are either desperate or impossible, and with resources that in human terms are inadequate and weak (for that would be rather to tempt God than to trust in Him)'.[119] Later, he became less cautious. When the marquis of Santa Cruz complained late in 1587 about the danger of leading the Armada against England in midwinter, for example, the king replied serenely: 'We are fully aware of the risk that is incurred by sending a major fleet in winter through the Channel without a safe harbour, but . . . since it is all for His cause, God will send good weather'.[120]

Naturally, although Santa Cruz remained unconvinced, other ministers at other times often shared the king's conviction that he could secure God's favour and thus make the impossible possible. In 1574, when Philip resurrected the idea of invading England at a time when his resources seemed fully committed in both the Netherlands and the Mediterranean, his bewildered commander in Brussels concluded that such apparent lunacy 'must be divine inspiration'. In 1588, after reviewing the dangers inherent in the king's Armada strategy, one of the fleet's squadron commanders concluded: 'But since it is Your Majesty who has decided everything, we must believe that it is God's will.' At much the same time, either he or one of his colleagues informed the papal agent in Lisbon:

> Unless God helps us by a miracle the English, who have faster and handier ships than ours, and many more long-range guns, and who know their advantage just as well as we do, will never close with us at all, but stand aloof and knock us to pieces with their culverins, without our being able to do them any serious hurt. So we are sailing against England in the confident hope of a miracle.[121]

From the king downwards, almost everyone in Spain seems to have anticipated that God would intervene directly whenever required, and miracles became an integral part of Spain's strategic culture. In December 1574 for example – after losing Tunis and La Goletta to the Turks, failing to take Leiden from the Dutch, and paying a fortune to end the mutiny among his Spanish veterans in the Netherlands – Philip informed his secretary: 'May God help us with a miracle. I tell you that we need one so much that it seems to me that He *must* choose to give us a miracle, because without one I see everything in the worst situation imaginable'.[122] In the course of the 1580s an adviser declared that 'miracles are especially essential in the duchy of Milan, where one struggles against necessity all the time', and after the Armada's failure an outspoken courtier noted that 'everyone relies on the miracles and supernatural remedies which God visibly provides for His Majesty – and may He continue to do so, because it cannot be denied that the cause is His'.[123]

This constant and overt reliance on miracles nevertheless made some of the king's advisers feel uncomfortable. 'I do not know whether God will always perform miracles,' warned Cardinal Granvelle in 1585. 'In the end, we cannot do so much with so little, and God will not always do miracles for us,' echoed the duke of Parma the following year.[124] In June 1588, after a storm had damaged some vessels of the Spanish Armada, driven others into Corunna, and scattered the rest, its commander Medina Sidonia decided that the age of miracles must have passed. The storm had been so severe, he told the king, that 'At any time it would be remarkable; but since it is only late June and since this is the cause of Our Lord, to whose care it has been – and is being – so much entrusted, it would appear that what has happened must be His doing, for some just reason.' Perhaps, the duke speculated, the Almighty had issued a warning that the enterprise should be abandoned? Philip flatly rejected this. 'If this were an unjust war [he replied], one could indeed take this storm as a sign from Our Lord to cease offending Him; but being as just as it is, one cannot believe that He will disband it, but rather will grant it more favour than we could hope . . . I have dedicated this enterprise to God,' the king concluded briskly. 'Get on, then, and do your part!' Remarkably, this display of blinkered intransigence seems to have convinced the duke: just two weeks later he reported jubilantly that 'God, since it is His own cause, and since He has not forgotten the great service that His Majesty wishes to offer with this enterprise, has been pleased to reunite the entire fleet, without the loss of a single ship, and with no loss for any of them. I hold this to be a great miracle.' Medina Sidonia, like his master, now looked forward confidently to victory.[125]

This textbook example of 'cognitive rigidity' highlights two critical weaknesses created by the king's messianic imperialism: a willingness to cast all caution to the winds and, equally dangerous, a failure to make contingency plans. Late in 1572 Secretary of State Zayas drafted a letter from the king congratulating the duke of Alba on his successful campaign and giving advice on the best way to crush the prince of Orange who, 'since he is hard pressed, I believe will cross to England'. Philip deleted this phrase, adding, 'I never wish to write down predictions, or what I think will happen'. The king likewise failed to devote serious thought to 'fall-back strategies': he rejected almost all the alternatives to a conventional war to end the Dutch Revolt between 1572 and 1576 (Chapter 4), and in 1588 he refused to consider (until long after it had happened) what the dukes of Medina Sidonia and Parma should do if they proved unable to join forces as planned (p. 267 below).[126] It is easy to criticize these failures, but Spain's strategic culture absolutely demanded such total optimism: since it had to be assumed that God fought on Spain's side and would therefore send success, any attempt to plan for possible failure could be construed as either 'tempting Providence' or denoting a lack of faith.

Nevertheless, as the eminent mathematician John von Neumann once observed, 'Failure must not be thought of as an aberration, but as an essential, independent part of the logic of complex systems. The more complex the system, the more likely it is that one of its parts will malfunction.' Messianic imperialism, by contrast, accorded no place to failure, no recognition that human affairs have a tendency to become disorderly or that their random deviations from the predicted pattern require constant correction – particularly in warfare where, as Carl von Clausewitz wrote, every strategy is carried out by individuals, 'the least important of whom may chance to delay things or somehow make them go wrong'.[127] Philip failed to take this into account.

Admittedly, many twentieth-century statesmen and strategists have made the same mistake: Germany's Schlieffen Plan before World War I, Hitler's Operation Barbarossa against Russia, and the Japanese attack on Pearl Harbor all lacked a fall-back strategy: failure to take Paris in the first case, failure to take Moscow in the second, and failure to destroy the entire United States Pacific fleet together with its fuel reserves in the third, all proved fatal because from that point onwards, strategy had to be replaced by confused improvisation, impassioned rhetoric, and the hope of a miracle.[128] Philip II, however, left more to chance – or 'Providence' – than most statesmen, thanks to his complete confidence that God would make good any deficiencies and errors. Philip's messianic claims precluded not only planning for failure, but also a willingness to make the compromises that ultimately had to be agreed, whether with Protestants or with Muslims. Philip could never, like Henry IV of France, change his religion when it suited him ('Paris is well worth a Mass'); and yet his reluctance to abandon or even to adapt his confessionally based policies when they ran into difficulties gave other states – France, the Ottomans, England, the Dutch and several Italian rulers – time to mobilize their resources in order to thwart Spain's strategic goals. They may not have been able to prevent the acquisition of Portugal and its overseas empire, but they could and did limit the benefits that Spain derived from it; and they also successfully challenged Philip's power elsewhere, first in the Netherlands and the Mediterranean, then in the North Atlantic and finally in Asia and the Americas.

Scarcely had the king died than a flood of tracts and polemics claimed that the power of the crown had waned both at home and abroad during his reign. In 1599, Rodrígo Vázquez de Arce, president of the council of Finance, graphically informed the Cortes of Castile that 'We can truthfully say that when His Majesty died, his royal person disappeared and so did the entire royal treasury.' Martín González de Cellorigo, a lawyer who worked for the Spanish Inquisition, in 1600 printed a celebrated 'Memorial' for the 'Restoration of Spain' which argued that the Spanish Monarchy 'has reached a state which all of us judge to be worse than ever before' and explicitly used (perhaps for the first time) the term 'decline'. Balthasar Álamos de Barrientos, another lawyer in government service, composed a blistering assessment of Spain's position that almost parodied Charles V's survey just half a century before. Having described at length the discontents of subjects in every state of the Monarchy except Castile – open rebellion in the North Netherlands and vehement anti-Spanish sentiment in the South; discontent in Portugal, Spanish Italy, Aragon and the Americas – Álamos de Barrientos relentlessly reviewed the hostility of almost all the Monarchy's neighbours. France, although now at peace, boasted a powerful king (Henry IV) who ruled a unified state full of disciplined veteran troops: she would welcome any opportunity to foster a war in Italy that would weaken Spain further. England's inveterate hatred had led it to support Spain's rebels, to interlope in the Americas and even to launch direct attacks on the peninsula. The larger independent states of Italy all resented Spanish dominance and longed to see it end; the smaller ones, including the Papacy, could no longer be relied on for support.[129] The contrast with the confident vision of Charles V fifty years earlier could hardly have been starker. Just as the emperor (although he had acquired several new territories in the Old World and the New) failed to pass on his inheritance intact to his son, so Philip (although he too had added further realms around the globe) proved unable to hand on intact all the lands he had inherited, let alone achieve his strategic goals. Above all he had lost a good part of the Netherlands and his influence in England. Why?

PART II: THE FORMATION OF GRAND STRATEGY

In the year 1600 one of Philip's senior diplomats, writing in Rome, shrewdly observed to a colleague:

> Truly, sir, I believe we are gradually becoming the target at which the whole world wants to shoot its arrows; and you know that no empire, however great, has been able to sustain many wars in different areas for long. If we can think only of defending ourselves, and never manage to contrive a great offensive blow against one of our enemies, so that when that is over we can turn to the others, although I may be mistaken I doubt whether we can sustain an empire as scattered as ours.

The empire on which the sun never set had begun to seem like the target on which the sun never set. In the same year Anthonis Duyck, one of the king's former subjects in the North Netherlands, having somewhat smugly reviewed the various defeats and failures of the 'arch-enemy' in his diary, likewise began to 'wonder whether the Spaniards might lose in the seventeenth century all the reputation that they gained in the sixteenth'.[1] Both writers believed that Philip had failed to achieve his strategic goals and that, in doing so, he had gravely weakened the overall security of the Spanish Monarchy.

Paul Kennedy's *Rise and fall of the Great Powers* offered three explanations for this failure. To begin with, it accorded great importance to the series of changes in the art of war in Europe sometimes termed the 'Military Revolution'. First came the development of more powerful gunpowder weapons in the fifteenth century which rendered useless the high thin walls, designed to deter assaults, which had for millennia formed the standard defence for human settlements. Starting in Italy in the 1520s, however, a new system of fortification appeared, with low thick walls built in star-shaped patterns of bastions and ravelins, surrounded by a wide moat. Every part of the new defences bristled with guns arranged in interlocking fields of fire, ready both to cut down any besiegers rash enough to attempt a frontal assault and to keep the enemy's artillery away from the walls. The new style of fortifications, called the 'modern style' in Italy and the

'Italian style' everywhere else, made it virtually impossible to capture any major stronghold quickly. In the Netherlands, Antwerp, surrounded by eight kilometres of walls studded with ten bastions, fell in 1585 only after a siege lasting a year; while Ostend, a seaport defended by bastions and powerful outlying redoubts, withstood investment for three years before it surrendered in 1604.

Partly in response to the need to mount a sustained blockade of enemy strongholds (while at the same time defending one's own bastioned fortresses), the size of armies began to increase rapidly. The armed forces of Habsburg Spain, for example, increased almost tenfold in the first half of the sixteenth century. Inevitably, this prodigious inflation of manpower, on top of the crippling cost of the new fortifications themselves, led to a dramatic leap in expenditure on war.[2] These various developments, according to Paul Kennedy, formed the principal reason why the Habsburgs' bid for mastery failed: thanks to escalating military costs they 'consistently spent two or three times more than the[ir] ordinary revenues provided' on war. Before total victory could be achieved, the state went bankrupt.

Kennedy also suggested that two other problems exacerbated Spain's military and fiscal crisis. On the one hand, he saw the Habsburg empire as 'one of the greatest examples of strategical overstretch in history': 'the Habsburgs simply had too much to do, too many enemies to fight, too many fronts to defend' – in the Netherlands, Germany, Italy, North Africa, the Mediterranean, the Atlantic, the Americas and, after 1580, around the shores of Africa and South Asia as well. In the age of the Military Revolution, he argued, no state could hope to fight wars on so many fronts and win. On the other hand, Kennedy noted that the Habsburgs mobilized even the limited resources available for this herculean effort inefficiently. Instead of husbanding every available ducat, time and again they squandered resources needlessly: crippling industrial growth with heavy taxes; maintaining numerous internal tariff barriers; minting a disastrously overvalued copper currency; expelling the Moriscos in 1609; investing huge sums of money in palaces and court splendour.[3] But is this the whole story?

Admittedly many contemporaries anticipated Kennedy's argument. According to an English tract, published just after the 1596 bankruptcy decree, Philip's campaigns had become simply too expensive to win.

> [His] warres on land, as those in the Lowe Countries . . . will cost him six times more than it costeth his enemies, for that before he hath raised a souldier in Spaine, and placed him in the frontiers of Artois, ready to fight against a Frenchman, it costeth him a hundreth duckets, where a French souldier will cost his king but ten.

Many others excoriated the inefficiency, the backwardness and the underdevelopment of the Spanish economy.[4]

Nevertheless, the accusation that the Spanish empire mobilized its resources 'inefficiently' – though true – is anachronistic. To begin with, a number of basic, permanent and normally insurmountable obstacles lay in the path of any 'bid for mastery' by an early modern European state. In the first place, no government of the period could reach into all areas or command all subjects within its borders. The typical polity of early modern Europe was not the homogeneous and unitary nation-state; rather it comprised a loose aggregation of territories formed over the course of centuries by marriage treaties, negotiated take-overs and formal mergers. In almost every case an act of association laid down in detail the separate identity and particular privileges of the various constituent parts. Valois and Bourbon France, Stuart Britain and the Spanish Monarchy all formed 'composite states' linked by dynastic rather than by national, geographic, economic or ideological ties. Failure to observe the terms of incorporation almost always led – often very swiftly – to disaffection and even to revolt, led by the local elite. In addition, each major component state retained its own economic, social and (above all) defensive interests long after incorporation, and they did not always coincide with those of the central government. Thus Charles V favoured war with Denmark in the 1520s and 1530s because its king had come to power by deposing his predecessor, married to Charles's sister, and the emperor felt that dynastic honour required him to act. The government of the Netherlands, however, desired peace with Denmark because the prosperity of the country's Baltic commerce (popularly known as the 'mother trade' because it nourished so many other forms of economic activity) depended upon safe passage through the Danish Sound. For similar reasons, the Brussels government wanted to preserve peace with England, another major trading partner, and opposed any attempt by either Charles or Philip to imperil cordial relations.[5]

Conflicting religious allegiances, especially after the rise of the Protestant Reformation, also limited government effectiveness in many early modern states. Several rebellions against Philip arose in large part from the opposition of confessional minorities – Protestants in the Netherlands, Muslims in Spain – to the policies of religious unification that his government sought to impose, and some international crises stemmed from his desire to stamp out Protestantism. The king's confessional goals, however, often conflicted with other interests. At the public level, Philip's unqualified commitment to advancing the Catholic cause deprived him of potential friends and made him unnecessary enemies: he broke with England, Spain's ally for almost two centuries, essentially over religious differences. At the private level, it set up a tension between principle and practice that caused severe problems. Philip firmly believed – and his many devout advisers frequently reminded him – that he served as God's lieutenant on earth and therefore had an obligation to pursue at all times policies consistent with the needs of the Catholic church. This formed a crucial 'boundary condition' that all his policies and decisions ultimately needed to satisfy. Sometimes, nevertheless, when dealing with either Protestant subjects or Protestant neighbours, the king apparently failed for a while to perceive when a policy – such as permitting changes in the ecclesiastical affairs of the Netherlands between 1561 and 1566 – infringed this key boundary condition. In time he saw his error and changed course, but by then it provoked widespread opposition because many of his subjects, assuming that the new policy reflected a trend rather than an aberration, had made a commitment – just as firm as Philip's own – to an incompatible and equally militant creed. In the case of England, the king likewise failed to indicate what compromises he could contemplate in order to maintain cordial relations with a Protestant state, and so led Elizabeth to draw the wrong conclusions both from his apparent indifference between 1560 and 1568 and again between 1574 and 1585, and from his suddenly threatening actions at the end of those periods of coexistence. By failing, whether through expediency or oversight, to emphasize his boundary conditions throughout, the king embarked on a course of confrontation that would lead to almost eighty years of war in the Netherlands and almost twenty with England. The precipitation of these two hugely expensive but largely avoidable conflicts – which between them set Spain on the road to decline – had little to do with the Military Revolution, strategic overstretch, or the poor deployment of resources. Rather they stemmed from Philip's imperfect understanding of his executive functions, from the acute stress that periodically reduced his policy options as it increased his cognitive rigidity, and from the messianic strategic culture that prevailed at his Court.

4 The 'Great Bog of Europe': the Netherlands, 1555–77[6]

The 'Political Testament' composed by Charles V for his son in 1548 devoted remarkably little attention to the Netherlands because, as the emperor freely admitted, he did not know what to do. Should he bequeath them, along with Spain, to his son; or should he leave them attached to the Holy Roman Empire? 'As we have seen and discovered, the people there cannot tolerate being governed by foreigners'; and yet if Philip became ruler of the Netherlands, 'you will not be able to reside there, or visit them often'. Charles therefore decided that the young man should 'come and see the country for yourself' and promised to make no final decision until he did so.[7]

Four major considerations complicated the exercise of effective control in the Low Countries by the central government. First, the geography of the provinces created unique problems. On the one hand, much of the countryside in the west and north lay below sea level, and included large numbers of rivers, lakes and marshes, while an elaborate system of dikes protected the extensive reclaimed lands where farmers maintained a perilous existence. Owen Feltham, an English travel writer, later called the Netherlands 'The great bog of Europe. There is not such another marsh in the world, that's flat. They are an universall quagmire . . . the buttock of the world, full of veines and bloud, but no bones.' By contrast, an unusually large proportion of the population in the western areas lived in towns: the Netherlands boasted over 200 towns, nineteen of them with a population of 10,000 or more (compared with only three in England); half of the inhabitants of the province of Holland were town-dwellers, a figure unmatched elsewhere in Europe. All early modern governments found it hard to control their towns, especially when they were fortified, and by the 1560s twelve Netherlands towns possessed a complete circuit of 'modern', Italian-style fortifications while a further eighteen boasted a partial circuit.[8]

A second factor further enhanced the power of the towns in the Netherlands: the central government had only recently achieved its definitive form. By 1548 Charles ruled seventeen separate provinces, of which the most powerful were Brabant and Flanders in the south and Holland in the north; but whereas these three (and a few others) had been administered from Brussels for a century or more, others (such as Gelderland) had been acquired only a few years before. The absence of an accepted collective name epitomized the political fragmentation of the area: documents of the day referred lamely to 'the Low Countries' or 'The countries over there' (*Les pays de par delà*, a term coined by the dukes of Burgundy who acquired several Netherlands provinces in the fifteenth century, to distinguish them from Burgundy itself: *Les pays de par deçà* – 'the countries over here'). The emperor therefore decided to strengthen the ties that bound the seventeen Dutch provinces that he ruled. In June 1548 he persuaded the Diet of the Holy Roman Empire to recognize them as a single political unit (a 'Circle' or *Reichskreis*), to exempt them from imperial jurisdiction and imperial laws (including the 'religious peace' that permitted all territorial rulers to choose the religious creed of their subjects), and to promise to send military assistance if the Netherlands were attacked. A year later, having decided to allow his son to inherit the Netherlands after all, he persuaded the seventeen provinces – individually and collectively – to accept that thenceforth they would all accept the same ruler, and to recognize Philip as his heir and successor. Each province, however, retained its own representative assembly (the 'States'), sending representatives when requested for meetings of a States-General; but collective decisions of that body only became binding when the assembly of each province gave approval. In addition, each province had its own laws and legal system, which rarely permitted appeals to the central courts, and many boasted a formal contract that detailed the 'privileges' which each ruler had to swear to accept before his authority became effective. Any violation of the agreement could (and often did) produce rebellion: as one of Philip's Spanish advisers later noted with alarm, 'we read in the chronicles that there have been thirty-five revolts against the natural prince, and after each of them the people remained far more insolent than before'.[9]

Had these two considerations constituted the only obstacles to the effective government of the Netherlands, no doubt the Habsburgs would in time have surmounted them – after all, Charles remained a remarkably popular ruler despite some isolated rebellions, most notably by Ghent in 1539–40. In the course of his reign, however, two further challenges reared their heads. On the one hand, Protestant doctrines found many adherents in the area: by 1530 at least thirty works by Luther had appeared in Dutch translation, and during Charles's reign at least 2,000 Netherlanders were executed for their religious beliefs and a far larger number were sentenced to fines, confiscation or exile. Nevertheless, when the emperor abdicated in 1555, partly due to relentless persecution heresy seemed to be losing ground. The only major outstanding problem that Philip inherited from his father in the Netherlands (as elsewhere) was therefore financial. Despite prodigious tax increases, Charles's expenditure far exceeded revenues and the short-term debt of the Brussels government soared from 1 million ducats in 1544 to 3.5 million in 1556. The following year Philip convened the States of Brabant (the richest province) and asked for new taxes, but they only agreed on condition that they themselves would supervise the collection and distribution of the money raised. The king bitterly regretted this precedent but, at war with France and the

Turks, he had no alternative; he also had to make the same concession early in 1559 in order to secure an even larger grant, the Nine Years' Aid (worth 3.6 million ducats), from the States-General.

Having secured these tax revenues, and having signed the peace of Cateau-Cambrésis with France, Philip returned to Spain in order to concentrate on the affairs of southern Europe. In itself, this need not have proved a crucial error: Charles had frequently been absent from the Netherlands, often for years at a time (1522–31, 1532–40 and so on), delegating extensive authority to one of his relatives as regent. However, Philip foolishly decided to introduce a number of innovations to take effect at his departure. He appointed an inexperienced regent, his half-sister Margaret of Parma, with extremely restricted powers: he ordered her to inform him of every matter of note and to take no decision without consulting him first; he even provided her with a list of candidates who were to be appointed in strict order to ecclesiastical benefices as and when they fell vacant. To ensure her compliance, Philip also ordered her to follow in all things the advice of Antoine Perrenot de Granvelle, son of a leading minister of Charles V and an experienced diplomat in his own right (he had served as one of Philip's three negotiators at Cateau-Cambrésis). Granvelle corresponded directly and regularly with the king, often criticizing Margaret. All this seriously undermined her authority, and before long the English and French governments withdrew their agents from Brussels 'because we have learned that so far everything is decided in Spain'.[10] A second innovation was Philip's decision to leave behind two tercios of Spanish veterans as a permanent garrison, both to guard against the possibility of French aggression and to serve as a 'rapid reaction force' should a crisis arise in north-west Europe. Many Netherlanders regarded their presence with deep suspicion, fearing that they might also be used during a domestic crisis. 'I do not believe that people are happy with so many novelties,' Count Lamoral of Egmont (a councillor of State and prominent Netherlands nobleman) advised his colleague William of Nassau, prince of Orange. 'The king is totally determined to retain the Spanish infantry and demobilize all the other troops: I leave you to guess his reasons.' Somewhat later Granvelle voiced these fears more clearly: 'People here universally display discontent with any and all Spaniards in these provinces. It would seem that this derives from the suspicion that one might wish to subject them to Spain and reduce them to the same state as the Italian provinces under the Spanish crown.'[11]

The political leaders of the Netherlands soon discovered an effective method of registering their hostility. Given the dependence of the Spanish garrisons on local taxes for their maintenance, and given the government's agreement that the provincial authorities would control both the collection and the distribution of these taxes, the States flatly refused to release any of the Nine Years' Aid until the Spaniards left. After much heart-searching the king crumbled and, early in 1561, the troops sailed home – despite Granvelle's warning that 'they serve as a brake on people here: please God, let no trouble start once they have gone'.[12] Events soon justified his fears. In 1559 Philip had secretly arranged with the pope to create a new episcopal hierarchy for the Netherlands, where only four bishops ministered to over three million people; under the 'new bishoprics scheme', fourteen more sees (including one archbishopric) would be added. In addition, two members of each new diocesan chapter would serve as inquisitors to crack down on heresy, thus supplementing the efforts of the undermanned and overworked apostolic inquisition in the area. The new bishoprics scheme remained a closely guarded secret for two years while a committee appointed jointly by the pope and the king worked out the new diocesan boundaries. By 1561 everything seemed ready and so, without warning, the pope published the scheme and named the new bishops (all of them proposed by Philip). Granvelle became both primate of the new hierarchy and a cardinal.

A huge outcry immediately broke out in the Netherlands. The political elite felt alienated by the secrecy with which the scheme had been devised; many senior clerics opposed the plan because finance for the new bishops would come from redistributing the revenues from existing ecclesiastical institutions (theirs!); and the towns, led by the cosmopolitan trading metropolis of Antwerp, objected vociferously to the expansion of the Inquisition on the grounds that it would damage their trade with Protestant countries. Philip thus achieved a feat that had escaped his father: previously the nobles, the clergy and the towns of each province had always been at each other's throats; the new bishoprics scheme now united them. This time the Netherlands elite exploited the factions at the king's Court. In the opinion of a French observer, 'The stubbornness of the [Netherlands] nobles in their quarrel rests upon the favouritism and divisions that exist at the Court of Spain . . . The duke of Alba and Ruy Gómez . . . spread their wings to the most distant lands such as the Netherlands, where the duke supports Cardinal Granvelle, and Ruy Gómez, who has been [the cardinal's] enemy since the days of the late emperor, favours his opponents'.[13] Granvelle's opponents in Brussels made full use of their contacts at Court – above all Ruy Gómez and Francisco de Erasso – to discredit him and to assure the king that, at the price of a few small concessions, all would again be well in the Netherlands. In the face of their tenacious and well-orchestrated opposition Philip crumbled yet again: first he abrogated the 'inquisition' idea; then he suspended the appointments to several new sees (including Antwerp); finally he agreed to recall Granvelle whom everyone (wrongly) suspected of masterminding the unpopular scheme.

In retrospect, this sequence of retreats clearly formed the prelude to the major rebellion in the Netherlands that began in 1566; why did Philip not realize the danger at the time and take a firmer stand? The principal explanation lies in the king's perceived need to accommodate his principles – no compromise on heresy, no concessions to opponents, loyalty to his subordinates – to a series of crises outside the Netherlands. In the summer of 1560 the Ottoman fleet ambushed a Habsburg expeditionary force sent by the viceroy of Sicily to the island of Djerba in North Africa, capturing some thirty galleys and 6,000 veteran troops. With-drawing the tercios from the Netherlands a few months later could thus be justified as shoring up the defences of Christendom against Islam in the Mediterranean. The same remained true in 1562–63: while the Netherlands political elite concentrated on destroying the new bishoprics scheme and securing the recall of Granvelle, Philip focused all his resources and attention first on sending an expeditionary force to help his brother-in-law Charles IX to defeat his Protestant subjects in the first of the French Religious Wars and then on relieving Oran (besieged by Muslim forces). In the words of a minister of Court, 'We talk of nothing here but the siege of Oran . . . and on its outcome depend many other things – even whether we [i.e. the king] stay here or return there [to the Netherlands]'.[14] Under such circumstances, Ruy Gómez, Erasso and their colleagues could claim that concessions – even religious concessions – in the Netherlands were justified on the grounds that they enabled Philip to uphold the Catholic faith elsewhere.

Philip wrongly believed those who assured him that these measures would restore sound government, and he therefore left the Low Countries to look after themselves while he concentrated on another major campaign in the Mediterranean: he sent no letters at all to Brussels between April and August 1564. By the end of the year, encouraged by their new independence and under pressure from a small number of Protestant supporters, the Netherlands leaders decided to ask the king to modify the remaining heresy laws and to tolerate Protestantism in the Low Countries just as his cousin Maximilian did in the Holy Roman Empire. In March 1565 Count Egmont travelled to Spain in order to secure this further concession; at Court he stayed with Ruy Gómez. In one sense, the count had picked a good moment: he arrived just as news came in that the Turks intended to take Malta, forcing Philip to concentrate on making plans for its relief. The king had also arranged an interview between his wife Elisabeth de Valois and her mother, Catherine de Medici queen regent of France, with selected ministers from each side in attendance, in order to resolve outstanding differences between the two crowns and to hammer out a common policy on extirpating heresy. Egmont's chances of success were compromised, however, by the waning influence of his principal court allies: Erasso had fallen under suspicion of fraud (a *visita* would later suspend him from office and impose a heavy fine), and much of Ruy Gómez's time now went on running the household of the unpredictable and unlovable heir to the throne Don Carlos. Besides, the king now realized that their conciliatory policy had increased rather than reduced his problems in the Netherlands: as he wrote petulantly to a trusted adviser: 'I greatly regret [the things] contained in the two papers that [Egmont] has given me. I think we should look more closely at the motives of those – either there or here – who have put him up to this'.[15]

For the moment, however, the king's hands were tied. 'I have so much on my mind', he lamented as he wrestled over what to tell Egmont, 'that I scarcely know what I am doing or saying.' He could not accept the count's demand for toleration; yet 'if we refuse outright we would never see the end of him'.[16] Philip sought to draft an ambiguous reply that would maintain the integrity of his principles without stirring up more trouble. He failed. Naturally, Philip's constant preoccupation with Mediterranean affairs had become well known in the Low Countries: the records of Margaret's council of State (on which Egmont and Orange sat) carefully monitored developments in southern Europe and drew the obvious conclusions. In April 1565, for example, Orange noted that 'The Turks press us hard this year, which we believe will mean that the king cannot come to the Netherlands'; the following month Egmont, newly returned from Spain, confirmed that 'being preoccupied with the war against the Turks, who are expected to attack Malta, His Majesty finds it impossible to come to the Low Countries this year'. The king's subjects throughout the Netherlands ardently followed the progress of the Mediterranean campaign, with the aid of foreign newsletters and even cheap printed maps of Malta, since everyone realized that the outcome of the siege would determine royal policy in the north. For months no word came from the king: apart from another ambiguous letter in May, Philip did not communicate with his ministers in the Netherlands until mid-October 1565 when he began his letter to Margaret of Parma with the feeble excuse: 'Madam my good sister: The great and varied matters of business which have come upon me for several months past have caused my long delay in replying to the several letters you have written me . . .'[17]

Philip's studied neglect of his northern possessions had allowed an extremely dangerous situation to arise. After Egmont's return, few enforced the heresy laws in the Netherlands and Protestant cells developed in several hundred communities, creating a contradiction between principle and practice that the king clearly could not tolerate. In his carefully crafted letters of October 1565, sent just after hearing of the relief of Malta, Philip therefore reaffirmed all his earlier policies: no toleration, full and immediate implementation of the new bishoprics, expansion of the Inquisition. By now, however, words no longer sufficed: a formal petition demanding the abolition of the Inquisition and the moderation of the heresy laws began to circulate in the Netherlands and soon attracted over 400 signatures from nobles and gentry. In April 1566 some 300 armed supporters of these proposals forced their way into Margaret's palace and asked that she meet their demands pending a formal decision from the king. Lacking troops, money and support, she reluctantly agreed, and within a few weeks crowds of thousands began to attend the open-air sermons delivered by Protestant – mainly Calvinist – preachers. Incredibly, Philip still failed to respond. Although over the winter of 1565–66 he considered travelling to the Netherlands in person with an army, news that the Turks would again send their main fleet west dissuaded him: in April they took Chios, the last Genoese outpost in the Aegean, and only in August 1566 did it become certain that their galleys had entered the Adriatic and so would probably not attack one of Philip's possessions. His silence concerning developments in the Netherlands provoked Egmont to warn him directly that 'the sluggishness with which Your Majesty takes decisions on the affairs of this country is damaging both our Catholic faith and your service'. From Rome, Pope Pius V bombarded the king with pleas to travel immediately to the Netherlands in order to restore order 'before it is too late'.[18]

In the absence of forceful leadership from the king and his demoralized servants, Calvinist preachers in the province of Flanders began to urge their audiences to enter Catholic churches and forcibly remove all images – stained glass, statues, paintings – in order to 'purify' the edifices for Reformed worship. When the first few outbreaks of iconoclasm went unpunished, the movement gathered momentum and by the end of the month some 400 churches and countless lesser shrines all over the Netherlands had been desecrated. Misled by the ease with which the Iconoclastic Fury occurred, Margaret of Parma hysterically warned her brother that half the population of the Netherlands was infected with heresy and that 200,000 people had taken up arms against her authority. She also asserted that only two options now remained open: either to allow full religious toleration, or to restore religious and political control by force.[19] Initially, Philip tried to do both. Confessing weakly that 'in truth I cannot understand how such a great evil could have arisen and spread in such a short time', he signed a letter to Margaret which abolished the Inquisition, suspended the laws against heresy and authorized her to pardon the opposition leaders (although after a few days he made a declaration before a notary that the concessions had only been made under duress and were therefore not binding); he also dispatched orders to recruit 13,000 German troops for service in the Netherlands and sent a bill of exchange for 300,000 ducats to pay for them.

As the agent of one of the Netherlands nobles at Court grimly predicted upon hearing of the iconoclasm: 'Sooner or later His Majesty cannot fail to exact vengeance for such great disrespect and if he does leave Spain it will be with more strength and power than any king ever took to the Low Countries'. Confirmation that Suleiman had invaded Hungary in person with the Turkish main army, and sent his fleet into the Adriatic instead of into the western Mediterranean, gave Philip more room for manoeuvre; then in September came the news that the sultan had died on campaign, provoking mutinies and provincial revolts in his empire. Now, at last, the king could concentrate – for the first time since his departure in 1559 – on the Low Countries. The change came not a moment too soon: as his Spanish advisers pointed out on hearing of the Iconoclastic Fury, 'If the Netherlands situation is not remedied, it will bring about the loss of Spain and all the rest'.[20] After a series of council meetings, Philip (who, exceptionally, attended in person) resolved to return to the Netherlands, preceded by a powerful army. Since the loyalty of all the coastal provinces of the Netherlands seemed suspect, the troops would have to travel from Spain to Milan, and thence across the Alps and overland; once they had ended the troubles, Philip would sail from Santander back to the Netherlands and supervise the restoration of order. At first the king intended his army to march before the winter snows closed the Alpine passes, but neither the duke of Savoy nor the duke of Parma accepted his invitation to serve as commander. So on 29 November Philip appointed the duke of Alba instead. This inevitably delayed the whole operation until the spring, and some feared that the Mediterranean might not remain at peace for another year, but Alba left Spain in April 1567 and led his force of 10,000 Spanish veterans across the Alps in June. He entered Brussels unopposed on 22 August 1567.[21]

Philip now at last had a golden opportunity to redress the damage that his neglect had caused. The Netherlands were at peace, with many rebels dead and the rest fled; a new religious war broke out in France in September, offering some security from that quarter; and at Santander a powerful fleet stood by, ready to carry him and his Court northwards. On 7 August, however, even before the duke reached Brussels, the king resolved to remain in Spain until the following spring. His desire to keep the decision entirely secret led him to encode personally much of the eight-page letter of explanation to Alba, which 'nobody knows that I am writing to you', and he reviewed in detail several implications of the change: Margaret of Parma would need to be replaced as regent in the Netherlands, and Philip raised the possibility of sending his young brother Don John, whom Alba could train so that he would be ready to take over after the king's visit; further funds would be required to maintain all the Spanish troops for the additional months, and the duke must find ways to secure them; the punishment of those implicated in the troubles, which Alba had been instructed to carry out at once, could now be delayed until the winter, in the hope that 'this might offer reassurance to the prince of Orange, so that he will want to return to those provinces (although I doubt it), for it would be a great thing to be able to deal with him as he deserves, because if we punish the others first it would rule out dealing with him for ever. Nevertheless', the king concluded, 'I remit all this to you, as the person who will be on the spot, with better understanding of the advantages and disadvantages which might arise in all this, and of whether to act swiftly or slowly in the matter of punishments, on which so much depends.'[22]

The king's decision to put off his departure and to leave Alba in charge a proved fatal error. The duke wasted no time in pressing ahead with 'the punishments': only five days after entering Brussels he set up a secret tribunal to try those accused of heresy and rebellion, and early in September he had Egmont and other Netherlands leaders arrested. Margaret of Parma, outraged by the detention of her former advisers, resigned almost immediately, forcing Alba to take over the civil government of the provinces himself. Orange, just as the king had feared, remained in Germany. Then, in the spring of 1568, the prince and his supporters launched a major invasion which Alba only defeated after mobilizing almost 70,000 troops, at vast cost, and campaigning for several months. Meanwhile in Spain, the behaviour of Don Carlos, heir to the Spanish throne, became so erratic and intemperate that the king arrested him and placed him in preventive custody. By the time Alba had triumphed in the Netherlands, Don Carlos was dead and so was Philip's queen, Elisabeth de Valois, whom he had intended to leave as his regent while he revisited Brussels. Moreover, at Christmas 1568 a serious rebellion broke out among the Moriscos of Granada, which spread rapidly the following year, and in 1570 the Turks resumed their Mediterranean offensive, invading the Venetian island of Cyprus. Philip could no longer leave Spain.

Instead the king reverted to the techniques of government by 'remote control' that had proved so inadequate in the past. He insisted – as in 1559 – both on ordering the implementation of difficult and delicate new policies and on circumscribing the independence of his lieutenant. Apart from impusing a much larger contingent of Spanish troops and requiring the full implementation of the new bishoprics scheme, the king ordered Alba to create a new legal tribunal to deal with those accused of rebellion (the 'Council of Troubles' tried some 12,000 cases between 1567 and 1573), to streamline the entire legal system and to introduce important new taxes to pay for it all. As Alba observed soon after his arrival in Brussels: 'If Your Majesty looks closely at what is to be done, you will see that it amounts to creating a New World'.[23] Although separated by 1,000 kilometres from events, Philip sought to supervise all these initiatives himself, imposing restrictive instructions on Alba and requiring detailed information from all his agents abroad in an effort to maintain personal control. 'I charge you always to tell me everything you know,' he hectored his ambassador in Paris, because 'I both want and need to know in detail what is happening there [in France] and in the Netherlands'. In 1568, worried again about the absence of news, the same diplomat received orders that 'to end the suspense in which the king finds himself' about developments in the Low Countries, Alba should send a weekly report on affairs 'which Your Lordship can forward to us here by various routes'. Ministers in Madrid longed (like their master: p. 52 above) for an airmail service: 'If Your Lordship knew how much store the king places on knowing what is happening there [in France] and in the Netherlands, I tell you that you would send it by air'.[24]

Although the king's interference irritated the duke profoundly, for a while he succeeded in creating his 'new world' in the Netherlands, thereby leaving Philip free to create a massive fleet (maintained jointly by the 'Holy League' he had signed with Venice and the Papacy) which in October 1571 inflicted a crushing defeat on the Ottoman navy at the battle of Lepanto. The Turks made good their naval losses remarkably swiftly, however, forcing the king to allocate an even larger share of his resources to the Mediterranean theatre in 1572. He intensified his pressure on Alba to finance his expensive regime entirely from local taxes, especially from a sales tax known as the *alcabala* or 'Tenth Penny'. Alba did his best: in March 1572 he moved detachments of troops into the premises of shopkeepers and merchants who had ceased business in protest at the sales tax (levied without the consent of the provincial states), but pleaded with the king to continue sending money from Spain to subsidize his army until his draconian measures took effect. Philip, preoccupied with Mediterranean defence, proved unsympathetic: 'With the Holy League and so many other things that must be paid for from here, it is impossible to meet the needs of the Netherlands to the same extent as we have been doing up to now.' Subsequent letters commanded the duke to start collecting the Tenth Penny forthwith since 'It is very necessary and indeed unavoidable to do so, because we cannot send you any more money from here . . . My treasury has reached the state where no source of income or money-raising device remains which will yield a single ducat.'[25]

Yet again, Philip's attempt to micromanage policy from a distance had created fatal tensions. As Alba anxiously pointed out to a senior colleague in Madrid: 'I have no doubt that the royal treasury must be in a desperate state, and for that reason I am going almost out of my mind as I see matters proceed in such a way that if some new problem, however small, were to arise, His Majesty's resources are so exhausted that he might not have the strength to resist'. The duke concluded by wishing that he could come to Court himself to 'throw myself at His Majesty's feet and beg him to look at what he is doing' – at this point, however, Alba thought better of his bluntness and crossed out the last few words, substituting 'and beg him to have these things carefully examined, because they endanger both God's service and his own'.[26]

Alba's regime had alienated almost everyone, both at home and abroad. In 1567 and again in 1569, on Philip's orders, the duke sent troops into France to help the government's forces to defeat its Protestant subjects; in 1569 he also confiscated all English property in the Netherlands and in 1571 he became involved – albeit reluctantly – in Philip's plan to invade England in support of a plot to dethrone Elizabeth Tudor. None of these policy initiatives earned him many friends in the states that surrounded the Netherlands. Moreover, although he had defeated the attempts of William of Orange and other rebels to overthrow his regime in 1568, some 60,000 Netherlanders had fled into exile abroad where they longed for the day when they could exact revenge. Forces loyal to Orange, based in England, attempted invasions and failed only because the duke placed some 1,200 Spanish veterans in strategic locations throughout Holland (companies guarded Brill, Haarlem, Leiden, Alkmaar and so on) to guard against surprise attack. But both the garrisons and the towns concerned complained that this placed an intolerable strain on their food resources and so in October 1571 Alba recalled the troops to the citadel of Utrecht, where they spent the winter in greater comfort. Everywhere in the Netherlands discontent with the regime mounted – by no means solely because of the duke's attempts to raise the Tenth Penny: in 1571 and early 1572 a plague epidemic ravaged the country, trade languished, bread prices soared, storms caused widespread flooding and heavy frosts and snows froze the rivers. In March 1572 a shrewd observer in Brussels reviewed the unprecedented economic crisis and predicted that 'If the prince of Orange had conserved his forces until a time like this, his enterprise would have succeeded'.[27]

This danger had not escaped Alba's attention and he resolved both to send 4,000 Spaniards back into coastal garrisons in Holland for the summer and to build a citadel in Flushing (the most important port in Zealand, controlling access to the river system of Flanders and Brabant, the richest provinces).[28] Unfortunately for him on 1 April 1572, while the Spanish troops detailed to guard the coast remained at Utrecht, a force of about 1,100 outlaws and exiles (popularly known as the 'Sea Beggars') made a daring descent on Brill.

Alba and his lieutenants reacted to the outbreak of rebellion with impressive speed and initiative. Philip's agents had already divined the Sea Beggars' intentions: on 3 February Don Guerau de Spes, formerly Spanish ambassador in England, arrived in Brussels and warned Alba that the Beggars intended to attack one of the islands of Zealand, and on 25 March his successor provided even more detailed intelligence, writing that they lurked off Dover, 'Broadcasting among themselves that they awaited the arrival of some friends so that, all together, they could attack Brill on the island of Voorne'. This letter reached Brussels on 2 April – just too late to be acted upon – but Count Bossu, governor of the province of Holland, had already heard rumours of the presence of enemy vessels off the coast and led a force of 200 men to Maassluis, which he reached at dawn on the 2nd. There, learning of the fall of Brill the previous day, he immediately summoned reinforcements from the Spanish garrison at Utrecht. Thanks to his prompt and vigorous action, by 4 April (the day news of the Beggars' landing reached Brussels) Bossu had assembled a force of some 1,200 veteran troops on the mainland less than ten kilometres from Brill.[29] By the time enough boats had been assembled to ferry the troops to the island of Voorne, however, contrary winds held them back; and by the time the wind changed, the Sea Beggars had received reinforcements and now outnumbered the Spaniards, who perforce withdrew.[30]

Bossu's garrisons along the Maas nevertheless managed to repulse almost every move made by the rebels to extend their base in South Holland. Even in Zealand, although the Beggars managed to take Flushing on 22 April, the government rushed reinforcements into Middelburg (the provincial capital) and some other strategic locations. The situation only deteriorated on 21 May with the defection to the Sea Beggars of the well-fortified port of Enkhuizen, for this opened North Holland – previously a safe area – to the rebels, at a time when the government had its forces fully committed further south.[31] With three enemy bridgeheads – Brill, Flushing, Enkhuizen – to contend with, Bossu now stood in desperate need of reinforcements, and he appealed to Alba for urgent assistance. Bitter disappointment awaited him.

Had the Sea Beggars' descent on Holland remained the only problem facing the duke in 1572, it would no doubt have been solved relatively swiftly; but, in the event, four other incursions followed the capture of Brill with breathtaking speed. Ever since the failure of their invasion in 1568, William of Orange and his brother Louis had laboured in exile to mobilize foreign support for their cause, even moving to France in 1569 to fight in person in the army of the Protestant opponents of Charles IX. The following year, despite several victories, Charles made peace with his rebellious subjects and the Protestant leader, Gaspard de Coligny, entered the king's council; Louis of Nassau travelled to Paris to join him. The French Protestants eventually promised to take part in a new invasion of the Netherlands to be organized by Orange, and on 24 May 1572, three days after the fall of Enkhuizen, a group of French Protestants led by Louis of Nassau took by surprise the city of Mons in Hainaut, defended by a powerful circuit of Italian-style defences (a simultaneous attempt to take nearby Valenciennes failed).[32] Two weeks later Orange's brother-in-law, Count van den Berg, crossed the frontier of Gelderland with an army raised in Germany and took several strategic towns including Zutphen, the regional capital, which likewise possessed new-style fortifications. On 7 July Orange himself crossed from Germany with another army and began to capture towns in Limburg, while five days later a second French Protestant force set out from Paris with the intention of reinforcing Mons. Most observers expected that Charles, influenced by Coligny, would shortly declare war on Spain.[33]

Faced by so many different threats Alba seems briefly to have panicked: according to a well-informed source, he sought the advice of 'some theologians who claim the ability to predict the future' while his advisers desperately consulted works of necromancy. In the light of this (and no doubt other) advice, he soon regained his self-control and took two crucial decisions.[34] First, although well aware that his master's resources were stretched to the limit by the war in the Mediterranean, on his own initiative the duke increased his armed forces in response to each new crisis from 13,000 in March to 67,000 in August 1572. Second, he decided that absolute priority must be given to the defence of the southern frontier in view of the danger of a French declaration of war. Accordingly, despite the steady progress of the rebels in the north, Alba not only refused to reinforce his hard-pressed subordinates there but even withdrew their best troops southwards: on 15 June he ordered Bossu to send him all the Spanish troops in Holland, and ten days later he instructed the governor of Gelderland to send him a regiment too.[35] Both commanders protested vigorously, predicting (correctly) that this would cause the loss of areas that would prove extremely difficult and expensive to recover later, and they delayed carrying out Alba's orders for as long as they could; but the duke insisted.[36]

His gamble began to pay off in late July when Spanish troops ambushed and almost wiped out the French Protestant force marching to reinforce Mons. Then the assassination of Coligny followed by the St Bartholomew's Day massacre of Protestants in Paris (23–24 August) temporarily ruled out further French intervention in the Netherlands.[37] Two days later, Alba – dressed (as was his custom on campaign) from head to foot in brilliant blue – finally set out for Mons and two weeks later, 'on one of the most beautiful days ever seen', he personally directed the repulse of a desperate attempt by Orange and his army to break through the siegeworks and relieve Mons. The prince fell back and advised the beleaguered garrison to make the best terms it could.[38]

This marked a turning-point in the revolt because, with Orange in full retreat and the danger from France neutralized, Alba and his massive army could now counter-attack. Several alternative strategies lay open. First, the duke could pursue Orange's main force and try to compel it into fighting; but that was not his style. In 1568, when the prince invaded the Netherlands with an army for the first time, Alba had acted with great caution. In the words of one of his field commanders:

The duke has laboured specifically to avoid fighting a battle, despite pressure from those who forget that victory is a gift of Fortune, which can benefit the Bad as well as the Good. If Orange were a powerful monarch who could maintain a mighty army for longer, I would be in favour of fighting a battle; but since it is certain that shortage of money will cause his forces to crumble, and that he will not then be able to regroup, I am against it.

In the event the duke's men skirmished for twenty-nine days continuously until Orange's army finally disintegrated and fled.[39] In 1572 other considerations reinforced Alba's prudent military approach: some fifty towns had declared for the rebels so that winning a single battle would not necessarily force their surrender (Plate 20). Yet attempting to reduce systematically every town in rebel hands likewise made little sense, since many boasted Italian-style defences and could withstand a siege for months. Alba therefore chose a strategy of selective brutality towards the rebellious towns, calculating that a few examples of terror would accelerate the process of pacification. At first the policy proved spectacularly successful. Mechelen, which had refused to accept a royal garrison in June and had then welcomed the prince of Orange's troops in August, was taken by storm and subjected to a horrifying sack which lasted three days. Even before the screams abated, the other rebellious towns in Flanders and Brabant made haste to surrender, 'So now the entire country on this side of the Maas is secure' (as Claude de Mondoucet, a French envoy in the duke's camp, noted with reluctant admiration).[40]

Since Orange's forces still controlled almost all the major towns along the rivers Maas and Rhine, the duke could not advance directly into Holland, but had to march north-eastwards into Gelderland and recapture the rebellious areas there in order to protect his lines of communication. In November, his forces moved against Zutphen, the strongest town in the area, which (like Mechelen) had not only refused to accept a royalist garrison but then promptly defected to the rebels. Once again, 'beastliness' paid off: after the brutal sack of the city, Alba proudly informed the king that 'Gelderland and Overijssel have been conquered with the capture of Zutphen and the terror that it caused'.[41] The rebel centres in Friesland, too, soon surrendered: this time the duke pardoned them all.[42]

Now, at last, Alba could deal with the provinces where the 'troubles' had started. No one seems to have envisaged great difficulties: even Mondoucet (no friend of Spain) believed that 'Since the population of Holland is not warlike and lacks spirit, every town will seek to surrender when the duke's army approaches'. Nevertheless, Alba resolved to make an example of one more rebellious centre in order to encourage the surrender of the rest. Naarden, the first town across the provincial boundary of Holland, obligingly declined to surrender when summoned early in December and, in the duke's own words, 'The Spanish infantry gained the walls and massacred citizens and soldiers. Not a mother's son escaped.'[43] Almost immediately, just as Alba had predicted, envoys from Haarlem (the nearest rebel stronghold) arrived at the camp; but they asked to negotiate,

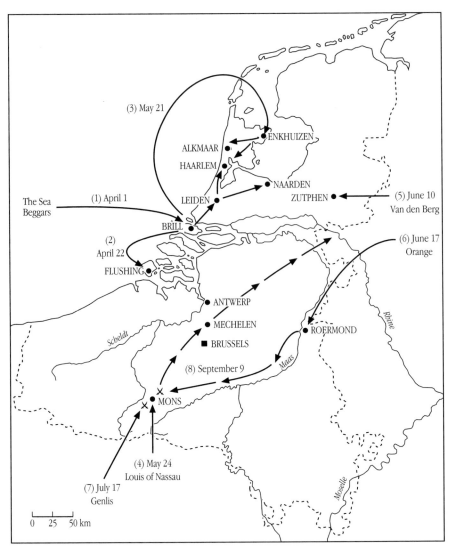

Plate 20 The 1572 campaign. The duke of Alba faced five separate invasions in the course of
1572. In April a small fleet carrying some 1,100 exiles, known as the Sea Beggars, captured the
small port of Brill in South Holland in the name of the prince of Orange. From there they
exploited local discontent in order to gain control of the key ports of Flushing in Zealand and
Enkhuisen in North Holland. In May another group of exiles and some French Protestant
supporters, led by Orange's brother Louis of Nassau, seized the heavily fortified city of Mons in the
south, and a month later a German force commanded by Count William van den Berg (Orange's
brother-in-law) seized the equally well-defended town of Zutphen in the east. Alba began to
withdraw troops from the outlying provinces in order to concentrate on the siege of Mons, which
encouraged several towns in Holland to declare for Orange. Meanwhile, in July, the prince
advanced with a large army from Germany into the eastern Netherlands, while another force of
French Protestants crossed the southern frontier: both aimed to relieve Mons. They failed. In July
the French were ambushed and almost annihilated; in September a desperate attempt by Orange
to break through the siegeworks miscarried. The prince and his troops retreated northwards,
leaving Mons – and the rest of the towns that had declared for him – to make the best terms they
could. By December Alba's army had pacified all but parts of Holland and Zealand.

instead of offering unconditional surrender. After the rigours of eight months of bloody campaign, the Spaniards refused to discuss terms and sent the delegates of Haarlem home to think again.

This proved to be a rash decision for two reasons. The rebel cause had put down far deeper roots in Holland and Zealand than in the other provinces. Haarlem, like other leading towns, had not been surprised by Orangist forces like Mechelen or Zutphen: rebel cadres within had declared spontaneously for the prince, opened the gates and allowed a large number of exiles (many of them from prominent local families) to return home to take charge. Then, assisted by local supporters, the new rulers purged and reformed the town's government, closed Catholic churches and allowed Calvinist worship, and sent delegates to the provincial Estates which assembled almost spontaneously and ruled most of Holland in the name of Orange. These circumstances naturally produced a greater determination to resist, because those who had flouted the king's authority in both politics and religion so flagrantly knew they could expect no mercy. If any doubted this, the fate of Naarden soon convinced them.[44] Moreover, for the strategic reasons noted above, Alba's troops arrived in the area last, which gave the rebel regime there far longer to generate a revolutionary fervour and tenacity and, equally important, to build and garrison new Italian-style fortifications (as at Haarlem and Alkmaar) and to begin flooding the surrounding areas to keep besiegers at bay (as at Leiden).[45]

On the other hand, by December Spain's forces were far weaker. The very success of Alba's campaign had dramatically reduced the size of his field army, both because the various 'actions' of the war, especially the sieges of Mons and Zutphen, caused relatively high casualties among the front-line troops, and because each rebellious town recaptured, whether by brutality or clemency, required a garrison. After Naarden, Alba's field army numbered scarcely 12,000 effectives.[46] To contemplate the siege of a town like Haarlem – which boasted a garrison of over 3,000 men and strong defences – with such a relatively small force would have been rash at any time; but in the depths of winter, with the possibility of having to dig siegeworks in the frozen earth, it seemed foolhardy in the extreme.[47]

Such conduct appeared all the more surprising in the duke of Alba, a general with thirty years' experience of command and a universal reputation for prudence.[48] Furthermore, in this particular instance, personal recollection should have reinforced his instincts because he had commanded the Habsburg forces at the unsuccessful siege of Metz, called off after three months in December 1552 mainly because the besiegers could no longer endure the cold.[49] Several reasons explain Alba's fatal disregard of this precedent. To begin with, after three months 'sleeping rough' at the head of his troops, the duke (now 66 years old) fell ill and had to stay behind at Nijmegen, leaving his inexperienced and arrogant son, Don Fadrique de Toledo, to take the fateful decision to reject Haarlem's offer to surrender on terms.[50] By the time the duke heard about it, the opportunity for clemency had passed. Even had he been present, however, Alba might himself have insisted on unconditional surrender. To begin with, the 'strategy of selective brutality' appeared to be working again: the delegation from Haarlem was followed by others equally anxious to make peace before the Army of Flanders approached their town. The entire revolt might therefore collapse, if only the Spaniards could persevere for a few more weeks.[51] Second, Alba worried that, if the rebellion continued into the spring of 1573, it might gain further assistance from Spain's enemies abroad – from France, England and the German Protestants. One of his few foreign allies had already warned him that 'it was not the prince of Orange or the counts of Nassau who made war in the Netherlands, but its neighbours, because of the hatred they bore towards His Excellency'. On this score too, Alba felt, one more show of force to end the uprising swiftly seemed worth the risk.[52] Third, and most pressing of all, perseverance with the war appeared to make financial sense. All early modern armies expected some wage arrears before they went into winter quarters, but in December 1572 Alba could pay nothing at all. Even before the 'troubles' started, he owed his Spanish troops one year's back wages and by December twenty months', while he owed the new (and more numerous) Netherlands units six months'. The German regiments had received nothing since they enlisted. So it seemed to the duke not only 'cheaper' to fight on; it also reduced the risk of mutiny by the troops who – although somewhat placated by the plunder gained at Mechelen, Zutphen and Naarden – suffered greatly because of the high cost of victuals in war-torn Holland.[53]

One thousand kilometres away in Spain, as in 1566 the king realized that his policies had misfired catastrophically. Already in the autumn of 1571, in response to Alba's repeated requests to be allowed to return to Court, Philip had appointed the duke of Medinaceli, a grandee with considerable military and administrative experience, to succeed; but he could not decide on either the right policy for him to follow or even the right moment for him to take over. The unfortunate duke therefore received contradictory instructions: those drawn up by Philip's French language secretary, reflecting the views of Ruy Gómez and many Netherlanders, urged Medinaceli to pursue a policy of reconciliation and gentleness; those prepared by the Spanish secretary of state, which incorporated the policy of Alba's allies at Court, commanded Medinaceli to collaborate with his predecessor and to follow his policies, forbidding him to attempt any new measures without express orders from Madrid. To inspissate the obscurity, the king's private secretary showed Medinaceli 'all the papers of complaints [against Alba] that I have in my possession (which we will be using in due course), for his information, preparation and secret knowledge, in order to convince him that he can report back here clearly'.[54]

As so often, Philip tried to do too many things at once. He decided that Medinaceli should go to the Netherlands by sea, together with a large fleet of vessels carrying reinforcements for the Army of Flanders; then he repeatedly delayed the fleet's departure from Spain, in case the troops could be used to assist a rising of English Catholics against Queen Elizabeth (p. 161 below). By the time they finally arrived in the Netherlands, in June 1572, Alba's policies had produced widespread rebellion which precluded his replacement, and so his designated successor, with little else to do, began to ingratiate himself with the leading Netherlands nobles and, as instructed, relayed their views directly to the king in a clandestine correspondence carried by his own special messengers. This, as Mateo Vázquez (who handled the correspondence) pointed out, 'enables Your Majesty to learn what is happening without anyone being aware of the fact' and the king enthusiastically authorized its continuation, adding, 'I want no one to learn of this'.[55]

It is worth lingering for a moment over this episode because it epitomized so many of the faults inherent in Philip's style of government. It made no sense to tie Medinaceli's departure to that of a fleet prepared for an entirely different purpose: even without the foolish attempt to link the fleet's departure to events in England over which Spain had no control, getting any major expedition to sea inevitably risked delay (when Philip finally authorized Medinaceli to sail, adverse winds held him back until 1 May 1572; almost immediately a storm struck his fleet and dispersed it to various ports; it only dropped anchor in the Netherlands on 13 June). Medinaceli could have travelled separately, either by sea or through France, and replaced the hated duke of Alba long before the outbreak of rebellion – thus perhaps neutralizing much of Orange's local support. Leaving the governor-designate in the Netherlands with no clear role to play made no sense either. He consistently advocated a conciliatory line, both in the council and in his secret letters to the king, but to no avail; Alba's arguments always prevailed. Thus at a meeting of Alba's council of war in September 1572, as the Spanish army moved on Mechelen, Medinaceli urged that as many innocent people as possible should be spared, to which his rival replied icily 'that he did not know who the innocent were, and if his lordship knew, he should tell him. And with that the council broke up.'[56]

Back in Spain, the king could not decide what to do. When he received news of the revolt, and of the probability of French involvement, Philip immediately ordered Don John of Austria, in command of the fleet of the Holy League, to remain where he was – at Messina in Sicily – and to undertake no action against Muslim forces until receiving further orders (thereby enraging both the Venetians and the pope). Furthermore, the king approved Alba's decision to follow the Habsburgs' traditional operational strategy of employing over-whelming force in order to achieve swift success (as in 1546–47 against the German Protestants, in 1543–44, 1552–53 and 1557–58 against France, and in 1568 against William of Orange's invasion) and, in spite of his recent litany of protests about the total exhaustion of his treasury, managed to raise large sums of money to finance the rapid increase in the size of the Army of Flanders. The great risk with this strategy, however, lay in the absolute need for *rapid* success: neither the economic nor the diplomatic situation of the Habsburg Monarchy could permit a massive military effort in one area indefinitely. That was the real reason why rejecting Haarlem's offer to negotiate proved so significant, for Spain's forces could not capture the city without a blockade and a blockade would take months, exhausting the king's resources and allowing his enemies elsewhere to exploit the situation. In the end, it is true, the town surrendered unconditionally – but only in July 1573, after a siege lasting seven months during which the Spaniards lost thousands of men, the rebels gained a number of strongholds elsewhere, and the king spent over 2 million ducats.

Long before this, Philip had lost patience with Alba and those at Court who supported him. 'I will never have enough money to assuage your appetite,' he informed the duke with uncharacteristic bluntness, 'but I can easily find a successor able and steadfast enough to end by moderation and clemency a war that you have not been able to end by force'.[57] In January 1573, since the initial success of the 'strategy of selective brutality' had discredited Medinaceli and the stalemate in the trenches before Haarlem now undermined Alba, the king decided to recall both dukes and informed Don Luis de Requesens, one of his childhood playmates and a man who had managed to remain unaffected by the factional rivalries at Court, that he should forthwith take charge in the Netherlands and attempt to end the war 'by moderation and clemency'. According to Philip's letter of appointment,

> Wars, misfortunes and other events have reduced the Low Countries to such a miserable state that, despite the successful course of the war in terms of capturing and recovering the towns in rebellion (which I trust in God will be swiftly and favourably completed), I am deeply concerned. For the discharge of my conscience, for the security and conservation of those provinces, and for the repair of so much damage, I am convinced that it is necessary to find a lasting settlement there.

In the king's opinion, finding an immediate and permanent solution to the Netherlands problem constituted 'the greatest and most important enterprise with which I have had, or could have, to deal'.[58] Unfortunately for the king's plans Requesens, serving at this time as governor of Milan, regarded his new appointment as a poisoned chalice: 'the position there is hopeless', he confided to his brother as he began a sustained campaign to persuade the king to find someone else for the post. Philip found it necessary to write no fewer than five long holograph letters – cajoling and hectoring by turns – before his reluctant nominee consented to leave Milan. Given the distance involved, each exchange took up almost a month and Requesens only rode reluctantly into Brussels in October 1573.[59]

This extraordinary series of delays in replacing Alba fatally undermined all chances of turning the fall of Haarlem (in July) to advantage. William of Orange's closest adviser, Philip Marnix, feared that the city's surrender might cause the collapse of the revolt and the duke of Medinaceli, still malevolently yet impotently monitoring Alba's conduct of the war, agreed. He warned the king:

Affairs have now reached the point where either they will be brought to a speedy conclusion or else they will last a long time; and, in my opinion, this depends on the decisions to be taken on how to proceed in Holland, because a lot of towns [there] remain to be reduced, besides the seas and Zealand . . .'[60]

Alba and his son as usual ignored Medinaceli, however, and instead frittered their chances away. Although they imposed only a relatively modest fine on Haarlem when it surrendered, they ordered the execution of some sixty burghers and 2,300 soldiers of the garrison in cold blood (Plate 21). Admittedly, shortly after this Alba offered a limited pardon to any rebels who surrendered, which again alarmed the Dutch leaders; but not for long. The duke's shortage of money caused the unpaid Spanish regiments to mutiny until he had paid at least a part of their wage arrears, depriving Alba of two weeks of prime campaigning season; and the massacre of so many defenders strengthened the resolve of other rebellious towns

Plate 21   The execution of the Haarlem garrison. Just as the Spanish army re-entered Holland in December 1572, Orange managed to rush German, French, English and Scots reinforcements into Haarlem, and the civic leaders who had declared for the prince a few months before therefore decided to reject Alba's demand for unconditional surrender. Seven months later, however, after the failure of all attempts at relief, the town placed itself at the Spaniards' mercy. They executed some sixty burghers and most of the garrison, over 2,000 men, sparing only some English and Germans. Walter Morgan, an English volunteer in Dutch service, who copied several contemporary prints of Spanish defeats and atrocities into his 'campaign journal', included a sketch of the mass executions at Haarlem in July 1573. It shows the burghers being hanged while the garrison is either beheaded in the market place or thrown into the river Spaarn (beside one of the bastions that had made the town so hard to capture).

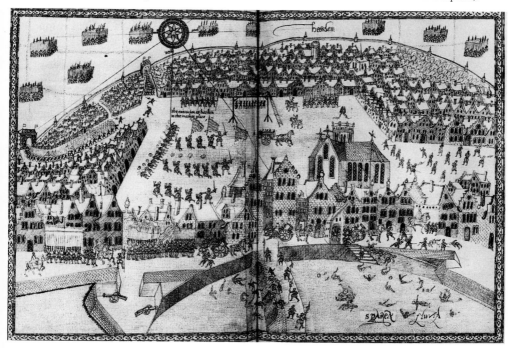

to resist. As Cardinal Granvelle, in semi-exile in Italy, sagely observed, 'the duke of Alba now complains that other areas have not surrendered spontaneously, but he should remember that there are soldiers defending the [other] towns who, fearing the same treatment as the garrison of Haarlem, will fight to the last man'.[61] The duke's second crucial error at this point was to move against Alkmaar, a relatively insignificant town in North Holland, but newly fortified in the Italian style and surrounded by flooded land. Alba anticipated that Alkmaar would prove an easy target, and indeed many of the town's inhabitants at first favoured surrender; but even his ingenious floating batteries and assault pontoons failed to take it. Equally serious, the abortive siege postponed by six more weeks the entry of Philip's forces into South Holland and Zealand, the core of the uprising.[62]

Meanwhile the Army of Flanders absorbed 500,000 ducats each and every month and the Mediterranean fleet almost as much again (Table 4). At the same time, France began again to undermine Spain's position: in Constantinople Charles IX's envoy secured from the sultan peace terms for Venice (March 1573) and a guarantee of protection for the Papal States (June 1573), leaving the king of Spain to withstand Turkish assaults in the Mediterranean virtually alone; meanwhile Charles and his younger brothers all sent assistance to the Dutch.[63] This dangerous financial and diplomatic conjuncture naturally led both Philip and his senior commanders to give active consideration to alternative strategies for winning the war against the Dutch.

The first and most obvious of these involved making peace with the Turks in order to concentrate on the Low Countries. In 1572 the king had held back his fleet until he could be sure that France did not intend to declare war on him; but from July onwards his commitment to the Holy League remained firm, and even news of Venice's defection did not change it. In the Netherlands, Alba despaired and launched several appeals for Philip merely to strengthen the fortifications of outposts that the Turks might attack:

> Because they cannot harm His Majesty on dry land, and still less can he harm them; so that everything spent on the League is wasted, and the fleet at risk . . . I beat my head against the wall when I hear talk about what we are spending here, since it is not the Turks who are disturbing Christendom but the heretics, and they are already within the gates.

To the duke (as to many others), defending the Netherlands seemed more important than attacking the Turks. Philip did not agree: to him it seemed that God's cause must be upheld against all-comers; and, besides, to seek peace from the Ottoman sultan would be to lose reputation. His Mediterranean fleet therefore remained on its war footing and, as if by way of reward, captured Tunis from its Turkish vassal later in the year.[64]

This did not mean, however, that the king eschewed all alternatives to subduing the Dutch Revolt by conventional means. For example, he and many of his ministers sponsored attempts to assassinate William of Orange in the hope that

The cost of war on two fronts, 1571–77

| Year | Money received from Castile (in ducats) | |
	By the Mediterranean fleet	By the Army of Flanders
1571	793,000	119,000
1572	1,463,000	1,776,000
1573	1,102,000	1,813,000
1574	1,252,000	3,737,000
1575	711,000	2,518,000
1576	1,069,000	872,000
1577	673,000	857,000
Total	7,063,000	11,692,000

Table 4   The cost to Spain of defeating the Turks at Lepanto in 1571 remained relatively low, thanks to contributions from Philip's Italian dominions as well as from his allies. The campaign of the following year, although it achieved nothing, cost twice as much; and after Venice made a separate peace in 1573 Philip's subjects had to shoulder almost the entire burden of Mediterranean defence. At the same time, the cost of suppressing the Dutch Revolt soared. Since the total revenues of the crown of Castile barely exceeded six million ducats, of which half went on servicing previous loans, the treasury quickly ran up huge debts. In September 1575 Philip issued a 'decree of bankruptcy' suspending all payments.

without him the revolt would founder. The technique had been employed frequently elsewhere in the recent past – in France against factional leaders (the duke of Guise, Anthony of Navarre, Gaspard de Coligny), in Scotland against King Henry Darnley. One of Alba's lieutenants, referring to the period between 1567 and 1570, claimed that 'All the time I was in Flanders I did nothing except try to find someone who would kill the prince of Orange'. In 1573 the duke sent 'Niccolo the Albanian' and others to murder both Orange and his brother Louis and, after the surrender of Haarlem, the duke spared William Balfour, one of the Scottish captains in the garrison, in return for his promise to kill Orange. (Balfour immediately betrayed his mission to the prince and continued to fight for the Dutch cause until his death.)[65] Later that year Gabriel de Zayas, Philip's secretary of state, again enquired hopefully about the possibility of assassination, and so did the Spanish ambassador in Rome, Don Juan de Zúñiga, in 1574.[66] The subject remained on Spain's agenda until Orange's eventual assassination in 1584; but, long before that, some realized that the prince's removal from the scene would no longer be enough to end the revolt. Don Francés de Álava, formerly Spanish ambassador in France and a stern critic of the policy of maximum force in the Netherlands, noted in the summer of 1574 that although 'ending the lives of Orange and [Count] Louis' offered obvious attractions, 'their deaths would not reconcile the spirits of that people [the Dutch] nor would it restore at a stroke the places which are in rebellion against Your Majesty'.[67]

Even as the attractions of this alternative waned, however, another suggested itself to Philip's strategists. Early in 1574 they decided to try their luck in South Holland, realizing (correctly) that the city of Leiden offered the key to success in crushing the rebellion, for its capture would both separate the rebels of North Holland from those of Zealand and weaken the stranglehold of the ports of Zealand on the trade of the southern provinces. Leiden possessed a substantial population, defended by redoubts and bastions as well as by many flooded fields, so that it could only be taken by blockade; but, assisted by a number of supporters in the area who provided advice and even maps, field commander Francisco de Valdés managed to invest the town in March. Almost at once, however, Louis of Nassau invaded the east Netherlands with another army raised in Germany, forcing most royal troops to abandon Holland in order to defeat him. Immediately after doing so, the victorious Spanish regiments, exasperated by their still unpaid wage arrears, mutinied anew: settling their claims took more than a month and cost over 500,000 ducats. The Army of Flanders did not resume the siege of Leiden until May.[68]

Not surprisingly, all this depressed Don Luis de Requeséns, who had finally taken over as governor-general. His first months in office had not been happy: although Alba had assured him before he left that victory lay just around the corner, he lied. Middelburg, the only loyal town left in Zealand, surrendered almost immediately after a long siege; while a fact-finding mission to Holland revealed that the 'reconquests' trumpeted by Alba consisted mostly of undefended villages.[69] Disillusioned, Requeséns warned the king that 'There would not be time or money enough in the world to reduce by force the twenty-four towns which have rebelled in Holland if we are to spend as long in reducing each one of them as we have taken over similar ones so far.'[70] He suggested a radical new strategy: the systematic inundation of Holland and Zealand.

The opportunity seemed perfect. The drainage mills on the dikes, ceaselessly keeping the water at bay, served as a constant reminder that most of the areas in rebellion lay below sea level; and few could forget the catastrophic consequences of previous inundations.[71] Furthermore, the rebels themselves had broken several dikes, to blockade the royalist garrison in Middelburg and to impede the siege of Alkmaar. Leiden began to flood areas around the town in November 1572, creating a 'moat' about 250 metres wide, and over the next fifteen months further deliberate inundations increased the flooded perimeter to over one kilometre.[72] When the Spaniards nevertheless persisted in their blockade of the town, the Dutch broke more dikes and opened the sluices along the rivers south of Leiden until the surrounding water became deep enough for a fleet of flat-bottomed barges to sail provisions into the city on 3 October 1574, forcing the Spaniards to withdraw.

Even before this débâcle, Valdés, the frustrated Spanish commander, had advocated more drastic measures, informing Requeséns:

When I first entered Holland with the army, I intercepted a letter written by the prince of Orange in his own hand [to one of his officials] . . . in which he wrote the following words: 'I had given orders that you should break the sluice at Maassluis in order to flood the area, but we have gathered together here . . . some learned men, and they find that if these sluices are broken, the whole countryside will be flooded without it being possible ever to reclaim it. So it would be better not to break them.' I thought I should let Your Excellency know this [Valdés continued] so that you will be aware that if, at any time, you might wish to flood this country, it is in your power. And since our enemies have taken the initiative in doing so, if they continue in their obstinate rebellion they indeed deserve to be flooded out.[73]

The suggestion, which bears a striking resemblance to the proposed United States air strikes against the dams and dikes of the Red River Delta during the Vietnam War (the 'Rolling Thunder' and 'Linebacker' campaigns), received the approval of the high command in Brussels, which began to make preparations to execute the plan in North Holland, at the time a low-lying peninsula protected from the North Sea only by a thin strip of sand dunes and popularly known as 'Waterland'. First, however, they forwarded it to the king for approval.

To their disgust, Philip – like President Johnson four centuries later – forbade the operation.

It is very clear [he wrote] that the severity, wickedness and obstinacy of the rebels has reached the level where no one can doubt that they are worthy of a harsh and exemplary punishment . . . And [we know that] we can easily flood Holland by breaking the dikes. But this strategy would give rise to a great disadvantage: that once broken, the province would be lost and ruined for ever, to the evident detriment of the neighbouring provinces who would have to build new dikes of their own . . . So that, in effect, it would not be wise to adopt this strategy, nor must we do so because (apart from the disadvantages already mentioned, great and manifest as they are) we should also recognize that it would earn for us a reputation for cruelty which would be better avoided, especially against our vassals, even though their guilt is notorious and the punishment justified.

Admittedly, Philip went on to sanction the burning of some rebellious areas by way of exemplary punishment (even suggesting the locations and the units that might be most appropriate), but first he wished the rebels to receive one last offer of clemency and so he drafted and sent two sets of instructions – one for each eventuality: negotiation or 'hard war' – and concluded his letter to Requeséns with an unusual offer: 'You, holding responsibility for these things, will do what you see to be most fitting to my service, and to the advancement of what lies in your hands.'[74] It seemed that at last the king had learned that the secret of effective military command lay in delegating operational decisions to his subordinates, but yet again the opportunity passed. By the time Philip's prohibition arrived in Brussels, Valdés and his lieutenants had already begun to break a few dikes in North Holland, but almost at once the Spanish troops mutinied once more and abandoned the province, rather than spend another winter in the field, and so

Requeséns could not make use of his unusually broad powers.[75] When Spanish forces finally entered Waterland in spring 1575, intending to burn all property and 'to kill as many people as we may come across' (just as the king had ordered), they found that the rebels had constructed and manned entrenchments that prevented further progress. The troops therefore withdrew.[76]

Philip had rejected on both moral and political grounds a military solution that might have ended the Dutch Revolt in a matter of weeks. Not surprisingly, however, Spanish statesmen from time to time reconsidered the idea of ending the revolt by 'flooding 'em back to the stone age'. Most notably, in 1602 one member of the Spanish council of State explicitly recalled the 'alternative' of 1574, while another claimed that Philip had then believed that opening the sea dikes would have terminated the revolt relatively swiftly. The new king, Philip III, found their arguments convincing and ordered the strategy to be implemented – but fortunately for the Dutch, this time no Spanish troops managed to enter Holland or Zealand.[77]

Another alternative strategy for ending the rebellion to which Philip II devoted more sustained attention involved creating a royal fleet in the North Sea. As the hostile French agent Mondoucet noted at the end of 1572, even if Alba managed to take Haarlem and the other inland towns of Holland, the prince of Orange still possessed a powerful fleet and several ports, by means of which he could keep his rebellion alive. Almost everyone seemed to recognize from the outset that the successful conclusion of the war required Spain to achieve naval mastery – indeed one of Philip's officials predicted unhelpfully (if correctly) that the Dutch Revolt could last fifty years unless Spain gained command of the seas – but less agreement existed on how to attain it.[78] Clearly the balance of naval power could not be redressed in the king's favour from local resources alone. From the outset, royalist operations in Holland and Zealand had been severely hampered by the lack of warships and munitions: the Sea Beggars captured the naval Arsenal at Veere – full of bronze and iron guns, powder and shot – in April 1572; fourteen ships just equipped for service at Enkhuizen in May; and eight more warships (with twenty-seven naval guns) at Zierikzee in August.[79] These gains, plus the extensive network of rivers, lakes and canals, allowed the rebels to move their forces around at will – both to overwhelm isolated royalist detachments and to send aid to towns that seemed ready to declare for them. Count Bossu, for one, realized that the royalists faced two distinct naval problems: they needed more warships to defend all possible targets in the threatened provinces; and to support these ships, they needed to control one or more suitable harbours where the vessels could shelter, refit and take on new provisions. In this respect, the loss of most major ports in Holland and Zealand proved critical because those two provinces possessed the only suitable deep-water facilities in the entire Netherlands: those of Flanders and Brabant either lay too far from the sea or held too little water to serve as adequate naval bases. 'If we do not recover Holland soon', Bossu grimly (and accurately) warned, 'we shall be hunted from the sea'.[80] Furthermore, although the small royal fleet in the Low Countries managed to score some successes in the early months of the war, each engagement with the rebels caused losses that could not be replaced and damage that could not be made good. Eventually not enough fighting ships remained to secure victory: one royal squadron met with defeat on the Zuider Zee in October 1573 and two more in the attempts to relieve Middelburg in January and February 1574. A further unsuccessful engagement in the Scheldt estuary the following May more or less eliminated the king's navy in the Netherlands.[81]

Now the king could only wrest command of the sea from the Dutch by the dispatch of a powerful naval squadron from Spain. Philip had long appreciated the value of a navy to defend his southern possessions: in the Mediterranean, thanks to a massive programme of construction, he managed to triple the size of his fleet from 55 to 155 galleys. At the same time, he issued a stream of orders designed to increase the quantity and improve the quality of ships laid down in the yards of Cantabria, whether for service northwards to Flanders, or westwards to America. But until the 1580s this shipbuilding programme did not include the construction of warships capable of operating effectively in the North Sea.[82] Accordingly, when Alba began to plead for the dispatch of fighting ships from Spain in order to defeat the rebels, he and the king thought at first in terms of galleys. However, an itinerary for the galleys to sail to Flanders prepared by the chief pilot of Spain turned out to be impractical: the shortest route was almost 1,000 kilometres, and the safest 1,300. Philip warned Alba to expect little help from this quarter.[83]

Instead, the king began to plan the dispatch of Spanish sailing warships to regain command of the North Sea. Since he lacked a High Seas fleet, the necessary vessels would have to be commandeered from the merchant marine and supplied with ordnance, munitions and soldiers by the crown. This technique had worked well enough in 1565–66, when the king commissioned his most experienced Atlantic commander, Pedro Menéndez de Avilés, to destroy all French bases in Florida and reassert Spanish control in the western Atlantic; but whereas twenty-five ships had sufficed to recover Florida, such a small force would make little impression on the Dutch.[84] So in February 1574 the king signed orders to create a fleet based on Santander both to clear 'the Channel [of pirates] and to recapture some ports in the Netherlands occupied by the rebels'; he also ordered the embargo of 224 ships in the ports of Spain, from which Menéndez would choose his task force, and the recruiting of 11,000 soldiers.[85]

Naturally this represented an impossible goal for a single campaigning season and provides another example of Philip's lack of strategic sense. To locate and load the artillery and other equipment required to turn a merchantman into a fighting ship took months and, for such a huge undertaking (as Menéndez and several of Philip's councillors pointed out), 'it could take years'. Moreover, once in northern waters, such a large fleet would need a safe harbour in which to shelter in case of need, and Philip no longer controlled one.[86] Gradually Menéndez came to realize this and in August suggested to the king that instead of going to the Netherlands he should merely cruise between Brittany and the Scilly isles, capturing and punishing all the 'pirates' he encountered; if storms threatened, the fleet could take refuge either in the Scillies or in some Irish port, and from that base a squadron could be sent directly to the Netherlands the following spring. The king immediately agreed to this ingenious plan – in effect a blockade of the Channel approaches – but he did not do so solely because the fleet as yet lacked the strength to gain control of the North Sea.[87] Earlier in the summer the Turks had sent a large fleet west which laid siege to the Spanish garrisons at La Goletta and Tunis; Philip knew that, should they fall, the defence of the Mediterranean might become more urgent than the recovery of Holland and Zealand. He therefore ordered the fleet to stay close to Spain in case it might be needed to keep the Turks at bay. In the end it made no difference because, even as he led his fleet out of Santander to patrol the Channel in September, an epidemic carried off Menéndez and many of his men. The king cancelled the entire expedition.[88] He had squandered over 500,000 ducats on it.[89]

This fiasco, coupled with the simultaneous loss of Tunis and La Goletta along with all their defenders and the failure of the siege of Leiden, led the king and his advisers to consider yet another alternative strategy: a negotiated settlement with the Dutch. Initially Philip had taken a hard line in the Netherlands for two reasons: 'for the conservation of religion, and to preserve the obedience of the [king's] vassals there in light of the example of France, where the rebels were treated with so much circumspection, pardoning them and even honouring them'.[90] The duke of Alba, at least, had no intention of making this mistake. 'Let this rebel [Orange] lay down his arms and beg for mercy, and then we can see what should be done,' he advised the king on one occasion; and on another: 'These troubles must be ended by force of arms, without any use of pardon, mildness, negotiations or talks: that will be the right time for clemency'.[91] As the situation deteriorated, however, the king wavered in his resolve. His decision in 1573 to recall Alba stemmed primarily from his conviction that force must henceforth be tempered by concessions in order to save the Netherlands for God and its sovereign, and in July of that year he tried to implement a more conciliatory policy even while the duke remained in charge. With his forces fully committed in the Mediterranean, the king told Alba that ending the war in the Netherlands as soon as possible and on almost any terms had now become his highest priority:

> [Although I rejoice at all your victories] it is essential that we bring affairs to a conclusion, as much to avoid the loss and destruction of those provinces as because of the impossible situation we face for money. So I request and require you most earnestly to arrange things so that we may gain days, hours and even moments in what must be done to secure [a peace].[92]

Yet again, this insistence on an immediate change of policy 1,000 kilometres away proved totally unrealistic. The courier carrying this crucial dispatch only arrived in the Netherlands six weeks later – long after the fall of Haarlem, which would have afforded an admirable opportunity for clemency – and by then the

Spanish army had begun to besiege Alkmaar. Its commander still failed to see the need for compromise; indeed he felt that he had been far too lenient in the past. 'If Alkmaar is taken by force, I am determined not to leave a human being alive, but rather to slit all their throats. Since the example of Haarlem, where all the burgers (except for forty or so) were pardoned, has not brought any benefit,' he told the king, 'perhaps an example of cruelty will bring in the rest of the towns [in revolt]'. Warming to his theme, Alba continued: 'I cannot refrain from beseeching Your Majesty to disabuse yourself of the notion that anything will ever be accomplished in these provinces by the use of clemency. Things have reached the point where many Netherlanders who until now have been begging for clemency now admit their mistake and believe that every living soul in Alkmaar should have their throats cut.'[93]

The duke's forceful statements highlighted the fact that the king's policies once again stood at variance with his principles. Under pressure from Ruy Gómez and the moderates, Philip had been on the point of issuing a 'General Pardon' for his rebels (albeit with numerous exceptions), but upon reading Alba's objections to clemency (which arrived after Ruy Gómez's death) he decided to hold it back for a while. He nevertheless remained perplexed by the confusing advice received from the various factions at his Court and in the Netherlands. In one of the tortuous holograph letters in which he sought to persuade Requeséns to take over from Alba, the king summarized the arguments he had heard. On one side stood the duke and his supporters, who saw the revolt as primarily religious and therefore impossible to end by compromise, since the king's conscience could not allow him to grant toleration. On the other side were the loyal Netherlanders and their supporters at Court who 'say that very few acted for reasons of religion, but rather through the ill treatment they have received in everything . . . and that the panacea is mildness, good treatment and a general pardon'. But who was right? The king confessed that:

> With so many different opinions I have found myself in a quandary, and since I do not know the truth of what is happening there I do not know which remedy is appropriate or whom to believe; so it seems to me safest to believe neither the one group nor the other, because I think they have [both] gone to extremes. I believe it would be best to take the middle ground, although with complete dissimulation.

To cover all eventualities the king decided to prepare two contradictory Instructions for Requeséns: 'those in Spanish seem to lean somewhat in one direction, while those in French very clearly go in the other'. He apologized for the difficulties this might cause, but concluded: 'I did not want to burst my brains emending them except for small things because your real instructions will be what you see and understand when you get there'. He did, however, expressly forbid Requeséns to make religious concessions or offer to pardon the rebel leaders.[94]

By the time Requeséns finally arrived in Brussels, informal negotiations with the enemy had already begun. Initially the local commanders on each side in South Holland exchanged letters merely about ransoms and the future treatment of prisoners (for up to that point those captured by both sides had been executed out of hand); before long, however, William of Orange took the opportunity to state his terms for a settlement. First, he insisted, there must be toleration for all Calvinists; second, all goods confiscated from the rebels must be restored; third, constitutional government must be reinstated and all foreign troops withdrawn; fourth and finally, the agreement must be guaranteed by a foreign ruler (such as the emperor or the king of France).[95] This unauthorized exchange of views with the rebel leader horrified the duke of Alba and he swiftly disavowed it; but, almost simultaneously, he decided to follow up reports that some individual rebel towns might be willing to make separate terms.[96]

The king's advisers in Madrid duly discussed these initiatives and concluded that, although 'without doubt if Your Majesty had the money to pacify matters there by force, it would be better', since sufficient funds could not be found, certain concessions would clearly be needed. The council of State therefore recommended that the General Pardon should be issued after all, exempting only Orange and his principal lieutenants, and that the unpopular new taxes and legal tribunals introduced by Alba should be discontinued. The king duly authorized these concessions. He also agreed that the talks with individual rebel towns should continue. Accordingly in the spring and summer of 1574, although various efforts to betray strongholds to the Spaniards failed, a succession of secret envoys shuttled between Brussels and Holland in order to ascertain the terms on which the Dutch might be willing to discuss an end to hostilities and a return to Philip's obedience.[97] Requeséns hectored the king to authorize substantial concessions (causing Philip to protest at one point that 'Flanders cannot be pacified in two days as he seems to think') and eventually formal talks with Orange and his supporters opened at the town of Breda in March 1575, just three years after the revolt began.[98]

After four months the two sides reached agreement on almost all their political differences, but this did not suffice. Requeséns concluded that Alba had been right all along: religion did indeed constitute the real cause of the continuing resistance of the rebels. 'If we were talking about a peace that could be settled by transferring four towns or four kingdoms', he wrote sadly in July 1575, something could surely be arranged; 'but it all depends on religion, which has caused this war'. And so, he gloomily predicted, 'I have no hope whatever for a settlement [since] . . . we cannot meet any of the [rebels'] demands on the religious question'.[99] Spain still refused to tolerate Protestantism in a reconciled Netherlands state, and the Dutch rebels would not recognize the king's authority again without it. Although victory had become militarily impossible, to Philip and his principal advisers a negotiated settlement remained ideologically unacceptable.[100] The conference at Breda in fact only served to strengthen the rebels by increasing their internal cohesion as they negotiated collectively, and by creating a new platform from which they could justify their cause.[101]

The history of Spain's efforts to suppress the Dutch Revolt between 1572 and 1575 thus offers partial support for Paul Kennedy's 'strategic overstretch' explanation of Spain's failure to secure European mastery. The bastioned defences of the key rebel strongholds, whether prepared in advance by the Habsburgs' own engineers (as at Mons) or improvised in haste by the Dutch (as at Alkmaar), indeed proved crucial in thwarting Spain's chosen strategy of deploying overwhelming force in order to secure a rapid victory. Once the reconquest became ensnared by the Military Revolution, it became impossible for Philip to support an army on this scale for long, especially when he remained heavily committed to the defence of the Mediterranean as well. As he told his secretary in July 1574: '[The fate of the Netherlands] is very much at risk, with so many troops and no money to pay them, and so we must send them some financial help without delay . . . Unless God performs a miracle, our affairs there cannot be improved without money.' Indeed, he sighed some days later, 'I think the Netherlands will be lost for lack of money, as I have always feared . . . We are running out of everything so fast that words fail me'.[102] After two years of secret preparation, in September 1575 the Castilian treasury ordered the suspension of all payments. Seen from the Netherlands, this marked the end of the road. As Requeséns wrote despairingly to his brother:

> The decree of bankruptcy has dealt such a great blow to the Exchange here [in Antwerp] that no one in it has any credit . . . I cannot find a single penny, nor can I see how the king could send money here, even if he had it in abundance. Short of a miracle, the whole military machine will fall in ruins so rapidly that it is highly probable that I shall not have time to tell you about it.[103]

No miracle occurred, however, and Requeséns's pessimism proved prophetic: in March 1576 he himself died of plague and in July the unpaid Spanish field army mutinied and abandoned Holland. In September the States of the loyal provinces, on their own initiative, began talks with the rebels of Holland and Zealand for a negotiated settlement to the civil war.[104]

Yet this neat model of military and economic determinism, although accurate as far as it goes, remains insufficient on three counts. First, it overlooks the facts that, despite his egregious errors in and after 1559, Philip managed to regain complete control in 1566–68; and that, despite provoking an even more serious rebellion in spring 1572, the royalists came within a hair's breadth of ending it by the end of the year. Second, it leaves no room for the numerous non-economic factors that thwarted the king's chosen strategy: his repeated failure to return to the Netherlands between 1560 and 1571 in order to supervise the creation of his 'new world' in person; Don Fadrique's rash insistence on unconditional surrender in the case of Haarlem at the end of 1572; and Alba's decision to besiege Alkmaar rather than (say) Delft in 1573. Finally, it does not explain the relative neglect of alternative strategies: Orange's assassination; systematic inundation; gaining naval mastery in the North Sea; and, above all, negotiating a settlement in at least one of Spain's major wars.

Great and small, all of these constituted political – not economic or military – failures. All of them, moreover, arose from two 'systemic' weaknesses in Philip's system of government. On the one hand, although the king possessed clear policy goals, he failed to indicate clearly the 'boundary conditions' that would identify the compromises that would be acceptable (as opposed to those that would not) when his agents experienced difficulty in executing his policies. Each new crisis, each new setback, therefore had to be handled *de novo*, first by his lieutenants in the field and then by the king himself, wrestling with his papers either alone or with just one or two advisers. On the other hand, time and again the plans carefully made in Madrid had become outdated by the time they reached the Netherlands: distance defeated the decision to offer major concessions in July 1573, to send a less abrasive governor-general in 1571 and again in 1573, and to send a fleet in 1574. With remarkably few exceptions – during the emergency of spring 1572 and again in October 1574 – Philip refused to confer adequate powers on his theatre commanders. Perhaps the slow pace of the Low Countries' War, in which each siege took so long that it left time for several exchanges of courier, fatally encouraged the king to micromanage operations; but examples of the same tendency abound in other areas – the Mediterranean, the Atlantic, even the Americas (pp. 70–71 above) – strongly suggesting that the desire to monopolize power lay in the king's nature, not in the specific circumstances of the Netherlands. Taken together, they created a 'strategic overstretch' of another kind: mental and political rather than economic and military.

Only the bankruptcy of 1575 seems to have forced Philip to make harsh strategic choices, perhaps because it led him to suspect that he had somehow misread God's plan. Now, at last, he prepared himself to 'endure the unendurable': in 1576, with his treasury still empty and the Dutch in control of virtually the entire Netherlands, the king reluctantly decided to purchase peace in the Netherlands at any price. He worked with ministers who favoured making far-reaching compromises in order to end the war, and his secret Instructions for the new governor-general, Don John of Austria, conceded that:

> If matters are in such a state that the States-General demand unilateral conces-
> sions before they will recognize your authority, it seems that, safeguarding
> religion and my authority *as much as may be*, since matters have reached these
> extremes, given the need to extinguish the fire and to prevent these people from
> more desperate action, so that everything is lost, *we shall have to concede everything
> necessary in order to bring about a conclusion and save what we can.*[105]

At first Don John seemed reluctant to obey and after only two months in the Netherlands threatened to reopen hostilities with the Dutch rebels. The king allowed him no latitude, however, sending an express letter in triplicate

> to tell you, as I have told you so many times before and as you have heard from me [in person], that you must avoid at all costs allowing negotiations to break down . . . I have to charge you, brother, to avoid a breach, and to accommodate yourself to time and necessity, which are the best counsellors you can have in such an urgent and difficult matter as this.

Don John duly crumbled and signed an agreement that required all Spanish troops and officials to leave the Netherlands for Italy, that halted religious persecution, and that empowered the States-General of the reunited Netherlands to determine their future religious and political organization.[106]

Meanwhile the king further decided both to disband a large part of the Mediterranean fleet, leaving it on a purely defensive footing, and to send an envoy to Istanbul with powers to conclude an immediate armistice with the Turks so that, for the first (and only) time in his reign, his entire monarchy was at peace.[107] A few months later, however, the situation changed again. In July 1577 Don John unilaterally broke with the Dutch and directly ordered the Spanish veterans to return from Italy to the Netherlands in order to defend him, claiming that such was the king's wish. When the news reached Spain, Philip immediately fired off orders to Italy forbidding his ministers to comply, and the troops therefore remained at their posts. Don John received another long rebuke: 'In no way does it suit to declare open war on the Netherlands provinces without my express communication and order', the king thundered.

> Instead you must follow the path that has been indicated. If matters reach such extremes, you must advise me of the fact, so that I can decide what seems best, according to the situation in which my other realms find themselves, and the resources and funds that I have to hand, in order to put such a resolution into effect; for without that, anything we do would be in vain.[108]

A few days later, however, perhaps reassured by peace in the Mediterranean and the providential arrival of a rich treasure fleet from America, Philip felt able to return to his underlying principles and ordered the tercios back. Civil war returned to the Low Countries and lasted until 1609, long after Philip's death; his grandson finally signed a peace which recognized the political and religious independence of the seven northern provinces of the Netherlands in 1648.

By that time Owen Feltham had no doubt that Spain's inability to regain control of the entire Netherlands had caused its downfall as a Great Power. The Dutch, Feltham wrote,

Are the Israelites passing through the Red Sea ... They have strugled long with Spain's Pharaoh, and they have at length inforced him to let them go. They are a Gideon's army upon the march again. They are the Indian rat, knawing the bowels of the Spanish crocodile, to which they got when he gap'd to swallow them. They are a serpent wreathed about the legs of that elephant. They are the little sword-fish pricking the bellies of the whale. They are the wane of that empire which increas'd in [the time of] Isabella and in [the time of] Charles the fifth was at full. They are a glass wherein kings may see that though they be sovraigns over lives and goods, yet when they usurpe upon God's part, and will be kings over conscience too, they are somtimes punisht with a loss of that which lawfully is their own. That religion too fiercely urg'd is to stretch a string till it not onely jars, but cracks; and in the breaking, whips (perhaps) the streiner's eye out.[109]

He might have added that the same combination of distance, religious intransigence and a failure to establish boundary conditions also doomed Philip II's attempts to triumph over his other major enemy in north-west Europe: Elizabeth Tudor.

5 *The 'British Problem', 1558–85*

The religious upheavals of the sixteenth century transformed international relations in western Europe in three important ways. First they created, at the heart of almost every state, a nucleus of zealots prepared to place the advancement of their religion above obedience to their rulers. Elizabeth I of England survived over twenty plots against her life; in France Henry IV succumbed in 1610 to the knife of his twentieth would-be assassin and religious opponents also murdered his predecessor Henry III (1589) as well as several faction leaders (Anthony of Navarre and Henry of Guise in 1563, Gaspard de Coligny and many other Protestant chiefs in 1572). Second, the growing ideological differences seriously complicated – in the sixteenth century as in the twentieth – regular diplomatic intercourse between parties divided by strongly held beliefs: Elizabeth expelled two Spanish ambassadors for supporting plots against her life hatched by Catholic opponents and recalled her last resident ambassador from Spain in 1568 when Philip refused to allow him to conduct Protestant worship in his own embassy. Finally, the Reformation disrupted the established pattern of international alliances. In the fifteenth and early sixteenth centuries Castile and the Netherlands had been the traditional allies of England, while France sided with Scotland, but the breach with Rome first by England and then by Scotland effected a diplomatic revolution. As Lord Burghley, Elizabeth's chief minister, observed in 1589: 'The state of the world is marvellously changed, when we true Englishmen have cause for our own quietness to wish good success to a king of France and a king of Scots.'[1]

This critical transition began in 1553–54 with the successful negotiations of Charles V to marry his son and heir, Philip, to Queen Mary Tudor of England. This diplomatic and dynastic coup not only created a powerful new Habsburg constellation in north-west Europe but also completed the encirclement of France: England and the Netherlands to the north; Franche-Comté and the empire to the east; Lombardy, Sardinia and Spain to the south.[2] In 1557 England followed Philip's lead and declared war on France and Scotland. In November 1558, however, Mary died childless and the English crown passed to her half-sister Elizabeth, who soon showed unmistakable signs of wishing to turn England into a Protestant state again. Many ministers urged Philip, whose title 'king of England' lapsed with his wife's death, to recover his position – both to maintain the Catholic faith there and to keep England within the Habsburg orbit, for without it 'the Low Countries, and in consequence Italy and the Americas, would stand in great danger of being lost'.[3] For a moment Elizabeth herself offered a solution, indicating just after her accession that she might view favourably an offer of marriage from Philip. Although his advisers in Spain rejected this initiative out of hand 'on account of her birth and for religious considerations', the king – resident in Brussels at this time – decided to test the waters, albeit with remarkably little enthusiasm. In January 1559, 'feeling like a condemned man wondering what is to become of him', he authorized his trusted ambassador in London, the count of Feria, to respond positively to Elizabeth – but only 'to serve God and to see if this might prevent that lady from making the changes in religion that she has in mind' (and only if the terms were better than those agreed when he married Mary Tudor). 'Believe me,' he later confided Feria, 'if it were not for God's sake, I would never do this. Nothing could or would make me do this except the clear knowledge that it might gain the kingdom [of England] for His service and faith'. After a few weeks, however, Elizabeth rejected her graceless suitor and began to implement the 'changes in religion' that would make England Protestant again.[4]

Philip now faced an awkward dilemma. Eight years of almost continuous war with France and the Turks, fought on several fronts with armies and navies of unprecedented size, had exhausted the Spanish Monarchy and the king had already been forced to reschedule his debts (p. 87 above). Under these circumstances a major new military undertaking such as an invasion of England to restore Catholicism, especially while the war with France continued, remained inadvisable. And yet, unless he acted swiftly, Elizabeth's new religious settlement might become entrenched and far more difficult to destroy at a later date. In a confidential holograph letter to Feria in March 1559 the king gave vent to his frustration:

> This is certainly the most difficult decision I have ever faced in my whole life . . . and it grieves me to see what is happening over there [in England] and to be unable to take the steps to stop it that I want, while the steps I can take seem far milder than such a great evil deserves . . . But at the moment I lack the resources to do anything.

Later in the letter, the king returned to his point in a more forceful and calculating way:

> The evil that is taking place in that kingdom has caused me the anger and frustration I have mentioned . . . but I believe we must try to remedy it without involving me or any of my vassals in a declaration of war until we have enjoyed the benefits of peace [for a while].[5]

Even as he wrote these words, however, others endeavoured to engineer a rebellion in England against Elizabeth. Feria informed the king of a plot to depose the queen in favour of a Catholic relative and begged for Philip's support, since 'No better opportunity could arise for a prince to gain reputation in the eyes of both God and the world'. 'All the water in the Thames would not cleanse the stains from my conscience,' Feria added, if the king failed to act. Shortly afterwards, Henry II of France proposed a joint invasion, to be followed by a partition of England between the two victors.[6]

The king referred these two proposals to his leading foreign policy advisers: Granvelle, Alba and Ruy Gómez. They, too, saw a marvellous chance to restore Philip's power in England and advised him both to keep in constant readiness the fleet that had been assembled to convey him back to Spain and to send money to Feria for use in case of need. They ruled out, however, any cooperation with France (on the grounds that the French could not be trusted to adhere to any agreement: earlier in the century, the councillors recalled, France had reneged on a treaty to partition Naples) and they advised against any unilateral action by Philip against Elizabeth. Their greatest fear was that civil war might break out in England between the Catholics and Protestants, and that one side or the other might appeal to the French for assistance. To avoid this, they recommended that Philip should make known to Elizabeth that he would protect her against all comers.[7] In the event, the king tried to leave his options open. He instructed Feria to

> arrange to advise me immediately, by all possible channels, of the current state of affairs, and I shall tell you what you have to do. In case a rebellion occurs so unexpectedly that you cannot consult me quickly enough, you should make yourself available as a mediator to pacify them, without declaring support for either of the parties until you have informed me and received my reply.

Only if the Catholics clearly held the upper hand could Feria provide them with financial support, albeit even then 'secretly and underhand' while seeming to 'smile upon the heretics, in order to avoid alarming them and to make sure they do not seek to call in the French'.[8]

Elizabeth, for her part, fully realized the vulnerability of her position. Although she had succeeded to the throne peacefully and with considerable support, she had done so as a Catholic (at least in outward manifestations). Once she felt able to reveal her Protestant sympathies, many Catholics both at home and abroad turned their thoughts to the claims of her cousin, the still impeccably Catholic Mary Stuart, brought up in France almost since birth and recently married to Francis, heir apparent to the French throne. In April 1559 Francis ratified the peace of Cateau-Cambrésis (which ended hostilities of France and Scotland against the Habsburgs and England) as 'king of Scotland, England and Ireland, and dauphin of France'. Elizabeth therefore played her matrimonial card again: she indicated that she would consider marrying one of Emperor Ferdinand's sons, hoping that this would guarantee Habsburg assistance in case of a French attack.

Plate 22   The Great Seal of Francis II and Mary Stuart. Mary Stuart had succeeded to the Scottish throne in 1542 when only one week old. Almost immediately her French mother took her to France, where she grew up at Court. In 1558 she married Francis, heir to the French throne, and when her cousin Mary Tudor died, the couple claimed to be sovereigns of England and Ireland (Mary was the granddaughter of Henry VIII's sister and did not recognize the title of the Protestant Elizabeth). Even after the peace of Cateau-Cambrésis ended the war between Scotland, France and England in April 1559 the couple retained all their titles and placed them on their seal: 'Francis and Mary, by the grace of God rulers of France, Scotland, England and Ireland.

Three events saved her from this fate. In June a group of Scottish Protestants entered Edinburgh and forced the regent, Mary of Guise, to flee; in July, Henry II of France was killed in a tournament; and in August Philip set sail for Spain. True, immediately after Henry's death, the new French rulers adopted the unambiguous style 'Francis and Mary, sovereigns of France, Scotland, England and Ireland' (see Plate 22) and prepared to send an expeditionary force to restore order in Scotland. True, also, several of Philip's senior advisers advocated exploiting the sudden change of regime in France in order to invade England; so did the pope, who even promised to invest Philip as king of England, so that his conquest would be legal.[9] But Philip declined. As late as 23 June 1559 he declared his intention of staying in the north 'at least until next January', sending a long paper of explanation to his sister Juana, regent in Spain; and he urgently requested funds both for his proposed intervention in England and for his continued residence in the Netherlands 'because without it everything here will be lost, and my person too'. He demanded a response 'by a special courier who will come for no other purpose'. The reply, when it eventually arrived, delivered a slap to the royal face: Juana flatly refused to send any money at all and her advisers found his requests so unrealistic that (as Philip noted ruefully) 'they had a good laugh' at his expense. The councillors had good cause: the Castilian treasury lay empty, many areas in the crown of Aragon verged on open insurrection, and Protestant cells had been discovered in Seville and Valladolid (the administrative capital). Above all, attempts to conclude a peace with the Turks had failed, raising fears of new attacks in the western Mediterranean. Spain urgently required her king to return and take personal control; under the circumstances, Philip's request for more money specifically to prolong his absence seemed ridiculous. On the other hand his Netherlands advisers continued to urge that he stay for at least a few months more in the north since his departure might precipitate 'developments that could do irreparable damage to His Majesty and his successors. It cannot be a good thing for him to leave the Netherlands with English affairs as they are at present and relations with France not settled. I am not sure that the needs of Spain are so great that they exceed ours.' [10] In the end, it all came down to money. On 24 June, the day after his urgent letter to Spain, a special financial commission convened by the king in Brussels advised him to expect no more money from the Netherlands: instead they argued that funding from abroad – that is, from Spain – would be essential to put his policies for northern Europe into effect. This seems to have made up Philip's mind: later that week he announced his intention to return to Spain, and in July he left Brussels for the coast. Even news of Henry II's death failed to produce a change of heart: he set sail for the land of his birth in August 1559.[11]

One cannot really blame Philip for this decision: he had little choice. He could no longer govern Spain and intervene effectively in the Mediterranean from Brussels, over 1,000 kilometres away; he lacked the money to do anything useful in the north; and, as Juana pointed out, the time had come to address directly the problems created in his southern kingdoms by the relentless demands of war and by his five-year absence. Philip's error lay in believing that he could intervene effectively in the affairs of Britain (or the Netherlands) from Spain: thanks to his first-hand experience as king of England, Philip came to regard himself as an expert on the subject. He could not understand, for example, why in 1570 the pope decided to excommunicate Elizabeth without consulting him first, 'knowing that I could give him better information and advice on that kingdom and on its affairs and people than anyone else'.[12]

The same confidence that he possessed an unrivalled comprehension of British politics also led him to overlook a second important obstacle: the different agenda of his various lieutenants in Brussels. The 'sub-imperial' policies pursued by its energetic agents abroad – especially by the regents in Brussels, responsible for a population of three million souls and a complex economy – proved a constant source of potential tension within the Habsburg Monarchy. Alba, for example, possessed very firm views on the 'British question'. He too had spent some time in England during which, like his master, he had noted both the complexity of Tudor society and the strength of Protestant feeling; also like his master, he seems to have concluded that no firm alliance could be maintained with such an unstable country (and ruler), so that the best policy was to placate Elizabeth so that she would remain neutral. He therefore opposed any attempt to undermine or dethrone the queen. Until he left Spain in 1567, any difference of opinion between the duke and his master had limited significance, because before taking a decision Philip could consult with others whose opinion on British affairs he also respected (above all Feria, who had served as his ambassador and married one of Queen Mary's attendants, keeping him in touch with more 'interventionist' English Catholic opinion). Once Alba arrived in Brussels, however, the differences became far more significant. In the first place, the duke's views received strong endorsement from his Netherlands ministers, all of whom desired peace with England, one of the country's principal trading partners, since on that depended the prosperity of the seventeen provinces and therefore the stability of the entire regime. Second, although Philip limited the authority of Margaret of Parma and sought to do the same with Alba, once a trade war began with England late in 1568 he could not avoid delegating greater powers to the duke. Alba now possessed not only greater authority when pressing his opinions upon Philip but also the means to thwart the execution of any 'interventionist' initiatives with which he disagreed.[13]

Inertia rather than policy decided the outcome of the first 'British crisis' of the reign, however. No sooner had Philip left the Netherlands than both England and France took major steps to secure a favourable solution to the Scottish problem. The French sent an expeditionary force to support Mary of Guise: it soon regained Edinburgh and drove the Protestants back beyond the Forth. Elizabeth retaliated by mobilizing a huge fleet – the largest until 1588 – which sailed to Scotland and cut off communications with France. To Cardinal Granvelle, Philip's principal adviser in the Netherlands, it seemed clear that to secure England 'we should do the same as we would to secure Brussels', but Philip remained unmoved: instead he concentrated on a combined operation against the North African island of Djerba. Luckily for him (and Elizabeth) storms dispersed a second French expeditionary force early in 1560, with heavy losses, and so Francis II called upon his brother-in-law Philip for assistance. 'Since we agree that this is all about religion', the French king asked that Philip should warn Elizabeth 'that if she did not abandon her protection of the Scottish heretics and accept the honest terms offered her, that he [Philip] would embrace God's cause and assist and favour the king his brother [Francis II] with all his strength and means'.[14] The appeal came too late: Elizabeth had already sent an envoy to ask Philip for assistance should her realm be attacked by the French, and in March 1560 the king agreed. 'Given the importance to us, and the danger that would follow to our dominions if she and her kingdom were lost', Philip ordered his Spanish veterans in the Netherlands to stand ready to help Elizabeth in case of French attack.[15] This sealed the fate of the French – and of the Catholic faith – in Scotland. Far from home, blockaded at Leith by the Scots on land and by England's navy at sea, in July Francis's 4,000 troops capitulated. A representative assembly quickly gathered in Edinburgh and introduced a Reformed church order.[16] Elizabeth had established her independence with little help from Philip (her enthusiasm for a Habsburg marriage cooled rapidly), and two subsequent events soon reinforced it. In December 1560 the death of Francis II left the French throne to his ten-year-old brother Charles IX and thus temporarily removed the threat of further French intervention across the Channel, and the next month all Spanish troops in the Netherlands sailed home in order to take the place of the veterans lost in the ill-fated Djerba expedition.[17]

Thanks to his decision to concentrate on Spain and the Mediterranean, Philip had lost his first and best chance to tame Tudor England and for the next few years, although Elizabeth remained vulnerable, the king neglected English (as well as Netherlands) affairs while he fought the Turks. A letter to his ambassador in London in 1562 typified the prevailing attitude. After acknowledging receipt of numerous dispatches, and asking for the flow of information to continue, he announced:

> If your letters have not been answered and the present does not deal with them as you desire, it is from no want of will on our part but because we have not yet been able to come to a resolution as to the steps to be taken to remedy the evils, which must be attacked at their roots . . . [They] must be deeply considered, jointly with the state of our own affairs. As soon as I arrive at a decision I will send full particulars.[18]

Philip seems not to have realized that his best chance of keeping Elizabeth dependent on him would be to make things harder for her – for example by covertly supporting her Catholic opponents in England and Ireland. Instead he did everything possible to protect her. In 1562, the leaders of the French Protestants (normally known as Huguenots) attempted to seize control of the person of Charles IX and, having failed, began an armed struggle to secure religious and political concessions that opened a quarter-century of civil war. Elizabeth rashly provided immediate assistance to the Huguenots, sending an expeditionary force to seize the port of Le Havre and thus rekindling the hostility of the French government towards her. Nevertheless Alba warned Philip that, since he lacked the resources for an invasion (thanks to the continuing Mediterranean crisis), he could not take advantage of Elizabeth's weakness; instead he should merely offer to mediate between England and France.[19] To seek the queen's deposition made no sense, Alba argued, because it would only benefit Mary Stuart – now back in Scotland – who was at this stage even less acceptable to Spain. Mary's Catholic credentials had become open to question. Although she subsequently played the role of Counter-Reformation martyr to perfection, it was a late development: in the 1560s almost all her Scottish ministers were Protestants and she eventually granted official recognition to the Reformed religion and married one of her Protestant subjects (the earl of Bothwell) according to the Reformed rite. Mary nevertheless remained a French princess: she wrote almost all her letters in French and in her will of 1566 all of the first seven (and ten of the first twelve) beneficiaries were her French relatives. Small wonder that Alba saw no advantage in toppling the unreliable but isolated Tudor queen simply to turn England into a French satellite under Mary Stuart. Philip therefore continued to protect Elizabeth without seeking anything in return. When in 1563 the council of Trent, 'at the instance or insistence of some English bishops and other Catholics', began to 'discuss the deposition of the queen of England' Philip ordered it to stop 'because it could cause very grave inconveniences, and awaken new feelings, and above all because it would be done at a time and season in which it would bear no fruit'. Even when a trade war broke out between England and the Netherlands later that year, Philip refused to allow it to spread to Spain; and when in 1565 Mary wrote to him for the first time, asking for aid against common enemies of the Roman church, the king offered her assistance only in Scotland.[20] In 1567, however, a group of Scottish nobles rebelled against Mary and imprisoned her. At the same time, Alba and his Spanish troops left Italy for Brussels to restore order, while the king announced his intention of sailing back to the Netherlands himself and began to assemble a fleet at Santander to transport him.

In the event Philip remained in Spain but his interest in the British question began to revive. In February 1568, for example, he wrote to ask his ambassador in London, Guzmán de Silva, if 'there is any hope of the queen some day coming to her senses and recognizing her error [i.e. her adherence to Protestantism], and also whether, in effect, there are any persons about her or in her council who may be able to lead her to this with credit and dignity'; he then added wearily, 'so far as we can judge her by her words and actions, she seems so wedded to heresy that it will be difficult for her to free herself from it; but if I could in any way profitably help her to this end I would do so with all my heart'.[21] The letter offered no hint of aggressive intent. At just this moment, however, an unfortunate diplomatic incident concerning Elizabeth's representative in Madrid set in train a major change of policy. Dr John Man, a Protestant cleric, had served the Tudors in minor diplomatic and administrative posts for over thirty years when in 1566 Elizabeth appointed him to serve as her ambassador in Spain. Although Man could speak Italian, French and Latin, as the only Protestant ambassador (indeed the only 'legal' Protestant) in Madrid he proved unable to navigate a safe course among his embittered Catholic compatriots at the Spanish Court. By the summer of 1567 his dispatches recorded the hostility of the count of Feria, Philip's former envoy to London and now (in Alba's absence) his principal adviser on English affairs, as well as 'the professed patron' to all the English Catholic refugees in

Spain. Before long, some of those exiles testified that Man had made invidious remarks about the Catholic faith and, one night at dinner, had insulted the pope (whom he called a 'canting little monk'). Perhaps in retaliation, Man's household received orders from the king to cease Protestant worship in the embassy and attend Catholic services instead. This infringed diplomatic convention (Catholic embassies in London always retained the right to celebrate Mass, and Guzmán de Silva was himself a priest), but Philip persisted and in March 1568 refused to grant Man further audiences and exiled him from Court until he received permission to go home. The king virtuously informed the pope that the ambassador's continued presence might cause offence to God 'whose service, and the observation of whose holy faith, I place far ahead of my own affairs and actions and above everything in this life, even my own'.[22]

Philip had picked an unfortunate moment for this gratuitous confessional gesture: two weeks after news of Man's disgrace reached London, Elizabeth learned that Mary Stuart, having escaped from prison and taken part in an unsuccessful bid to regain power in Scotland, had sought refuge in England. Her agents immediately placed the Scottish queen in custody and soon arranged a 'trial' at which her Scottish enemies presented evidence that she had murdered her second husband, thus apparently neutralizing (at least for a time) the threat that Elizabeth's enemies might seek to place her on the English throne. At the same time, another civil war broke out in France, which for the next two years again eliminated the risk of French intervention in British affairs.

Even more unwisely, Philip now replaced his experienced and urbane ambassador in London, Guzmán de Silva, with the fiery and inexperienced Don Guerau de Spes. Admittedly Philip urged his new envoy to steer clear of Mary and in September 1568, having received an urgent plea for help from the Scottish queen, referred the matter to the moderate Alba: 'I have refrained from taking any decision or answering her autograph letter, of which I enclose a copy, until you tell me what you think of her business and in what way, and to what extent, I should assist her'.[23] Spes, however, proved unable to resist the opportunity to plot: he worked indefatigably to win Mary's confidence and to put her in touch with dissident English Catholics, whose desire to overthrow Elizabeth he also encouraged; and with equal energy he strove to exaggerate and exploit any English slight or action that seemed to prejudice Spanish interests. In retrospect, it seemed to at least one diplomat that amicable relations with Elizabeth could have been preserved if only Guzmán had remained at his post.[24]

The 'cold war' with England began over relatively minor issues. The duke of Alba's successful campaign to defeat William of Orange in 1568 (p. 122 above) cost a great deal of money, and most of it came from Spain, transferred by letters of exchange issued by bankers in Madrid and payable in Antwerp; however, with millions of ducats changing hands, most bankers needed to transfer some part of the money for their loans in specie. In November 1568 French pirates chased five ships carrying one such instalment of cash being shipped by some of the crown's

Genoese bankers from Spain to their Netherlands agents, and forced them to seek refuge in English ports. Spes, in London, asked Elizabeth to protect the precious cargo, either by providing a naval escort direct to Antwerp or else by permitting it to be transported overland to Dover; the queen agreed and, since the pirates continued to threaten, most of the bullion was brought ashore. But there it stayed. No sooner had the treasure ships taken refuge in England than news arrived that a trading fleet under the command of John Hawkins of Plymouth had been set upon and largely destroyed by a larger Spanish force at San Juan de Ulúa in the Caribbean. Spain claimed a monopoly of trade both with and within the Americas, and so automatically regarded people of all other nations as pirates (in 1565–66 French colonies in Florida had been destroyed, and all survivors either executed or imprisoned: see p. 14); Elizabeth, however, could not agree. Instead, although she solemnly promised Guzmán that she would do everything in her power to prevent Hawkins from sailing, she formally addressed him as 'General' of the fleet and even loaned him two warships from her navy by way of an investment.[25] Elizabeth's Court, just like Philip's, contained several factions with different policy aims, and some of the queen's advisers favoured a more aggressively Protestant policy – England's intervention in Scotland in 1560 and in France in 1562 had been their doing. Now they favoured confiscating the bullion aboard the Spanish ships in order to hamper Alba's campaign against their co-religionists in the Netherlands and news of the attack on Hawkins (in which the queen and several of her councillors had invested) provided the pretext of retaliation for doing so. Nevertheless, these incidents could easily have been resolved: on the one hand, the money (which represented only a fraction of Alba's total budget) did not belong to Spain but to its bankers; on the other, the queen would have to explain why her warships had accompanied Hawkins to the Caribbean despite her express assurances to the contrary. Almost single-handed, however, Spes turned a crisis into a war. In December he asserted (wrongly) that Elizabeth had confiscated the treasure and urged Alba to embargo all English property in the Netherlands in retaliation; he also asked the king to do the same in Spain. Both swiftly obliged and, when she heard of it, the queen reciprocated; she also placed Spes under house arrest.[26]

Direct intercourse between England and Spain now virtually ceased. Elizabeth had eventually recalled Dr Man but had not replaced him, so she lacked a voice at Philip's Court to explain her intentions; Spes remained in detention and almost incommunicado for six months.[27] Philip now took a decision that exacerbated the difficulties created by distance: in the absence of his own diplomatic links, he resolved to involve the duke of Alba in Brussels, and to a lesser extent his ambassador Don Francés de Álava in Paris, in the formation of policy towards England. This dramatically increased the length of time required to take and implement decisions. Moreover, at just this moment, a new problem arose to distract the king from dealing with the crisis in the north: the Moriscos of Granada rebelled at Christmas 1568 and efforts to subdue them tied down a large army and consumed valuable resources for almost two years.

Nevertheless, early in 1569 Philip asked Álava to ascertain 'if by chance that queen wishes to go further with her madness [*locura*]' and to assure Mary Stuart that, as long as she remained a staunch Catholic, 'I will treat her as a true sister, just as if we were children of the same mother, and as such I will help and assist her as much as lies in my power'. He began to consider – for the first time in ten years – ways to restore Catholic worship in England by force 'since it appears to me that, after my special obligation to maintain my own states in our holy faith, I am bound to make every effort in order to restore and preserve it in England as in former times'.[28] The arrival of news in March 1569 that Elizabeth had also confiscated Portuguese shipping, sent assistance to the French Protestants, and opened negotiations with some German princes for the defence of the Reformed religion encouraged the king in such thoughts 'because if she means to break simultaneously with me and with France . . . clearly God must be allowing it on account of her sins and unfaithfulness, so that she will be lost'. Meanwhile Don Guerau de Spes smuggled out of his captivity a grandiose plan to topple Elizabeth and replace her with Mary Stuart, a project for which he coined the term 'the Enterprise of England'.[29]

Alba exploited his position as Philip's security adviser for British affairs in order to create his own diplomatic links with England. Early in 1569 he sent over Christophe d'Assonleville, a Netherlands minister who had already undertaken several missions to London, in order to ascertain the queen's true intentions and to do what he could to restore harmonious relations. D'Assonleville's information, and the contacts he established, impressed the king and for a time he virtually delegated the 'British problem' to Alba 'since you are on the spot'. Little did he realize that the duke never saw the point of replacing Elizabeth Tudor with Mary Stuart and therefore strove first to delay and then to sabotage all the king's plans to achieve this. This fundamental policy difference between Brussels and Madrid was perhaps Elizabeth's greatest asset during the series of crises that lay ahead.[30]

Long before d'Assonleville returned to Brussels, Alba warned the king that open war with England would be a mistake: Orange's recent invasion had exhausted the Netherlands so that his government lacked 'the ships and many other things necessary for a fresh war', and in any case he considered that the success of the Huguenot rebels in France made it imperative to use any spare resources to help Charles IX (a major expeditionary force left the Netherlands to fight in France early in 1569). The duke therefore suggested that Philip should write an emollient letter to Elizabeth, asking why she felt aggrieved and how good relations could be restored. The king immediately complied.[31] In mid-June Alba requested powers to follow up this conciliatory approach himself but, although Philip again obliged, postal delays held his letter of authorization back for three months; and by the time it arrived other actors had appeared on the stage. In July 1568 Pope Pius V began to pressure Philip to invade England and restore Catholicism. Since the king showed little interest, early the following year Pius presented the duke of Alba with a golden sword (the mark of a warrior for the faith) and, when this too produced no effect, in November 1569 he sent a letter that explicitly called on Alba to invade England. By then, although not yet privy to this papal summons, Philip had also become impatient with Elizabeth and decided that the time had come 'to use force where reason has failed'. He drew encouragement from a rebellion against the queen by the Catholics of northern England, from the containment of the Morisco revolt, and from the victories of the French crown over its Protestant rebels (thanks in part to Spain's military assistance): taken together, these three developments seemed to create a favourable situation for a more active policy against England. Furthermore the king considered that the long delay in securing restitution of the treasure seized by 'that woman' had 'already begun to affect our prestige'. Late in 1569 Philip informed Alba that he now favoured sending money to Elizabeth's northern rebels, encouraging the Irish Catholics to revolt, and actively supporting Mary Stuart's claim to the English crown. Yet again, however, his nerve apparently failed him: conscious that he wrote far from events, the king concluded his letter with a disclaimer: 'I only mention all this so that you will know what we are thinking here and so that, with your great prudence, and bearing in mind the state of affairs in all areas, you can consider what would be most appropriate.'[32]

The duke's 'great prudence' dictated otherwise. Although sharing Philip's frustration at the queen's refusal to return the confiscated money, or even to discuss doing so, he resolutely rejected all talk of an open breach. By the time Philip's letter arrived he had already poured sarcasm on the pope's invitation to invade England:

> Such is the zeal and enthusiasm of His Holiness for the service of God, and so holy is his intention, that we might with justice judge him a heavenly rather than an earthly being since he places – as it is right to place – all trust in God. And if our sins did not get in the way of God's purpose, no one could doubt that, without considering any human agency, we could have total confidence of success if we undertook any enterprise of this sort in this way. However, since worldly affairs form such a large part of us, His Holiness should not marvel if we might also want to make use of human agencies, so let me tell you what I think about these in as few words as possible . . .

The duke conceded that 'It would be easy for His Majesty to conquer England if the English had only their own forces with which to defend themselves'; but of course as soon as Philip started to attack England, France and the German princes would attack Philip's possessions. Perhaps, the duke continued, France and Spain could carry out the invasion together and then partition the kingdom; but this too seemed impractical, because the victors would inevitably squabble over the exact division (he again cited the failed agreement to partition Naples earlier in the century). And, in any case, Alba despaired of replacing Elizabeth with another ruler who would restore Catholicism because it would be hard to find someone acceptable to both monarchs.[33] Neither sarcasm nor reason deterred the pope, however: in February 1570, without consulting the king, he excommunicated Elizabeth and absolved her subjects from their obedience, sending copies of his sentence to the duke of Alba a month later (also without telling the king) along with orders both to ensure its diffusion in England and to take steps to depose her.[34]

By then Philip's patience had finally run out. In January 1570 he angrily reminded Alba that Elizabeth had confiscated not only the treasure of his bankers but also the goods of his subjects in England; she had welcomed his rebels (perhaps 30,000 Dutch exiles, mostly Protestants and many of them implicated in the rebellions of 1566 and 1568, resided in England); she had broken off all trade; and she had licensed attacks on any ships sailing through the Channel under Spanish colours. 'By contrast, the damage which she, her kingdom and her subjects have received from us is so little that it hardly counts . . . so that one could justly say that she has declared war on us, but we are at peace with her.' This unequal situation, the king insisted, could not be allowed to continue: a way of harming Elizabeth, and thus of bringing her back to peaceful coexistence, had to be found. His letter also contained, for the first time perhaps in over a decade, a 'messianic' element. Philip reiterated his belief that God's service 'required' him to intervene in order to liberate the Catholic queen of Scots and to restore Catholicism in England – especially since 'God has already granted that by my intervention and my hand that kingdom has previously been restored to the Catholic church once'. This confidence that God intended him to annex England made Philip ready – perhaps for the first but certainly not the last time in his reign – to throw caution to the winds. He informed Alba that:

> Even though human prudence suggests many inconveniences and difficulties, and places before us worldly fears, Christian certitude and the confidence that we must justly have in the cause of God will remove them, and inspire and strengthen us to overcome them. Certainly we could not avoid remaining with great guilt in our soul, and great regret, if because I failed that queen [Mary] and those Catholics – or, rather, the faith – they suffered and she was lost.

The king briefly reviewed several possible strategies for achieving these ends (conveniently forgetting that Alba had already scornfully rejected most of them): an outright invasion by his various forces; a joint invasion with the French; and an assault on Ireland (representatives of the Irish Catholics had recently arrived in Spain to secure his support). As usual he solicited Alba's assessment of these plans, but this time he also ordered him secretly to provide both the English Catholics and Mary Stuart with money, arms and munitions, and to send military advisers to help train her supporters. To facilitate this, Philip enclosed a letter of credit for 300,000 ducats.[35]

Alba remained totally unconvinced by both the spiritual blackmail and the strategic alternatives and he drew up a detailed rebuttal modelled on his reply to the pope two months earlier. He even adopted the same tone of heavy sarcasm towards Philip's messianic imperialism: 'Even though the principal means must come from God, as Your Majesty very virtuously and piously suggests, nevertheless since He normally works through the resources He gives to humans, it seems necessary to examine what human resources would be needed to carry out your wishes'. Alba began by ruling out an immediate invasion, with or without the French, on the grounds both of cost and of the troubled international situation; he also pointed out that, although the English Catholics begged for assistance, they had made it very clear that they did not want deliverance to come by means of a foreign army; finally he noted that the rising of the northern Catholics had 'gone up in smoke' (as he had always predicted, he added smugly). The duke felt more positive about sending financial support to Elizabeth's disaffected subjects in Ireland (especially since it was something 'which Your Majesty will be better able to do than I') as well as in England. He therefore recommended 'putting in order and assembling', in both Spain and the Netherlands, 'all that we can, both ships and everything else [for a future invasion] – albeit with some other excuse' in order to avoid alarming Elizabeth. Needless to say, he expected all funds for this purpose to come from Spain.[36]

News that the king of France had begun peace talks with the Huguenots temporarily cooled the king's ardour, because an end to the civil wars (which duly occurred in August) would leave Charles IX free to assist Elizabeth if Spain attacked. In addition, the king's tour of Andalusia (to restore confidence in the wake of the Morisco rebellion) and news of the Turkish invasion of Cyprus (beginning in July 1570) distracted him from other matters. So Philip sent Elizabeth a message that the traditional Anglo-Spanish friendship would never be broken through a fault on his part; and he warned Spes to cease his plotting. He also passed the initiative for coordinating policy back to Alba, telling Spes: 'English affairs depend so entirely on those of Flanders and the duke of Alba is managing them with so much prudence and consideration, to the benefit of my interests, that you will continue to follow the instructions he may give you'.[37]

In September 1570 ninety of the ships assembled by Alba set sail, not for England but for Spain, carrying Philip's future wife, his niece Anna of Austria. Although Elizabeth feared the worst, ordering her entire navy to sea as the Spanish fleet sailed through the Channel, everything passed off amicably. The duke's moderation appeared to have prevailed. Philip nevertheless took two important steps that kept hostilities going: he declared himself willing to assist the Irish Catholics, welcoming to his Court Thomas Stukeley, an Anglo-Irish adventurer who planned to lead an invasion to drive the English from his homeland; and he approved a suggestion from Spes that he should maintain contact with both discontented English Catholics and with Mary through a Florentine banker in London, Roberto Ridolfi, who enjoyed the pope's confidence and handled the funds secretly sent from Rome to England. Unfortunately for all of them, Ridolfi – virtually the only channel through which the various conspirators in England could communicate – was almost certainly a double-agent who shared all his information with Elizabeth's ministers.[38]

Philip's first ploy almost immediately produced excellent results: early in 1571 Elizabeth sent a special envoy to Spain, urging the king not to support her Irish rebels, asking if she might send a new ambassador and declaring her willingness to negotiate a settlement of all outstanding issues.[39] Instead of using Stukeley as a bargaining counter, however, the king decided to support the plan to overthrow Elizabeth in favour of Mary queen of Scots. The full story of the 'Ridolfi plot' can probably never be told because too many important documents have been lost and much of the information that survives was extracted under torture (or the threat of it). Two distinct – indeed incompatible – plans seem to have been under discussion. According to the subsequent testimony of Mary's ambassador at the English Court, the Scottish queen would be spirited from her prison and taken to the coast, where a fleet manned by sympathetic Englishmen and led by John Hawkins – the same man who had been set upon and almost killed at San Juan de Ulúa scarcely two years before – would 'convey' her to safety in Spain. There she might marry Philip's brother, Don John of Austria, while her young son James would be betrothed to Philip's daughter Isabella. This Elizabeth later claimed she could have tolerated ('hir Majesty thynketh it no just cause to be offended with those devises tendyng to hir [Mary's] liberty', according to Lord Burghley); what appalled her was clear evidence that Mary had also wished to dethrone her.[40]

Ridolfi left England in March 1571 armed with 'instructions, commissions and letters' from his numerous contacts and, having visited Alba and the pope, arrived in Madrid at the end of June and met with the king, Feria and various other ministers. In July the council of State debated the English question and unanimously agreed with Feria's proposal that Elizabeth should be either captured or killed in the autumn while she was on her annual progress through the Home Counties. This, they anticipated, would unleash a general rising of English Catholics, to be led by the duke of Norfolk, whom Mary would marry. This in turn would serve as a signal for Alba to send a fleet, reinforced by the flotilla under the duke of Medinaceli already standing by at Santander (pp. 130–31 above), to escort 6,000 troops drawn from the Army of Flanders across to England to assist Norfolk. Alba would be sent 200,000 ducats specifically to prepare this task force. One week later, after carefully considering the recommendations and conversing further with Ridolfi, Philip wrote to apprise Alba of his plan.[41] A month later, however, the king introduced various significant refinements: first, Feria signed a contract with an agent of John Hawkins promising that Hawkins's squadron of sixteen ships, then at Plymouth, would sail to the Netherlands in September and help ferry over Alba's troops; second, the king increased the number of troops scheduled for the expedition to 10,000 and designated Harwich in Essex as the landing zone.[42] Third, he authorized Alba to send money to Scotland to help Mary's supporters there to create a diversion (although Philip forbade him to send troops 'in order to avoid open war with the queen of England'); and finally he granted Stukeley permission to lead his diversionary attack on Ireland.[43]

These changes made the plan dangerously complicated, yet the entire initiative still remained with Norfolk and a bunch of assassins: until the latter killed the queen, and Norfolk brought his supporters out, the squadrons in Plymouth, Santander and Zealand could not join forces, let alone start embarking Alba's troops. Yet, apart from the documents circulated by Ridolfi, no reliable evidence existed either that Norfolk (a Protestant, not a Catholic!) wished to lead a rising against Elizabeth or that any significant body of English Catholics would follow him if he did. As the scale of these problems dawned upon him, Philip changed his plans yet again. In August 1571 he informed Alba that, even if the plot to kill Elizabeth did not take place, or took place and failed, he must still invade. Realizing that the duke would probably object strenuously to this (as he had to every other suggestion that force be used against Elizabeth), Philip fell back once again on messianic imperialism:

> No one can deny that this venture involves many and great difficulties, and that if it goes wrong we will incur considerable inconveniences (as you prudently pointed out [in a recent letter]) . . . In spite of all this I desire to achieve this enterprise so much, and I have such complete confidence that God our Lord, to whose service it is dedicated (because I have no personal ambition here), will guide and direct it, and I hold my charge from God to do this to be so explicit, that I am extremely determined and resolved to proceed and participate, doing on my side everything possible in this world to promote and assist it.

Such rhetoric left Alba unmoved. Upon receiving the king's letter he replied suavely but firmly that an invasion was at this stage out of the question because, 'as I have already told Your Majesty, I have not begun to make any preparations'; furthermore he declared himself unwilling to hazard his troops in England unless they had guarantees of substantial local support.

The separate agendas of Madrid and Brussels now came into full play. As governor-general of the Low Countries, Alba earnestly desired a settlement with Elizabeth, not open war; he therefore even discouraged the king from sending troops to Ireland before the English Catholics rose, on the grounds that 'once that happens, Ireland will fall by itself'. Once more, in desperation, Philip played the messianic card: on 14 September he again urged Alba to launch the invasion – even if Norfolk had been arrested, even if Hawkins failed to materialize – because 'I am so keen to achieve the consummation of this enterprise, I am so attached to it in my heart, and I am so convinced that God our Saviour must embrace it as His own cause, that I cannot be dissuaded. Nor can I accept or believe the contrary.'[44] It was a poor substitute for strategy.

As it happened, unknown to either Philip or Alba, the plan had no chance of success. Thanks to the information supplied by Ridolfi (whether voluntarily or not) and by Hawkins (deliberately), by 5 September 1571 Elizabeth's ministers possessed enough incriminating evidence to arrest Norfolk and to order Mary to be more closely confined and prevented from speaking with anyone. A letter written by Lord Burghley late that night and sent to Mary's keeper 'hast, post hast, hast, hast for lif, lif, lif' instructed him to 'have some good speeche to the queen of Scottes' both about her plans to escape and flee to Spain, and to 'provoke hir to answer' about 'hir labors and devices to stir up a new rebellion in this realm [of England] and to have the king of Spain assist it'. Subsequent interrogation of the plotters soon provided most of the missing details.[45] Eventually Elizabeth had Norfolk executed and subjected Mary to far stricter confinement (she punished few others because – as Alba had always claimed – virtually no evidence existed that the Catholics of southern England harboured any wish to change their allegiance). Ridolfi, wisely, never again crossed the Channel and, after performing various diplomatic missions for his native Florence, died in 1612. Stukeley went off to fight at Lepanto and thence made his way to Rome to find other backers for his Irish schemes.[46]

Thus perished another major opportunity to overthrow Tudor England. Admittedly the revolt of the Moriscos tied down some of Philip's resources, but Alba commanded a victorious army throughout the period, and until Queen Anna's voyage to Spain he also possessed a respectable fleet. France remained riven by civil war, and thus incapable of interfering, until the summer of 1570. Rapid assistance for the rising of the northern Catholics late in 1569, or modest support for the Irish Catholics at almost any time, would have placed Elizabeth under almost intolerable pressure to negotiate an end to the trade war and perhaps to provide guarantees for good behaviour in the future. However, as in 1559–60, Philip's relative isolation in Spain and his imperfect grasp of British affairs – exacerbated this time by the separate agenda pursued by his trusted lieutenant in Brussels – prevented him from exploiting Elizabeth's weaknesses. Instead, deluded by his religious zeal and by his assurance that he could 'give better information and advice on that kingdom and on its affairs and people than anyone else' (p. 151 above), he placed all his trust in a grandiose plan that had virtually no chance of success yet still managed to alienate and discredit his few supporters at Elizabeth's Court.

The Ridolfi plot proved a turning-point in Anglo-Spanish relations. In the short term, Elizabeth made haste to sink her differences with France, signing a defensive alliance in April 1572 that promised French assistance should England be attacked by a foreign power; in the long term, she never trusted Spain and her monarch again. She began to spend heavily to improve the defence of her realm and she openly welcomed and succoured rebels against Philip, whether in the Netherlands, in America or (after the Spanish annexation of 1580) in Portugal. She also tolerated, and sometimes directly supported, privateering activity against Spanish interests: no fewer than eleven major English expeditions sailed to the Caribbean between 1572 and 1577, plundering Spanish property and killing or ransoming Spanish subjects. Finally, in 1577, she provided the resources that enabled Francis Drake to sail to the East Indies via Cape Horn in order to open a direct route to the 'Spice Islands'. Drake's 'famous voyage', which turned into a circumnavigation of the globe, lasted three years and caused extensive damage to Spanish goods and ships as his flotilla sailed up the coast of South America and proved that the Pacific was no longer a 'Spanish lake'.[47]

The duke of Alba recognized that the plot had turned England from a neutral observer into a covert enemy, but 'regarded the queen as quite justified in what she had done and is still doing' against Spain and urged Philip to meet all Elizabeth's conditions for a restoration of peace. At first the king resisted – early in 1574 he asked his new lieutenant in the Netherlands, Don Luis de Requeséns, to evaluate the feasibility of a fresh invasion, commissioned a survey of the southern coast of Ireland and apparently toyed with the idea of sending a part of the fleet assembled in Santander for the reconquest of the Netherlands to capture an Irish port – but later that year he followed Alba's advice and concluded a full settlement of all outstanding differences with England.[48] Indeed, in an attempt to restore harmonious relations, Philip conceded more than Elizabeth had required: where she had asked only that those whom she had exiled from England should be expelled from the Netherlands, Philip ordered the expulsion of *all* English Catholics and even decreed the closure of the English seminary at Douai. His 'reward' came the following year: when storms drove a fleet of fifty vessels carrying Spanish troops to the Army of Flanders to take shelter in English ports, they received courteous treatment, and Elizabeth temporarily moderated her support for the Dutch.[49]

In fact Philip had few alternatives: the war in the Mediterranean and after 1572 also in the Netherlands (the designated launching pad for the invasion of England), absorbed prodigious amounts of money (see Table 4 on p. 135 above). As the papal secretary of state put it, 'I do not see how His Majesty can undertake the necessary expenditure [for the Enterprise of England], while he has to pay for the campaign against the Turks'. As long as the Mediterranean war continued, he believed, Philip lacked both the time and the money to attack England.[50] Pope Gregory XIII, however, who succeeded Pius V in 1572, shared his predecessor's interest in restoring England to the Catholic church and decided that even though Philip could no longer act alone he could at least favour the anti-Elizabethan designs of others. Early in 1575 he authorized Nicholas Ormanetto, his nuncio in Spain and a man who had worked alongside the king to re-Catholicize England in the 1550s, to persuade Philip either to send Don John of Austria to the Netherlands, with orders to invade England and regain it for the faith, or (failing that) to lend his support to an assault on Ireland under papal aegis.[51] To Ormanetto's delight, the king once again sounded out his military commander in the Netherlands about mounting an invasion, and meanwhile declared himself willing to fund and transport a papal force of 2,000 men to Ireland.[52]

1575 was a Jubilee year which brought many English Catholic exiles to Rome. Early the following year two of their leaders, William Allen and Francis Englefield, presented the pope with a memorial demonstrating that England could easily be won back for the faith by sending some 5,000 musketeers, commanded by Thomas Stukeley (then also in Rome), from Italy direct to

Liverpool. This, they argued, would provoke a general rising of the English Catholics (particularly numerous in Lancashire), allowing the expeditionary force to liberate Mary Stuart from captivity and proclaim her queen of England. She would then marry a consort nominated by Philip. The pope immediately endorsed this bold plan, again termed 'The Enterprise of England'; and it also received enthusiastic endorsement from the Spanish ambassador at the papal Court, Don Juan de Zúñiga, who hailed it as a bargain since Philip needed to provide only a subsidy of 100,000 ducats and his blessing.[53] The king expressed great enthusiasm for the project in principle, and even sent Zúñiga half the subsidy requested, but he soon claimed that it was too late in the year to mount an invasion before the winter made navigation too hazardous and that any diversion of his resources – severely restricted after the state bankruptcy in September 1575 – would imperil the defence of the Mediterranean.

The pope persisted, however, and in August 1576 again asked Philip to undertake the invasion. At first the king remained cautious: 'Nobody desires more than I that the matter be put in hand, but when and how depend on the way things go in Flanders, and on many other considerations', he wrote. Four months later he approved the plans hatched by Don John of Austria, newly appointed governor-general of the Netherlands, to invade England the following year should the opportunity arise; but this scheme, too, aborted. By the time Don John arrived in the Low Countries in November 1576, the entire royal army there had either mutinied or deserted so that he lacked both the authority and the resources to undertake any major enterprise.[54] For a moment he and the king toyed with the idea of sending the Spanish veterans in the Netherlands back to Spain by sea, and making a surprise descent upon an English port, and the pope enthusiastically welcomed this course of action; but when early in 1577 news arrived that a major Turkish fleet might sail west that summer, the king ordered the veterans to return overland to Italy instead in order to help defend the Mediterranean.[55] The pope perforce fell back on the troops gathered in Italy for the 'Enterprise': 600 men under Stukeley's command left Porto Ercole in February 1577 and reached Lisbon shortly afterwards.

Both Don John and Gregory XIII continued to bombard Philip with pleas to persevere with the invasion of England, and other ministers also chimed in – according to the Spanish ambassador in Paris, 'everything evil comes from England' – but their pleas only served to make Elizabeth aware of the conspiracy being hatched against her, since some crucial letters on the subject were intercepted and deciphered. As Zúñiga lamented: 'The worst is that the queen now knows what we had planned and feels the same indignation as if the enterprise had taken place.'[56] In the event, Stukeley and his men grew tired of waiting and in 1578 joined Sebastian of Portugal's 'crusade' to conquer Morocco where, at the battle of Alcazarquivir, like Sebastian, most of them perished. Only a few survivors made their way back to the Iberian peninsula whence, the following year, Philip reluctantly allowed them to sail to Smerwick, a large but remote natural harbour in County Kerry, where they fortified a promontory overlooking the bay, called the 'Castello del Oro' (the Golden Castle), and launched an appeal to Catholic Europe for reinforcements.[57]

Philip's attempts to orchestrate from Spain a complex operation against Elizabeth in conjunction with the Papacy thus proved no more successful than his earlier efforts to 'go it alone'. A combination of confusion, suspicion and delay – which would recur in the 1580s – frustrated every intention. Serious structural obstacles repeatedly thwarted detailed strategic planning between Madrid and Rome: the difficulties of coordinating a campaign quickly enough to be put into effect the same year, and the danger of a security leak if it took longer; disputes over the best strategy to follow and over who should choose the next ruler of England;[58] the propensity of both pope and king to change their minds – and their plans – without consulting each other;[59] and the temptation to withhold promised funds in order to pressure the other party to accept those changes.[60] All would reappear a decade later. The rhetoric and the strategic goals of 1575–79 would also re-emerge during the planning of the Armada campaign: the euphemisms used at this time (such as 'the Enterprise of England' and 'the principal business') recurred; while the commitment to replace Elizabeth Tudor with Mary Stuart, and the argument that 'His Majesty will never be at peace until England is conquered', both remained articles of faith at the Court of Spain.[61]

Nevertheless Philip still stopped short of promising to overthrow Elizabeth: as he constantly reminded the pope, he had fully committed his resources elsewhere. Admittedly, in 1577 he managed to extricate himself from the Mediterranean war, which allowed him to reduce his defence establishment there dramatically; but he exploited this advantage to send the treasure and troops to the Netherlands that enabled war against his Dutch rebels to resume.[62] The following year, Sebastian's death at Alcazarquivir left Philip as the closest male heir to the Portuguese empire and brought to the fore the traditional priorities of the Spanish crown. In the stirring phrase of a royal chaplain, Fray Hernando del Castillo:

> Uniting the kingdoms of Portugal and Castile will make Your Majesty the greatest king in the world . . . because if the Romans were able to rule the world simply by ruling the Mediterranean, what of the man who rules the Atlantic and Pacific oceans, since they surround the world?

Philip and most of his courtiers saw the unification of the peninsula as a vital step on Spain's road to global mastery. According to one councillor, acquiring Portugal 'would be the principal, most effective, and decisive instrument and remedy for the reduction of the Netherlands to obedience' as well as a useful means of controlling England. As Hernando del Castillo tersely put it: 'The gain or loss [of Portugal] will mean the gain or loss of the world'.[63]

Philip apparently paid heed. Scarcely had Lisbon fallen than he resolved to seek a measure of revenge for the depredations of Drake in the Pacific, and for Elizabeth's aid to the Dutch, by sending assistance to the papal contingent in

Ireland. In September 1580, after consulting the duke of Alba (who, as usual, strongly opposed the venture), Philip authorized Juan Martínez de Recalde to convey some 800 Spanish and Italian volunteers to Smerwick. Unfortunately for them, however, shortly after Recalde departed, Elizabeth's military and naval forces surrounded the Castello del Oro and, although the troops within surrendered in return for a promise that their lives would be spared, the English immediately massacred all but twenty-three of them in cold blood.[64]

Their king scarcely felt their loss amid the wealth and resources gained in Portugal and her overseas empire. Above all, he gained ten fighting galleons constructed in the 1570s by the Portuguese crown for the defence of seaborne trade, together with the great natural harbour of Lisbon in which to station them. Apart from the English navy, which at the time numbered scarcely twenty fighting ships (some of them very old), Philip now possessed the best warfleet in the western world. Its qualities were soon demonstrated. Most of the Azores archipelago refused to recognize the Spanish succession, instead acknowledging the claim of Dom Antonio, prior of Crato, Sebastian's illegitimate cousin; but in 1582 an expeditionary force of sixty ships, led by the royal galleons and commanded by the resourceful and experienced marquis of Santa Cruz, sailed from Lisbon and destroyed Dom Antonio's larger fleet (prepared in France and containing some English and Dutch vessels) in a battle off the island of São Miguel. Only the island of Terceira now held out, garrisoned by Portuguese, French and English troops; and in 1583 an even larger Armada, consisting of 98 ships and over 15,000 men (again commanded by Santa Cruz), carried out a skilful combined operation that reconquered it.[65]

Jubilation at the marquis of Santa Cruz's success reached such heights that, according to some Spaniards, 'even Christ was no longer safe in Paradise, for the marquis might go there to bring him back and crucify him all over again', while Cardinal Granvelle urged that the time had now come to take up other enterprises that would advance God's cause – 'and all the more so, since in doing His work we are also doing our own'.[66] Nor did celebration stop at verbal hyperbole. A mural of Santa Cruz's victory off São Miguel soon filled one wall of the Hall of Battles in the Escorial; a special medal commemorating the union of the two great world empires bore the legend THE WORLD IS NOT ENOUGH (Plate 2 above); while a bowl commemorating the Terceira campaign of 1583 (found among the wreckage of a Spanish Armada vessel that foundered off Ireland five years later) shows Spain's warrior patron saint with new attributes. St James still rides a charger, with his sword-arm raised to strike down his foes; but these foes are no longer cowering infidels but the swirling waves of the Ocean Sea, waves now subdued by Spain along with the human enemies who sought refuge amongst them (Plate 23).[67] The euphoria even affected Santa Cruz who, flushed by his success, pointed out to the king in August 1583 that:

> Victories as complete as the one God has been pleased to grant Your Majesty in these [Azores] islands normally spur princes on to other enterprises; and

Plate 23　'The Terceira Bowl'. One of the officers aboard the Armada ship *La Trinidad Valencera* took with him a souvenir of an earlier campaign, the victorious combined operation led by the marquis of Santa Cruz to capture Terceira island in the Azores in 1583. The base of the bowl shows St James the 'Moor-slayer', Spain's patron saint, subduing the waves of the Ocean Sea with a suitable Latin inscription. In the event the bowl sank when the ship ran aground off Kinnagoe Bay in northern Ireland, and there it remained until excavated almost four centuries later.

since Our Lord has made Your Majesty such a great king, it is just that you should follow up this victory by making arrangements for the invasion of England next year. [68]

Meanwhile, in Scotland, a group of Catholics led by the duke of Lennox, favourite of the 16-year-old James VI, in 1582 hatched a plot to restore Catholicism and sought the assistance of co-religionists abroad – in the Netherlands, France, Italy and Spain. In the event, a Protestant splinter group seized James later that year and Lennox lost his influence. [69] The continental Catholic leaders did not give up, however: in the summer of 1583 various meetings took place in Paris between the papal nuncio and the Spanish ambassador in France, the duke of Guise (leader of the French Catholics), and some British exiles to plan an invasion of southern Scotland or northern England. In August Gregory XIII offered to contribute 400,000 ducats to the cost of the venture and sent an envoy to Madrid to secure Philip's support.[70]

The king remained as reluctant as ever to cooperate in a joint venture with the French. He did, however, commission maps and surveys of the English coast; he ordered close study of previous attempts to invade England (from the Romans and Saxons down to the Ridolfi plot and the Smerwick landing); and he asked both Santa Cruz and the prince of Parma, governor-general of the Netherlands since the death of Don John in 1578, whether they could provide support for the invasion from the forces at their command.[71] Parma proved reluctant, but Santa Cruz and his entourage swiftly assembled a dossier that ruled out a descent on ports in remote (albeit Catholic) areas such as Liverpool or Milford Haven and instead advocated a landing in irresistible force as close to London as possible.[72]

In October 1583 Philip yet again changed his mind and pulled out, stating coyly that 'the season of the year is now so far advanced that it excludes any other designs that we may have had'. He decided to send the victorious veterans of the Terceira campaign to the Netherlands via Italy, instead of holding them in readiness for a descent upon England.[73] The pope and the duke of Guise persisted, however. In November Don Juan de Zúñiga, now the king's chief adviser on foreign affairs, received a diffident letter from the Spanish ambassador in Rome containing the news that 'His Holiness has proposed that His Majesty should marry the queen of Scots, saying that in this way he can once more become king of England'. He added, no doubt for Zúñiga's eyes alone: 'The pope expressly told me to write this to His Majesty, but through embarrassment I have chosen to do so through you.' Inevitably, the king saw the letter and scribbled: 'I do not feel any embarrassment at being told what should be done; but I do feel it with something so inappropriate as this – the more so because I know that I could not fulfil the obligation of either governing that kingdom [of England] or of going there, having so many other duties that it is impossible to fulfil even those as I would wish.'[74] The king seemed no more eager to marry Mary Stuart than – twenty-five years before – he had been to marry Elizabeth. He did, however, countenance the support offered by his ambassador in London, Don Bernardino de Mendoza, to a new plot (devised by Francis Throckmorton) aimed at eliminating Elizabeth and replacing her with Mary Stuart, who would then marry a Catholic prince favourable to Spain.

Philip's attention and resources throughout the 1580s increasingly centred upon developments in north-west Europe. In 1581 his Dutch rebels declared Philip deposed and chose Francis Hercules, duke of Alençon (and later Anjou), brother and heir presumptive to Henry III of France, as their sovereign ruler with the style 'prince and lord of the Netherlands'. He soon moved to the Low Countries accompanied by a powerful French army and a substantial supply of French gold; he also announced his betrothal to Elizabeth Tudor. Meanwhile some of his Dutch supporters transferred the strategic enclave of Cambrai, an imperial fief previously ruled by Philip, to French control.[75] In 1582 another French expeditionary force entered the Netherlands to support Anjou and the Dutch, while followers of Dom Antonio received permission from Henry III to raise an army and navy to defend the Azores.

Alarmed and offended by these acts of open aggression, Philip decided to retaliate by stirring up Henry III's discontented subjects. He had already made contact with the militantly Catholic duke of Guise – money had changed hands in 1578 and they had discussed the joint invasion of England in 1583 – but now the subsidies became more regular and more substantial, and Philip promised his protection against the French Protestants should Henry die.[76] Shortly afterwards, Philip also proposed an alliance to the Huguenot leader Henry of Navarre, offering to pay a subsidy and even to marry Henry's sister Catherine in return for Navarre's re-conversion to Catholicism and a declaration of war against Henry III.[77] Finally, he favoured the attempts of the maverick duke of Montmorency to build an independent power base in south-west France, signing a draft treaty for mutual military assistance in September 1583.[78] Meanwhile, Philip's forces in the Netherlands, under Parma's able command, began to make spectacular progress: they regained the key ports of the Flemish coast – Dunkirk and Nieuwpoort – in 1583 and some major cities of the interior – Bruges and Ghent – in 1584. That same year first the duke of Anjou and then William of Orange died, and Parma daringly decided to besiege Antwerp, the largest city in northern Europe, boasting a population of 100,000.

To support these various undertakings, the king began to show greater financial foresight. In spring 1582 he ordered his treasury officials to prepare an imperial budget for the two succeeding years, in order to assure a more stable and predictable flow of money to all the government's various undertakings. In the summer of 1583, at his command, they did the same again.[79] In 1584 the king decided to send 2 million ducats in cash – half in silver 'pieces of eight' and half in gold – from Barcelona to Milan, where it formed a strategic reserve both to finance Parma's reconquest of Flanders and Brabant and to subsidize the French Catholics, and for almost two years consignments of 600,000 ducats travelled punctually in overland convoys to the Netherlands every four months, with more periodically shipped to France. Yet more money was apparently stored in strong-boxes in the royal palace in Madrid.[80]

The steady stream of Spanish successes – in the Azores, the Netherlands and France – alarmed Elizabeth. Some of her councillors, including the earl of Leicester (her favourite) and Sir Francis Walsingham (her secretary of state), had long regarded war with Spain as inevitable at some point and therefore favoured a pre-emptive strike by England before Philip could concentrate his resources. In 1581 (the year after the Smerwick incident) a consortium of courtiers and others raised money for a naval expedition to support Dom Antonio, temporarily a refugee in England: Francis Drake, newly returned from his circumnavigation, offered to lead it to the Azores. When Mendoza threatened in August that Spain would regard open support for the 'Portuguese pretender' as a *casus belli*, however, calmer heads prevailed and Elizabeth ordered the ships, ordnance, men and victuals to be 'discharged'. 'All the flagges etc with the armes of Portugal' were sold to Dom Antonio, who promptly moved to France.[81]

Some of the English vessels assembled for the expedition nevertheless joined Dom Antonio in a private capacity on his unsuccessful Azores venture, while others sailed on the troublesome voyage led by Edward Fenton in 1582, with orders to establish an English trading base in the Moluccas (under licence from Dom Antonio) and to send home rich cargoes of spices. The venture did not prosper. Fenton's chief pilot, Thomas Hood, rejoiced in unorthodox methods of navigation: 'I give not a fart for all their cosmography', he boasted, 'for I can tell more than all the cosmographers in the world'. Not surprisingly he guided his little fleet, not to the Moluccas, but first to Africa and then to the River Plate, where a Spanish squadron closed in at a time when the crews were drunk. The damage sustained proved so severe that most ships had to return home, although one collided with the coast of Brazil, delivering the men aboard to the native inhabitants who (according to rumour) enslaved the fittest and ate the rest.[82]

Meanwhile, in England, Mendoza's involvement in the Throckmorton plot led to his expulsion early in 1584 for 'conduct incompatible with his diplomatic status' (namely, seeking to encompass the queen's death), and increased the pressure of the 'war party' at Elizabeth's Court for more overt action against Philip. Anjou's death in June 1584 strengthened their hand yet further because, although incompetent and unprepossessing, the duke had fulfilled two important political functions. First, his role as 'prince and lord of the Netherlands' had virtually guaranteed French support for the Dutch; now his death jeopardized it, especially after the assassination of William of Orange the following month. Anjou's mother, Catherine de Medici, predicted that without the two leaders the king of Spain would quickly complete the reconquest of the Low Countries and 'after that . . . he will not fail to attack this kingdom [France] and England'.[83] Second, Anjou had ranked as heir presumptive to his childless brother Henry III and, because the Salic Law restricted succession to the French crown to the nearest male relative of the monarch, his death left the Protestant Henry of Navarre as the new heir presumptive.

In Spain, the death of Anjou caused both rejoicing and concern. It removed a thorn in Parma's side in the Netherlands, allowing him to concentrate on the siege of Antwerp without fearing another 'stab in the back' from France. In February 1585 his engineers completed a massive fortified bridge across the Scheldt below Antwerp, in order to prevent the arrival of relief. But the prospect of Navarre's succession to the French crown raised the spectre of an openly hostile regime in Paris which might challenge Philip's authority in all areas. As soon as he heard the news of Anjou's death, the king commissioned Don Juan de Zúñiga to work out the best policy to prevent this. Several cogent analytical papers came back within the week, all starting with the premise that 'Your Majesty is obliged to make sure that no heretic succeeds [to the throne of France], both because you have a duty always to defend and protect the Catholics and because any heretic must necessarily be an enemy of Your Majesty'. Zúñiga perceived three ways of achieving this goal: open military intervention; an alliance with Henry III; or a secret alliance with the French Catholics. Since a declaration of war would prove ruinously expensive, and since Henry had shown himself to be 'ill-willed and unstable up to now', Zúñiga recommended the third course of action – alliance with the French Catholics. At the same time, he noted that the Catholics had no credible candidate for the throne, should Henry die childless, and he therefore advocated marrying the duke of Savoy to one of Philip's adolescent daughters, since they were the oldest surviving grandchildren of Henry II of France and thus possessed a potential claim to the throne: married to the powerful and ambitious duke of Savoy, the Infanta would find a willing champion (see Table 3 on p. 79 above). The king entirely agreed: he lost no time in offering an alliance to the French Catholic leader, Henry of Guise, and the following year the duke of Savoy married Philip's daughter Catalina.[84]

Guise also considered a Protestant king totally unacceptable and he created a paramilitary organization, the 'League', dedicated to securing a Catholic succession. While Henry III negotiated with the Dutch about continuing French support for their struggle against Philip, Spanish envoys opened negotiations with Guise for a closer alliance. The offer of funds to help keep the League's army prepared, and of military assistance should civil war break out, culminated in a treaty signed at Guise's palace at Joinville on 31 December 1584 that guaranteed both objectives. In return, the League leaders promised to do their best to further Spain's designs elsewhere in Europe.[85] Philip began to reap the benefits almost immediately: in March 1585 Henry III not only refused an invitation to assume Anjou's mantle in the Netherlands but also signed a formal agreement with Guise (the treaty of Nemours) which ceded several important towns to the League's control, and promised to work towards extirpating Protestantism.[86]

This further round of Spanish successes greatly increased Elizabeth's sense of isolation. In October 1584 her Privy Council had conducted a major review of the Netherlands situation and concluded that, in the wake of the death of Anjou and Orange, the rebels' prospects seemed hopeless without foreign aid. Almost unanimously the council urged the queen to intervene.[87] Still she procrastinated, however, hoping that Henry III would take up Anjou's commitments; but she conceded that, if no aid came from other quarters, England would have to provide assistance.[88] When, therefore, in March 1585 Henry indicated that he would not help the Dutch and news of the treaty of Joinville arrived, English ministers began to negotiate with envoys sent by the Republic to forge a formal alliance.[89]

Although anxious to delay open support for Philip's rebels as long as possible, fearing that (as Mendoza had threatened) it would provoke all-out war with Spain, in August 1584 Elizabeth nevertheless agreed to sponsor another semi-private naval attack on Spanish overseas interests, creating a special fund 'to be issued from tyme to tyme' on the orders of a commission consisting of Burghley, Walsingham and Lord Admiral Howard. The money went to Sir Francis Drake who, by the end of November 1584, had assembled a fleet of 15 ships (two of them the queen's warships) and 20 pinnaces, with 1,600 men (500 of them soldiers) for an expedition to the East Indies. The total cost was estimated at £40,000 (about 160,000 ducats), of which the queen agreed to contribute almost half in cash and ships.[90] The following month, however, Elizabeth changed her mind and suspended the project – although she allowed a small colonizing expedition to sail to America (a precarious settlement briefly took root at Roanoke in North Carolina), and Drake continued to keep his force in being.[91] In April 1585, as a gesture of support to the Dutch, she suspended all English trade with the Spanish Netherlands.

Meanwhile the siege of Antwerp continued. In Madrid, Philip and his ministers hoped that its capture might cause the collapse of Dutch resistance and discussed how best to second the efforts of Parma and his troops in the trenches. Granvelle (who had since 1579 served as a senior minister in Madrid) argued strongly that the sudden seizure of all Dutch shipping in Spain and Portugal, followed by a prohibition of the rebels' lucrative trade with the Iberian peninsula, might bring the revolt to a swift end.[92] Although it would inevitably harm the economy of both the Iberian peninsula and the Spanish Netherlands, the king appears to have been ready to order an embargo in September 1584; but news of the death of Anjou and Orange the previous July and the possibility that the revolt might collapse without them anyway caused a change of plan.[93] Yet the rebel cause did not founder. Instead, Antwerp continued to resist and Granvelle repeated that: 'In my opinion Holland and Zealand could easily be reduced if we deprive them of the trade with Spain and Portugal; and I am sure that in the end, when everything has been discussed, we shall have to do it'. The ideal time, he suggested, was either the autumn, when the Iberian ports would be full of Dutch vessels coming to collect wine, olive oil and other newly harvested crops, or the spring, when they brought Baltic grain; and he recommended the blanket seizure of all foreign vessels, except for those of Catholic states: 'I would arrest all of them, and afterwards we can discuss which should be released and which should not.'[94]

Elizabeth's prohibition of trade with the Spanish Netherlands in April 1585 played right into Granvelle's hands. Philip now decided to implement the policy advocated by the cardinal for so long and the following month ordered the embargo of all foreign ships in Iberian ports, save only the French (on account, he claimed, of their small size). Characteristically, he carried it out in a complex and clandestine manner.

Do it [he told his agents in the ports] in such a way that, for the present, it will be understood that ships belonging to the rebels of all my states, and those from Hanseatic [ports] and Germany, and from England, will be embargoed on the grounds and with the pretence of wanting to create a great fleet. Having done this, once they have been embargoed and detained, we will know what we have in all areas [of the peninsula] and can better ordain what should be done.[95]

Accordingly, again as Granvelle had suggested, in July the king ordered the release first of all German and Hanseatic vessels (with compensation for the period of detention) and later of the English, leaving only the Dutch, whose vessels he eventually either incorporated into royal service or else sold by auction.[96]

In one respect, the gambit worked extremely well: Dutch trade with the Iberian peninsula temporarily collapsed as scores of Holland and Zealand vessels suffered arrest and the Republic immediately halted further sailings to Spain and Portugal. The total of Dutch ships leaving the Danish Sound – most of them bound for Iberian destinations – fell by 30 per cent and stayed low for three years.[97] The decision to embargo non-Dutch ships as well proved a disaster, however, for when a party of Spanish officials came to arrest the English vessel *Primrose* near Bilbao, the master decided to fight his way out, taking with him to England not only the Spanish boarding party but also a copy of the embargo decree and the magistrate who had attempted to enforce it.[98]

The Spanish government never seems to have paused to consider how the inclusion of English and Hanseatic along with Dutch vessels might be interpreted in London. Granvelle, the architect of the scheme, did not care: on one occasion he dismissed the English as 'ordinarily of an unpleasant nature who hate foreigners . . . I dislike them intensely and the best of them is not worth a fig'. But even Granvelle knew that it would be foolish to halt trade with England at the same time as with the Netherlands: far better, he argued, to release the English ships after verifying their identity because later on, in the absence of the Dutch, 'we shall soon have our ports full of them'. That, he thought, would be the optimum time to put a second embargo into effect.[99]

Elizabeth and her ministers of course knew none of this. Her councillors lost no time in studying the exact wording of the embargo decree served on the *Primrose* and immediately noted that it affected only ships from Protestant lands since it expressly exempted the French. To Sir Francis Walsingham, the queen's ever-suspicious secretary of state who detected international conspiracy everywhere, this seemed deeply sinister:

> The late arrest that . . . hath ben made in Spayne of our shippes and the shippes of othirs well affectid in relligion, with a spetyall excepcion (though cullorable) of the French . . . cannot but be interpretid as a manifest argument of secreat intelligence and mutuall concurrency lykely to be betwin the French and the Spaniard for the ruyne and overthrow of the professours of the Ghospell.[100]

The Spaniards aboard the *Primrose*, when interrogated in London, offered little reassurance on Philip's intentions: one of them informed his captors that 'hearing that the Hollanders seake ayde in England and fearing least [= lest] they shalbe ayded', the king of Spain 'meaneth by this arreste to feare the Englishe from

ayding them'. Moreover an intercepted letter from a Spanish merchant in Andalusia to his partner in Rouen spoke unequivocally of 'the state of war that now
exists with England'.[101]

Temperatures in England already ran high: in the wake of the Throckmorton
plot (in which Spain had been deeply involved) and Orange's assassination (which
everyone knew had been carried out at Philip's behest) the Privy Council made
contingency plans for an interim administration should Elizabeth die, and drafted
a 'Bond of Association' which pledged that, should she perish by violent means,
Mary Stuart would automatically and immediately be executed. Meanwhile military and naval preparations went ahead apace.[102] Walsingham devised 'A plott for
the annoying of the king of Spayne' which involved seizing all Spanish vessels
off Newfoundland and sending Drake back to the West Indies – even though
Walsingham recognized that these 'inconveniences' would force Philip to declare
war.[103] Not all Englishmen longed for war, however. Between September 1583
and September 1584 English merchants imported from the Iberian peninsula
goods worth almost £30,000 (two-thirds through London, where 132 vessels
landed goods from Spain and Portugal in the course of the year) and exported
goods worth about £20,000 (about 80,000 ducats): hostilities with Spain would
end this trade and ruin them.[104] But their fears seem to have weighed little with
the queen and her ministers as they assessed the potential consequences of Parma's
apparently inexorable progress in the Netherlands, of first Philip's and then
Henry's treaty with the French Catholic League, and above all of the embargo.
For the first time in her reign, perhaps, a clear majority of the council now
favoured war.

In June 1585 Elizabeth invited Dom Antonio to return to England (he arrived
in September), and later that month she commissioned a small English squadron
to sail to Newfoundland with orders to attack the Iberian fishing fleet (it later
returned to England with many boats and about 600 captive mariners). Shortly
afterwards the Privy Council drew up regulations for the issue of licences for any
subjects affected by the embargo, allowing them to make good their losses by
plundering any ship sailing under Philip's colours, as if a state of war existed
between the two countries.[105] In July 1585 Drake again received permission to
purchase stores and press men for his voyage 'into forraine parts'.[106] News of
Philip's decision to release all English ships affected by the embargo failed to
change the queen's mind: on 20 August, at her palace of Nonsuch, she signed a
formal treaty with the Dutch envoys which, together with a supplementary treaty
three weeks later, promised to provide over 6,000 regular troops for their army,
to pay one quarter of their defence budget, and to supply an experienced councillor to coordinate government in the rebel provinces and to lead their army. In
return the Republic promised to place three strategic ports under English control,
which would serve as sureties until the queen's expenses could be repaid once
Spain had recognized their independence.

The treaty of Nonsuch came too late to save Antwerp, which fell on 17 August;
but within a month (as Parma angrily noted) over 4,000 English troops had

arrived at Flushing, one of the three Dutch ports ceded to Elizabeth by treaty.[107] Meanwhile, Drake's squadron of twenty-five ships (two of them the queen's warships) and eight pinnaces, carrying 1,900 men (1,200 of them soldiers), sailed from Plymouth. On 7 October 1585 they arrived off Galicia and for the next ten days launched raids on several villages in the vicinity of Bayona, desecrating churches, collecting booty, and taking hostages.[108]

Why exactly Drake chose to raid Galicia remains unclear: neither his commission nor his instructions seem to have survived. Perhaps he needed to take on stores following a hasty departure from England; perhaps, as one of his officers later wrote, he wished to undertake some initial act of bravado 'to make our proceedings known to the king of Spain'.[109] Either way, no sovereign state could overlook such an act of naked aggression. Don Diego Pimentel, a senior Armada commander captured in 1588, told his interrogators then that:

> The reason why the king undertook this war [against England] was that he could not tolerate the fact that Drake, with two or three rotten ships, should come to infest the harbours of Spain whenever it pleased him, and to capture its best towns in order to plunder them.[110]

Elizabeth's succession of aggressive acts in the summer of 1585 in response to Philip's embargo decree – kidnapping the fishing fleet, welcoming Dom Antonio, issuing letters of marque, sending soldiers and subsidies under treaty to assist rebellious subjects, and now invading the peninsula – sent an unmistakable message. On 13 October, as soon as he heard of Drake's actions in Galicia, the imperial ambassador in Madrid warned his master that 'with this act the English have removed their mask towards Spain'. Two weeks later his French colleague reported that the English had 'sacked' Bayona, killed some clerics and done damage 'approaching 300,000 crowns'; and the Venetian ambassador, having described the same outrages, also forwarded a list of the twenty-six ships captured by the 'English pirates' off the coasts of Spain.[111] All three diplomats concluded that Elizabeth's actions amounted to a declaration of war.

Philip's foreign policy towards England had thus backfired yet again. As in 1559–60 over Scotland and in 1568–74 over the treasure ships, the king and his ministers had consistently underestimated the political acumen, the determination and the 'luck' of Elizabeth. In part, these repeated failures arose from Philip's preoccupation with other matters and from his isolation from the political scene in northern Europe: the war in the Mediterranean until 1577, the Morisco rebellion in 1568–71, the Dutch Revolt after 1572, the chance to annex Portugal (including the Azores) between 1578 and 1583, and finally the opportunity to intervene in France after 1584 all diverted attention from England. At the same time the expulsion of Ambassadors Spes and Mendoza, and Philip's insistence that any permanent English representative in Spain be a Catholic, reduced his information on the balance of factions at Elizabeth's Court, while his travels around Spain distracted him further: he was at Barcelona celebrating the wedding of his daughter to the duke of Savoy when he signed the embargo order, at Monzón (a remote town of Aragon) when news of Drake's attack on Galicia arrived, and at Tortosa (at the mouth of the Ebro) when he finally decided to retaliate.

Nevertheless, for the first time since 1556, a major European ruler had, in effect, declared war on Spain, and Philip had mainly himself to blame for it. He had repeatedly broken one of the cardinal rules of Grand Strategy: that, usually, 'less is more'. Although each major state must maintain a substantial military force to protect its strategic interests in key areas, peripheral challenges are best met through non-military means – indeed the trick is to do as little as necessary to defeat each challenge. Alba had it right: Elizabethan England was inherently unstable and so should be left alone as far as possible to pursue a policy of 'glorious isolation'. Given the existence of an influential 'peace party' among Elizabeth's councillors until at least 1584, and given the permanent uncertainty surrounding the succession should the childless queen die, there is no reason to doubt that the skilful deployment of non-military instruments would have minimized English interference abroad whilst enhancing Philip's reputation for resolve and strength. Now, however, having repeatedly failed – and been seen to fail – to bring England back into the Habsburg orbit by diplomacy and plots, and having in effect provoked Elizabeth to attack him openly, Philip found himself faced with the much more costly option of meeting force with force.

6 *The 'Enterprise of England', 1585–88*

Pope Gregory XIII made one last effort before his death to interest Philip II in the invasion of England. This time he worked through the grand duke of Tuscany, who in February 1585 sent Luigi Dovara, an agent with considerable experience of negotiating at the Court of Spain, to offer financial support for a new 'enterprise'.[1] In July, shortly after Dovara's arrival in Madrid, Philip also received an appeal from the new pope, Sixtus V, loftily calling on Spain to undertake some 'outstanding enterprise' for the faith, such as another attack on Elizabeth. This seems to have irritated the king, for he scribbled angrily on the back of the letter:

> Doesn't [the reconquest of] the Low Countries seem 'outstanding' to them? Do they never consider how much it costs? There is little to be said about the English idea: one should stick to reality.[2]

For a while, Sixtus obligingly shifted his attention to the possibility of recapturing Geneva, once possessed by the dukes of Savoy and now the citadel of Calvinism; but in August he again proposed that Spain should invade England as a prelude to the final reduction of Holland and Zealand. Once more Philip rejected the idea, albeit slightly less firmly. After emphasizing the cost and the long duration of the war in the Netherlands – 'all because I will not yield an inch over religion' and 'in order to maintain obedience there to God and his Holy See' – the king urged his ambassador in Rome, the count of Olivares, to make the pope see the problem from Spain's point of view:

> Let His Holiness judge whether I can undertake new enterprises, with this one [the Dutch war] in its current state . . . because one cannot deal effectively with more than one thing at a time; and let him consider whether reducing the pressure there [in the Netherlands] for anything else would be right, or a service to Our Lord . . . because the war is fought against heretics, which is what the pope wants. He should not think me idle as long as it continues.

Nevertheless, he conceded,

> If God is pleased to end that war, as (with His favour) one may hope, then there
> would be a way to satisfy [the pope's] holy zeal – and my desire, which is no
> different from his – in some other area. You must not tell him all this in a way
> that totally closes the door to every proposal similar to the one he has just made,
> but instead make him understand that, as long as I am so busy with the war in
> the Netherlands, which is as holy as a war can be, I could not (even though I
> wish to) find the money for others.

Almost immediately Philip wrote to his son-in-law, the duke of Savoy, approving
his plan to recapture Geneva, as suggested by the pope.[3] Dovara, still at the
Spanish Court, had almost abandoned hope when news arrived on 11 October
1585 that Drake's forces had landed in Galicia four days earlier.[4]

The responses of Spain's leaders to this outrage varied. In Lisbon the marquis
of Santa Cruz, captain-general of the Ocean Sea since June 1584, drew up a
memorandum of necessary defensive measures to prevent further attacks on the
peninsula, to clear the seas of hostile vessels, and to safeguard Spanish America
against the possibility (soon to become reality) that Drake might continue his
depredations there.[5] Archbishop Rodrigo de Castro of Seville, however, roundly
condemned the document (copies of which, he claimed, 'circulated in the streets
and squares' of his city) as craven and pusillanimous. What was the point, he
enquired in November, of chasing after Drake, a fine sailor with a powerful fleet?
Surely the best way to end the English menace would be to attack England and,
since Drake would probably be absent from home waters for some months, 'if we
are going to undertake a campaign against England there will never be a better
time'. The king, who saw this letter, agreed. On the dorse he wrote: 'the decision
has already been taken'.[6]

It had indeed: on 24 October 1585, just over two weeks after Drake's forces
landed in Galicia, Philip dictated letters to inform both the pope and the grand
duke of Tuscany that he accepted their invitation to undertake the conquest of
England, and entrusted the letters to Luigi Dovara for personal delivery. The king
sounded only two notes of caution. First, 'Although His Holiness and His Majesty
agree and are of the same mind about this enterprise, the lack of time (since
putting the venture into effect requires extensive preparations) excludes the
possibility of doing it in 1586, and so it will have to be delayed until 1587.'
Second, because the total cost of the enterprise seemed likely to exceed 3 million
ducats, while the war in the Netherlands already stretched Spain's finances to the
limit, the king declared himself 'happy to contribute what he can, but states that
it cannot be more than a third – or at the most a half – of the cost. The rest will
have to come from [Rome and Florence]'. In all other respects, however, Philip's
response seemed positive, even enthusiastic.[7]

The king now commissioned his principal adviser on foreign affairs, Don Juan
de Zúñiga, to prepare a thorough review of Spain's security priorities in the light

of recent developments. Like his earlier analyses of the impact of the duke of Anjou's death (pp. 171–2 above), Zúñiga's position paper represented Spanish strategic planning at its best. He identified at the outset four major enemies – the Turks, the French, the Dutch and the English – and reasoned that the Turks, although previously Spain's foremost antagonist, had committed so many re-sources to their struggle with Persia that Philip need only maintain a defensive posture in the Mediterranean; while the French, also formerly a major threat, now seemed so thoroughly mired in their own civil disputes that, although it might be necessary to intervene at some stage in order to prolong them, the cost to Philip would probably not be high. This left the Dutch and the English. The former had been a thorn in Spain's flesh since the rebellion of 1572 because every Spanish success seemed to be followed by some countervailing reverse; but at least the problem, although costly and humiliating, remained confined to the Low Countries. The English menace was quite different: it had arisen recently and it threatened the entire Hispanic world, for Elizabeth clearly supported the Dutch and Dom Antonio as well as Drake. Zúñiga argued that England had now openly broken with Spain and that 'to fight a purely defensive war is to court a huge and permanent expense, because we have to defend the Indies, Spain and the convoys travelling between them'. An amphibious operation of overwhelming strength, he reasoned, represented the most effective form of defence, and also the cheapest. The immediate diversion of resources to the Enterprise of England might temporarily compromise both the reconquest of the Netherlands and also the security of Spanish America; but Zúñiga felt the risk must be taken because, so long as England remained uncowed, no part of Philip's Monarchy would be safe.[8]

Events soon vindicated Zúñiga's analysis. On the one hand, Parma reported a massive build-up of English forces in Holland, paid for by English subsidies, culminating in December 1585 with the arrival of Elizabeth's Favourite, the earl of Leicester, to serve as governor-general of the rebellious provinces. On the other hand, a constant stream of information poured back to Spain on the destruction caused by Drake in the Canaries, in the Cape Verde Islands and finally in the Caribbean (where he sacked first Santo Domingo, then Cartagena and finally St Augustine).[9] According to one of Drake's companions, the expedition caused 300,000 ducats worth of damage 'upon the co[a]ste of Spaine' and '300 millions' in the Indies; while, in Germany, Elizabeth's envoy Sir Horatio Pallavicino gloated that Drake's voyage had damaged Philip in two distinct ways: by reduc-ing his revenues as well as by increasing his costs, 'since it is most certain that one year of war in the Indies will cost the Spaniards more than three years of war in the Netherlands'. In Madrid, Cardinal Granvelle spoke for almost everyone when he fretted, 'I keenly regret that the queen of England makes war on us so boldly and dishonestly, and that we cannot get our own back'.[10]

Small wonder, then, that the king became increasingly anxious to secure the pope's agreement for an outright attack on England. On 6 November 1585, two weeks after his initial favourable response, Philip instructed Ambassador Olivares to ascertain whether Sixtus V truly desired the invasion of England, or whether the proposal merely emanated from the grand duke of Tuscany and the late Gregory XIII, whereas the new pope 'himself inclines rather to some other enterprise'.[11] When confirmation on this point duly arrived, the king dictated and signed two letters which committed him not only to carry out the conquest of England but also to employ – as intended in both 1571 and 1575–77 – the Army of Flanders to achieve it. On 29 December 1585 he invited the prince of Parma, fresh from his triumphant reconquest of most of Flanders and Brabant, to propose a suitable strategy for invasion. Four days later he authorized Olivares to discuss with the pope certain political questions arising from the operation – how would the invasion be justified to the world; what role would His Holiness and the grand duke play; who would rule England after the death of Mary Stuart (still the obvious successor to Elizabeth and explicitly recognized as 'my sovereign' by many Catholics) – and to propose that Parma should command the expeditionary force.[12]

It was, of course, one thing to decide that the England must be invaded, and quite another to make it happen. Nevertheless, nine English governments had been overthrown or seriously undermined by seaborne invasions in the five centuries since the Norman Conquest of 1066, with at least seven other successful landings of major forces, and many more lesser raids (as well as seaborne assistance against England sent to Scotland or Ireland). Philip II and his ministers compiled a careful list of these various operations, and studied them. They concluded that three strategies offered a reasonable prospect of success (Plate 24). The first consisted of a simultaneous combined operation by a fleet strong enough both to defeat the opposing English navy and to shepherd across the Channel an army sufficient to accomplish the conquest (as William I had done in 1066 with spectacular success). The second possible strategy involved assembling an army in secret near the Channel while launching a diversionary assault on Ireland which would draw off most of England's defenders, leaving the mainland relatively open to invasion by the main force (the Smerwick operation of 1579–80 seemed to show the way). Finally, a surprise assault might be essayed (as, most recently, Edward of York had done in 1471 and Henry Tudor in 1485).[13] That all these possible strategies received consideration in 1586–88 reflects great credit on the vision and competence of Philip and his 'national security advisers'; that they tried to undertake all three of them at once does not.

Confusion began to creep in when in January 1586 the king invited Santa Cruz to assess how many ships and men would be needed to protect the coasts of Spain and Portugal from further humiliating raids by 'pirates' like Drake. The marquis obliged the following month, but accompanied his list with an eloquent plea that the best way to defend the peninsula against the threat from England would be to attack England itself, and (somewhat presumptuously) offered 'to serve Your Majesty myself in the enterprise in the firm hope that, being so much in Your Majesty's service, I will emerge just as victorious from it as in the other things that I have done for you'.[14] The proposal met with an enthusiastic reception, and

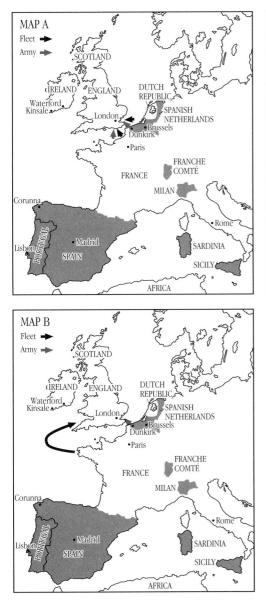

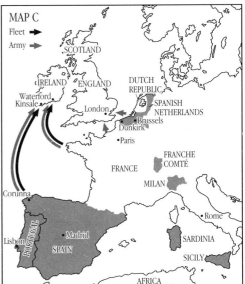

Plate 24 Three proven invasion strategies against England. A study of the numerous successful invasions of England suggested to Philip II and his advisers that three strategies enjoyed a fair chance of success: a combined operation in strength across the Channel (A); an attack by an invasion force assembled in secret on the continent while the English navy was distracted elsewhere (B); and finally a surprise attack (C). Variations on these plans had either overthrown or seriously undermined at least nine English governments since 1066.

Philip invited the marquis to prepare and send 'a paper showing the way in which you believe this could be effected, should circumstances permit'.[15]

This marked a radical departure in Spanish strategic thinking towards England, because all previous plans had involved an invasion launched from the Netherlands, not from the Iberian peninsula. Santa Cruz seized his opportunity and, aided by the provisioner-general of the navy, in March sent a detailed proposal entitled: 'The fleet and army that it would seem necessary to assemble for the conquest of England'. Unfortunately neither the proposal itself nor the covering letters that survive reveal the precise strategy envisaged, but given the size of the forces proposed – 510 ships, carrying 55,000 infantry and 1,600 cavalry, with all their supporting equipment, munitions and artillery – a direct descent upon some point in England or Ireland must have been intended (without any involvement of Parma's troops from Flanders). Evidently Santa Cruz aimed to emulate William the Conqueror, with an invasion in overwhelming strength.[16]

Before this plan could be considered, however, reports of Drake's sack of Cartagena and later of Santo Domingo, and fears that the English intended to establish a fortified base in the Caribbean, led the king to authorize immediate and drastic action. In April he ordered Santa Cruz to join forces with the transatlantic convoy escorts and sail straight to the Caribbean, there to seek out and destroy Drake and his fleet. For the first (but certainly not for the last) time, the marquis disobeyed: he informed the king that he needed more ships and supplies in order to take on the English, and he refused to leave port until he had them.[17] After many fruitless exchanges with his recalcitrant admiral, the king decided to send just the escort vessels across the Atlantic (they left Seville in May), while in July Santa Cruz sent six galleons from Lisbon to the Azores in order to await and protect the fleets returning from America and Portuguese India.[18]

Philip did not forget the 'principal enterprise', however. Orders went out to raise troops in Andalusia to reinforce the fleet in Lisbon, and to embargo and arm suitable ships in the Cantabrian ports in order to form two new squadrons: one composed of large merchantmen, the other comprising smaller vessels and pinnaces.[19] Meanwhile, in Rome, Ambassador Olivares raised again with the pope the question of financial support for the invasion of England. Sixtus responded by welcoming Philip's zeal, approving the venture, and urging haste; but he absolutely declined to contribute one-third (let alone one-half) of the cost. As the ambassador ruefully admitted, 'The reports flowing in from all parts concerning the preparations that Your Majesty is making, which may be for this venture, have done much harm', because the pope argued that, since Spain clearly intended to press ahead anyway, it could do so without a papal subsidy. Sixtus offered 300,000 ducats, in lieu of the million requested.[20]

While the king pondered this disappointing response, a messenger arrived at Court with Parma's long-awaited proposal for the invasion of England. The 28-page document began by regretting the lack of secrecy surrounding the king's intentions. The prince asserted that even ordinary soldiers and civilians in the

Netherlands now openly discussed the best way to invade England. Nevertheless, he believed that three basic precautions might still save the enterprise. First, the king of Spain must have sole charge 'without placing any reliance on either the English themselves, or the assistance of other allies'. Second, the French must be prevented from interfering, either by sending assistance to Elizabeth or by intervening in the Netherlands. Third, sufficient troops and resources must remain behind to defend the reconquered Netherlands against the Dutch once the assault force had left.

After meeting these conditions, Parma suggested detaching a force of 30,000 foot and 500 horse from the Army of Flanders and ferrying it across the Channel aboard a flotilla of seagoing barges to launch a surprise attack on England. Provided his precise intentions remained a secret, 'given the number of troops we have to hand here, and the ease with which we can concentrate and embark them in the barges, and considering that we can ascertain, at any moment, the forces which Elizabeth has and can be expected to have, and that the crossing only takes 10 to 12 hours without a following wind (and 8 hours with one)', the prince felt sure the invasion could be undertaken with a fair chance of success. 'The most suitable, close and accessible point of disembarkation [he concluded], is the coast between Dover and Margate', which would permit a rapid march on London. In essence, this represented the third alternative invasion strategy: a surprise assault.

Only two paragraphs of the letter addressed the possibility of naval support from Spain, and even then only in the context of 'the worst case scenario': that somehow details of the plan had become known in England. In that case, Parma suggested, since Drake's exploits had forced the king to mobilize a fleet to protect the Atlantic, perhaps this new navy might 'either sail suddenly up here in order to assist and reinforce the troops who have already landed [in Kent] and keep open the seaway between the coasts of Flanders and England; or else – if your fleet is large, well-provided, well-armed and well-manned – it could create a diversion which will draw the English fleet away [from the straits of Dover]'. This corresponded to the third alternative strategy for invading England, the one later favoured by Napoleon: a naval decoy to facilitate an attack by a relatively unprotected invasion army.[21]

To some extent, the long delay before Parma's proposal arrived at Court reduced its appeal. The king had asked for it in December 1585; yet Parma only complied four months later, entrusting it to a special messenger, Giovanni Battista Piatti, who travelled to Court by a circuitous route (via Burgundy and Italy). It therefore did not reach the royal cipher clerks until 20 June and four more days elapsed before the king's advisers had debriefed Piatti about the exact amount of shipping available in the ports of Flanders to ferry a major army across the open sea, and about the possible advantage of seeking a landing place closer to London.[22] Then the king turned the dossier over to Don Juan de Zúñiga, already responsible for coordinating the preparations advocated by Santa Cruz, and Zúñiga in turn seems to have consulted Bernardino de Escalante.

The archives of Philip's government are full of letters and memorials written by men like Escalante. Born in Laredo, the son of a prominent naval captain, he had sailed to England with the king in 1554 and spent fourteen months there before enlisting as a soldier in the Spanish army in the Netherlands. He later returned to Spain, went to university and evidently studied geography as well as theology, for he later wrote an excellent treatise on navigation. After his ordination, he served as an inquisitor until in 1581 he became major-domo to the fire-eating archbishop of Seville, Don Rodrigo de Castro. Over the next twenty years, Escalante sent over twenty papers of advice to the king, most of them concerned with the war with England, and some clearly influenced by Castro's aggressive attitude. Moreover he managed to send these papers directly to the king's desk, as well as meeting with Secretary of State Idiáquez to discuss his suggestions.[23]

In June 1586 Escalante reviewed the various alternative invasion strategies in detail and even drew a campaign map to illustrate them – the only one concerning the Enterprise of England to survive (see Plate 25). First (on the left of the map) he noted that a fleet from Lisbon might undertake a daring voyage through the North Atlantic directly to Scotland, where it would regroup before launching its main attack ('The seas are high and dangerous,' Escalante warned, 'but through Jesus Christ crucified everything is possible'). An attack into the Irish Sea might offer a second potential strategy although the Royal Navy, whose forces (labelled 'the enemy') appear in the map at the entrance to the English Channel, made this a high-risk operation too. No less dangerous would be a surprise attack from Flanders to Dover, and on to London (defended by 'E Greet Tuura' [The Great Tower]). Escalante therefore suggested a combination of the two distinct strategies advanced by Santa Cruz and Parma. A Grand Fleet of 120 galleons, galleasses, galleys, merchantmen and pinnaces, together with an army of 30,000 infantry and 2,000 cavalry, should be concentrated in Lisbon and launched against either Waterford in Ireland or Milford Haven in Wales. At the same time the Army of Flanders should be reinforced, first to tie down the English expeditionary force in Holland, and then to cross the Channel in small ships in preparation for a surprise march on London while Elizabeth's forces dealt with the distant bridgehead established by the Armada.

This ingenious scheme, backed up by a wealth of detail on the political and physical geography of the British Isles, clearly convinced Don Juan de Zúñiga, because his own letter of advice to the king largely reiterated the plan proposed by Escalante. Zúñiga merely added the observation that, since Spain would gain no advantage from the direct annexation of England ('because of the cost of defending it'), the newly conquered realm should be bestowed upon a friendly Catholic ruler. He suggested Mary Stuart – but recommended that she should marry a dependable Catholic prince, such as Parma.[24]

The king added little to these suggestions when on 26 July 1586 he sent a 'masterplan' to both Brussels and Lisbon commanding the concentration of forces for a dual assault on the Tudor state. Although this document has unfortunately

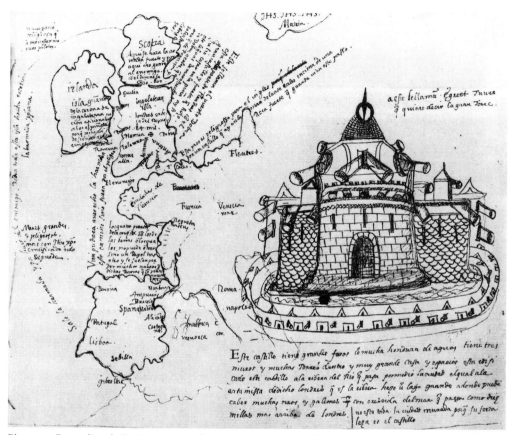

Plate 25   Bernardino de Escalante's map of how to invade England. The only surviving 'campaign map' for the Enterprise of England was drawn up in June 1586 by the priest and former soldier Bernardino de Escalante. He used it to illustrate the various possible invasion strategies discussed in a memorial he sent to Court: dismissing expeditions via either Scotland or the Irish Sea, Escalante favoured a landing in southern Ireland to draw off the Royal Navy while Philip's troops in the Netherlands made a surprise attack in Kent and marched on London, defended only by 'E Greet Tuura' (which Escalante remembered only imperfectly from his brief sojourn in England during the 1550s).

not so far come to light, its contents can be deduced from subsequent correspondence between Brussels, Madrid, Lisbon and Rome.[25] A formidable Armada would sail from Lisbon in the summer of 1587 – one year later – carrying all available troops together with most of the equipment (above all a powerful siege train) needed for the land campaign, directly to Ireland. There it would put ashore assault troops and secure a beachhead (probably at Waterford), thus drawing off Elizabeth's naval forces and neutralizing their potential for resistance when, after some two months, the Armada suddenly left Ireland and made for the Channel. At that point, and not before, the main invasion force of 30,000 veterans from the Army of Flanders would embark on its secretly assembled flotilla of small ships and, under Parma's personal direction, leave the Netherlands for the coast of Kent while the Grand Fleet cruised off the North Foreland and secured local command of the sea. Parma's men, together with reinforcements and the siege train from the fleet, would then land near Margate, make a dash for London and seize the city – preferably with Elizabeth and her ministers still in it.[26]

One wonders whether Philip and Zúñiga realized the full implications of their ambitious plan. In retrospect, Santa Cruz's proposal contained much merit. The events of 1588 proved that, once they got their Armada to sea, the Spaniards experienced little difficulty in moving 60,000 tons of shipping from one end of the Channel to the other, despite repeated assaults upon it. And the Kinsale landing of 1601 (p. 279 below) showed that they could secure and fortify a beachhead in southern Ireland. Likewise, Parma's concept of a surprise landing in Kent had much to recommend it: time and again, his troops had shown their mettle under his leadership, and the largely untrained English forces, taken by surprise, would probably have failed to withstand the Army of Flanders once it got ashore. The Armada's undoing ultimately arose from the decision to unite the fleet from Spain with the army from the Netherlands as an essential prelude to launching the invasion.[27]

Why did they do it? Zúñiga had played an outstanding role in coordinating the naval campaigns of the Mediterranean for almost twenty years, and had been closely involved in the abortive plans to invade England a decade before. Philip, for his part, had also participated in planning many victorious campaigns in the past, most notably the conquest of Portugal and the Azores between 1580 and 1583, and had seen active service in the campaigns of 1557 and 1558. He also possessed direct experience of the route his fleet would follow: in July 1554 he had sailed from Corunna to Southampton, his journey taking just one week, and five years later he had sailed back relatively easily from Flushing to Santander. But both men remained essentially armchair strategists: technical, tactical and operational considerations all remained a closed book to them. Moreover, as usual, Philip refused to move closer to the action: he ignored suggestions that he should return to Lisbon in order to supervise the assembly of the fleet in person, so it took at least a week before Santa Cruz received a solution to each problem referred to the king, and between two and three weeks in Parma's case. More serious, Philip normally remained ignorant of the problems that his commanders chose not to refer to him, or referred to him late. Worse still, he declined to brief either of them properly: both received the masterplan of July 1586 by mail (though Parma's copy went with the same messenger, Piatti, who had brought the prince's own suggestions to Court). Neither could thus oblige Philip to explain precisely how two large and totally independent forces, with operational bases separated by over a 1,000 kilometres of ocean, could attain the accuracy of time and place necessary to accomplish their junction. Finally, both Zúñiga and Granvelle, the only ministers in Madrid who possessed the authority and the knowledge to raise objections, died in the autumn of 1586, so no one could impress upon the king that there should be a 'fall-back strategy' in case joining forces proved impossible.[28]

For the time being, however, Spanish public opinion seems to have become unanimous that invading England represented the only sure way to preserve the security of Spain, the Netherlands and the Americas. After hearing of Drake's sack of Santo Domingo, the president of the council of the Indies argued that only a direct strike on England would safeguard the Americas; and even the prudent duke of Medina Sidonia, when asked his opinion on mobilizing a High Seas fleet, urged 'that this should be set in hand at once, and in earnest, and let it be understood that it will not suffice simply to oppose what the English send: [the fleet] will need to go into the Channel'. The duke also recommended that 'in all parts – in Italy, as in Vizcaya, Guipúzcoa, Portugal and Andalusia – preparations and activity should be undertaken, because it will become known in England and will make them draw in their horns'.[29] The king entirely agreed: a stream of commands flowed from his desk to set in motion the plan adopted in July 1586. Orders went out for the new defensive squadrons raised in northern Spain to sail to Lisbon, for troops to be raised all over Spain to man the new fleet, and for Naples and Sicily to send soldiers both by land along the Spanish Road to join Parma and by sea to join Santa Cruz.[30] To transport the latter, and to convey stocks of artillery and munitions to Lisbon, Philip also commanded the embargo of suitable merchant ships and the addition of sundry galleys and four heavily gunned galleasses from Naples to serve as escorts.[31]

With rare single-mindedness, the king now gave the Enterprise of England his undivided attention. On the one hand he cancelled or forbade other ventures that might reduce available resources. In 1586 he rejected a plan submitted by the council of the Indies (in the wake of the devastation caused by Drake's raid) to improve the defences of the Caribbean: 'No one regrets the damage and no one desires a remedy more than I do, if only we had a way to execute it as we wish,' he informed the council, 'but your plan presents a lot of problems, and the biggest one is the lack of money with which to pay for it all'. In 1588 Philip likewise turned down the request of his viceroy of India for the dispatch of 'more troops, ships and munitions than normally leave each year' in order to attack the sultan of Acheh, because 'the large number of ships of all sorts, troops, munitions and military equipment' assembled for the Armada 'consume so much that it was not in any way possible (even though we have tried very hard) to send more than five ships' to Goa. He also vetoed a proposal to construct a fortress at Mombasa in East Africa, once more in order to avoid diverting resources required for the Enterprise of England, and rejected a request from the Spanish colonists of the Philippines to launch an invasion of China.[32] On the other hand he strengthened economic sanctions against his European enemies. In May 1586 he prohibited all trade from England to Spain: English goods arriving even on neutral shipping would now be regarded as contraband. In July he extended the measure to Portugal.[33] In January 1587 he ordered a new embargo of all shipping from the Netherlands, to be followed by a detailed search to ascertain if any came from the rebellious provinces; in March he forbade the import of Dutch goods aboard Dutch ships, and in August aboard neutral ships as well.[34]

The king also continued to implement his Grand Strategy in non-military ways. In September 1586 he approved the support offered by Don Bernardino de Mendoza, now his ambassador in Paris, to Catholic conspirators led by Anthony Babington who intended not only to murder Elizabeth and replace her with Mary Stuart but also to kill or capture her leading councillors – Burghley, Walsingham, Hunsdon, Knollys and Beale (although, interestingly enough, Philip wanted Burghley to be spared). The king promised to 'send assistance, both from Flanders and from here in Spain . . . as soon as news arrives that the principal deed that Babington and his friends wished to undertake in England had been carried out'. He feared that the involvement of so many people might compromise the venture but hoped that 'God would be pleased to permit what they plan . . . [since] the time has perhaps arrived when He will advance His cause'. The king ordered Mendoza to persevere, albeit with a warning that less information should be committed to paper.[35] In fact Walsingham already knew all about the plan and, as soon as he had sufficient evidence to incriminate all the participants (especially Mary), Babington and the rest were arrested, tortured and executed, while plans were laid to put Mary on trial for treason.

Philip's diplomats elsewhere proved more successful. In May 1587, after pro- longed negotiations, his ambassador to the Catholic Swiss cantons concluded a treaty which (in return for some pensions and customs concessions) guaranteed the security of Franche-Comté and the duchy of Milan, and secured the right of Spanish troops to pass through the cantons from Italy to Germany and the Netherlands.[36] In Rome, Olivares worked tirelessly not only to persuade the pope to part with 1 million ducats towards the costs of the conquest, but also to grant Philip the right to choose the next ruler of England. Both points provoked tortuous and acrimonious negotiations. On the question of finance, discussions focused not only on the total amount payable by the pope, but also on the event that would trigger the transfer of funds (the departure of the Armada from Lisbon, or the landing of the invasion force on English soil?), and on the risk that, if Sixtus died unexpectedly, his successor might refuse to honour the commitment. To secure the last point, in November 1586 the king insisted that all the cardinals must forthwith swear that, should they be elected pope in the event of Sixtus's death, they would honour his promise to pay. The king acknowledged the risk that this involved:

> Even though my desire to arrange this may lead to a breach of secrecy, because it may require a meeting of the College of Cardinals, nonetheless it is a point of such importance that it should not be forgotten. Because if we are not protected, we may find ourselves deceived.

Shortly after this, Olivares secured a promise that 1 million ducats would be paid as soon as proof arrived that Spanish forces had landed in England.[37] He also reached a temporary solution to the 'investiture' problem: Mary Stuart would be placed on the English throne and Philip would then – and only then – announce her successor. The pope promised in advance to accept without reservation the king's choice.[38]

However, Mary Stuart's execution on a charge of treason by her English captors in February 1587 nullified this arrangement. At first, armed with family trees and dynastic treatises, Philip now set out to prove that he was himself heir presumptive to the English throne by virtue of his descent from the house of Lancaster. In the end his advisers dissuaded him from making this claim public, on the grounds that it would alarm all – even his allies – who feared any increase in Habsburg power: instead, once more after long and bitter argument, the pope agreed that after the successful invasion of England Philip would nominate, subject to papal approval and investiture, a ruler pledged to restore and uphold the Catholic faith there (the king apparently intended to 'invest' his daughter Isabella, after she had married one of her Austrian cousins).[39] Until then the post-conquest administration would be entrusted to William Allen, superior of the English College at Douai, assisted by members of various religious orders aboard the Armada and with Parma's army, and by local Catholics. Together they would superintend the restoration to the church of all lands and rights lost at the Reformation.[40]

In other ways, the elimination of Mary Stuart simplified matters for Philip. Above all, the French Catholics reacted violently to the news (she was, after all, a dowager queen of France, sister-in-law of Henry III and cousin of the duke of Guise). In Rouen, rioters seized English ships and goods; in Paris, outraged clerics delivered inflammatory sermons that called for revenge, and exhibited pictures outside their churches that luridly portrayed the atrocities committed against English Catholics by the Elizabethan regime.[41] Everywhere Philip's agents sought to exploit the 'judicial murder' of an anointed queen (who had not even been Elizabeth's subject) in order to justify the king's plans to overthrow the 'English Jezebel'.

Strangely enough, they failed only in Scotland, thanks largely to Mary's 'phantom will'. In May 1586 the queen of Scots had written to Don Bernardino de Mendoza, that she intended to 'cede and grant by Will my right to the succession of this crown [of England] to the king, your master'. Almost certainly, she never executed such a deed, although Philip had the archives of Rome, Paris and Simancas ransacked to find some trace of it. Six months later, Mary informed the pope that she also wished to leave to Philip 'all the rights and interests I may have in the government of the kingdom of Scotland, since my son remains obstinately outside the [Catholic] church'. A copy of this letter likewise reached the king, who annotated it. After Mary's death he emphasized the 'affinity' that linked his family and hers (Mary had been Philip's sister-in-law and a playmate of his late wife, Elisabeth de Valois), and even began to pay her legacies from his own funds. Elizabeth's agents, however, intercepted Mary's letters and sent copies of the relevant items to her son and successor, James VI. The young king, realizing that his mother planned to deprive him of the Scottish throne as well as of his expectation of the English succession, made clear his support for Elizabeth.[42] Any residual temptation to side with Philip evaporated when news leaked out of

Spain's support for various plots by Scottish Catholics to overthrow James.[43] Even the execution of his mother scarcely shook James's loyalty to Elizabeth: although he launched a torrent of protests, he continued to pocket his annual English subsidy of £4,000 (about 16,000 ducats), and he imprisoned a Spanish envoy sent to woo him. The loyalty of some of James's subjects seemed less sure: in spring 1588 the Catholic Lord Maxwell began a rebellion in south-west Scotland with the declared intention of providing the Spaniards with a base; and in August alarming rumours reached York that some Scottish border lords 'have said openly [that] so soune as they shall here that the Spaniardes be landed in anie parte of Scotland, they will ryde straight into England, though the kinge saye no'.[44] Elizabeth found it prudent to maintain an army of 6,000 foot and 400 horse on the Scottish border for almost a year.[45]

The queen took her revenge in Istanbul, capital of the Ottoman empire. She made use of every opportunity to curry favour with the sultan – for example by repatriating a hundred Turkish galley slaves freed by Francis Drake during his West Indies raid – and tried to persuade him to wage war on Spain again. Although she failed, her representative in Istanbul did persuade the Turks that they had nothing to gain from renewing the truce with Spain: Philip's agents went home empty-handed in April 1587. The government in Madrid therefore remained fearful that the sultan might attack a Christian base in the western Mediterranean as rumours (all later proved false) spread that he had made peace with the Persians (September 1587), that he had promised Elizabeth that he would attack Spain if Philip attacked England (January 1588), and that his fleet had set forth for a campaign in the Mediterranean (June 1588).[46]

The centre of Philip's diplomatic energies nevertheless remained France, and here he triumphed. Following the treaty of Nemours in March 1585 (p. 172 above), Henry III permitted the Catholic League to take possession of several strategic towns and in April 1587 Guise's cousin, the duke of Aumâle, seized three cities in Picardy, near the frontier with the Netherlands and also close to the Channel.[47] These successes, liberally financed by Spanish subsidies, provided a 'shield' of friendly forces that would prevent Henry from sending aid either to Elizabeth or to the Dutch. An attempt to secure control of a deep-water harbour close to England failed, however. A spy in Guise's household overheard a conversation about the need 'for some way to capture the town of Boulogne, which was said to be necessary for them to receive and shelter the fleet they expected from Spain' and warned the town's governor. Aumâle's attempt to seize the town therefore failed; instead Elizabeth sent Admiral Howard there with a naval squadron as a token of her support.[48]

Naturally, Philip's military, naval, economic and diplomatic activities all over western Europe did not go unnoticed. Foreign envoys at Madrid filled their dispatches with news of them; Elizabeth's spies in Italy, Spain and Portugal picked up much of the detail; members of the papal Curia seem to have talked of little else. Most of the queen's advisers now agreed that England formed the most likely target and so, besides intensifying her diplomatic efforts in Edinburgh and

Istanbul, Elizabeth took a number of more practical steps to thwart Philip's plans. Between 1585 and 1588, the Navy Board built or purchased sixteen new vessels and repaired the rest, until 'there is never a one of them that knows what a leak means'; the Privy Council also ordered the embargo of all ships in English ports and, from these, special commissioners chose 64 armed merchantmen, 33 supply vessels and 43 private pinnaces to serve with the queen's ships.[49] At the same time, repairs to the fortifications along the south coast resumed; and orders went out to disarm known Catholics.[50] More assertively, at the request of the French Protestants the queen also provided money to raise troops in Germany for an invasion of the Guise heartland, Champagne and Lorraine. All through the spring of 1587 this threat detained the field army of the duke of Guise, and from September also a detachment of the Army of Flanders, in the east of France. Admittedly, the 11,000 German mercenaries who eventually crossed the Rhine met with ignominious defeat, but their menace prevented Guise from making another effort to gain Boulogne – a significant failure from Philip's point of view, for had his Armada been able to wait there (rather than off Calais) in 1588, while Parma embarked his army, the enterprise might have taken a very different course.[51]

Elizabeth's other 'preventive measure' proved equally effective: at the queen's command, Sir Francis Drake began to prepare a new naval expedition. In November 1586 he invited citizens of the Dutch Republic 'to provide cash and credit for the preparation and maintenance of 25 warships' which he intended 'to employ in a voyage to assist the king of Portugal, Dom Antonio, or on some other service'. In December he hinted that the fleet might sail to the Caribbean again, and promised to return 70 per cent of all 'prizes and conquests' to his backers. But late in March 1587 the queen revealed the 'other service': in order to impede the junction of the forces for the Armada coming to Lisbon from Italy and Andalusia, she instructed Drake to sail into any port containing Philip's ships and destroy them, as well as any naval stores he could find. Although shortly afterwards, no doubt influenced by the moderate voices among her councillors, she changed her mind and authorized Drake only to attack Philip's shipping on the High Seas, his fleet of twenty-three ships – six of them powerful galleons from the Royal Navy – had already left. On 29 April they entered the harbour of Cadiz by surprise and captured or destroyed some twenty-four Spanish vessels, some of them large, together with considerable quantities of food and stores destined for the Armada.[52]

It remained a close-run affair, however, because Philip had just acquired an unimpeachable source of information concerning Elizabeth's plans. In January 1587 Sir Edward Stafford, the English ambassador in Paris, declared himself ready to serve Spain in any way possible (short of encompassing the queen's death), and for the next eighteen months he proved as good as his word. He sent back to his own government a constant stream of information suggesting that Philip harboured only pacific intentions against England and that Elizabeth could safely reduce her spending on defence; and he repeatedly revealed confidential information received from England to the Spanish ambassador in Paris (see pp. 221–3 below). Thus, as soon as he became aware of the plan to send Drake's fleet against Spain, Stafford told Mendoza; more significant, as soon as he ascertained (in spite of all attempts by the English government to keep it secret) Drake's intended destination, he also told Mendoza. Only distance prevented Stafford's warning from arriving at the Court of Spain until the day after Drake struck Cadiz: although the courier took only eleven days to ride from Paris to Madrid, he arrived on 30 April, one day after Drake. Had he arrived sooner, or had Drake been delayed a few days more by adverse winds, thanks to Stafford's treachery his reception might have been very different.[53]

Instead, having 'singed the king of Spain's beard', Drake lurked off Cape St Vincent for a month, interdicting all movement by sea between the Mediterranean and Andalusia, as well as between Andalusia and Lisbon.[54] Then he sailed away to the Azores in order to intercept (as Stafford had also warned) the returning fleets from America and India. His exploits there – capturing the rich East India carrack *São Felipe* in June, burning some settlements on the islands of Cuervo and Flores in July – caused panic throughout the Iberian peninsula. All summer long, ambassadors at the Court of Spain filled their reports with rumours about new deeds planned or executed by 'el Draque'.

Philip could not decide what to do next. In June he ordered the large squadron of ships bringing munitions from Italy, which had taken refuge from Drake in the ports of Andalusia, to sail to Lisbon guarded by galleys and the escort galleons of the Indies fleet, there to join forces with the vessels assembled by the marquis of Santa Cruz; Santa Cruz was ordered to await their arrival before sailing to the Azores in pursuit of Drake. But contrary winds confined the Andalusian fleet to harbour and on 5 July Santa Cruz asked permission to sail with only the ships in Lisbon; the king agreed on the 10th, and also sent orders to Andalusia that although most of the ships there should leave for Lisbon as soon as they could, the Indies escorts should go straight to the Azores. Santa Cruz received his instructions on the 15th and set sail that night. The commander of the Andalusian squadron, Don Martín de Padilla, did not receive his orders until the 20th because he and his entire fleet had already left for Lisbon, but he then at once ordered the Indies escorts to set course for the Azores. Meanwhile, in the Escorial, the king received news that more English raiders lurked off the Iberian coast and became fearful that the Indies escorts, if they travelled alone, might be intercepted and overwhelmed; on 14 July he therefore ordered them to remain with Padilla. This order reached its destination somewhat later on the 20th, and the ships were accordingly recalled. Next, news reached the king that a fleet of Barbary corsairs had been sighted passing through the straits of Gibraltar, and he feared it might attack Cadiz in the absence of the galleys; so on 20 July Philip ordered Padilla to return to Cadiz as soon as he had escorted the transports to Lisbon. Finally on 30 July, after receiving further alarming reports about the corsairs' strength and intentions, the king commanded the galleys to return to Cadiz from wherever they might be. As it happened, Padilla had reached Lisbon on 4 August and received the order there four days later. He left that same night.[55]

This amazing chapter of contradictions shows Philip's strategic style at its worst. Convinced that he alone had 'complete information on the present state of affairs in all areas' (p. 71 above), the king could not resist attempting to micromanage operations. The more reality diverged from his plan, the more things he saw that needed to be changed. No doubt his ill-health in the spring of 1587, which seriously delayed the transaction of business (p. 44 above), complicated matters, but gradually Philip recognized that the entire Enterprise of England required rethinking. On the tactical level, since a state of war now clearly existed with Elizabeth, he decreed that English seamen captured by his ships should no longer be treated as pirates (until this point their captains, masters and pilots had been beheaded, and their crews sent to the galleys).[56] On the strategic level, some at Court began to question the wisdom of a direct amphibious assault on an enemy who seemed so powerful by sea; but the government did not agree. In the words of Philip's new foreign policy adviser, Don Juan de Idiáquez, 'with the English established in Holland and Zealand, together with their infestation of the Americas and the High Seas, it seems that defensive measures cannot deal with everything. Rather, it obliges us to put their house to the torch' in order to force them to withdraw from 'the Netherlands, that voracious monster which gobbles up the troops and treasure of Spain'.[57] Meanwhile a prominent councillor of War delivered a similarly belligerent message to the papal nuncio in Madrid: the 'Enterprise of England', he asserted, remained essential to assure the safety of the fleets sailing between Spain and the Americas, 'and also for [the king's] reputation, to avoid being subjected every day to similar accidents like [the Cadiz raid]'.[58] But how best could that be achieved? Spain had clearly forfeited the element of surprise: surely, the king reasoned, Elizabeth must now expect an imminent invasion. So he made two important changes to the strategy laid down in July 1586. First he resolved to combine all the shipping at his disposal – Santa Cruz's galleons (whenever they returned from the Azores), the powerful fleet from Andalusia, and the various squadrons created to defend Spain's northern coasts – in a single Grand Fleet which would either overwhelm or drive off all opposition; second he ordered it to sail, not to Ireland, but directly to the Channel in order to escort Parma's invasion army across to the coast of Kent. The former merely represented a reversion to the traditional Habsburg strategy of attacking in overwhelming strength; the latter introduced a critical new dimension.[59]

Ever since receiving his copy of the masterplan, Parma had repeatedly expressed doubts in his letters to the king concerning the need for a fleet from Spain and pressed for details both on its itinerary and on its proposed junction with his forces. In February 1587 Philip at last addressed these concerns (in a remarkably convoluted sentence), but still offered no solutions:

> I note what you say about the need to make the Channel safe, because of the risk of sending a fleet like ours to sail between France and England at the appointed time (which often sees very bad weather in the Channel) without having a safe port in either, nor in Flanders (except for Dunkirk, which apart from being the only one available is not suitable for ships of large draught), which would force

it to face the weather; leaving aside the general advantages, and the more detailed knowledge of those coasts, that the enemy fleet will have. All these are points of substance, and I am looking into them.[60]

Either his illness in the spring, or the trauma of Drake's raid, seems to have prevented further consideration of these 'points of substance'. Instead, in June 1587, the king suddenly decided to revert to Parma's original plan of April 1586 – a surprise attack – informing his nephew that:

> Because the Armada here must first deal with meeting and protecting the fleets coming from the Americas, I do not think it will be possible for it to reach the Channel before your own crossing. This should not matter, but rather conforms with what is already arranged, because neither the person you sent here [Giovanni Battista Piatti], nor you after his return, asked for the Armada to come before, but only after . . . The best course seems to me that, almost at the same time, or as close to it as possible, we attack in three directions: an invasion by you and your forces; a diversion via Scotland, thanks to the men and money that the Catholics of that kingdom have requested; and an attack by this Armada on the Isle of Wight or Southampton.

Parma responded with his usual firmness that this new strategy would not work either. Now that the element of secrecy had been lost, he declared, he lacked sufficient warships to defend his transports: he could never be certain of the whereabouts of the English fleet; although an attack by the Armada on the Isle of Wight would draw off some of the queen's warships it would certainly not tie down all of them; and, given the need to concentrate all his shipping at one point for the embarkation process, Elizabeth's spies would be able to guess in advance the exact time of the invasion.[61]

This hard-hitting critique, received at Court in late August, seems to have impressed the king because on 4 September he signed detailed instructions for both Santa Cruz and Parma to follow a totally – fatally – different strategy. The idea of invading Ireland or the Isle of Wight now disappeared. Instead,

> With all his forces and fleet, the marquis will sail in the name of God straight to the English Channel and go along it until you have anchored off Margate head, having first warned the duke of Parma of your approach. The said duke, according to the orders he has received, on seeing the passage thus made safe by the Armada either being off the said headland or else cruising in the mouth of the Thames (if time allows), will immediately send across the army he has prepared in small boats, of which (for transit alone) he has plenty.

The king insisted that, until Parma and his men had made their crossing, the Armada 'should do nothing except make safe the passage, and defeat any enemy ships that might come out to prevent this'. He also confidently asserted that 'from

Margate, you can prevent any junction between enemy warships in the Thames and the eastern ports, with those in the south and west, so that the enemy will not be able to concentrate a fleet which would dare to come out and challenge ours'. Parma, for his part, having received advance warning of Santa Cruz's approach, should 'be so well prepared that, when you see the Narrow Seas thus secured, with the Armada arriving off the said headland [Margate] . . . , you will immediately send the whole army over in the boats you have prepared'. Philip expressly forbade Parma to set out from the Flemish coast until the fleet arrived.[62] Once again, the king sent both sets of detailed and binding instructions by courier, rather than with a trusted messenger able to brief the two theatre commanders in more detail on their role, to answer their questions and to provide feedback on the state of their readiness and morale.[63]

Shortly before receiving these orders, however, Parma suddenly (and, in hindsight, inexplicably) became more optimistic. He now suggested to the king that, after all, if Santa Cruz could get his Armada as far as the Channel approaches it might draw the Royal Navy down to Plymouth, creating a window of opportunity for him to launch a surprise attack on the coast of Kent just as he had originally planned; he also indicated that he would have everything entirely ready for the crossing by early December. The king was overjoyed by this news and on the 30th wrote to override the strict prohibition on independent action in his recent instructions, authorizing Parma to invade alone as soon as it seemed safe to do so 'without waiting for the Armada, because in this case the diversion it will cause [by its approach] will suffice to cover your crossing, which is our principal end'. Santa Cruz, he promised, would sail almost immediately to provide support and reinforcements.[64] Unknown to Philip, however, the marquis had limped back to Lisbon the previous day with his ships severely damaged by storms, his crews depleted by disease, and his provisions almost all consumed by the ten-week operation. Santa Cruz deemed another sortie by the Armada to be out of the question for the time being.

Far away in the Escorial, Philip simply refused to believe this. Convinced that Santa Cruz exaggerated his problems, the king continued to urge Parma in the strongest possible terms to cross to England at once, if he could, recklessly (and totally improperly) promising that the Armada would be ready to sail within a few days. At the same time he directed a stream of rebukes and exhortations to Santa Cruz: 'There is no more time to waste in requests and replies,' he informed the marquis curtly; 'just get on with the job and see if you cannot advance the agreed departure date [25 October] by a few days'. As the deadline approached, with little sign of progress, Philip raged impotently that 'so much time has been lost already that every further hour of delay causes me more grief than you can imagine. And so I charge and command you most strictly to leave before the end of the month.' The Venetian ambassador at Court, Hieronimo Lippomano, obtained a copy of Santa Cruz's measured refutation of one of these unrealistic tirades and paused to speculate on why the king should refuse to believe his most experienced admiral, while noting 'how difficult it is for him to change plans, once he has decided on something'. He correctly highlighted two factors: Philip's knowledge of international affairs led him to see operations in each theatre in a wider context, increasing his anxiety to act before the favourable situation changed; and his supreme confidence 'in the course of his good fortune', which led him to assume that God would reward his efforts if he performed his own part to the full.[65]

Meanwhile, in the Netherlands, just possibly exploiting the knowledge that his co-commander was still not prepared, Parma boasted to the king on 14 November that:

> Everything here will be ready and in being by the 20th., and . . . I am entirely resolved, in the name of God and with His holy assistance, to put to sea myself on the 25th . . . And unless we hear that there is an [enemy] fleet in the Channel that might prevent us from crossing, and if God is pleased to bring us safely to land and favour us . . . I hope we shall be able to give a good account of ourselves to Your Majesty.[66]

Now the king panicked lest Parma should undertake his solo venture and then become stranded without the fleet from Spain. He therefore fired another barrage of letters urging Santa Cruz to put to sea even if he could lead only 48 seaworthy ships (10 December), and then even if he had only 35 (21 December). The king did not give up until January, when the marquis pointed out that intelligence received from his spies in England clearly showed that Parma and all his forces remained in Flanders.[67]

After this interlude of order, counter-order and disorder which confused everyone – foreign ambassadors and spies as well as the king's own ministers (see Chapter 7 below) – the king returned to inflexibility. Early in 1588, despite strident objections from Bernardino de Escalante and others about the danger, Philip reiterated the 4 September plan with its fatal requirement that the invasion could take place only after the two commanders had linked up in the Narrow Seas: Parma must not stir until the fleet from Spain arrived off Margate; the Armada should attempt nothing against England until it had 'joined hands' with Parma.[68]

It is easy to see why Philip felt so desperate. The cost of his armed forces placed a tremendous strain on his finances: the Armada cost 30,000 ducats a day, and Parma's army a further 15,000.[69] Whereas a few years before he had been able to plan multimillion-ducat budgets two years in advance, and possessed a substantial cash reserve (p. 170 above), by March 1588 the king had to sell his late wife's jewels in order to raise funds and throughout the year he asked for, and received, weekly statements of the amount of money in the treasury and personally determined which obligations should be met and which must wait (Plate 26). In April 1588 his secretary of state, trying to maintain the favourable international situation, accused the president of the council of Finance of sabotaging the entire operation because he had failed to send enough money to Lisbon to allow the

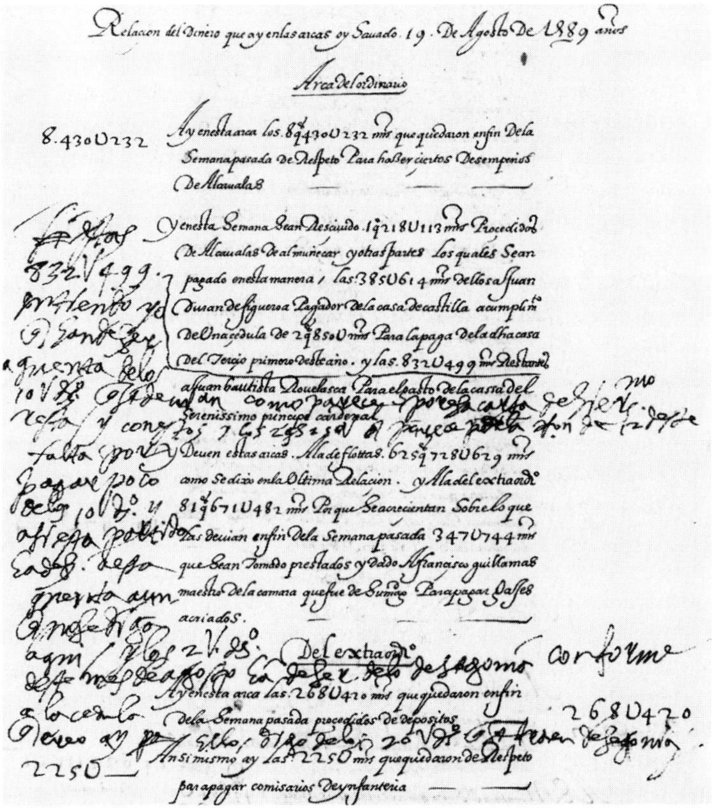
Relacion del Dinero que ay enlas arcas oy Sauado. 19. De Agosto De 1589 años

Arca del ordinario

8.430U232 Ay enesta arca los 8q430U232 mrs que quedaron enfin Dela Semana pasada De Respeto Para hazer ciertos Desempeños De Alcaualas

Plate 26 A 'Relación de sábado', 1589, annotated by Philip II. The cost of the Armada placed such a strain on the royal treasury that in 1588 Philip called for statements every Saturday stating the amount of cash in hand and the outstanding obligations that needed to the met. All sums were given in maravedis, a small unit of account which made the totals seem large, but with 400 maravedis to the ducat the king normally had only 20,000 ducats at his disposal (less than the cost of the Armada for one day). Small wonder that he struggled to find ways of delaying some payments.

Armada to sail. In June Philip told his councillors that 'finding money is so important that all of us must concentrate only on that and on nothing else, because whatever victories we may win, I do not know what will come of them (unless God performs a miracle) without money'.[70] Above all, the king feared that although he had managed to neutralize all his other enemies for the present, the uniquely favourable international situation might not last: above all, 'next year we might find ourselves with a Turkish fleet attacking Italy, should the sultan make peace with the Persians', while the French might reconcile their differences and make peace in order to prevent Spain from annexing England.[71]

In the event, Philip's diplomatic luck held. At a meeting with the Spanish ambassador in late April 1588 the duke of Guise, on behalf of the French Catholic League, agreed to engineer a general rebellion the moment he heard of the Armada's departure. The immediate payment of 100,000 ducats to the League's leaders clinched the deal. But as time passed, temperatures rose: one of Guise's supporters, the archbishop of Lyon, advised the duke to emulate Charles Martel – who in the eighth century as 'mayor of the palace' had seized power from the impotent Merovingian kings of France and founded his own (Carolingian) dynasty

– and depose the last of the Valois.[72] The Paris Catholics began to agitate for a take-over of the city and when, on 12 May 1588, Henry III deployed his Swiss Guards to preserve order, the entire capital erupted into violence, erecting barricades against the king's troops and forcing him to flee. The 'Day of the Barricades' made Guise the master of Paris and shortly afterwards he became 'lieutenant-general of the kingdom'; from Madrid, the French envoy warned his master that 'The corruption of these times and Spanish money will make a mark on the subjects of Your Majesty that will not easily be effaced, and a wound in your kingdom that will not heal'. Philip had in fact intended that Guise should capture Henry and force him to make concessions (including free access to ports like Boulogne and Calais); but even without that crowning achievement the towns of Picardy, as well as Paris, remained under League control. As the Armada approached the Channel, the French economy ground to a halt: 'I never did see, nor no man hath seen it, since France was France, that ever money was impossible to be gotten as it is here now among all sorts, for all traffick ceaseth and for money there is none to be seen'. Neither Henry III nor the French Protestants could now save Elizabeth.[73]

Philip's diplomacy also – rather more surprisingly – divided England from her Dutch ally. The king pursued three approaches to this end. First, he strove to isolate the Dutch diplomatically in order to limit their capacity to threaten the Spanish Netherlands once Parma had left for England, and in this he seems to have achieved total success: a Dutch assessment in August 1587 lamented: 'We have no league or alliance with other Protestant princes; rather, we alienate them daily'.[74] Second, Elizabeth herself indicated a willingness to discuss terms for the with-drawal of her forces from the Netherlands, provided the initiative could seem to come from Spain (in order to save face with her Dutch allies). Third, and apparently independently, King Frederick of Denmark offered his services as a mediator between Philip and his northern enemies. Philip authorized Parma to explore both of these peace initiatives, since they might reduce (even temporarily) English aid to the Dutch and perhaps secure some restitution for goods seized by English privateers on the High Seas and in the Americas – but without either reducing the military pressure on the Dutch, or ruling out the possibility of a direct assault on England. Early in 1587 Dutch troops captured an envoy sent by Parma to Denmark, bearing full details of his talks with Elizabeth's ministers. This forced the queen to show her hand and she now announced her intention of beginning formal talks with Spain and begged the Dutch to join in.[75] Her appeal divided the Republic. The inland provinces which bore the brunt of the war against Spain – and even some towns in Holland – favoured discussions, but the States-General held firm and refused to send delegates to the peace talks.[76] The queen persisted, however, and in February 1588 her commissioners arrived in Flanders with authority to negotiate a peace with Spain on two conditions: toleration for Protestants in the Netherlands and withdrawal of all foreign troops. Needless to say, Philip had no intention of making these concessions, but he instructed Parma to pretend that they might form a basis for discussion, in order to divide the Dutch further and to confuse Elizabeth. Despite the death of Frederick of Denmark, formal talks began at Bourbourg (near Dunkirk) in May. Parma, under orders to keep the talks going at all costs (even though he knew they would lead nowhere), exploited to the full the divisions among the English commissioners, even encouraging one of them, Sir James Croft (a long-time Spanish pensioner and informant), to break ranks and discuss terms for a complete English withdrawal from the Netherlands.[77] Once more, Spanish propaganda made much political capital out of 'perfidious Albion' with the already suspicious Dutch. It is true that Elizabeth also gained something from the talks (above all an observation post in Flanders from which to monitor Parma's military preparations), but she lost far more by forfeiting the trust of the Dutch.[78]

By July 1588, as the Armada finally prepared to sail to the Channel, Philip had orchestrated a major diplomatic triumph. In the admiring words of the imperial ambassador:

> At the moment, the Catholic King [Philip II] is safe: France cannot threaten him, and the Turks can do little; neither can the king of Scots, who is offended at Queen Elizabeth on account of the death of his mother. The one [monarch] who could have made trouble was the king of Denmark, who has just died, and his son is young and so has other things to deal with – although this is not true of the Protestant princes of the Empire, who may incline in favour of the queen [of England]. At the same time, Spain can be assured that the Swiss cantons will not move against him; nor will they allow others to do so, since they are now his allies.

In short, he concluded, no foreign power could now prevent the execution of the king's Grand Strategy.[79]

He might have added that the king and his ministers had also done their best to mobilize public – and divine – support. In Lisbon, the 'nun of Lisbon' (reputed a saint but later unmasked as a fraud) blessed the Armada as it prepared to leave; one of the fleet's commanders informed the pope's envoy that they sailed 'in the confident hope of a miracle'; and Pedro de Ribadeneira, a leading Jesuit, composed an 'Exhortation to the soldiers and captains who sail on this campaign to England' which confidently asserted that: 'We are not going on a difficult enterprise, because God our Lord, whose cause and most holy faith we defend, will go ahead, and with such a Captain we have nothing to fear'.[80] In Rome, the pope issued a special indulgence to all who sailed on the Armada and even to those who simply prayed for its success, while Cardinal Allen completed two tracts for circulation among English Catholics: the first, *A declaration of the sentence and deposition of Elizabeth, the usurper and pretensed queen of England*, purported to be a papal bull but in fact merely summarized the second, *An admonition to the nobility and people of England and Ireland, concerning the present wars made for the execution of His Holiness' sentence, by the high and mighty King Catholic of Spain*, calling on all Catholics to offer every assistance to the 'liberators' when they arrived and to

The military strength of Philip II and his enemies, 1587–88

PHILIP II

Spain, North Africa, Portugal
On the Armada: 19,000 troops
In garrisons: 29,000 troops
Fleets: 130 ships with the Armada at Lisbon, 22 galleys defending the Mediterranean.

Italy
Milan: 2,000 troops
Naples: 3,000 troops and 28 galleys
Siciliy: 2,000 troops and 10 galleys

Overseas
5,000 soldiers in Portuguese Asia
8,000 soldiers in Spanish America

Netherlands
27,000 troops ready to invade England
40,000 troops in garrisons throughout the Netherlands
81 ships and 194 barges for the invasion of England

ENEMIES

England
45,000 troops on land at the peak of the Armada crisis
15,000 men with the Royal Navy
6,000 troops in the Dutch Republic
197 ships scattered along the south coast

Dutch Republic
17,500 troops
67 ships scattered along the Flemish and Frisian coasts

Table 5   By dint of enormous efforts to mobilize all his resources, Philip managed to support some 135,000 troops in 1588, of whom 19,000 (almost all Spaniards) sailed aboard the Armada and another 27,000 stood ready for embarkation in Flanders (see Table 6 below). He also maintained 130 ships in Lisbon, 60 war galleys in the Mediterranean, and a motley flotilla of ships and barges in the ports of Flanders. His enemies could not match these totals: their forces were far inferior in both quantity and quality, and they remained dispersed long after it became clear where Philip intended to strike.

abandon their allegiance to Elizabeth. Allen finished both works in April and sent them to Antwerp for printing; they would cross to England for distribution with Parma's troops. In Madrid, while the population joined in massive religious processions every Sunday and holiday, and at other times followed a small published church-by-church guide to gain the Armada indulgence, the king's printer brought out a detailed 'True relation of the Armada' which listed all the ships, the guns and the officers aboard, sending copies for translation to Naples, Rome, Milan, Cologne and Paris. Philip intended the document both to intimidate his enemies and to impress his allies: all Europe would know that the conquest had been achieved by Spanish arms and treasure (perhaps rendering more acceptable the king's claim to choose England's next monarch). And in the Escorial, according to one source, the entire royal family spent three hours daily in relays before the Holy Sacrament, praying for the Armada's success.[81]

By the spring of 1588, thanks to his single-minded concentration on the mobilization of the resources of his entire Monarchy (and of most of his allies), Philip had managed to assemble 130 ships and 19,000 troops in Lisbon, with 300 more small ships and 27,000 veterans waiting in Flanders. The rest of his empire boasted impressive defences. At the same time, the strength of his enemies had been dramatically reduced. The Dutch lacked the forces both by land and sea to offer effective opposition, and Elizabeth's forces by land were stretched to the limit: all her veteran troops remained in the Netherlands and soldiers she could neither spare nor afford guarded the Scottish frontier in case of an invasion (see Table 5). Although she eventually divined that Philip's fleet from Spain would need to join the Army of Flanders before trying to land, Elizabeth never grasped until it was too late that they planned to storm ashore in Kent rather than in Essex. When, on 6 August, the Armada duly anchored off Calais, just 40 kilometres from Parma's forces at Dunkirk and within sight of the designated landing area – having overcome all the problems posed by the Military Revolution, strategic overstretch, bureaucratic inefficiency, information overload and distance – Philip's Grand Strategy seemed on the point of success. The king knew it: 'Things hang in the balance, and not just these affairs [of northern Europe] but of all areas,' he wrote. 'Please God, let the events up there be for His cause, and may He assist us as is so necessary.' After all the crises, he felt confident that 'nothing on my part remains to be done': everything now depended on executing the plan he had conceived and shaped with such care over the previous three years – and on a few miracles to which, he felt, his prodigious efforts in God's cause entitled him. All he could do now was wait and pray.[82]

PART III: THE EXECUTION OF GRAND STRATEGY

In 1588, most observers saw the Homeric duel between Philip and Elizabeth in religious terms: the king's belief that God would decide its outcome was shared by his adversaries. Thus in the Netherlands, when the duke of Parma warned Valentine Dale, an English diplomat, that a single battle lost by his queen would end the Tudor regime, Dale retorted tartly that one battle rarely sufficed 'to conquere a kingdome yn another countrie', as Parma should know himself, 'by the difficulties of the recoverie of that which is the king's owne by succession and patrimonie. "Wel", sayd he [Parma] "that ys yn God's hand." "So it is", quoth I'.[1]

By the summer of 1588, Philip had concentrated the formidable military and naval resources of his Monarchy on achieving his objectives in north-west Europe, and simultaneously used diplomacy, inducements, economic pressure, deception and propaganda (the key ingredients of every Grand Strategy) to weaken and isolate his opponents. Even his enemies believed that the odds overwhelmingly favoured Spain. Sir Walter Raleigh, discussing the events of 1588 a quarter of a century later, asked 'Whether England, without helpe of her fleete, be able to debarre an enemie from landing' and concluded 'I hold that it is unable so to doe'. He further argued that the troops assembled by the queen in Kent were 'of no such force as to encounter an armie like unto that, wherewith it was intended that the prince of Parma should have landed in England'.[2] These impressive achievements, taken together, should have proved more than adequate to defeat England and end the Dutch Revolt; but they did not.

The explanation for this failure lies in the execution – as much as in the formation – of Philip's strategic goals, and above all in the twin problems of 'friction' and 'chance' that, according to Carl von Clausewitz's remarkable study *On war*, frequently prevent military and naval plans from being carried out as intended. According to Clausewitz, writing in the 1820s, friction (a term he borrowed from physics) encompasses all those 'factors that distinguish real war from war on paper':

Everything in war is very simple, but the simplest thing is difficult. The difficulties accumulate and end by producing a kind of friction that is

inconceivable unless one has experienced war . . . Countless minor incidents –
the kind you can never really foresee – combine to lower the general level of
performance, so that one always falls short of the intended goal . . . The military machine – the army and everything related to it – is basically very simple
and therefore seems easy to manage. But we should bear in mind that none of
its components is of one piece: each part is composed of individuals . . . the
least important of whom may chance to delay things or somehow make them
go wrong.

Earlier on in his work, Clausewitz used another felicitous simile to summarize the
role of chance and contingency in war:

Absolute, so-called mathematical, factors never find a firm basis in military
calculations. From the very start there is an interplay of possibilities, probabili-
ties, good luck and bad that weaves its way throughout the length and breadth
of the tapestry. In the whole range of human activities, war most closely
resembles a game of cards.[3]

The same 'interplay' dominated military calculations in early modern Europe.
Machiavelli devoted much attention to the influence of 'Fortune' on war and
statecraft in *The Prince*; while according to Count William Louis of Nassau, one of
the king's leading enemies, 'The outcome of war depends on chance, just like a
game of dice'.[4] In the execution of Philip II's Grand Strategy in 1587–88, friction
and chance played a prominent role in three distinct areas: in the lack of secrecy
surrounding Philip's intentions, which some considered 'the worst-kept secret
in Europe', allowing Elizabeth the opportunity to prepare an effective defence;
in the unsuccessful efforts of the duke of Parma to 'join hands' with the Armada,
which many observers at the time and afterwards condemned as inadequate and
blamed for the overall failure; and in the technical and tactical disparity that
emerged when the English and Spanish fleets came to blows, allowing Elizabeth's
'Navy Royall' to outmanoeuvre the Armada, thereby preventing Medina
Sidonia from 'joining hands' with Parma, without which the invasion – and thus
the entire Grand Strategy – could not succeed. Each aspect merits detailed
consideration.

This is not to claim that the entire fate of the 'Habsburg bid for
mastery' depended upon chance. In the lapidary phrases of a recent study of
strategy:

Even stunning operational success cannot overcome defective strategic
policy . . . It is more important to make correct decisions at the political and
strategic level than it is at the operational and tactical level. Mistakes in
operations and tactics can be corrected, but political and strategic mistakes live
forever.[5]

Nevertheless, when an ambitious strategy apparently comes so close to success – the Schlieffen Plan in 1914 or Operation Barbarossa and Pearl Harbor in 1941 spring to mind, as well as the Armada in 1588 – historians must devote close examination to the details of execution, because not all 'mistakes in operations and tactics can be corrected' in time, so that some of them may also 'live forever'.

7 The Worst-kept Secret in Europe?

The conjunct armament [i.e. combined operations] goes against the enemy like an arrow from a bow. It gives no warning where it is to come, and leaves no traces where it has passed. It must wound, too, where it hits, if rightly pointed at a vulnerable part . . . The enemy, in the meantime, like a man in the dark labouring under the weight of an unwieldy shield, moves slowly to and fro, distracted and at a loss which way to go to guard against the stroke of an invisible hand.

Thomas Molyneux, *Conjunct expeditions* (London, 1759)[6]

Only intelligence – the use of covert means to ascertain an enemy's exact plan, above all his intended target – can effectively parry the 'stroke of an invisible hand'. Once Elizabeth and Philip II moved to the brink of war in 1585, the security of Tudor England depended in large measure upon acquiring a steady stream of reliable information about Spain's intentions – and Elizabeth knew it. Among the State Papers for 1586 in the Public Record Office in London lie two copies of a document in Spanish entitled 'Summary copy of a statement prepared by the Marquis of Santa Cruz . . . and sent to His Majesty [Philip of Spain] today, 22 March 1586' (see Plate 27). They are exact copies of the overall logistical plan prepared by Philip's foremost naval commander for the invasion of England (see p. 184 above).[7]

No one should be surprised by this remarkable breach of security, for several other governments – including France, the Papacy, Venice and Urbino – gained their own copies of the same item.[8] Moreover this constituted but one in a long series of leaks concerning the Enterprise of England. According to the duke of Parma, at the same time, soldiers and civilians in the Netherlands began to discuss openly how Spain could best invade and conquer England.[9] Similar conversations occurred in most capitals of western Europe. Sometimes the information rested upon hearsay, but often enough it derived directly either from genuine 'leaks' by a Spanish official or from copies of state papers made by a spy (like the Santa Cruz strategic plan). In March 1588 even the Spanish battle-plan became known abroad: a sketch of the distinctive crescent-shaped formation in which the Armada

Plate 27 Plan for the invasion of England. The Public Record Office in London possesses two copies of the detailed calculations made by Santa Cruz, assisted by Bernabé de Pedrosa (an expert on naval logistics), of the ships, men, supplies and equipment needed for a successful invasion of England. The spy who transcribed the document – of which the original may now be found in the archives of Simancas in Spain – noted that it had been sent 'today, Saturday 22 March 1586'. The copies were probably made by a Flemish valet in Santa Cruz's household, whose brother worked for the English spymaster Sir Anthony Standen, and they no doubt travelled from Lisbon to Madrid, where Ambassador Gianfigliazzi of Tuscany forwarded them to Standen in Florence. Thence they reached Secretary of State Walsingham in England, who could thus read Santa Cruz's proposal only a few weeks after the king himself.

would sail up the Channel, with the position of each ship duly marked, fell into the hands of at least three ambassadors, one of whom claimed to have obtained his copy 'from the original which lay on His Majesty's table' (see Plate 28).[10]

Paradoxically, however, these remarkable and recurrent breaches of security only partially compromised the integrity of Philip's Grand Design. The king later boasted that 'although speculation occurred concerning what might take place, the plan remained concealed until the course of the campaign revealed it', and he was right: when the Armada at last set sail against England only he and his two senior commanders knew either its precise target or its exact purpose (and even Medina Sidonia seems not to have been told the place of disembarkation).[11] Others might guess, but they usually erred. In October 1587 several ambassadors at the Court of Spain expressed their frustration about the complete secrecy that sur-

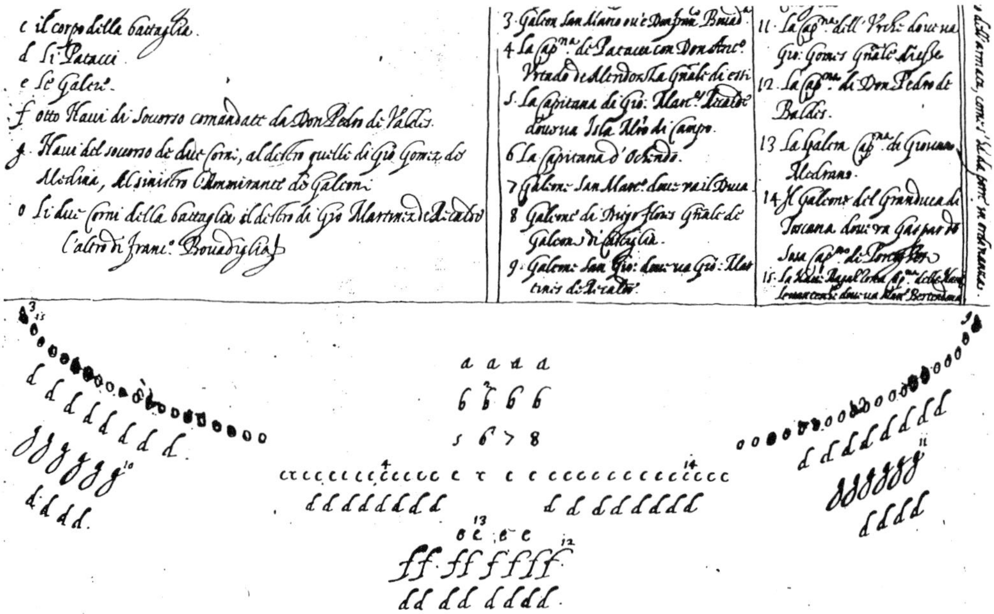

Plate 28 Battle plan of the Spanish Armada, sent to the grand duke of Tuscany on 25 March 1588. The Tuscan ambassadors at the Court of Spain obtained valuable intelligence for their own government. Gianfigliazzi's successor, Vincenzo Alamanni, managed to see and copy the 'design' of the Armada as early as March 1588 – two months before it put to sea. The Papal Nuncio did not secure a copy until June, his Venetian colleague only the following month. The plan corresponded exactly to the Armada's order of battle as it entered the English Channel.

rounded the Armada: 'The discretion of His Majesty and his ministers is such that it is impossible to know what the outcome will be,' complained the Mantuan envoy. In February 1588 the Tuscan representative lamented that: 'We have not yet divined where this fleet will go: some think it will attack Holland and Zealand, others Ireland; some [think it will go] straight to England, others by way of Scotland'. Three months later – just before the Armada left Lisbon – the French resident in Madrid, Longlée, still thought that 'the principal design of these forces is to take Zealand, preventing any relief from getting through'. The English fleet, he asserted, would only be attacked if it tried to interfere with the reconquest of the Dutch Republic.[12] The Mantuan ambassador, one of the first to divine the true Spanish strategy – namely a junction of the Armada from Spain with an expeditionary force from the Netherlands as the prelude to a descent upon England – later became convinced, like Longlée, that the fleet instead intended to exploit a plot to surrender the port of Flushing in Zealand to the king; and although the envoy of Ferrara had also correctly guessed the Grand Strategy at an early stage, the large number of other observers who considered the real goal to be Holland and Zealand eventually shook his confidence. Even the imperial ambassador, Khevenhüller, normally the most perceptive diplomat in Madrid, at one point deemed it all a hoax: 'In 1587 I was right when I predicted that the Armada would not leave that year, now in 1588 I do not trust myself to make a prediction.

But . . . I believe that all these preparations are more to facilitate and preserve a good peace than for any other reason.'[13] Sir William Winter, one of England's most experienced admirals, agreed: Parma's military preparations, he thought, aimed either to secure a peace 'most for his master's advantage' or else to assault Holland and Zealand. Finally the earl of Leicester, governor-general of the Dutch Republic and Elizabeth's Favourite, believed that Spain wished to make peace with England in order to concentrate on supporting the French Catholics.[14] All of these distinguished observers would soon have to eat their words.

Two questions arise from this remarkable confusion: how did so much classified information on Philip's strategic plans come to be generally available; and why did so many expert observers nonetheless manage to misinterpret it? In part, the paradox resulted from the absence of direct diplomatic links between England and Spain. Elizabeth recalled her last resident ambassador from Spain in 1568 and expelled the last Spanish ambassador to Tudor England in 1584. After this, only a few *ad hoc* diplomatic contacts took place and the envoys exchanged seem to have had little access to state secrets until the summer of 1588, when a conference convened at Bourbourg in Flanders to discuss the issues that divided the two powers. There, almost two whole weeks before the Armada arrived in the Channel, Valentine Dale (one of Elizabeth's peace commissioners) heard from an unimpeachable source that Parma was preparing to invade England. When Dale asked point-blank at an audience on 18 July if he intended to carry out the papal sentence of deposition against the queen, the duke replied that, although he served Philip II and not the pope, if his master commanded him to invade, then 'as a servant and a soldier' he must obey; adding

> yn myne opinion yow have more cause to desyre [peace] than we, for that yf the king my master doe lose a battayl he shal be able to recover hyt wel enough without harme to himselfe, being far enough off yn Spayne; and if the battayl be lost of your side, yt may be to lose the kingdom and all.

Incredibly, Queen Elizabeth missed the significance of even this indiscretion, for in response she merely required her commissioners to ask Parma again 'plainly whether or not he had any commandement from the king to invade her realm' and to secure 'immediate satisfaction from him under his own hand' that 'he has no direction from the king of Spain or the pope to invade'.[15] Receipt of this insouciant reply enraged Dale: that same day – 5 August 1588 – he fired off at least five letters to his friends on the Privy Council upbraiding them for their blindness.

> Her Majestie coulde have no playner advertisement then that of the duke's speache that he was a servant and a soldior to doe his master's commandement and then if his master would command hym to execute the pope's sentence he must not refuse hit. And when he said the queen had nede to loke to hit bycause one battaile lost yn England woulde be the losse of her crowne . . . he coulde speake no playner, except he had sayd 'I wil gyve her a battail yn England'.

He also reminded his correspondents of the large concentrations of troops 'which are here yn readiness expecting the navie of Spayne, to be transported into England' and, referring to Henry VIII's cross-Channel invasion in 1544, asked 'is yt not playne enough without a globe? Should a man have demanded whether King Henrie went [= would go] to Boulogne when his armie was yn readines?' But it was already too late: the very next day the Armada anchored off Calais.[16]

The business of intelligence in the sixteenth century consisted of the same three divisions as today – acquisition, analysis and acceptance – and Valentine Dale's frustrating experience highlights the crucial importance of all three. Simply gaining useful information (as he had done) did not suffice; governments also needed to grasp its significance and then react accordingly.[17] In the sixteenth century, 'acquisition' generally fell into one of two categories: intelligence from intercepted communications or from individuals. Most of it seems modest by modern standards. Since it is far easier to intercept radio signals than couriers, espionage proved relatively unsuccessful against Philip II's communication systems, particularly in the case of operational intelligence (because of the need to intercept large numbers of messages over an extended period of time in order to piece together the relevant details of an enemy's plans). Furthermore interrogation of enemy personnel in the sixteenth century rarely produced the spectacular results claimed by the 'spy-catchers' of the twentieth. Nevertheless, the intelligence services of early modern European states still scored occasional triumphs. Thus the capture of Odo Colonna, a junior officer in the Spanish Army of Flanders, by a Dutch raiding party in December 1587 provided rich rewards because Colonna (although serving incognito) was no ordinary subaltern. His uncle, a cardinal, knew all about Philip's designs because, from the first, the king had shared his plans for the conquest of England with Pope Sixtus V. At first, details leaked to members of the Sacred College through papal indiscretion – at Christmas 1586 the Spanish ambassador, kneeling piously as usual at the front of the congregation at pontifical Mass, overheard Sixtus bring the two cardinals assisting him up to date with Spain's plan to conquer England. Worse followed in 1587 when the king demanded a formal promise binding the pope and his successors to recognize Philip's rights to the crown of England and to contribute 1 million ducats to the conquest. The matter came before three meetings of the papal Consistory to which Cardinal Colonna belonged, and although the king had his way – the pope and the cardinals eventually consented – dozens more people now knew the secret.[18] All this and more Odo Colonna passed on to his Dutch captors, who lost no time in notifying the English government; but, as with the duke of Parma's indiscretion to Valentine Dale, at first no one in London seems to have grasped its significance.[19]

The testimony of the Spaniards captured on the Armada itself could hardly be ignored, however. Just after the Grand Fleet entered the Channel, Sir Francis Drake took the flagship of the Andalusian squadron, *Nuestra Señora del Rosario*, more or less intact. It carried a large sum of money (which he and his crew immediately appropriated), a welcome supply of powder and shot (redistributed among the English fleet), and some 250 prisoners (most of them immediately sent to London for interrogation). Only Don Pedro de Valdés, one of the Armada's eight squadron commanders, stayed with Drake. He had been present at all meetings of the council of War and now for ten days he ate at the same table and slept in the same cabin as Drake, who apparently debriefed him exhaustively on the technical and tactical strengths and weaknesses of the enemy fleet.[20] Meanwhile, ashore, the English Privy Council interrogated some forty other captives from the *Rosario* on 12 August. They asked, for example, 'Whether the intention of the fleet was to invade and conquer England or no'; 'Where they should have landed; and whether their meaning were to take the City of London; and what they meant to have done if they had taken it?' Apart from unanimous confirmation that the fleet had intended to join forces with Parma before launching the invasion, the answers to these questions possessed only marginal interest to Elizabeth's ministers by the time they were recorded, for the Armada had already been repulsed. More relevant were question 7 – 'What they have heard or know of any help or succour that they should receive upon their landing in England' – and question 15 – 'Whether there be any other preparation to come hereafter for the defence of this fleet'. Their responses proved alarming: on the first issue the prisoners answered that they expected between one-third and one-half of the population of England to support the invasion; on the second they replied that a considerable reserve fleet was in preparation in Lisbon for dispatch against England.[21] It seems likely that this information – although false – contributed directly towards the ruthless treatment of the Armada survivors forced ashore on the coasts of Ireland in the following month: fearing that they might constitute the advance units of a second fleet, and with fewer than 750 English soldiers stationed in all Ireland, as a panic measure the government decided 'to apprehend and execute all Spaniards found, of what quality soever'.[22]

Such intelligence coups remained few. Although England regularly sent ships to cruise off the coast of Spain in order to intercept merchant vessels and interrogate (and sometimes abduct) their masters and crews, most of those captured had no access to strategic information; and even the light they could shed on operational matters was usually limited.[23] Moreover they often became, in effect, double-agents for they could pick up as much data as they gave. Thus the unfortunate magistrate captured aboard the *Primrose* at Bilbao in 1585 returned to Spain with precious details on the Royal Navy's preferred tactics; two master-mariners captured in 1586, and taken back to England for questioning, on their release provided valuable detail on Elizabeth's preparations and even the names of some of Elizabeth's spies in Spain; others supplied a detailed description of the English warships, listing the guns aboard and comparing them with Armada vessels.[24]

Elizabeth's government therefore relied, for most of its knowledge about Philip's plans, on its agents and friends overseas. Some data came from the couriers who carried diplomatic messages between England and the continent: ministers routinely debriefed them on what they had seen and heard.[25] More originated with 'Englishmen abroad' who reported their impressions by letter. One of the most exact accounts of the invasion transports assembled in the ports of Flanders by the duke of Parma came from an English sailor who arrived at Dunkirk to unload a consignment of good English beer for the diplomats at Bourbourg (whose patriotic stomachs churned upon imbibing the local brew). His experienced mariner's eye quickly noted the numbers, strengths and weaknesses of the duke's fleet, which he promptly wrote down and sent back to London.[26] Foreign well-wishers also contributed some intelligence: thus the Protestant rulers of northern Europe regularly passed on any information that came their way about Catholic designs against their English ally.[27] And from Portugal the queen could count on information supplied by those who sympathized with the 'Portuguese pretender', Dom Antonio, a refugee at the Tudor Court after 1585. The papers of Sir Francis Walsingham, Elizabeth's secretary of state and principal 'spymaster', contain a number of detailed reports on the preparation of the Armada sent from Lisbon by Philip's disaffected new subjects.[28]

These agents too, however, rarely enjoyed access to secrets of state: although they could supply information on the mobilization of Philip's resources, they could neither fathom their purpose nor foretell the likely moment or manner of their deployment. For this, Elizabeth's government needed to penetrate the communications network of Spain and its allies. Admittedly, reading the mail of people close to, though still outside, the centres of government could provide valuable operational information: the location of the writer's unit and what it planned to do; recent movements of troops and munitions; the state of local morale. Thus an intercepted letter from an Italian merchant in Brussels to a friend in Spain on 30 June 1588 provided not only precise details on the programme for the embarkation of Parma's troops in Flanders but also a copy of the pope's special indulgence for all who joined the 'crusade' to conquer England – thus revealing beyond all doubt, for those who would listen, the Armada's principal objective.[29] Yet although events would confirm every detail in this letter, it remained barely distinguishable from the host of other, contradictory messages, most of them equally plausible, intercepted by the queen's agents.

Elizabeth's ministers desperately needed information from the pen of the king himself in order to evaluate the other material; but this they rarely managed to intercept. Part of the problem lay in the fact that Philip and his envoys abroad wrote their letters in complex codes. For example, each secretary of state normally used a 'general cipher' for his correspondence with ministers abroad, and these changed as a matter of routine every few years; in addition, they employed a special cipher to communicate with groups of senior officials (for example with the governor-general in Brussels and the ambassadors in London, Paris and Vienna, and each of these ministers used the same cipher when they corresponded among themselves). Furthermore, individuals in particularly sensitive circumstances abroad might be given a totally different – unique – cipher. Finally, at times of acute uncertainty, distinct codes might be used for alternate paragraphs in the same letter.[30] Even these precautions did not always suffice, however. Occasionally, a key might be lost (all Spain's ciphers had to be changed in 1564, for example, after the waylaying of an ambassador's servant); or an enemy might intercept a ciphered copy of a document already possessed *en clair* (a high risk during peace negotiations, where both sides would discuss copies of the same documents).[31] Finally a corrupt official might give or sell codes to an enemy: in 1576 and 1577 the Dutch managed to decode almost all intercepted letters exchanged between Philip and his agents in the Netherlands, apparently due to the betrayal of cipher keys by the chief clerk of the Spanish secretary of state.[32] But could codes be broken without help of this sort? The evidence is ambiguous. According to a mathematician and geographer in Spanish service, 'until today, no cipher has been found that cannot be deciphered and understood'; and yet French ambassador Laubespine and Elizabeth's chief minister Burghley – both men of outstanding intelligence – frankly admitted that they could not break codes without a key.[33] Sir Francis Walsingham, who maintained a team of cryptanalysts, seems to have been more successful. His greatest triumph concerned a ciphered letter of March 1588, sent in duplicate by Philip's ambassador in Rome, to report to his master a detailed conversation with the pope about the continuing delays in the Armada's departure, Parma's involvement in the enterprise, the amount of support to come from the papal treasury, and the investiture of the next ruler after Elizabeth's deposition. One copy somehow reached Walsingham, and by early June (if not before) his experts had produced an almost perfect deciphered copy that revealed all the essential elements of Philip's Grand Strategy against England.[34]

Precisely to avoid these various mishaps, the king and his ministers normally wrote down as little as possible that might reveal their plans to a third party. The perils of committing operational plans to paper had been graphically demonstrated to Philip many years before. Early in 1552 Habsburg agents captured near Trieste a French courier coming from Istanbul. His papers included a long letter from the French ambassador at the Ottoman Court to his master in Paris, outlining in detail the sultan's campaign plans for the year – including the crucial intelligence that the Turks would *not* launch an attack in Hungary but instead proposed to concentrate on naval operations off the Italian coast. Since the letter had not even been ciphered, the Habsburgs could act immediately and deploy their forces in the most effective manner, enabling them to survive (albeit by only a narrow margin) the combined attack launched later that year by the French, the Turks, several Italian princes and the German Protestants.[35] It provided a valuable lesson in intelligence procedure that Philip and his advisers rarely forgot. Thus in September 1586 the king criticized his ambassador in Paris for committing too many sensitive details to paper. 'In future', the king chided, 'it would be better and more secure to entrust these secret matters to persons of confidence who will handle them by word of mouth, without writing them down'.[36] And he normally followed his own advice meticulously: for example, although Philip sent full details of the proposed invasion strategy for England to the duke of Parma via a special messenger in July 1586, subsequently he referred in writing only to 'the plan agreed [*la traza establecida*]' or 'the appointed place [*la plaza acordada*]'.[37]

Spain's enemies therefore needed to gain direct access to the documents 'on the king's desk', or to the ministers who made and discussed policy. The Santa Cruz memorandum of March 1586 (see Plate 27) must have been copied by a spy in the marquis's household in Lisbon – and by a spy who knew his job, for he sent two copies, lest one should be lost. Even today the spy's identity is unknown, but he was probably the 'Fleming' in the marquis's household whose brother served as a courier for Sir Anthony Standen, alias 'Pompeo Pellegrini', a talented master of espionage based in Florence. The network functioned as follows: Standen's agent took documents and information from his brother (and perhaps others) in Lisbon to Madrid where he gave them to the Tuscan ambassador, Gianfigliazzi, who forwarded them to Florence where Standen picked them up for transmission to Walsingham in London.[38] When Gianfigliazzi returned to Tuscany, Standen made a personal journey to Madrid and Lisbon in order to verify for himself the strength and purpose of the Armada, sending a stream of highly informative dispatches back to England via Florence: thus in July 1587 he found out for certain that Santa Cruz would lead his fleet from Lisbon to the Azores and not against England by somehow managing to read the king's Instruction to the marquis even though it 'was only knowne to the one and the other'; and in June 1588 he even succeeded in obtaining exact information on the Armada's ultimate destination – London – apparently the only outsider to do so.[39]

Sir Anthony Standen was but one of several special agents deployed by Walsingham. In spring 1587 the secretary drew up a 'Plotte for intellygence owt of Spayne' which included establishing a clearing house in Rouen for all Spanish news coming to merchants in Le Havre, Dieppe and Nantes; securing 'intellygence at Brussells'; and maintaining 'two intellygensers in the work of Spayne, one of Finale, another of Genua'. These various initiatives duly bore fruit. News of the death of the marquis of Santa Cruz in spring 1588 reached London via Walsingham's agent in Genoa within the month.[40] A man who called himself 'Captain Jacopo da Pisa' sent Walsingham numerous letters from Lombardy between September 1586 and March 1587 filled both with news received from the Iberian peninsula and with details on the movement of troops, treasure and diplomats through Milan, the principal marshalling yard for the resources of the Spanish empire in Europe.[41] Burghley sent Stephen Powle first to Germany and then in May 1587 to Venice in order to collect information about Philip's designs against England, and over the next ten months he sent back to London bi-weekly reports on political and military developments. Other agents of the English government laboured elsewhere in the peninsula, and Burghley made it his business 'frequently [to] reade the advices which commonly come from Italye'.[42]

For Italy served as the centre of all European intelligence in the later sixteenth century. Even when receiving information from an English pilot working 'undercover' aboard the Armada itself, one of Walsingham's agents advised that 'spies should be sent into Italy to discover the truth [of all this]'.[43] Ten independent Italian states normally maintained a resident ambassador at the Court of Spain, because the preponderant influence of Spain within Italy made it essential for them to keep track of Philip's intentions. Naturally, the majority of each envoy's correspondence dealt with local matters – especially territorial disputes, either with one of the Spanish dominions in Italy or with another Italian potentate (for smaller states often asked Philip to serve as mediator – but developments elsewhere that might distract the king of Spain, especially if they could result in hostilities, also received careful note. And since war with England would clearly affect the Italian states, their ambassadors strove almost as hard as Walsingham to divine Spain's true intentions.[44]

Each major stage in the formation of Philip's Grand Strategy against England became known in the courts of Italy with astonishing speed. Thus in October 1585 when, in response to Drake's sack of some coastal towns in Galicia, the king informed both the pope and the grand duke of Tuscany of his readiness to undertake the Enterprise of England (p. 180 above), some members of the diplomatic corps actually anticipated this decision. The envoy from Lucca informed his government in August, two months before the English struck at Galicia, that:

> The enterprise of the conquest of England has been decided upon for next year, and I understand that King Philip has already requested the pope to intervene with the king of France, asking that he should not hinder the operation but favour it.[45]

The news may have been premature, but the ambassador had certainly detected which way the wind blew. In any case, Philip's decision in late October became known in Rome and Florence about a month later, and in Venice, Mantua and Turin shortly after that.

As already noted, the blueprint for mobilizing an amphibious expedition against England prepared by Santa Cruz early in 1586 was swiftly intercepted and transmitted to most Italian courts as well as to London; and news of Philip's resolution to mobilize resources throughout the Iberian and Italian peninsulas leaked out soon afterwards. Indeed the Mantuan ambassador got word of the decision almost as it left the king's desk:

> I learned today that His Majesty is extremely annoyed by the news of Drake's progress in the Indies, and that some ten days ago he dispatched twelve couriers . . . with orders to embargo ships. And it is said that His Majesty is entirely resolved to undertake the Enterprise of England.[46]

How did the ambassadors secure such remarkably accurate intelligence? Although, understandably, they rarely revealed their precise sources, they seem to have used three major techniques of information-gathering: their own observations, data from paid informers, and information from well-wishers. To begin with, envoys sometimes claimed to have seen a document that they then either summarized or copied.[47] Occasionally, an ambassador may even have chanced to see something 'which lay on His Majesty's table'. However, in 1575 the king reviewed precisely this risk with his private secretary after an embarrassing security leak: neither considered it feasible. 'It is not to be believed that anyone could come and read the papers on Your Majesty's table,' asserted the secretary, and the king concurred: 'It would not have been possible to see the documents, because I always keep them concealed. It just would not have been possible.'[48] Most of the items 'which lay on the His Majesty's table' reported in ambassadorial dispatches, especially when a copy was enclosed, probably came by way of a member of the king's own staff. Cardinal Granvelle once complained that 'nothing is discussed in Madrid without the princes of Italy and even others finding out', and he blamed minor officials, several of whom were caught over time betraying secrets: in 1556 an under-secretary was found to have sold documents on Spain's bargaining position during negotiations with France, while in the 1560s Philip's Flemish valet allegedly rummaged through his master's pockets while he slept and sent details on his plans to the Netherlands opposition.[49] In 1567 the French ambassador hoped to discover Spain's intentions towards the Netherlands 'by means of a friend of the secretary of a certain lord; but the said secretary replied that his master warned him, with his hand on his sword, that he would kill him with a hundred blows if the enterprise on which they are presently engaged should become known'.[50] In 1581 the chief official of the State Department, Juan del Castillo, born in the Netherlands of a Spanish father, was arrested and charged with sending intelligence and even cipher keys to the Dutch in return for an annual pension of 300 ducats from William of Orange.[51] Sometimes, however, even ministers could be indiscreet. In 1584 Granvelle (then president of the council of Italy), irritated by the knowledge that someone was betraying secrets to the Venetian ambassador, planned to provide some false information on a pending promotion in order to trace the leak; to his horror, however, he discovered that the council's secretary had himself already given – or sold – a copy of the relevant document to the ambassador over dinner.[52]

Some diplomats paid for such useful information while others received it free. In April 1586 the duke of Medina Sidonia volunteered to the imperial ambassador full details about the naval preparations just authorized by the king, including their purpose – the conquest of England – while in the summer of 1598 a 'well-informed person' at the Escorial sent regular reports to the nuncio in Madrid about the declining state of the king's health.[53] Sometimes ambassadors shared the information they acquired. Fourquevaux – representing France and thus perhaps viewed with suspicion by most Spaniards – regularly consulted his diplomatic colleagues to ascertain what they knew about Philip's policies; in 1585, the nuncio in Madrid provided the Mantuan ambassador with a copy of a papal brief that called upon Philip to invade England; and the following year, when the Savoyard ambassador discovered that the king had decided upon a Grand Strategy that combined a fleet from Spain with the Army of Flanders, he immediately shared the knowledge with his Venetian counterpart.[54] Since each envoy usually forwarded to his government in unciphered letters the information he obtained, Elizabeth's agents in Italy enjoyed multiple opportunities for interception.

The efforts of the diplomats in Madrid did not, of course, stand alone. Philip's ministers elsewhere could also be indiscreet, and well-placed agents could learn much from them: the household of Santa Cruz in Lisbon harboured at least two spies – not only Sir Anthony Standen's 'Fleming' but also a confidant of the papal collector in Portugal, Mutio Buongiovanni, whose lively reports contained a great deal of classified material (all sent to Rome in unciphered dispatches). In addition, in the spring and summer of 1588, details of Philip's final strategy leaked out from the duke of Parma in Brussels, from Don Bernardino de Mendoza in Paris, from Cardinal Allen in Rome and from the duke of Medina Sidonia in Lisbon. The Armada had indeed become the 'worst-kept secret in Europe'.[55]

Details of Philip's Grand Strategy might also have been available to the English government from the correspondence of the two non-Italian representatives in Madrid – the French and imperial envoys – but, for very different reasons, their intelligence proved of limited use to England. The imperial ambassador, Hans Khevenhüller zu Aichelburg, count of Frankenburg, probably acquired the best information of any diplomat at the Spanish Court because he enjoyed a number of advantages. To begin with, since he represented Rudolf II, head of the junior Habsburg line and Philip's brother-in-law (and nephew and cousin), many ministers regarded him as a friend; since he was an aristocrat (in contrast to the career diplomats and patricians from Italy) he could deal with courtiers as an equal; and since he served in Madrid continuously from 1574 to 1606, he had built up many reliable contacts. In addition he possessed a perfect command of Spanish, even writing parts of many dispatches in that language, so that he missed little of what he heard and saw.[56] Finally, whenever his own resources proved insufficient to establish the truth, Khevenhüller could call upon the dowager Empress María, Rudolf's mother and Philip's sister, who had retired to a Madrid monastery but kept in close touch with the Court, and upon Rudolf's younger brother the Archduke Albert, who as viceroy of Portugal supervised all preparations for the Armada at Lisbon.[57] Although the imperial embassy staff remained small – only 4 or 5, compared with 14 or 15 for Mantua – Khevenhüller could usually rely on the good offices of the empress or the archduke to procure copies of almost any document that he thought his master might require: thus his detailed report on the Armada's progress, sent to Rudolf on 14 September 1588, came from copies of letters sent by Philip to inform María, and shown by her to Khevenhüller.[58] But Prague lay too far from London to be of much use to Elizabeth's government: by the time a courier had travelled from Madrid to Prague, a journey of between four and eight weeks, and then from Prague to London, which took at least four weeks more, the news would usually be out of date.[59]

Paris would have been far more useful for English intelligence but two considerations seriously compromised the value of the information available there: Pierre de Ségusson, lord of Longlée, the French envoy in Madrid, was both underfunded and unreliable; and Sir Edward Stafford, the English ambassador in Paris, became a Spanish spy. Appointed in 1583, but denied the rank of ambassador, Longlée rarely had enough money to employ spies of his own (on one occasion Henry III forbade him to send letters by express messenger because it cost too much), and therefore often lacked information available to other ambassadors.[60] In March 1586, for example, he remained blissfully unaware that, six months before, Philip had taken the decision to invade England, and his master had to instruct him to find out about the facts on his own doorstep:

I have seen the Advertisements that Your Majesty [Henry III] has received from Italy and other places suggesting that the king of Spain is presently assembling large forces which are thought to be intended for the invasion of England . . . concerning which Your Majesty commands me to keep my eyes open for anything affecting your service and to keep you informed.[61]

Longlée seems to have developed his own agenda, however. In January 1587 he sent a trusted emissary to see the nuncio in Madrid and, in strict secrecy, let it be known that he personally favoured sending the Armada against England in order to extirpate Protestantism both there and in the Netherlands. He hoped that the venture could be mounted jointly by France and Spain, but if not he still desired the pope to throw his whole weight behind it. The nuncio, while noting that Longlée seemed a man of deep faith, whose 'household resembles a monastery', remained dubious about his sincerity; however, two months later the French envoy called in person and once again expressed his personal support for the Enterprise of England.[62] This private resolve may explain Longlée's otherwise inexplicable errors and omissions when reporting on the Armada to his superiors in Paris. As late as January 1588 he still claimed to have no clue concerning the Grand Fleet's real purpose: 'As for the place at which all these armed forces, both here and in Flanders, will strike, so far it has been beyond my power to penetrate any deeper'.[63] Such insights would scarcely help the spies maintained by the English government in Paris – especially since Spanish agents often knew which documents Longlée had secured and so could work to discredit them.[64]

Unfortunately for Elizabeth, the leading spy in Paris was her own ambassador. On the surface Sir Edward Stafford boasted superb qualifications, both social and professional, for England's foremost diplomatic posting: his late stepmother (Mary Boleyn) had been Elizabeth's aunt; his mother served as lady-in-waiting to the queen; his brother-in-law (Howard of Effingham) served both as admiral of England and as a privy councillor. Furthermore he had cut his diplomatic teeth in France during the negotiations for the queen's marriage to the duke of Anjou. His appointment as ambassador to the French Court in 1583 came as no surprise. Stafford's only real disadvantage lay in his poverty. He complained several times that he lacked funds to discharge his responsibilities properly and asked the queen to lend him money even if she could not afford to pay his salary; but she gave him no satisfaction and he ran up huge debts. Then in 1586, if not earlier, he seems to have found an alternative source of funds. Three independent contemporary accounts accused Stafford of selling information to the duke of Guise, leader of the French Catholic League. But still his debts mounted – largely through immoderate gambling. He squandered not only his salary and the cash from Guise but also a substantial sum sent to him by the queen to distribute among her French supporters. In January 1587, desperate for money, Stafford approached Don Bernardino de Mendoza and offered to provide information on Elizabeth's plans.[65]

From this point on, Stafford repeatedly supplied Spain with precise details on (for example) the strength, movements and objectives of the Royal Navy just as soon as he found them out. Stafford passed on to Mendoza advance warning of Drake's Cadiz raid in April 1587, of a planned attack on Lisbon in March 1588 and of the concentration of the English fleet at Plymouth in May 1588 – strategic information on which the security if not the survival of the Tudor regime depended – just as soon as it arrived from London. It is true that he exaggerated the firepower of the Royal Navy on at least one occasion, and one could argue that he did so in order to alarm, and perhaps deter, Philip; but, equally, Stafford may have believed the information to be true, since it came directly from his brother-in-law Admiral Howard.[66]

Further evidence of Stafford's treachery appears in the information on Spain's preparations and intentions that he himself sent back to London. For a man who enjoyed almost constant contact with the Spanish ambassador (as well as with the rest of the diplomatic corps in Paris), Stafford should have been able to transmit a constant stream of high-grade intelligence on Philip's plans to his government, just as other ambassadors did.[67] Curious to relate, however, such information featured only rarely in his dispatches. Instead he played up the hostility of the French to England, especially after the execution of Mary Stuart, making the League seem to be Elizabeth's principal enemy. On the relatively few occasions when he did mention Spain, Stafford went out of his way to stress the restraint, the pacific intentions and the moral rectitude of the king of Spain. Perhaps his most egregious attempt to deceive his own government came in January 1588 when he informed Elizabeth that the Spanish Armada had been disbanded. A copy of his letter reached Admiral Howard, who expressed incredulity:

> I cannot tell what to think of my brother[-in-law] Stafford's advertisement; for if it be true that the King of Spain's forces be dissolved, I would not wish the Queen's Majesty to be at this charge that she is at; but if it be a device, knowing that a little thing makes us too careless, then I know not what may come of it.

In May 1588 Stafford suggested that the Armada was aiming for Algiers. Shortly afterwards he at last referred to a letter he had seen in Mendoza's study, men-

tioning an enterprise against England; but he suggested that anything left out in
the open there would clearly be meant only to deceive, thus constituting one more
indication that the Armada had some other purpose. In June he told Walsingham
that he thought the Armada would sail for the Indies; in mid-July he asserted that
bets of six to one were being made in Paris that the Armada would never reach the
Channel; and on 31 July, with the Grand Fleet off the Lizard, Stafford still insisted
that it remained too damaged ever to leave Corunna. To advise his government
repeatedly that Spain no longer intended to launch an invasion, at a time when he
must have known that every effort was being made to get the Armada to sea,
constituted treason of the basest sort. Since Philip secured all these benefits in
return for payments to Stafford that totalled just 5,200 ducats, Sir Edward must
surely be regarded as the intelligence bargain of the century.[68]

Naturally Elizabeth and her ministers did not depend totally on Stafford for
their news from France: other independent agents also reported directly to
Walsingham, many of them resident in Paris, but the queen paid them poorly. A
fifteenth-century treatise, *Le Jouvencal*, had recommended that 'a prince should
spend one-third of his revenues on spies', but Queen Elizabeth laid out barely 5
per cent of hers – £11,000 (about 44,000 ducats) annually in the critical years
1584–87.[69] The general calibre of agents available therefore remained low. Some
of them started out in the service of the queen's enemies until, having been
captured as they went about their business, they secured their liberty in return for
becoming a double-agent. Others were recruited in gaol, especially if they languished there for debt, and earned release by spying on their fellow-prisoners.
They then went on to spy elsewhere and received payment as and when they
turned in some apparently valuable nugget of intelligence. A better recipe for
stimulating false or exaggerated information could scarcely have been devised: not
surprisingly, Walsingham, widely known to fear an international Catholic conspiracy directed against England, was bombarded by his agents with reports of
plots, assassination attempts and invasion plans; Burghley, by contrast, who held
a less apocalyptic world-view, tended to receive rumours of peace and evidence of
Spanish moderation from his men.[70]

The detailed and accurate signals received from Italy must be seen in the context
of this chaotic background noise, for successful intelligence operations depend, as
noted above, not only on acquisition but also on analysis and acceptance. It is hard
to assess the Tudor government's success in analysing foreign data, because so
many key documents have disappeared: the relevant volumes in the 'State Paper'
series in London contain far more incoming than outgoing letters (and precious
few evaluations or policy statements); and although the private archives of both
Burghley and Walsingham help to fill this gap, many lacunae remain. Nevertheless, the surviving evidence indicates clearly enough some grave deficiencies in
Elizabeth's secret service.

The queen boasted of her ability to hear and see everything (Plate 29). She, as
well as Burghley and the earl of Leicester, had known Philip and some of his older

Plate 29   The 'Rainbow portrait' of Queen Elizabeth I, perhaps by Geeraerts or Critz, is one of 110 known contemporary pictures of Elizabeth of England. In stark contrast to the understated portraits of Philip II (such as Plate 4), the queen liked to be portrayed in colourful majesty. The painting also used code, or (in the phrase of the treatise of Cesare Ripa's *Iconologia* of 1592) made 'images signify something different from what one sees at first in them'. Key symbols here include the eyes and ears on Elizabeth's gown, implying that she could see and hear everything.

ministers personally, while Walsingham had served as ambassador in France and so possessed first-hand experience of the 'field work' required for gathering intelligence.[71] Nevertheless, England faced the same difficulties as all states, however well informed, in trying to avoid strategic surprise. The failure of United States forces to predict and prepare for the Japanese attacks on Pearl Harbor and the Philippines on 7/8 December 1941 offers a helpful parallel. After all, as Roberta Wohlstetter observed in her brilliant study of the available evidence, 'Never before' had a government possessed 'so complete an intelligence picture of the enemy'. American cryptanalysts had broken not only the main Japanese diplomatic codes but also some of those used by Japanese agents in American and other foreign ports; American naval leaders had at their disposal radio traffic analysis of transmissions in Japanese military and naval codes which enabled them to pinpoint the location of the various Japanese fleet units; British intelligence placed their own findings at the United States' disposal; finally, the US embassy in Tokyo, naval attachés and observers in East Asian ports, and the Far Eastern correspondents of several American newspapers all provided extremely accurate reporting of Japan's actions and intentions almost up to the last moment.[72] And yet, despite this abundance of information, the Japanese attacks on Pearl Harbor and the Philippines still took the United States by surprise. Why? Wohlstetter advanced several explanations: previous alerts before the attack had proved to be false alarms and so numbed responses to subsequent signals of further danger; American forces believed a sabotage attack to be the most likely Japanese strategy; Japan managed to conceal certain key intelligence while providing convincing 'disinformation' for American collection. More important than any of these, however, was 'the very human tendency to pay attention to the signals that support current expectations about enemy behavior'. 'Human attention', she noted, 'is directed by beliefs as to what is likely to occur, and one cannot always listen for the right sounds.'[73]

All of these factors also came into play in England in 1585–88, exacerbated by the extraordinary fluidity of Spanish planning: a landing in Scotland, a surprise attack on the Isle of Wight, a sudden solo assault by Parma's army on the coast of Kent, as well as amphibious assaults from Lisbon on Algiers and Larache instead of on England – Philip gave all of these strategies serious consideration at some point. Moreover, as already noted, the various ambassadors duly detected each proposal and passed it on to their principals, creating a cacophony of background noise that disguised the king's true intentions.[74] Few could accept that the most powerful monarch in Christendom could be so irresolute; still less that, after so much apparent vacillation, he would adopt the most obvious of all strategies, the one that everyone had been talking about for months, and would choose for his target the most obvious place, where the Romans, Saxons and others had already landed.[75]

When in late December 1587 Queen Elizabeth ordered her fleet to put to sea, her Instructions to Admiral Howard revealed almost total confusion about Philip's intentions. The document began firmly enough: 'Being sondry wayes most credibly given to understand of the great and extraordinary preparations made by sea as well in Spayn by the king there as in the Lowe Countreys by the duke of Parma'; but then uncertainty set in – 'and that it is allso ment that the sayde forces shall be employed in som enterprise to be atempted eyther in our dominiones of England and Irland or in the relm of Scotland'. The document therefore envisaged a large number of possible scenarios and tried to guard against every conceivable threat. Drake would take one part of the fleet 'to ply up and downe between the relm of Irland and the west parte of this relm' in case the Spanish fleet should seek to attack Ireland, south-west England or the west coast of Scotland; meanwhile Howard should 'ply up and down, somtymes toward the north and somtymes towards the south' to guard against a descent from either Spain or Flanders on the east coast of either England or Scotland. If Parma moved against a Dutch seaport, however, Howard should 'doo your best endevor to impech any such attempt'; while if the Armada appeared in the Channel approaches, he should send reinforcements to Drake.[76]

Paradoxically, given the poor security reigning at his Court, Philip could have found no more effective way of confusing his enemies about his true intentions than by constantly changing his mind, for every change seemed to cast suspicion on the accuracy of the last piece of intelligence, making 'analysis' and (above all) 'acceptance' extremely difficult.[77] Moreover, the confusion brought out the worst in Elizabeth. On the one hand, the continuing state of high alert reinforced her parsimonious instincts. The cost of war in the sixteenth century rose constantly, and England had already spent heavily to support the struggle of the Dutch Republic against Spain: £400,000 (roughly 1.6 million ducats) in the three years 1585–88. Elizabeth had also sent subsidies to the French and German Protestants. The cost to her treasury of all-out war with Spain could scarcely be less than £400,000 a year – precisely double her ordinary revenues! So the queen seized upon every excuse to delay until the last moment full mobilization against the possibility of invasion.[78] On the other hand, the blizzard of information coming in from her agents and friends abroad compromised her ministers' ability to make decisions once the immediacy of the threat finally became clear – exactly the same problem that confronted Philip and his ministers (see Chapter 2 above). In June 1588, for example, the normally punctilious Walsingham apologized to a correspondent for not replying to letters because 'I had never more business lying on my handes sithence I entered this chardge, then at this present'. He was right: the series 'State Papers Holland' (which formed but one part of Mr Secretary's concerns) in the Public Record Office includes six volumes for 1586, eight for 1587 and ten for 1588.[79]

To be sure, Elizabeth and her ministers did not leave everything until the last moment. They embargoed all merchant shipping (both native and foreign) in English ports in October 1587, and took over all vessels that might play a useful role in the kingdom's defence; the following month they sent out commissioners to tour the coastal shires and determine what defensive measures would be required to resist invasion. In April 1588 the Privy Council named 'overlords' to superintend coastal defence, ordered surveys of the places deemed most likely to serve as beachheads for both the Armada and Parma's forces, and commanded the county militias to begin serious training (three days every fortnight). All three measures came too late. The 'overlords' could not agree on the best strategy: whether to 'answer' the enemy 'at the sea side', or to leave only a few garrisons in coastal strongholds and withdraw most of the troops to a more defensible point inland, there to 'staye the enemy from speedy passage to London or the harte of the realme'.[80] Some of the surveys lacked rigour: the sketch of Weybourne Hope in Norfolk, 'made in haste this first of May 1588', even lacked a scale – 'reason would a scall', the draftsman wrote apologetically, 'but tyme permyts not'. And time did not permit extensive construction of new fortifications either: Elizabethan England in the Armada year boasted very few defences capable of resisting artillery bombardment.[81] Finally, the county militias may have begun regular training but relatively few men carried firearms and, at least in the northern shires, even they received only one pound of powder for each fortnight's training so that 'they have been driven hetherto for the most part to traine with false fires' (that is to say, they could prime their firearms but lacked charge and bullet for target practice). The quality of the militia, both there and elsewhere, often caused despair: the men of Dorset, it seemed to their commander, 'will sooner kill one another than annoye the enemye'.[82]

Even the mounting trail of indiscretions – above all Cardinal Allen's *Admonition*, received by Burghley on 22 June 1588, and Don Bernardino de Mendoza's French translation of the Armada's 'Order of battle', which specified that it 'sailed against the English fleet' – only gradually revealed to Elizabeth the exact nature of the peril that threatened to engulf her.[83] On 26 June she warned her principal military commanders that Spain intended 'not onlie of invadinge, but of makinge a conquest also of this our realme' with 'an army put alredie to the seas'; and on 18 July, when news arrived that the Armada had left Lisbon, she ordered her troops in Kent to move towards the coast in order to prevent the Spaniards from landing.[84] On 27 July the queen finally grasped that Philip's Grand Strategy consisted of 'the setting out of the great armie by sea in Spaine to ioyne with the said force in Flaunders in the execucion of the said attempt'; but she mistook the 'appointed place', informing her county commanders that the enemy's main force would land in Essex (whereas Philip had selected Kent) and instructing them to send their levies to Brentwood. Even then, work on the fortifications at Tilbury, intended as the linchpin of England's defence by land, only began on 3 August, by which time scarcely 4,000 poorly armed men remained to defend Kent.[85] On the 5th, when the Essex levies arrived at Tilbury with 'not so much as one meal's provision of victual with them', orders went out to stop all further contingents where they stood 'except they had provisions with them'.[86]

It seems little enough to meet a crisis of such magnitude, but Elizabeth could do no more. Her coffers lay empty: England's export trade had passed through a severe crisis in 1586–87 and tax revenues had consequently fallen, while subsidies to the Dutch and spending on the navy had drained all her reserves. On 29 July Burghley, the lord treasurer, calculated that he needed to find almost £40,000 (160,000 ducats) to pay and feed the crews aboard the ships mobilized against the threat of invasion (petulantly observing, 'I marvel that where so many are dead on the seas the pay is not dead with them'), with over £10,000 (40,000 ducats) more due to the Ordnance Office and sundry creditors. He had no idea where this money could be found, because although some London merchants had offered to lend, 'I find no probability how to get money here in specie, which is our lack, but by [foreign] exchange . . . which will not be done but in a long time'. Burghley concluded on a melancholy note: 'A man would wish, if peace cannot be had, that the enemy would not longer delay, but prove, as I trust, his evil fortune'.[87]

Philip soon obliged. Two days later, having secured the diplomatic isolation and economic strangulation of England with consummate skill, his Armada entered the Channel. One week later it anchored off Calais, within sight of the still unsuspecting 'appointed place' for the landing, ready to escort Parma's invasion transports from Dunkirk to the Downs, a distance of only 70 kilometres. His adversaries, by contrast, resembled Thomas Molyneux's 'man in the dark, labouring under the weight of an unwieldy shield, mov[ing] slowly to and fro, distracted and at a loss which way to go to guard against the stroke of an invisible hand'.

'Intelligence', it has been noted, is an excellent 'force multiplier', but can seldom be a 'force equalizer'.[88] The odds between a global empire and a small but vulnerable jewel set in a silver sea remained simply too great to be overturned by superior intelligence alone. Thanks to his simultaneous ability to maintain huge military and naval forces for almost two years, and (through a remarkable combination of disinformation and irresolution) to safeguard until the last moment a vital element of surprise, Philip's enterprise may indeed have become 'the worst-kept secret in Europe'; yet, at least in strategic terms, it still stood a reasonable chance of success. As Molyneux wrote in his 1759 study of 'combined operations': 'A strong army in a good fleet, which neither infantry or cavalry are able to follow, cannot be hindered from landing where they please, whether in England, France or any other country, unless they are prevented by a fleet of equal or sufficient strength'.[89]

What, however, constituted 'sufficient' strength in August 1588? After all, as a diplomat in Paris shrewdly observed, the English did not need to destroy the Armada in order to thwart Spain's Grand Strategy: they only had to prevent it from linking up with the forces assembled in Flanders in preparation for the invasion.[90] And, for that, everything depended upon two things: the ability of Parma's forces in Dunkirk and Nieuwpoort to join the Grand Fleet when it arrived in the Narrow Seas, and Medina Sidonia's capacity, at least temporarily, to control the 70 kilometres of sea that separated Dunkirk from Dover.

8   *Was Parma Ready?*[1]

In the middle of August 1588 a remarkable scene took place in the town square of Dunkirk in Flanders. The duke of Parma, surrounded by his most illustrious officers, issued a public challenge 'not as captain-general of the armies of Philip II, his uncle, but as Alexander Farnese, to satisfy anyone who blamed him for the failure of the Enterprise of England'. No one present replied.[2] Although for the time being this challenge silenced all criticism of Parma ashore, naturally it had no effect aboard the Spanish Armada. The fleet had been driven away from Calais by English fireships on the night of 7/8 August, and then attacked and bombarded at close range by the entire Royal Navy in a battle off the Flemish coast, forcing it to sail northwards with the English in hot pursuit. Morale was low and, according to the Armada's senior military officer Don Francisco de Bobadilla, everybody began 'saying "I told you so" or "I knew this would happen"'. Don Francisco dismissed this as 'trying to lock the stable door after the horse has bolted'; but even he ventured a guarded criticism of Parma's performance. While admitting that many serious defects had been exposed since the expedition left Lisbon, he noted that 'In spite of all this, the duke [of Medina Sidonia] managed to bring his fleet to anchor in Calais roads, just seven leagues from Dunkirk . . . [so that] if, on the day that we arrived there Parma had come out, we should have carried out the invasion.'[3] Other members of the Armada's high command proved more outspoken. Maestre de Campo Don Diego Pimentel, captured by the Dutch after the battle off Gravelines, when asked about the fleet's plans should the duke of Parma's forces not be able to join the fleet, replied bitterly that:

> They had never once thought that the duke, with 100 ships, a multitude of coasters and barges, and an army of around 40,000 men, would not be able to sally forth as planned; and that it seemed strange to him that the duke, having such strength, should not have come out, or had not at least sent out enough barges with musketeers to drive back the warships of Holland and Zealand to enable his own warships to get out.[4]

In September accusations began to fly thick and fast. According to Ambassador Bernardino de Mendoza in Paris, virtually everyone in France believed that Parma had deliberately tried to sabotage the enterprise. In Italy the duke of Savoy (Philip's son-in-law) offered to take over command of the Army of Flanders because (according to the Spanish ambassador in Turin) in light of 'the accounts, which seem worse every day, of how badly Parma has carried out his orders (whether through malice or carelessness) to be ready and to aid Medina Sidonia, it seems impossible to the duke (and to everyone else who considers the matter) that Your Majesty can leave him in the Netherlands'; while a Venetian military expert surmised that 'Parma has reason to be, after King Philip, the most desperate man in the world'. In October the Florentine ambassador in Madrid reported that 'all the Spaniards, and especially those who returned on the Armada' both 'in public and in private' blamed its failure on 'the delays of the duke of Parma . . . so the poor gentleman will need a good excuse'.[5]

The duke already realized his peril: the Armada had hardly moved into the North Sea when he wrote to urge his uncle, Cardinal Farnese, who watched over the family's interests in Rome, to provide immediate refutation 'if it should happen that, either to exculpate the duke of Medina Sidonia or for some other reason, the Spaniards wish to blame me for the misfortunes that have befallen their nation'; and in October he sent a special envoy to Italy in order to defend his conduct.[6] Unfortunately, he chose for this mission Count Niccolo Cesi, a somewhat blunt soldier raised in the Farnese household who seems to have blamed Medina Sidonia instead. The outraged Spanish ambassador in Rome (who happened to be Medina's cousin) wrote to chide Parma for his disloyalty and pettiness: 'It was God's will, not your fault – and not Medina's'. And in any case, the ambassador added tartly, 'explanations of how each commander behaved are due to His Majesty and to nobody else'.[7]

The duke had already taken care of this, too. On the very day of the battle off the Flemish coast he penned a preliminary 'explanation' to his master:

> Those who came here off the fleet and have tried to give the impression that we were not ready – because they could not see guns and munitions on my ships, nor the troops aboard – are mistaken. Everything was prepared as it should have been for the Channel crossing . . . Nothing would have been gained by embarking in advance because the ships are so small that there is not even room to turn round. Undoubtedly the men would have sickened, the food would have putrefied and everything would have perished.

Nevertheless the king and his ministers remained doubtful. When Secretary of State Don Juan de Idiáquez acknowledged receipt of this letter he began by noting acerbically that it had been written at Bruges, 'which is a long way from Dunkirk'.[8] Before long diplomats at the Court of Spain noted that 'many people are talking about the duke of Parma, since it seems to some that he has not done everything he should', and so in November Idiáquez became more direct. Having assured the duke that 'you have no truer servant in any country than me', and after dismissing 'the lies sowed by the ignorant, the malicious, and those who are looking for an excuse', he regretted that there remained a 'cloud to dispel' because some continued to assert that Parma would have needed two weeks to embark his forces. Therefore, Idiáquez continued disarmingly but firmly:

> So that we, your servants, can (when occasion arises) counter with confidence and with substance the confusion over whether your army and its transports were or were not ready when the Armada arrived, please will Your Excellency tell me clearly on which day of August you intended to cross, had the fleet not sailed away?[9]

This time Parma's reply proved more cautious. He devoted several paragraphs to disowning the conduct of Niccolo Cesi who, he claimed, had been sent to Rome merely because Cardinal Farnese had fallen ill and it seemed important to have someone at the papal Court to protect his reputation; he had never intended to blame others. Next he defended the readiness of his forces.

> On Monday 7 August, which was the day that [Medina Sidonia's] Secretary Arceo arrived [with the news that the Armada had reached Calais] and the day I left Bruges, I had 16,000 infantry embarked in Nieuwpoort; and when I arrived at Dunkirk, which was on Tuesday the 8th, the troops who were to embark there had arrived before dawn and were beginning to board, and they finished that same day together with the munitions and all the other things which were ready and prepared. We were embarking at top speed [*a furia*], and we would certainly have finished. Had we not called a halt in view of the news we received of the Armada, we could well have begun to sail out that same night, and joined the Nieuwpoort contingent together with that from Dunkirk in order to effect their task [i.e. the invasion] that night and part of the next day, because they lacked nothing that they needed.

He concluded defiantly: 'My statement that we needed no more than three days to embark and be ready to sail forth was not made without justification.'[10]

Some doubts still lingered, however. In June 1589 the duke felt moved to send copies of all the relevant Armada documents to Court – nine letters from Medina Sidonia to Parma; six letters back (and Parma's instruction to one of the messengers); memoranda of the artillery, munitions and food prepared for the embarkation; all major letters to the king – together with another attempt at exculpation. Perhaps rashly Parma also added some barbed comments about the unwisdom of the entire enterprise, provoking a long response from the king which (in effect) told him to stop complaining and to concentrate instead on current matters.[11] And there the issue seems to have rested, at least for Philip and his ministers.

So where did the truth lie? The disappearance of several key papers complicates the search for certainty: the government's archives in Brussels and Simancas, as well as the Parma family papers in Naples and Parma, have all suffered major losses.[12] Furthermore, on the one hand, the surviving testimony of the duke himself might have been biased, since upon its acceptance depended his reputation and perhaps even his life; while the favourable opinion of those in his entourage might be explained by a sense of personal loyalty or even by bribes.[13] On the other hand, Parma had already made a number of enemies who, both then and later, welcomed every opportunity to discredit him. Juan Moreo, who had played a prominent part in negotiating the treaty of Joinville and later served as chief liaison officer with the French Catholic League, noted in 1586 that 'the duke of Parma has assumed great authority over His Majesty's affairs, and handles them very imperiously'. A month later the new inspector-general of the Army of Flanders, Juan Bautista de Tassis, likewise complained of Parma's proprietorial attitude and his resentment of criticism. Both men renewed their complaints subsequently, contributing to the king's later decision to recall Parma and subject his entire administration to a rigorous *visita* (or judicial review), and so their hostile retrospective evaluation of Parma's conduct in 1588 also remains suspect.[14]

The critical issue, however, is not whether absolutely everything in Flanders had been perfected for the Enterprise of England in the first week of August 1588, but whether enough had been done to permit the invasion force to join up with the Armada, had it been able to remain in (or return to) the Narrow Seas. The question 'Was Parma ready?', on which the success of the entire venture depended, can only be answered by examining in detail the strategic, logistical and operational evidence and the testimony of friends and foes alike.

In 1586, in response to Philip's request for a blueprint for the invasion of England, Parma had proposed a surprise attack on the coast of Kent by a force of 30,000 infantry and 500 cavalry drawn from the Army of Flanders carried by a fleet of barges guarded by a small escort of warships. The king eventually rejected this relatively simple strategy in favour of a combined operation that involved dispatching a powerful warfleet from Spain which would drive away the Royal Navy and, taking up station off Margate (a location subsequently referred to, for security reasons, as 'the appointed place'), protect Parma's army while it crossed from the ports of Flanders to the coast of Kent. The Armada would provide the firepower both afloat and, in the shape of the magnificent siege-train it carried, ashore; Parma would supply the invasion troops and their equipment, together with the landing craft to transport them. Neither force could succeed without the other.[15]

Philip's final instructions to Medina Sidonia, signed on 1 April 1588, made clear that Parma's invasion force could only set forth after the fleet had secured local command of the sea; and a personal letter added the warning that:

> As for ships to land troops, remember that the duke of Parma has a large number of these – barges, coasters and other vessels suitable for this effect;

but all his vessels are of this type, and not of [sufficient] size and force to fight. That is why he must wait until the Armada arrives and secures his crossing.[16]

Medina seems to have missed this point completely. In June, as his fleet approached Cape Finisterre, he blithely informed Parma that 'I am coming to find Your Excellency, and will write to you when I enter the Channel to tell you where this fleet is, so that Your Excellency can lead his [ships] out'. Medina even sent an extra pinnace 'so that Your Excellency can use it to tell me the state in which you find yourself, when you can come out, and where we can meet'. The king, upon reading a copy of this letter, immediately spotted the error, and scribbled in the margin, 'This cannot be unless he [Medina] makes it safe first.' He lost no time in firing off an anguished protest:

> I will not repeat here what I have told you so often, except to say that . . . the main point [of the plan] was to go on until you could join hands with the duke my nephew . . . I am sure you will have done this, and proceeded to that location and made safe the duke's transit, because his ships are not able to come out and meet you further off until you have cleared the crossing of enemies: they are merely transport vessels, not fighting ships.

Even this apparently clear statement seems to have missed its mark, for Medina remained utterly convinced that Parma could bring out his ships to meet him off 'Cape Margate'. Immediately after leaving Corunna, one month later, he once again erroneously informed the king that 'the intention is that the duke of Parma should come out with his ships to the place where I arrive [that is, to the coast of Kent] without making me wait for him for a moment. On this depends the whole success of the campaign.'[17]

Medina also sent a messenger to Flanders as soon as he had cleared the coast of Spain. As he led the fleet into the English Channel one week later he complained to the king that he had still not heard a word from Parma, 'which amazes me', so that 'we are travelling almost with our eyes closed'.[18] Accordingly he wrote again to Flanders as the fleet sailed past Portland Bill on 1 August to 'ascertain from Your Excellency what I should do, and where I should wait, in order for us to join forces', and with the same courier Don Francisco de Bobadilla sent a letter urging Parma 'to come out in person as soon as you see this fleet in the anchorage that it should reach [i.e. "the appointed place"], even if it cannot be with all the ships and troops that you have'. Off the Isle of Wight on 4 August, still without word from Flanders, Medina wrote once more to remind Parma that 'Your Excellency should be ready to put to sea and find me' literally at a moment's notice. Off Beachy Head on the 5th, after three days of long-range bombardment 'from dawn until dusk' without being able to force a fleet action, it occurred to Medina that perhaps the small warships assembled by Parma in Dunkirk might be able to close with the English and engage them until his bigger vessels could get alongside and board.

He therefore dispatched a fourth messenger to beg Parma to send him '40 or 50 flyboats or other small and light warships' immediately.[19]

In spite of all this, no word had come from Flanders by the next morning, when the Armada sighted the French coast near Boulogne. What should Medina Sidonia do now? The English fleet remained only five kilometres astern, so that anchoring off the Kent coast near Margate – as Philip had instructed – no longer made sense. So the duke resolved to

> steer a course for the Calais roads, which we reached at 4 p.m. There were different opinions on whether to anchor in that roadstead, and most favoured going on; but the duke, understanding from the pilots he brought with him that if he proceeded further the currents would force him out of the Channel and into the North Sea, determined to anchor before Calais, seven leagues from Dunkirk, where Parma could come and join him. And so at 5 p.m. he ordered the whole fleet to drop anchor.[20]

Medina now wrote to ask Parma once again for the '40 or 50 flyboats' so that 'we can hold off the fleet of the enemy until Your Excellency can come with all the rest [of your forces] and we can capture some port where this Armada can anchor in complete safety'.[21]

Medina Sidonia's assumptions here betray a fatal lack of familiarity with the realities of naval warfare: one cannot imagine his predecessor, Santa Cruz, making the same elementary mistake. It never seems to have occurred to the duke that all his messengers had either to run the gauntlet of the hostile ships lurking in the Channel, or else to make for the French coast and hope to find a relay of horses ready to convey them overland all the way to Flanders. It was foolish to assume that they would arrive – let alone return with an answer – much before the Armada reached 'the appointed place'. In the event, the first messenger dispatched in June in 'a well-armed pinnace with oars' made good time, reaching Flanders in eleven days; but the storms that dispersed the Armada off Corunna soon made nonsense of his message. The envoy sent from the Bay of Biscay on 25 July in an 'armed pinnace with six oars' took only seven days to reach Parma, who at once began to mobilize his invasion forces. The next messenger, however, took five days to travel from Portland Bill and only reached Parma's headquarters on the 6th. Later that same day, the messenger dispatched from the fleet off the Isle of Wight arrived; and the following morning news came that the Armada had already reached Calais! So although Medina repeatedly expressed regret at his slow progress, and sought by every means to increase his speed exactly as Philip had exhorted him to do, from the perspective of the Army of Flanders he arrived far too soon.[22]

Parma's efforts to make contact with the fleet met with no better success. On 21 June Captain Francesco Moresin, dispatched by Medina off Cape Finisterre, arrived in Flanders with news that the Armada had begun its journey towards the Channel. Then came silence.[23] Parma did not discover until 21 July – ironically the very day they set sail again – that Medina Sidonia and his ships had been sheltering in Corunna for the previous month. On the 30th he sent another vessel with messages for the fleet, and more followed on 31 July and on 1, 2 and 5 August.[24] Only the last one reached its destination: after a whole day at Calais, Medina Sidonia finally received a letter from Parma that must have made his heart miss a beat, for it was dated 3 August, and only replied to his letter of 25 July, revealing Parma's total ignorance of the fleet's proximity.[25] Medina's spirits would have sunk even further had he known the reaction of Parma and his entourage to his later letters: not only did they totally reject Medina's plea to send out the small warships on their own 'because of the risk that they would be lost, along with all the men on board, before they reached the Spanish fleet'; but they remained adamant that Medina should defeat the English fleet and take up station off Margate 'in order to secure the passage from Dunkirk to England for all the soldiers assembled in Flanders' according to the king's masterplan.[26]

Clearly, given the almost total breakdown in communications between the two commanders, Parma could not possibly have had his men aboard the ships on 6 August, ready to meet Medina 'at a moment's notice', because he did not know until that day that the Armada had even entered the Channel, let alone reached Calais. His critics aboard the fleet – Bobadilla, Pimentel and the rest – simply failed, like Medina Sidonia, to understand the situation. Idiáquez and most of Philip's other ministers therefore exculpated Parma on this count; but they remained extremely interested in the date at which Parma *could* have been ready, had the Armada somehow managed to stay off Calais.[27]

No one at the time denied that an impressive force for the invasion of England had been assembled in Flanders. By late June 1588 some 27,000 men waited restlessly in their cramped billets near the coast (see Table 6).[28] Parma had prepared a meticulous embarkation schedule, including the precise itinerary and the sequence for each unit's march to either Nieuwpoort (for the 18,000 Walloons, Germans and Italians) or Dunkirk (for the 9,000 Spaniards, Irish, Burgundians and cavalry); and he had supervised two 'rehearsals' to ensure that everyone understood their role.[29] On 2 August, on receipt of Medina Sidonia's message that he had arrived off the Lizard, Parma placed his forces on alert; and on the 6th, on learning that the Armada's approach continued, all units began to move to the ports. The fact that almost 27,000 men managed to embark within the following thirty-six hours – no mean feat for an army in any age! – testifies to the military effectiveness of both Parma and his troops.[30]

Many obstacles had been overcome in order to achieve this goal. To begin with, concentrating those 9,000 Spaniards and Italians in Flanders required the organization of a complex itinerary, by sea to Genoa and thence via Lombardy, over the Alps and along the Spanish Road to the Low Countries.[31] Moreover, conditions in Flanders – ravaged by almost a decade of war – caused heavy losses once the troops got there: in February 1588 Parma estimated that the newly raised Spanish and Italian units had diminished by more than one-third, with many more men sick.

The invasion force for England, 1588

'Nation'	Units	Men
Spaniards	4 tercios	6,000
Italians	2 tercios	3,000
Irish	1 tercio	1,000
Burgundians	1 regiment	1,000
Walloons	7 regiments	7,000
Germans	4 regiments	8,000
Cavalry	22 companies	1,000
Total		27,000

Table 6   Philip expected the principal invasion force for the Enterprise of England to come from his Army of Flanders, and organized the dispatch of substantial reinforcements from most of his dominions – Spain, Spanish Italy, Franche-Comté and the Netherlands – as well as welcoming Catholic soldiers from Germany and Ireland. In addition, thousands more troops garrisoned the loyal towns and fortresses of the Low Countries, ready to defend them should either the Dutch or the French attempt an attack during the absence of the invasion army.

This high wastage continued. The tercio of Don Antonio de Zúñiga, which had entered the Low Countries from Italy 'not only without arms but also without clothes, and they came badly treated', numbered 2,662 men in July 1587 but only 1,500 by April 1588. Of the 9,000 Italian infantry who marched to Flanders in the summer of 1587, only 3,615 remained the following April.[32] Moreover, once arrived, every unit required food, clothes and lodgings – in a country where food prices stood at unprecedentedly high levels – as they waited month after month for the fleet. The king's repeated insistence, from September 1587 onwards, that the Armada's departure was 'imminent' (even though other correspondents tended to be less sanguine) compelled Parma to keep his entire invasion force close to the coast, in areas that had been devastated and depopulated by bitter fighting, for almost a year.[33] In the words of an English observer:

> [It] may justly give cause of wonder how so many lyvynge in a wasted and greately spoyled country . . . should notwithstandinge be victualled . . . I observed in our journey from Ostend to Burbourghe all round about, viewinge ye contrie for ye space of 40 miles [about 70 kilometres] in length, and somewhat more, that ye villages were desolated, and raysed in a manner to the grounde, noe inhabitante to be founde in them, scarcely any houses but here and there scattered standinghe to dwelle in.[34]

Parma scored a major logistical triumph in maintaining almost 30,000 men amid this unpromising environment – albeit at great personal cost: his household accounts and correspondence reveal numerous loans taken out in 1587–88 from a remarkable variety of sources (he even borrowed from the nuns of St Catherine of Siena and the Jesuit College in Rome).[35] He performed another minor masterpiece in equipping them all for the invasion. According to Alonso Vázquez, specially constructed magazines at both Nieuwpoort and Dunkirk overflowed with munitions and provisions, with more stored in nearby houses and monasteries; according to a Dunkirk diarist, the Greyfriars convent in the town alone housed 1,000 tons of gunpowder.[36] It had a narrow escape on 6 March when a small Dutch boat sailed into Dunkirk, allegedly carrying butter and cheese. The harbour was 'full of vessels from the front to the back', forcing the new arrival to anchor some way off, so that when the bombs concealed in its hold exploded that night they only destroyed two of Parma's ships, severely damaging five more and breaking all the glass windows in the town.[37] Stockpiling continued unabated: 7,000 pairs of wading boots, accoutrements for 3,000 horses, straps to keep horses stable on ships . . .[38] Some English spies at Bruges in March saw men loading 'powder, bullett, match, a great sort of bridges for horses with crosseledges, scalling ladders, mattockes, spades, shovells and hatchets'; others near Dunkirk in June spotted forty 'flatte bottome boats . . . prepared a purpose to carry horse[s], for they have within them both racke and manger and other necessaries'; others still noted ovens to bake bread aboard some ships.[39] Lacunae of course remained. Only two weeks before the Armada arrived Don Luis de Queralt, the commander of one of the newly raised Spanish tercios scheduled for the invasion, begged Parma to 'order that we should be given weapons because (as your highness well knows) we lack them'. A previous complaint had produced arms for two companies, and Queralt promised that 'I shall get the troops out once or twice a week, as I have already begun to do, and place them in formation and drill them as much as I can'; but he could not yet complete the training of the rest of his men.[40] All armies have their weak links, however: notwithstanding the shortcomings of some of Queralt's men, everyone agreed that Parma's invasion force was in superb shape for the enterprise.

Evidence concerning the ships assembled to carry the troops is more equivocal. As Sir William Winter, with a lifetime of naval experience behind him, observed:

> Whereas it is said that the prince [of Parma]'s strength is 30,000 soldiers, then I assure your honour it is no mean quantity of shipping that must serve for the transporting of that number and that which doth appertaine to them, without the which I do not think they will put forth; 300 sail must be the least; and, one with another, to be counted 60 ton.[41]

At first, Parma possessed nothing like this total. Indeed his initial plan of April 1586 had devoted little attention to marine matters: he wrote vaguely of using barges without specifying either numbers or size, and ministers in Madrid had to ascertain these details from the messenger who brought the plan to Court. Then in November 1587 the duke nonchalantly suggested that the barges – on which the success of the whole plan now depended – might not be capable of sailing to England after all: 'I am not convinced that the barges can perform the service that we expect of them because, although they sail the seas, they are light and small ships that need very calm weather and can do nothing . . . but go where the winds take them'. The meticulous care that Parma devoted to planning every movement of his troops overland contrasted sharply with his casual attitude towards the far more complex task of transporting them across the Channel to England.[42]

Eventually, however, a flotilla of suitable size took shape. Undoubtedly the duke exaggerated when he claimed in the autumn of 1587 that he had enough ships for the crossing: according to his own records, only 67 vessels then lay in Dunkirk harbour, and they lacked 370 guns and 1,630 sailors.[43] By June 1588, however, an English spy reported some 70 merchant ships of between 50 and 60 tons' burthen embargoed in Dunkirk 'and most of them now laden with vitayle'. In addition, 'There be at Dunkirk twelve great ships of seven or eight score [= 140–160] tonne apeece; of which twelve, thre[e] of them have twenty peces of cast ordinance of fawcons and fawconnets, ten of a side; the rest have but thre cast peces of ordinance and a fowler a side'. He also saw twelve 'flyboats' of around 80 tons, eight of them armed with six small cast-iron guns, and eight more ships of between 40 and 50 tons' burthen, five of them armed with six pieces and the rest just with stern- and bow-chasers. 'All these men of war are redie and their sayles aborde,' claimed the English report, as were a considerable number of merchant-men. However, 'It is not apparant . . . where there should be had halfe [the] saylers sufficient to man the foresayd ships'; furthermore, 'These ships be open and have no defence when they be borded.'[44]

According to the records of the Flanders fleet itself, by the summer of 1588 almost 100 vessels – 26 warships (several displacing over 150 tons), 21 barges, together with perhaps 50 merchant ships – some hired in Hamburg – rode in Dunkirk harbour. Almost 200 more boats, most of them barges, waited in and around Nieuwpoort.[45] As soon as he heard of the Armada's departure from Lisbon, Parma ordered all seamen to report to their ships upon pain of death, and a week later (according to an English source) he 'came to Dunkirke and viewed the fleete, and rowed out of the mouth of the haven to viewe it'.[46]

A number of experienced English seamen thus seemed convinced that Parma's fleet lay more or less ready to sail by July 1588. Dutch observers agreed: on 14 July, on the basis of detailed reports, the States of Zeeland concluded that Parma's forces stood ready to embark for any destination he chose: 'with his ships in such readiness that they could set sail in 10 to 12 days'.[47] On 7 August Parma apparently wrote to tell Medina (as he later told the king) that his forces would be ready to put to sea in just two more days.[48] Some Spanish eyewitnesses, however, saw matters in a different light. Don Juan Manrique de Lara, colonel of one of the German regiments scheduled to embark at Nieuwpoort and a member of Parma's council of war, complained just afterwards that 'We found the ships unfinished and none of them contained a single piece of artillery or anything to eat'.[49] Two envoys sent by Medina Sidonia to ascertain the situation in Flanders – the inspector-general of the fleet, Don Jorge Manrique, and the duke's secretary, Hierónimo Arceo – concluded that Parma could not be ready in time and frantically exhorted him to greater efforts. Only Arceo, however, seems to have committed his complaint to paper, informing Medina Sidonia that Parma would not be ready for two more weeks.[50] According to Alonso Vázquez, 'although it is true that the magazines of Dunkirk and Nieuwpoort contained large quantities of provisions and munitions, with the rest of the equipment and gear that had been prepared, they were not embarked; nor were many ships equipped as they should have been, on account of the speed that he [Parma] required, although they were ready to go [*con las vergas en alto*].' Vázquez concluded: 'In my opinion, speaking as an eyewitness, it was rash to hazard such a powerful army in weak and defenceless vessels like those prepared by Parma.'[51] Don Carlos Coloma, a subaltern at Dunkirk in 1588, subsequently penned an equally damning verdict in his memoirs: 'Whatever its cause, it is certain – and I saw for myself – that during this time [the summer of 1588] the preparation of the fleet in Dunkirk proceeded very slowly, so that when it was necessary to embark the Spanish infantry, not even the flagship . . . was ready to sail.' Nevertheless, Coloma continued, as soon as Parma heard that the Armada had reached Calais,

> He resolved to embark, notwithstanding all other considerations and all dangers. The sergeant-majors of the tercios immediately distributed the embarkation orders, which were obeyed at once, albeit with much laughter among the soldiers [*aunque con harta risa de los soldados*] because many of them were required to embark in ships on which no shipwright or ship's carpenter had worked. They were without munitions, without provisions, without sails.[52]

The patent disparity between these assessments and those of the English and Dutch spies is at first sight hard to reconcile. To begin with, however, the incompleteness of Parma's flagship, upon which several Spanish observers commented, can be discounted: Alonso Vázquez specifically stated that it lacked only some of its 'cageworks' and a lick of gold paint, adding that many a ship had lost more of its superstructure in a storm and still successfully completed its journey. The charge that other vessels lacked provisions and sails was likewise refuted not only by Vázquez but also by another contemporary, Antonio Carnero: 'I know from trustworthy persons who were both present and involved, that only two or three ships were not ready.' Carnero continued:

> Those who say that victuals were lacking are wrong, because a vast quantity of baked bread, biscuit, herring and flour was ready to be sent wherever the army might be. It was not embarked since it was not necessary to do so, [both] because the troops were to cross in a single tide of six hours, in which time few provisions would be consumed, and because special boats were designated to take the victuals as soon as the troops were aboard.[53]

Perhaps, for a relatively short journey, troops could even be crammed aboard boats 'like sardines' – as occurred for a later celebrated cross-Channel expedition from Dunkirk, in 1940, as well as in other amphibious operations by the Army of Flanders (see Plate 30).

Plate 30 Sketch of Spanish troops (1605). Great uncertainty surrounds the adequacy of the ships and supplies assembled by the duke of Parma to transport his troops to England in the summer of 1588. Some soldiers complained that they were crushed into the appointed boats without food. Parma, however, anticipated that the Channel crossing would only take between eight and twelve hours, so that on the one hand few provisions would be needed for the actual journey (and in any case he had embarked these on other ships) and, on the other hand, the troops could be packed fairly tightly into the boats. This drawing of how the Spanish army crossed the Rhine, in order to make a surprise attack on Holland, showed some possibilities.

The records of the Flanders fleet itself reveal a stream of payments for preparing the ships, right down to painting their names in gold, and adding a sea-horse at the prow. Parma's flagship had a 'royal standard' of red damask bearing the Spanish coat of arms on one side and a depiction of Christ crucified, flanked by the Virgin Mary and St John the Baptist, on the other; other ships would fly ensigns of yellow taffeta displaying the cross of Burgundy (also shown in Plate 30), the arms of the seventeen provinces of the Netherlands, and of Spain. The flags were all 'scattered with flames of fire', as a sign that they would be unfurled in war; furthermore, according to an English source, the Spanish companies at Dunkirk 'sett up their ensignes in the shippes wherein they were to embarke' in readiness. Parma also made his own preparations: in May 1588 his personal treasurer purchased the materials to make a special 'rain cape for His Highness, decorated with silver thread'.[54]

The balance of opinion on the readiness of the ships thus also favours Parma – not least because the criticisms of unpreparedness came mainly from those who recorded their recollections later (Vázquez and Coloma) and entirely from landsmen with limited experience of how swiftly a vessel could be made seaworthy. No doubt some ships did indeed remain unready on 8 August 1588, but the majority must have been prepared because, on the one hand, so many Dutch and English sailors deemed them to be so and, on the other, the embarkation of almost the entire invasion force actually took place. If serious problems had arisen in this area, Don Jorge Manrique and other well-placed observers would surely have mentioned them in their detailed reports to the king.[55]

Once again, it is easy to forget how many obstacles had been overcome in order to create this invasion fleet at Dunkirk and Nieuwpoort. To begin with, Parma had originally envisaged launching the invasion of England from Antwerp, where he had captured the seventy or so armed vessels (some of them large) that defended the city during the siege of 1584–85. Although the Dutch continued to blockade the River Scheldt, the duke hoped to be able to bring out a fleet led by his flagship, the galleon *Sant Alessandro* of some 600 tons' displacement (armed with fifty bronze guns) and a large galley (specially built by a team of carpenters brought from Genoa), together with some thirty other warships (including eight new 'flyboats'), and various troop transports. Opinions on their value differed. One English intelligence report early in 1588 ranked the '31 brave ships of war' riding before Antwerp 'as good as any on our side', whereas according to another, 'it is a common opinion that she [Parma's flagship] will never be able to brook the sea before she be new made [i.e. totally rebuilt]. The rest are ordinary poor things'.[56]

Whatever their effectiveness, however, everything depended upon getting the *Sant Alessandro* and her consorts out of the Scheldt. Parma's capture in August 1587 of the port of Sluis at the mouth of the estuary, containing a considerable number of additional seagoing vessels, opened up the possibility of the big ships sailing down the Scheldt, where they would 'liberate' the flotilla confined in Sluis before proceeding to Nieuwpoort and Dunkirk to embark the invasion army. Parma carried out a personal reconnaissance of the estuaries and channels along the north coast of Flanders but found that between 130 and 140 Dutch ships lay in wait just below Antwerp to forestall precisely this manoeuvre. He reluctantly concluded that none of the Antwerp ships could reach Sluis in safety by that route. Resourceful as ever, the duke decided to leave the larger warships where they lay, in order to pin down the Dutch blockaders, and move the rest to Sluis along the inland waterways. Pioneers worked to deepen the canals and to break some dikes in order to increase both the level and the flow of water until in March 1588 all the smaller craft from Antwerp and other ports along the Scheldt moved to Ghent. Thence over 100 ships (including the large galley) eventually reached Sluis. At the same time, some 200 seamen recruited in Hamburg and Lübeck arrived overland to reinforce the crews aboard the flotilla.[57]

Inevitably the Dutch noticed these developments and almost immediately placed another blockade squadron before Sluis, ruling out any thought of a sortie from there too.[58] So Parma set his pioneers to work again, this time to deepen the

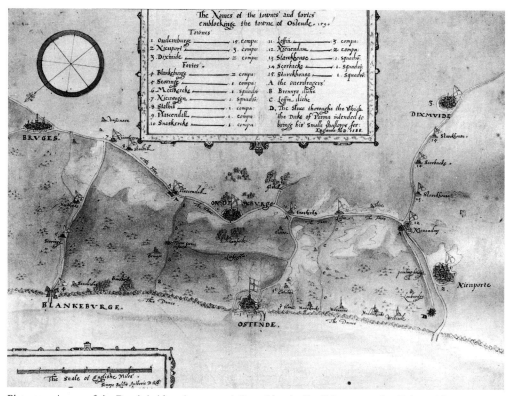

The Names of the townes' and forts'
emblockinge the towne of Oslende. 1590

Townes		
1 Oudemburge	— 14. compa:	— 3. compa:
2 Nieuport	— 5. compa:	12 Nieuendam. — 2. compa:
3 Dixmude	— 2. compa:	13 Slackehouse — 1. squadri:
		14 Scorbacke — 1. squadri:
Fortes .		15 Starckhouse — 1 Squadri:
4 Blankeburge	— 2. compa:	A the ouerdragers'
5 Scormes	— 1. compa:	B Brennye diche
6 Meelkercke	— 1. squadri	C Lessin diche
7 Nieuuegen	— 1. squadri:	D. The sluce throroughe the whiche
8 Stalhill	— 1. compa:	the Duke of Parma intended to
9 Plascendall	— 1. compa	bringe his' smalle shalloppe for:
10 Snaskercke	— 1. compa:	England. Ao: D. 1588.

Plate 31   A map of the Dutch-held enclave around Ostend by the English cartographer Robert Adams in 1590 reveals the topography of one of the embarkation areas for the invasion army two years earlier. Near Nieuwpoort (on the right) Adams has marked 'the slu[i]ce throroughe the whiche the Duke of Parma intended to bringe his smalle shallopps for England'. The duke's headquarters, at Bruges, appear at the upper left; the other port of embarkation, Dunkirk, is off the map to the right.

rivers and to dig new canals in order to link Sluis with Nieuwpoort. On 5 April they opened a 'cutt' 10 metres wide and almost 2 metres deep which, even though the larger and better-armed vessels had once again to be left behind, allowed the barges and other flat-bottomed craft to reach the seacoast (see Plate 31).[59]

All in all it was a most impressive achievement. Against heavy odds, by the beginning of June 1588, seven merchantmen and 173 flat-bottomed craft, divided into three squadrons, now rode in Nieuwpoort harbour, ready to join the warships and transports at Dunkirk, and as soon as he received news of the Armada's arrival off Calais, Parma not only started to board his troops in the Flemish ports, but also ordered the ships in the Scheldt to move downstream in order to draw off more Dutch blockade ships.[60] However, the total tonnage prepared at the two ports of embarkation remained relatively small – the largest of the warships displaced only 180 tons, the average merchantmen under 150, most barges barely 100 – so that the overall displacement of the 26 warships, 55 merchantmen and 194 barges prepared for Parma's 27,000 troops can scarcely have exceeded 30,000 tons.[61]

This total must be put in perspective. Sir William Winter, as already noted, thought that 30,000 men and their provisions would require 300 ships with an average displacement of 90 tons, or 27,000 tons in all. Parma seems to have met that target. Perhaps, however, Winter underestimated: after all, the Dutch assembled no fewer than 1,450 vessels for their surprise seaborne attack on Flanders in 1600, a total displacement of over 150,000 tons for the 100-kilometre journey of their 18,000 troops. Even so, small ships predominated, many of exactly the same type (barges normally used on inland waterways) as those assembled by Parma; only sixteen warships accompanied the Dutch expedition.[62] Furthermore the records of the port of Dunkirk reveal that local merchants at this time frequently used ships built for inland use for trade with Dover and the Downs.[63] The available data thus fully confirm Parma's claim that his ships, both at Dunkirk and at Nieuwpoort, were 'ready enough' for embarkation: on a purely technical level, if the Dutch could effect a seaborne invasion with barges in 1600, and if Dunkirkers could sail them to England for trade, Parma could also use them to carry his army across the Channel.[64]

As soon as Philip's decision to invade England became public knowledge, Parma recognized that his forces would be unable to cross to England in safety until the Armada from Spain arrived in the Channel. As late as November 1587 he apparently still contemplated launching a surprise attack as soon as the Grand Fleet approached and drew off the Royal Navy (see p. 197 above), but the following month he mentioned for the first time the appearance of a Dutch blockade squadron off the Flemish coast and warned the king that the Armada would now also need to clear the way for his forces to come out and reach 'the appointed place'. From now on he repeatedly drew attention to this problem in his letters to the king. In April 1588 he lamented that:

> The enemy have . . . been forewarned and acquainted with our plans, and have made all preparations for their defence; so that it is manifest that the enterprise, which at one time was so easy and safe, can now only be carried out with infinitely greater difficulty, and at much larger expenditure of blood and trouble. I am anxiously awaiting news of the departure of the duke of Medina Sidonia with his fleet . . . [to protect] my passage across, so that not the smallest hitch should occur in a matter of such vital importance. Failing this, and the due cooperation of the duke with me, both before and during the landing, as well as afterwards, I can hardly succeed as I desire in Your Majesty's service.

In June, on receipt of Medina Sidonia's letter asking where the two forces should meet (p. 233 above) Parma angrily observed to the king that 'Medina seems to believe that I should set out to meet him with my small ships, which is simply impossible. These vessels cannot run the gauntlet of warships; they cannot even withstand large waves.' The king only received this particular communication on 7 August – the very day that nemesis (in the shape of the English fireships) struck his fleet – and perceptively (if vainly) annotated this passage: 'Please God let there not be some slip-up here.'[65] Philip and Medina Sidonia had totally failed to grasp Parma's precise situation.

Don Bernardino de Mendoza and others believed that these various excuses masked the fact that Parma had systematically (but covertly) striven to sabotage an enterprise that he regarded as doomed to failure. Certainly, although the king first requested a plan of operations from Parma on 29 December, the duke did not comply until 20 April, offering the somewhat lame excuse that he had been 'busy'; and he furthermore chose to send his plan with a personal messenger who took virtually the longest possible route to the Spanish Court, overland through Luxemburg, Franche-Comté and Italy and then by galley to Spain. In consequence, the plan only arrived in Madrid on 20 June with the result that, as Parma must have realized, the invasion could not possibly take place in 1586 – thus buying him a whole extra year in which to continue the reconquest of the Netherlands. Then in 1587 and again in 1588 the duke bombarded his master with complaints about the role he had been assigned, about the lack of secrecy, about the absence of the promised support from Spain, and (occasionally) even about the wisdom of persisting with the enterprise.

This hardly amounts to 'sabotage', however, because whatever his inner misgivings Parma worked ceaselessly (as demonstrated above) both at collecting men, supplies and ships close to viable ports of embarkation, and at concealing his true intentions from the Dutch and English in order to minimize the risk of them being bottled up. Thus besides shifting his troops and ships around, he also stayed away from Brussels, his administrative capital, for a whole year, moving relentlessly about Flanders and Brabant both to superintend preparations for the invasion in the four designated ports and also to spread confusion concerning his target.[66] In this he proved entirely successful. On 12 July 1588, when the Dutch admiral cruising off the Flemish coast suddenly realized that Parma's entire army could sail out from Dunkirk and Nieuwpoort at any moment, he commanded only 24 ships, whereas 32 ships cruised off Sluis, 135 blockaded Antwerp and a further 100 stood guard further north around the entrance to the Zuider Zee and the Eems.[67] Moves by the Dutch federal government to concentrate more vessels off Flanders ran into bitter opposition from the political leaders of Holland and Zealand who, as late as 10 August – two days after the battle off Gravelines – still feared that Philip really intended to attack them.[68] As Lord Henry Seymour, commanding the English squadron in the Narrow Seas, correctly remarked: 'I think they [the Dutch] desire more to regard their own coast than ours', while Admiral Howard of Effingham noted with irritation as he closed with the Spanish fleet that 'There is not one Flushinger nor Hollander at the seas'.[69]

The nature of the Dutch blockade has been much misunderstood: their vessels did not lurk, as often stated, at the very entrance to the harbours of the Flemish coast. Rather, as Alonso Vázquez noted:

Whenever Parma wanted to join his two fleets [in Nieuwpoort and Dunkirk], it would be easy for him to do so, because the seacoast was clear of enemy ships. They could not come inshore because of the guard mounted by the places that secured it, besides the many currents and sandbanks created by the tides in the entire Narrow Seas.[70]

Contemporary cartography makes the position clear. A map prepared in 1586 shows the 'banks of Flanders', with the safe routes for shipping considerably offshore (Plate 32); and subsequent views of the approaches to Dunkirk show the Dutch blockade ships some distance offshore and the larger Dunkirk ships anchored securely between a large sandbank, 'Het Schuurken', and the batteries on the shore.[71] According to a detailed description of the two ports, sent to (and annotated by) Philip in 1583, the roadstead between Dunkirk and Nieuwpoort could easily shelter a large fleet, while that off Mardijk (between Dunkirk and Gravelines) could be used for an embarkation.[72]

The capacity of the two harbours has also been misrepresented, with some contemporaries (including Medina Sidonia) suggesting that Parma's fleet could only have emerged at a spring tide.[73] But Parma explicitly denied this:

Although with some winds the water level falls and we need spring tides, very few vessels are affected; and even supposing this should happen and we could not use them, but could undertake the task with the rest, I have never . . . thought of waiting for the spring tides or of holding back for a moment for this reason.

According to a description of the ports specially prepared in 1583 for Philip, Dunkirk harbour contained four metres of water at low tide and more than five at high tide, with five and almost six respectively at Nieuwpoort, and about one metre more during the March and August spring tides. Moreover, ships displacing up to 300 tons could and did enter Dunkirk on a regular basis at this time.[74]

Even so, getting Parma's entire fleet to sea from the two Flemish harbours would not have been easy. As Antonio Carnero noted in his memoirs, it seems unlikely that the 300 vessels assembled could have moved out on a single tide: the first ships would therefore have needed to wait in the roadstead for the rest.[75] But this might not have proved as difficult as it sounds, for not only did the Dutch blockade squadron off the Flemish seacoast lack numbers: it also lacked firepower.

In January 1584 the prince of Orange had asked the States-General to sanction the construction of 'ten good warships' of between 180 and 400 tons but they refused, authorizing instead only a few small coastal protection vessels.[76] It is true that between November 1587 and July 1588 the Republic commandeered 180 vessels for its defence, but only 55 of these reinforced the Zealand fleet (responsible for blockading Flanders), the largest displacing but 300 tons; more significantly, in July 1588 the Royal Navy peremptorily rejected the 23 warships sent

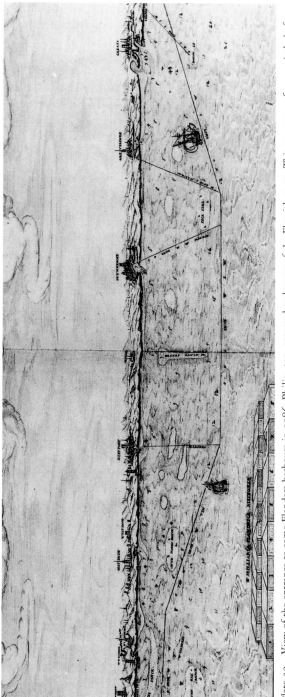

Plate 32   View of the entrance to some Flanders harbours in 1586. Philip, too, accumulated maps of the Flemish coast. This one comes from an 'atlas' of 1586, consisting of twenty-four sea charts covering the coast of continental Europe from Reval in the Baltic to La Rochelle. All views are done from an imaginary 'crow's nest' position out to sea and show the spires and other 'leading marks' before each port, together with any sandbanks and other hazards: in the case of the coast between the Scheldt and the Calais, above, the sea-lanes leading to and connecting each port – including Dunkirk and Nieuwpoort – are clearly shown. The atlas was probably prepared by the Dutch cartographer Aelbert Haeyen, who expected it to be published by the States of Holland; however, the publication of Waghenaer's *Mariner's Mirror* in 1585, with a licence that prevented anyone from bringing out a rival product for ten years, forced Haeyen to look elsewhere. He therefore sent – or more likely sold – his work to Spain.

by Holland to assist in England's defence as too small and too poorly equipped to be of service.[77] Although the States-General later hired two substantial merchant-men – one displacing 600 tons, the other 750 – the cost of manning them was deemed so high that they never put to sea. Indeed the expense of crews for even the smaller ships was such that neither Holland nor Zealand managed to pay their sailors any wages between January and November 1588.[78]

So by early August, when the Armada arrived off Calais, Parma's forces faced a mere 35 Dutch ships, albeit reinforced by some 1,200 musketeers specially trained for warfare at sea.[79] Some 40 larger vessels lay in reserve, but they too were relatively small and their total displacement scarcely exceeded 7,000 tons: only two displaced over 300 tons, and the largest of them carried but 20 guns (all of 9-pounder calibre or less).[80] The navy maintained by the States of Holland likewise included few powerful ships – the largest carried 14 guns; only four carried 10 or more – and in any case they did not appear off Dunkirk until late August, long after this crisis had passed.[81] The English Narrow Seas squadron under Seymour, for its part, remained mostly at the Downs.

Hardly surprisingly, Justinus of Nassau and his inadequate force proved unable to close the port of Dunkirk totally. Parma managed to send out one ship on 17 February 1588, four on 1 March, one on 1 May, three on 7 June, one each on 30 and 31 July and 1 and 2 August, three on the 5th and three more on the 12th – all to seek out the Armada – while two Armada vessels entered Dunkirk to take on stores and left again shortly afterwards. Lord Burghley, upon reading about this, scribbled angrily in the margin: 'Wherefore serveth Justin and his shipps of Zeeland?'[82]

In defence of 'Justin' it should be recalled that maintaining a close blockade in the age of sail always proved extremely difficult. Storms could and did blow ships off station, allowing enemy vessels to slip out. This happened frequently off Dunkirk in the unusually inclement days of July 1588, and again at the beginning of August when a 'tempest forced all the ships of war . . . that lay before Dunkirk and Nieuport to come in'. Although they had returned by the 4th, on 16 August Seymour wrote that 'The weather has been such as no man hath been able to look upon the coast of Flanders this seven or eight days past'.[83] Even in less boisterous conditions it might prove difficult to intercept a fast-moving blockade-runner: in early July, for example, Seymour lay in wait for one of Parma's ships to emerge but admitted that it was 'a hundred to one she may escape me'. Meanwhile the 'great gallee' apparently managed to get out of Sluis with 100 Italian soldiers and 200 oarsmen aboard (although storms drove it to Texel, where it fell into Dutch hands).[84]

So on 8 August 1588, as Parma's meticulous embarkation process neared completion, Justinus and his thirty-five small and poorly gunned ships found themselves off Dunkirk virtually alone, 'with no Holland ships in sight'. He warned his masters, the States of Zealand, that he was too weak to withstand alone the entire power of the enemy concentrated in the area.[85] What chance existed, then, that Parma's invasion force might have got to sea?

The available evidence demonstrates that an impressive army stood ready by the coast of Flanders; that a fleet of transport vessels capable of carrying all of them in relatively calm seas lay more or less ready in the harbours of Dunkirk and Nieuwpoort; and that, once the order to embark had been given, the process took just thirty-six hours to complete. At that point Parma's army might have got to sea in one of three distinct ways: first, the Armada could have either defeated, diverted or cowed the enemy fleets – Dutch and English alike – so that they could not threaten the Army of Flanders in their poorly defended barges; second, Medina could either have taken shelter in a secure anchorage in the Channel until news arrived that Parma had his forces entirely ready to set sail without making him 'wait for him for a moment'; or, third, once at Calais he could have sent enough ships to Dunkirk to drive off the Dutch and escort Parma's fragile flotilla first to the main fleet and then across to Margate (much as he had successfully chaperoned his own lumbering and poorly armed supply vessels all the way up the Channel). By the time Medina reached Calais, however, the first option was clearly closed: although the Royal Navy had failed to halt or defeat the enemy, it had established beyond question its tactical supremacy in combat. As for the second alternative, the port of Calais – the only one available by the time the Armada reached the Narrow Seas – could not accommodate Spanish galleons (in 1598, while the city lay temporarily in Spanish hands, a large troopship sent from Spain proved unable to enter the port, and others that did enter could not get out again because of an Anglo-Dutch blockade).[86] The only anchorage in the area large enough to accommodate both the Armada and Parma's fleet remained the Downs; and to reach it, Parma's flotilla first needed to 'join hands' with the Armada.

Most commentators have dismissed the third alternative – proceeding to Dunkirk – on the grounds that (to quote a contemporary, Luis Cabrera de Córdoba) 'it was not possible to join the Flanders fleet with the Armada because the galleons drew 25 to 30 feet of water [between 8 and 10 metres], and the seas around Dunkirk were far more shallow'.[87] But Cabrera was in Spain, not Flanders, at the time; and he seems to have overlooked a number of facts. First, detailed contemporary surveys of the Flemish coast indicated two safe anchorages within the sandbanks, one of them specifically deemed suitable for a fleet seeking to embark an army (see p. 245 above).[88] Second, within living memory ten large galleons had in fact come inshore – close enough to provide an effective bombardment during the battle of Gravelines in 1558 – proving that deep-draught warships could indeed approach Dunkirk. Surely, thirty years later, given the small size and the light armament of the Dutch blockade ships, ten Armada galleons (which actually drew far less than Cabrera's eight metres!) would have sufficed to bring out Parma's army in safety.[89] Failing that, even just the four shallow-draught galleasses, each armed with over fifty guns (including two 35-, two 36- and two 50-pounders), could easily have cleared a path from Dunkirk to Calais. With no certainty when Parma's army could be ready, and having already lost several of his capital ships, however, Medina Sidonia no doubt felt he should not risk detaching some of his best fighting vessels when the English fleet – now united and superior to his in numbers – lay less than two kilometres behind him, poised to attack again at any moment.[90]

Yet without some assistance from the Armada, as he had repeatedly stated, Parma could not break the blockade on his own. Some sources claim that he made an attempt to drive off the Dutch squadron with a task force of 1,000 select musketeers aboard ten warships, and that it failed with the loss of all hands.[91] Yet even had this ploy succeeded (as, given Justinus's weakness, it might have done), Parma still required the Armada's protection for the Channel crossing in the teeth of Seymour's powerful squadron in the Downs – the precise place scheduled for the landing. His army of victorious veterans, honed by years of combat experience (as one of their English adversaries admitted) into 'ye best soldiers at this day in Christendom', represented a unique asset that, once lost, could never be replaced.[92] Just as Justinus of Nassau could not withstand single-handed the entire power of Spain so Parma could not, once the Dutch blockade squadron had taken up station, venture his forces against Spain's enemies by sea unsupported.[93]

Instead, on 6 and 7 August, as Parma marched his troops to the ports and began to embark them, and the Armada rode anxiously at anchor off Calais and took on some supplies, the English concentrated their fleet: Seymour's squadron and some reinforcements from London sailed across to join Howard, Drake, Hawkins and the rest to windward of the Spanish fleet. On the night of the 7th, as the tide began to run north, the English sent eight fireships towards the Armada. Some were intercepted, but to avoid the rest Medina ordered his vessels to slip their cables and take evasive action. This achieved what English gunfire had previously failed to do: the Armada scattered, allowing the queen's ships to get in among the fleet and fire their big guns at close range. On 8 August, as Parma's men continued to board, they could hear the sounds of battle out to sea; but the sounds grew fainter as the two fleets sailed into the North Sea. Gradually Medina Sidonia and his lieutenants gathered their fighting ships together, allowing the Armada to re-form, but now the wind blew strongly from the south, forcing them to retreat. By the 12th they were level with the Firth of Forth, and the English turned for home, satisfied that Medina would no longer risk leading his fleet back to the straits of Dover, but would attempt to return to Spain around the north of Scotland and Ireland.

As it happened, the strong winds that drove the Armada into the North Sea, followed by Seymour's squadron as well as the main English fleet, also blew the Dutch off station again for almost a week. Seymour could not get his squadron back to the Downs until the 11th. In theory this created a 'window of opportunity' for the invasion. But if even galleons could not withstand the gales of the Narrow Seas that week, what chance had Parma's crowded barges which could 'not even withstand large waves'? After that, even though Parma kept his forces on stand-by until the end of the month, the chance to invade and conquer England vanished.[94] On strategic, logistical and operational grounds, it was therefore entirely reasonable for Alexander Farnese to have offered, shortly after the

Armada's hasty departure from the Flemish coast, 'to satisfy anyone who blamed him for the failure of the Enterprise of England'; and it was equally reasonable for all those present to remain silent, because clearly naval technology (combined with the weather) had rendered Parma's logistical triumphs and meticulous embarkation schedules redundant. The guns of Elizabeth's navy had destroyed Philip's masterplan beyond repair.

9 *The Guns of August*[1]

In particular I must warn you that the enemy's intention will be to fight at long distance, on account of his advantage in artillery . . . The aim of our men, on the contrary, must be to bring him to close quarters and grapple with the weapons they hold in their hands; and you will have to be very careful to carry this out. So that you will be well informed, I am sending you some reports from which you will see the way in which the enemy employs his artillery to fire low and sink his opponent's ships; and you will have to take such precautions as you consider necessary in this respect.[2]

As usual, Philip II was well informed: his summary of how the Royal Navy would defeat the Spanish Armada in August 1588 proved impeccable – the English did indeed keep their distance and fired low, while the Armada never found a way to close and grapple. This predictable outcome, which sealed the fate of Philip's Grand Strategy, raises two important questions: how had the English developed their distinctive, superior tactical doctrine, and why could the Armada not follow suit?

England's achievement in 1588 has seldom been in doubt: its ships thwarted Philip's design to invade and conquer the realm, by driving the Armada away from its planned junction with Parma. Exactly how much damage the Spaniards suffered, by contrast, is hotly disputed. Even before the climactic battle off Gravelines on 8 August, however, all four galleys attached to the fleet failed to reach the Channel;[3] one squadron flagship, the *Santa Ana* of the Biscay squadron, became separated from the fleet and sought refuge in Le Havre (where she eventually had to be abandoned); another flagship, the *Nuestra Señora del Rosario* of the Andalusian squadron, collided with her consorts twice during the first day's action and suffered such damage that she had to surrender; a third warship, the *San Salvador*, was also abandoned and captured that same day because her powder magazine exploded; and the flag galleass likewise collided with another ship, lost her tiller and, before she could regain control, ran aground and became thoroughly disabled. Admittedly the English played little part in most of these events, but the loss of an entire squadron (the galleys), of three squadron flagships, and of another prime fighting ship before the decisive encounter reflects little credit on Spanish seamanship; and it certainly helped the English, who made full use of the copious stores recovered from their two prizes – particularly the 229 barrels of powder and the 3,600 'cannon, demi-cannon and culverin shot', which they immediately distributed among the queen's ships.[4] Then, on 8 August, during the battle itself, the English sank one Spanish ship by gunfire and inflicted such extensive damage on two more, both powerful Portuguese galleons, that they ran aground and had to be abandoned. Far more losses occurred on the long journey back to Spain: perhaps one-third of the remaining Armada ships sank or were abandoned – several (if not most) of them specifically because of damage inflicted by the English in action.[5] Yet Elizabeth achieved all this in return for the loss of only eight small private vessels, deliberately sacrificed as fireships to disrupt the Armada's formation at a total cost of £5,111 10s. – 'perhaps', as one naval historian suggested, 'the cheapest national investment that this country has ever made'.[6] So how and when had England acquired the ability to defend her shores even against, in the words of Sir John Hawkins, 'the greatest and strongest combination, to my understanding, that ever was gathered in Christendom'?[7]

Certain elements of the explanation stemmed from the common heritage of all sixteenth-century Atlantic states. By 1500 the 'full-rigged ship' – one of the greatest technological inventions of medieval Europe, originating in the Iberian peninsula and spreading northwards in the course of the fifteenth century – had become the most important sailing vessel all along the Atlantic coast. With its great holds, it served the needs of the burgeoning European economy; with its superb sailing qualities, it facilitated voyages of discovery and overseas coloniza- tion; with its powerful construction, capable of absorbing the recoil of outgoing gunfire as well as the impact of incoming rounds, it opened the way for the artillery broadside.

An effective cannonade, however, also required the invention of hinged gunports in the hull, for heavy artillery could be safely deployed only on a ship's lower decks. Although visual evidence reveals the existence of gunports as early as the 1470s, the first sailing warships capable of firing 'great ordnance' only appeared after 1500. During the first two decades of the sixteenth century, England, Scotland, France and Denmark all began to build vessels displacing around 1,500 tons and heavily armed with gunpowder weapons, some of them large. The size and armament of the English fleet rose particularly swiftly: by the 1540s the 'Navy Royall' comprised 53 vessels, including 15 'great ships', with a total displacement of some 15,000 tons and almost 200 heavy guns (9-pounder calibre and above).[8]

Fifty years later the picture had changed in several significant respects. In 1595, although the Royal Navy included only 38 fighting ships, 23 of them exceeded 400 tons' displacement, and the total for the fleet approached 20,000 tons.[9] More striking still, the total of heavy guns aboard the ships had more than tripled – to over 600 – and 250 of them fired a ball weighing 16 pounds or more.

All these weapons could inflict devastating damage at close quarters.[10] Further-more the ships that bore them possessed a remarkable consistency of construction. Beginning in 1573 the queen's shipwrights introduced a new design – known as 'race-built' – that involved a reduction in the 'castles' fore and aft, sleeker lines, and a longer gundeck. These changes produced two important advantages: they effected a revolution in armament, for the castles had carried the majority of the anti-personnel weapons, while the longer gundecks permitted a significant increase in the weight of the broadside; and the sleeker lines gave the English warships a distinct edge over their competitors, allowing them to sail faster and to manoeuvre – and bring their guns to bear – with (for that age) remarkable dexterity. The first of the faster 'all-big-gun battleships' of the Tudor navy was called (in an uncanny parallel with the similarly innovative capital ship of the Edwardian navy in the early twentieth century) the *Dreadnought*. Launched in 1573, she displaced 700 tons and carried 31 tons of ordnance (not counting the weight of the gun carriages and tackles).[11] The ability to carry heavy artillery equivalent to almost 5 per cent of total displacement was unprecedented, but this record did not last: in 1590 the new ship *Defiance*, also 700 tons, carried 53 tons of ordnance, equivalent to over 7.5 per cent of her displacement. Equally impor-tant, a remarkable programme of rotation for the queen's ships began in 1577, to 'reform' (in the phrase of its mastermind, Sir John Hawkins) older vessels to a 'race-built' design: in 1592 the 'reformed' *Swiftsure* (650 tons) bore 43 tons of ordnance, or almost 7 per cent of her displacement (see Figure 3).[12]

These measures did not come cheap yet Elizabeth, despite her celebrated reputation for parsimony, spent heavily on warships (her navy acquired sixteen vessels between 1585 and 1588 and repaired the rest), on maintaining a perma-nent cadre of trained officers and men, and on creating a massive stockpile of ordnance specifically for use on sailing warships. During the war years 1585–1604 her navy received over £1.5 million (about 6 million ducats) from her treasury.[13] Although this figure may seem puny when set beside the spending levels achieved by Philip – 10 million ducats on the Armada alone in 1585–88 and almost 40 million ducats in France and the Netherlands between 1588 and 1598 – no other early modern state regularly devoted 30 per cent of its defence spending to the navy.[14]

Thanks to all this, in 1588 Elizabeth's capital ships constituted the most powerful navy afloat anywhere in the world. It was not, however, the largest. Although she possessed eighteen capital ships, Philip boasted slightly more: ten Portuguese galleons, most of them recently built and all of them heavily armed; eight newly built guardships of the transatlantic convoys that sailed annually between Seville and the Caribbean (each displacing 700 tons but carrying only 24 guns – a battleship armed like a cruiser, as it were); and four Neapolitan galleasses (each weighing around 750 tons and mounting 50 guns, including six heavy pieces mounted on the fore- and stern-castles).[15] Together these royal vessels totalled twenty-one – but they belonged to three distinct nautical 'families', each designed for a different purpose, and few of them had operated together before.[16]

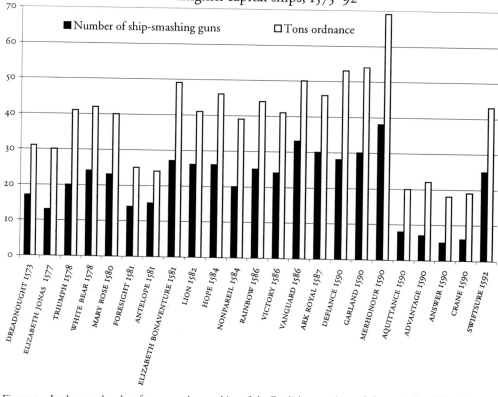

English capital ships, 1573–92

■ Number of ship-smashing guns □ Tons ordnance

Figure 3 In the two decades after 1573 the warships of the English navy changed dramatically. Older ships were 'reformed' and new vessels were laid down according to a design that allowed them to sail faster, to carry far more ordnance and to fire it more rapidly. Starting with the *Dreadnought* in 1573, the weight of the artillery carried by Elizabeth's ships increased from over 4 per cent to around 7 per cent – and the weight of munitions, carriages and tackle increased the figures still further. Source: Parker, 'The *Dreadnought* revolution of Tudor England', 287–8.

Elizabeth's warships, by contrast, had been served by the same officers and crews for years, patrolling the Narrow Seas, showing the flag off the coast of Ireland, and (in the case of several ships) cruising in Spanish waters. By August 1588, they had been mobilized and had been at sea for most of the previous eight months, giving all aboard a thorough (perhaps excessive!) familiarity with their vessels. Moreover Elizabeth could also count upon the assistance of some privately owned galleons whose technological sophistication rivalled that of her own warships. Thus Howard's flagship, the *Ark Royal*, displacing 1,100 tons and carrying 32 guns, had begun life as a private ship (the *Ark Raleigh*, built for Sir Walter by the queen's master shipwright, Richard Chapman); the *Edward Bonaventure* (450 tons and 30 guns), owned by the earl of Oxford, was built in 1574 according to the design of the queen's ship, *Foresight*; and the *Galleon Leicester* (600 tons and 42 guns), owned by the earl of Leicester, was built in 1578 in express imitation of the

Revenge by the queen's master shipwright, Matthew Baker (this ship may have been the first ever to be built according to formal plans). These private warships – for they were no mere merchantmen – all fought effectively against the Armada alongside the queen's ships.[17]

Philip proved less fortunate in this regard. Most of the 'fleet auxiliaries' embargoed for the Armada campaign had been built to carry bulk cargoes: Spain and Portugal did not, at this stage, engage in the sort of aggressive commerce raiding in the Atlantic that gave rise to the *Edward Bonaventure* and her consorts. For Spain's crusade against England, these embargoed merchant ships (which came from almost every continental port between Ragusa and Rostock) required extra ordnance, powder and shot from the government: thus the *Gran Grifón*, a 950-ton grain transport from Rostock in the Baltic, carried 27 guns (all iron and none larger than 6-pounder) when she was embargoed in Spain in 1587; but she sailed against England with 38 (the new ones all bronze and including four 10-pounders). However, converting a ship built to carry bulk cargoes into an effective warship involved more than just cutting more gunports into the hull and supplying additional cannon: the crew needed to be retrained and the ship's entire structure required reinforcement in order to withstand the recoil from firing heavy ordnance. The *Gran Grifón*, which figured prominently in several actions, foundered off Fair Isle on the way home because (according to her commander) she had been damaged not only 'by the many guns which some of the English ships fired against her' but also 'by the [recoil of the] guns she fired against them'.[18]

The English fleet in 1588 apparently suffered no such problems. One of Elizabeth's captains claimed that at the battle off Gravelines, on 8 August, 'Out of my ship [the *Vanguard*: 850 tons, 37 guns] there was shot 500 shot of demi-cannon, culverin and demi-culverin; and when I was furthest off in discharging any of the pieces, I was not out of the shot of their harquebus [within small arms range: about 50 metres], and most times within speech of one another [close enough to shout abuse: perhaps 20 metres in naval combat]'.[19] This picture of relentless bombardment by heavy artillery at very close range is confirmed by the surviving Spanish accounts, all of which remarked on the constant and effective artillery barrage maintained by the queen's ships: to some, the English seemed able to fire three rounds in the time it took the Armada to fire one; to others, it seemed to 'rain shot'; and men who had been at the battle of Lepanto claimed they saw 'twenty times as much great shot . . . plied as they had there'.[20] More specifically, a gunnery officer on Medina Sidonia's flagship reported '107 direct hits on the hull, masts and sails by cannon shot'; Juan Martínez de Recalde, in the vice-flagship, thought 1,000 rounds had been fired against him; while some claimed that another Portuguese galleon 'had been shot through 350 times' before it ran aground.[21] All the Spanish survivors commented on the close range of the action – 'within musket shot and sometimes arquebus shot'.[22]

Unfortunately, few of the English Ordnance Office's operational records for 1588 appear to have survived, and so these impressions cannot be substantiated

Shot and powder expended by Royal Navy ships on the Cadiz and Caribbean raids, 1595–96

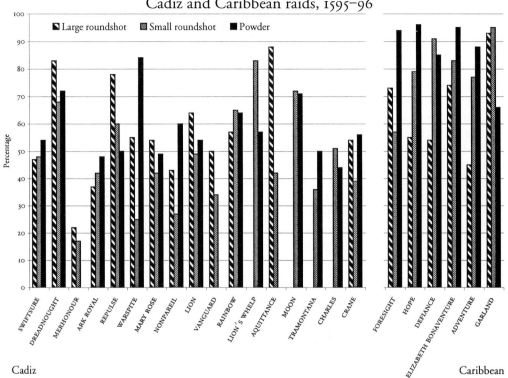

Figure 4 In 1595–96 Elizabeth sent almost her entire fleet to sea against Spain: seventeen warships led an expedition to take Cadiz, while six more sailed to the Caribbean. The records of powder and shot supplied to, and used by, each royal ship show a prodigious use of ammunition (the smaller vessels – the *Charles*, *Lion's Whelp*, *Moon* and *Tramontana* – carried no heavy ordnance). Some ships fired over 550 heavy-calibre rounds and three tons of powder in the course of the campaign – a triumphant vindication of the new 'race-built' design pioneered by English shipwrights. Source: PRO WO 55/1627 'The booke of the remaynes of Her Majesty's shippes returning from the seas', 1595–6.

beyond all doubt. However the full accounts for 1595–96 – the first to survive, covering both the raid by Howard and Essex on Cadiz and the voyage of Drake and Hawkins to the Caribbean – provide strong support.[23] The former involved seventeen of the queen's ships, leading a fleet of over 120 English and Dutch vessels; the latter included six. The Ordnance Office carefully noted the quantities of shot and munitions issued to each royal ship at the start of the campaign, the total used ('the waste spente at the seas'), and also the amount returned (Figure 4). These reveal that not only did the 308 heavy guns aboard the royal ships discharge a total of 3,976 rounds and 554 tons of powder during the Cadiz campaign, they fired most of it on a single day (21 June 1596 OS) when, according to a contemporary account, 'infinite store of shot was spent between our ships, the town and galleys, much to their damage and nothing to our loss'.[24] Much the same pattern marked Drake and Hawkins's last expedition to the Caribbean shortly before. The six royal vessels on the expedition received a total of 4,910 roundshot for their 142 big guns and fired 3,303 (67 per cent) of them; they also received 194 tons of powder and used all but 2 tons (99 per cent).[25] Although by modern naval standards firing 550 heavy-calibre rounds and almost 3 tons of powder per ship in the course of a campaign may seem modest, in the sixteenth century it was unprecedented. Whether the English employed the same tactics in 1588 – and all the evidence suggests that they did, since by the end of the action the entire fleet had run out of both powder and shot[26] – clearly by the end of the sixteenth century a new type of naval warfare had emerged in England.

Why could the Armada not follow suit? After all, the technique of long-range naval battery originated in the Iberian peninsula. The Instructions provided in 1500 by King Manuel of Portugal (Philip's grandfather) to the commander of a fleet dispatched to the Indian Ocean specified that, upon meeting any hostile ships, 'you are not to come to close quarters with them if you can avoid it, but only with your artillery are you to compel them to strike sail . . . so that this war may be waged with greater safety, and so that less loss may result to the people of your ships'.[27] The precision of the orders suggests that the tactics described were not new in 1500. Over the next half-century, however, Portuguese tactical doctrine for war at sea changed. In 1555 Fernando Oliveira, in his influential treatise *The art of war at sea* (the first manual of naval warfare ever published), still asserted that 'at sea we fight at a distance, as if from walls or fortresses, and we seldom come close enough to fight hand-to-hand' and recommended 'a single and straight [*singella e dereyta*] line' as the ideal combat formation. But he also advised captains to carry heavy weapons only at the prow, like a galley, with lighter pieces, mostly muzzle-loaders, on the broadside, and warned that: 'It is never safe at sea to allow opponents on your beam; rather you should always keep them ahead when you are fighting . . . Never expose your broadside to them.'[28]

For Oliveira, the 'single and straight' line of warships resembled an advancing formation of galleys, with their heavy guns to the fore. Theorists of naval warfare in Spain agreed. Writing in about 1540, Alonso de Chaves expressly advised battle fleets 'to sail in wings [*en ala*] because all [the ships] can see their enemies and fire their artillery without impeding each other. They must not sail in line [*en hila*], with one behind the other, because that would cause serious harm, since only the ships in the van can fight'.[29] In the 1580s Spain's Atlantic fleet clearly still deployed in a crescent, just like galleys, so that all except the ships on each wing (or 'horn' as the Spaniards now called it) could normally fire only their bow- and stern-chasers.[30] Nevertheless, like galleys, a crescent of sailing warships could still inflict grievous harm on an adversary. Thus, in July 1582, a large Spanish fleet – including some of the same ships and the same officers who later sailed against England – defeated a superior French and English naval force in a battle off São Miguel in the Azores largely through firepower. The senior Spanish infantry officer (a veteran of Lepanto) considered that the battle had been fought 'with the greatest fury ever seen' and several participants commented on the large number of rounds exchanged; one of the principal galleons involved had only a single barrel of powder left at the end of the action. According to one account, the 'sides, masts and rigging' of the enemy flagship 'were so shattered by the battery we gave them that she sank'; according to another, most of the victorious galleons had also suffered so much damage that they got home only with difficulty.[31]

So Philip's ships could, on occasion, deploy their artillery effectively and cause damage to their foes, yet they did not do so in 1588. The problem does not seem to have been a failure to fire. It is possible to be fairly precise about this because the clerk aboard every hired ship received strict instructions to keep a record of the powder, shot, match and lead used every day, 'stating in detail the pieces of artillery that were fired, their calibre and weight, and the powder and ball consumed', on behalf of the ship's master (who was responsible for everything he received from government agencies); and one or two of the soldiers aboard also noted down these same details on behalf of the Ordnance Office.[32] Despite the disorder aboard some ships during the battle, and the disorganization of the surviving papers of the Armada, reasonably accurate records can be reconstructed for nine ships (see Figure 5).[33] Every case offers a striking contrast with the records for Elizabeth's ships: only a small fraction of the powder and shot expended in action and huge quantities returned at the end of the campaign.

Only the Portuguese galleons, the sole purpose-built sailing warships in the fleet, seem to have maintained a high rate of fire. Juan Martínez de Recalde, in the 46-gun *San Juan*, reported firing 140 rounds on 31 July (although he received 300 incoming rounds), 130 on 3 August, and 300 rounds on 8 August (against, he thought, 1,000 incoming); while, according to a gunnery officer aboard Medina Sidonia's 48-gun flagship, the *San Martín* fired 120 rounds on 31 July, 120 again on 2 August ('of which some must have caused much damage to the enemy's ships'), 130 on 3 August and 300 on 8 August.[34] Medina Sidonia's special envoy to the king, Don Balthasar de Zúñiga, claimed that after the battle off Gravelines 'they had no ammunition left, not even two roundshot with which to withstand the enemy'; and the duke himself asserted that by then the fleet 'had no artillery balls to fire'.[35] But this could not have been entirely correct, because all of the nine ships for which full information survives (see Figure 5) possessed copious supplies of both powder and shot long after 8 August and the same seems to have been true of others. Medina Sidonia himself provides a crucial clue, for on 4 August he begged the duke of Parma to send him 'a couple of ships with powder and shot of the calibre specified in the memorial attached'. That memorial has apparently not survived but, according to Medina's campaign journal, he asked Parma for 'balls of 4, 6 and 10 pounds, because many of them had been expended during the skirmishes'.[36] Likewise the surviving records – both archaeological and archival – of the various Spanish ships reveal that they fired mostly small shot, even though only larger-calibre ammunition stood much chance of inflicting serious damage on Elizabeth's ships. Thus of the 314 iron shot fired during the 1588 campaign by

Shot expended by ships of the Spanish Armada, 1588

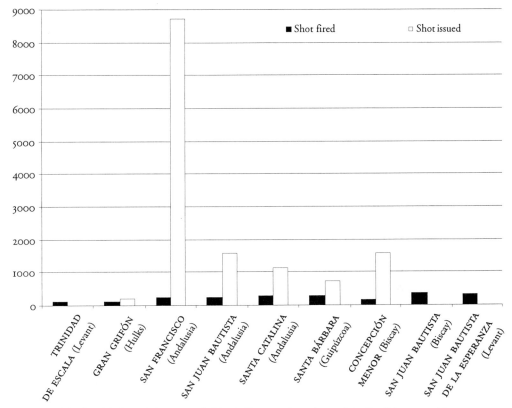

Figure 5   The Spanish Armada kept remarkably similar records to those of the English navy, with one exception: Philip II's clerks noted the issue of shot and other munitions to vessels hired from the private sector but not for the crown's own vessels, whereas the queen's servants appear to have done exactly the reverse. No account apparently survives on the gunnery performance of the galleons of Portugal or Castile, which by common account bore the brunt of the fighting in August 1588. The detailed records assembled for some other ships, however, reveal a consistent pattern: vast quantities of munitions supplied – no doubt some of them for subsequent re-distribution – but remarkably little used. In several cases we know not only the number of rounds issued, but also the number fired day by day and the quantity returned to government store when the fleet got back to Spain. The contrast with Elizabeth's ships (Figure 4) could hardly be more striking. Source: Parker, 'The Dreadnought revolution of Tudor England', 278–9.

the *San Juan Bautista de la Esperanza* (Levant squadron) 'in the fight with the English vice-flagship as well as in others', 41 weighed 5 pounds, 13 weighed 3 and 4 pounds, and 260 weighted 2 pounds or less. Of the 1,640 rounds fired by the nine ships for which detailed records survive, only 175 (11 per cent) exceeded 9 pounds and none exceeded 20 pounds.[37]

This must partially explain why the Armada's substantial expenditure of powder and shot apparently inflicted so little harm on the Royal Navy. Several historians have noted that the English government's own 'Dockyard Survey' of the queen's ships recorded only damage to sails, rigging, masts, boats and superstructures – and precious little of that – with not a single mention of structural damage to hulls.[38] This should occasion no surprise, because responsibility for repairing the hulls of the queen's ships lay with the treasurer of the navy, not with the dockyards, and his accounts for the year 1588 show substantial expenditure on 'the groundinge, gravinge, repairinge and preparinge at Chatham of all her highnes' ships' after the Armada campaign. These structural repairs required over 4,000 metres of planking (ranging from 2 to 9 centimetres thick); 99,500 nails and 1,000 treenails; 15,400 pounds of ironwork; 85 loads of oak and elm timber; and wages for 948 'shipwrights, sawyers and pulleymakers' who worked an average of 35 days each.[39] This total is the largest repair bill found in any of the accounts submitted by the treasurers of the navy during the entire period of the Spanish War, and it indicates that Elizabeth's warships returned to port after the Armada campaign in need of considerable repair.

Nevertheless, these figures must be placed in perspective. First, the total cost only ran to £3,500 (about 14,000 ducats) – the amount required to build or repair just one new warship – in a record expenditure for the year of over £92,000 (roughly 368,000 ducats).[40] Second, although the account provides no detail about which ships received what repairs, something about the scale and nature of the operation can be deduced from the materials supplied. The majority of the planking was 2 and 4 centimetres (some 3,000 metres), which can only have served for the superstructures; the 500 metres of 6-centimetre planks probably went into internal decks; but repairs to the ships' hulls would have required 8-centimetre planking, and of this less than 200 metres were purchased. Likewise the large number of iron nails would have gone into the superstructures, because fastening the hull required treenails – of which only 1,000 were supplied. Third, 85 loads (roughly 85 tons) of timber would not go far, since constructing an Elizabethan galleon required at least 500 loads. Furthermore, the same account reveals that far more repairs took place *before* the campaign against the Armada. Early in 1588, just for Howard's squadron, contractors supplied almost 8,000 metres of planking (over 1,000 metres of it 8-centimetre), 9,000 treenails, 56 'great beams', and 262 loads of oak, elm and maple.[41] In view of all this it seems safe to affirm that Philip's ships failed to inflict serious damage on their adversaries in 1588, even though during the engagement on 8 August (at least) some of them had fired repeated artillery salvoes at very close quarters ('within speech of one another'. Why?

Recent attempts to explain this failure have centred on three technological issues: the larger size, the poor performance, and the inferior gunnery of the Spanish vessels. There is less to these charges than meets the eye. The debate on the relative size of the ships stems largely from the different (and somewhat arcane) systems of measuring vessels at the time; for contemporaries the contrast seemed less significant. Thus in 1586 four Portuguese captains captured and interviewed by John Hawkins compared one of the queen's ships – the *Hope* – with the flagship of the Portuguese squadron: 'it was only slightly smaller than the galleon *San Martín*,' they said, and a comparison of displacements, rather than capacity, confirms this.[42] However, whatever the size, observers on both sides agreed that English 'race-built' galleons, both royal and private, could manoeuvre far more rapidly than their adversaries. Don Diego Pimentel claimed that the English had been 'able to tack four or five times in the time it took us to go about once'; while, according to another senior officer, in comparison with some of their English adversaries, even the swiftest ship in the Armada 'appeared to be standing still'.[43] Moreover, many of Philip's vessels probably did exceed the queen's ships in size, because they were bulk cargo vessels: after all, one of the Armada's primary functions was to transport the munitions, equipment and reinforcements that Parma required for a successful invasion; Elizabeth's fleet simply had to fight.

The evidence concerning gunnery is more complicated. To begin with, even the galleons of Portugal carried a mixed bag of weaponry. Thus the 1,000-ton *San Juan* on which Recalde sailed, built in 1586 and reputed 'the best-gunned ship in the Armada' because 'her artillery was the most uniform in type and weight, being armed with guns made for the purpose', nevertheless carried nothing larger than a 20-pounder, with eight more pieces throwing between 16- and 18-pound shot. Most of the other big guns were periers (stone-throwers), and the majority of the *San Juan*'s 46 guns fired 10 pound balls or less. Moreover (despite the paean to uniformity) her ordnance consisted of no fewer than nine different calibres of iron and six more of stone shot. Among the flagships of other squadrons, the 1,100-ton *Santa Ana* (Guipúzcoa) carried 47 guns, but only three fired 16-pound balls or more; the 1,000-ton *Nuestra Señora del Rosario* (Andalusia) carried 46 guns, of which nine threw 16-pound balls or more; and the 600-ton *San Cristóbal* (Castile) carried 32 guns, the largest two 12-pounder periers.[44] In fact the entire Armada lacked heavy artillery: fewer than 150 of the 2,431 guns known to be aboard the fleet fired 16-pound shot and above, and these belonged to at least twelve different calibres, the heaviest of them siege pieces unsuitable for use at sea. The Royal Navy, by contrast, boasted 250 heavy guns, all belonging to the same three calibres.

Many other guns on the Spanish Armada may also have been ill-suited for use at sea because they rested upon two-wheel carriages with long trails, whereas the queen's ships (at least) used compact four-wheel carriages. Even the first known survey of the Royal Navy, in 1515, recorded that the large guns aboard Henry VIII's warships rested on 'trotills' or 'on four wheels'; and examples of such carriages have been excavated from the wreck of the *Mary Rose*, one of those very ships, which sank thirty years later. By the 1570s, when systematic records begin to survive, the Ordnance Office constructed 'carriages for sea service' with 'truckells' quite differently, and kept them quite separately, from 'land carriages'.[45] This does not seem to have been the case on the Spanish ships. Some guns aboard the Armada were definitely mounted upon very large two-wheeled carriages, some of them expressly intended for land use. Thus in April 1588 Don Pedro de Valdés, commander of the Andalusian squadron, noted that 'The hulk named Santa Ana has a culverin of 31 quintals and 93 pounds of Naples which, because it is very long and is on a land carriage, cannot be used on the said hulk because there is not sufficient space for it.' Valdés therefore ordered the gun to be brought aboard his own, much larger, flagship, *Nuestra Señora del Rosario*, together with 30 rounds and appropriate loading equipment.[46] Excavation of the *Trinidad Valencera*, a Venetian transport embargoed for service with the Armada and wrecked on the coast of Northern Ireland, revealed a massive sea-carriage with a long trail, making an assemblage 6 metres long on a deck barely 12 metres wide.[47] Whether these inappropriate mountings prevailed throughout the fleet is not known, because so far only details of new carriages supplied to the Andalusian squadron have been found; but those had only two wheels, each apparently standing 72 centimetres high.[48]

One last technical factor may have influenced the outcome of the Armada campaign. Many Spanish vessels had fewer gunners than the queen's ships they faced – although only incomplete statistics survive on each side. Thus the number of gunners aboard Elizabeth's warships varied between twenty and forty, while those aboard the ships of the Armada's Andalusian squadron rarely exceeded ten.[49] The former, moreover, were purpose-built warships, the latter merchantmen embargoed as they prepared to sail to America; and in any case, writing some years later, Sir Walter Raleigh held that 'every piece at least requires foure gunners to attend it'.[50] Admittedly Alonso Vanegas, a gunnery officer aboard the Spanish flagship, claimed that a gun captain and his assistant, with six soldiers, served each piece aboard the *San Martín*, under the overall command of a master gunner (*condestable*) and six artillery officers; while Medina Sidonia's battle orders for his ship allocated two artillery officers to each side of the main gundeck, and a senior officer with four assistants (two on each side) on the other.[51] However, as Colin Martin has pointed out, if six soldiers permanently worked each of the flagship's 48 guns, no fewer than 288 of the 302 soldiers aboard would have been tied down. Furthermore, Medina Sidonia's battle orders also stipulated that, once at action stations, all soldiers would serve as infantry, fully armed for combat, with muskets, arquebuses and slow match at the ready; they could hardly then double up as gunners.[52] Elizabeth's captains, by contrast, expected everyone – gentlemen, gunners, sailors – to participate equally in any activity required.[53]

Technology, however, cannot entirely explain the unequal performance of the two fleets in August 1588. Commanders on both sides reckoned that some twenty vessels in each fleet bore the brunt of the action, fighting as well as they could, while the rest tried to keep out of trouble.[54] Moreover the armament (like the size) of those twenty vessels perhaps did not differ greatly: the *San Salvador* and the *Rosario*, although they played no part in the action, carried several guns that their English captors reckoned as cannon, culverin and demi-culverin. The real issue, as noted above, was not how many big guns the Armada carried, but how often and how effectively they fired them.[55]

Philip had not assembled his fleet with a view to fighting and winning a close-range naval duel as a prelude to landing an invincible expeditionary force: rather, as already noted, his Grand Strategy assigned it the role of an armed convoy that would transport supplies and reinforcements to the rendezvous with Parma's army. The king's instructions to the fleet commanders – first Santa Cruz and then Medina Sidonia – stressed that battle should be avoided at almost any cost.

> Since the success of this business consists of going for the root, even if Drake should have set out for these waters with a fleet in order to divert and hinder [you], as some reports from England claim, you are not to be deflected from your journey, but rather continue it without seeking out the enemy.

Admittedly the king allowed three exceptions:

> If [Drake] follows you and comes close, you may in that case attack; and also if you run into Drake and his fleet at the mouth of the Channel, because if the [English] forces are divided, it would be very good to defeat them in this way so that they cannot unite.

And if, finally, the Armada reached the Narrow Seas and found Elizabeth's entire navy defending the coast, then – and only then – Medina was permitted to attack.

Philip's advice on how to win in these circumstances did not correspond to reality, however, and he offered no advice on how exactly Medina should force the English to come close enough to be boarded.[56] In 1587, Philip had prudently allowed Santa Cruz a measure of latitude to disregard his tactical instructions if necessary:

> Since the outcome of wars, and especially of wars at sea, are so subject to fluctuations in the weather and to the uncertainty of the information available to those who command armies and navies, I have absolutely nothing certain to tell you or precise orders to give concerning what should be done with the fleet. Since you are so competent and expert in both, it seemed best to delegate all this to you so that, according to the opportunities that occur, both for the navy to fight and for the pursuit of the pirates [i.e. the English], and in all the other things that may occur during your voyage, you will do whatever seems to you most appropriate.[57]

In 1588, however, Medina received no such dispensation. Instead Philip personally placed at the duke's right hand a naval adviser renowned for his caution.[58] At first sight, Diego Flores de Valdés possessed impressive credentials for the job. He had participated in a peacetime expedition to England in 1554 (bringing Philip II from Corunna to Southampton in order to marry Mary Tudor) and served as second-in-command of the fleet that in 1565 expelled the French from Florida. He had also commanded without mishap the great convoys sailing between Spain and the Caribbean eight times between 1567 and 1580. Since the king saw the Armada in much the same light, and since Flores's experience in this regard was second to none, his posting to the flagship seems less surprising.[59] Nevertheless, his record as commander of the flotilla sent to chase the English from the South Atlantic in 1581–84 had been lacklustre and, early in 1588, on hearing of Flores's appointment to command the squadron of Castile, at least one person warned the king that he would do better to appoint 'a man who is not so timid and so afraid of fighting'.[60]

The advice proved prescient, for throughout the Armada campaign Diego Flores consistently advocated policies that were 'timid' and many subsequently blamed him for the failure of the entire enterprise. His critics included the Armada's second-in-command, Admiral Juan Martínez de Recalde, who had more combat experience than anyone in either fleet – Spanish or English – since he had participated in several naval engagements in the 1570s and in the Terceira campaign. He had also commanded two troop convoys sailing from Spain to Dunkirk (one of which sheltered for a while in the Solent), as well as an amphibious expedition to Smerwick in Ireland.[61]

Recalde's strategic vision differed radically from that of both Philip II and Diego Flores. On 29 July 1588, even before sighting the English coast, the admiral wanted to 'ensure that the enemy comes out to fight, and to incite him to do so', and he therefore advocated a surprise attack on the port of Plymouth, where the English fleet was by then known to be refitting: 'Although I am no friend of bravado, we should try it as we pass before the port [of Plymouth],' he wrote. At a council of war the next day, Recalde and others tried to convince the duke to sail straight to Plymouth and there either bottle up or destroy the English fleet: according to one witness, the council 'agreed that yf they could passe the haven with twenty shipps abrest they would followe that advise'. That same night however – perhaps intentionally – Medina took a decision that prevented this: he ordered the Armada to take in sail and wait, allegedly to rally all his fleet. He subsequently justified his action (to an irate Recalde) by claiming that although the attack on Plymouth 'was discussed by the council, it was not decided upon, nor was it advisable'.[62] This crucial delay gave the English fleet time to get to sea and to gain the weather gauge.

On 1 August, since the English remained resolutely to windward, Recalde urged Medina to turn the Armada around and launch an outright attack, 'and better to do it today than tomorrow, because we are using up our resources while our enemies are increasing theirs'. In another note that day he argued vociferously for attack again: 'We should put all our eggs in one basket, and the sooner the better'. Yet again, the duke remained faithful to Philip's Instructions and kept sailing up the Channel. On the 4th, Recalde offered to lead the entire rearguard of the Armada in pursuit of the English in order either to drive them away or confine them in the Solent, the anchorage between the Isle of Wight and the English mainland. At the same time he strongly opposed proceeding any further up the Channel, where the Armada would lack an adequate anchorage, until the duke of Parma confirmed that he knew of the fleet's approach and had his forces ready for the invasion.[63] For the third time Medina Sidonia rejected his admiral's advice.

Little did Recalde realize that the duke had no choice. In June, as his fleet approached Cape Finisterre, Medina forwarded to the king a copy of his letter to Parma reporting that he had 'consulted the pilots and other experts aboard this fleet who are familiar with the whole coast of England, and asked them to decide in which port this Armada might shelter' while he waited for news that Parma had his forces ready.[64] Philip immediately responded: 'The main point [of the plan] was to go on until you could join hands with the duke my nephew,' he chided. 'I am sure you will have done this, and proceeded to that location and made safe the duke's transit'. If the campaign had gone according to plan Medina would not have received this message until it was too late since the king sent it to Flanders for delivery: it would have remained just another of Philip's misguided but ineffective attempts at micromanagement. As it happened, however, Providence afforded the king an unexpected – and, as it turned out, fatal – opportunity to interfere, because shortly afterwards storms drove the fleet to seek refuge in Corunna, where it remained for a month. Medina Sidonia therefore received a copy of Philip's letter there, together with another admonition a few days later to proceed to Flanders as fast as possible.[65] He dared not disobey now.

The difference of opinion on both strategy and tactics between Recalde and Medina Sidonia reached crisis proportions once the fleet anchored off Calais. The duke's 'log' noted that many of his advisers wanted to 'go on', rather than stop short of both Dunkirk and the Downs; and the admiral later recorded that the decision to halt was taken 'much against my will, because in entering the North Sea the venture was finished'. Recalde felt so strongly that he refused direct orders to attend a meeting of the council of war. When on 7 August the prince of Asculi, a grandee on the general staff, came to summon Recalde to council on Medina Sidonia's flagship, the admiral 'replied that now was not the time to go there and leave his ship, and that his opinion was worth little or nothing. And the prince replied that because his own vote did not count, and because of the confusion that prevailed on the flagship, he [too] had left'. When Medina summoned him again two days later, after the fireship attack and the battle off Gravelines, Recalde at first refused to go 'through anger at seeing the little courage of all and the confusion on the [flag]ship; and because his opinion had not counted for much in some of the earlier meetings [of the council] he did not want to go'. Recalde obeyed the duke's second summons, but only to object to the 'dreadful resolution' to return to Spain around the British Isles, rather than try again to reach Parma.[66]

Would the alternative operational plans proposed by Recalde have snatched victory from the jaws of defeat? Undoubtedly he was right to oppose sailing at full speed towards the Dover straits without some indication that Parma was ready: Medina's expectation that his messengers to Flanders would arrive – let alone return with an answer – in less than a week was patently absurd (p. 234 above). Perhaps, had Philip appointed him to succeed Santa Cruz, Recalde would have received the same discretionary powers to 'do whatever seems to you most appropriate' and might therefore have shortened sail as he advanced up the Channel. This change alone, however, would not have tipped the scales. On the one hand, had the Armada taken refuge in the Solent it would have become vulnerable to a fireship attack similar to the one the English later unleashed off Calais. On the other hand, neither confining the Royal Navy to Plymouth nor 'chasing' it would obviate the need for the fleet to ferry the invasion transports in Flanders across to the coast of Kent, and for that the English fleet had to be defeated or at least cowed. Everything depended on the Armada's ability to fight and win. Recalde clearly believed that this could be achieved – but was he right?

The course of the battle off Gravelines on 8 August, when the two fleets finally engaged fully, offers little support for Recalde's confidence. During the protracted close-quarter combat on that day, the Spanish ships did not manage either to board or to inflict substantial harm on a single English vessel, whereas many of them received extensive damage. Had the engagement occurred in the Channel the previous week, there seems no reason to suppose that the outcome would have been different.[67] Given the inequality in firepower, boarding offered the Armada's only chance of success, and everyone knew it. Thus on 3 August, after four days of heavy skirmishing, Martín de Bertendona tried 'to close with and board the English flagship . . . passing among many English ships, firing cannon at them without stopping in order to reach their flagship . . . and board it'. He failed. The following day Medina Sidonia complained that:

> The enemy's fleet has come to bombard me so that we have had to turn and face them, and most days they have bombarded us from morning until night, without ever letting themselves to go alongside our armada, even though for my part I have done everything possible and given them every occasion – sometimes our ships have been in the middle of their fleet, all to the end that one of their ships should board and so bring on the battle.[68]

English naval writers agreed on the crucial role of boarding. Sir Walter Raleigh later drew attention to the naval battle off São Miguel in 1582, at which the victory of Philip's fleet had hung in the balance until one ship managed to grapple the enemy flagship and thus brought on a general mêlée in which boarding could take place. Had Howard of Effingham allowed this to happen in 1588, Raleigh believed he would have been lost too.[69] It is easy to see why: the Spanish fleet carried almost 20,000 soldiers – more than enough to overwhelm all the queen's ships, which carried only sailors and gunners, had the two fleets become entangled. Howard and his subordinates fully realized this, which is why they took care to avoid contact with any Spanish vessel; but their success in doing so stemmed from more than just tactical skill.

Elizabeth's naval experts had also grasped the vital equation later adumbrated by Admiral 'Jackie' Fisher, the patron of the later and more famous *Dreadnought*: 'Strategy should govern the types of ships to be designed. Ship design, as dictated by strategy, should govern tactics. Tactics should govern details of armament.'[70] Like Fisher, they realized that to protect England effectively against foreign invasion by more numerous opponents required a fleet of ships capable of using stand-off gunnery to keep its enemies at bay until their ships had been either disabled or driven away. They also realized that a government with a coastline to defend that declared war and only then started to mobilize its navy ran grave risks, for a wooden capital ship exceeded the size of many a country house, carried more artillery than a fortress, and required over a year to construct; even after that, it took time to train the officers, gunners and crews for combat. Philip II had started late: having maintained a powerful fleet of galleys and galleasses in the Mediterranean throughout his reign, he only began to create a High Seas fleet in the 1580s – between 1582 and 1584 he ordered nine galleons to be constructed at Santander to serve as escorts for the American treasure fleets, and between 1583 and 1586 he had six more large galleons built for the defence of Portugal. Late in 1587 he authorized a crash programme of cannon-founding at Lisbon – even agreeing that the new guns need not bear the royal arms, in order to save time and money – although in March 1588 he still feared (rightly, as it turned out) that too many of his ships either had too few guns or lacked sufficient guns of heavy calibre.[71] He failed, however, to devise an effective operational doctrine for his new armament.

Philip also failed to devise realistic contingency plans. Admittedly he recognized that, since Elizabeth had enjoyed ample opportunity to improve her defences on land, Parma's army might become bogged down in Kent. Parma's final instructions (this time only sent aboard the fleet, perhaps so that the duke would not have a chance to complain before putting them into effect) therefore decreed that the presence of Spanish forces on English soil should be used to secure three concessions. First, Catholics throughout the realm must be granted toleration and freedom of worship. Second, all English troops must withdraw from the Netherlands, surrendering directly to Spanish forces the towns they held (especially Flushing, which controlled the sea approaches to Antwerp). Third, England should pay a war indemnity – although Parma might drop this demand in return for the main concessions.[72] Philip also foresaw that his fleet might not, in the end, manage to join forces with Parma: then (but only then) he authorized Medina to return and occupy the Isle of Wight. He only turned his thoughts to other possibilities on hearing of the battle of Gravelines and his reaction dramatically illuminates the shortcomings of his overall style of command. On 31 August 1588 he prepared a long memorandum telling the two dukes what they should do if the Armada took refuge in either Scotland or Emden (refit, and discuss ways of effecting the invasion the following year), or if it started on the journey back to Spain (put some troops ashore near Waterford, in order to create a bridgehead for operations the following year). On 15 September, even more unrealistically (as the battered remnants of the fleet anxiously neared the coast of Spain), his ministers drafted orders for Medina Sidonia to land in Scotland, ally with the local Catholics, and winter there.[73]

These attempts by men with no direct experience whatsoever of naval warfare to dictate complex operational choices 1,000 kilometres (and at least two weeks) away highlight once more a critical structural defect in Philip II's Grand Strategy. To be sure, the king's improvised hybrid Armada succeeded (albeit only just) against Dom Antonio's equally heterogeneous force off the Azores in 1582; but the integrated fleet of Elizabeth presented a very different type of challenge because, from the 1570s onward, her naval experts deliberately sought to link her simple yet realistic defence strategy with the appropriate tactics and thus (just as Admiral Fisher later advocated) with an equally appropriate ship design: the heavily gunned 'race-built' galleon. Philip and his advisers, by contrast, devoted little thought to such matters: although the king acquired much useful information on English naval tactics he failed to see their significance (an ironic parallel with Elizabeth's inability to draw the correct conclusions from her intelligence about Philip's intentions). Instead he devised a Grand Strategy that depended for success on operational brilliance by his subordinates – and then proceeded to tie their hands, forbidding both Medina and Parma to depart from their detailed instructions. The king relied on miracles rather than on ministers to overcome any deficiencies. 'I have dedicated this enterprise to God,' he scolded Medina when the duke wanted to abandon the enterprise. 'Get on then and do your part' (p. 107 above). Philip's flawed 'management style' frustrated the Armada's success far more than the loss of secrecy, the lack of communication between the two theatre commanders and the technical differences between the two fleets. His refusal to delegate, his 'zero-defects mentality', his self-generated information overload and his messianic outlook produced grave strategic errors that rendered operational success almost impossible.

10   *After the Armada*

Philip II's attempt to conquer England in 1588 affected different people in different ways. The mother of Thomas Hobbes, the future political philosopher, 'fell in labour with him upon the fright of the invasion of the Spaniards'; by contrast the future High Court judge James Whitelocke, then a freshman at Oxford, dismissed in his journal 'the terrible shew of the sea armada from Spaigne' as just 'a little distemper to the quiet course of study'.[1] Some of their compatriots developed a sudden urge to learn Spanish: the first Spanish–English dictionary came out shortly afterwards (compiled with the aid of some Armada prisoners), as did translations of several Spanish works, especially military.[2] For the thousands of English sailors who died aboard the victorious fleet and for their families, however, the Armada proved a catastrophe; while for their government it almost brought bankruptcy – in July, as he listed the outstanding obligations that he could not pay, Lord Treasurer Burghley insensitively marvelled that, although the number of men aboard the fleet dwindled through disease and death, their wage bill did not (see p. 227 above). Even success had its cost: England now faced an implacable foe who would need to be opposed with a well-maintained navy at sea as well as with subsidies and expeditionary forces on the continent. As Secretary of State Walsingham sighed in 1589 of the expensive Dutch alliance: 'I wyshe that our fortune and theirs were not so straytely tyed as yt is, so as we cannot well untye withowt great hasard'.[3] England fought on for another fifteen years, plunging the Tudor state deep into debt.

The impact of the Armada upon Spain, of course, far exceeded this. Philip II himself put the cost of the abortive enterprise at 10 million ducats, and the taxes voted to make good the deficit provoked rioting in some cities of Castile and depopulation in parts of the countryside.[4] Other losses proved less easy to remedy: almost all of Spain's experienced naval commanders died, became prisoners or suffered disgrace (of the eight squadron commanders who left Lisbon in May 1588 only one, Martín de Bertendona, remained at his post in December); and at least half of the soldiers and sailors who sailed for England perished before the year ended – a total of perhaps 15,000 men. Even in hospital, survivors continued to die of illnesses contracted during the journey, while the families of the missing

moved forlornly from one northern port to another in search of news. According
to one friar at the Escorial, 'it was the greatest disaster to strike Spain in over six
hundred years', while another deemed it a misfortune 'worthy to be wept over for
ever . . . because it lost us the respect and good reputation that we used to have
among warlike people . . . The grief it caused in all of Spain was extraordinary:
almost the entire country went into mourning . . . People talked of nothing else.'[5]
Criticisms of the king and of his expensive policies, which had largely ceased since
the conquest of Portugal, now recommenced. Some blamed him for choosing a
strategy that 'could never have worked'; others even attributed the failure to his
personal sins. The 'nun of Lisbon' began to have nationalist dreams, claiming that
'the kingdom of Portugal does not belong to Philip II but to the Braganza family',
until the Inquisition arrested her (and found that her 'stigmata' washed off with
soap and water); while in Madrid the widely reported dreams of Lucrecia de León
also turned to politics – criticizing Philip for oppression of the poor, squandering
tax revenues on the Escorial, and failing to maintain the greatness of Spain – until
the Inquisition arrested her too.[6]

The scale of the disaster, and the criticisms it occasioned, affected the king. On
31 August, when the first news arrived from Parma that the junction with Medina
Sidonia had not taken place, Secretary of State Idiáquez could not

> exaggerate the grief caused by seeing something that cost so much time, money
> and trouble – and is so important to the service of God and His Majesty –
> placed in jeopardy, just at the point where it was about to bear fruit. His
> Majesty has felt it more than you would believe possible, and without some
> remaining hope in God that all this might have achieved something for His
> cause . . . I do not know how he could bear such a great blow. Certainly this
> leaves no time to think about anything else, nor to think of it without excessive
> grief.

The passage of time brought no relief. Four days later, a courier from France
brought more detailed news concerning the Armada's ignominious northward
flight. The ministers blanched, and debated which of them should break the
news to the king. The choice fell upon Mateo Vázquez; but even he elected to
work through an intermediary, forwarding a letter from a (singularly tactless)
courtier which suggested that 'when we consider the case of King Louis IX of
France, who was a saint and was engaged on a saintly enterprise [the Seventh
Crusade in 1250], and yet saw his army die of plague, with himself defeated and
captured, we certainly cannot fail to fear greatly for the outcome [of our enter-
prise]'. This proved too much for the king: 'I hope that God has not permitted so
much evil,' he scribbled angrily on the letter, 'for everything has been done for
His service'.[7]

Even when news of the disaster that had befallen the fleet began to arrive, about
a month later, the king's stoicism persisted. In October, for example, he ordered
prayers for the fleet's success to cease, to be replaced by a solemn thanksgiving

Mass in each diocese that not everything had been lost and a new round of devotions 'by all clerics, and other suitably devout persons . . . entrusting to Our Lord most sincerely in their private and secret prayers all my actions, so that His Divine Majesty may direct and guide them to whatever may serve Him, the exaltation of His church, and the good and conservation of Christendom – which is what I desire'.[8] As reports of the losses relentlessly multiplied, however, Philip came to feel that God had abandoned him. One day in November 1588 – as on at least one occasion during the crisis of 1574 (p. 43 above) – he confided to his secretary that he longed for death because:

> Very soon we shall find ourselves in such a state that we shall wish that we had never been born . . . And if God does not send us a miracle (which is what I hope from Him), I hope to die and go to Him before this happens – which is what I pray for, so as not to see so much misfortune and disgrace . . . Please God let me be mistaken, although I do not think I am. Rather we shall have to witness, quicker than anyone thinks, what we so much fear, unless God returns to support His cause.[9]

The king's depression did not last long, however. Two days later he ordered the council of State to discuss the correct policy to follow in the light of the Armada's failure; and when they forwarded a report that unanimously rejected a defensive posture (on the grounds that it would cost almost as much as a new offensive but would do nothing to bring the war to an end), and instead urged the concentration of forces for a new expedition that would 'sail straight to England and try to conquer it', the king welcomed it with enthusiasm.

> I rejoiced greatly to read all that these papers said, which corresponds perfectly to what one might expect from those who said it, and to the intention that has inclined me to this enterprise since the beginning, for the service of Our Lord, the defence of His cause and the benefit of these realms . . . I undertake to deal swiftly with everything necessary to achieve all this, and to remember all the things that are necessary . . . I shall never fail to stand up for the cause of God and the well-being of these kingdoms.

The king now asked the Cortes to vote a new tax to cover the cost of these measures. Here too he met with a favourable response: 'Everything possible must be done . . . to defeat [the English], to repair the recent loss, and to restore the reputation of our nation,' the proctor from Toledo asserted, and in 1590 the assembly voted a new tax of 8 million ducats payable over six years.[10]

Almost immediately a Spanish High Seas fleet began to take shape. The Armada of 1588 had included few royal ships – the galleons of Portugal; the Mediterranean galleasses; the escort vessels from the transatlantic convoys – but now the king ordered the construction of new galleons with a more stream-lined design and a 22-gun broadside, while his captain-general of artillery called for 'Each ship to carry guns that are appropriate to its size and weight, and of a sort that can do damage from a distance because of their good range, and from close range wreak notable destruction on the enemy fleet.' By 1591, 21 new galleons and 500 tons of naval ordnance had entered service, and in that year Spain's reconstituted navy drove the main English fleet away from the Azores, where it had hoped to intercept the returning treasure fleet, and captured the *Revenge*. By 1598 Philip's Atlantic fleet numbered 53 royal warships. To the Italian political philosopher Giovanni Botero, writing at this time, the Spanish Monarchy appeared a sort of thalassocracy whose component parts, although separated from one another, 'should not be deemed disconnected because . . . they are united by the sea. There is not a dominion, however distant it may be, that cannot be defended by naval force'.[11]

The king and his ministers had learned a good deal from the strategic and tactical miscalculations of the 1570s and 1580s. Almost immediately, however, developments elsewhere began to compromise their new plan. In January 1589 news arrived that Henry III had murdered the duke of Guise, Philip's client and ally, the previous month. Everyone immediately recognized that the task of defending the Catholics of France now devolved upon Spain, and that 'the amount of money required will ruin the preparations we are making here' to attack Elizabeth again. They therefore resolved that aid to the League should remain clandestine for as long as possible because, as one councillor put it:

> The temptation to declare war on France is great; nevertheless, when we consider the state of this Monarchy, the open war with England (so powerful at sea), and the pressure that our rebels and enemies [in the Netherlands] will bring to bear on His Majesty, we must not declare war on France under any circumstances.[12]

The king agreed: he continued to restrict his support for the French Catholic cause to discreet (albeit substantial) financial assistance. His only change of policy concerned the duke of Savoy's seizure of the strategic French enclave of Saluzzo at the end of 1588: having initially resolved to order its return, in the light of Guise's murder he now agreed that Savoy should retain it.[13] In all other respects Philip continued to concentrate on England.

His plan of campaign soon became just as unrealistic as that of the preceding year. In May 1589, as part of his new strategy to 'wage war in the enemy's own house', he sent money to enable Parma to prepare men and ships for a surprise attack on the Isle of Wight that would create a diversion while a new fleet from Spain sailed up the Channel to deliver the *coup de grâce*. The decision to involve the Army of Flanders once again flew in the face of almost all the advice tendered to the king: even before the Armada set forth the previous year Bernardino de Escalante, the soldier-priest who had played a large part in devising the initial strategy (see p. 186 above), sent an urgent warning against making a junction between Parma and Medina Sidonia the essential prelude for the invasion; and afterwards he, like many other commentators (including some participants), blamed this requirement for the failure of the enterprise.[14]

In the event the new plan remained a dead letter because a massive (if misman-aged) Anglo-Dutch fleet attacked both Spain and Portugal for most of the summer of 1589, twice putting ashore an expeditionary force (something the Armada had totally failed to do) and causing widespread panic, while another English squadron lay off the Azores hoping to ambush the returning treasure fleets.[15] In addition, a Catholic fanatic murdered the French king, transforming the entire strategic scene. In many ways Henry III had served Philip's purposes well. Although fundamentally hostile to Spain, Henry lacked the resources to do much, especially after the death of his brother Anjou in 1584: his Protestant and his Catholic subjects despised and distrusted him in almost equal measure, and the royal treasury lay empty. The only scenario that might have seemed preferable to Philip would have been Henry's death, leaving a healthy young son to be brought up by the Guise family during a lengthy minority; but Henry, like all his brothers, sired no legitimate male children and so after his death a good number of his French subjects and all of his Protestant neighbours immediately recognized his nearest male relative, Henry of Navarre the Huguenot leader, as King Henry IV.

Philip could not accept this – indeed he did not even recognize Henry's title to Navarre (he himself claimed to be its king and referred to Henry dismissively as 'Vendôme') – and so warned the duke of Parma of the critical implications of these developments in France:

> My principal aim [there] is to secure the well-being of the Faith, and to see that in France Catholicism survives and heresy is excluded . . . If, in order to ensure this exclusion and to aid the Catholics so that they prevail, you see that it is necessary for my troops to enter France openly [then you must lead them in].

This would inevitably mean both postponing the surprise attack on the Isle of Wight – even had it proved feasible – and scaling down the war against the Dutch; so, the king continued prudently, since

> The affairs of France create obligations that we cannot fail to fulfil because of their extreme importance; and since we must not undertake too many things at once, because of the risk that they will all fail (and because my treasury will not allow it), it seems that we must do something about the war in the Nether-lands, reducing it to a defensive footing.

Philip therefore ordered that the elite troops of the Army of Flanders should be maintained on stand-by, ready to intervene in France immediately should need arise.[16]

Parma, fearing the strategic dilemma that now threatened to engulf him, responded with the suggestion that the king should open peace talks with the

Dutch, offering to permit the private exercise of Calvinist worship in certain towns of Holland and Zealand for an indefinite period if 'the rebels' promised to 'return to obedience' (which he construed as ordering the demobilization of their armed forces and the open toleration of Catholic worship). The king's councillors in Madrid debated this peace plan indecisively in November 1589: on the one hand, they recognized that to concede toleration to the Dutch would forfeit 'the claim His Majesty has made, and the reputation he has won at the cost of so much treasure and so many lives, not to concede one jot or tittle in matters of religion'; on the other, they lamented, 'to attempt to conquer the rebellious provinces by force is to speak of a war without end'. The king agreed: he resolved to ask the pope either to start contributing directly to the cost of fighting the Dutch ('since this war is being waged solely for religion') or to permit peace talks to begin. In the meantime Parma received authorization to see whether the rebels might be willing to negotiate a settlement.[17]

Yet again, however, new strategic pressures intervened. In February 1590, Henry of Navarre's decision to blockade Paris (the League's capital since the Day of the Barricades, p. 200 above) raised the possibility that unless the French Catholics received open and substantial military aid their resistance might collapse. The Spanish council of State now debated a number of possible strategies: a descent by Parma and the Army of Flanders in the north to relieve Paris; landing an expeditionary force from Spain in Brittany in the west; and a thrust by land forces from Aragon into Languedoc or Béarn in the south. The council felt that one operation would not be enough to save the Catholic cause, whereas three would overtax Spain's resources; they therefore suggested that the fleet destined for a new assault on England should instead land troops in Brittany, while the Army of Flanders should invade northern France instead of attacking the Isle of Wight.[18] Navarre's crushing victory over his Catholic opponents at Ivry in March 1590 confirmed the need for action and, immediately upon hearing of the battle, Philip informed Parma that 'the strategy for assisting the French Catholic cause that I have followed, although the correct one until now, will not serve any longer'. He commanded the duke to invade France at once with 20,000 men. They left the Netherlands in late July and entered Paris in triumph in September. One month later an expeditionary force of 3,000 men from Spain arrived at St Nazaire in Brittany both to reinforce the French Catholics there and to create a fortified base for future operations against England.[19] The king saw no alternative to these expensive commitments. As he explained to one of his wealthiest subjects, as he requested a donation:

> Everybody knows about the great, continuous and unavoidable expenses that I have incurred for many years past to defend our holy Catholic faith and to conserve my kingdoms and lordships, and how they have grown immensely through the war with England and the developments in France; but I have not been able to avoid them, both because I have such a specific obligation to God

and the world to act, and also because if the heretics were to prevail (which I hope God will not allow) it might open the door to worse damage and dangers, and to war at home.

At least the king decided to reconsider his position on the Dutch problem: in November 1590 he informed the pope that he stood ready to concede toleration to his rebels for a limited time in return for recognition of his sovereignty, and requested the appointment of papal and imperial intermediaries to handle negotiations to secure this. He even hoped for a cease-fire during the talks.[20]

Naturally, he hoped in vain. As in 1576 (see p. 144 above) the king's decision to offer important concessions – made only when he really had no alternative – came too late. Although the Dutch went through the motions of negotiating, as soon as Parma intervened in France they launched a series of campaigns which recovered much of Gelderland and Overijssel in 1591–92. So Philip now found himself with not one but three 'voracious monsters gobbling up the troops and treasure of Spain'.[21] In 1591 a fourth appeared: a ham-fisted attempt by the government to extradite a fugitive from justice in Zaragoza provoked major rioting which turned into open rebellion in September. The following month, with remarkable promptitude, a royal army of 14,000 troops invaded Aragon and swiftly restored order – but only at a cost of almost 1.5 million ducats, diverted from the funds earmarked for Philip's wars abroad.[22]

The rapidly worsening strategic position of the Monarchy alarmed the king. In January 1591, even before the troubles in Aragon, Philip regretted that the affairs of his Monarchy 'do not depend on my will, or on my wanting it, but rather on many other matters that are hard to arrange. Everything is in a terrible state unless God remedies it'. The following month Mateo Vázquez warned his master that 'if God had placed Your Majesty under an obligation to remedy all the troubles of the world, He would have given you the money and the strength to do so'; while in September 1591 Escalante advised that under no circumstances should Spain intervene openly in France or use force in Aragon – rather, all available resources should remain reserved for operations against England. Escalante compared the Anglo-Spanish struggle to that of Rome against Carthage, and argued that only a direct attack on England would stop Elizabeth and her subjects from supporting the Dutch, ravaging the Indies, and attacking Spanish ports and ships. Admittedly, Philip's decision to intervene openly in France achieved important short-term results (without it, the League would almost certainly have collapsed in 1592); but now the two sides in the French civil war stood fairly evenly matched so that Spain – just as Escalante had predicted – faced the prospect of another 'war without end' to sustain. In this stressful situation, as in earlier crises, the king oscillated between bitter fatalism and messianic euphoria. He may never have seen Escalante's (somewhat verbose) admonition; but to Vázquez he replied grandly:

I know you are moved by the great zeal you have for my service to say what you did, but you must also understand that these are not matters that can be abandoned by a person who is as conscientious about his responsibilities as you know me to be.

'The cause of religion', the king concluded, 'must take precedence over everything'.[23] Like his Bourbon descendants two centuries later, Philip seemed to have learned nothing and forgotten nothing.

If the principles of Philip's Grand Strategy remained the same despite the Armada's failure, so did the practice. He continued to rely on God to intervene in case Spain's resources alone proved inadequate. Thus in October 1596 he deployed precisely the same arsenal of spiritual blackmail that he had used in the past against Alba, Santa Cruz and Medina Sidonia, in order to persuade the dispirited commander of his new High Seas fleet to sail immediately against England.

I tell you again and order you expressly . . . to leave in the name of God and do what I have ordered in the voyage and in the whole campaign. Although I see that the season is advanced, and the risks that this poses, we have to trust in God (who has done so much for us) in this. To stop what we have begun now would be to show weakness in His service, to spend money without profit, and to find ourselves without troops in time of need. Since these are definite disadvantages, it would not be sensible to allow them. It is also [our] Christian duty to put into effect what we have done and you, in any case, must aid me now to achieve it. May God guide you, and I trust in Him that there will be much to thank Him – and you – for.[24]

Furthermore, the king still permitted no debate over his perception of Spain's strategic needs. When Admiral Bertendona went to Court in June 1589 and requested an opportunity to give his sovereign some advice 'in case there should be a campaign against England next year', Philip characteristically replied: 'you can tell me about it in writing, since there is no opportunity to do it in person'. Equally characteristically, shortly afterwards he asked Bertendona to send him detailed information on naval affairs, 'because I would like to be informed of what occurs to you for when we take a decision on the matters you raise'.[25]

Although after the death of Mateo Vázquez in 1591 the volume of Philip's surviving personal papers dwindles dramatically, making it harder to generalize about his intentions, nothing suggests a major change in his outlook or his priorities. He took some anti-tax riots in Castile and the revolt of Aragon in his stride, and when some proctors in the Cortes of Castile protested in 1596 against the heavy expenditure on foreign wars, pointing out that 'although the wars against the Dutch, the English and the French are holy and just, we must beg Your Majesty that they may cease', Philip firmly rebuked the representatives of the people for their presumption.

They should and must put their trust in me, in the love I have for these kingdoms, and in the long experience I have in governing them, [and accept] that I shall always do what is in their best interests. Speak to them at length in this vein and advise them that they are never, on any pretext, to come to me with such a suggestion again.[26]

He also took more practical steps to neutralize this opposition: 'the theologians of Madrid should be forewarned', he wrote, 'so that if the deputies of the Cortes should turn to them for advice, they may include in their opinions a full account of my case' (more sinister, he also expected the theologians to report the intentions of their advisees to his agents). The government furthermore ordered theologians in the other towns represented in the Cortes 'to assure the consciences of the scrupulous' and to mobilize support for royal policies both through personal meetings and through written (sometimes published) tracts.[27]

These repeated efforts at spiritual blackmail reflected a perceptible reduction in Philip's ability to get things done. In the early 1590s, every morning he discussed financial and domestic business with his chamberlain, Don Cristóbal de Moura, who also dressed him and massaged his feet; after lunch he handled Italian and Aragonese business with the count of Chinchón; and he spent every afternoon and evening with his principal secretary of state, Don Juan de Idiáquez, dealing with foreign affairs. As the years passed, the king spent more time at prayer, more time asleep, and more time sick: illness prevented him from transacting business in May and June 1595, in March and April 1596, in spring 1597 and for most of 1598, the year of his death. After 1595 he spent most of his days in the sixteenth-century equivalent of a wheelchair – a sort of lounger with movable positions from vertical to horizontal – in which he ate, worked and slept, wearing loose garments that did not put pressure on his arthritic joints (Plate 33). He could not manage to stand for the last two years of his life. Although in 1594 he began to make use of Prince Philip for routine decisions, and although after 1597 the prince signed all outgoing orders, the king relied increasingly on Moura to convey his commands to all ortgans of state and his meandering apostils on incoming documents gave way to those of his chamberlain who now decided 'the business of all his kingdoms, councils, armies, fleets, ministers and treasury'.[28]

Moura and his ailing master could not always produce the results they wanted: they and their overworked associates encountered with increasing frequency the response 'I obey but I do not execute.' Thus in 1596 the king intervened personally to command the governor of Milan to expel the small Jewish community from the state (something he had attempted unsuccessfully in the past), adding with his own hand the threat that 'If this is not done at once, it will be necessary to send someone from here to do it'; three months later, however, another letter was required, promising to 'discover and punish whoever is to blame for these delays'.[29] In October 1597 the sailors aboard the High Seas fleet refused direct orders to set sail against England: astonished observers witnessed the commander-in-chief, Don Martín de Padilla, whose ship (alone) had put to sea, coming back

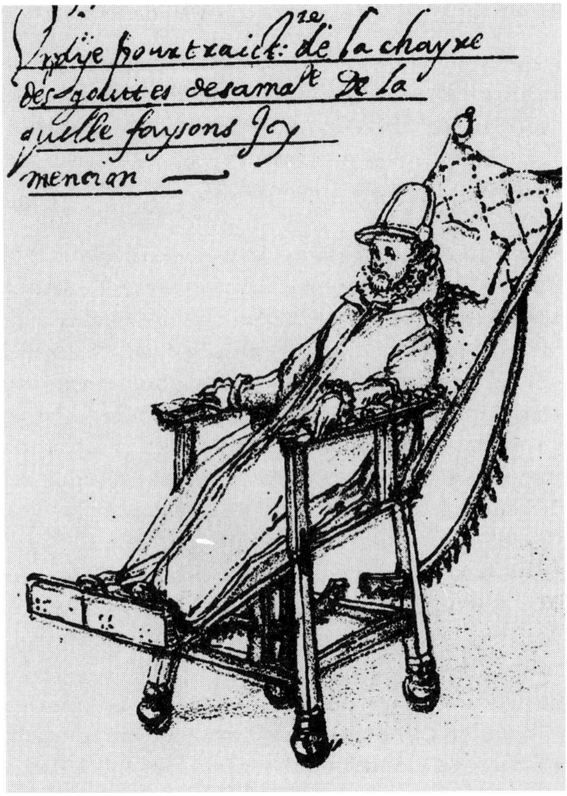

Plate 33 Philip II in his 'wheelchair' and 'babygro suit', from Jehan Lhermite's *Passetemps*. Philip lived longer than any other member of his dynasty, but for his last two years arthritis prevented him from standing up. His Flemish valet, Jehan Lhermite, described and illustrated the special loose-fitting garments that the king wore in order to ease the pressure on his joints, and also the ingenious chair with various settings that enabled him both to sit and sleep without having to stand. From this contraption – in which he also travelled between his various palaces – he governed his world-wide empire until his last illness in 1598.

in a skiff and being rowed from one ship to another 'going to extraordinary lengths to force them out of the harbour . . . on account of the ill-will they felt towards the enterprise, seeing how late in the season it was and the great dearth of everything necessary for a successful outcome'.[30]

Meanwhile, mutinies disabled the king's armies both in France (forcing his commanders to make a truce with Henry IV in 1593) and in the Netherlands (where at least twenty military revolts occurred between 1589 and 1598). In 1595, a beleaguered theatre commander of the Army of Flanders invited his superiors 'to consider the misery and desperation of the poor soldiers in Friesland and Gelderland, and how much courage they will have to resist the enemies' forces with empty stomachs'. Spanish troops in Brittany wasted one opportunity after another for lack of support, and armies sent to reinforce the French Catholic bases in Burgundy and Languedoc both failed miserably.[31] Philip's only success in this period was to prolong the Irish rebellion against Elizabeth: in May 1596 its leader, the earl of Tyrone, had been on the point of making peace when Spanish agents arrived bearing promises of aid, closely followed by some much-needed munitions. England took its revenge two months later, when a large amphibious force captured Cadiz and held it unchallenged for two weeks. As the invaders sailed away they smugly noted that the fires they had started in the city 'kept on burning in our view until Wednesday night following, at which time we lost sight thereof'. In addition, the invaders took away with them two of Philip's new galleons (and two more only escaped the same fate because their crews set fire to them first). Spain's merchant fleet at Cadiz, preparing to sail to America, lost twenty-eight ships and goods worth 4 million ducats.[32]

Eventually, as in 1575–76, prodigal expenditure on too many fronts led first to financial and then to moral collapse. In November 1596, Philip once again suspended all payments from his treasury and began to recognize the unavoidable need to make peace, at least temporarily, with some of his enemies. The following year he accepted papal offers to mediate a settlement with Henry IV of France, and the peace signed at Vervins in May 1598 in essence confirmed the terms agreed at Cateau-Cambrésis thirty-nine years before. Admittedly Philip lost no territory, but he had spent millions of ducats – and sacrificed numerous outposts in the Netherlands to the Dutch – in order to oblige Henry of Navarre to become a Catholic again.[33] Later in 1598 he also signed an act bequeathing the Netherlands to his daughter, Isabella, betrothed to his nephew Albert (son of Maximilian and María, whom Charles V had once considered making rulers of the Netherlands: pp. 88–9 above). They were to be independent of Spain in all matters except foreign policy and defence, for Philip intended to maintain the Army of Flanders at full strength both to defend the new sovereigns against the Dutch, and as a weapon to use in the continuing war against England. The king hoped that the partial severance of the link between Spain and the Netherlands – under discussion since the 1540s – would restore a balance of power in Europe and therefore reduce the international pressure on his Monarchy.

Philip III, who succeeded in September 1598, continued his late father's policies: he confirmed the transfer of the Netherlands to his sister and brother-in-law and supplied them with the resources to mount a new offensive against the Dutch; he avoided war with France (even in 1600 when Henry IV attacked his other brother-in-law, the duke of Savoy); and he made new efforts to defeat England. All these initiatives failed. In 1599 a new Armada intended to attack England had to be diverted to defend the Azores against a powerful Anglo-Dutch fleet. In 1601 when Spain finally managed to put an army ashore to support the Irish rebellion led by the earl of Tyrone against Elizabeth, it landed at Kinsale, far from the rebels' bases and (in effect) lured Tyrone to defeat by forcing him to march hundreds of miles in the depths of winter to Kinsale, where the English lay in wait. The Spaniards capitulated soon afterwards and went home, leaving the Irish leaders to surrender and do homage to Elizabeth. Meanwhile mutinies continued to paralyse the Army of Flanders and in 1600 the Dutch inflicted heavy losses at the battle of Nieuwpoort. Undeterred, Philip III continued his efforts to achieve victory in the Netherlands and in 1602 promised (in terms reminiscent of his father) that 'in order to restore those provinces entirely to the Catholic faith and to ensure that they do not leave obedience to . . . this crown, I will devote and venture everything that God has entrusted to me, and my own person'. England, however, was different: following the death of Elizabeth in 1603 Philip concluded first a cease-fire and then a peace with her successor, James VI of Scotland, which more or less restored the pre-war situation. Philip received no promises of toleration for English Catholics or of English abstention from trade in the East and West Indies. But at least the peace left Spain free to concentrate – for the first time since 1585 – on the Netherlands. Despite some highly successful campaigns there, however, in 1609 Philip III signed a Twelve Year Truce which explicitly recognized the rebellious provinces 'as if they were a sovereign nation', with no obligation either to admit Spanish sovereignty or to tolerate any religion besides Calvinism – the two issues on which Spain had insisted since 1572. Nor would they agree to keep the peace outside Europe.[34]

Philip II's strategic achievements fell far short of expectations, and the pessimistic assessments of his Monarchy by Balthasar Álamos de Barrientos and Martín González de Cellorigo just after the king's death (p. 108 above) contained much truth. Despite huge sacrifices of men, money and prestige he failed to preserve the territories he had inherited from his father: the seven northern provinces of the Netherlands never again accepted Habsburg rule or papal authority and their ships traded with impunity from the 1590s onwards in the Americas, Africa and Asia, forcing Spain to spend heavily on defence. England, too, remained defiantly outside both the Habsburg orbit and the Catholic church, and its vessels also sailed to America and to Africa: privateering at the expense of Philip's subjects enriched many Elizabethans. Even in the Mediterranean, Dutch and English merchants defied Spanish prohibitions and traded with both Christian and Muslim states, forming clandestine alliances with many of Philip's enemies. Spanish influence in Germany reached its nadir in the 1590s when the princes of the empire mobilized against the Army of Flanders as it attempted to winter in Westphalia; and although Philip's pressure forced Henry of Navarre to reconvert to Catholicism in order to end the French Religious Wars, he remained Spain's implacable foe. To be sure, Philip added both the Portuguese empire and the Philippines to his possessions, but by the end of the reign it had become clear that he could not defend the former adequately and within another decade the latter had entered a semi-permanent state of siege. Both cost far more to defend than they ever produced in revenues for the crown. Finally, within Spain, a devastating plague epidemic struck a population already weakened by a run of bad harvests: in the words of Mateo Alemán's mordant novel of 1599, *Guzmán de Alfarache*, 'the hunger that rose from Andalusia met the plague that descended from Castile'. Perhaps 10 per cent of the kingdom's population died and men began to write openly of 'the decline of Spain'.

To what extent, historians may wonder, did the policies of Philip II contribute to this series of disasters, and to what extent were they the inevitable consequences of structural factors? Might another strategic culture, a different Grand Strategy, or a better execution of policy have secured a different outcome?

Conclusion: Agent and Structure

It cannot be a law that all nations shall fall after a certain number of years. God does not work in that sort of way: they must have broken some law of nature which has caused them to fall. But are all nations to sink in that way? As if national soil, like the soil of the earth, must lie fallow after a certain number of crops. And will England turn into Picts again after a certain number of harvest years? Or will a nation find out at last the laws of God by which she may make a steady progression?

(Florence Nightingale, letter from Egypt, 1849)[1]

In the decade after the Armada many searched for some 'law of nature' that would explain Spain's various strategic failures. Don Martín de Padilla, the unsuccessful commander of the armadas of 1596 and 1597, noted that:

Although our desire to reduce the Netherlands and England to the obedience of God and Your Majesty is, of itself, good, it seems that God has not wanted to accept this service, a circumstance that must arouse great concern because Our Lord does not usually inflict such reverses except for very good reasons. We have attributed past losses to material causes – sometimes blaming the councillors, sometimes the storms and other things – keeping our eyes on the stone that harmed us and not on the arm from which it came. Therefore the deductions we drew from one failure only set us up for another, thinking that if last year we went wrong by leaving too late, next year we would succeed if we got ready earlier; and so God permitted the selfsame errors that caused the past reverses to cause the next ones.[2]

Many Spanish analysts did indeed tend to 'keep their eyes on the stone that harmed us' – even in the 1620s and 1630s, men continued to ascribe the Armada's fate in 1588 solely to material factors such as the inferior design of Spanish galleons – but Padilla himself had already drawn a different conclusion. Immediately after the humiliating English capture and sack of Cadiz he warned Philip:

281

No power exists that can maintain continuous wars, and even for the greatest monarch it is important to conclude wars rapidly. There will be many who would consider this desirable, saying that the policy we now follow will never end the war and that the expenditure in men and money is enormous; and that if another cure is not found the patient will soon die.

Padilla therefore recommended concentrating all the king's resources for a while on just one objective – another all-out attack on England – which would force Elizabeth to make a peace favourable to Spain, ushering in what 'will with reason be called a happy and golden century'. He was disappointed: although some detected a 'siglo dorado', few considered it happy.

After Philip's death Padilla addressed another withering assessment of Spain's strategic culture to the new king.

I have been much grieved for some years past to see that, for motives of economy, expeditions are undertaken with such small forces that they principally serve to irritate our enemies, rather than to punish them. The worst of it is that wars thus become chronic, and the expense and trouble resulting from long continued wars are endless.

Other ministers took up Padilla's theme. According to the duke of Sessa, an experienced diplomat,

We flit so rapidly from one area to another, without making a major effort in one and then, when that is finished, in another . . . I do not know why we eat so many snacks but never a real meal! I would like to join everything together, so that we could perhaps do something worthwhile – either in Ireland or in North Africa – but I fear that, as usual, we shall do both and thus only lose time, men, money and reputation.

For both Padilla and Sessa, the central defect of Spanish Grand Strategy lay in taking on too many commitments, which fatally compromised the government's ability to succeed in any of them. Admittedly, Philip II had tried to concentrate all his available resources on delivering a rapid knock-out blow whenever a new problem occurred: against the French in Florida in 1565–66, in the Netherlands in 1566–67 (with total success) and again in 1572–73 (with almost total success), against Portugal and the Azores in 1580–83 (again with total success), and against England in 1586–88. If the initial blow miscarried, however, he seemed incapable of cutting his losses; instead, his forces continued to fight on several fronts, despite the fact that the Monarchy's other commitments could not be ignored indefinitely, and despite the risk that (as the duke of Alba put it in 1573 'if some new problem, however small, were to arise, His Majesty's resources are so exhausted that he might not have the strength to resist'.[3]

*   *   *

Why, then, did Philip wait so long before concluding settlements that could have been made years (if not decades) before? First, and most obvious, no political leader likes to lose; but there is more to this simple statement than meets the eye. International relations analysts have found that 'prospect theory' helps to explain why statesmen act with such tenacity to retain what they have: government policy, they argue, is shaped by individuals who – like most people – tend to think in terms of gains and losses, rather than of assets. Because the psychological world is not symmetrical, however, most people seem prepared to take more risks to avoid a loss than to make a gain. Three interesting implications have been suggested for international relations, both today and in the sixteenth century: first, statesmen – like other people – may be disposed to pay a higher price and run higher risks when they face losses than when they seek gains; second, and in consequence, measures of deterrence are more likely to succeed against statesmen trying to make gains than against those driven by the fear of losses. Third and finally, conflicts tend to be more common – and to last longer – when both sides believe that they are defending the status quo, because each believes it will suffer losses unless it takes strong if not aggressive action.[4]

Prospect theory is particularly relevant in the case of Philip II because of the geographically fragmented nature of his Monarchy, created by inheritance rather than by conquest – or, in the aphorism of the time, *Bella gerant alii. Tu, felix Austria, nube* ('Others make war; you, happy Habsburgs, marry'). The marriage of Maximilian of Habsburg with Mary of Burgundy had linked the lands of the house of Austria in east central Europe with the distant Netherlands; while the marriage of their son Philip with Juana of Trastámara eventually added equally distant Castile (with its acquisitions in North Africa and the Americas) and Aragon (with outposts in Sardinia, Sicily and Naples). By 1519 their son Charles V had succeeded to all these scattered territories and aspirations, and added the imperial dignity as well. Little, however, linked his vast dominions except the dynasty: the emperor's various possessions had no common language or currency, no common institutions or laws, and no imperial defence plan or imperial economic system. Although Philip II did not succeed his father as emperor, in 1580–83 he enforced his inherited claim to the crown of Portugal and its global empire, thereby acquiring yet another major polity with its own separate system of government. Fear of forfeiting any part of these exposed acquisitions led the king to persevere in losing ventures. Moreover, thanks to the 'domino theory' which suggested that failure to defend or deter adequately in one area would foment challenges elsewhere (pp. 89–90 above), he normally seemed prepared to pay a high price to avoid even limited defeats.

As a Spanish diplomat observed in 1600, 'I believe we are gradually becoming the target at which the whole world wants to shoot its arrows' – that is, the empire on which the sun never set had become a target on which the sun never set. The geographical dispersion of Philip's dominions created difficulties in most areas. For example Ambrosio Spínola, commander-in-chief of the Army of Flanders, once pointed out that:

I have noticed something that will seem strange there [in Spain], which is the fact that our [Dutch] enemies can easily wage war defensively, but Your Majesty cannot. This is because of the great advantages they enjoy with the rivers, so that they can travel with their armies in two days to places which the army of Your Majesty can only reach in fifteen, and so have time to fortify themselves in whatever place they choose before Your Majesty's forces can arrive.

Despite repeated attempts to remind them of this asymmetry (to say nothing of the endless unsuccessful campaigns) the Spanish Habsburgs continued to insist that the war in the Netherlands must be won at all costs – despite pressing commitments elsewhere. In 1606 the duke of Lerma (Philip III's principal adviser) explained to an envoy from the Netherlands that Spain could not possibly send any more money to finance the war against the Dutch because of the cost of equipping two fleets to defend shipping in the Atlantic and the Caribbean, 'to pay the garrisons maintained by His Majesty in all parts', to subsidize the emperor's war against the Turks, and to pay pensions and maintain troops in Italy. Yet Lerma (and the king) still balked at negotiating with the Dutch, even though they knew that the war could not be won.[5] This dogged determination only crumbled later that same year with the discovery that the treasury could neither meet its obligations from available revenues nor raise any further loans. Just like his father in 1574–75 and 1596–8, Philip III authorized serious negotiations to find a settlement with the Dutch only when a decree of bankruptcy became inevitable.[6]

The Habsburgs, however, really had no alternative to accepting the consequences of the astonishing success of their dynastic policies. No one seriously suggested that Charles V should renounce the imperial crown in 1519, because the honour would then pass to his French rival; and the only serious discussion (in 1544) about sacrificing one of the empire's outlying possessions in order to buy peace for the rest merely revealed that the emperor's various advisers could not agree which part he should surrender (see pp. 88–9 above). In a perceptive letter of 1565, Don Luis de Requeséns observed:

It may be that there are old men in Castile who believe we were better off when we held no more than that realm . . . and in truth if they could [they would] return . . . to that time when there was a king in Aragon and another in Naples and a lord in Flanders and another in Burgundy and a duke in Milan, and would likewise distribute what the king of France has now joined together. I confess that this would be better for the kingdoms, although not for the authority and greatness of kings; but supposing that the world, or at least Christendom, did come to be reduced into only the power of His Majesty [Philip II] and of the King of France, and what is ours could not be otherwise unless it belonged to our enemy – it [would still] be necessary to conserve [what we have], which requires having allies.[7]

If diplomacy was a 'zero sum game', Requeséns concluded, it was far better to command than to cajole or cringe.

In February 1580 the stern Jesuit, Pedro de Ribadeneira, made much the same point when he warned the government of the dangers of annexing Portugal. It would, he asserted, involve a war that 'pitted Christians against Christians, Catholics against Catholics', raise higher the taxes in Castile which already meant that 'although the king is so powerful and so feared and respected, he is not as well liked as he used to be', and allow the king's enemies abroad to find and exploit a 'fifth column' of discontented subjects within the peninsula; nevertheless, Ribadeneira conceded, the only thing worse than fighting to secure Portugal would be to let someone else acquire it! Even though uniting the peninsular kingdoms under a single ruler would threaten the European balance of power (just as Charles V's election as Holy Roman Emperor had done in 1519), allowing the Lusitanian inheritance to pass to someone else would point a dagger at the heart of Spain itself.[8] The death of the childless Henry III of France in 1589 likewise created an impossible dilemma for Philip: most observers recognized that intervention to secure the succession of an acceptable candidate would involve a huge outlay and, even if successful, would arouse animosity abroad; and yet not intervening would, as in Portugal a decade earlier, allow the installation of a sworn enemy, dedicated to challenging if not to diminishing Spanish power.

Philip never seems to have appreciated that his gains – however acquired – might appear to his neighbours to threaten the international status quo. For example, in 1570 the king's representative read a statement to the Cortes of Castile that sought to justify both the government's achievements since the last meeting of the assembly (four years before) and some new tax demands: having noted Philip's continual residence in the kingdom and his efforts to defend both justice and the faith at home, the speech addressed four policy initiatives that had cost a great deal of money – the expedition to expel French Protestant colonists from Florida in 1565–66, sending the duke of Alba to the Netherlands in 1567 and defeating Orange's invasion the following year, mobilizing an army against the Morisco rebels of the Alpujarras, and finally sending troops into France to defeat the Huguenots in 1569. To Philip – and no doubt to the deputies in the Cortes – these four items all seemed similar; to his neighbours, however, they did not. The brutal treatment of the French settlers in America (many were murdered and the rest brought back to prison in Spain) caused a rift between Paris and Madrid that lasted five years (until Philip released the survivors as part of the celebrations for the victory of Lepanto); the arrival of Alba and the creation of a powerful standing army in the Netherlands alarmed Elizabeth of England and helped to alienate her from Spain; and the Spanish expeditionary force in France, although it played a prominent part in the Huguenots' defeat, unsettled the ministers of Charles IX (they made peace with their former enemies in 1570). These misperceptions resembled those of the United States and the USSR in 1961–62 preceding the Cuban Missile Crisis: President Kennedy believed the deployment of Jupiter missiles in Turkey to be a prudent measure of defence whereas Chairman Khrushchev saw it as a threat requiring drastic counter-measures, including sending missiles to Cuba.[9]

Ideology – in the sixteenth century as in the Cold War – reinforced the propensity of statesmen to take risks in order to avoid losses. The Providential vision of Philip and his ministers not only gave them a further reason to accept the various gifts provided by Fortune but also reinforced their determination to defend these 'windfalls' at all costs. As they saw it, they had all come from God and so should not be rejected; they also feared that abandoned areas might fall into the hands of heretics. Thus the crown consistently repudiated arguments that both the Philippines and Ceylon should be abandoned, despite the fact that they constituted a permanent drain on the Monarchy's finances, because to do so would deliver the native population to the Protestant Dutch. In Europe, a good part of Philip's resolve to depose Elizabeth, to fight a war without compromise in the Netherlands, and to support the French Catholic League stemmed (as he so often said) from his desire to advance the cause of the 'true church'.[10] It happened that these goals coincided with Philip's perception of Spain's political interests, and this congruence 'between God's service and mine' no doubt played a part in his numerous decisions to go to war. After the failure of that initial effort, however, the congruence ceased. In each case, political considerations called for a rapid compromise and a negotiated peace; only religious concerns required hostilities to continue – but since for Philip that took precedence, Spain fought on. As the king wrote in 1586 (with a rare touch of humour) when Sixtus V suggested that Spain would have to attack England anyway in order to retaliate against Elizabeth's attacks, whether or not the Papacy helped him to finance it:

> I reject the opinion they have [in Italy] that necessity compels me to undertake this enterprise, because although over there they hold the law of vengeance to be general and immutable, they are also so knowledgeable about political expediency that they cannot fail to realize (for it is easily understood) that if I gain command of the sea, and create a navy that will keep it clear, and secure the Atlantic convoys and the Americas, I could avoid embarking on such a difficult enterprise because I would be safe and sure of not being open to attack. His Holiness really needs to understand that; and also that if I want to undertake the venture, properly supported, it is with no other cause or aim beyond the sadness I feel to see the persecution that afflicts the church there, and the duty that all of us have to serve Our Lord.[11]

Such convictions lay at the root of the king's remarkable confidence that, whenever his plans ran into difficulty, God would 'return to support His cause' and produce the miracle that would enable him to overcome all obstacles because it was all done for 'the duty that all of us have to serve Our Lord'.

Philip saw himself, if not as King David, then certainly as Moses: one of the few men capable of hearing, understanding and executing God's will. Like Moses, he expected God to provide a miracle when the goals he had set seemed unattainable by purely human means: he expected the Red Sea to part before him (and, after the victory of Lepanto, at least one of his ministers thought it had done so: see p. 101 above); above all he felt confident that he could see a pillar of cloud by day and of fire by night guiding him, and those over whom he ruled, to the Promised Land. The danger with this view lay in the fact that 'In the end, we cannot do everything with nothing', as the duke of Parma complained to his master in 1586, 'and one day God will grow tired of working miracles for us'. But Philip seldom realized when the gaps between ends and means had become too large to be bridged by 'ordinary' miracles. Even after the events of 1588 seemed to indicate that (again in Parma's words) 'God is sworne Englishe', the king continued to believe that, since he fought for God's cause, he should tolerate no compromise, allow no deviation and eschew all fall-back strategies.[12]

Warfare therefore came to be seen as the 'normal' state of the Monarchy. As Philip IV later put it: 'With as many kingdoms and lordships as have been linked to this crown it is impossible to be without war in some area, either to defend what we have acquired or to divert our enemies', and from his accession in 1621 until his death in 1665 – as between 1577 and 1607 – Spain's forces fought continuously on at least one front.[13] Not surprisingly, the continuous strain of war produced a fatalism in those who made policy. When, for example, in 1619 Don Balthasar de Zúñiga (Philip III's principal adviser on foreign policy) considered whether Spain should go to war with the Dutch again when the Twelve Year Truce ran out, he realized that he would make the wrong choice whatever he did:

> Whether we do it [break the Truce] or do not do it, we can be sure that we shall find ourselves in a bad situation because, when matters reach a certain stage, every decision taken will be for the worst, not through lack of good advice, but because the situation is so desperate that it is not capable of remedy; and whatever policy is selected discredits whoever chose it.

Six years later, Zúñiga's nephew and successor as Philip IV's chief minister, the count-duke of Olivares, rebuked with equal fatalism a colleague who suggested that the ship of state was sinking:

> I do not consider a constant and despairing recitation of the state of affairs to be a useful exercise, because it cannot be concealed from those who know it at first hand. To make them despair of the remedy can only weaken their resolution . . . I know the situation, I lament it, and it grieves me, but I will allow no impossibility to weaken my zeal or diminish my concern. For as the minister with paramount obligations it is for me to die unprotesting, chained to my oar, until not a single fragment is left in my hands.[14]

Fighting a major war in the sixteenth century, as today, demanded efforts of enormous magnitude and left few reserves of energy or insight to deal with the even more complex problems of how to achieve a satisfactory final outcome:

indeed, the longer the conflict continued, the more likely it became that the minutiae of fighting the war would divert statesmen from planning how to win the peace. Olivares, like Philip II before him, therefore tended to fix his attention on tactical and logistical issues, on coordinating complicated military and naval operations, rather than on ensuring that those issues and operations would bring peace. He regularly attempted to micromanage strategy, disconcerting and discouraging his subordinates while at the same time neglecting 'the big picture'.[15]

Some saw such personal failings as paramount in Spain's failure. Philip II appeared repeatedly in the dreams of the teenage Madrid clairvoyant Lucrecia de León between 1587 and 1590. The images she later reported were not flattering: crowds jeered at the king because he had impoverished them; his strength failed and his subjects longed for a new ruler to lead them; most hurtful of all, a placard by the chair where he slumbered announced 'He did not do nearly enough for the faith'. In one dream, even his daughter Isabella belittled his achievements:

> Look, Your Majesty, Spain is lost . . . Your Majesty is aware of the fame my grandfather, Emperor Charles V, left behind. The name of the Catholic Monarch [Ferdinand] also lives, even though he has been dead many years, and the names and glories of the holy kings of France are known everywhere. As for you, it is only said that you have impoverished your kingdom.

In another of Lucrecia's dreams Philip appeared as a new Roderick, the last Visigoth king whose licentious life was popularly believed to have caused the loss of Spain to the Moors in 711 AD. Don Juan de Silva, a discontented courtier, also blamed Philip for everything: in 1589 he confided to a friend that 'a man of leisure and insight told me that if one considers in detail the actions of His Majesty since he began to reign . . . one could not ascribe any gain by our enemies to [their] "luck", nor attribute any of our own successes to diligence – a melancholy thought'. Ten years later, just after the king's death, the Jesuit Juan de Mariana penned the most damning personal indictment of all while writing about the Armada's failure in his treatise *Of kings and kingship*:

> Great loss was suffered on the coasts of England: we sustained that blow, that ignominy, which many years will not be able to efface. That was the retribution exacted for grave delinquencies in our nation and, unless memory fails, it was the vile lusts of a certain prince which enraged the Divinity. This prince had forgotten the sacred personage he was, and the advanced age and even senility he had reached; and the rumour spread abroad that he had dissipated himself beyond reason in licentiousness.[16]

The wide range of explanations offered for Philip II's failure – from those of Padilla, Sessa and Spínola on the one hand to Lucrecia, Silva and Mariana on the other – raises in an acute form one of the principal historiographical debates of our time: the role of agent versus structure in historical causation. Some recent scholars have ascribed everything to structural factors. According to Henry Kamen,

> Philip was never at any time in adequate control of events, or of his kingdoms, or even of his own destiny. It follows that he cannot be held responsible for more than a small part of what eventually transpired during his reign . . . He was 'imprisoned within a destiny in which he himself had little hand'. He could do little more than play the dice available to him.

This is an extreme view. As John Lewis Gaddis has pointed out, 'History is always the product of determined *and* contingent events: it is up to historians to find the proper balance between them'.[17] But where does that 'proper balance' lie in Philip's case?

Studies of other rulers of large states under stress reveal many cases in which the role of the agent equals – and sometimes perhaps exceeds – that of the structures. The experience of the Mogul emperor Akbar (1556–1605), for example, suggests that a dramatic increase in data does not inevitably cause 'information overload'. Akbar created an elaborate information-gathering system, with imperial agents collecting and processing the data gathered by the 'newswriters' placed in every sub-district throughout the empire; the emperor and his provincial governors also maintained sets of secret agents and writers, who acted as a 'control' on the rest; and a dense network of runners and camel-borne messengers transported a mass of official documents, orders and reports across the country under the control of the postmasters. An eminent historian has characterized the Mogul state as an 'exercise in surveillance'; but, although Akbar was no less absolute than his contemporary Philip, the Mogul emperor did not insist on seeing all the data for himself or on using it to micromanage policy.[18]

Nevertheless, the delays in communication caused by distance, coupled with the rapid increase in the amount of available data, produced significant confusion in most sixteenth-century capitals. English ministers, for example, complained about the inefficiency of their government in terms that would have won immediate recognition from their Spanish counterparts. Thus in 1596, as Elizabeth vacillated over whether or not to send more troops to fight in France, one of her courtiers expressed sentiments remarkably similar to those of Don Martín de Padilla a few months earlier (p. 282 above): 'We had never in this court so busy a time . . . We are to provide for the saving of Ireland, the contenting of France, the winning of the Low Countries to such conditions as they are yet far from, and the discovering and preventing of designs which are now more and greater than ever.' Somewhat later, another of the queen's ministers lamented – as Philip's servants had done (pp. 65–6 above) – that 'It hath been always our custom to seek still to put off the time and never to endeavour the preventing of our mischiefs till they be fallen upon us, which maketh that afterwards they are not either at all to be remedied, or at least not without great difficulty'.[19]

Of course rulers of large states could experience high stress even in peacetime. Roman emperors in the first and second century AD, whether at home in their palaces or on progress through the provinces, appear to have been workaholics, endlessly taking decisions as they tried to maintain order and justice. Eighteenth-century Chinese emperors rose before dawn and sometimes forced their councillors and secretaries to work more than twenty-four hours at a stretch in order to keep on top of their paperwork.[20] The administrative habits of the emperor Yung-cheng (1723–35) offer an uncanny parallel to those of Philip II: on the one hand, Yung-cheng tried to avoid audiences and to transact all government in writing; on the other, he developed two systems of imperial communication, one for routine matters handled by the 'outer court' (the permanent bureaucracy) and the other for more sensitive issues contained in secret letters sent directly to the emperor and handled by him with a select group of confidential advisers. Some matters, indeed, he dealt with alone in stream-of-consciousness rescripts written in his distinctive imperial vermilion ink – 'informal, rambling, and spontaneous', commenting on a sudden fall of snow in the capital ('[It is] the benevolence of heaven . . . Why has such happiness come to me?'), chiding an official for leaving too many unused extra folds at the end of his report, and concluding, 'I have written these [thoughts] as they came to me to let you know'. According to a fascinating recent study, 'behind Yung-cheng's earnest and frenzied attention to governing there flourished an imperial preference for handling things independently and sometimes haphazardly or even capriciously'.[21]

At least Yung-cheng, although disorganized, knew how to delegate. Other leaders, especially at times of crisis, did not. Jefferson Davis, President of the Confederate States of America between 1861 and 1865, who was said to have 'ink instead of blood in his veins', proved another inveterate meddler. He acted as his own secretary of war and general-in-chief, issuing a stream of narrow instructions that hampered his generals' freedom of action and even giving orders to subordinates directly instead of through their commanding generals; he spent an inordinate amount of time justifying his decisions whenever they ran into criticism or failure; and he insisted on compartmentalizing the entire structure of command so that he retained control of all decisions. In the words of one of his officials, 'The radical vice of Mr Davis's whole military system is the separate departmental organization, each reporting only to him'. Some have ascribed the Confederates' defeat in large part to Davis's personal shortcomings.[22]

The best parallel for assessing the relative roles of agent and structure in the failure of Grand Strategies is offered by Nazi Germany because, to quote John Lewis Gaddis again, 'It is hardly possible to imagine Nazi Germany or the world war that it caused without Hitler'.[23] Soon after gaining power in 1933 Adolf Hitler deliberately created a labyrinthine system of competing structures in the Nazi state in order to protect his own central role and oblige everyone to turn to him for decisions. In 1938 he extended the system to the armed forces by appointing himself minister of war and gathering around him a special military bureau which mediated his orders to the various service chiefs, but he once again made sure that only he had the full picture. The following year the new operational advisory staff accompanied the Führer eastwards on a train (the 'Führer special') to follow the progress of the war in Poland; in 1940, during the conquest of western Europe, they moved to a converted farm in the Eifel; and after 1941 (following the invasion of Russia) they took over a fortified complex, the 'Wolf's Lair', in a forest in East Prussia. In the memorable phrase of Hitler's chief of operations staff, Alfred Jodl, 'The Führer's headquarters was a cross between a cloister and a concentration camp', and its various remote locations naturally – and intentionally – isolated the supreme commander and his staff from the immediacy of events. According to Jodl's deputy, Walter Warlimont: 'Hitler was, so to speak, in a little corner sheltered from the blast; neither he nor his immediate entourage got any direct information either of the severity of the struggle on the main front on the one hand or of the blazing effects of the air war on the German cities on the other'.[24]

This isolation produced two important consequences. First, in an apparent attempt to counteract his seclusion, Hitler often allowed direct access to a wide range of people. According to Jodl, speaking soon after the war:

> There were endless ways through which the Führer was informed about military matters. Every individual and every office could hand in reports direct to the adjutant's department. The photographer sent out by the Führer to take pictures at the front found it expedient to use this opportunity to report to the Führer on military matters also. When I objected to this, the Führer answered, 'I do not care from whom I hear the truth; the main thing is that I hear it.'[25]

This was not quite true. Admittedly Hitler, like Philip II, accepted advice from all quarters while he was making up his mind on an issue; but thereafter access to Supreme Headquarters was carefully controlled and those who entered soon realized that news and views that criticized the Führer's previous decisions were not welcome. In September 1942 Jodl discovered this for himself. Hitler sent him east to goad forward the commanders in the Caucasus who appeared to have become bogged down. He returned with an account of the difficulties he had witnessed – snow-covered passes and so on – which fully explained the lack of progress.

> I didn't send you, Jodl [Hitler hissed], to hear you report on all the difficulties. You were supposed to represent my view. That was your job. Instead you come back completely under the influence of the front-line commanders. You are nothing but their megaphone. I didn't need to send you there for that.

Jodl's hackles rose and he argued back; two days later, he heard that he would be replaced. Stunned by this rebuke from his hero, Jodl immediately recognized his error: 'One should never . . . try to point out to a dictator where he has gone wrong, since this will shake his self-confidence, the main pillar upon which his personality and his actions are based.'[26]

Theatre commanders proved no more successful in changing Hitler's mind: when summoned to make a presentation or report at headquarters, none seemed able to resist the overpowering influence of the Führer's presence. Thus Heinz Guderian – son of a Prussian general, pioneer of armoured warfare, and a conspicuously successful commander in Poland, France and Russia – arrived at the Führer's headquarters in August 1941 intent on persuading Hitler to sanction a quick thrust on Moscow, instead of transferring his armoured forces southwards. In the course of a morning with Hitler, however, Guderian changed his tune '100 per cent', later offering the excuse that 'Having become convinced by his interview that the Führer was firmly resolved to execute the drive to the south, it was his duty to make the impossible possible in order to put these ideas into effect'.[27]

The problem, as another of Hitler's generals shrewdly put it, lay in the fact that 'The Führer was interested in the very big issues, and also in the tiniest details. Anything in between did not interest him. What he overlooked was that most decisions fall into this intermediate category.' Within that vast terrain, Hitler's intervention tended to be erratic and unpredictable. 'In my view,' Chief of Staff Franz Halder wrote in 1941, 'the situation resulting from the Führer's interference is intolerable for the Army. These individual instructions by the Führer produce a situation of order, counter-order and disorder, and no one can be held responsible but he himself personally.'[28] Hitler nevertheless remained incorrigible. According to Jodl, in January 1945 the military signals system attached to the Führer's headquarters in Berlin handled 120,000 phone calls, 33,000 teleprinter messages and 1,200 radio messages each and every day. It seems unlikely that any command centre at that time – let alone any supreme commander – could process effectively such a volume of traffic in order to implement a coherent strategy. Only someone with total confidence in their mission, like Hitler, would even try.[29]

Writing shortly after Philip II's death, Sir Walter Raleigh attributed the king's failure to achieve his goals to a similar overweening confidence. With reference to the Armada, Raleigh suggested that: 'To invade by sea upon a perilous coast, being neither in possession of any port, nor succoured by any party, may better fit a prince presuming on his fortune than enriched with understanding.' Philip did not entirely disagree: he felt sure that, thanks to his special relationship with God, he 'understood matters differently' from other people and therefore felt able to discount 'the difficulties and problems that spring up'.[30] It is not hard to see why. Despite all the structural problems that beset his Monarchy – distance and fragmentation; information overload; 'imperial overstretch' (to use Paul Kennedy's useful term again) – the king came remarkably close to achieving his goals. With but a minimal rewrite of history (or, in Philip's terms, with only a minor miracle) the outcome at several key junctures could have been very different. Had the king returned to the Netherlands at any point between 1562 (when opposition to the 'New bishoprics' scheme became subversive) and 1568 (when the unpopularity of Alba's regime made a new rebellion highly likely), the Low Countries' Wars might have been entirely avoided; had Alba conceded magnanimous terms to the defenders of Haarlem when they surrendered 'at discretion' in 1573 (or had an earlier attempt on Orange's life succeeded) other rebellious towns might also have sought terms. The drain on Philip's resources would then have ceased, enabling him to intervene more effectively elsewhere. Likewise, had any of the plots against Elizabeth's life in the 1570s and 1580s succeeded – whether or not they involved Spain – Mary Stuart would almost certainly have become the next queen of England and drawn closer to Spain in order to secure Philip's support against her Protestant subjects. Alternatively, if the king had adopted a strategy (any strategy) for the conquest of England that did not require the Armada to join with Parma's army in advance; had Medina Sidonia not received at Corunna Philip's letter forbidding him to wait in the Channel until news arrived that Parma was ready; or had the Armada been commanded by a fighting admiral – whether Santa Cruz or, after his death, Recalde – it might have secured at least the temporary command of the sea required for Parma's crossing to the relatively undefended coast of Kent. As it was, in August 1588 Philip's remarkable – and remarkably coordinated – military, naval, diplomatic and economic efforts against England almost succeeded: Parma managed to embark his army within 48 hours, and Medina Sidonia led his fleet (more or less intact) to Calais, and kept it there for 36 hours. And, finally, had either Sebastian of Portugal or Henry III of France not met a violent death while still young and childless, Philip could have continued to profit from their incompetence without so obviously threatening the European balance of power.

'Counterfactual' calculations have, of course, been scorned by many historians – especially by those who believe that major events must stem from major causes. Two centuries ago, however, Samuel Johnson eloquently demolished these doubts:

> It seems to be almost the universal error of historians to suppose it politically, as it is physically true, that every effort has a proportionate cause. In the inanimate action of matter upon matter, the motion produced can be but equal to the force of the moving power; but the operations of life, whether private or publick, admit no such laws. The caprices of voluntary agents laugh at calculation. It is not always that there is a strong reason for a great event. Obstinacy and flexibility, malignity and kindness, give place alternately to each other, and the reason of these vicissitudes, however important may be the consequences, often escapes the mind in which the change is made.[31]

Nevertheless the long-term consequences of these 'vicissitudes' must not be exaggerated. We must also consider 'second-order counterfactuals' – that although some things might have happened differently, the long-term result might have remained unchanged. In Philip II's case, even success in the Netherlands and against England could not have altered his unpromising genetic legacy.

The fatal inheritance

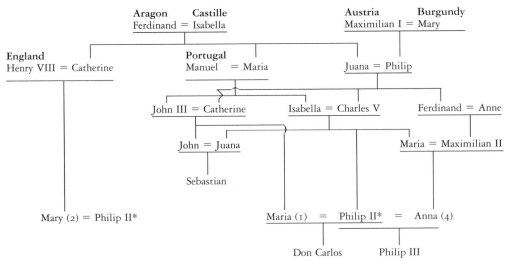

Table 7 Both the Portuguese and the Spanish royal families earnestly sought to unite the entire Iberian peninsula under one sceptre; and to that end, generation after generation, they intermarried. Although this inter-breeding eventually produced the desired effect – in 1580 Philip of Spain succeeded to the Portuguese throne – it involved a hidden cost: the gene pool of the dynasty became dangerously reduced. Don Carlos, for example, Philip II's unstable son, could count only four – instead of eight – great-grandparents.

After all, the Portuguese inheritance only came to Spain thanks to repeated intermarriage of the two ruling dynasties (see Table 7). Don Carlos, Philip's mentally unstable eldest son who (fortunately for the Monarchy) predeceased his father, descended from several generations of in-breeding between the two families; likewise Philip III's father and mother were already uncle and niece before they married, and his mother's parents were also cousins. Sooner or later, such endogamy would produce a ruler totally incapable of governing the Monarchy (as in the event happened with Carlos II in the late seventeenth century), and in a hereditary state the deleterious consequences could not be avoided.[32]

No hegemony, of course, lasts for ever. The Mogul empire expanded rapidly under Akbar and his successors, but began to disintegrate a century later; the Ch'ing empire ruled by Yung-cheng collapsed less than two centuries later in revolution, followed by decades of fragmentation under warlords and foreign occupation. The odds are stacked heavily against creating and – even more – against conserving hereditary empires. In either case, however, ascribing everything to structures and nothing to agents – to write a history without either heroes or villains – seems perverse. An elaborate simile used in one of the funeral sermons preached after Philip's death in 1598 takes us to the heart of the matter:

The life of a king resembles that of a hand-loom weaver . . . You may think that the weaver's life is easy, because he works at home, sheltered, close to his loom; but in reality the task is very hard. He labours with his arms, but see his feet working the pedals while his eyes remain glued to the cloth lest it become tangled. His attention is divided among the many threads, some going here and others there, keeping his eye open lest any break so it can immediately be tied . . . Such is the life of a king: writing with his hands, travelling with his feet, his heart attached to threads – one to Flanders, another to Italy, another to Africa, another to Peru, another to Mexico, another to the English Catholics, another to preserving peace among Christian princes, another to the problems of the Holy Roman Empire. So much attention required by the various states and threats! If the thread to the Indies should break, the king must hurry to tie it, and the same if the thread to Flanders should break.

A king's life, the preacher concluded, involved endless activity, constant strain, and permanent uncertainty about when or where the next crisis would arise.[33]

Even if we accept this sympathetic picture of Philip's ceaseless toil at the loom of state, it is legitimate to wonder why he did not produce more cloth. Admittedly his unwieldy inheritance, distance, and the rising number of decisions required of him created deep structural problems, but other statesmen have proved better at delegation, and have not always placed ideological commitment above rational calculation. Surely he could have exploited the serious weaknesses that beset most of Spain's enemies throughout the later sixteenth century to better advantage: Germany divided uneasily between Protestant and Catholic; England ruled by a woman who, although an adroit politician, lacked a clear successor and needed to accommodate a large religious minority; above all, France – his father's nemesis – seriously weakened by repeated religious wars. Yet despite these uniquely favourable international circumstances Philip failed both to preserve what he had inherited and to achieve the dynastic and confessional goals that he had set. Even if it is a law (as Florence Nightingale feared) 'that all nations shall fall after a certain number of years', the decline of Philip's global Monarchy so soon after its creation by the union of crowns in 1580 must be ascribed to the limitations of the royal weaver rather than to the structure of his loom, the configuration of his cloth, or the weakness of its component threads. Above all, his invincible confidence that God would provide, leading him to 'play down the difficulties and problems that spring up', gave rise to a potentially dangerous form of messianic imperialism which became the basis of Grand Strategy. Perhaps it was inevitable. As has been written of Hitler and Stalin, who also adopted an 'emotionally based ideological romanticism',

There seems to have been something about authoritarians that caused them to lose touch with reality. Being a communist provided no greater safeguard against tilting at windmills than being a fascist. The explanation is not difficult to discern: autocratic systems reinforce, while discouraging attempts to punc-ture, whatever quixotic illusions may exist at the top.[34]

The authoritarian character of Philip II, although far less sinister than that of the later dictators, constituted both the greatest strength and the greatest weakness of his Monarchy.

Notes

Abbreviations Used in the Notes

AA	Archivo de la Casa de los Duques de Alba, Madrid, Manuscript Collection (with *caja* and folio)
ACA	Archivo de la Corona de Aragón, Barcelona
	CA Consejo de Aragón
AGI	Archivo General de Indias, Seville
AGNM	Archivo General de la Nación, Mexico
	CRD Cédulas reales duplicadas
AGPM	Archivo General del Palacio Real, Madrid
AGRB	Archives Générales du Royaume/Algemeen Rijksarchief, Brussels
	Audience Papiers d'État et d'Audience
	CC Chambre des Comptes
	MD Manuscrits Divers
	SEG Secrétairerie d'État et de Guerre
AGS	Archivo General de Simancas
	CJH Consejos y Juntas de Hacienda
	CMC Contaduría Mayor de Cuentas (with *época* and *legajo*)
	CS Contaduría del Sueldo (with *época* and *legajo*)
	Estado Negociación de Estado
	Estado K Estado Francia
	GA Guerra Antigua
	SP Secretarías Provinciales
AHN	Archivo Histórico Nacional, Madrid
	OM Órdenes Militares
Álava	P. and J. Rodríguez, *Don Francés de Álava y Beamonte. Correspondencia inédita de Felipe II con su embajador en París (1564–1570)* (San Sebastián, 1991)
AMAE	Archive du Ministère des Affaires Etrangères, Paris
	MDFD Mémoires et documents: Fonds divers, Espagne
AMC	Archivo de la Casa de los Duques de Medina Celi, Seville, Manuscript Collection
APO	J. H. de Cunha Rivara, *Archivo Portuguez-Oriental* (6 vols, Nova Goa, 1857–76)
ARA	Algemene Rijksarchief, The Hague
ASF *MP*	Archivio di Stato, Florence, *Mediceo del Principato*

ASG *AS*	Archivio di Stato, Genoa, *Archivio segreto*
ASL	Archivio di Stato, Lucca, Archivio diplomatico
ASMa *AG*	Archivio di Stato, Mantua, *Archivio Gonzaga*
ASMi	Archivio di Stato, Milan, Cancellaria spagnuola
ASMo *CD*	Archivio di Stato, Modena, *Cancellaria ducale, sezione estera: ambasciatori Spagna*
ASN *CF*	Archivio di Stato, Naples, Sezione diplomatica-politica *Carte Farnesiane*
ASP *CF*	Archivio di Stato, Parma, *Carteggio Farnesiano*
ASV	Archivio Segreto Vaticano
	LP Lettere principi
	NS Nunziatura Spagna
ASVe *Spagna*	Archivio di Stato, Venice, *Senato: dispacci Spagna*
BAV *UL*	Biblioteca Apostolica Vaticana, *Urbinates Latini*
BCR	Biblioteca Casanatense, Rome
BL	British Library, London, Department of Western Manuscripts
	Addl Additional Manuscripts
	Cott. Cotton Manuscripts
	Eg. Egerton Manuscripts
	Harl. Harleian Manuscripts
	Lans. Lansdowne Manuscripts
	Sloane Sloane Manuscripts
BMB	Bibliothèque Municipale, Besançon, Manuscript Department
BMO	J. Calvar Gross, J. I. González-Aller Hierro, M. de Dueñas Fontán and M. del C. Mérida Valverde, *La batalla del Mar Océano* (3 vols, Madrid, 1988–93)
BNL	Biblioteca Nacional, Lisbon
BNM	Biblioteca Nacional, Madrid, Manuscript Section
BNP	Bibliothèque Nationale, Paris, Manuscript Department
	Ms. esp. Manuscrit espagnol
Bod.	Bodleian Library, Oxford, Department of Western Manuscripts
	Rawl. Rawlinson Manuscripts
Bouza	F. J. Bouza Alvarez, *Cartas de Felipe II a sus hijas* (Madrid, 1988)
BPM	Biblioteca del Palacio Real, Madrid, Manuscript Collection
BPU *Favre*	Bibliothèque Publique et Universitaire, Geneva, Collection Manuscrite Édouard Favre
BRB	Bibliothèque Royale, Brussels, Manuscript Section
BSLE	Biblioteca del Real Monasterio de San Lorenzo de El Escorial, Manuscripts
BZ	Biblioteca de Zabálburu, Madrid, Manuscripts (with *caja* and folio number)
Cabrera	L. Cabrera de Córdoba, *Historia de Felipe II, rey de España* (4 vols, Madrid, 1876 edn; vols I–II originally published in 1619)
CCG	E. Poullet and C. Piot, *Correspondance du Cardinal de Granvelle 1565–1586* (12 vols, Brussels, 1877–96)
CDCV	M. Fernández Alvarez, *Corpus Documental Carlos V* (5 vols, Salamanca, 1974–81)
CGT	L. P. Gachard, *Correspondance de Guillaume le Taciturne* (6 vols, Brussels, 1849–57)
Co.Do.In.	*Colección de documentos inéditos para la historia de España* (112 vols, Madrid, 1842–95)
CSPF	*Calendar of state papers of the Reign of Elizabeth, Foreign series*
CSPScot	*Calendar of state papers relating to Scotland and Mary Queen of Scots*

CSPSp.	M. A. S. Hume, *Calendar of letters and state papers relating to English affairs preserved in, or originally belonging to, the archives of Simancas: Elizabeth* (4 vols, London, 1892–99)
CSPV	H. F. Brown, *Calendar of state papers . . . Venice*, VIII (London, 1894)
Documentos . . . El Escorial	J. Zarco Cuevas, G. de Andrés and others, *Documentos para la historia del monasterio de San Lorenzo El Real de El Escorial* (8 vols, Madrid, 1917–62)
Donà	M. Brunetti and E. Vitale, *La corrispondenza da Madrid dell' ambasciatore Leonardo Donà (1570–1573)* (2 vols, Venice–Rome, 1963)
Encinas	*Cedulario Indiano recopilado por Diego de Encinas* (1596: ed. A. García Gallo, 4 vols, Madrid, 1945–46)
Epistolario	Duke of Berwick y Alba, *Epistolario del III duque de Alba* (3 vols, Madrid, 1952)
FD	C. Fernández Duro, *La Armada Invencible* (2 vols, Madrid, 1888)
Fourquevaux	C. Douais, *Dépêches de M. de Fourquevaux, ambassadeur du roi Charles IX en Espagne, 1565–72* (3 vols, Paris, 1896–1904)
GCP	L. P. Gachard, *Correspondance de Philippe II sur les affaires des Pays-Bas* (5 vols, Brussels 1848–79)
GPGP	A. Gonzalez Palencia, *Gonzalo Pérez, secretario de Felipe II* (2 vols, Madrid, 1946)
Groen van Prinsterer, *Archives*	G. Groen van Prinsterer, *Archives ou correspondance inédite de la maison d'Orange-Nassau* (1st series, 8 vols and supplement, Leiden 1835–47; 2nd series, I, Utrecht, 1857)
HHStA	Haus-, Hof- und Staatsarchiv, Vienna
Herrera Oria	E. Herrera Oria, *La Armada Invencible. Documentos procedentes del Archivo General de Simancas* (Valladolid, 1929: Archivo Histórico Español, II)
HMC Bath	Historical Manuscripts Commission *Calendar of the manuscripts of the Most Honourable the Marquess of Bath*, V (London, 1980)
HMC Downshire	Historical Manuscripts Commission *Calendar of the manuscripts of the Most Honourable the Marquess of Downshire*, III (London, 1938)
HMC Rutland	Historical Manuscripts Commission *Twelfth Report* (London, 1888), appendix, part IV, 'Manuscripts of His Grace the duke of Rutland'
HMC Salisbury	Historical Manuscripts Commission *Calendar of the manuscripts of the Most Honourable the Marquess of Salisbury*, III (London, 1889)
Hunt *HA*	Huntington Library, San Marino, California, *Hastings Manuscripts*
IVdeDJ	Instituto de Valencia de Don Juan, Madrid, Manuscript Collection (with *envío* and folio number)
KB	Koninklijke Bibliotheek, The Hague, Manuscript Section
KML *MSP*	Karpeles Manuscript Library, Santa Barbara, *Medina Sidonia Papers* CC *Casa de la Contratación* CR *Cartas de reyes*
Laubespine	L. Paris, *Négociations, lettres et pièces diverses relatives au règne de François II, tirées du portefeuille de Sébastien de L'aubespine* (Paris, 1841)
Laughton	J. K. Laughton, *State Papers concerning the defeat of the Spanish Armada* (2 vols, London, 1895–1900)
Longlée	A. Mousset, *Dépêches diplomatiques de M. de Longlée, résident de France en Espagne, 1582–90* (Paris, 1912)
Maura	G. Maura Gamazo, duke of Maura, *El designio de Felipe II y el episodio de la Armada Invencible* (Madrid, 1957)
Mondoucet	L. Didier, *Lettres et négociations de Claude de Mondoucet, résident de France aux Pays-Bas (1571–1574)* (2 vols, Paris, 1891–92)
NMM	National Maritime Museum, Greenwich

NS	New Style (dates according to the Gregorian calendar)
Nueva Co.Do.In.	*Nueva Colección de documentos inéditos para la historia de España* (5 vols, Madrid 1892–4)
OÖLA *KB*	Oberösterreichisches Landesarchiv, Linz, *Khevenhüller Briefbücher*
OS	Old Style (dates according to the Julian Calendar)
PEG	C. Weiss, *Papiers d'État du Cardinal de Granvelle* (9 vols, Paris, 1841–52)
PRO	Public Record Office, London
	AO Audit Office
	E Exchequer
	PRO Transcripts from other archives
	SP State Papers
	WO War Office
RAH	Real Academia de la Historia, Madrid, Manuscript Collection
RAZ	Rijksarchief Zeeland, Middelburg
Reivindicación	F. Pérez Minguez, *Reivindicación histórica del siglo XVI* (Madrid, 1928)
RSG	N. Japikse, *Resolutiën der Staten-Generaal van 1576 tot 1609* (14 vols, The Hague, 1917–70)
Riba	C. Riba García, *Correspondencia privada de Felipe II con su secretario Mateo Vázquez 1567–91* (Madrid, 1959)
Serrano	L. Serrano, *Correspondencia diplomática entre España y la Santa Sede durante el pontificado de San Pio V* (4 vols, Madrid, 1914)
Sigüenza	José de Sigüenza, *La fundación del Monasterio de El Escorial* (1605: Madrid, 1988)
UB Leiden *HS Pap.*	Universiteitsbibliotheek, Leiden, Manuscript Collection

Note: full titles of all works cited will be found in the bibliography, at pp. 407–33 below.

Preface

1. Sorensen, *Decision-making in the White House*, xi, xiii (from Kennedy's preface).

2. Gaddis, *We now know*; Lebow and Stein, *We all lost the Cold War*.

3. For an important example of how such a study should be undertaken, see Hess, *The forgotten frontier*.

4. See von Ranke, *Sämmtliche Werke*, XXXIV, 144–50 (an appendix to his 'History of the Italian and German peoples, 1494–1535', originally published in 1824. I thank Paul Bushkovitch for bringing this passage to my attention.) For the location and nature of the sources on which this study rests, see pp. 397–402 below.

5. Fortescue, *Correspondence of King George the Third*, IV, 350–1: George III to Lord North, 11 June 1779. Philip II frequently made the same calculation, and also justified his rejection of 'the scale of a tradesman' by reference to 'Divine Providence' (see pp. 99–107 above). On the need to consider each statesman's interaction and convergence with society, see Jarausch, *The enigmatic chancellor*, ix.

6. Braudel, *The Mediterranean*, 21; for the moment in 1944 at which Braudel, then a prisoner-of-war in Germany, suddenly hit upon the idea of three 'speeds', see Braudel, 'Braudel antes de Braudel', 94. For a recent forthright statement that all major events must have major long-term causes see Israel, *The Dutch Republic. Its rise, greatness and fall*, 169.

7. See the important insights of Beyerchen, 'Clausewitz'; Roth, 'Is history a process?'; and Beaumont, *War, chaos and history*, chaps 1–2.

8. *Memoriën . . . Hooft*, I, 182.

Introduction: Did Philip II Have a Grand Strategy?

1. Braudel, *The Mediterranean*, II, 1236; Koenigsberger, *Politicians and virtuosi*, 80, 82 (from his splendid essay, 'The statecraft of Philip II', first published in 1971); Kennedy, *Rise and fall*, 35–6.

2. Definitions from Wheeler, 'Methodological limits', 10; Kennedy, *Grand strategies in war and peace*, 2–3 (Liddell Hart); Cowley and Parker, *The reader's companion*, 448 (Luttwak). Mies van de Rohe quoted in Hopf, *Peripheral visions*, 240–1.

3. For various interpretations of the changing Grand Strategies employed by Roman emperors, see Ferrill, 'Grand Strategy', Luttwak, *Grand Strategy*, and Wheeler, 'Methodological limits'.

4. Kennedy, *Rise and fall*, 36. Fernández Álvarez, *Felipe II*, 775–87, agreed. Lutz, *Christianitas Afflicta*, 208–9; and Elliott, 'Foreign policy and domestic crisis', made much the same point for the preceding and subsequent periods. Wheeler, 'Methodological limits', 23, 218–19 and 227–32, brilliantly demonstrates that although the Romans, like Philip II, 'lacked a coherent strategy in the sense of a great "master plan" for empire, this does not exclude strategy in general for how to defend it' (229–30).

5. Quotations from BL *Eg.* 592/38–48v, 'Discurso astronómico' (anonymous), at fo. 44 (in fact only five 'hours' separate Madrid and Cuzco, but the idea of using time-zones to measure size seems strikingly modern); and Salazar, *Política española*, 24. According to González Dávila, *Teatro*, 1, the king of Spain was 'head of the most extensive empire that any king in the world has ruled'. (Cited in Lisón Tolosana, *La imagen del rey*, 19–23.)

6. Camden, *Historie*, book IV, 131. The 'empire on which the sun never set' conceit, used by Vergil, was apparently first applied to the Habsburgs by the city of Messina in 1535, to celebrate Charles V's victorious return from the conquest of Tunis (Gil, 'Visión europea de la Monarquía', 66). For subsequent uses see Elliott, *Count-duke*, 47–8.

7. See Losada, *Sepúlveda*, 64–74 and 94–100; Niccoli, *Prophecy and people*, 113–20 and 168–88; Headley, 'The Habsburg world empire', 93–127; idem, 'Rhetoric and reality', 241–69; Parry, *The Spanish theory of empire*; and Bosbach, *Monarchia universalis*.

8. Not all the texts went into print immediately: Campanella's *De monarchia hispanica discursus* remained unpublished until 1640 (at Amsterdam); Valdés, *De dignitate regum*, approved for publication in 1595, only came out in 1602 (at Granada); Borrell, *De regis catholici praestantia*, completed in 1597, appeared in print only in 1611 (at Milan); Salazar de Mendoza, *Monarchia de España*, written between 1598 and 1600, saw publication only in 1770. However López Madera, *Excelencias de la monarchia y reyno de España*, did appear in 1597 (at Madrid). On these (and other) universalist writers from the late sixteenth century, see Fernández Albaladejo, 'Imperio de por sí'; idem, ' "De Regis Catholici Praestantia" '; Díez del Corral, *La Monarquía hispánica*, 305–56 (on Campanella); and Pagden, *Spanish imperialism*, chaps 2–3. Admittedly not all Spanish political theorists advocated universal monarchy; some indeed (Soto, Covarubbias, Vázquez de Menchaca) explicitly denied its usefulness: see Pagden, *Lords of all the world*, 53–61. Nevertheless, even Covarubbias dedicated one of his works, the *Practicorum quaestionum liber* of 1556, to 'Philip the Great' (see Fernández Albaladejo, 'Imperio de por sí', 174–5).

9. Details from Checa, *Felipe II*, 271–2 and 486 (see yet more imperialist examples in those locations).

10. Bouza Álvarez, 'Retórica da imagem real', 39 (and plate 2 above); W.

Bigges, 'A summarie and true discourse of Sir Francis Drake's West Indian Voyage' (1589), in Keeler, *Sir Francis Drake's West Indian voyage*, 245–6 and 315 (and plate 3 above).

11. IVdeDJ 62/916, Duarte Nunes de Leão to Gabriel de Zayas, 8 Aug. 1585. Although Checa, *Felipe II*, 281–2, cites this document, my reading of the text – including the Latin inscription (which is a play upon Vergil, *Aeneid*, VI, 797: 'Extra anni solisque vias') – differs from his. Tanner, *Last descendant*, 163, records and reproduces another 'imperialist' medal from this period whose obverse displayed Philip II's face and the reverse a globe with a yoke above it held by two hands and the legend SIC ERAT IN FATIS. Some found this presumptuous: see BAV *UL*, 1115/61, 'Aviso' from Madrid, 26 July 1586.

12. On Spain's external influence, see Deswarte-Rosa, *Ideias e imagens*, 55–122 ('Roma desfeita'); and Bouza Álvarez, *Locos*, 40 (on early modern Spain's export of jokes and comedians all over the European continent).

13. *CDCV*, IV, 127, Philip II to Charles V, 16 Nov. 1554 (see also the similar statement from 1558 in Rodríguez-Salgado, *Changing face*, 161); ASMo *CD Carteggio di Principi, Spagna*, 1, unfol., Philip II to the duke of Ferrara, 30 June 1572. At this time, in the Netherlands, the duke of Alba was convinced that the French were preparing to invade (see *Epistolario*, III, 119–20 and 160, Alba to Philip II, 23 May and 18 July 1572), and he was absolutely right: see Sutherland, *The massacre of St Bartholomew*, chaps 13–14.

14. *BMO*, II, 254, Philip II to the count of Olivares, Spanish ambassador in Rome, 22 July 1586; and Pereña Vicente, *Teoría de la guerra*, 62, from a funeral oration in 1598, quoting a letter from Philip to the corregidor of Toro.

15. The attempt to invade England in 1587–88 seemed an aberration, but even here Philip II's aide and biographer, Luis Cabrera de Córdoba, claimed 'self-defence': 'The king did not go to war against the queen and the kingdom of England because of ambition or an insatiable desire to increase his Monarchy through the conquest of new states . . . The war against England, although an offensive act on Spain's part (because we struck the first blow), was defensive in its motive and was entirely just, being waged against someone who had broken the peace without cause, caused injury by force and deception, [and] destroyed the Catholic faith . . . Matters eventually reached such a state that these disgraceful insults provoked King Philip, who was obliged to avenge them, into action' (Cabrera, III, 220–1).

16. This 'security dilemma' is well analysed by Trachtenberg, *History and strategy*, 64–5. See also Howard, *The lessons of history*, 81–96, on the ambiguous position of Edwardian Britain at the beginning of the twentieth century.

17. Quotations from Scott, *The Somers collection*, 164–70; MacCaffrey, *Queen Elizabeth*, 338–9; and Pincus, 'Popery', 18 (see also other fears of a Spanish 'universal monarchy' voiced by Englishmen ibid., 18–19).

18. Sutherland, *The massacre of St Bartholomew*, 265, quoting Coligny; Groen van Prinsterer, *Archives*, 2nd series I, 11, Henry of Navarre to Leicester, 8 May 1585; Longlée, 308, letter to Henry III, 23 Sept. 1586; and *Le Soldat français* (1604), quoted with numerous other contemporaneous tracts by Bitton and Mortensen, 'War or peace', 129.

19. Quotations from Danvila y Burguero, *Moura*, 650–1, Philip II to Gregory XIII, 10 Aug. 1580; and Berwick y Alba, *Documentos escogidos*, 286, Philip II to Granvelle, 10 July 1581, holograph. The different strategic perceptions of the popes and the Habsburgs during the early modern period are brilliantly illuminated by Lutz, *Christianitas Afflicta*; Repgen, *Die*

20. BL *Addl.* 28,263/487–8, Philip II to Vázquez, 25 Dec. 1588 ('para la defensa es menester ofender'). See also the arguments of Luis de Torres (1571) in Serrano, III, 324–9, and of Don Juan de Zúñiga (1585), on p. 181 above, that attack was the cheapest form of defence.

21. See BZ 90/35 'Primer discurso sobre lo que la Armada de Su Magestad podría hacer', 28 Nov. 1571 (anonymous); BNM Ms 783/149–56, Alba to Don Juan de Zúñiga, 17 Dec. 1571.

22. AGS *Estado* 1239/51, marquis of Ayamonte to Philip II, 16 June 1574 (I thank Mario Rizzo for bringing this document to my attention).

23. Torres Lanzas and Navas del Valle, *Catálogo,* II, clxxxiii–iv; Guillén Tato, *Museo Naval,* XVIII, fos 146–60, 'Relación'; Bishop Ribeiro Gaio quoted, along with other similar contemporaneous proposals, in Boxer, 'Portuguese and Spanish projects'.

24. For further detail on these and other projects see Headley, 'Spain's Asian presence', 638–45; Díaz-Trechuelo, 'Consecuencias', 1535–6; and Parker, 'David or Goliath?', 253–7.

25. Hair, *To defend your empire*; Boxer, 'Portuguese and Spanish projects'.

26. See Rizzo, 'Finanza pubblica', 311. Philip II may at times have used Spanish Italy as a 'laboratory of government', testing policies and initiatives there before implementing them elsewhere: see the suggestive article of Musi, 'L'Italia nel sistema imperiale', in Musi, *Nel sistema imperiale,* 51–66, at pp. 61–2.

27. See the admirable surveys by Peña Cámara, *Nuevos datos* (quotation, from Benito Arias Montano in 1571, at p. 8 note); and Ramos, 'La crisis indiana'.

28. *Co.Do.In.,* XXXVII, 84, Alba to Philip II, 6 Jan. 1568; Gilissen, 'Les phases'; and van de Vrught, *De criminele ordonnantiën.*

29. Craeybeckx, 'La Portée fiscale'. The calculation of the tax was indeed ingenious: the government took the average rent for a house to be 6.25 per cent of its capital value, so that one had to multiply by 16 in order to calculate its total worth ($16 \times 6.25 = 100$); they then set the tax rate for income from property at 16 per cent of the income. So a house rented in 1569–70 for 62.5 florins was valued at 1,000 florins, and the government took 16 per cent of the rent, or 10 florins – precisely the 'hundredth penny' of its notional value. Income from other investments was estimated at 4.5 per cent, and the multiplier and tax rate to produce the 'hundredth penny' therefore became 22 instead of 16 ($22 \times 4.5 = 99$). This method of calculation prevented owners from wilfully undervaluing their assets. See also Parker, *Dutch Revolt,* 114–17; and Maltby, *Alba,* 214–22. The government in Madrid also decreed some changes in the fiscal administration of both Naples and Sicily in 1570–71: see Muto, 'Modelli', 293 and 295.

30. AGNM *Bandos* I/1, printed ordinance of 1 Nov. 1571. In fact unsuccessful earlier attempts to levy the *alcabala* (a well-established Castilian tax) in the Americas had been made, and even this one did not take effect until 1574 in Mexico, 1575 in New Galicia, 1576 in Guatemala, and 1591 in Peru: see Sánchez Bella, *La organización financiera,* 52–3, and the text of these later decrees in Encinas, III, fos 429–45.

31. Duviols, *La lutte,* 337, noted parallel efforts against religious deviants in Granada, the Netherlands and Peru in 1568–71. For a parallel argument that the Grand Strategy of the Roman empire can, in the absence of a surviving 'blueprint', be deduced from its policies, see Wheeler, 'Methodological limitations'.

32. Canestrini and Desjardins, *Négociations diplomatiques,* IV, 737: Cavriana to Vinta, 3 Mar. 1587; Laughton, I, 361: Hawkins to Walsingham, 31 July 1588 OS. See also ibid., II, 59: Howard to Walsingham, 8 Aug. 1588

OS. ('All the world never saw a force such as theirs was.')

33. Groen van Prinsterer, *Archives*, 2nd series I, 213: William Louis of Nassau to Maurice of Nassau, 17 Jan. 1593: 'le plus grand Monarche du monde'. Details of Spain's military achievements appear in Parker, *The Army of Flanders*, and Thompson, *War and government*. The work cited is Charles de Mansfelt, *Castra dei* (Brussels, 1642).

1   *The Largest Brain in the World*

1. McNamara, *In retrospect*, xxi.
2. Ibid., 277. See also specific examples of this dilemma at pp. 108, 177 and 273.
3. The reign of Elizabeth offers an uncanny parallel. She reigned longer than any English monarch between Edward III (who began as a minor) and George III (who ended insane); had she lived only as long as her mother and her half-brother, she would never have become queen; had she only reached the age of her half-sister and grandfather she would have died before Mary Stuart: see Black, *Convergence or divergence?*, 118. The extinction of the direct line of the Jagiellon (1572), Avis (1580) and Valois (1589) dynasties underscored the fragility of hereditary monarchies.
4. AGS *Estado* 153/155, Gaspar de Quiroga to Philip II and reply, undated [= 1574]; *Co. Do.In.*, XXXII, 556–7, Alba to Gabriel de Zayas, 7 Sept. 1580. The duke asked for nightly reports on the king's health. Two days later he asked that the reports should bear the hour as well as the date; three days later he claimed that 'of all the things that have happened to me in this world, nothing has revealed my weakness until now, when the rulers who love us best give us concern about

their life and death' (ibid., pp. 563 and 571). The duke's concern was soon vindicated: although Philip recovered, Queen Anna died the following month.

5. *CCG*, X, 137, Morillon to Granvelle, 11 Apr. 1583; Longlée, 272, letter to Henry III, 19 June 1586; *CSPV*, VIII, 407, Lippomano to the Doge and Senate, 22 Oct. 1588.
6. AGS *CJH* 27/214, countess of Francavilla to Ruy Gómez da Silva (her son-in-law), 21 Nov. 1557 (concerning Bartolomé Carranza); other quotations from Feros, '"Vicedioses, pero humanos"', 110–12; and Vargas Hidalgo, 'Documentos inéditos', 399.
7. Kamen, *Philip*, v, Philip II on 29 Nov. 1578. Philip may have seen himself as a martyr to God's cause by the end of his reign, however: see Rocca, 'Court and cloister', chap. 1. For the anecdotes quoted here, see Herrera y Tordesillas, *Historia general*, II, 46–7; and Velázquez, *La entrada*, fos 79–80. The king also regularly issued pardons on Good Friday: see Las Heras, 'Indultos', 129–30.
8. On the French captives, see AGS *Estado* 553/112 and *Co.Do.In.*, CII, 322–5, Philip II to Alba, 27 Nov. 1572, and 21 Oct. 1573. On those executed by the 'council of Troubles', see Parker, *Dutch Revolt*, 108 and 292 note 35.
9. BL *Addl.* 28,263/7, Philip II memorandum, undated (=1574–75). On the *fueros* of Aragon, see Gil, 'Aragonese constitutionalism'.
10. *CCG*, X, 126, Granvelle to Bellefontaine, 3 Apr. 1583.
11. See Parker, *Philip II*, 175, and Kamen, *Philip*, 257. On the seven recorded attempts to assassinate Philip II, see Álava, 211–12 (two 'Flamencos' in 1567); *CSPSp.* II, 94 (a Venetian in 1568) and 137 (William Cecil in 1569); Herrera y Tordesillas, *Historia general*, II, 7 (three Frenchmen in 1571); Kamen, *Philip*, 199 (an attempt in Lisbon in 1581); IVdeDJ 21/148–57, correspondence of Vázquez with Philip II in Mar. 1583

(another Frenchman); and *CSPV*, VIII, 174, Gradinegro and Lippomano to Doge and Senate, 25 June 1586 (a Portuguese woman). Sometimes the king did tighten security: in 1568, he increased his guard from 10 to 100 horsemen when he travelled between his palaces (Fourquevaux, III, 100: letter to Catherine de Medici, 17 Aug. 1568); in 1577 and again in 1589 (following the assassination of Henry III of France), he brought armed guards when he visited the Escorial (Sigüenza, 76 and 127).

12. Kamen, *Philip*, 214–15; Muro, *Vida*, appendix 12, Esteban de Ibarra to Mateo Vázquez, [Apr.] 1578: Ibarra recalled the attempted assassination of Ferdinand the Catholic in Barcelona in 1492. Elizabeth's speech is best rendered in Green, '"I my self"'.

13. Quotations (from 1584 and 1585) in Rodríguez-Salgado, 'The Court of Philip II', 241, and Parker, *Philip II*, 177. On Philip as a striking exemplification of Castiglione's ideal, see Jenkins, *The state portrait*, 31–4.

14. Santullano, *Obras completas de Teresa de Jesús*, 1394: Teresa to Doña Inés Nieto [1576–77]; Donà, 75–8, letter to Venice, 1 Sept. 1570; Porreño, *Dichos y hechos* (1628), quoted with other interesting material in Feros, '"Vicedioses pero humanos"', 110.

15. Donà, 677–81, letter to Venice, 17 Apr. 1573; BCR Ms 2417/39, Don Juan de Silva to Esteban de Ibarra, 13 Aug. 1589 (for the context of this remark see pp. 66–7 above); González Olmedo, *Don Francisco Terrones*, xl, from Terrones's funeral oration for Philip II, 19 Oct. 1598.

16. Furió Ceriol, *El concejo y consejeros del príncipe* (1559), 95; council sizes from Alvar Ezquerra, *Felipe II*, 16–21. The Venetian ambassador in 1557 reported that Philip II's household numbered 1,500 officials (Firpo, *Relazioni*, VIII, 150); a list of 1566 put it at 1,450, with a further 450 in the households of the queen, the prince, and Princess Juana (BAV *UL* 829/4/652–63); and BPM Ms II–2291,

unfol., Antonio de Rojas, governor to Don Carlos, to Granvelle, 12 May 1560, estimated the total number of courtly 'mouths' to feed at 4,000.

17. Alvar Ezquerra, *Felipe II*, 22. See also Fernández Alvarez, *Madrid bajo Felipe II*. On the configuration of the Madrid palace during Philip's reign, see Barbeito, *El Alcázar de Madrid*, 33–83 and Orso, *Philip IV*, 13 and 122–42. Some critics alleged that the remodelling of the palace in the 1580s enabled the king to 'take refuge there during the winters, and his success can be seen from the fact that he avoids audiences there better than in either the Pardo or the Escorial' (BAV *UL* 1115/108–9, newsletter from Madrid, 10 Jan. 1587).

18. Rodríguez-Salgado, 'The Court of Philip II', 218. See also the examples cited in Kamen, *Philip*, 198, and the charming account of Philip on his way to hear Mass deliberately walking slowly so that his subjects could speak to him or give him their petitions in person: Donà, 319, letter to Venice, 3 July 1571.

19. Riba, 105–6, Vázquez to Philip II, 23 Apr. 1577, summarized by Rodríguez-Salgado, 'The Court of Philip II', 219. Espinosa planned to see the king 'carrying the memoranda, so he can speak about them as he holds them in his hand' – a suggestion made by the perplexed monarch the previous day when he failed to understand the document on its own: see note 116 below.

20. Riba, 394–5, Vázquez to Philip II and reply, 30 Apr. 1586: the irritated king made the same point three times in the same paragraph.

21. Archivum Romanum Societatis Iesu, Rome, *Epistolae Hispaniae* 143/293–4v, holograph report by Acosta, 16 Sept. 1588. Admittedly the king had known Francisco de Borja well – both as a courtier and minister before he took religious vows (in 1548) and afterwards as confessor to both his grandmother and his sister Juana – and so had a personal interest; but

many of the other exchanges reported by Acosta seem a waste of time.

22. Riba, 44, Philip II to Vázquez, 23 May 1576. For other examples of how long individual audiences could last, see the blow-by-blow accounts in Fourquevaux, II, 427–30; Donà, 75–8, 159–65 and 220–4; and Mosconi, *La nunziatura*, 72–8 and 81–5. Speciano obtained fourteen audiences during his thirty months at Court (Apr. 1586–Nov. 1588), and his subsequent descriptions of the business transacted took up five or six pages each in his dispatches to the Curia: these meetings must therefore have lasted at least an hour each.

23. Donà, 373, letter to Venice, 2 Nov. 1571 (see also the subsequent account of the same incident in Sigüenza, 43).

24. Fourquevaux, II, 388–9, letter to Charles IX, 12 Nov. 1571. Philip also muttered something more specific, but Fourquevaux missed it: 'The said king then, with a smile, said something so softly that I could not hear it'. Fourquevaux's detailed report of this audience contains other interesting details. First, like Acosta's audience in 1588, it demonstrates that, contrary to the assertions of many historians, Philip II did not always merely listen; second, since the king always seemed so well informed, Fourquevaux found it prudent before each audience to visit both the leading Spanish ministers and some other ambassadors at Court in order to ascertain what Philip might already know about French affairs; and third he noted the dismissive nomenclature used by the king about his opponents – he did not refer to Jeanne d'Albret as queen of Navarre (Spain had annexed most of that kingdom in 1512) but as 'madame de Vendosme', and he referred to Count Louis merely as 'Ludovic', without any title. Philip had good cause for concern: Jeanne travelled to Paris expressly to arrange the marriage of her son, the future Henry IV, with Charles's sister Marguerite de Valois, and Louis of Nassau sought to involve the French king in his plan to start a new rebellion in the Netherlands: for his success in this, see pp. 124–5 above.

25. Donà, 39–40 and 198, letters to Venice, 6 June 1570 (Philip replied 'con poche parole, ma veramente esquisite como è di suo costume') and 4 Feb. 1571 ('three or four words'). See also the remarks of Giovan Maria Cecchi on Philip's taciturnity in audiences, quoted in Bouza Álvarez, 'Guardar papeles, I', 5. On the king's amnesia after audiences, see IVdeDJ 53/5/15, Philip II to Vázquez, 27 Jan. 1576. Interestingly, the king and his senior ministers warned their own envoys *never* to communicate with other governments in writing for precisely this reason – it allowed longer to prepare a reply! (See *Epistolario*, III, 257, Alba to Monteagudo, Philip II's ambassador at the Imperial Court, Nov. 1572, minute.) The Venetian Council of Ten also forbade its ambassadors to negotiate in writing for much the same reason: see Donà, 733, letter of 5 Sept. 1573.

26. Maura, 38, Philip II to the duke of Medina Sidonia, 29 Oct. 1578; see also Álava, 56–7, Zayas to Álava, Jan. 1572, telling him to write down the comments he wished to convey to the king in person. Philip knew, however, that audiences played an important role in maintaining contact between a conscientious ruler and his subjects: see his advice to his son in the 'Raggionamenti', quoted in *Reivindicación*, 174–5.

27. Fourquevaux, II, 18 and 21, letters to Charles IX and Catherine de Medici, 18 Nov. 1568. See another example, from 1569, ibid., II, 87–8. Fourquevaux could draw on extensive experience, having twice been the prisoner of the Spaniards and having previously served as ambassador in Scotland, Ireland and Germany. See also Donà, 393–4, letter to Venice, 26 Nov. 1571: an extraordinary ambassador arrived from Venice to congratulate Philip on Lepanto, but

decided not to ask for an audience until the king returned from the Escorial, because 'His Majesty does not want ambassadors to come and worry him' there.

28. Mosconi, *La nunziatura*, 16–17, Novara to Rusticucci, 18 Oct. 1586. The reports of ambassadors at the Court of Spain to their home government frequently commented on the difficulty of obtaining an audience with the king (see, for example, Fourquevaux, II, 347: his replacement arrived on 23 Feb. 1572 but could not present his credentials until 15 Mar.). It could also be hard to find a moment with the principal ministers: in Mar. 1588 the Mantuan ambassador was summoned by Secretary of State Idiáquez to join him at Mass in the church of San Jerónimo, near the palace, because 'he had business to discuss'! (ASMa *AG Spagna*, 601 unfol., Aqui to Mantua, 14 Mar. 1588.) See also ASV *NS* 19/263, Novara to Rusticucci, 11 June 1587, reporting his meeting with Idiáquez in a cloister after Mass.

29. BL *Eg.* 330/4–20, 'Copia de carta que escrivió al Señor Rey Phelipe II Don Luis Manrique', *c.* 1577 (fo. 8); BNM Ms 18718 no. 55 'Papel a Philippo II', also *c.* 1577 (quote from fo. 99v graciously provided by Antonio Feros). On the novelty of written court culture in the later sixteenth century, see Bouza Alvarez, 'Leer en palacio'.

30. Riba, 25–6, Vázquez to Philip II, 21 Mar. 1576 (Philip had acted as regent of Spain for the first time in 1543 – precisely thirty-three years before). On Ávalos, see Carlos Morales, *El consejo de Hacienda*, 116.

31. Bouza Alvarez, *Del escribano a la biblioteca*, 81–2, quoting Mendoza; *CCG*, X, 190, Granvelle to Morillon, 7 May 1583. On the king's deliberate 'invisibility', see Checa, 'Felipe II en El Escorial', 17–21; Elliott, 'The Court of the Spanish Habsburgs', 148–9; Bouza Alvarez, *Del escribano a la biblioteca*, 84–5; and Feros, 'Twin souls: monarchs and favourites', 33–5.

32. Sigüenza, 57; Firpo, *Relazioni, VIII*, 257 (Lorenzo Priuli in 1576).

33. Until recently only the council of the Indies had received detailed study: Schäfer, *El consejo real y supremo de las Indias*, with a collection of conciliar documents for Aragon, mostly from 1587–88, in Riba y García, *El consejo supremo de Aragón*. Now see Arrieta Alberdi, *El consejo supremo de la corona de Aragón*; Carlos Morales, *El consejo de Hacienda*; and Fernández Álvarez, *Felipe II*, 47–74.

34. BL *Addl.* 28,399/20, Philip II to viceroy of Sicily, 20 Jan. 1559; Alvar Ezquerra, 'Unas "reglas generales"'. See the wide range of councils with which Ambassador Don Juan de Zúñiga corresponded from Rome in *Nueva Co.Do.In.*, I–V (his correspondence just for 1574!). Sánchez-Bella, *La organización financiera*, 4, Philip II to the Audiencia of Charcas, 15 Oct. 1595.

35. For 1566 see Cabrera, I, 491–2; ASG *AS* 2412A, unfol., Sauli to Genoa, 29 Apr. 1566 (Philip's attendance at the council seemed 'cosa molta insolita'); and UB Leiden *Hs Pap.* 3/2, Alonso de Laloo to Count Hornes, 22 July 1566. According to HHStA *Spanien Varia* 1b/r/20, 'Aviso' of 28 Apr. 1566, the king 'always brought in and took out the papers [to the meetings], not leaving them in the hands of his secretaries'.

36. Others used the same system: Juan Martínez de Recalde and the duke of Medina Sidonia exchanged *billetes* during the Armada campaign (p. 264 above) and Charles I of England wrote comments – sometimes quite rude! – on memoranda from his ministers: see examples in Sharpe, *The personal rule*, 203–4.

37. Mateo Vázquez seems to have seen the king for two hours at a time in the 1580s – see IVdeDJ 55/XI/123 and 190, Vázquez to Philip II, 29 July and 16 Sept. 1588, with royal replies allocating a two-hour slot in which to transact business – and of course Vázquez was just one of several

secretaries transacting council business with the king. For an idea of what the 'arch-secretary' handled at these meetings, see IVdeDJ 101/105–19, Vázquez's notes on the matters discussed each day that he met with the king, Oct. 1585–Mar. 1586. For a description by Juan Ruiz de Velasco, the king's valet, of how the king and Vázquez dealt with matters at these meetings, see Parker, *Philip II*, 33.

38. ASG *AS* 2416, unfol., Sebastián de Santoyo to Ambassadors Fiescho and Passano, 31 July 1579.

39. AGS *GA* 155/193, royal apostil to a consulta on Indies business dated 10 Mar. 1583. See also ACA *CA* 36/312, consulta of the council of Aragon to Philip II [1583], sending an emergency order already in final form directly 'for Your Majesty to sign, if he wishes'. (Mateo Vázquez commented: 'The letters have been signed and it was very good to send them in order to save time'.) Heredía Herrera, *Catálogo*, I, 649, council of the Indies to Philip II, 26 Aug. 1589, reveals once more the king's sanction for the practice of sending the outgoing letter for signature along with the consulta that recommended it 'in cases of urgent necessity'. See also the interesting case in *BMO*, II, 254, Philip II to the count of Olivares, 22 July 1586, minute, which the king wanted to change. Idiáquez added: 'The underlined passage was removed from the ciphered text, changing the characters totally so that they could not be read' – in other words, the final version had been encrypted before the king had even read the draft. The same seems to have happened with ibid., II, 338, Philip II to Mendoza, 5 Sept. 1586.

40. BZ 144/11, Vázquez to Philip II, 20 May 1574. See also Vázquez's repeated attempts during the Armada emergency to bring a letter from the duke of Infantado to the king's attention: p. 68 above.

41. AGS *Estado* 570/139, Pérez to Juan de Escobedo (Don John's secretary), Apr. 1576, minute; BNP *Ms. Esp.* 132/

179–80, Pérez to Juan de Vargas Mexía, 26 Jan. 1579, original. On Pérez's other deceptions and on his fall, see Parker, *Philip II*, chap. 8, Kamen, *Philip*, 162–8, and Mignet, *Pérez*, 21–32.

42. Herrera Oria, 152: Idiáquez and Moura to Medina Sidonia, 22 Feb. 1588, discussed in Martin and Parker, *Spanish Armada*, 148. Interestingly, the duke's letter appears to be missing from the state archives.

43. On the *sumiller de corps* ('groom of the Stole'), from whose sight palace etiquette demanded that the king 'should never withdraw', see Feros, 'Twin souls: monarchs and favourites', 37–8.

44. *GPGP*, II, 485, Pérez to Philip II and reply, undated [Apr. 1565].

45. IVdeDJ 67/211, Requeséns to Don Juan de Zúñiga, 14 Apr. 1574, explaining why he had decided to write directly to the king, 'closing my eyes to the fate that normally awaits absentees'. This initiative caused problems at Court: on the one hand, Mateo Vázquez had to decode the 'secret' letters himself (IVdeDJ 44/57, Vázquez to Philip II and reply, 11 Apr. 1574); on the other, since writing replies inevitably involved consulting others, he then had to prepare 'sanitized' versions of Requeséns's letters to circulate – see, for example, IVdeDJ 68/287a, Philip II to Vázquez, 28 June 1574: 'Make a précis and think about who should see it . . . according to who wrote the letters to which he [Requeséns] replies'.

46. See IVdeDJ 68/231–2, Requeséns to the marquis of Los Vélez, 23 July 1575, giving the history of his relations with every member of the council of State and noting his success in avoiding the 'passions between Ruy Gómez and the duke of Alba'. This heart-searching was occasioned by the fact that Requeséns had received no letter from the Court for nine months, which he could only assume indicated that someone had turned the king

against him. The nature of 'faction' in the courts of sixteenth-century Europe is hotly debated. For Spain, see Boyden, *The courtier and the king*, chap. 5; and Martínez Millán, *La corte de Felipe II*, especially the introduction and chap. 2. For England, see Adams, 'Favourites and factions'.

47. Muro, *Vida*, 115, Vázquez to Philip II, 3 July 1579. On the fall of Pérez, see Parker, *Philip II*, chap. 8, and Kamen, *Philip*, 163–8.

48. GCP, I, 358, Pérez to Tomás de Armenteros, 30 June 1565, about the contradictory letters sent to the Low Countries by the king in April (working with his Spanish advisers) and in May (drafted by his Netherlands officials).

49. Thompson, *War and government*, 79. Although Thompson's charge holds good for some periods, from time to time Philip II endeavoured to ensure that the council of Finance monitored both the income and expenditure handled by several other councils: see Carlos Morales, *El consejo de Hacienda*, 233–49. On Erasso, 'to whose hands and management almost everything is now entrusted', see Laubespine, 66, letter to Francis II, 4 Aug. 1559; and Carlos Morales, 'El poder de los secretarios reales'.

50. Fourquevaux, II, 88, letter to Catherine de Medici, 6 July 1569; AGS *Estado* 148/181, count of Chinchón to the governor of Milan, 12 Dec. 1566; IVdeDJ 81/1251, Requeséns to Zúñiga, Nov. 1572.

51. AMAE *MFMD Espagne* 239/126–35, Philip II to Diego de Covarrubias [autumn 1572], copy. Fourquevaux had already noted that the 'excessive power' delegated by Philip II to Espinosa seemed 'contrary to his nature and his custom' (Fourquevaux, II, 55, letter to Charles IX, 28 Feb. 1569). In his 'Instruction' of 1543, Charles V had warned his son: 'Do not bind yourself to, or become dependent on, any individual, because although it may save time it will do you no good' (*CDCV*, II, 109). Philip's words

to Covarrubias sounded remarkably similar: perhaps he remembered – or had even read again – what his father had told him.

52. The critical matters handled by these juntas largely escaped the scrutiny of the conciliar system and, until recently, the attention of historians: see Lovett, *Philip II*; idem, 'Juan de Ovando and the council of Finance,'; idem, 'The Castilian bankruptcy of 1575'; and Carlos Morales, *El consejo de Hacienda*, 113–78.

53. BL *Addl.* 28,263/222, Philip II to Mateo Vázquez, 14 Apr. 1579. See also BZ 144/16, same to same, 6 Nov. 1574: 'Since I wrote to you, something has come up that I need to talk to you about, so be ready from 1 o'clock onwards for when I call you, which will be when I can . . .'

54. BL *Addl* 28,399/20, Philip II to the viceroy of Sicily, 20 Jan. 1559, copy. See also AGS *Estado* 1049/107, Philip II to the viceroy of Naples, 13 Feb. 1559, minute (interestingly enough, the secretary had omitted the passage about 'sending letters directly to me' but the king noticed and ordered its insertion 'as in the other letters'). For Requeséns's direct correspondence, see p. 77 above.

55. BL *Addl* 28,357/45, Philip II to the governor of Lombardy, draft, 29 Aug. 1574; BZ 141/108, Philip II to Mateo Vázquez, 1 May 1586 (the 'offender' was the marquis of Almazán, viceroy of Navarre). This passage indicates that even Vázquez did not open letters addressed to the king 'en su mano'.

56. BL *Addl* 28,363/83, consulta of the count of Barajas, president of the council of Castile, 25 May 1587, with royal response.

57. Two further examples: Lagomarsino, 'Court factions', for the influence of Fray Lorenzo de Villavicencio on Philip II's response to the development of heresy in the Low Countries; and Loomie, *The Spanish Elizabethans*, chap. 3, for Hugo Owens. For some general reasons why the reports of outsiders are likely to impress

government ministers, see Halperin, *Bureaucratic politics*, 143–4 (quoting George F. Kennan).

58. Encinas, II, 311–15, repeated royal orders to various ministers in the Americas to allow everyone the freedom to write to him (1551, 1573, 1575, 1586 and 1595).

59. IVdeDJ 44/37–44, papers sent by Mendieta in Apr. 1587, forwarded to Vázquez on 29 Dec. and sent by him to the king on 7 Jan. 1588; and BZ 143/7, Vázquez to Philip II and reply, 9 Jan. 1588, about his meeting with 'un Acosta, jesuita'. On Mendieta, see Phelan, *The millenarial kingdom*; for an earlier letter of Mendieta to the king, see p. 58 above. On Acosta's mission to Spain in 1587–88, see Headley, 'Spain's Asian presence', 642–3.

60. Laubespine, 49, letter to the cardinal of Lorraine, 27 July 1559.

61. Carlos Morales, *El consejo de Hacienda*, 74 and 224; Schäfer, *El consejo . . . de las Indias*, 140; Thompson, *War and government*, 38. The councils did not work on Sundays or in Holy Week, however, and observed over fifty holidays: see Arrieta Alberdi, *El consejo . . . de Aragón*, 242–3.

62. Andrés, 'Diurnal', 17–22; IVdeDJ 97, 'Libro de memoriales' (20 Aug. 1583 to 31 Dec. 1584).

63. The hundreds of minor emendations made by the king to the letters sent to the Doria family have been noted by their editor, Rafael Vargas Hidalgo: pending their publication, see the report in the Spanish periodical *ABC*, 7 Oct. 1995, p. 59. Compare the testimony of Dean Rusk, United States Secretary of State, about the outgoing traffic of his department in the 1960s: 'Of the thousand or so cables that go out of here every day, I see only five or six and the President only one or two' (quoted in Halperin, *Bureaucratic politics*, 292).

64. Riba, 36, Philip II to Vázquez, 30 May 1576 ('Hoy no os he podido llamar por echar de my papeles, que lo menos ha sido firmar casi 400 firmas'). From 1543 until 1554 (when he

became king of England), Philip signed his Spanish letters 'Yo el príncipe'. Thereafter, although he signed letters written in French 'Phle', those to the pope and to Portugal 'El Rey', and those in German 'Philipp', his official style in Spanish remained 'Yo el Rey' – witness his testimony to the Spanish Inquisition during the Carranza trial in 1562 (surely the only time the king had to give evidence under oath): when asked to state his name, Philip replied 'Yo el Rey'! See Tellechea Idígoras, *Carranza*, III, 182–8 and 404–5. In 1593 he contemplated changing the 'Nos' (we), with which edicts customarily began, to 'Yo' (I): see Bouza Álvarez, 'Monarchie en lettres d'imprimerie', 209.

65. ASVe Senato: dispacci Spagna 20/68–72, Lippomano to Venice, 14 Apr. 1587 (partial précis in *CSPV*, VIII, 266); ACA *CA* 36/325, consulta of the council of Aragon, 25 Mar. 1594 (with the royal decree written and initialled by Prince Philip); AGNM *CRD* 1bis/43, Philip II to the viceroy of Mexico, 24 Sept. 1597 (announcing that because of the difficulty he now experienced in writing, and because Prince Philip 'is now a man and enjoys good health' who was 'beginning to learn about the business of government', he would henceforth sign royal letters. See also *Documentos . . . El Escorial*, II, 49, clause 16 of the codicil to Philip II's will, 23 Aug. 1597). Birch, *Memoirs*, 82, Anthony Standen to Lord Burghley, 8 Sept. 1592 (ironically, Burghley worked in a very similar way, preferring to read and write things himself rather than use secretaries: see Smith, 'The secretariats of the Cecils').

66. IVdeDJ 61/130 Philip II to Pedro de Hoyo, Apr. 1567; BL *Addl.* 28,699/114, Philip II to Mateo Vázquez, 2 May 1577. Normally, although the king could read papers in the countryside, he could not annotate them there: *CCG*, XII, 514–15, Philip II to Granvelle, 7 Aug. 1579. Two years later, however, he did manage to write

while in his carriage, and Granvelle chided him for working too hard (loc. cit., 621–2, Granvelle to Philip II, 27 Mar. 1581).

67. IVdeDJ 51/162 and 180, Vázquez to Philip II and reply, 11 Apr. and 15 Oct. 1578.

68. IVdeDJ 51/187 and 55/XI/121–2, Vázquez to Philip II and reply, 26 Jan. 1581 and 27 July 1588. For other examples of writing at ten without having broken off for dinner, see IVdeDJ 53/VI/17 and 21/253, same to same, 15 May 1577 and 14 July 1578.

69. Kamen, *Philip*, 251: Philip II memorandum, 3 Feb. 1584. For early examples of not reading incoming mail in full, see AGS *Estado* 524/4 and 6, Granvelle and Margaret of Parma to Philip II, 10 and 12 Mar. 1563, both with instructions to his secretary 'Sacadme los puntos'.

70. BZ 148/187, Vázquez to the marquis of Almazán, 17 July 1588, minute; BZ 143/88, Philip II to Vázquez and reply, 14 June 1588.

71. Longlée, 366, letter to Henry III, 30 Apr. 1588 (the king was then 61 years old); BRB *Ms* II.1028/270–v, 'Passetemps de Iehan Lhermite', describing and illustrating the clocks with candles attached (still to be seen in Philip's study at the Escorial); BL *Addl* 28,700/156, Vázquez to Philip II and reply, 14 Feb. 1587; and IVdeDJ 45/122–34 consultas for 12, 15, 16 and 18 Jan. 1596. IVdeDJ 45/122–256 and 349–548 contain numerous reports of the Junta Grande and the Junta de Gobierno for 1588–98. A study of these steering committees is urgently required; in the meantime see the discussion in Lovett, *Philip II*, 201–7.

72. Vargas Hidalgo, 'Documentos inéditos', 418, nuncio to Rome, 2 Aug. 1598; Feros, 'Lerma y Olivares', 210–11.

73. IVdeDJ 55/IX/79–82, Vázquez to Philip II and reply, 4 May 1586; BZ 146/219, council of Finance to Philip II, 14 June 1588, with royal reply on the 18th; and BZ 143/97, Vázquez to

Philip II and reply, 18 June 1588. A few months later, when it again seemed to the king that Vázquez was forwarding too many consultas, he told him not to send more ('unless they are urgent') until he started returning those he already had: IVdeDJ 55/XI/251–2, Vázquez to Philip II and reply, 18 Nov. 1588. Cf. President Kennedy doing the same in 1962: Sorensen, *Decision-making in the White House*, 18.

74. IVdeDJ 55/XI/149–50, Vázquez to Philip II and reply, 4 Aug. 1588. See the interesting comments of Sir Ian Jacob on Winston Churchill's 'priority system': Wheeler-Bennett, *Action this day*, 179.

75. Ricotti, 'Degli scritti di Emanuele-Filiberto', 94; Berwick y Alba, *Documentos escogidos*, 100–1, Córdoba to Alba, 1 Feb. 1571; AA 32/42 and 44, Córdoba to Prior Don Hernando de Toledo, 4 Aug. 1574 and 14 Sept. 1575.

76. Quotations from Johnson, *Managing the White House*, 19 and 35; see also Neustadt, *Presidential power*, 131–3, and Drucker, *The effective executive*, 149–50. Neustadt notes that such 'exposure to detail' can go too far, citing the examples of Presidents Herbert Hoover (1929–33), who personally read and approved every letter sent by the Budget Bureau to executive agencies, and Jimmy Carter (1977–81), who read between 300 and 450 pages of memoranda a day during his presidency (ibid., 336 n. 4 and 230). Johnson (*Managing the White House*, 177), likewise criticized the misconceived 'intrusions into detail' by President Lyndon Johnson (1963–69).

77. Wheeler-Bennett, *Action this day*, 178. See also Johnson, *Managing the White House*, 217 (President Richard Nixon, 1969–74, 'much preferred spending three minutes reading a memo to hearing someone out in person for a quarter of an hour'); and Drucker, *The effective executive*, 29–30 ('People are time-consumers and most people are time-wasters').

78. Quotations from Wheeler-Bennett, *Action this day*, 20 and 22 (Lord Normanbrook), 186–7 (Sir Ian Jacob) and 50 (Sir John Colville). Recently published documents reveal that the Soviet leader V. I. Lenin (1917–24) also 'treated his vast realm like a private estate, ordering remote provinces on one day to ship logs, specified to a fraction of an inch . . ., and on another, to deliver sheep and pigs' (Pipes, *The unknown Lenin*, 13, 81–2 and 136–7).

79. Donà, 350, letter to Venice, 23 Aug. 1571; Firpo, *Relazioni*, VIII, 669; Pérez de Herrera, *Elogio*, 92; van der Hammen, *Don Felipe el Prudente*, fo. 186.

80. Neustadt, *Presidential power*, 129–30. The author advised Presidents Truman and Carter, and President Nixon's advisers claimed to have studied the first (1960) edition closely. Johnson, *Managing the White House*, 133–4, praised President Kennedy's insistence on receiving data directly from a very wide range of sources and his refusal 'to take the chance that his subordinates were screening out criticisms, alternatives or information on his or their errors' (see also pp. 11 on Roosevelt and 63–4 on Truman, and the further examples in Sorensen, *Decision-making in the White House*, 36–9, and in Halperin, *Bureaucratic politics*, chap. 9). Margaret Thatcher agreed: close advisers (she wrote), whether or not members of the government, must be allowed direct access more or less when they wished 'if a prime minister is not to be the prisoner of his (or her) in-tray' (Thatcher, *The Downing Street years*, 135). President Bill Clinton in the 1990s maintained a special 'zip code' and a personal fax number that allowed trusted 'outsiders' to communicate directly to his private office any matters that they thought he should know. The dramatic consequences of 'tailoring' information to suit the perceived preferences of the central government of Wilhelmine Germany

appear in Lebow, *Between peace and war*, 126–30 and 140.

81. BZ 144/33, Vázquez to Philip II and reply, 6 Dec. 1574. For an example of a secret correspondence, Mateo Vázquez's exchanges with the duke of Medinaceli in 1572–73, see pp. 130–1 above; for examples of intercepted and opened letters see p. 54 above.

82. IVdeDJ 55/IV/65, Vázquez to Philip II and reply, 29 Aug. 1581. The king claimed that such secrecy was necessary 'because if it is known that meetings are taking place, once people see who is involved they will guess the subject'.

83. Fourquevaux, II, 304: letter Charles IX, 19 Dec. 1570. See also ibid., pp. 389–90, to same, 12 Nov. 1571 ('He is a prince who keeps [his thoughts] in his heart and does not say what he thinks'); and Donà, 233 and 509, letters to Venice of 14 Mar. 1571 ('nel cuori [of Philip and his ministers] non posso penetrar') and 16 July 1572 (on their 'misterio di exquisita taciturnità').

84. Solórzano y Pereira, *Política indiana*, V, 166, quoting the marquis of Montesclaros, viceroy of Peru 1607–15.

85. See the regional examples in Céspedes del Castillo, 'La visita como institución indiana'; Rizzo, 'Finanza pubblica'; Peytavin, *La Visite*; and Lefèvre, 'Le Tribunal de la Visite'. For a *visita* of a council, see Carlos Morales, *El consejo de Hacienda*, 94–9; and of an overseas institution, see Phelan, *The kingdom of Quito*, part III.

86. Antonio Clementino in 1577 quoted in Bratli, *Philippe II*, 224. See two examples quoted in Salazar, *Política española*, 112–13.

87. See, for example, AGS *Estado* 139/201, corrected cédula of 1560 in favour of Francisco de Erasso, the most powerful secretary at this time: the king had spotted that the total of the rewards accorded exceeded the sum of the parts. See a further example,

from the records of the council of the Indies, cited in Parker, *Philip II*, 34–5.

88. BL *Addl* 28,263/432, Mateo Vázquez to Philip II and reply, 11 Aug. 1587. On Piedrola, see Kagan, *Lucrecia's dreams*, 95–101, and p. 34 above.

89. See, by way of example, Riba, 54–5: Vázquez to Philip II and reply, 3 Sept. 1576 (the king repeated three times that he needed more information before taking a decision); BL *Addl* 28,700/339, Philip II to Vázquez, 25 May 1590 ('until I am better informed, I do not wish to comment on this matter': Vázquez was to find out more 'and give me a report on it all, so that I can see what should be done'); BL *Addl* 28,528/30–1, Vázquez to Philip II and reply, 9 Apr. 1582 (concerning a letter from Vespasian Gonzaga, of which 'I could not make out a single word': would Vázquez make a copy); and BL *Addl* 28,702/96–8, Granvelle to Philip II and reply, 3 Mar. 1582 (translate into Castilian a letter from Mary queen of Scots 'which is very badly written').

90. See, for example, the testy 'Do this again, without the underlined bit which no one will understand': IVdeDJ 55/X/181, Philip II to the duke of Albuquerque, Oct. 1587, draft. For another example of the king correcting the diplomatic style of an improperly drafted letter, see BL *Addl.* 28,263/236, Philip II to Mateo Vázquez, 3 Feb. 1581.

91. BL *Addl* 28,361/110, corrected draft of the Pragmatic, 11 Sept. 1586, returned to Mateo Vázquez who (sarcastically?) endorsed the file 'Coronets and courtesies'. Numerous drafts of the *Pragmática en que se da la orden y forma que se ha de tener y guardar en los tratamientos y cortesías de palabra y por escripto* (finally issued on 8 Oct. 1586), festooned with royal apostils, fill fos 31–145 of this volume.

92. AGS *Estado* 949/191–5, 'Lo que Su Magestad resolvió' (on allocating the vast number of benefices left vacant by Cardinal Granvelle); BZ 134/1, undated Philip II memorandum (*c.*

1571), and BZ 135/77 royal, apostil on the count of Barajas to Vázquez, 16 Apr. 1579 (concerning palace etiquette); BZ 85/65, Don Juan de Zúñiga to Philip II and reply, 1585 (on coaches); IVdeDJ 45/464, Junta Grande to Philip II and reply, 10 June 1592 (on how the city of Valladolid should receive him); IVdeDJ 55/VIII/ 25, Vázquez to Philip II and reply, 4 Oct. 1585 (on lodgings); ACA *Generalitat* 929/120–3v, Philip II to viceroy, standing committee of the Estates and council in Barcelona, 23 Apr. 1564 (concerning the division of the new royal palace in Barcelona between the Inquisition and the standing committee of the Estates, specifying which windows, rooms and corridors could be used by each); and IVdeDJ 7/46 (numerous papers from the 1590s on applicants for minor offices in the palace). See also IVdeDJ 61/338, Pedro de Hoyo to Philip II and reply, undated (1567) on making appointments ('but do not let anyone know I am doing this, so that they will not interrupt me, because I need peace and a lot of time').

93. On papal fury at the new court etiquette, see Mosconi, *La nunziatura*, 61–5; Hübner, *Sixte-Quint*, I, 381–5; AGS *Estado* 951/181, Francisco de Idiáquez to Philip II and reply, undated [winter 1586–87]; and González Novalín, *Historia de la Iglesia*, III.2, 70–1. See also the report of discontent among Philip's courtiers over the new style in BAV *UL* 1115/ 108–9, 'Aviso' from Madrid, 10 Jan. 1587; and ASMa *AG Spagna* 600a, unfol., Cavriani to Mantua, 6 Mar. 1587. See also Kamen, *Philip*, 231.

94. AGS *GA* 198/98, Antonio de Guevara to Andrés de Alva, 14 June 1587. Some twenty years before, when the king's valet Sebastián de Santoyo fell ill, he jested that whereas most convalescents craved water to help their recovery, he craved ink: Bouza Álvarez, 'Cortes festejantes', 192–3.

95. IVdeDJ 61/19, Pedro de Hoyo to Philip II and reply, 22 May 1562 (for

another similar exchange, see *PEG*, VI, 144, Philip II to Granvelle, 7 Sept. 1560); BL *Addl* 28,350/233, Philip II to Hoyo, mid-Dec. 1565; AA 5/69, Philip II to Alba, 7 Aug. 1567 (see p. 122 above); and *Addl* 28,263/2, holograph transcript by the king of two letters from Antonio de Guaras, 11 and 19 Apr. 1574 (admittedly the king proceeded to correct certain errors made by Guaras; but this too could have been done with less effort on his part).

96. BL *Addl* 28,263/62–3, Philip II to Mateo Vázquez, 27 Oct. 1576. See also IVdeDJ 51/49, Philip II to Vázquez, 30 Aug. 1575: 'I have been waiting for the dossier that you have to send for Juan Vázquez until now, which is 11 p.m., and I cannot wait any longer, because of my eyes and my head – all the more so because I must go to church tomorrow for Mass.' Two more pages of stream-of-consciousness followed. On 11 Apr. 1578 he began 'after 9:30 p.m.' a letter to Mateo Vázquez, the last of several that day, announcing that he was too busy and tired to transact any more business – yet in the next half-hour he covered almost three sides of octavo paper with some 500 words (IVdeDJ 51/162, Vázquez to Philip II and reply, 11 Apr. 1578). For another example of late-night verbal diarrhoea, from 1565, see Kamen, *Philip*, 99.

97. AGS *Estado* 165/24, 'Lo que Su Magestad es servido' (the word was 'de' in 'de detener'); AGS *Estado* K 1567/46B, 'Avisos de Londres'; IVdeDJ 55/XII/40, Philip II to Mateo Vázquez, 28 Apr. 1589.

98. AGS *Estado* 137/227, Princess Juana to Philip II, 14 July 1559, with royal reply 'quiero . . . hazer lo que sé que mas me combiene, que es irme sin andar aprovechándome de parecer de nadie'; AGRB *MD* 5480/232, Granvelle memorandum, 14 Aug. 1579, about the reconciliation of the Walloon provinces of the Low Countries (*CCG*, XII, 567, provides

an incorrect identification and an inaccurate transcript.)

99. I am grateful to Eliot Cohen, Ronald Meijers, David van Deusen and Marjoleine van Doorn-Claassen for sharing their expertise on this point with me. See also Barnard, *The function of the executive*; Chandler, *Strategy and structure*, 1–51; and Drucker, 'The coming of the new organization' and *The effective executive*.

100. On Philip's admirable reasons for appointing Medina, see Pierson, *Commander of the Armada*, 83–6.

101. On Alba, see *CDCV*, III, 109, Charles V's Instruction to Philip, 4 May 1543: 'in matters of state and war . . . he is the best man we have in Spain'. On the commanders he trained, see González de León, 'The road to Rocroi', chap. 1.

102. AGS *Estado* 2843/1, 'Parescer' of the council of State, 11 Sept. 1577; HHStA *Belgien PA* 90/109, Philip II to Parma, 31 Oct. 1578.

103. On the proposed punishment of Alba, see IVdeDJ 36/40, 'Lo que a Su Magestad ha parecido advertir sobre la relación de los excessos que se dize se han hecho en los Estados de Flandes' [8–10 Mar. 1574] and BL *Addl* 28,702/244–74, various 'relaciones' of accusations labelled 'B' to 'F'. The appropriate response is discussed in IVdeDJ 45/329, the reports of the 'Juntas grande y particular', 15 Mar. 1574; and ibid., 44/57–60, Mateo Vázquez to Philip II, 11 and 15 Apr. and 14 June 1574. The king's advisers recommended banishing Alba from the Court, but the king demurred: 'Although making this gesture would give me great satisfaction, I do not wish to do it without further advice.' Later on he did banish Alba's former advisers, but for a totally different reason (see Maltby, *Alba*, 271–82). In Parma's case, likewise, the king eventually withdrew his support and ordered his recall, but only when Parma systematically refused to carry out orders to intervene in France: see Parker, *Dutch Revolt*, 228–30.

104. ACA *CA* 33/1, Philip II to Juana, his regent in Spain, 8 Sept. 1556 (vetoing one of her suggestions for the position of justiciar of Aragon on the grounds that the man had opposed a recent piece of government legislation); *BMO*, II, 378, Philip II to Parma, 19 Oct. 1586.

105. For Alba, see AA 160/18, 'Los agravios' (a list of Alba's grievances since his nomination on 29 Nov. 1566); for Toledo, see Ramos, 'La crisis indiana', 51–61; for Pedro Menéndez, see ASG *AS* 2415, unfol., Sauli to Genoa, 18 July 1574; for Don Juan, see BPU *Favre* 28/97–101, Philip II to duke of Sessa, 27 Dec. 1576.

106. On Requeséns's sad story, see p. 132 above. Don John of Austria insisted on meeting with the king before moving from Italy to the Netherlands in 1576, but he disobeyed Philip's express command in order to do so: see GCP, V, xvi–xix. According to ASMa *AG Spagna* 601, unfol., Cavriano to Mantua, 2 Mar. 1588, the king rejected Medina Sidonia's request to 'come and kiss his hands' on his way to Lisbon.

107. *BMO*, III, 1964, Bertendona to Philip II, 15 Feb. 1588. Disagreements continued throughout the Armada campaign: see pp. 264–5 above.

108. KML *MSP CR* 5/82, Philip II to Medina Sidonia, 11 Mar. 1588: 'Creed que de tal manera considero la importancia desta jornada, que si yo no fuera menester tanto acá, para acudir a lo que para ella y otras muchas cosas es menester, holgara mucho de hallarme en ella; y lo hiziera con gran confiança que me havía de suceder muy bien'.

109. Bouza, 114: Philip II to Catalina, 27 Aug. 1586. Philip may have recalled that the prestige of his father Charles V had suffered gravely because of his presence at the failed sieges of Algiers (1541) and Metz (1552).

110. See for example *CDCV*, III, 593, Charles V to Philip II, 2 Apr. 1552 (urgent pleas for money and men carried by Alba); ibid., IV, 147, same to same, 7 Dec. 1554 (about letters, instructions and communications from Philip brought by Erasso); and Kervijn de Lettenhove, *Relations politiques*, I, 55–9 (Philip's Instructions to Ruy Gómez, going to Mary in England and Charles in Spain, 2 Feb. 1557).

111. Admittedly Philip entrusted the plan of 26 July 1586 (pp. 186–7 above) to the same confidential messenger – Giovanni Battista Piatti – who had brought Parma's invasion scheme to Court earlier in the year, and Piatti seems to have received a briefing from the king and his ministers (AGS *Estado* 2218/56, Don Juan de Idiáquez to Parma, 27 July 1586); but this seems to have been a rare reversion to the standard practice of the 1550s.

112. Drucker, *The effective executive*, 142 (a brilliant insight). For a couple of practical examples, see pp. 162–3 and 267 above.

113. See pp. 170 and 180 above. For other examples of strategic planning, see *CCG*, X, 174–8, Granvelle to Idiáquez, 6 May 1583, discussing position papers (not included in the dossier) on the overall strategy of the Monarchy; and ibid., XI, 617–32, papers prepared by Don Juan de Zúñiga on the foreign policy problems facing the Monarchy in June 1584 (pp. 171–2 above).

114. IVdeDJ 56, paquete 6–2, unfol., Hernando de Avalos to Vázquez, with royal apostil, 25 Mar. 1576; ibid. 53/3/65 and 53/4/169, Philip II to Vázquez and reply, 8 June 1574 and 12 Sept. 1575. For later examples, see ibid. 53/5/25 and 55/IX/151–2, ibid., 10 Feb. 1576 and 4 Nov. 1586.

115. IVdeDJ 53/3/76, Mateo Vázquez to Philip II and reply, 26 July 1574.

116. BL *Addl* 28,699/103, Philip II to Mateo Vázquez, 22 Apr. 1577. Juan Fernández de Espinosa, the author, duly arrived 'with the memorandum in his hand' the following day for an audience: see p. 18 above.

117. AGS *CJH* 249, carpetas 16–18 contain numerous *Relaciones de sábado* from 1588, almost all bearing tortured royal annotations and computations. For an earlier example of Philip's attempts to fathom his financial problems directly, see *PEG*, VI, 156–65, a seven-folio holograph financial statement by Philip II (apparently based on AGS *Estado* 139/294 'Relación de las consignaciones', 6 Oct. 1560, with long royal comments).

118. *GPGP*, II, 524–5, Gonzalo Pérez to Philip II and reply, 13 Aug. 1565. The king's anxiety on this score continued to the end of his life: as late as 1593 he agonized over appointing the best candidate to be justiciar of Aragon since 'it is so important to get it right': ACA *CA* 33/9, consulta of the council of Aragon [23 May 1593].

119. Kervijn de Lettenhove, *Relations politiques*, I, 59, Philip II's Instructions to Ruy Gómez, 2 Feb. 1557. In the event Charles refused, but agreed not to renounce the imperial title for a while.

120. Cabié, *Ambassade*, 432–3. See also Fourquevaux, I, 11, letter to Catherine de Medici (the Infanta's grandmother), 26 Sept. 1566.

121. AGS *Estado* 527/5 and 146/147, Gonzalo Pérez to Philip II and reply, [24] Mar. and [10] Apr. 1565.

122. IVdeDJ 51/172 and 51, Philip II to Mateo Vázquez [undated, but 1574] and 19 July 1575.

123. IVdeDJ 53/3/56 and BZ 144/34, Vázquez to Philip II and reply, 13 May and 10 Dec. 1574.

124. IVdeDJ 44/119, Mateo Vázquez to Philip II and reply, 10 Mar. 1575. See also BZ 144/61, same to same, 31 May 1575: 'There are so many things [to do] that I do not know how I get through each hour.' See other examples in Kamen, *Philip*, 273.

125. See the perceptive remarks on the impact of stress on policy-making in Lebow and Stein, *We all lost the Cold War*, 331–8 (quotations from p. 331).

See also Holsti, *Crisis, escalation, war*, chap. 1; Breakwell and Spacie, *Pressures facing commanders*, 11 and 26 (based on interviews with over 100 commanders and staff officers); and the case-studies in Part II above.

126. IVdeDJ 55/XII/4, Philip II to the Junta Grande, 13 Jan. 1589 (arthritis) and 55/XI/249, Vázquez to Philip II and reply, 15 Nov. 1588 (stomach ache); BL *Addl* 28,700/151 and 155, Vázquez to Philip II and reply, 7 and 9 Feb. 1587 ('flu'). One day in 1580 he reported to his daughters that his stomach ached after eating too many melons: Bouza, 50.

127. IVdeDJ 55/IX/155, 93 and 217, Vázquez to Philip II and reply, 8 Nov. and 7 June 1586, and 17 Oct. 1588. See an earlier complaint about his sight failing him at night in Kamen, *Philip*, 209. Ironically, his glasses (*antojos*) may have come from England: see *CSPSp*, II, 674, Bernardino de Mendoza to Philip II, 14 May 1579, announcing the dispatch of a pair.

128. BL *Addl* 28,357/13, Philip II to Alba, 28 July 1573. Oliveros de Castro and Subiza Martín, *Felipe II*, 197, suggest that the various ailments were related to chronic malaria; but even so, the trigger seems to have been psychological stress.

129. BL *Addl.* 28,363/220, comment of Juan Ruiz de Velasco on a letter from Zayas to Mateo Vázquez, 12 May 1587; BL *Addl* 28,376/33–4, Andrés de Prada to Don Juan de Idiáquez, 17 May 1587.

130. BL *Addl* 28,363/116–17 and 112, Ruiz de Velasco to Mateo Vázquez, 20 and 30 June 1587 (the latter replying to a Vázquez note of 17 June); Riba, *El consejo supremo de Aragón*, 51, count of Chinchón to Mateo Vázquez, 19 Sept. 1587.

131. IVdeDJ 38/70, Diego de Espinosa to Philip II and reply, undated [= spring 1569]. The king continued: 'Do not be sad at what I have written, for since I cannot unburden myself with anyone but you, I cannot refrain from doing

so.' See also pp. 143 and 271 above and p. 404 n. 5 below.

2   *Distance: Public Enemy Number 1?*

1.   Van Creveld, *Command in war*, 264–5.
2.   Spengler, *Der Untergang des Abendlandes* (1918), and Satow, *A guide to diplomatic practice* (1917), both quoted by Kern, *The culture of time and space*, 160 and 275. I have learned a great deal from Kern's brilliant study, especially from Chapter 10, 'Temporality of the July Crisis', and I thank Robert Tomilson for bringing it to my attention. On the dramatic impact of the telegraph on the relations between government, generals and the public in wartime, see Dean, '"We live under a government of men and morning newspapers"'.
3.   BSLE Ms I. III. 30/122v, from the 'Raggionamento' of Philip II. See the perceptive analyses of the problems posed by distance in early modern Europe in Braudel, *The Mediterranean*, I, 354–94; and Delumeau, *Vie économique et sociale*, I, 23–79.
4.   See Devos, 'La Poste au service des diplomates espagnols'; and Alcázar Molina, 'La política postal española' (the contract of 1516 is discussed at pp. 227–9). See also Allen, *Post and courier service*, 91–106; Lunitz, *Diplomatie und Diplomaten*, 163–77; Fagel, *De Hispano-Vlaamse Wereld*, 310–23; and Brayshay, 'Royal post-horse routes'.
5.   See *Epistolario*, I, 647–9 and 654, Alba to Margaret of Parma, 16 June and 10 July 1567 for the 'Spanish Road' courier chain; and *Epistolario*, III, 121–3, Alba to Philip II, 24 May 1572 for the decision to send duplicates.
6.   Carter, *Secret diplomacy*, 269.
7.   Fourquevaux, II, 127–8 and 142, letter to Charles IX and report attached, 31 Oct. 1569 (see also the account in Álava, 372, Philip II to Don Francés de Álava, 4 Nov. 1569);

Fourquevaux, II, 206–7, letter to Catherine de Medici, 3 Apr. 1570 (the courier carried the marriage contract between Charles IX and Elisabeth of Austria, negotiated in Madrid and sent to Paris on 18 Jan.); and Mulcahy, 'Two murders'.

8.   Fourquevaux, II, 338, letter to Charles IX, 31 Mar. 1571. For examples of letters entrusted to Spanish couriers, see ibid., 172, 206, 241 and so on. Admittedly Spanish ministers sometimes entrusted letters to French couriers, but only when they contained nothing compromising: see, for example, Álava, 354 and 380, Philip II to Álava, 4 July 1569 (announcing that he was not sending a new cipher to his ambassador because the package would be carried by Fourquevaux's servant) and 15 Dec. 1569 (stating that he would not reply to Álava's recently received letters 'because this will be carried by a courier of Fourquevaux').
9.   Donà, 298–9, 303–4, 316–18 and 372–5, letters to Venice on 7, 15 and 28 June, and 2 Nov. 1571, about incoming news; and 234–5, 390–1 and 491–2, letters on 14 Mar. and 26 Nov. 1571 and 18 June 1572 (among many others) about giving letters to Pérez in advance. See also IVdeDJ 60/335, Antonio Pérez to Philip II, 6 June 1571, announcing that at 3 p.m. he had received news that the Holy League had been signed on 20 May.
10.   Lorenzo Sanz, *Comercio de España*, I, 34; Burkholder and Johnson, *Colonial Latin America*, 70–1.
11.   Couto, *Da Ásia: decada X*, 17–18, 27–31 and 150–1; Ruiz Martín, *Lettres marchandes*, 401, Simón Ruiz to Baltasar Suárez, 26 Aug. 1585; AGS *SP* 1551/274–81, bishop of Malacca to Philip II, 31 Dec. 1588.
12.   AGNM *CRD* II/15–36 and 240–3. The only other detailed record of letters received came in 1588 (fos 181v–6v), but many of these had been affected by Drake's activity and the Armada, both of which interfered with the departure of the annual

convoys. For examples of 'naves de aviso', both from the Americas announcing the dispatch of the fleet, and from Andalusia warning of some hazard, see Lorenzo Sanz, *Comercio de España*, I, 37–8; and Andrews, *The last voyage of Drake and Hawkins*, 12–19.

13. Data from Paris based in BNP *Ms. esp.* 132; and from Venice based on Pierre Sardella's calculations from the 'diaries' kept by Marino Sanudo of Venice between 1497 and 1532 (which recorded the date on which each letter received in Venice was written and the time it arrived), summarized by Braudel, *The Mediterranean*, I, 362–6.

14. *GPGP*, II, 557: Philip II to Pérez, n.d. [=4 Oct. 1565]; and *Reivindicación*, 416. See another example on p. 123 above, and compare Charles V's wish, a generation earlier, that a courier bearing an important dispatch to his brother 'could fly': Lanz, *Korrespondenz*, II, 361, to Ferdinand, 11 Jan. 1530.

15. UB Leiden, *Hs Pap.* 3/4, Alonso de Laloo to Count Hornes, 20 Sept. 1566, reported the journey of 'un correo spañol' from Brussels to Segovia in ten days, and of 'Jacques correo' in only nine days. *Epistolario*, III, 133–4, Alba to Philip II, 12 June 1572, noted the arrival of another courier (travelling the other way) in ten days. In 1633 a courier left Irún on 16 June and arrived in Brussels on the 22nd, '230 leagues in 6 days' – over 150 kilometres a day – which seems to constitute the early modern overland record: AGS *Estado* 2240, unfol., certificate of Juan de Arbalayz.

16. Donà, 373, letter to Venice, 2 Nov. 1571. News of the battle on 7 Oct. arrived in Madrid at 2 p.m. on the 31st: see p. 19 above. Strangely, the king had to make do with Donà's detailed account for almost two months after this: see BL *Addl* 28,528/11, Philip II to Don Juan de Zúñiga, 25 Nov. 1571, complaining that he had only just received the full story on Lepanto. Donà, 493, letter to Venice of 18 June 1572.

17. *CCG*, X, 50, Foncq to Granvelle, 7 Feb. 1583; BL *Addl.* 35841/146–7v, Anthony Standen to Jacopo Manucci, 28 May 1588.

18. RAH Ms 9–1–4–A60/125, bishop of Osma to Granvelle, 1 Feb. 1557; Donà, 74–5, letter to Venice of 1 Sept. 1570; AA 8/45, Philip II to Alba, 8 July 1573, received 19 Aug. (see p. 140 above).

19. For details, see (respectively) Álava, 257, Zayas to Álava, 10 Sept. 1568; Allen, *Post and courier service*, 79–80; Álava, 316–17 and 341–2, Philip II to Álava, 20 Mar. and 25 June 1569; Preto, *I servizi segreti*, 294–7. In 1572 the frequency with which couriers were robbed in France provoked a formal protest from the Spanish secretary of state to the French ambassador: Fourquevaux, II, 420, letter to Charles IX, 12 Feb. 1572.

20. Woltjer, *Friesland in hervormingstijd*, 3, Count Aremberg to Margaret of Parma, 15 Sept. 1566 ('ceulx de pied ont meilleur moyen de faire diligence que les autres'); AGS *CJH* 75, unfol., Gregorio de Guzmán, corregidor of Palencia, to Philip II, 30 May 1566.

21. *CSPSp.*, IV, 637–41 and 644. In the 1640s, when Spain again supported an Irish rebellion, letters from Spanish agents in Ireland could take between three and eight months to reach Madrid, and the replies could take up to eleven months to arrive: Ohlmeyer, 'Ireland independent', 96.

22. *CSPSp*, II, 2–3, Diego Guzmán de Silva to Philip II, 10 Jan. 1568 (acknowledging receipt of the king's letters of 14–15 Oct. 1567) and vice versa, 4 Feb. 1568 (Guzmán's letters of 1, 7 and 15 Nov. 1567 only arrived on 26 Jan.); IVdeDJ 37/65, Don Luis de Requeséns to Don Juan de Zúñiga, 28 Aug. 1575; AGS *Estado* 688/93ff, Don Guillén de San Clemente to Philip II, 1 Aug. to 1 Dec. 1581 (eight letters). For other examples of various postal calamities, see ASP *CF* 108, unfol., Tomás de Armenteros to the duke of Parma, 27 Aug. 1564, reporting that he would have to send

letters from Brussels to Italy via Lorraine because plague afflicted Switzerland; OÖLA *KB* IV/245v and 261, Khevenhüller to Rudolf II, 13 May and 23 July 1587 lamenting that a courier carrying letters for him had been imprisoned in France, so that he lacked news of the imperial Court; and ASG *AS* 2418/3/333, Spinola and Doria to the Doge and Senate, 1 May 1587, also complaining that three couriers carrying letters from Madrid to Genoa had been robbed in France.

23. AGNM *CRD* XLVII/153v–4v, Philip II to Audiencia, 4 July 1570, copy, expediente 256; *BMO*, II, 34, Parma to Philip II, 28 Feb. 1586. See the excellent study of MacKay, 'To obey and comply', and pp. 151–2 and 157–63 above on 'sub-imperial' agendas in the Spanish Monarchy.

24. For example, on 18 Nov. 1574 Requeséns sent a letter to Philip II in triplicate, one via the Spanish Road and two via the Spanish ambassador in Paris, who sent one overland by the normal post route and the other to Nantes and thence by sea to Spain. The original (sent overland) arrived at Court on 18 Dec. (exactly one month later), the duplicate (sent via Nantes) on 10 Jan., the triplicate (sent by Italy) on 20 Jan.: see AGS *Estado* 560/12, endorsement. Requeséns explained his system to the king in a letter of 10 Sept. 1575 (*Estado* 564/108). Details such as these are elusive because Philip normally ordered duplicates to be destroyed once the original arrived: BZ 144/17, Vázquez to Philip II and reply, 7 Oct. 1574 ('This dossier from Requeséns came by way of Italy. I believe it is a duplicate: if it is, you can burn it'). Merchants also routinely sent duplicates: see p. 57 above.

25. Newsletters compiled by merchants or magistrates in the leading European cities carried items relayed from other centres: see BAV *UL* 1056, 'Avvisi dell'anno 1588' for an excellent collection.

26. *Epistolario*, III, 99–101, Alba to Don Antonio de Toledo, 27 Apr. 1572 ('Los negocios de aquí están en muchos peores terminos de lo que escribo a Su Magestad'); AGS *Estado* 551/27, Joachim Hopperus, French language secretary at Court, to Philip II, 22 Apr. 1572, enclosing several letters about the loss of Brill; *Estado* 553/95 and 99, Philip II to Alba, 30 Apr. 1572, minute (royal apostil noting that he had found out from Hopperus), and 17 May 1572, minute (saying that 'we heard about Lumey's descent before your letters arrived'); *Epistolario*, III, 91 and 133, Alba to Philip II, 26 Apr. 1572, with news of the Brill, and 12 June 1572, apologizing for his silence; and pp. 124–6 above. For another powerful viceroy striving unsuccessfully to control the flow of information to his master, see Merritt, 'Power and communication', 126–7 (Strafford in Ireland in the 1630s).

27. AGNM *Mercedes* V/215–215v, decree of Viceroy Luis de Velasco, 21 Jan. 1561.

28. See Cumming, 'The Parreus map'; and (for the 1580s), pp. 201 and 221–3 above. Although we lack a study of Philip II's diplomatic corps, see the useful overview in Carter, 'The ambassadors of early modern Europe'; and also the case-studies of Levin, 'A Spanish eye on Italy'; Fernández Álvarez, *Tres embajadores*; and Jensen, *Diplomacy and dogmatism*.

29. *Co.Do.In.*, XCVIII, 483, Philip II to count of Luna, 8 Aug. 1563; *Co.Do. In.*, XXXII, 189–497: between 1 July and 30 Aug. 1580 Alba wrote no fewer than seventy-two letters to Philip II; *BMO*, III, 1868–69, report of Santa Cruz to the count of Fuentes, *c.* 4 Feb. 1588. The papal nuncio believed that Santa Cruz's sources were superior to the king's, mainly received from Mendoza in Paris: English affairs 'are known earlier and better in Portugal than here [Madrid]' (ASV *NS* 32/82, Lodi to Rusticucci, 8 Mar. 1586). Philip agreed: on one occasion he suggested sending Mendoza a copy of the information gathered by

Santa Cruz's agents: *BMO*, II, 474, Philip II to Mendoza, 17 Dec. 1586, minute with royal apostil.

30. Plaisant, *Aspetti e problemi*, 103, Instruction to the count of Lodosa, 21 Nov. 1595; Álava, 370, Zayas to Álava, 3 Sept. 1569 (asking to receive copies not only of the ambassador's missives to other ministers but also a copy, or at least a summary, of the letter to which he replied). For the critical importance of 'sharing information' in any large enterprise, see Drucker, 'The coming of the new organization', 49; Destler, *Presidents*, 52–82; and Fukuyama and Shulsky, *The 'virtual corporation'*, 29.

31. See *Co.Do.In.*, CII, 35n for evidence that Zúñiga drafted his brother's letters, which Requeséns merely copied out and sent. For the frequency of their correspondence, see *Nueva Co.Do.In*, V, 290–2, Requeséns to Zúñiga, 28 Sept. 1574, and *passim*.

32. RAH Ms 9–1–4–A60, Requeséns to Granvelle, 3 June 1557; Granvelle's reply of 15 Nov. reproduced in Bouza Álvarez, 'Guardar papeles, I', 4; and Martínez Millán, 'Un curioso manuscrito'. On 'factions' at Court, see p. 25 above.

33. Alba's Academy has been virtually forgotten, but see the fascinating sketch by Bouza Álvarez, 'Corte es decepción', 459–61, with numerous quotations from the witty and highly indiscreet correspondence of Don Juan de Silva with his fellow 'academicians'.

34. Zúñiga's incoming letters from other ministers between 1571 and 1583 (when he returned to Spain) take up twenty-nine boxes in BZ alone (*cajas* 62–92, though not box 85), with more in BPU: see the inventory in Bouza Álvarez, 'Guardar papeles, II'. AGS *Estado* 1539–40 contains the incoming correspondence of Cristóbal de Salazar in Venice. For examples of 'inter-office correspondence' among Philip II's ministers in Madrid, see Bouza Álvarez, 'Guardar papeles, I', 8–9.

35. Individual and total costs from AGS *Estado* 146/189 'Lo que se a gastado en los correos'; and Le Glay and Finot, *Inventaire sommaire... Nord*, V, 322 (£7,543 for maintaining the courier service in Lorraine and Franche-Comté in 1588–90). See the heavy expenditure on *correos* in the accounts of Don Luis de Requeséns, ambassador in Rome 1563–68: IVdeDJ 22/2/D21, 'Relación de gastos', and the data in Jensen, *Diplomacy and dogmatism*, 128–9; Allen, *Post and courier service*, 50–1; and Fernández Álvarez, *Felipe II*, 102–4.

36. See the selections of Ruiz's correspondence published by Gentil da Silva, *Stratégie des affaires*; Vázquez de Prada, *Lettres marchandes*; Ruiz Martín, *Lettres marchandes*; and the general remarks of Lorenzo Sanz, *Comercio de España*, 26–42.

37. For the theory, see Encinas, II, 313, Philip II to the viceroy of Peru, 14 Sept. 1592; for the practice, see IVdeDJ 60/307, Antonio Pérez to Philip II and reply, undated, concerning a letter from the duke of Alba to Don Antonio de Toledo [1572–73]; ibid., 51/17, Philip II to Vázquez, 17 July 1573, concerning letters about the Netherlands; and ibid., 21/716, royal apostil on Fray Antonio de San Pablo to Vázquez, 17 Nov. 1581. For other examples, see González de Amezúa, *Isabella de Valois*, II, 133n, Philip's order to have a secret copy made of a letter written to his wife by her mother; IVdeDJ 60/259, Antonio Pérez to Philip II, undated (but 1566–67), discussing letters written by Baron Montigny, resident at Court, which had been opened 'on Your Majesty's orders'; and AGS *Estado* 149/176–7, letters written by the marquis of Berghes and his secretary, also at the Spanish Court, in Mar. 1567, intercepted and read by Philip II's ministers. Of course Philip II was not alone in this practice: Preto, *I servizi segreti*, 294–7, records numerous examples of Italian governments opening other people's

mail; while Potter, *Secret rites*, 39–40, and Firth, 'Thurloe and the Post Office', document the opening and copying of all diplomatic and a selection of other mail entering and leaving London in the 1640s and 1650s.

38. Longlée, 390–401: the originals and decrypts. Alfred Mousset, editor of the volume, found Longlée's cipher key and made his own transcript of the documents, revealing that the Spanish codebreaker (Luis Valle de la Cerda) had made many mistakes (see pp. l–li).

39. Phelan, *The millenarial kingdom*, 78.

40. BL *Eg*. 1506/21–2, Quiroga to Philip II and reply, 16 July 1574 ('Yo lo vi por mis ojos'). For a striking feat of memory – when the king managed to identify (and provide the 'full bibliographic record' for!) one book missing from a consignment of 473 sent in 1566 to the Escorial – see Antolín, 'La librería de Felipe II', 480.

41. AGNM *CRD* II/184 (expediente 337), Philip II to the viceroy and Audiencia of New Spain, 29 June 1588; *APO*, III, 826, Philip II (signed by his son) to Viceroy Dom Francisco da Gama, 26 Jan. 1598.

42. *CCG*, I, 469–74, Granvelle to Philip II, 15 Sept. 1566, with appreciative comments by the king. Four years later the duke of Alba likewise evaluated from his own experience the various possible itineraries for the journey of Philip's bride, Anna, from Vienna to Spain: *Epistolario*, II, 423–4, Alba to Philip II, 15 Sept. 1570.

43. See Maltby, *Alba*, 195, and pp. 149 and 158 above. See also the council of State's debate on the issue of a General Pardon for the Dutch rebels in 1574, which included a detailed discussion of what had happened after the Comuneros rising in Castile, fifty-two years before: AGS *Estado* 561/25, consulta of 24 Feb. 1574. See also ibid., 561/77, Requeséns to Philip II, 12 May 1574, and the document cited in Bouza Álvarez, 'Guardar papeles, I', 6. In 1569 Philip recalled that the rivalry between Catherine de Medici

and the Cardinal of Lorraine closely resembled her rivalry with the cardinal's father in 1546–47: Álava, 342, Philip II to Álava, 25 June 1569. A decade later he even discussed with Mateo Vázquez an incident that he thought might have happened when he was in his mother's womb! (Muro, *Vida*, appendix 43 and facsimile). See other examples at pp. 116 and 138 above.

44. See the definitive edition of Kagan, *Spanish cities of the Golden Age*.

45. Guevara, *Comentarios de la pintura*, 219–21. See also Kagan, *Spanish cities*, 44–5.

46. BSLE, Ms K.I.1: each map measures approximately 19 by 28 inches. The calculation of 1:430,000 comes from Vázquez Maure, 'Cartografía de la península', 62. For a discussion of how the maps were made, see Parker, 'Maps and ministers', 130–4. That article also discusses two similar projects initiated slightly earlier by Philip II for the Netherlands: a series of cityscapes by Jacques van Deventer and a corpus of topographical maps by Christophe's Grooten. In 1566 Philip also ordered 'a map and description' of Naples to be sent to him, because 'every day things crop up' that can only be understood and dealt with effectively if '[we] know the distances between the places of that kingdom, and its rivers and boundaries' (BCR Ms 2174/43–v, Philip II to viceroy of Naples, 1 Feb. 1566; see also a similar order at fo. 132–3, 11 Mar. 1575).

47. See details in Fernández Álvarez, *Felipe II*, 23, and Kagan, *Spanish Cities*, 47. BNM Ms 5589/64: 'Ynterrogatorio,' mentions '13 or 14 volumes' of 'relaciones'; AGS *Estado* 157/104, 'Instruction and memorandum for the relations to be made and sent to His Majesty for the description and history of the communities of Spain'; and ibid., 157/103, Philip II to the corregidor of Toledo, Oct. 1575, minute, explaining that 'if we were to send a person to compile the descriptions required, it could

48. See Bouza Álvarez, 'Monarchie en lettres d'imprimerie', 213.

49. For details, see Benson, 'The ill-fated works of Francisco Hernández'; López Piñero, *Ciencias y técnica*, 217–19; Goodman, *Power and penury*, 65–72; and González García, *Archivo General de Indias*, 178–9. See also Bouza Álvarez, *Del escribano a la biblioteca*, 90–100, for an overview of the king's various surveys; Miranda, *España y Nueva España*, 20–1, 56–9 and 69–71, for a useful list of royal subsidies to scientists and other scholars; and Vicente Moroto and Esteban Piñero, *Aspectos de la ciencia aplicada*, 399–406, on López de Velasco.

50. López de Velasco, *Geografía y descripción*; and idem, *Demarcación*. The original of the latter work, with beautiful hand-coloured maps, may be studied in the John Carter Brown Library, Providence, RI, *Cod. Span.* 7. (I thank John Headley for bringing it to my attention.) In a volume based on Velasco, in 1601 Antonio de Herrera y Tordesillas's *Descripción de las Indias occidentales* explicitly recognized that the area between the Caribbean and the Philippines represented 'a hemisphere and half of the world, with 180 degrees' (see the erudite discussion of these works in Headley, 'Spain's Asian presence', 629–33).

51. See the richly documented studies of Cline, 'The *Relaciones geográficas*'; Edwards, 'Mapping by geographical positions'; and, most recently, Mundy, *The mapping of New Spain*, and Sacchi, *Mappe del nuovo mondo*.

52. See Vicente Maroto and Esteban Piñero, *Aspectos de la ciencia aplicada*, 81, 403–6 and 437–43; and AGI *Mapas y planos, Mexico* 34, 'Juizio astrológico del eclipse de la luna que aconteció en 17 de noviembre, año 1584'. See also Lamb, 'The Spanish cosmographic juntas', 60 (although she dates the eclipse 'October 1584'). Goodman, *Power and penury*, 67, reports that the observations were

also coordinated with colleagues in China.

53. See AGNM *CRD* II/22, expediente 62, Philip II to viceroy of New Spain, 12 Mar. 1583 (asking about Dominguez's maps); Goodman, *Power and penury*, 82 n. 12 (the eclipse ended at 7.31 p.m., according to Jaume Juan's 'clock with wheels', but at 7.22 according to the observed position of a fixed star, and at 7.20 according to the observed elevation of the moon).

54. UB Leiden *Hs Pap.* 3/3 Alonso de Laloo to Count Hornes, 31 Aug. 1566.

55. Gordon, *Power/knowledge*, 52, an interview with Foucault in 1975; *CCG*, IV, 558, Granvelle to Morillon, 11 May 1573, quoting Don Pedro de Toledo, viceroy of Naples 1532–53.

56. De Reiffenberg, *Histoire*, 413, complaint by the knights of the Golden Fleece, 1546 (the knights said exactly the same about Charles V: see pp. 415–16); BPM Ms II–2291, unfol., Gonzalo Pérez to Granvelle, 16 Apr. 1560; Berwick y Alba, *Discurso*, 75, Pérez to Requeséns, 1565; and p. 120 above.

57. See Díaz-Plaja, *La historia de España*, 603, quoting Requeséns in 1571; IVdeDJ 68/231–2, Requeséns to the marquis of Los Vélez, July 1575; Berwick y Alba, *Discurso*, 75, Requeséns to Zúñiga, 1575. When Cardinal Granvelle, president of the council of Italy, likewise complained in 1582 that he had received no replies from the king (then in Portugal) to his various letters 'for months' a minister at Court unhelpfully replied that 'it must be because he is so busy': BMB Ms *Granvelle* 32/41–2, Idiáquez to Granvelle, 26 Feb. 1582.

58. Laubespine, 562, mémoire of 26 Sept. 1560 (see also an earlier complaint in Gachard, *Bibliothèque Nationale à Paris*, II, 119); Fourquevaux, II, 338, letter to Charles IX, 31 Mar. 1571 (see also earlier complaints ibid., 92 and 251); and Binchy, 'An Irish ambassador', 371, quoting the cardinal of

Como to Nuncio Ormanetto, 2 July 1577.

59. See AGRB *Audience* 239/123, listing the dispatches of 31 Aug. 1566; and (for example) *BMO* III, 344–58, twenty-two letters on Armada business dispatched on 15 May 1587. See also the figures on p. 28 above.

60. On Simancas and Barcelona, see Kamen, *Philip*, 238–9; on Rome, see García Hernán, 'La iglesia de Santiago', 307–14. Copies of Philip's various orders creating the post of archivist at Simancas, and requiring the heirs of former ministers to deposit state papers there, may be found in AGPM *Cédulas reales* I/1–2, orders dated 5 May 1545 to 4 Aug. 1555. For later examples of Philip sending material to Simancas see IVdeDJ 60/321, Antonio Pérez to Philip II and reply, undated (but late 1566: 'see if you or Gonzalo Pérez have any original documents which it would be good to send to Simancas'); AMAE *MDFD* 237/28, Certificate by Diego de Ayala, archivist of Simancas, 19 Mar. 1581 (acknowledging receipt of the original affidavit by the governors of Portugal recognizing Philip of Spain as their lawful sovereign); and Bouza Álvarez, 'Guardar papeles, I', 8. In 1556 Alba created a government archive in Naples too: see Maltby, *Alba*, 98.

61. *CCG*, XI, 272, Granvelle to Margaret of Parma, 21 Sept. 1584; ASV *NS* 19/192, Novara to Rusticucci, 3 May 1587 (the nuncio noted that the pope had already reprimanded Philip once for this, and asked that he should do so again); BCR Ms 2417/39, Don Juan de Silva, count of Portalegre, to Esteban de Ibarra, 13 Aug. 1589. (Bouza Álvarez, 'La majestad de Felipe II', 64–5, cites this document at length from another copy dated 1597; I have used the autograph original with some corrections in Silva's own hand.)

62. On Granvelle, see van Durme, *Cardenal Granvela*; on Silva, see Bouza Álvarez, 'Corte es decepción'.

63. IVdeDJ 21/740, notes by Philip and Mateo Vázquez on a letter from the general of the Jeronimites, 12 Sept. 1589; and ibid., 21/374, Jerónimo Gassol to Philip II and reply, 8 July 1591. The king's use of 'Fabius' was noted by Gachard, 'Notice de la collection'.

64. BZ 143/111, Mateo Vázquez to Philip II and reply, 28 June 1588, about a letter from the duke of Infantado (Vázquez first brought the duke's letter to Philip's attention on 14 June, but the king replied that 'I dare not read papers as long as this just now': BZ 143/88); IVdeDJ 55/XI/153, same to same, 10 Aug. 1588. Cf. the observation of Drucker, *The effective executive*, 11: the executive always has to deal with 'matters of importance to someone else'.

65. Neustadt, *Presidential power*, 130–1. See also Sorensen, *Decision-making in the White House*, 32: 'Under any president, life in the White House is a series of deadlines'.

66. AGI *Indiferente General* 738/82, royal apostil on a consulta of 5 July 1568. The unfortunate Legazpi had been dispatched entirely without maps, being instructed to get hold of Portuguese charts whenever he could, 'even by buying them', in order to find out where he was going (see Quirino, *Philippine cartography*, x). The king's command became part of the Ordinances for the government of the Americas issued in 1571, which ordered the council of the Indies to keep all maps in its archive (González García, *Archivo General de Indias*, 180).

67. Quotations from BZ 144/39, Mateo Vázquez to Philip II and reply, 28 Dec. 1574 (Vázquez, for his part, had lost the copies of Philip's instructions to his sister Juana in 1554); Riba, 179, Philip II to Vázquez, undated but 1578; and Rodríguez de Diego and Alvarez Pinedo, *Los Archivos de Simancas*, 127 (reproducing the king's anguished holograph note of July 1581). For other examples of the king losing things see AGPM *Cédulas reales*

2/46, letter to Luis de Vega, 2 Mar. 1558 ('We have lost your last letter, please send a copy'); IVdeDJ 60/321, Antonio Pérez to Philip II, undated (but late 1566: hunting for a missing letter mentioned by Granvelle); Bouza Álvarez, 'Leer en palacio', 40 (a misplaced book); and BZ 144/31, Philip II to Vázquez, 25 Nov. 1574 (losing a consulta).

68. Groen van Prinsterer, *Archives*, 1st series I, 426, Chantonnay, Spanish ambassador in Vienna, to Granvelle (his brother), 6 Oct. 1565; AGS *Estado* 527/5, Philip II to Gonzalo Pérez [24 Mar. 1565]. See also pp. 119–20 above.

69. Schelling, *Arms and influence*, 227; Barnard, *The function of the executive*, 194.

70. AGNM *Mercedes* V/248–9v, Licence of Viceroy Velasco to Francisco de Ibarra, 2 Jan. 1561, rehearsing Philip II's order of 29 Dec. 1557; and AGNM *CRD* 1bis/20–1, cédulas of 11 Sept. 1569 and 13 June 1571. For the 'perverse interlock' between greater certainty at the top and less at the bottom in any chain of command, and vice versa, see van Creveld, *Command in war*, 274.

71. BPU *Favre* 28/83–101v, Philip II to Sessa, 27 Dec. 1576 – the holograph postscript qualification appears on fo. 95. For other examples of delegating responsibility for major policy choices see pp. 122 and 137 above (whether or not to delay arresting rebels in 1567 or to flood Holland in 1574); and IVdeDJ 60/127, Antonio Pérez to Philip II and reply, 10 May 1578 (alternative instructions given to Juan de Marliano for truce talks with the Turks, allowing him to choose the most appropriate set upon reaching his destination).

72. AGS *Estado* K 1448/197, Philip II to Bernardino de Mendoza, 28 July 1588 ('pues agora es el tiempo de avisarme de todo por momentos').

73. *BMO*, III, 1274, Philip II to Santa Cruz, 21 Oct. 1587: 'Creedme, como a quien tiene entera noticia del estado en que se hallan al presente las cosas en todas partes'.

74. AGS *Estado* 165/146, Philip II to Medina Sidonia, 14 Aug. 1588; and *Estado* 2219/91, Notes by Idiáquez on 15 Sept. 1588. See also *Estado* 146/144 and 2219/77, Philip II to Medina Sidonia and Parma, 7 Aug. 1588 (the day of the fireships' attack off Calais) exhorting both commanders to follow the strategy the king had devised. See also pp. 265 and 267 above.

75. *GPGP*, II, 524–5, Gonzalo Pérez to Philip II and reply, 13 Aug. 1565 (see also other royal expressions of concern that 'we get it right' at pp. 41 and 316 n. 118 above); Donà, 340, letter to Venice, 1 Aug. 1571; FD, II, 221–2, Medina Sidonia to Philip II, 30 July 1588.

76. KML, 'Instructions' of Elizabeth to Howard, 20 Dec. 1587 OS, original (admittedly she then added: 'Of all your doings and proceedings in the said service, and such intelligences as you shall receave, we require you to advertise us from tyme to tyme'; but that too contrasted with Philip II's frantic demands for instant transmission of all news: see, for example, note 72 above). Hunt *HA* 30881/87v–8, Lord Huntingdon to Privy Council, 23 June 1588 OS, minute.

77. Watts, 'Friction in future war', 91; and Jablonsky, *The owl of Minerva*, 33–6. Watts (75–7) notes the interesting parallel between his strategic model and Friedrich von Hayek's observation that modern economies also exceed the grasp of any individual mind.

78. Exodus, 18: 13–23 (quoting from the *New Jerusalem Bible* [New York, 1985], 103–4). Figures on the July crisis calculated by Holsti, *Crisis, escalation, war*, 81–5 (Holsti used only published papers in his calculations, and drew attention to the fact that many more documents from both Vienna and Berlin have been destroyed. See also the data on July 1914 presented by Lebow, *Between peace and war*, 119–47. By contrast, in the 1980s, the British prime minister's

office received between 4,000 and
7,000 letters *per week*: Thatcher,
Downing Street years, 19.

79. Guilmartin, *A very short war*, 157.
Guilmartin (involved at Koh Tan and
later an outstanding military historian) views 'information saturation' as
the principal problem in modern warfare: see ibid., 32–3, 109–10 and
157–9.

80. See, for example, Elizabeth Tudor's
failure, almost until the last moment,
to realize that Spain really did intend
to invade and conquer her realm: p.
227 above.

81. Thus, once they had decided to invade
England, Philip II and his ministers in
1586–88 tended to see the Armada as
the solution to all of their problems:
see chap. 6 above.

82. This section draws heavily on Jervis,
Perception and misperception, 117–202;
Lebow, *Between peace and war*, 101–19;
and Holsti, *Crisis, escalation, war*,
chaps 1, 4 and 8 (see some spectacular
examples of motivated bias at pp.
206–10).

83. BPU *Favre* 30/73v, Philip II to Don
Luis de Requeséns, 20 Oct. 1573,
copy of holograph original: 'Spero en
Dios . . . que os dara mucha salud y
vida, pues se empleara en su servicio y
en el mío, que es lo mismo'.

3   *'With God on Our Side'*

1. Plaisant, *Aspetti e problemi*, 111,
Don Mendo Rodríguez de Ledesma to
Philip III, 14 Sept. 1600; Fernández
Álvarez, 'Las instrucciones políticas',
175, Francisco de Erasso to Philip II
and reply, 20 Feb. 1559; BZ 144/39,
Mateo Vázquez to Philip II and reply,
28 Dec. 1574.

2. See the full text in *CDCV*, II, 569–
601. The emperor had provided
political advice for his son before –
in 1539 (ibid., 32–43) and 1543
(ibid., 85–118); but it lacked the
comprehensive quality of the 1548
'Instructions', composed when the

emperor stood at the height of his
success. Fernández Álvarez (ibid.,
569) is surely right to detect the
influence of Nicholas Perrenot de
Granvelle in this remarkable document. See also Beinert, 'El testamento
político de Carlos V'; and Fernández
Álvarez, 'Las instrucciones políticas'.

3. *CDCV*, II, 572–3.

4. Ibid., 575. Charles V had perceived
himself to be surrounded by 'envy'
since at least 1528: see Rassow, *Die
Kaiser-Idee Karls V*, 20.

5. AGS *SP* 2604, unfol., Margaret of
Parma to Philip II, 13 Aug. 1564,
about Ferdinand's death, bears a royal
apostil about 'the special affection that
I held for His Majesty'. See in general
Fichtner, *Ferdinand I*, 220–35 and
259, and the letters between the two
monarchs published in *Co.Do.In.*, II,
419–592, many concerned with the
correct religious policy to be pursued.

6. IVdeDJ 55/IX/97–8, Mateo Vázquez
to Philip II and reply, 17 June 1586.

7. On the Augsburg family compact,
see Fichtner, *Ferdinand I*, 167–8 and
175–7; Rodríguez-Salgado, *Changing
face*, 33–40; and Lütz, *Christianitas
Afflicta*, 81–7.

8. Charles made Philip his 'Vicarius
generalis imperii' in Jan. 1556, but
Ferdinand refused to follow suit
when he became emperor: *Co.Do.In.*,
XCVIII, 24–8, Ferdinand to Aquila,
Philip's ambassador, 22 July 1558.
Philip tried again in 1562 to persuade
Ferdinand to concede the title, but
without success: see the king's correspondence with the count of Luna,
his ambassador at the imperial Court,
ibid., 293–8 and 309–10. See also
Lutz, *Christianitas Afflicta*, 322–3 and
408–23.

9. Quotations from Firpo, *Relazioni, III*,
373–4, Cauallier to the Doge and
Senate, 22 July 1564; and HHStA
Spanien Varia fasz. 1b/n/2v, 'Aviso' of
23 Nov. 1564.

10. Fourquevaux, II, 141–7, Fourquevaux's account of the negotiations with
Philip's ministers and 'don Dietrichstein', the imperial ambassador in

Madrid, Aug.–Nov. 1569; Serrano, III, 253, Don Juan de Zúñiga to Philip II, 7 Mar. 1570. See also Philip's firm but affectionate letters to Maximilian exalting their 'union and brotherhood': for example *Co.Do.In*, CIII, 432, letter of 5 Feb. 1570.

11. See Rill, 'Reichsvikar und Kommissar'. Maximilian's first priority, of course, was to maintain the peace of the Holy Roman Empire and to minimize the risk that conflict elsewhere might polarize opinions in Germany, which explains his efforts to maintain peace in Italy, France, the Baltic and the Netherlands: see Lanzinner, *Friedenssicherung*, and Luttenberger, *Kurfürsten, Kaiser und Reich* – I thank Mark Choate and Jason Lavery for these references. A modern study of relations between Philip II and the Austrian Habsburgs is much needed, though see the important monograph of Edelmayer, *Maximilian II., Philipp II., und Reichsitalien.*

12. *CDCV*, II, 575–7. Interestingly, Charles's predecessor, Ferdinand of Aragon, had advised him in 1516 that an alliance with the papacy would form the best guarantee of Spanish dominance in Italy: see Ferdinand's 'political testament' printed in Doussinague, *Política internacional*, 675–81.

13. *Co.Do.In.*, II, 430–1, Philip II to Ferdinand, 20 Nov. 1556; the king went on to note with satisfaction that God had punished the pope for his 'unjustified action' by allowing Spanish forces to advance 'almost to the gates of Rome'. See also Dandelet, 'Roma hispanica', 71–2, and Fernández Álvarez, *Felipe II*, 764–5.

14. Details from Dandelet, 'Roma hispanica', 82, 109 and 114. Pensions to the cardinals exceeded 30,000 ducats in most years: see ibid., 83, 113–14, 131 and 135. The 1591 total comes from García Hernán, 'La curia romana', 641.

15. See Dandelet, 'Roma hispanica', 118–22, on the use of troops and grain to influence the outcome of elections in

1590–92; Lynch, 'Philip II and the Papacy', for a useful survey; García Hernán, 'La curia romana', for an important pontificate; and Borromeo, 'España y el problema de la elección papal de 1592', for a case study from late in the reign.

16. BCR Ms 2174/76v–7, Philip to Ambassador Zúñiga, 17 July 1569. See also Philip's complaints on p. 7 above.

17. *CDCV*, II, 577–9. The emperor discussed two other states, but their circumstances soon changed dramatically: the republic of Siena, which Charles hoped would prove loyal, declared against him in 1552 and was invaded, occupied and finally ceded to the duke of Florence; while the duchy of Parma, at loggerheads with the Habsburgs in 1548, shortly afterwards became one of their most loyal allies. I thank Mark Choate, Giuseppe Galasso, Michael Levin, Giovanni Muto and Mario Rizzo for valuable suggestions and references concerning the relations between Spain and Italy. On the system, see Musi, *Nel sistema imperiale*; Rivero Rodríguez, 'Felipe II'; and (later on), Storrs, 'The Army of Lombardy'.

18. AGS *Estado* 560/36, Requeséns to Philip II, 7 Nov. 1574, quoting with approval Ferrante Gonzaga, governor of Milan and an intimate of Charles V.

19. Serrano, II, 42, Philip II to Requeséns, Spanish ambassador in Rome, 16 Feb. 1567. For another example, see Álava, 336, Zayas to Álava, 16 May 1569.

20. See Doria, 'Un quadrennio critico, 1575–78' (see p. 379, for estimates of investment in Philip II's loans); Bitossi, *Il governo dei magnifici*, 46–61 (for the 'civil war' of 1575–76); and Emmanuelli, *Gênes et l'Espagne dans la Guerre de Corse.*

21. Von Aretin, 'Die Lehensordnungen in Italien im 16. und 17. Jahrhundert', 57–9.

22. For Savoy's rewards, see AGS *Estado* 1270/123, Terranova to Philip II, 25 Nov. 1592, and Plaisant, *Aspetti e problemi*, 100–2. Quotation from AGS

Estado 1249/122, Juan Manrique to Antonio Pérez, 19 May 1578. For the subsidy of 12,000 ducats (raised to 15,000 in 1600) paid to the duke of Urbino, see Cano de Gardoquí, 'España y los estados italianos independientes', 526 and 537. Plaisant, *Aspetti e problemi*, 116–17, prints the text of an agreement to place a state (Modena) under Spanish protection in 1600.

23. Spanish service, however, did not make most Italian princes rich: Parma spent almost 50,000 ducats a year of his own in the Netherlands, and ended his fourteen-year term as governor-general there with debts of almost 800,000 ducats (more than twice his duchies' total revenues): see Romani, 'Finanza pubblica e potere politico', 27 and 38. On Colonna, see Rivero Rodríguez, 'El servicio a dos cortes'.

24. For the use of the 'Tusón' as a reward, see ASMa *AG* 583/310 and 334, Philip II to the new duke of Mantua, 19 Mar. and 7 Nov. 1588. In the same year, having received an interest-free loan of 300,000 crowns towards the cost of the Spanish Armada, Philip ordered all disputes between Milan and Mantua to be settled in the duke's favour: see ibid., fos 304 and 314, Philip II to the governor of Lombardy, 24 Feb. and 30 Mar. 1588; and *AG* 601, unfol., Aqui to Mantua, 14 Mar. 1588.

25. Rizzo, 'Poteri, interessi e conflitti geopolitici nei territori della Lunigiana', quoting a letter from the marquis of Ayamonte, governor of Milan, in 1577. Fernand Braudel coined the phrase 'pax hispanica' to describe Philip II's control of Italy: see his chapter 'L'Italia fuori d'Italia' in Einaudi, *Storia d'Italia*, II, 2156.

26. Even the chief cipher clerk of the pope was in Spanish pay during 1580 (Philippson, *Ein Ministerium unter Philipp II*, 56); and so were some of Gregory XIII's guards (Dandelet, 'Roma hispanica', 108). On Spain's occasional use of assassins (for example against the lord of Piombino in 1589),

see Angiolini, 'Diplomazie e politica', 452 n. 73.

27. ASV *LP* 41/96, Philip II to Gregory XIII, 7 Mar. 1584. See also a similar pleas, ibid., 46/65–6, Philip II to Sixtus V, 23 Dec. 1588. For an example of mutually hostile allies, consider the Gonzaga and the Savoia, both of whom coveted the marquisate of Monferrat.

28. Serrano, II, 447–9 (Philip II to Zúñiga, 19–20 Aug. 1568); ibid., II, 459–61, III, 89–91 and 239–41 (Zúñiga to Philip II, 17 Sept. 1568, 13 June 1569 and 28 Feb. 1570); *CCG*, XI, 118, Granvelle to Don Juan de Idiáquez, 19 Aug. 1584. In the latter case, Spain supported Lucca: see ASL *Offizio sulle differenze dei confini*, 269, unfol., Ambassador Portico to Lucca, 31 May and 26 July 1586 (enclosing copies of relevant letters from Idiáquez and Granvelle). For two further examples of Spanish arbitration, see *CCG*, XI, 247–8, Granvelle to Idiáquez, 19 Sept. 1584 (between Savoy and Tuscany); and Plaisant, *Aspetti e problemi*, 102 (between Savoy and Monaco, 1595). See also other declarations by Philip that he desired above all things to preserve the peace of Italy in Romero García, *El imperialismo hispánico*, 111–56; Donà, 524, letter to Venice of 24 July 1572; and pp. 4–6 above.

29. AGS *Estado* 2855, unfol., consultas of 27 Oct. 1588 and 10 Jan. 1589. See also ASV *LP* 46/76v, Philip II to Sixtus V, 1 Nov. 1588; Altadonna, 'Cartas de Felipe II a Carlos Manuel', 168–71, letters of 23 June, 1 Nov. and 23 Dec. 1588; and Cano de Gardoquí, *La cuestión de Saluzzo*. In 1595 the king ordered his new ambassador to Savoy to 'restrain somewhat the great enthusiasm of the duke to undertake enterprises' (Plaisant, *Aspetti e problemi*, 108, secret instruction to Lodosa, 21 Nov. 1595). See also Chapter 10 above.

30. Vigo, *Uno stato nell'impero*, 14, quoting Guicciardini; Arnold, 'Fortifications and the military revolution',

31. *CDCV*, II, 580–1.

32. See Calabria, *The cost of empire*, 79; Rizzo, 'Finanza pubblica', 324 and 355–6; and Riley, 'The State of Milan', 173–202. On the finances of Sicily, see Koenigsberger, *The practice of empire*, 124–43.

33. For the three states that 'demobilized' see Costantini, *La Repubblica di Genova*, 52; Partner, 'Papal financial policy', 52; and Angiolini, 'Diplomazie e politica', 458. On the size of Philip II's galley fleet, see Parker, *Spain and the Netherlands*, 122–33, and Ribot García, 'Las provincias italianas', 110–13.

34. BNM Ms 783/191–2, Requeséns, governor of Milan, to Don John of Austria, 16 Apr. 1572; AGS *Estado* 1235/207, 'Relación de los castillos del Estado de Milán', June 1572. The outposts – Pontremoli in Lunigiana, Nice across the border in Savoy, and so on – are listed in Rizzo, 'Competizione politico-militare'. See also the quotations in Rizzo, 'Centro spagnolo e periferia lombarda', 324; and Ribot García, 'Milán, plaza de armas de la Monarquía', 206.

35. For a sample, see the thousands of transit permits for horses, arms, armour and specie registered in ASMi *Cancellaria spagnola*, XXI vols 18–22 ('patenti') for 1585–89, and for the movement of troops and their equipment and pay ibid., XXII vols 32–5 ('mandati') for 1585–87. Consider also the following: between 1569 and 1571, Milan exported to Spain (for the war of Granada) and the fleet, 20,000 arquebuses, 17,300 helmets, 6,000 corselets, almost 5,000 pikes and almost 4,000 quintals of gunpowder (AGS *Estado* 1232/95, 'Relación').

36. On Alba's march see Parker, *Dutch Revolt*, 99–105, and idem, *The Army of Flanders*, 61–7 and 81 (see also

211, quoting Alessio Beccaguto. The engineer was right: the Gonzaga fortress of Casale resisted a Habsburg siege in 1628–29 and again in 1630, seriously compromising Spain's stature in Italy.

pp. 278–9 for a list of other marches of Spanish veterans from Italy to the Netherlands); on Lepanto, see Parker, *Spain and the Netherlands*, 122–33. On the fortifications network constructed by the Habsburgs, see Tosini, 'Cittadelle lombarde de fine '500', and Ribot Garcia, 'Las provincias italianas', 104–6.

37. See the definitive account of this episode in Edelmayer, *Maximilian II., Philip II., und Reichsitalien*. Ironically, the Carretto dynasty which ruled Finale soon died out and its last member assigned the fief to Philip II; Spain took possession in 1602. See Cano de Gardoquí, *La incorporación del marquesado de Finale*; *Atti dei convegni internazionali sulla storia del Finale*; and Storrs, 'Army of Lombardy, II,' 15.

38. *Nueva Co.Do.In.*, I, 38–40, Ayamonte to Zúñiga, 13 Jan. 1574 (the client was Fabricio Correggio); and Rizzo, 'Poteri, interessi e conflitti' (on the unrest in Lusola, a small fief in the Lunigiana).

39. *CDCV*, II, 579–80. See further similar sentiments at p. 584. Again, Ferdinand of Aragon had given remarkably similar advice to Charles in 1516: see Doussinague, *Política internacional*, 681.

40. *CDCV*, II, 584–7 and 590.

41. BPM Ms II–2320/6, Granvelle to Juan Vázquez, 29 May 1559. See the interesting discussion of the treaty in Rodríguez-Salgado, *Changing face*, 325–30; and in Russell, *Peacemaking in the Renaissance*, 242–55.

42. Koenigsberger, *Politicians and virtuosi*, 88, Philip II to Margaret of Parma, 15 July 1562; Álava, 205, Philip II to Álava, 27 Nov. 1567. Philip sent troops from Spain to fight in France in 1563 and from the Netherlands in 1569; he also prepared another expeditionary force in Spain ready to intervene in 1570.

43. Quotation from Lalanne, *Oeuvres complètes de . . . Brantôme*, IV, 304–6; and Álamos de Barrientos, *Discurso político*, 44–5. For further detail on Philip's policy towards France see

Chapters 6–7 and 10 above; on the confused but critical last decade, see Tenace, 'Spanish intervention in Brittany'.

44. Philip II's Scandinavian policy has been little studied: see, however, Hildebrand, *Johan III och Europas katolska makter*, 154 and 287–313 (in 1557 John III's mother, Bona Sforza, left her extensive Italian estates to Philip II and her son entered into complex negotiations to secure compensation: my thanks to Jason Lavery for this reference); Boratynski, 'Estebán Batory'; and Ruiz Martín, 'El pan de los países bálticos'. See also pp. 200–1 above on Danish attempts to broker a peace between Spain and England in 1588.

45. Charles V had attempted to resolve this problem with the 'New Laws' of 1542, but they had provoked rebellion; then in 1551–52 he permitted public debates on policy to be held at Valladolid and Seville. See the excellent summary in Hanke, *The Spanish struggle for justice*, chap. 8.

46. *CDCV*, II, 106 (Instructions of 1543) and 573–4 (Instructions of 1548).

47. Parker, *The Army of Flanders*, 134.

48. See Carlos Morales, *El consejo de Hacienda*, 82, 77–8 and 121.

49. We lack a reliable history of Philip II's finances, partly because the surviving documentation is at once so abundant and so chaotic; but see Ulloa, *La hacienda real de Castilla*. For the particular issue of debt rescheduling, see Castillo, 'Dette flottante et dette consolidée en Espagne'; Lovett, 'The Castilian bankruptcy of 1575'; idem, 'The General Settlement of 1577'; and, from the bankers' point of view, Doria, 'Un quadrennio critico, 1575–78'. Naples has been better served: see Calabria, *The cost of empire*.

50. *PEG*, V, 606, Philip II to Granvelle, 24 June 1559. Charles V scarcely mentioned Spain in his 'Political Testament'. On the significant westward shift of the Habsburg empire's centre of gravity during the 1550s, see Lutz and Müller-Luckner, *Das römisch-*

deutsche Reich, 277–8; Kohler, *Das Reich im Kampf*, 22–6; and Rodríguez-Salgado, *Changing face*, 339–56.

51. IVdeDJ 67/121, Requeséns to Zúñiga, 30 Oct. 1575. See Requeséns's similar lament two weeks later, cited on p. 143 above; and Chapter 4 above for further details on the collapse of Philip II's policies in 1575–6.

52. See Tenace, 'Spanish intervention in Brittany', 426–7.

53. For the link between bankruptcy and peacemaking in 1559, see Russell, *Peacemaking in the Renaissance*, 242–55; in 1575–77, see Braudel, *The Mediterranean*, 1150–61, and Skilliter, 'The Hispano-Ottoman armistice of 1581'; and in 1597–98, see Tenace, 'Spanish intervention in Brittany', chap. 10. Of course, many subsequent governments experienced much the same phenomenon: even in the twentieth century, despite the more sophisticated understanding of economics and public finance, most of the European states that fought World War I also bordered on bankruptcy (and some defaulted): see Hardach, *The First World War*, 144–69; Balderstone, 'War finance'; and Neal, *War finance*, III, 5–225.

54. *CDCV*, II, 591–2.

55. Details in Chabod, 'Milán o los Países Bajos?' Late in 1547 a prominent minister proposed the marriage of María to Emanuel Philibert of Savoy, making them joint rulers of the Netherlands (in return for which, Emanuel Philibert would cede Piedmont to Philip: ibid., pp. 356–64); but María's marriage to Maximilian had already been arranged. For other discussions of broad policy, see Chabod, 'Contrasti interni e dibattiti sulla politica generale di Carlo V'. On other proposals to exchange Milan, see Vigo, *Uno stato nell'impero*, 21, 26.

56. See the opinions quoted in Chabod, 'Milán o los Países Bajos?', 341, 364, 369–70.

57. Quotations from Gachard, *Retraite et mort de Charles-Quint*, II, 43, Philip II's

Instructions to Bartolomé Carranza, 5 June 1558; and BL *Addl* 28,702/96–100, Granvelle to Don Juan de Idiáquez, 3 Mar. 1582; and AGS *Estado* 2023/24 and 124, consultas of the council of State on 21 Mar. and 20 July 1600. For Philip II's fear of France, see Sutherland, 'The origins of the Thirty Years War', 594–6; and the general remarks of Israel, *Empires and entrepôts*, 163–9, and idem, *The Dutch Republic. Its rise, greatness and fall*, 131–2. For similar expressions from a later period, see Israel, 'Olivares, the Cardinal-Infante and Spain's strategy'.

58. Quotations from AGS *Estado* 554/89, Philip II to Alba, 18 Mar. 1573; ibid. 2843/7, consulta of the council of State, 5 Sept. 1577. For a later example, see the stirring phrase of Don Balthasar de Zúñiga, chief minister of Philip IV: 'A monarchy that has lost its reputation, even if it has lost no territory, is a sky without light, a sun without rays, a body without a soul', quoted by Elliott, 'Managing decline', 93.

59. AGS *Estado* 2851, unfol., opinion of Almazán, 22 Nov. 1588; and *Estado* 2855, unfol., 'Lo que pareçió sobre los quatro papeles principales', Nov. 1589.

60. HHStA *Spanien Varia* 2/59–62, report of Christophe d'Assonleville on his mission to England, Dec. 1558; AGS *Estado* 137/95–7, 'Apunctamientos para embiar a España' (points 7 and 8), undated. The king forwarded the second document, with comments, to his regent in Spain: AGS *Estado* 521/20–1, Philip II to Juana, 29 June 1559.

61. *CCG*, I, 314–18: Granvelle to Philip II, 19 June 1566; ASN *CF* 1706, Miguel de Mendivil to Margaret of Parma, 22 Sept. 1566 (from *Cahier van der Essen* XXXIV/18–19); Serrano, II, 60, Cardinal Alexandrino to Nuncio Castagna, 6 Mar. 1567; Fourquevaux, II, 34, letter to Catherine de Medici, 23 Dec. 1568 ; and IVdeDJ 6/12/6, Requeséns to Zúñiga, 23 Sept. 1572.

62. Quotations from IVdeDJ 76/491–503, 'Relación' by Juan de Ovando, Apr. 1574, and ibid., 51/33, Vázquez to Philip II with reply, 20 June 1574. See also ibid., 53/3/87, same to same, 4 July 1574, and ibid., 44/136, same to same, 31 May 1575. For a classic statement of the apparent 'interdependence of commitments' of modern superpowers, see Schelling, *Arms and influence*, 55–6.

63. AGS *Estado* 2843/7, 'Parescer' of the council of State, 7 Sept. 1577, opinion of Quiroga, supported by Aguilar and the president of the council of Castile (another copy of this document at *Estado* 570/103bis). The same view was expressed equally forcefully in 1578: see, for example, *Estado* 570/2, consulta of 3 Feb. 1578; *Estado* 578/121, opinion of the duke of Sesa, 22 June 1578; and AHN *Inquisición* libro 284/156–8, opinion of Quiroga, 30 July 1578. Events vindicated these fears in 1585, when a rebellion broke out in Naples and the insurgents warned the viceroy to 'have an eye to events in the Netherlands': Villari, *La rivolta antispagnola a Napoli*, 49–51.

64. Quotations from AGS *Estado* 2023/124, consulta of the council of State on 20 July 1600; Alcocer, *Consultas del consejo de Estado*, 261: vote of the count of Chinchón – fully buttressed by historical examples stretching back to 1559 – in the council of State's consulta 'Sobre el remedio general de Flandes', 26 Nov. 1602; and AGS *Estado* 634/73, 'Papeles tocantes al buen govierno', 1 Jan. 1605, by Juan Andrea Doria. See also the 'domino theory' deployed in 1635 by the count-duke of Olivares: 'The greatest dangers [facing the crown] are those that threaten Lombardy, the Netherlands and Germany, because a defeat in any of these three is fatal for this Monarchy; so much so that if the defeat in those parts is a great one, the rest of the Monarchy will collapse, for Germany will be followed by Italy and the Netherlands, and the Netherlands

65. BPM Ms II-2291, unfol., count of Feria to Granvelle, 7 Sept. 1560; BMB Ms *Granvelle*, 8/189, Pérez to Granvelle, 19 Feb. 1564.

66. *Actas de las Cortes*, III, 16, speech of Francisco de Erasso, 1570; *Co.Do.In.*, CII, 68, Zúñiga to Philip II, 2 Apr. 1573.

67. Bouza Álvarez, 'Portugal en la Monarquía hispánica', 70, G. B. Gesio to Philip II, 20 Sept. 1578. See also p. 166 above. On the fall in remittances to the Netherlands, see Parker, *The Army of Flanders*, 293.

68. Casado Soto, *Discursos*, 193. See also the identical sentiments of a Spanish minister half a century later: 'Our first concern should be to settle the problems of Spain, rather than to save the other provinces, because if the war [in the peninsula] lasts for long everything will be lost; whereas by regaining Catalonia and Portugal, everything can be sustained and we can recover what has been lost [elsewhere]' (AHN *Estado libro* 969, unfol., Don Miguel de Salamanca to Olivares, Brussels, 14 July 1641, minute).

69. García Hernán, 'La curia romana', 645, Philip II to Diego de Espinosa, 8 Feb. 1564. On the start of the war in 1550–51, see Lutz, *Christianitas Afflicta*, 40–2; on the collapse of the peace talks in 1559, see Rodríguez-Salgado, *Changing face*, 298–302. For Ferdinand of Aragon's aggressive Mediterranean policy, see Doussinague, *Política internacional*, 487–93.

70. For appeals to place the Netherlands before the Mediterranean, see *Epistolario*, III, 289–91 and 300, Alba to Philip II, 12 Feb. and 7 Mar. 1573; *Co.Do.In.*, CII, 378, Requeséns to Zúñiga, 22 Nov. 1573; AGS *Estado* 1066/6, Granvelle to Philip II, 6 Feb. 1575; and pp. 133–4 above. For the

king's defence of his strategic choices, see AGS *Estado* 554/84, 'Las razones que concurren para no se poder dexar la Jornada de Levante' [early Mar. 1573]; and *Estado* 554/89, Philip II to Alba, 18 Mar. 1573. See also *Estado* 2843/3, Philip II to Don John, 31 Jan. 1577, insisting that peace must be preserved in the Netherlands as long as the Turks threatened Italy. For the truce of 1578, see p. 145 above. For later efforts to undermine Turkish power, see the examples in Oliveira e Costa and Gaspar Rodrigues, *Portugal y Oriente*, 321–7.

71. Serrano, I, 310, Philip II to Requeséns, his ambassador in Rome, 1 Aug. 1566. See also an earlier paean of self-praise in AGS *Estado* 119/40, Philip II to Juana, 10 June and 2 July 1557, summary.

72. *PEG*, VI, 149, Philip II to Granvelle, 7 Sept. 1560; Serrano, I, 316–17, to Requeséns, 12 Aug. 1566; *CCG*, XII, 339–41, to Parma, 17 Aug. 1585; KML *MSP: CR* 6/174, to Medina Sidonia, 15 Dec. 1590; IVdeDJ 51/1, Vázquez to Philip II and reply, 8 Feb. 1591 (Vázquez's proposal in Parker, *Philip II*, 181). See yet more similar quotations in *Reivindicación*, 151–2, and García Hernán, 'La curia romana', 645.

73. Álava, 221, Philip II to Álava, 19 Feb. 1568; and *Co.Do.In.*, CIII, 432, to Maximilian II, 5 Feb. 1570. For further examples of his advice to other (as he saw it, weaker) Catholic rulers, see Álava, 221–4, Philip II to Álava, 19 Feb. 1568; and Fourquevaux, II, 167–72, letter to Charles IX, 5 Jan. 1570.

74. See Checa, *Tiziano*, 59–60, 259, and Tanner, *Last descendant*, 202–6 and 217–18. On the propaganda value of portraying monarchs at prayer, see Potter, *Secret rites*, 159; on the role of 'emotionally based ideological romanticism' among twentieth-century statesmen, see Gaddis, *We now know*, 291.

75. For a list of chronicles on the king and his deeds, see Bordejé y Morencos, *El escenario estratégico*, 39–41, and Kagan,

'Felipe II'; for other aspects of propaganda see three fine articles by Bouza Álvarez, 'La majestad de Felipe II', 'Retórica da imagem real', and 'Monarchie en lettres d'imprimerie'.

76. On the *Antiapologia*, possibly written by Pedro Cornejo, see Timmer, 'Een verweerschrift'. Lord Burghley's annotated copy of *La felicissima Armada* is now in the British Library (Printed books: 192 f. 17 (1) t.p.): see a sample page in Whitehead, *Brags and boasts*, 67.

77. On papal reluctance to engage in polemics until the 1530s, see Edwards, 'Catholic controversial literature', 201–4; on the Catholic pamphleteers in and around the Netherlands, see Vermaseren, *De katholieke Nederlandsche Geschiedschrijving*. On the publicity for 1588, see Gómez Centurión, 'The new crusade'; idem, *La Invencible*, chap. 2; and pp. 201–3 below.

78. The sermon, delivered by Cardinal Reginald Pole, is printed in Anon., 'The chronicle of Queen Jane', 158 (I thank Glyn Redworth for this reference). On Portugal see Cabrera, II, 633–4. See also quotations in Pereña Vicente, *Teoría de la guerra*, I, 63–4; in Tanner, *Last descendant*, 167–8; and in the twenty-nine funeral orations for Philip II noted by Vargas Hidalgo, 'Documentos inéditos', 453–61. Interestingly, between 1587 and 1590, however, a group of the king's critics in Madrid suggested that a 'second David' was about to appear, in order to rescue Spain from the house of Habsburg: see Milhou, *Colón y su mentalidad mesiánica*, 245–9, and Kagan, *Lucrecia's dreams*, 73 (and indeed all of chap. 3).

79. AMAE *MDFD* 237/59, Philip II to Olivares, his ambassador in Rome, 30 Sept. 1585, original: a most remarkable letter. The 'rex et sacerdos' link is suggested both by Fernández Albaladejo, '"Imperio de por sí"', in idem, *Fragmentos de Monarquía*; and by Lisón Tolosana, *La imagen del rey*, 103–6. For evidence that some saw Philip as a saint, see Vargas Hidalgo, 'Documentos ineditos', 399.

80. See the bold comprehensive statements of the king's patronage rights in Encinas, I, fos 83–179. See also AGS *GA* 72/164, royal cédula of 27 Mar. 1569 forbidding any devotional work to be printed in Spain without royal licence; and Setton, *The Papacy and the Levant*, IV, 912, on Philip's insistence that papal bulls could only be published in his dominions with royal permission (the 'exsequatur').

81. AGS *Estado* 946/148, Philip II to Olivares, 22 Aug. 1585, minute; BL *Addl* 28,346/270, same to same, 24 Feb. and 27 June 1586, copies; AGS *Estado* 947/84, same to same, 11 Dec. 1586 (see also fo. 87, a list of the cases that the pope wished to review); and ASV *NS* 33/235, Philip II to Sixtus V, 2 Apr. 1587, holograph. For an example of the king's personal intervention in patronage, see Heredía Herrera, *Catálogo*, I, 674: consulta of 14 June 1590, and royal reply. For an example of Philip virtually demanding a Spanish cardinal at once, see García Hernán, 'La iglesia de Santiago', 329.

82. See the original letters of recommendation in the Archivo General del Ministerio de Asuntos Exteriores in Madrid, *Embajada de la Santa Sede*, legajo 1 onwards (with microfilm copies in the Spanish embassy in Rome: I thank Michael Levin for this information); BCR Ms 2174/133, Philip II to viceroy of Naples, 11 Mar. 1575; *Co.Do.In.*, XCVII, 417–18, Don Juan de Zúñiga to the archbishop of Santiago, 4 Apr. 1568, Rome, minute (mentioning Pius V's complaint).

83. Hergueta, 'Notas diplomáticas'; and AGS *Estado* 951/93, Philip II to Olivares, 23 Oct. 1588.

84. AGS *Estado* 946/141a, Philip II to Olivares, 31 Mar. 1585, minute with holograph corrections by the king; Checa, *Felipe II*, 293–4.

85. See the detailed consideration of this parallel in von der Osten Sacken, *San Lorenzo*, 207–40; Tanner, *Last descend-*

ant, 162–82; and Mulcahy, *The decoration of the royal basilica*, 131–3.

86. See the remarkable pages on this subject in Eire, *Madrid to purgatory*, 264–5, 284–5 and 338–47; and Rocca, 'Court and cloister'.

87. Estal, 'Felipe II y su archivo hagiográfico'; von der Osten Sacken, *San Lorenzo*, 160–3; Eire, *Madrid to purgatory*, 266–8 and 331–4. See also Checa, *Felipe II*, 284–99 ('Pietas Austriaca').

88. See BAV *UL* 1115/108–9, newsletter from Madrid 10 Jan. 1587 ('está todavía recogido en el cuarto nuevo [of the Madrid palace]; avía mandado hazer este quarto con fin de recogerse en él los inviernos'; and Fray Mateo de Ovando, *Sermón funebre* for Philip II in 1598 (the late king 'devotíssimo, recogido, y todo empleado en la veneración y culto divino. Recogióse a su nido de San Lorenzo . . .'), quoted by Checa, 'Felipe II en El Escorial', 17. On the meanings of 'recogido', see van Deusen, '*Recogimiento*', 1–66.

89. BZ 141/84, Philip II to Mateo Vázquez, 19 Feb. 1586; IVdeDJ 55/IX/111, 26 July 1586; and BZ 143/6, 4 Jan. 1588. For the king's total seclusion during his 'retreats', see Fourquevaux, II, 3–7, Memoir of Oct. 1568, and Sigüenza, 92 (Holy Week, 1579). See further examples of daily religious devotions delaying the king's business at: *CCG* XII, 534–5 [Sept. 1579], the king received a letter going to Mass, but did not read it until after it ended; ibid., XI, 277–8, 22 Sept. 1584, the king could not read Granvelle's letter because he went to vespers to commemorate the anniversary of his father's death. Nevertheless the king did occasionally read important papers while in church (Donà, 372–3, letter to Venice, 2 Nov. 1571: Philip reading newly arrived letters 'right after the incense'; and IVdeDJ 68/287a, Vázquez to Philip II and reply, 28 June 1574: 'I have seen all these, although in haste and most of them during vespers'); and he once told his daughters that he could not go

to matins 'because I had a lot to do' (Bouza, 57, letter of 15 Jan. 1582). Cf. Margaret Thatcher's account of doing business on the back of her hymn sheet one day during a service: Thatcher, *The Downing Street years*, 76.

90. We shall probably never know, because his will commanded that all his letters to and from Fray Diego de Chaves, his confessor, should be burnt after his death without being read: see *Documentos . . . El Escorial*, II, 48, codicil of 23 Aug. 1597. No part of this correspondence seems to have survived, so we have nothing to set beside his grandson Philip IV's soul-searching letters to Sor Maria de Ágreda. On sleeping in time of sermon, see Bouza, 90.

91. In 1938, when he addressed a rally in Vienna, the city where he had grown up, Adolf Hitler declared, 'I believe it was God's will to send a youth from here into the Reich, to let him grow up, to raise him to be the leader of the nation so as to enable him to lead back his homeland into the Reich'. He saw other victories and deliverances (such as escapes from assassination) as 'fresh confirmation of the mission given me by Providence to continue toward my goal'. See Bullock, *Hitler and Stalin*, 569 (Vienna 1938) and 846 (after surviving the July bomb plot, 1944).

92. Groen van Prinsterer, *Archives*, 2nd series I, 84, François de la Noue to an English correspondent, 17 Aug. 1588; for Espinosa's assessment of Lepanto in 1571, see note 99 below. Various 'providentialist' medals of 1588 are reproduced in Rodríguez-Salgado, *Armada 1588–1988*, 276–7 and FD, I, 217–18. For examples of English 'providentialism' see Wiener, 'The beleaguered isle'; McKenna, 'How God became an Englishman'; McGiffert, 'God's controversy with Jacobean England'; Cressy, *Bonfires and bells*, chaps 7, 9 and 10; and Woolf, *The idea of History in early Stuart England*, 4–8. On the Dutch, see Groenhuis, *De predikanten*, 77–107.

93. See Fleischer, 'The lawgiver as

Messiah'. I thank Sanjay Subrahmanyam for drawing to my attention the messianic impulses of both Safavid and Mogul rulers in the later sixteenth century.

94. On Manuel, see Thomaz, 'Factions, interests and messianism'; on Ferdinand, see Suárez Fernández, 'La situación internacional en torno a 1492'. On Charles V's messianic imperialism from the 1520s onwards see Bataillon, *Erasmo y España*, 226–31; Yates, *Astraea*, 1–28; and Sánchez Montes, *Franceses, protestantes, turcos*, 42–51.

95. Salazar, *Política española*, proposition 3; Campanella quoted by Pagden, *Spanish imperialism*, 51. See also the discussion of the views of Francisco Vázquez de Menchaca in the 1560s by Fernández Albaladejo, '"Rey Católico"', 210, and Pagden, *Lords of all the world*, 56–62. See the interesting evidence of a growing religious obsession among 'ordinary' Spaniards in the later sixteenth century in Eire, *Madrid to purgatory*, 188–215.

96. Sigüenza, 8; *PEG*, V, 643, Philip II to Granvelle, 24 Aug. 1559. Interestingly the king went on to say that losing his states for lack of money 'would be the saddest thing I can imagine, and one which I would regret more than anything else – much more than if I lost them in a battle'.

97. AGS *Estado* 527/5, Philip II to Gonzalo Pérez, undated [Mar. 1565]; and IVdeDJ 37/155, Vázquez to Philip II and reply, 22 Jan. 1576.

98. IVdeDJ 55/X/52, Vázquez to Philip II and reply, 24 Mar. 1587; IVdeDJ 55/XII/16–17, same to same, 16 Feb. 1589.

99. BL *Addl* 28,704/270v–1, Espinosa to Alba and Don Juan de Zúñiga, 4 Dec. 1571, on the victory, 'la mayor después de la del Vermejo'. Fernando de Herrera's canticle on Lepanto also compared the victory with the drowning of Pharaoh's army in the Red Sea (see López de Toro, *Los poetas de Lepanto*, 233–42). In Italy the victory unleashed a host of prophecies: see Ginzburg, 'Due note sul profetismo cinquecentesco', 207–12; and Olivieri, 'Il significato escatologico di Lepanto'. On the messianic ambitions of the Spanish Court at this time, see Jedin, *Chiesa della storia*, 703–22; and García Hernán, 'Pio V y el mesianismo profético'. For the 'emperor of the east' project, see García Hernán, *La Armada española*, 67–8.

100. AGRB *Audience* 1728/2/77, Alba to Count Bossu, 29 Aug. 1572. Philip II was equally moved: according to the French ambassador, when he arrived for an audience the day after receiving news of the massacre, the king 'began to laugh, with signs of extreme pleasure and satisfaction', and he confessed to his own ambassador in Paris (the source of the news) that 'I had one of the greatest moments of satisfaction that I have had in all my life': Kamen, *Philip*, 141, quoting St Gouard to Charles IX, and Philip II to Don Diego de Zúñiga, both on 18 Sept. 1572. The king also looked forward to news of more massacres elsewhere in France and the Lord did not disappoint him: see Benedict, 'The St Bartholomew's massacres in the provinces' (massacres in at least twelve other French cities, and anti-Protestant 'incidents' in eight more).

101. Quotations from BL *Eg.* 1506/16–17, Gaspar de Quiroga, bishop of Cuenca and Inquisitor-General, to Philip II and reply, 8 Mar. 1574; and IVdeDJ 51/31, Mateo Vázquez to Philip II, 31 May 1574. On the prayer chain, see Bouza Álvarez, 'Monarchie en lettres d'imprimerie', 214–15, and Sigüenza, 69.

102. BZ 144/30, Vázquez to Philip II, 24 Nov. 1574 (the king replied 'When you come here [to see me], tell me what you heard about La Goleta and from whom'); Manrique quoted in Bouza Álvarez, 'Servidumbres' (I thank Professor Bouza for drawing this and other references from his article to my attention ahead of publication); IVdeDJ 51/181, Mateo Vázquez to Philip II, 28 Dec. 1578.

See also other criticisms from this period on pp. 20–1 above.

103. Cueto, '1580 and all that', 156, Cristóbal de Moura to Philip II, 25 Nov. 1578; IVdeDJ 51/105, Mateo Vázquez to Philip II and reply, 22 Aug. 1583; Freitas de Meneses, *Os Açores*, II, 83, Figueroa to Philip II, 3 Oct. 1582. Philip also thought about the queen and St Anne in 1588: see Kamen, *Philip*, 273. See also the long list of saints whose intervention Philip sought in his will: Eire, *Madrid to purgatory*, 284 n.

104. The sonnet of Hernando de Acuña (d. 1580), first published in his *Varias poesías* (Madrid, 1591), is taken from Rivers, *Poesía lírica*, 108–9 (my thanks to Santiago García-Castañón for this reference). See the brilliant analysis of the messianic imperialism of the soldier-poets by Terry, 'War and literature'. Other expansionist writers of this period are discussed in Fernández Armesto, 'Armada myths'.

105. Details from Kagan, *Students and society*, 83, 92–4. See also Martínez Millán, 'Un curioso manuscrito', which records the promotions envisaged by Cardinal Espinosa between 1566 and 1572: many of the candidates were graduates of the *colegios mayores*.

106. Álava, 97–8, to Alba, 17 Mar. 1568, and 352, Zayas to Álava, 27 June 1569. Another example of heavy religious humour occurred when Álava sent a copy of the Augsburg Confession to Madrid: Zayas referred to it as the 'Augsburg Confusion' (ibid., 316).

107. AGS *Estado* 531/91, Fray Lorenzo de Villavicencio to Philip II, 6 Oct. 1566 ('humbly' seems curiously incongruous amid such threats); Cueto, '1580 and all that', 167; ASV *NS* 32/181–3, Nuncio Novara to Rusticucci, 4 July 1586. A decade earlier, Don Luis Manrique (p. 20 above) had also used 'providential' arguments to try and change the king's mind. For a similar suggestion that President Truman's deliberate appointment of men who held principles like his own may have reduced his administration's flexibility, see Johnson, *Managing the White House*, 64; see also Halperin, *Bureaucratic politics*, 161.

108. *Monumenta historica societatis Iesu*, LX, *Ribadeneira*, II, 105–11, letter to Don Juan de Idiáquez, Dec. 1588. On Ribadeneira's political philosophy, see Bireley, *The Counter-Reformation Prince*, chap. 5. For another example of open and outspoken clerical criticism of the king at this time, see *CSPV*, VIII, 396, Lippomano to Venice, 1 Oct. 1588.

109. Quotations from ASV *NS* 19/15, Lodi to Rusticucci, 25 Apr. 1586; ASF *MP* 4919/88, Alemanni to Florence, 6 Feb. 1588. See the similar sentiments of the ambassadors of Lucca (ASL *Anziani*, 644, Compagni to Republic, 26 June 1588) and Ferrara (ASMo *CD* 15, Ripa to Ferrara, 5 Mar., 30 Apr. and 23 July 1588.) A few people, however, showed less constancy. As early as July 1588, after storms had driven the Armada back to Corunna, the nuncio began to wonder whether 'these impediments which the devil creates' might not be a sign that 'God does not approve of the enterprise'; and in November he noted that the fleet's various misfortunes had 'disturbed everyone, since they can almost openly see the hand of God raised against us'. ASV *NS* 34/415–18 and 583–5, Novara to Montalto, 6 July and 8 Nov. 1588.

110. For the hope that 'God would return to support his cause' see *BMO*, II, 338–9, Philip II to Don Bernardino de Mendoza, 5 Sept. 1586, minute (about the failure of the Babington plot to assassinate Elizabeth Tudor); and Kamen, *Philip*, 298. For 'God has done this', see BZ 166/92 and 100, Hernando de Vega to Philip II and reply, 9 and 11 Nov. 1586 (upon learning that the annual Indies fleet had arrived safely at Seville).

111. For details on these two cases, see Parker, *Dutch Revolt*, 64–5, and García

Vilar, 'El Maquiavelismo', 620–42. For Philip's use of theologians in the 1590s, see p. 277 above.

112. Horozco y Covarrubias, *Tratado de la verdadera y falsa profesía*, fos 37–8; Díaz Jimeno, *Hado y fortuna*, chap. 7; Kagan, *Lucrecia's dreams*; and idem, 'Politics, prophecy and the Inquisition'. Kagan argues that the three principal 'plaza prophets' of 1588 were manipulated by domestic opponents of the king. Certainly all three were arrested soon after the Armada's failure. See also an example of consulting necromancers in 1572 at p. 126 above; and the suggestion that Philip brought troops to the Escorial in 1577 because of a prediction that fire would consume a royal palace that year (Sigüenza, 76–7: in fact a bolt of lightning *did* cause a fire at the palace that summer).

113. Huerga, 'La vida seudomística', 62–3; and RAH Ms 9–2320/5v, Creswell to Philip III, 1602: 'el santo varón . . . me dixó que aquella Armada iría en humo' – so perhaps he did indeed enjoy a hotline to heaven.

114. For everyday examples of this complex but important phenomenon in action see, for continental Europe: Ozment, *Protestants*, 196–204; and Theibault, 'Jeremiah in the village'; and for England and its colonies, Donagan, 'Understanding Providence'; von Greyerz, *Vorsehungsglaube und Kosmologie*, 80–118; Hall, *Worlds of wonder*, 77–80, 91–4 and 116; Worden, 'Providence and politics'; and idem, 'Oliver Cromwell'. Perhaps the most remarkable example is presented by Gillespie, 'Destabilizing Ulster 1641–2', 116–19, which shows that in the earlier seventeenth century, Irish Protestants identified themselves with Israel and Irish Catholics with the Maccabees.

115. Burnet, *Memoires of the dukes of Hamilton*, Charles I to Hamilton, Dec. 1642 (I thank Ian Gentles for bringing this reference to my attention); and Halliwell, *Letters of the kings of England*, II, 383–4, Charles I to Prince

Rupert, 31 July 1645. See also Charles's uncompromising earlier statement, when only the Scots defied him, that 'I will rather die than yield to these impertinent and damnable demands': Ohlmeyer, *Civil war and Restoration*, 77, Charles to Hamilton, 11 June 1638. Charles's grandmother Mary Stuart had also met a martyr's death.

116. Thomas Beard, *The theatre of God's judgements* (1597), quoted with splendid examples of Cromwell's acceptance of this philosophy in Sproxton, *Violence and religion*, 52 and 59–61. See also Armitage, 'The Cromwellian Protectorate', 540–1.

117. Davis, 'Cromwell's religion', in Morrill, *Oliver Cromwell*, 187. For three examples (among many) of this attitude among Philip II and his advisers, see: IVdeDJ 53/3/33, Vázquez to Philip II and reply, 27 Apr. 1574 ('pues Dios nos ayuda y haze tanta merced', wrote the king, 'agora es menester que nosotros nos ayudemos'); BL *Addl* 28,702/24–5, Idiáquez to Granvelle, 24 June 1580 ('Parezçe que Dios nos ayuda si nos sabemos ayudar'); and IVdeDJ 51/105, Vázquez to Philip II, 22 Aug. 1583 ('el cuidado, zelo y asistencia con que Vuestra Magestad acude a las cosas del servicio de Nuestro Señor hazen que Él acuda como vemos a las de Vuestra Magestad').

118. BZ 146/219, council of Finance to Philip II, 14 June 1588 with long royal response of the 18th, copy; and BZ 143/111, Mateo Vázquez to Philip II and reply, 28 June 1588.

119. *BMO*, I, 62, Philip II to Alba, 14 Sept. 1571; see p. 162 above for other similar statements and for the context. Pereña Vicente, *Teoría de la guerra*, 70–1, offers an interesting consideration of this correspondence. Devout Protestants at this time also believed 'it is no greater fault to have confidence in man's power than it is to[o] hastily to despair of God's work': Feuillerat, *The prose works of Sir Philip Sidney*, III, 180, Sidney to Walsingham, 24 Mar. 1586

(ironically, discussing the best way to oppose Philip II).

120. AGS *Estado* 165/2–3, Philip II to Archduke Albert, 14 Sept. 1587. Perhaps the triumphant November voyage of the Dutch Armada a century later vindicated Philip II, however, by showing that God *could* send good weather when He chose. See Israel and Parker, 'Of Providence and Protestant winds'.

121. IVdeDJ 37/59 Requeséns to Zúñiga, 11 Oct. 1574 ('quizá deve de ser inspiración de Dios'); *BMO*, III, 1964, Bertendona to Philip II, 15 Feb. 1588; Mattingly, *Defeat*, 233 (quoting the papal collector, Buongiovanni, to Rome, in May 1588).

122. IVdeDJ 144/36, Vázquez to Philip II and reply, 11 Dec. 1574 ('Dios nos ayude en todo, que yo os digo que es tanto menester que a mi parece que se ha de ser servido con hazer milagro, porque sin el yo veo todo en los peores termynos que puede ser'). Even before these reverses, the king felt that 'Unless God performs a miracle, which our sins do not merit, it is no longer possible to maintain ourselves for {more than a few} months, let alone years' (IVdeDJ 53/3/56, Vázquez to Philip II and reply, 13 May 1574).

123. BNM Ms 9444/252v–3, Scipio de Castro's 'Instructions' to the duke of Terranova, *c.* 1583 (my thanks to Mario Rizzo for this reference); *BMO*, III, 478, Idiáquez to Medina Sidonia, 3 June 1587; BCR Ms 2417/37–42, Don Juan de Silva to Esteban de Ibarra, 13 Aug. 1589 (other extracts from this letter appear on pp. 66–7 above). For examples of blind faith in miracles earlier in the reign, see Olivieri, 'Il significativo . . . di Lepanto', 260, 262.

124. *CCG*, XII, 126–7, Granvelle to Margaret of Parma, 15 Nov. 1585; AGS *Estado* 590/23, Parma to Philip II, 28 Feb. 1586 – and, in another letter of the same day, 'God will grow weary of working miracles for us' (*Estado* 590/22).

125. Quotations from Maura, 258–61, Medina Sidonia to Philip II, 21 and 24 June 1588; Herrera Oria, 210–14, Philip II to Medina Sidonia, 1 July 1588; and KML *MSP: CR*, 5/353, Medina Sidonia to Archduke Albert, 15 July 1588, minute.

126. AGS *Estado* 553/112, Philip II to Alba, 27 Nov. 1572, minute; *Estado* 2219/84, Philip II to Parma, 31 Aug. 1588, and fos 85–6 'Apuntamiento en materia de armada que Su Magestad mandó hazer para que se considere y resuelva entre el duque de Parma, su sobrino, y el duque de Medina Sidonia' (four foolscap sheets). Admittedly Philip's Instructions to Parma (dated 1 Apr. 1588) contained advice on what to do should he not capture London after getting his forces ashore (see p. 267 above) but not on what to do should the Armada not arrive.

127. Von Neumann's elegant paraphrase of 'Murphy's Law' quoted by Campbell, *Grammatical man*, 73. See also Thomas, 'To err is human', 561 – 'Mistakes are at the very base of human thought, embedded there, feeding the structure . . . We are built to make mistakes, coded for error' – and the interesting essays on this subject in Beaumont, *War, chaos and history*. Clausewitz quoted p. 206 above.

128. The Schlieffen Plan of 1914 did not even provide for success: it failed to specify what would happen if Paris fell but required defending, as the Russian armies slowly but surely began their march on Berlin (I thank Holger Herwig for this observation).

129. Ulloa, *Hacienda real*, 831, quoting Vázquez; González de Cellorigo, *Memorial*, 94; Álamos de Barrientos, *Discurso político*, 31, 42–52. (This tract, although not published until the nineteenth century, circulated widely in manuscript. It has sometimes been attributed to Antonio Pérez.) See also the remarkably similar pessimistic survey by the duke of Medina Sidonia from 1598 printed in Pierson, *Commander of the Armada*, 217–18.

4 *'The Great Bog of Europe': the Netherlands, 1555–77*

1. IVDJ 82/444 duke of Sessa (Spanish ambassador in Rome) to Don Balthasar de Zúñiga (Spanish ambassador in Brussels), 28 Sept. 1600, minute; and Mulder, *Journael van Antonis Duyck*, II, 785 (my thanks to Ben Cox for this reference, which forms the conclusion to Duyck's diary for the year 1600).

2. See the details in Parker, *Military revolution,* chap. 1 and 'Afterword'.

3. See Kennedy, *Rise and fall,* chap. 2. Inevitably, this is a gross oversimplification, but I hope it fairly represents Kennedy's main argument, which offers both a brilliant synthesis of much current research on the subject and a chapter that is logically satisfying and beautifully crafted.

4. Anon., *The edict and decree of Phillip king of Spain*, sig. C3 (part of 'The answere to the edict'). The creative arithmetic of the extract – 10 to 100 is not a sixfold increase! – is typical of the period. Some idea of the legion of writers (known as *arbitristas*) who stressed the urgent need to overhaul the Spanish economy may be gained from Correa Calderón, *Registro de arbitristas*.

5. See Elliott, 'A Europe of composite monarchies', and pp. 91–2 above.

6. My thanks for encouragement and suggestions for this chapter go to Steven Glick, Fernando González de León, John F. Guilmartin, Michael Handel, Don Higginbotham, Jeffrey McKeage, W. H. McNeill, Williamson Murray, Jane Ohlmeyer and Henk van Nierop. I also owe a particular debt of gratitude to critiques by my graduate students at the University of Illinois and by the members of Professor Murray's military history seminar at the Ohio State University.

7. *CDCV*, II, 591 (see also pp. 88–9 above). The following paragraphs rest upon Parker, *Dutch Revolt*, 19–41.

8. Feltham, *Brief character*, 1–2, 5 (probably written in the 1620s); Brulez, 'Het gewicht van de oorlog', 394.

9. BL *Addl* 28,388/68, Don Luis de Requeséns, at the time governor-general of the Netherlands, to Don Gaspar de Quiroga, Aug. 1575.

10. Laubespine, 623–4, Francis II to La Forest (his agent in Brussels), Oct. 1560. (See also ibid., 47, Laubespine to Lorraine and Guise, 27 July 1559, already suggesting that no ambassador would be needed in Brussels.) Ramsay, *City of London*, 86–8, notes Elizabeth's decision to close the English embassy in Brussels in 1559.

11. Japikse, *Correspondentie van Willem I, prins van Oranje*, I, 143–4, Egmont to Orange, 1 July 1559; Groen van Prinsterer, *Archives*, 1st series I, 152, Granvelle to Philip II, 10 Mar. 1563.

12. *PEG*, VI, 166, Granvelle to Philip II, 12 Sept. 1560. For details on the Djerba disaster, see Vilar, *Tunez*, 459–62; and Braudel, *The Mediterranean*, 973–87.

13. BNP *Fonds français* 15,587/3–7, Mémoire of Laubespine (former ambassador to Philip II) to Catherine de Medici, autumn 1563, quoting the views of François Baudouin who had just returned from the Netherlands. For details of the linkages between the king's servants in Spain and the Netherlands, see the fine study of Lagomarsino, 'Court factions'. On Erasso, see Carlos Morales, 'El poder de los secretarios reales'.

14. AGRB *Audience* 475/84, Josse de Courtewille, Philip's French language secretary, to Viglius, president of the Netherlands Privy Council, 24 May 1563.

15. *GPGP*, II, 487, Philip II to Gonzalo Pérez [Mar. 1565].

16. AGS *Estado* 527/5, Philip II to Pérez [24 Mar. 1565]. Pérez was at the time sick in bed, and so all discussion of how to deal with Egmont had to be carried out in writing, thus revealing

exactly how the king gradually made up his mind what to do. See other quotations from these exchanges on p. 42 above; and the brilliant account in Lagomarsino, 'Court factions', 98–120. On the king's extraordinary silence, see *PEG*, VIII, 192 and 263 (no letter received from the king between Apr. and Aug. 1564).

17. Groen van Prinsterer, *Archives*, I, 369, Orange to his brother Louis, 3 Apr. 1565; Wauters, *Mémoires*, 268, Hopperus's account of Egmont's speech to the council of State in Brussels, 5 May 1565; Theissen, *Correspondance française de Marguerite d'Autriche,* 91, Philip II to Margaret, 17 Oct. 1565. See also AGRB *Audience* 779/120,178 and 225, minutes of the meeting of the Netherlands council of State on 26 Jan., 28 June and 3 Oct. 1565, recording news of military developments in the Mediterranean. I thank Paul Regan for drawing to my attention the cheap maps of Malta, printed by Cock in Antwerp.

18. Gillès de Pélichy, 'Contribution', 103–4, Egmont to Philip II, 30 May 1566, holograph; Serrano, II, xxxvi, provides chapter and verse for Pius's efforts. See also AGRB *Audience* 476/139, Viglius to Charles de Tisnacq, Philip's principal Netherlands minister in Madrid, 19 Aug. 1566, minute: 'These evils have arisen through a lack of timely decision and action'. For the 1566 campaign in the Aegean and Adriatic see Braudel, *The Mediterranean*, II, 1030–5.

19. AGS *Estado* 530, unfol., and Enno van Gelder, *Correspondance française de Marguerite d'Autriche,* II, 326–32, Margaret to Philip II, 27 and 29 Aug. 1566. Margaret's dramatic figures came back to haunt her a year later: when she urged Alba to reduce his forces the duke angrily reminded her of those earlier alarmist assessments: AGRB *Audience* 244/72–76v, Alba's instruction to Francisco de Ibarra, 8 Aug. 1567.

20. UB Leiden *Hs. Pap.* 3/5, Alonso de Laloo to Count Hornes, 29 Sept. 1566; other views cited on p. 90 above.

21. For the suggestion that Mediterranean affairs held Alba back, see Fourquevaux, I, 147–8, letter to Charles IX, 9 Dec. 1566, and 172–9, letter to Catherine de Medici, 18 Jan. 1567. For his march, see Parker, *Dutch Revolt*, 88–90 and 99–105.

22. AA 5/69, Philip II to Alba, 7 Aug. 1567. The nuncio found out about this decision four days later: see Serrano, II, 177, Castagno to Alessandrino, 11 Aug. 1567; the English ambassador divined it the previous day (Cambridge University Library, Ms Mm–3–8/89, Dr Man to Cecil, 10 Aug. 1567 ('Heare is yet no certen notyce geven of the kynges goyng towardes Flaunders. Whan it will bee, or wheather it will bee at all, God knowithe'). For a discussion of whether or not Philip ever intended to leave, see Serrano, II, li–lx, and Parker, *Dutch Revolt*, 292 n. 28.

23. *Co.Do.In.,* XXXVII, 84, Alba to Philip II, 6 Jan. 1568.

24. Álava, 203–4, 273–4 and 291, Philip II to Álava, 27 Nov. 1567, and Zayas to same, 2 Nov. 1568 and 12 Jan. 1569. For Alba's restrictive Instructions, see *Co.Do.In.*, IV, 349 and 354, Alba to Erasso and to Philip II, 26–27 Apr. 1567.

25. *CCG,* IV, 594–5 and AGS *Estado* 553/94, Philip II to Alba, Feb. and 20 Apr. 1572, minutes. See a similarly hectoring letter on 16 Mar. at AGS *Estado* 553/40. For details on the Turks' rapid recovery after Lepanto see the exciting new evidence in Imber, *Studies*, 85–101.

26. *Co.Do.In.,* LXXV, 190–1, Alba to Zayas, 12 Feb. 1573.

27. AGRB *Audience* 339/169–71, Esteban de Ibarra's order to withdraw garrisons, 28 Oct. 1571; *CCG*, IV, 146–52, Morillon to Granvelle, 24 Mar. 1572.

28. AGRB *Audience* 340/31, Alba to Bossu, 13 Feb. 1572; and AGS *Estado*

551/94, 'Relación de lo que se trató en el consejo' (in Brussels).

29. BL *Addl* 28,702/261–4 'Relación sobre los abusos' (this source also claimed that a captured Sea Beggar captain revealed that 'the rebels were discussing a descent on Brill or one of the islands' long before it happened); AGRB *Audience* 404/139, Zweveghem to Alba, London, 25 Mar. 1572; *Audience* 340/68, Alba to Bossu, 2 Apr. 1572, minute. The capture of Brill became known in Brussels two days later: see *Audience* 340/70, Alba to Wacken, 'Vendredy Sainct' [=4 Apr.] 1572, minute, noting the arrival of the news 'this morning'.

30. AGRB *Audience* 340/72, 79, 81 and 105, Bossu to Alba, 2, 3, 4 and 7 Apr. 1572. See also correspondence on the subject in the *Nieuwe Rotterdamsche Courant, Zaterdagse Bijvoedsel*, 22 June and 1 July 1988.

31. AGRB *Audience* 344/21 and 29, Bossu to Alba, both dated 23 May 1572. On the superior fortifications of Enkhuizen, see Groenveld and Vermaere, 'Zeeland en Holland en 1569', 163.

32. See *Co.Do.In.*, LXXV, 104–6, Julián Romero to Gabriel de Zayas, 22 Sept. 1572, noting that sixteen days' battery had made virtually no impression on the city's walls. Another source reported sixty guns deployed against Mons: *CCG*, IV, 383, 447, Morillon to Granvelle, 28 July and 28 Sept. 1572.

33. See the standard account of the Nassau brothers' negotiations with the Huguenots in van Herwerden, *Het verblijf van Lodewijk van Nassau in Frankrijk*, with a few additional data in Jouanna, *Le Devoir de révolte*, 154–6. For fears that France would declare war, see the pessimistic letters in March, *El Comendador Mayor de Castilla*, 153–5, Requeséns, governor of Lombardy, to Don Juan de Zúñiga, 29 June 1572; and *Epistolario*, III, 160–3, Alba to Philip, 18 July 1572. In Madrid, Ambassador Sauli of Genoa also believed that France would soon

declare war: ASG *AS* 2414, unfol., letters to Genoa of 25 May, 27 June and 2 July 1572; and Donà, 487–9, letter to Venice of 12 June 1572.

34. *CCG*, IV, 351, Morillon to Granvelle, 10 Aug. 1572.

35. AGRB *Audience* 344/83, Alba to Bossu, 15 June 1572, minute, and *Audience* 313/303–4, council of Gelderland to Alba, 28 June 1572, protesting against his order of the 25th to recall Meghen's regiment. Meanwhile, in the light of the capture of Zutphen, the governor of Friesland refused to release any troops to Holland: *Audience* 297/162, Baron Billy to Alba, 16 June 1572.

36. AGRB *Audience* 344/88, 135, 169, Bossu to Alba, 17 June, 5 and 18 July 1572 (the last in reply to Alba's express order 'ceste troisième fois': ibid., fo. 164, Alba to Bossu, 17 July, minute). Bossu finally complied a week later, reporting that the rebels had immediately occupied all places abandoned by the Spaniards: ibid., fo. 174, Bossu to Alba, 26 July 1572.

37. *Epistolario*, III, 169, Alba to Philip II, 19 July 1572, vividly described the defeat of the French column; Estèbe, *Tocsin pour un massacre*, analyses the events before, during and after 24 Aug.; Groen van Prinsterer, *Archives*, 1st series, III, 505 and IV, cii, Orange to Count John, 21 Sept. 1572, lamented the impact of St Bartholomew on his cause.

38. *CCG*, IV, 413, Morillon to Granvelle, 2 Sept. 1572, and Eguiluz, *Milicia, discurso y regla militar*, fo. 68, both recorded Alba's gay attire; *Epistolario*, III, 203, Alba to Philip II, 9 Sept. 1572, described the battle outside Mons; *Co.Do.In.*, LXXV, 104–6, Romero to Zayas, 22 Sept. 1572, noted Orange's letter advising Mons to surrender; and *CCG*, IV, 479, Morillon to Granvelle, 31 Oct. 1572, explained why it did so.

39. ASP *CF* 109, unfol., Don Sancho de Londoño (the senior field officer in Alba's army) to the duke of Parma, 21 Nov. 1568; see also the admiring

account of Alba's proceedings by Don Bernardino de Mendoza, an eyewitness: *Comentarios*, 441. Don Juan de Zúñiga later praised Alba's refusal to stake everything on the outcome of a battle (*Nueva Co.Do.In.*, I, 133–9, letter to Requeséns, 6 Feb. 1574).

40. Mondoucet, I, 56, letter to Charles IX, 5 Oct. 1572; and *Epistolario*, III, 239, Alba to Don Juan de Zúñiga, [27] Oct. 1572. Even as the sack of Mechelen continued, delegates from Oudenaarde, Dendermonde, Leuven, Diest and Tongeren all sent delegates to surrender and ask for mercy. See Orange's dispirited account of the collapse of his cause in the south: Groen van Prinsterer, *Archives*, IV, 3, letter of 18 Oct. 1572. See also Parker, 'The laws of war'.

41. *Epistolario*, III, 251, Alba to Philip II, 28 Nov. 1572. See also the confirmation in Mondoucet, I, 98–102, letter to Charles IX, 20 Nov. 1572.

42. See details of the 1572 Friesland campaign in Slicher van Bath, *Een Fries landbouwbedrijf*, part i; and also University of Texas at Austin, Humanities Research Center, *Kraus Catalog* 124/36, a remarkable series of twenty-one sketches of the operations undertaken by Baron Billy, governor of Friesland. On the fall of Zutphen, see the account in AGRB *Audience* 313/226, 239 and 253, Baron Hierges to Alba, 10, 11 and 14 June 1572.

43. Mondoucet, I, 106–10, letter to Charles IX, 25 Nov. 1572; *Epistolario*, III, 261, Alba to Philip, 19 Dec. 1572. See also the account of Mendoza, once again a participant: *Comentarios, 477*.

44. See the perceptive consideration of this point by Israel, *The Dutch Republic. Its rise, greatness, and fall*, 179–80. See also van Someren, *Correspondance*, 27–37, 154–7 and *passim*, with details on the prince's supporters in, and plans for, the province in 1570–71.

45. On the improvised new defences of Haarlem, with bastions and sconces beyond the medieval walls, see the contemporary drawings and prints in Gemeentearchief Haarlem, *Stedelijke Atlas*; and BNM Ms *Res* 200/38 (reproduced in Parker, 'Maps and Ministers', colour plate 4).

46. *Epistolario*, III, 275 and 290, Alba to Philip, 8 Jan. and 12 Feb. 1573, on the loss of veterans; *Co.Do.In.*, LXXV, 236–40, Alba to Zayas, 8 July 1573, on the problems caused by having to garrison each loyal town.

47. Mondoucet estimated that Alba's field army in early December had shrunk to 8–10,000 foot and 1,200–1,500 horse (Mondoucet, I, 119–22: letter to Charles IX, 9 Dec. 1572). The number of defenders is deduced from *Epistolario*, III, 472, Alba to Philip II, 28 July 1573.

48. Many contemporaries commented on this prudence; so does the admirable modern biography by Maltby, *Alba*, 37–8, 55–6, 60–1 and 268–70.

49. See ibid., 79–81, and the sources on p. 332. Even twenty years later Cardinal Granvelle, on hearing of the decision to besiege Haarlem in winter, said that he 'could still feel in my bones the chill I felt before Metz' (*CCG*, IV, 553–6, Granvelle to Morillon, 18 Mar. 1573).

50. AGS *Estado* 559/43, 'Relación del suceso y presa de la villa de Harlen', on Fadrique's foolish refusal to negotiate with Haarlem. Others later blamed him as 'the cause of all the damage here': see the blistering condemnation in *Nueva Co.Do.In.*, V, 224–35, Requeséns to Philip II, 19 Sept. 1574.

51. Wouter Jacobszoon, a monk who had taken refuge in Amsterdam, which remained loyal to the king, recorded the arrival of the booty-laden Spaniards on 3 Dec. 1572, the day after the sack of Naarden, closely followed by deputies from Haarlem 'and other places . . . all asking about their own town'. See van Eeghen, *Dagboek*, I, 90.

52. *CCG*, IV, 516, Morillon to Granvelle, 30 Nov. 1572 (quoting the Elector of Cologne); *Epistolario*, III, 250–3, Alba to Philip, 28 Nov. 1572. The same point was made by the perceptive French agent: see Mondoucet, I,

110–13, letter to Charles IX, 28 Nov. 1572. Events vindicated all this pessimism: as the revolt continued, foreign assistance grew.

53. *Epistolario*, III, 249 and 268, Alba to Philip, 19 Nov. and 22 Dec. 1572, warning of his financial plight. Wouter Jacobszoon frequently noted the high price of victuals in his 'journal': see van Eeghen, *Dagboek*, I, 105, 131, 134 and 151.

54. AMC legajo 250, unfol., contains the contradictory Instructions in French and Spanish (30 Oct. and 8 Nov. 1571). For other contradiction caused by having both French and Spanish secretaries deal with the same issue, see p. 25 above. The secret correspondence, which eventually helped to bring Alba down (see pp. 38 and 314 n. 103 above), is discussed in IVdeDJ 44/88 and 91, Vázquez to Philip II and reply, 4 Oct. and 21 Dec. 1572 (quotation from the first of these documents).

55. IVdeDJ 44/88, Vázquez to Philip II and reply, 4 Oct. 1572. See also Lovett, 'A new governor', 91–2; and Janssens, 'Juan de la Cerda', 222–7.

56. *Co.Do.In.*, XXXVI, 119–30, 'Relación de lo que ha pasado en algunos consejos', July to Nov. 1572, full of the heated exchanges between the two dukes (quotation from p. 126).

57. Berwick y Alba, *Discurso*, 65.

58. BPU *Favre* 30/30, Philip II to Requeséns, 30 Jan. 1573, copy (another copy, in Granvelle's handwriting, may be found at AGRB *MD* 5480/15–16; précis in GCP, II, 308–9).

59. See details in Lovett, 'A new governor', 99–100, and March, *El Comendador Mayor de Castilla*, chap. 16. Copies of Philip's fascinating holograph letters dated 30 Jan., 5 Apr., 21 June, 14 Aug. and 30 Oct. 1573 (the originals were destroyed when Requeséns died) may be found in BPU *Favre* 30/30–74; and copies of his instructions (dated 3 Oct.) in *Co.Do.In.*, CII, 277–306. Some of

Requeséns's replies were printed in *Co.Do.In.*, CII, 35–8, 45–6, 64–5, 74–6 and 103–6.

60. Gerlo and de Smet, *Marnixi epistulae*, I, 194–7 and 199–200, Marnix to Count Louis, 8 June 1573, and to Count John of Nassau, 2 July 1573; and IVdeDJ 32/139, Medinaceli to Mateo Vázquez, Maastricht, 20 July 1573, holograph (apparently the only surviving example of the duke's secret correspondence with the king).

61. *Epistolario*, III, 472–3, Alba to Philip II, 28 July 1573; Gerlo and de Smet, *Marnixi epistulae*, I, 202–3, Orange to Marnix, 1 Aug. 1573, holograph; and BNM Ms 783/469–71, Granvelle to Don John of Austria, 28 Aug. 1573 (Granvelle did not argue that the garrison should have been spared, merely that 'it was not wise to dispose of them before the end of the war: there would have been plenty of time to dispose of them afterwards'). For an interesting Dutch appreciation of Alba's strategy of selective brutality, and of the reasons why it failed, see Grotius, *De rebus belgicis*, 65. On the events at Haarlem, see Parker, *Dutch Revolt*, 159–60; Spaans, *Haarlem*, 42–6; and Groenveld and Vermaere, 'Zeeland en Holland en 1569', 158–9.

62. On the siege of Alkmaar, from 21 Aug. to 8 Oct. 1573, see Schöffer, *Alkmaar ontzet*, chaps 2–3 (Anthony Anthonisz's Italian-style walls are described at pp. 42–9). For the duke's misguided boast ('no téngolo por negocio dificultoso'), see AGS *Estado* 8340/242, Alba to Don John of Austria, 18 Sept. 1573. He may have been misled by the 1569 report of his engineers that Alkmaar lacked strong defences and could easily be bombarded from some higher ground nearby; the new bastions only went up in 1572–73 (see Groenveld and Vermaere, 'Zeeland en Holland en 1569', 159). Van Nierop, 'The Blood Council', mentions the initial desire of many citizens to surrender.

63. For some details, see Devos, 'Un projet de cession d'Alger'; Juste, *Les*

Valois et les Nassau; and Parker, *Dutch Revolt*, 149.

64. *Co.Do.In.*, LXXV, 190, Alba to Zayas, 12 Feb. 1573. For more expressions of the need to make peace in the Mediterranean in order to concentrate on the Netherlands, and of the king's counter-arguments, see p. 89 above.

65. Details in Berwick y Alba, *Discurso*, 76, 116–17 (statement of Francisco de Ibarra. Although this is undated, Ibarra arrived in the Netherlands with the duke in 1567 and left in 1570; he clearly wrote this document after his departure.) See also *Epistolario*, III, 310–11, Alba to Zayas, 18 Mar. 1573; *CGT*, VI, 1–2, Juan de Albornoz (Alba's principal secretary) to Zayas, 12 Feb. 1573; and Evans, *The works of Sir Roger Williams*, 130 (on Balfour).

66. *CGT*, VI, 2–4, Zayas to Albornoz, 17 July and 21 Oct. 1573; IVdeDJ 47/325, Requeséns to Zúñiga, 25 Nov. 1573; Berwick y Alba, *Discurso*, 124–5, Zúñiga to Philip II, 1574. Earlier, Zayas had favoured the assassination of other perceived enemies of Spain, such as a refugee Spanish heretic in Paris and the French Protestant writer and philosopher, Peter Ramus: see Álava, 257, Zayas to Álava, 10 Sept. 1568: 'será santíssima obra acabar al herege español y al Pedro Ramos'. The St Bartholomew's Day massacre must have made Zayas a happy priest.

67. Álava, 50, Álava's paper of advice to Philip II, 20 June 1574. In 1580 the king eventually declared Orange an outlaw and placed a price of 25,000 crowns on his head. An attempt on his life made by one of Philip's vassals in 1582 almost succeeded; a second ended it in 1584. See the documents on the various assassination plans assembled in *CGT*, VI.

68. Details from Fruin, *The siege*, see especially pp. 18, 85–9, and map II (an example of the assistance provided to Valdés by Dutch Catholic supporters of the crown).

69. *Co.Do.In.*, CII, 350–1 and IVdeDJ 67/205 and 211, Requeséns to Zúñiga, 15 Nov. 1573 and 12 Jan. and 14 Apr.

1574, on the lies that Alba and his relatives had told him; for interesting first-hand evidence of these lies, see AGS *Estado* 2852, unfol., Instruction of Alba to Juan Bautista de Tassis, sent to find Requeséns and portray the Netherlands situation in falsely favourable terms (undated, but Oct. 1573, original). See also BL *Addl* 28,388/38, Granvelle to Zúñiga, 19 Mar. 1574, criticizing Alba's policies.

70. *Nueva Co.Do.In.*, V, 368, Requeséns to Philip II, 6 Oct. 1574.

71. The idea was not entirely new for, as soon as he heard about the fall of Brill, Duke Emanuel Philibert of Savoy (who had governed the Netherlands in 1556–59) advised the king that if all other measures failed he should 'break the dikes and drown them [the rebels] before they can get established'. The king noted: 'I am not sure it will be so easy to drown them' (AGS *Estado* 1233/76, Juan de Vargas Mexía, ambassador in Turin, to Philip II, 22 May 1572). The constant danger of inundation in Holland during the 1570s is well described in Hart, 'Rijnlands bestuur'.

72. For the flooding of Walcheren – apparently the first such episode in the war – see AGRB *Audience* 343/84–5, Wacken and Beauvoir to Alba, Middelburg, 27–28 June 1572. On the flooding of areas around Leiden, on the building of a ravelin and sconces, and for the heroic relief, see the excellent account, based on local chronicles and the archives of the Rijnland Drainage Board, by Hart, 'Rijnlands bestuur', 20–5; and the splendid cartographic representations in van Oerle, *Leiden*, II, maps 34–7. Van Hoof, 'Met een vijand als bondgenoot', asserts that although the idea of using water-power for military purposes was present in 1573–74, the idea of making systematic use of it only dates from the 1670s. This ignores the Spanish evidence. See also Scholten, *Militaire topografische kaarten*, 32–4; and Brand

and Brand, *De Hollandse Waterlinie*, 39–80.

73. AGS *Estado* 560/91, Valdés to Requeséns, 18 Sept. 1574. On Orange's letter (to Marnix) see Fruin, *The siege*, 84–5. This whole episode is discussed, and the key documents printed, by Waxman, 'Strategic terror'.

74. AGS *Estado* 561/122, Philip to Requeséns, 22 Oct. 1574. On the Vietnam parallel, see Hays Park, 'Rolling Thunder'; idem, 'Linebacker'; and Pape, 'Coercive air power'. The remarkably similar logic used by the United States government for rejecting the strategic bombing of the Red River dikes in 1966 appears in Gravel, *The Pentagon papers*, IV, 43–8, memorandum of John T. McNaughton, Assistant Secretary of Defense, 18 Jan. 1966. The innate weakness of a strategy of 'destroying in order to save', which is so often either self-defeating or morally abhorrent (or both), was admirably perceived by von Clausewitz, *On war*, 577–612.

75. For the decision to destroy a few dikes, see AGS *Estado* 560/1, Requeséns to Philip II, 6 Nov. 1574; ibid., fo. 40, Electo [leader] of the Spanish mutineers to Valdés, 24 Nov. 1574; AGRB *Audience* 1733/2 fo. 411, Baron Hierges to Requeséns, 29 Nov. 1574; and Hart, 'Rijnlands bestuur', 23, 26–7. Some doubted the effectiveness of opening the sea-dikes: see *CCG*, V, 512–14, Amsterdam City Council to Requeséns, 8 Nov. 1574, claiming that many 'innocent' areas would be flooded and thus lost to both the king and the Catholic church, whereas the leading rebellious cities would remain unaffected. On the other hand, the consequences of systematic inundation may be judged from the history of the Zijpe polder, flooded by the Dutch to save Alkmaar in 1573: reclamation only began in 1597 and continued for over a century: see Zijp, 'Hoofdstukken'.

76. AGS *Estado* 562/74, Requeséns to Philip, 10 May 1575. On the 1575

campaign in Waterland, see van Nierop, 'The Blood Council'.

77. Alcocer, *Consultas del consejo de Estado*, 258–64, 'Sobre el remedio general de Flandes', 26 Nov. 1602, 'votos' of the marquis of Velada (who recalled the 1574 debate with uncanny accuracy) and the count of Chinchón; and ibid., 280–1, Philip III's approval. In the 1620s Augustus Bredimus, an engineer, and in the 1630s Michel van Langren, a geographer, both proposed diverting the course of the Rhine in order to flood parts of South Holland and thus open the rest to Spain's troops: AHN *Estado libro* 714, unfol., 'La Junta en 8 de febrero, 1627', on the Bredimus plan (this volume contains a number of interesting 'alternative strategies' discussed in 1627–28); and AGRB *Conseil privé espagnol* 1573/227–9 and 264–6, 'Aviso' of van Langren. Neither plan seems to have received serious consideration.

78. Mondoucet, I, 130, letter to Charles IX, 21 Dec. 1572; BNM Ms 1749/361–79, memorial of Alonso Gutiérrez, 23 Oct. 1577. For some other Spanish appreciations of the need to achieve naval mastery at this time, see AGS *Estado* 1236/24, Requeséns to Philip II, 23 Feb. 1573; IVdeDJ 67/203, Requeséns to Zúñiga, 14 Dec. 1573; *Nueva Co.Do.In.*, I, 31–2, Zúñiga to Requeséns, 9 Jan. 1574; IVdeDJ 76/505–6, anonymous memorandum on the need to control the North Sea, 1575; AGS *Estado* 578/119–21, opinions voiced at the council of State, 14–23 June 1578; *CCG*, X, 239, Granvelle to Broissia, 7 June 1583; and XII, 169, Granvelle to Charles of Mansfeld, 18 Apr., 1586. Even poets advocated creating a navy because conquering the Dutch by land 'would be to confront the impossible': see Aldana's 'Octavas' in his *Obras completas*, 17–56, especially pp. 33–4 and 40–1.

79. See Mendoza, *Comentarios*, 449 (on Veere); *Epistolario*, III, 115, Alba to Philip II, 23 May 1572 (on

Enkhuizen); and *CCG*, IV, 369, Morillon to Granvelle, 16 Aug. 1572 (on Zierikzee).

80. See AGRB *Audience* 344/95 and 135, Bossu to Alba, 20 June and 5 July 1572.

81. By March 1574 barely 1,000 sailors manned the royal fleet in the Scheldt – only thirty ships, many of them small: see AGRB *Audience* 1690/1, unfol., 'Relación de . . . el Armada de Su Magestad que está en Amberes'. For its cost, see AGS *Estado* 557/38, Requeséns to Philip, 25 Jan. 1574 (including an interesting comparison with the cost-basis of the king's Mediterranean fleet). See also Gerlo and de Smet, *Marnixi epistulae*, I, 191–3, Marnix to John of Nassau, 5 May 1573, listing the ships and guns gained from the royal fleet in a battle off Zealand.

82. Spain had in fact managed to send battle squadrons into the North Sea in the 1550s, especially in conjunction with the Royal Navy while Philip was king of England; but by 1572 this capacity had been lost. On the development of an Atlantic fleet see the data provided by Casado Soto and Thompson in Rodríguez-Salgado and Adams, *England, Spain and the Gran Armada*, 70–133, especially pp. 70–1 and 98–9; Thompson, *War and government*, part 3; Barkman, 'Guipuzcoan shipping in 1571'; Pi Corrales, *Felipe II*; and Goodman, *Spanish naval power*.

83. For Alba's expectations, and their disappointment, see *Epistolario*, III, 267–70 and 305–6, Alba to Philip II, 22 Dec. 1572 and 18 Mar. 1573. The chief pilot's opinion is printed in *Co.Do.In.*, LXXV, 35–8. The potential for using galleys based in Flanders was amply demonstrated by the success of the squadron operated by Federigo Spinola in the early seventeenth century out of Dunkirk: see Gray, 'Spinola's galleys'.

84. Two expeditions sailed to regain Florida, one of eight ships in 1565 and the second of seventeen ships in 1566:

see Lyon, *The enterprise of Florida* (*passim*). Even this venture cost 275,000 ducats (ibid. pp. 181–3). See also the documents concerning the embargo of forty-seven ships for the king's planned expedition to Flanders in 1567 quoted in Parker, *Dutch Revolt*, 292, n. 28, and the accounts in AGS *CS* 2a/197.

85. See the documents cited in Pi Corrales, *España*, 89, 103 and 181–4, and 191–6.

86. IVdeDJ 53/3/64, Philip II to Vázquez, 17 May 1574 (on Menéndez's pessimism). See also AGS *Estado* 557/84, Requeséns to Philip II, 5 Mar. 1574; *Estado* 2852, unfol., Menéndez to Juan Bautista de Tassis, 31 Aug. 1574; and *Estado* 2546/83, Requeséns's Instruction to Tassis, 6 Sept. 1574 (on where Menéndez might land).

87. *BMO*, I, 92–6, Menéndez to Philip II and reply, 15 and 24 Aug. 1574.

88. Pi Corrales, *España*, 214–17, Menéndez to Pedro Menéndez Márquez, 8 Sept. 1574 (with the remarkable news that Philip had ordered his fleet – 150 ships and 12,000 men – 'to assist where it was most needed': the Netherlands or the Mediterranean); and 218–21, Philip II to Requeséns, 24 Sept. 1574.

89. 'More than half a million' spent on the 'Armada de Santander' in the course of 1574 according to the president of the council of Finance: IVdeDJ 24/103, 'Parecer de Juan de Ovando', 25 Mar. 1575 (but see also AGS *Estado* 561/83, Zayas to Requeséns, 25 June 1574, claiming the fleet had already cost 600,000). Other details on the fleet from Pi Corrales, *España*, chaps 5–10. Requeséns took the news to abort the venture relatively well: 'I really do not know', he told the king philosophically, 'how it would have been possible to do everything in the time available, even if Menéndez had had the winds and the sea at his command' (AGS *Estado* 560/8, Requeséns to Philip, 6 Nov. 1574). Fifty ships from the fleet did leave in 1575, but their

orders envisaged only the transport of troops to Flanders: see p. 164 above.

90. AHN *OM* 3510, unfol. [Luis de Torres] to Granvelle, Monreale, 27 Oct. 1577, reviewing Spain's strategy in the Netherlands over the previous decade. For Philip's condemnation of the French policy of concessions, see p. 93 above.

91. Quotations from *Epistolario*, III, 474–8, Alba to Philip II, 29 July 1573; and AGS *Estado* 554/146, Requeséns to Philip II, 30 Dec. 1573 (citing Alba's 'hawkish' views).

92. AA 8/45, Philip II to Alba, 8 July 1573; the dorse recorded the date of receipt (19 Aug.), yet the duke did not reply until the 30th. Actually even Alba had inclined briefly towards mercy slightly earlier: see p. 133 above.

93. *Epistolario*, III, 493 and 502–4, Alba to Philip II, 30 and 31 Aug. 1573.

94. BPU *Favre* 30/71–4, Philip II to Requeséns, 20 Oct. 1573, copy of the holograph original; *Co.Do.In.*, CII, 323, Philip II to Alba, 21 Oct. 1573; ibid., 277–306, Instructions for Requeséns; and AGS *Estado* 554/146, Requeséns to Philip II, 30 Dec. 1573, regretting the prohibitions they contained.

95. See *CGT*, III, 81–7, copies of four letters from Orange to Julián Romero (they had served together in 1559–60), 7–10 Nov. 1573; the originals may be found in BPU *Favre* 60/43–9. See also Gerlo and de Smet, *Marnixi epistulae*, I, 213–18, Orange to Marnix, 28 Nov. 1573. Orange had made his terms clear several months earlier: see Rowen, *The Low Countries*, 45–6, Orange to his brothers, 5 Feb. 1573.

96. See GCP, III, 437 n. 2, Noircarmes to Alba, 14 Nov. 1573, and Alba's reply on the 22nd; ibid., 437–8, Noircarmes to Requeséns, 24 Dec. 1573, with Requeséns's reply of the 29th (which expressly prohibited any contact with Orange); and 450–1,

Requeséns to Philip II, 30 Dec. 1573 on why the talks must be discontinued. See also BPU *Favre* 60/65–7, Noircarmes to Alba, together with the explanatory note by Juan de Albornoz (Alba's principal secretary) to Requeséns, 24 Dec. 1573.

97. AGS *Estado* 561/25, 'Consulta de negocios de Flandes', 24 Feb. 1574 (see also p. 321 n. 43 above). On the General Pardon, see Janssens, *Brabant in het verweer,* 208–29; the exploratory talks of 1574 are expertly surveyed by Gachard in *CGT*, III, xxxvif and 373–430; the various attempts to betray towns by van Nierop, 'The Blood Council'.

98. IVdeDJ 67/287a, Vázquez to Philip II and reply, 28 June 1574. For an example of harassment in the cause of peace, see AGS *Estado* 560/12, Requeséns to Philip II, 18 Dec. 1574. For evidence that the council of State recognized the justice of some of the Dutch demands, see AGS *Estado* 568/38 and 49, consultas of 23 and 27 Jan. 1575.

99. IVdeDJ 67/106, Requeséns to Zúñiga, 9 July 1575; and ibid., fo. 271, Requeséns to the count of Monteagudo (Spanish ambassador in Vienna), 6 Mar. 1575. AGS *Estado K* 1537/23, Requeséns to Don Diego de Zúñiga, 23 Mar. 1575, copy, gives a good overview of his negotiating position at Breda.

100. The same dilemma undermined peace talks in 1577, 1579, 1589, 1598, 1607–9, 1629 and 1632: see details in Parker, *Dutch Revolt*, 182, 195 and 223 for the sixteenth century; and in Israel, *The Dutch Republic and the Hispanic world,* 11, 225 and 242 for the seventeenth.

101. As yet no adequate study of the Conference of Breda exists, but see Janssens, *Brabant in het verweer*, 230–54. On the role of the talks in strengthening the internal cohesion of the Dutch, see Lademacher, *Die Stellung des Prinzen von Oranien*, chap. 3.

102. IVdeDJ 53/3/87 and 77, Philip II to Mateo Vázquez, 4 and 18 July 1574.
103. IVdeDJ 37/72, Requeséns to Zúñiga, 12 Nov. 1575.
104. See details in Parker, *Dutch Revolt*, 173–8.
105. GCP, IV, 425–6, note written by the king and given to Don John of Austria before he left Madrid on 18 Oct. 1576: enphasis added. See also the documents from earlier in the year cited in Kamen, *Philip*, 156.
106. AGS *Estado* 2843/3, Philip II to Don John, 31 Jan. 1577. For the sequel, see Parker, *Dutch Revolt*, 181.
107. On the settlement in the Netherlands, see Parker, *Dutch Revolt*, 179–82; on the demobilization of the fleet, see BPU *Favre* 28/83–101, Philip II to the duke of Sessa, 27 Dec. 1576 (two long letters). In fact William of Orange managed to obtain a copy of Don John's Instructions, thus greatly enhancing his ability to exploit Spain's temporary weakness: see Sutherland, 'William of Orange', 222–4.
108. Porreño, *Historia del Sereníssimo Señor Don Juan,* 212: Don John to the officers and soldiers returned from the Netherlands, 15 Aug. 1577; AGS *Estado* 1247/133, Philip II to Ayamonte, governor of Lombardy, 28 Aug. 1577; and AGS *Estado* 571/56, Philip II to Don John, 1 Sept. 1577. The king, however, had already begun to waver. The previous day he signed a letter warning the governor of Lombardy to get the Spanish veterans – who were about to depart for Spain – ready to return to the Netherlands if necessary (IVdeDJ 47/16, Philip II to Ayamonte, 31 Aug. 1577) and a few days later he resolved to send them (AGS *Estado* 2843/7, consulta of the council of State, 5 Sept. 1577, noting that he had already issued the orders). For these same events from his brother's point of view, see the important letters at IVdeDJ 36/20–1, Don John to Don Juan de Zúñiga, 6 and 30 Sept. 1577.
109. Feltham, *Brief character*, 90–3.

5 The 'British Problem', 1558–85

1. Wernham, *Making of English foreign policy*, 1. Many thanks to Glyn Redworth for reading and commenting on this chapter.
2. Lutz, *Christianitas Afflicta*, 208–9, provides the best discussion of the implications of the Tudor marriage. He notes that it affected not only France, but also Charles's brother Ferdinand because it ended all hope that the latter might inherit the Netherlands and made it clear that the Spanish Habsburgs would be more powerful than their Austrian cousins. Small wonder that in 1553 Ferdinand tried to interest Mary Tudor in marrying one of his sons (Fichtner, *Ferdinand I*, 178–9).
3. HHStA *Spanien Varia* 2/59–62, report of Christophe d'Assonleville, Dec. 1558. For further 'domino theories', see pp. 89–90 above.
4. See AGS *Estado* 8334/186, '[Lo] platicado y conferido por los del consejo de Estado' [Jan. 1559] (the slur on Elizabeth's birth referred to Henry VIII's 'adulterous' marriage to Anne Boleyn); AMC 7/249/11–12, Philip II to Feria, 10 and 28 Jan. 1559, holograph; and González, 'Apuntamientos', 405–7, Philip to Feria, 10 Jan. 1559. See also Rodríguez-Salgado, *Changing face*, 319, and Rodríguez-Salgado and Adams, 'The count of Feria's dispatch'.
5. AMC 7/249/12, Philip II to Feria, 21 Mar. 1559, holograph. Two days later Philip formally announced that he would not marry Elizabeth Tudor. Some also saw Philip's marriage to Mary Tudor in 1554 as a 'sacrifice' for religion and defence: *CoDoIn*, III, 350, Ruy Gómez to Erasso, 29 July 1554.
6. AGS *CJH* 34/477 Feria to Ruy Gómez de Silva, 6 Mar. 1559, holograph. On the partition plan, see Rodríguez-Salgado, *Changing face*, 332.
7. Fernández Álvarez, *Tres embajadores,*

222–3, 'Paresçer' of Alba, Granvelle and Ruy Gómez, mid-Mar. 1559. In the event Philip sent 20,000 ducats to Feria, and promised 40,000 more (ibid., 43).

8. Ibid., 268, Philip II to Feria, 23 Mar. 1559.

9. See Romano, 'La pace di Cateau-Cambrésis', 540; Merriman, 'Mary, queen of France', 45–8; and Rodríguez-Salgado, *Changing face*, 331–7.

10. Fernández Álvarez, *Tres embajadores*, 64, Philip II to Juana, 23 June 1559, and 253–4, her reply of 13 July (with irritated royal apostils); BPM Ms II–2320/124, Granvelle to Juan Vázquez de Molina, 21 July 1559.

11. See the brilliant reconstruction of Philip's policy towards England during 1558–59 in Rodríguez-Salgado, *Changing face*, 323–53. Note also the important corroboratory evidence in IVdeDJ 67/1, Don Luis de Requeséns to Andrés Ponce, Jan. 1574, minute (claiming that the king could have supported at least two plots in 1559) and KB Ms 78 E 9/12–15, 'Parecer sobre las cosas . . . de Inglaterra', confirming that Alba did indeed compose the document of 10 July 1559, cited by Rodríguez-Salgado at p. 333.

12. Teulet, *Relations politiques*, V, 59–60, Philip II to Don Francés de Álava, 26 June 1570. This offers a striking confirmation of Robert Jervis's remarks on the distorting impact of first-hand experience on statesmen: Jervis, *Perception and misperception*, 240–52.

13. On the lessons drawn by Philip (and doubtless Alba) from their residence in Britain, see Redworth, 'Felipe II', 106; on the different perspectives of Brussels and Madrid in the 1560s, see Ramsay, *The queen's merchants*, 200. The same divergence recurred during the government of Don John of Austria and the duke of Parma (pp. 54–5 and 145 above), and even more under the Archdukes: see Allen, 'The strategy of peace'.

14. Fernández Álvarez, *Tres embajadores*, 73 Granvelle to Gonzalo Pérez,

5 Dec. 1559; Laubespine, 387, Francis II and the Guises to Laubespine, 21 May 1560.

15. Fernández Álvarez, *Tres embajadores*, 242–6, Philip's instruction to M. de Glajon, Mar. [?] 1560. See also ASP *CF* 107, unfol., Tomás de Armenteros to Parma, 26 Feb. 1560; and AGRB *Audience* 778/34, minutes of the council of State, Brussels, 25 Oct. 1560. These sources entirely contradict the account, based exclusively on English records, presented by Wernham, *Before the Armada*, 256.

16. The role of distance in France's Scottish failure emerges clearly from Laubespine, 14 (Instruction of Francis II to an envoy going to Edinburgh, 16 July 1559, asking for 'an express courier to be sent every five or six days to keep me aware of all that is happening') and 423–4 (commanders at Leith to Catherine de Medici, 9 July 1560, apologizing for their surrender but reminding her that they had received no relief and languished '300 leagues away from the place from which we had expected counsel and advice'). Distance also affected English policy: Elizabeth almost sabotaged her successful Scottish policy by foolishly trying at the last moment to make a safe-conduct for French withdrawal conditional on the return of Calais: fortunately for her (and the Scots Protestants) a deal had been struck at Leith before her new demands arrived (see MacCaffrey, *Shaping of the Elizabethan regime*, 66–7).

17. For more on Philip's 'British policy' in 1560–61, see *PEG*, VI, 5–8 and 91–4, Granvelle to Philip II, 16 Jan. and 20 May 1560, and 152, Philip II to Granvelle, 7 Sept. 1560. Spain's financial predicament appears clearly in the king's holograph 'Memorial de las finanzas de España', ibid., 156–65. See also Romano, 'La pace di Cateau-Cambrésis', 542–6, and Fernández Álvarez, *Felipe II*, 343–70.

18. *CSPSp.*, I, 228, Philip II to Alvaro de la Quadra, 9 Feb. 1562.

19. KB Ms 78 E 9/24–8, 'Parecer de Su

Excelencia sobre cosas de Inglaterra y Scocia' (Aug. 1562); AGRB *Audience* 778/211, minutes of the council of State, Brussels, 13 Jan. 1563, also discussed offering mediation.

20. *Co.Do.In.*, XCVIII, 481–2, Philip II to Luna, his ambassador at Trent, 8 Aug. 1563 (he also wrote in similar vein to the pope). On the trade war of 1563–65 see Ramsay, *City of London*, 191–283; AGRB *Audience* 779/38, minutes of the council of State, Brussels, 20 May 1564; and Wells, 'Antwerp and the government of Philip II', 277–300. On Mary's first letter, see de Törne, *Don Juan d'Autriche*, I, 7–18 (note that Philip declared himself willing to discuss Mary's marriage either to his son Don Carlos or his cousin Archduke Charles).

21. *CSPSp.*, II, 3, Philip II to Guzmán de Silva, 4 Feb. 1568.

22. Serrano, II, 360, Philip II to Don Juan de Zúñiga, his ambassador in Rome, 8 Mar. 1568. See the excellent account of this incident in Bell, 'John Man'. See also Man's own account of how Feria became his enemy (and his alarming prediction that Philip might stop off in England on his northward voyage) in Cambridge University Library, Ms Mm–3–8/83, Man to William Cecil, 15 June 1567.

23. *BMO*, I, 1–4, Philip's Instructions to Spes, 28 June 1568; *CSPSp.*, II, 71, Philip II to Alba, 15 Sept. 1568. However, Guzmán de Silva had by then already begun a secret correspondence with Mary (ibid., 74, Guerau de Spes to Philip II, 24 Sept. 1568, reporting the arrival of two ciphered letters from Mary to Guzmán, which Spes could not read 'as the latter has not left his cipher or even told me that he had one with her').

24. *CSPSp*, II, 89, Spes to Philip II, 18 Dec. 1568; Donà, 445, letter to Venice, 11 Mar. 1572.

25. For Elizabeth's promises regarding Hawkins, see *CSPSp.*, II, 1, 17 and 73–4, Guzmán de Silva to Philip II, 3 Jan. and 27 Mar. 1568, and Spes to

Philip II, 24 Sept. 1568. For the truth see Williamson, *Hawkins of Plymouth*, 100–56.

26. For details see Read, 'Queen Elizabeth's seizure of the duke of Alva's pay-ships'; the subsequent account by Spes in *BMO*, I, 71–2 (noting that two of the five 'pay-ships' managed to reach Antwerp); and the analysis of Ramsay, *The queen's merchants*, 90–111, and MacCaffrey, *Shaping of the Elizabethan regime*, 188–95.

27. For the general decline in England's embassies and other sources of foreign intelligence under Elizabeth, see Wernham, *Making of English foreign policy*, 58, and Haynes, *Invisible power*, 13–14.

28. Álava, 301–2 and 317, Philip II to Álava, 18 Feb. and 20 Mar. 1569; *CSPSp.*, II, 109, Philip II to Alba, 18 Feb. 1569; and Gómez del Campillo, *Negociaciones con Francia*, XI, 394, Philip II to Mary Stuart, 28 Feb. 1569.

29. Álava, 317, Philip II to Álava, 20 Mar. 1569; AHN *OM* 3511/4, 'Consideraciones de Don Guerau de Spes sobre la forma que podría tener para la empresa de Inglaterra', London, 31 May 1569 (this is the original document summarized in *CSPSp.*, II, 157–8). See also Kouri, *England*, chap. 4, on the assembly of all the major Protestant princes at Erfurt in Sept. 1569; and Thorp, 'Catholic conspiracy'.

30. See *CSPSp.*, II, 122–32, d'Assonleville's report of Mar. 1569, 160–3, Alba to Philip II, 12 June 1569 (requesting full powers to negotiate with Elizabeth), and 177, Philip II to Alba, 19 July 1569 (delegating them). Ramsay, *The queen's merchants*, 200, pointed out that the English government never seems to have realized its advantage: it always assumed that Alba slavishly followed the policies decreed by Philip in Spain.

31. *CSPSp.*, II, 132–3, Alba to Philip II, 10 Mar. 1569, and 150, Philip II to Alba, 15 May 1569; and *Co.Do.In.*, XC, 187–9, Philip II to Elizabeth,

undated but probably also 15 May 1569.

32. *BMO*, I, 34–5, Pius V to Alba, 3 Nov. 1569, and 38–9, Philip II to Alba, 16 Dec. 1569. For proof that the pope did not tell Philip of his commission to Alba, see ibid., 43, Philip II to Alba, 22 Jan. 1570.

33. *BMO*, I, 35, Alba to Don Juan de Zúñiga, Philip's ambassador in Rome, 4 Dec. 1569. See also ibid., 36, Alba to Philip II, 11 Dec. 1569, and the interesting discussion of the duke's position in Maltby, *Alba*, 197–8.

34. See the excellent discussion of the pope's motives in Edwards, *The marvellous chance*, 403–7, suggesting that the trigger was an anonymous letter from England calling for excommunication in the name of all English Catholics. Its author may well have been Roberto Ridolfi, who later ensured that the Bull became known in England. Pius only told the Spanish ambassador in Rome of his intention to excommunicate Elizabeth six weeks after he had done so: see Serrano, III, 291, Zúñiga to Philip, 10 Apr. 1570 (he signed the Bull on 25 Feb. and sent it to the duke of Alba on 30 Mar.).

35. *BMO*, I, 42, Philip II to Alba, 22 Jan. 1570: a most remarkable letter which, in the original, covers twenty-two sides of paper.

36. *BMO*, I, 43–7, Alba to Philip II, 23 and 24 Feb. 1570 (Maltby, *Alba*, 200–1, mis-dates these documents to 1571).

37. Teulet, *Relations politiques*, V, 57, Philip II to Álava, 17 May 1570; *CSPSp.*, II, 254–5, Philip II to Spes, 30 June 1570.

38. Whether or not Ridolfi was a double-agent, he certainly betrayed all the conspirators. (i) From the start, Ridolfi, his English contacts and Spes all used the same cipher (*CSPSp*, II, 111, Spes to Alba, 29 Feb. 1569), so that once Elizabeth had acquired the key from one of Ridolfi's servants, she could read everybody's mail. (ii) Ridolfi regularly wrote unciphered

letters to Mary as he moved from Brussels to Rome and Madrid, keeping her up to date on the progress of the plot, and thereby (since all Mary's mail was intercepted and read) keeping Elizabeth up to date too. On the probablility that Ridolfi had been 'turned', see Edwards, *The marvellous chance*, 86.

39. *BMO*, I, 52–3, Elizabeth to Philip II, 20 Mar. 1571, and 54–5, account of a meeting between Elizabeth's envoy (Sir Henry Cobham) and Feria, 8 June 1571. These documents make clear that Cobham had been authorized to arrange a new exchange of ambassadors, and to pave the way to a settlement of the trade dispute; the account in Wernham, *Before the Armada*, 308, seems too harsh.

40. Quotations from Collinson, *The English captivity*, 42–3, Burghley to Shrewsbury, Mary's custodian, 5 Sept. 1571; details of this aspect of the plot from *CSPScot*, IV, 30–2, bishop of Ross to Burghley, 9 Nov. 1571. If Mary had somehow managed to reach Hawkins, he would presumably have 'conveyed' her back to gaol.

41. AGS *Estado* 823/150–8, consulta of the council of State, 7 July 1571 (a remarkable document which records the substance of each councillor's views at two meetings of the council, and a further interview with Ridolfi, all on the same day); and AA 7/58, Philip II to Alba, 14 July 1571 (ordering immediate invasion and the capture or killing of Elizabeth, just as the council had recommended the previous week). For the Spanish naval component, see AGS *GA* 187/157, Martín de Bertendona (who was to have commanded the fleet) to Philip II, 5 Aug. 1586; and *Co.Do.In.*, XXXVI, 5–7, review of Medinaceli's fleet of forty-four vessels, held back at Santander throughout 1571 in order to take part in the invasion (see pp. 130–1 above).

42. *BMO*, I, 57–8, Philip II to Alba, 4 Aug. 1571; and *CSPScot*, IV, 274–5, 'Five cases shewed against the queen of Scottes', Apr. 1572, charge 2 (an

admirable summary of the plot). For Hawkins, see Williamson, *Hawkins of Plymouth*, 177–88, and González, 'Apuntamientos', 364–5, 'Lo que se ha tractado' between Feria and George Fitzwilliam, in the name of 'Juan Aquins', 10 Aug. [1571] (original at BZ 153/153). In return for his bogus offer Hawkins apparently managed to secure the release of many of his shipmates captured at San Juan de Ulúa in 1568.

43. ARA *Staten Generaal* 12,548, loketkas 14B/14, Philip II to Alba, 30 Aug. 1571. Some of this money – unlike the army and the fleet – did actually arrive: see *CSPScot*, IV, 60–1, 168–9 and 226–8. For Stukeley's involvement, see Tazón, 'The menace'. Edwards, *The marvellous chance*, chap. 5, suggests that Stukeley too might have been a double-agent. This seems less likely, although at a suspiciously early stage he did recommend a deal with Hawkins, 'who is very much my friend' (AHN *OM* 3511/10, Stukeley to Philip II, Madrid, 15 Mar. 1570).

44. *BMO*, I, 57–64, Philip II to Alba, 4 Aug. 1571, the duke's reply on the 27th, and Philip's final effort to get action on 14 Sept. (for further quotations from this letter, see pp. 105–6 above). See also ARA *Staten Generaal* 12,548, loketkas 14B/14, Philip II to Alba, 30 Aug. 1571, and to Spes on the same day, summarized in *CSPSp.*, II, 333–4.

45. Collinson, *The English captivity*, 42–3, Burghley to Shrewsbury, 5 Sept. 1571, a most important document. It may have been written upon receipt of Hawkins's letter of the previous day, enclosing a copy of his 'contract' with Feria: see the text in Williamson, *Hawkins of Plymouth*, 185–6. Some of Elizabeth's information on Spain's intentions also came from Florence (see de Törne, *Don Juan d'Autriche*, II, 94n; and IVdeDJ 67/1, Requeséns to Andrés Ponce, Jan. 1574), and from Scotland (see *CSPScot*, IV, 110–1, 'Artykles of the Lord Seton's negotyatyng wythe the duke of Alva').

46. On the later career of Ridolfi, see Edwards, *The marvellous chance*, 373–7; on Stukeley, see Tazón, 'The menace'. On events in England in 1569–71, see MacCaffrey, *Shaping of the Elizabethan regime*, 199–295. For an overview of the plot, see Kretzschmar, *Invasionsprojekte*, 5–45. Elizabeth probably did *not* know that Philip had planned to assassinate her as well as depose her.

47. See the documents in Pollitt, *Arming the nation*, and idem, 'Contingency planning'. The proclamation restoring trade between England and Spain, dated 30 Apr. 1573, is reproduced in *BMO*, I, 76.

48. IVdeDJ 67/1, Requeséns to Andrés Ponce de León, Jan. 1574, copy, all about a new project to invade England, and quoting Alba's justification of Elizabeth's hostility. For the Irish dimension in 1574, see Pi Corrales, *España*, 106–8 and 186–91; for the Santander fleet, see pp. 130–1 above.

49. De Törne, *Don Juan d'Autriche*, II, 66–7, for the concessions of 1574–75; PRO *SP* 12/105/123, Walsingham to Burghley, 6 Oct. 1575, reporting the arrival of '48 sayle of Spanyshe men of warre' off the coast of Devon, and the Spanish documents about their voyage in *BMO*, I, 100–6.

50. De Törne, *Don Juan d'Autriche*, II, 322, cardinal of Como to Ormanetto, 18 Mar. 1573.

51. See the documents quoted in Voci, 'L'impresa', 346 and *passim*.

52. See Voci, 'L'impresa', 356–62. For the amazed and despairing reaction of Don Luis de Requeséns in the Netherlands to the king's revived interest in invading England, see p. 106 above.

53. Voci, 'L'impresa', 267–72, discusses this episode on the basis of the Vatican records alone. For a fuller account (which apparently Voci did not use), see the masterly reconstruction in de Törne, *Don Juan d'Autriche*, II, 80–88. The plan of Feb. 1576, entitled *De facilitate speditionis pro recuperanda Anglia* – a title typical of the exiles' exuberance – is printed in both Latin

and in English translation by Renold, *Letters of William Allen*, 284–92. See also AGS *Estado* 1072/92, Don John of Austria to Philip II, 14 Apr. 1576, on Englefield's efforts to enlist Spanish support for an attempt to rescue Mary. *BMO* contains nothing on the plans to attack Elizabeth between 1575 and 1578.

54. De Törne, *Don Juan d'Autriche*, II, 88–91 and 101–2, Philip II to Zúñiga, 16 Apr. and 23 June 1576; Kamen, *Philip*, 159, Philip II to Gaspar de Quiroga, 24 Aug. 1576; Voci, 'L'impresa', 372–8; Kretzschmar, *Invasionsprojekte*, 47–63; AGS *Estado* 570/126–8, letters and papers of Philip II 'sobre lo de Inglaterra', Nov. 1576.

55. Voci, 'L'impresa', 379–86; AGS *Estado* 2843/3, Philip II to Don John, 31 Jan. 1577, minute.

56. AGS *Estado* K 1543/112, Vargas Mexía to Philip II, 12 Dec. 1577 (see also *Estado* K 1547/135, Gerónimo de Curiel to Philip II, 10 Jan. 1578, along the same lines); BL *Cott. Cal.* C. V/97v–98, Escobedo (Don John's secretary) to Philip II, 9 Apr. 1577, original, ciphered with decrypt and English translation; Gerlo and de Smet, *Marnixi epistulae*, 94–9, Marnix to Count John of Nassau, 28 July 1577 (about these letters); and de Törne, *Don Juan d'Autriche*, II, 102 n., Zúñiga to Philip II, 9 Aug. 1576.

57. Kretzschmar, *Invasionsprojekte*, 200–12 offers a detailed account of the discussions surrounding the Smerwick expedition. See also *CCG*, X, 540–1, Granvelle to Philip II and reply, 12 Sept. 1579; and ASV *NS* 24/612–65, receipts for papal funds supplied to the Smerwick expeditionary force.

58. Voci, 'L'impresa', 363 and 375.

59. Ibid., *passim*, offers countless examples of sudden changes of plan, over and above those mentioned above: should the target be England or Ireland? Should the launching-pad be Spain or Flanders? Should the expedition include the combined forces of Spain and the Papacy or of just one?

60. De Törne, *Don Juan d'Autriche*, II, 101–2.

61. Ibid., II, 68 n. (letter of 4 Mar. 1575), 173 n. (27 Apr. 1578) and 208 n. 2 (30 Aug. 1578), all exemplify this point of view.

62. The king first received news of a truce with the Turks late in 1577: see BL *Addl* 28,359/359, Pedro Velásquez to Gaspar de Quiroga, 20 Nov. 1577, Naples. On developments in the Netherlands, see Parker, *Dutch Revolt*, 183–6.

63. Quotations from Bouza Álvarez, 'Portugal en la Monarquía hispánica', 82 (Castillo); and BSLE Ms P. I. 20, fos 44–5, Giovanni Battista Gesio to Philip II, 16 Nov. 1578. See also the equally forceful views of Pedro Salazar de Mendoza and of Philip himself quoted in Pereña Vicente, *Teoría de la guerra*, 76–7; and the further examples of expansionist literature from these years on p. 102 above.

64. On the numerous reports of Drake's progress that reached the king, see *BMO*, I, 143–64; for Philip's knowledge of English support for Orange, see ibid., 206–7; for Alba's disapproval of the Irish venture, see *Co.Do.In.*, XXXII, 507–10, 530–1 and 559–62; for events at Smerwick, see O'Rahilly, *The massacre at Smerwick*.

65. On Dom Antonio, son of a clandestine marriage rather than a natural child, see Durand-Lapié, 'Un roi détrôné'. On the war for the Azores, see Fernández Duro, *La conquista*, and Freitas de Meneses, *Os Açores*. On the company of English defenders at Terceira, see Cerezo Martínez, 'La conquista', 19–23.

66. BNP *Fonds français*, 16,108/365, St Gouard (French Resident at the Court of Philip) to Catherine de Medici, 20 Aug. 1582; *CCG*, X, 331–2, Granvelle to Idiáquez, 21 Aug. 1583.

67. For a discussion of new ways of portraying St James at precisely this time, see IVdeDJ 62/917, Duarte Nunes de Leão to Zayas, 17 Aug. 1585.

68. *BMO*, I, 395–6, Santa Cruz to Philip

II, 9 Aug. 1583 (see the king's reply dated 23 Sept., ibid., 406). See also the poems and other triumphalist commemorations in Fernández Duro, *La conquista*, 94–175, and the quotations on p. 102 above.

69. See the interesting account in Hicks, *Letters and memorials*, xlix–lv. See also *CSPSp*, III, 382–4, Granvelle to Philip, 4 July 1582; and Carrafiello, 'English Catholicism'.

70. *BMO*, I, 406–9, Philip II to Olivares, his ambassador in Rome, 24 Sept. 1583 (with supporting documents), in reply to the pope's letter of 16 Aug. proposing the Enterprise of England; Hicks, *Letters and memorials*, lviii–lx; and Kretzschmar, *Invasionsprojekte*, 173–7 and 212–15.

71. *BMO*, I, 405–6, Philip II to Parma, 12 Sept. 1583, asking his urgent advice about a possible invasion; and *CCG*, X, 367–9, Granvelle to Idiáquez, 23 Sept. 1583. Parma forwarded a careful survey of the English coasts, prepared by Robert Heighinton (a Catholic exile) for William Allen, two months later: *BMO*, I, 420–1, Parma to Philip II, 30 Nov. 1583; AGS *Estado K* 1565/120, Don Bernardino de Mendoza to Philip II, 28 Nov. 1587. See also a survey of Channel ports sent by Parma in Oct. 1583: *BMO*, I, 412–13. Francis Throckmorton, who sought Spanish aid for his plot to murder Elizabeth, was found in Nov. 1583 to possess a list of ports and havens that an invading army could use: this may have been a copy of Heighinton's paper.

72. Lyell, 'A commentary', 14–25.

73. AGS *Estado* 1257/121, Philip II to the governor of Milan, 11 Oct. 1583; and Kretzschmar, *Invasionsprojekte*, 212–15, account of Bishop Sega to Gregory XIII.

74. NMM Ms *PH* 1B/435, Olivares to Zúñiga, 24 Oct. 1583, deciphered with royal holograph apostil. The best account of the 1582–83 invasion plan remains Kretzschmar, *Invasionsprojekte*, 64–109, with supporting documents from the Vatican archives. See also the

documents in *BMO*, I, 372–416, and NMM Ms *PH* 1B/432v–4v, on Philip's invasion plans at this time.

75. See Parker, *Dutch Revolt*, 197, 205–7; and Holt, *The duke of Anjou*, 157–9.

76. See de Törne, 'Philippe II et Henri de Guise'; AGS *Estado K* 1573/12, 21 and 24, Guise's receipts for Spanish subsidies, 24 Sept. 1582 and 24 Jan. and 5 May 1583; Teulet, *Relations politiques*, V, 261–3, Philip II to Juan Bautista de Tassis, his ambassador in France, 24 Sept. 1582. See also Martin, *Henry III*, 120–6.

77. Ritter, *La Soeur d'Henri IV*, I, 256; and Martin, *Histoire de France*, IX, 520–2.

78. Davies, 'The duc de Montmorency', and idem, 'Neither politique nor patriot?'.

79. Budget projections in IVdeDJ 76/161–2, Hernando de Vega, president of the council of Finance, to Philip II and reply, 24 Mar. 1582 (copy); and 68/286, same to same, 22 Aug. 1583 ('It is good that you have begun to discuss this large provision [of money], and therefore proceed with it and ensure that you do not forget about it, since it will be the remedy and relief of everything for the two years to come, 1584 and 1585'). For the background to these papers, see Parker, *The Army of Flanders*, 240–1. See also AGS *CJH* 223/1, budget for 1585, dated 6 Oct. 1584, extensively annotated by Philip II.

80. AGS *Estado* 2217/85, untitled paper of 25 May 1584 on sending the 2 million; ibid. 2218/28 and 49, Philip II to Parma, 1 July 1585 and 18 July 1586, for the payment by 'tercios' (four months) in advance. In November 1584 the first Japanese Christians to visit Spain reported seeing twelve chests containing gold and silver coins in the Madrid palace: see Sande, *De missione legatorum iaponensium*, 208 (my thanks to Francis X. Rocca for supplying a xerox copy of this item).

81. BL *Lans.* 31/197–203v, Lord Burghley's papers on the abortive expedition 'to serve Dom Antonio king of Portugal', Aug. 1581.

82. Details from Taylor, *Troublesome voyage*; and Donno, *An Elizabethan in 1582*, 151. Surprisingly enough, Thomas Hood survived and prospered: see Johnson, 'Thomas Hood's inaugural lecture'.

83. See BNP *Cinq Cents Colbert* 473/589, Catherine to Michel de Castelnau, French ambassador in London, 25 July 1584 (my thanks to Mack Holt for this reference). See also *CCG*, XI, 617–19, Zúñiga's first paper of advice on French policy in the wake of Anjou's death, 27–28 June 1584, pointing out that Parma could now concentrate on fighting the Dutch without fearing further French intervention.

84. On the rejoicing see *CCG*, XI, 58–9, 70–1 and 86–7, Idiáquez to Granvelle, 3, 7 and 11 Aug. 1584; and AGRB *MD* 5459/193, same to same, 14 Aug. 1584. On the formation of policy, see *CCG*, XI, 621–32, Zúñiga's second and third papers of advice, together with a cover note to Don Juan de Idiáquez, 28 June 1584 (quotation from p. 622). At the same time, Zúñiga recommended partitioning France in order to prevent a Huguenot succession: see AGS *Estado* 2855, unfol., 'Para mayor declaración de lo que se ha respondido a los puntos que vinieron en la memoria', June 1584.

85. AGS *Estado K* 1448/38a, Philip II to Juan Bautista de Tassis, 4 Jan. 1586. See the important – and apparently unknown – holograph letters, reports and instructions of Tassis on the negotiations at Joinville in AGS *Estado* 2846/79 and 86–9; see also Tassis's subsequent 'Commentarii', 445–57. One clause of the treaty required the surrender to Spanish agents of Dom Antonio, who in 1584 had taken refuge in Catholic Brittany.

86. See the detailed analysis of Jensen, *Diplomacy and dogmatism*, chaps 2 and 4; and also Chevallier, *Henry III*, 576–7. On 4 May 1585 Guise signed a receipt for 300,000 escudos from Spain: AGS *Estado* 1573/40.

87. See PRO *SP* 83/23/59–60, 'The resolution of ye conference had uppon the question of whyther his Majesty shuld presently releve the States of ye Low Countryes of Holland and Zelland or no' (holograph notes by Lord Burghley, 20 Oct. 1584 OS); ibid., fo. 61, Burghley's notes rehearsing Spain's past aggression against Elizabeth; and the summary in *CSPF*, XIX, 95–8. See also the account of this debate in MacCaffrey, *Queen Elizabeth*, 337–40; and Thorp, 'William Cecil and the Antichrist'. In brief, Burghley realized that aid to Holland would lead to a direct attack by Spain on England, but by this time thought it better to be attacked while one continental ally remained: see also his fears quoted on p. 6 above. Arrival of the news of Joinville in England reported in Wernham, *Before the Armada*, 370. On the interlock of events in 1585, see Baguenault de Puchesse, 'La politique de Philippe II', 34.

88. *CSPF*, XIX, 149–51, Elizabeth's Instructions to William Davidson, 13 Nov. 1584 OS; and *RSG*, IV, 515, meeting of the States-General, 8 Dec. 1584, to hear Elizabeth's offer.

89. BL *Harl.* 168/102–5, 'A consultacion . . . touchinge an aide to be sent in to Hollande againste the king of Spaine' (18 Mar. 1585 OS). See the excellent account of the tortuous negotiations in Oosterhoff, *Leicester and the Netherlands*, 38–40. On the disunity of the Republic at this time see van der Woude, 'De crisis in de Opstand'.

90. PRO *SP* 12/46/159, 171 and 178 (with copies in PRO *AO* 1/1685/20A), document the issues of money in 1584, starting with £3,500 paid to Drake in Aug. 1584. See also BL *Lans.* 43/11, John Hawkins's 'project for distressing Spain', 20 July 1584 OS, and 41/5 Burghley's memorandum entitled 'The charge of the voyage to the Moluccas', 20 Nov. 1584 OS.

91. By May 1585 the Spanish government knew of Elizabeth's plans to send another expedition to the East Indies: see *CCG*, XII, 58, Granvelle to

Margaret of Parma, 29 May 1585. For details on the preparations, see Adams, 'Outbreak of the Elizabethan naval war', 50–8.

92. On Granvelle's early demands for an embargo, and the reasons why it could not be implemented (the grain brought by Dutch ships kept the population of Lisbon from starving), see BL *Addl* 28,702/96, Granvelle to Philip II, 3 Mar. 1582; *CCG*, X, 43–5, Foncq to Granvelle, 31 Jan. 1583; 224, Granvelle to Bellefontaine, 23 May 1583; and 331–2, Granvelle to Idiáquez, 21 Aug. 1583.

93. *CCG*, XI, 65–6 and 102, Granvelle to Idiáquez, 5 Aug. 1584 ('Lo del arresto de los navios al mes de setiembre y serrar el comercio es tan necessario que ninguna cosa mas, si queremos acabar'), and 15 Aug. 1584. On the change of plan, see AGRB *MD* 5459/206 and 222, Granvelle to Idiáquez, 19 and 24 Aug. 1584; and *CCG*, XI, 177–9, same to same, 1 Sept. 1584, hoping to see it effected in October.

94. *CCG*, XI, 177–9 and 204–5, Granvelle to Idiáquez, 1 and 6 Sept. 1584, and the quotation from pp. 367–8, Granvelle to Charles de Mansfelt, 27 Oct. 1584. See other letters on the same subject – Granvelle was nothing if not persistent – ibid., 336–8, 340–1, 347–9 and 354–5, all to Idiáquez, 14, 17, 18 and 21 Oct. 1584; and *CCG*, XII, 58 and 70, Granvelle to Margaret of Parma, 29 May and 22 June 1585.

95. *BMO*, I, 476–7, Philip II order of 25 May 1585. It is worth stressing those words 'with the pretence [*con color*]', because several scholars have argued that the embargo was indeed intended to provide ships for naval operations (like the embargoes of vessels ordered in 1582, 1583 and 1586–88); but this does not appear to have been the case. For an alternative view, see Rodríguez-Salgado and Adams, *England, Spain and the Gran Armada*, 6, 56 and 241.

96. *BMO*, I, 490–1, order of 3 July 1585;

and AGS *GA* 80/125, 'Copia del apuntamiento que Antonio de Erasso dió a Don Cristobal de Moura', 20 July 1585 (some argued that the English should not be released because of the *Primrose* incident, but the king correctly pointed out that 'the ships that are here were not guilty of the crime'). For the eventual sale of the Dutch vessels, see KML *MSP: CC* 7, 'Cuentas del valor de las urcas de estrangeros que por mandado de Su Magestad se arrestaron'.

97. Kernkamp, *De handel op den vijand*, I, 153–60; Snapper, *Oorlogsinvloeden*, 32–8; and Israel, *Empires and entrepôts*, 193–4. *BMO*, I, 490–1, Philip II to Antonio de Guevara, 3 July 1585, mentioned 123 Dutch ships detained in Lisbon, Setubal and Andalusia alone (see also *BMO*, I, 481–90, for other papers on the ships embargoed).

98. PRO *SP* 94/2/78–84, Philip II to the corregidor of Bilbao, 29 May 1585, original with two distinct English translations.

99. Granvelle expressed his contempt for the English in a letter to Margaret of Parma on 11 Sept. 1572: *CCG*, IV, 420.

100. Bain, *The Hamilton Papers*, II, 650–1, Walsingham to Edward Wotton, 11 June 1585 OS. Note that the captured Spanish magistrate claimed to have lost, in the scuffle aboard the *Primrose*, one of the letters authorizing him to seize the English ship: PRO *SP* 12/179/32–3v, interrogation of Francisco de Guevara. Walsingham and his colleagues therefore did not have the entire picture.

101. PRO *SP* 12/179/36–8, Examination of the well-informed Bilbao merchant Pedro de Villareal, 13 June 1585 OS (he also confirmed that Spain sent regular subsidies to the French Catholic League: someone later underlined all information in his testimony concerning France); and PRO *SP* 12/180/59A, captured letter from Juan del Hoyo, merchant, 5 July 1585 NS.

102. Collinson, 'The Elizabethan exclusion crisis', 87–92 (on arrangements for

the 'interregnum'); Cressy, 'Binding the nation'; and Pollitt, *Arming the nation*.

103.   PRO *SP* 12/177/153–4, 'A plott', spring 1585, draft.

104.   BL *Lans.* 41/103–68, statements of goods imported and exported through English ports to Spain and Portugal. The government's interest in measuring the Iberian trade at precisely this time is interesting: did it perhaps wish to assess the possible economic impact of war with Philip? See also the helpful introduction to Croft, *The Spanish Company*, and idem, 'English commerce with Spain'.

105.   Durand-Lapié, 'Un roi détroné', 640, Leicester to Dom Antonio, 24 May 1585 OS; PRO *SP* 12/179/48, Commission to Bernard Drake, 20 June 1585 OS, copy; Corbett, *Papers relating to the navy*, 36–8, 'Articles set down . . . for the merchants, owners of ships and others whose goods have been arrested in Spain, and have licence from the Lord Admiral to reprise upon the Spaniards', 9 July 1585 OS. Adams, 'Outbreak of the Elizabethan naval war', 46, notes that the issue of letters of reprisal began three days later.

106.   PRO *SP* 46/17/160, Elizabeth's warrant, 1 July 1585 OS, and fo. 172, Privy Council warrant, 11 July 1585 OS. Piecing together the history of Drake's expedition is complicated by the absence of the Privy Council Register for 1582–86.

107.   See Oosterhoff, *Leicester and the Netherlands*, 39–45.

108.   For details see *BMO*, I, 518–19 and 539, Pedro Bermudez to the Court, 7 Oct. 1585, and Licenciado Antolinez to Philip II, 14 Nov. 1585. Almost all ambassadors in Madrid obtained and forwarded to their governments a copy of Bermudez's letter. For the English side, see Keeler, *Sir Francis Drake's West Indian Voyage*.

109.   See the discussion of motives, and the citation of sources, in Rodríguez-Salgado and Adams, *England, Spain and the Gran Armada*, 59.

110.   *Breeder Verclaringhe*.

111.   OÖLA *KB* 4/137, Khevenhüller to Rudolf II, 13 Oct. 1585; Longlée, 192, letter to Henry III, 28 Oct. 1585; *CSPV*, VIII, 123 and ASVe, *Senato: dispacci Spagna* 18, unfol., Gradinegro to Venice, 25 Oct. 1585.

6   The 'Enterprise of England', 1585–88

1.   ASF *MP* 2636/123–4, Instructions to Dovara, 28 Feb. 1585, and 5022/357ff., his correspondence with the grand duke. The reasons for Dovara's presence at Court puzzled other ambassadors: see ASMo *CD* 14, unfol., Varano to Ferrara, 29 June 1585; ASMa *AG* 600a, unfol., Cavriano to Mantua, 2 Jan. 1586; ASL *Offizio sulle differenze*, 268, unfol., Portico to Lucca, 29 June, 21 Sept. and 19 Oct. 1585, etc. Its significance at first eluded even the perceptive Spanish ambassador in Rome: see Olivares's apology to Philip II for failing to mention Dovara's mission: RAH Ms 9–5516, unfol., 'Relación de nueve cartas', letter of 28 July 1585. For Dovara's previous visits to Spain, see his correspondence with royal ministers in AGS *Estado* 1452.

2.   *BMO*, I, 478, royal apostil on a letter from Olivares to Philip II, 4 June 1585, received 2 July. Similar testy phrases recur in the king's reply to Olivares on 2 Aug.: *BMO*, I, 496. Sixtus may have been 'inspired' by a paper from William Allen that urged the new pope to support the 'enterprise' while the English Catholic community still possessed the strength and enthusiasm to support it: see Mattingly, 'William Allen'.

3.   AGS *Estado* 946/85–8 and 103–4, Olivares to Philip II 13 July (about the 'empresa de Ginebra'); and 28 July 1585; *BMO*, I, 496 and AGS *Estado* 946/229 Philip II to Olivares, 2 and 22 Aug. 1585 (from which the quotations come). See also Altadonna,

'Cartas de Felipe II a Carlos Manuel', 157, Philip II to Savoy, 23 Aug. 1585, approving the idea of an assault on Geneva as suggested by the pope (see also the king's letters on the subject dated 22 Aug. 1585: AGS *Estado* 1260/211, to Count Sfondrato, his ambassador to Savoy, and 1261/90, to the duke of Terranova, governor of Milan).

4. News of Drake's landing was sent to the Court, then at Monzón in Aragon, on the day it occurred, 7 Oct. 1585 (*BMO*, I, 519), and Don Juan de Zúñiga and other ministers began to discuss 'the excesses committed by the English ships' four days later (ibid., 521). For Santa Cruz's new command, see AGS *CS* 2a/280/8–15, Instruction and patents dated 23 June 1584.

5. *BMO*, I, 529–31, 'Memorial' sent by Santa Cruz to Philip II, 26 Oct. 1585.

6. IVdeDJ 23/385, 'Parecer del Cardenal de Sevilla sobre lo del cosario' (15 Nov. 1585), forwarded to Philip II by Hernando de Vega, president of the council of the Indies, on 30 Nov. This and Santa Cruz's Memorial are discussed in the excellent article of González Palencia, 'Drake y los orígenes del poderío naval inglés', in *Reivindicacíon*, 281–320.

7. *BMO*, I, 536–7, 'Lo que se responde a Su Santidad'. In fact this document, although forwarded to Olivares on 6 Nov. 1585, clearly relates to the letter sent with Dovara to the grand duke of Tuscany on 24 Oct. (ibid., 528; see also note 20 below). Equally clearly, it refers to the Enterprise of England, and not to some 'enterprise of Algiers', as the editors of *BMO* assert (p. 536). It is true that the document does not include the word 'Inglaterra' (nor, for that matter, 'Argel'), only 'la empresa'; but it evidently meant England because that was the only 'empresa' for which the grand duke had authorized Dovara to secure Philip II's support. (See ASF *MP* 2636/123–4, Instructions to Dovara, 28 Feb. 1585, and also AGS *Estado* 1452/20, Philip II to Florence, 27

July 1585.) The assertion of Rodríguez-Salgado, 'The Anglo-Spanish war', 7–8 and 34–5, that at this stage Philip only agreed to 'some enterprise' (perhaps Algiers, perhaps England) therefore seems incorrect.

8. Villari and Parker, *La política de Felipe II*, 110–15, Zúñiga to Philip II, undated but late 1585. Zúñiga handled all the papers concerning Drake's raid on Galicia: see *BMO*, I, 521.

9. News of the build-up of English forces in Holland following the treaty of Nonsuch came in two letters from Parma to Philip II dated 30 Sept. 1585 (AGS *Estado* 589/81 and AGS *SP* 2534/212). Parma also knew, from intercepted letters between the Dutch and the English Court, that these troops formed part of a new commitment by Elizabeth; but he did not yet know that a formal treaty had been signed. News of Drake's destructive progress seems to have arrived at regular intervals, maintaining the king's irritation at a high level: see *BMO*, I, 533–4, 539–40, 547–8 and 551–2.

10. *HMC Bath*, V, 71–2, Thomas Bayly to the earl of Shrewsbury, 27 July 1586 OS (also claiming that Drake had intended to attack Iberian vessels fishing off Newfoundland again, but the winds had been against him); PRO *SP* 81/4/201, Pallavicino to Walsingham, 11 Sept. 1586 OS, Frankfurt, in Italian; and *CCG*, XII, 133–5, Granville to Charles de Mansfelt, 29 Nov. 1585.

11. *BMO*, I, 535, Philip II to Olivares, 6 Nov. 1585. It should be recalled that Dovara received his commission during the pontificate of Gregory XIII; the fear that his successor might be of a different mind seems perfectly reasonable. In fact Olivares confirmed Sixtus's resolve on 15 Nov.: see *BMO*, I, 553, Philip II to Olivares, 2 Jan. 1586.

12. *BMO*, I, 550, Philip II to Parma, 29 Dec. 1585; ibid., I, 553–4, Philip II to Olivares, 2 Jan. 1586; BL *Cott. Vesp.* CVIII/412ff., letters of William Allen in 1585-86 addressing Mary as 'my

sovereign'. Some surprise has been expressed at the hiatus between the king's decision on 24 Oct. 1585 and his letter of commitment on 2 Jan. 1586, leading to the suggestion that he changed his mind in the interim (Rodríguez-Salgado, 'The Anglo-Spanish war', 7–8). However, two obvious considerations explain the delay: the need to assess the strategic implications for the king's other policies (as pointed out in Zúñiga's memorandum); and the need to make sure of the new pope's enthusiastic support – something that could only be established after Dovara, who carried the king's response of 24 Oct., reached Rome. Indeed, the king initially forbade Olivares to discuss the 'enterprise' with the pope until Dovara arrived: see *BMO*, I, 535, Philip to Olivares, 6 Nov. 1585, and note 20 below.

13. I am grateful to Paul C. Allen for discussing this point with me. See the list of successul invasions in Rodger, *Safeguard*, 429; for evidence that Philip II gave such precedents careful attention, see AHN *OM* 3512/27–8 and 30.

14. *BMO*, I, 566–7, Philip II to Santa Cruz, 26 Jan. 1586 (but note that the letter was signed in Valencia, not in San Lorenzo); 564, Santa Cruz to Philip II, 13 Feb. 1586 (note that the correct date is 'February' and not 'January': see *BMO*, II, ix–x); and ibid., II, 11–18, 'Relación de navíos' and letters from Santa Cruz to Philip II and Zúñiga, 13 Feb. 1586.

15. *BMO*, I, 566, Idiáquez to Santa Cruz, 26 Feb. 1586 (noting again that the true date was 'February' and not 'January': see *BMO*, II, ix–x).

16. *BMO*, II, 45–74, prints the 'Relación' of 22 Mar. 1586 in full. Ibid., 44, Santa Cruz to Philip II and to Idiáquez, 22 Mar. 1586, stated that (i) the 'Relación' was sent in response to Idiáquez's letter of 26 Feb., and (ii) 'the business is such that it is absolutely impossible to deal with or discuss it in writing' – so probably no

details on the strategy to be followed were committed to paper. The marquis showed commendable wisdom, for copies of his 22 Mar. 'Relación' fell into the hands of several foreign agents – including those of Venice, Urbino, France and, most dangerous of all, England: see p. 209 above.

17. *BMO*, II, 83–7, Idiáquez and Philip II to Santa Cruz, 2 Apr. 1586; and 93–4, Santa Cruz to Philip II, 9 Apr. 1586.

18. Ibid., xix–xxiii, give a good overview of the changes in the king's strategy.

19. See the relevant orders in *BMO*, II, 103–6, 113, 147–8 and 164–5. See also AGS *CMC* 1a/1735–6 and 2a/1208, on the embargo of ships to form the squadron of Vizcaya between 10 Apr. and 7 May 1586.

20. *BMO*, II, 26–33, Olivares to Philip II, 24 Feb. 1586. Olivares noted that since Dovara remained in Florence – he only left for Rome four days later: see ASF *MP* 2636/123, grand duke to Sixtus V, 28 Feb. 1588 – the ambassador had decided to speak to the pope on the basis of the information in Philip's letter of 2 Jan. Olivares also reported that he had *not* yet mentioned Parma as a possible commander (ibid., 26).

21. *BMO*, II, 108–11, Parma to Philip II, 20 Apr. 1586, and II, 195–6, 'Lo que dixo Juan Bautista Piata de palabra'.

22. Piatti's journey took so long because he travelled overland to Italy and thence by sea to Spain. Perhaps the disturbed state of France and the extreme sensitivity of his mission dictated this circuitous route; but, equally, Parma may have wished to buy time – his letter argued that the optimum season for the invasion would be October 'and if not this year, then it will be necessary to delay it until the same time next year'. A messenger sent via the Spanish Road in late April would be unlikely to return with plans to mount an invasion only six months later! (Parma did not, of course, know that the king had already scheduled the invasion for 1587.)

23. See Casado Soto, *Discursos*, 110–27, for Escalante's 'discurso' of June 1586, composed at El Escorial; and 52, 82, 147 and 157 for evidence of his 'hotline' to the king and his minsters.

24. *BMO*, II, 212, 'Parecer' of Don Juan de Zúñiga (June/July 1586). Zúñiga may, of course, have considered other papers of advice too, for several other 'experts' sent their opinions to the king: see, for example, the copies of four anonymous discourses written in 1586 'Sopra l'impresa d'Inghilterra' preserved in BAV *UL* 854/225–57v, 258–85, 286–8v and 289–303. The last two, written in Spanish and addressed directly to Philip II, are particularly interesting: the former, for example, suggested (perhaps for the first time) a junction at or near Dunkirk between the Armada and the Army of Flanders as a prelude to invasion (fo. 288); the latter advocated a landing in force from the Armada at Dover and an advance down the Thames to London (fo. 296v). Bustamente Callejo, 'Consejos del capitán laredano', printed another invasion plan sent to the king in 1587.

25. Although no copy of the masterplan has yet come to light, its existence is clearly indicated in *BMO*, II, 333, Philip II to Parma, 1 Sept. 1586: 'On 26 July I replied at length and in detail to the letter brought by Giovanni Battista Piatti, as I believe you will have seen before receiving this'; and ibid., 387, Parma to Philip II, 30 Oct. 1586, replying to 'your royal letter of 26 July which he [Piatti] brought me'. A similar letter probably went out to Santa Cruz because, at precisely this time, the king apologized for falling behind with his other work 'because I had so much to do for Flanders, Italy *and Portugal* the day before yesterday, yesterday and today': IVdeDJ 55/IX/111, Mateo Vázquez to Philip II and reply, 26 July 1586 (emphasis added).

26. In the absence of Philip II's letter of 26 July 1586, the *traza* (plan) has been reconstructed from the following: *BMO*, II, 387–8, Parma to Philip II, 30 Oct. 1586; 471–2, royal reply of 17 Dec. 1586; 535–6, Parma to Philip II, 17 Jan. 1587; and 624, Idiáquez to Medina Sidonia, 28 Feb. 1587. After the death of his father in Sept. 1586, Alexander Farnese became duke of Parma.

27. It is interesting to note that precisely the same error was made by Spain and France in 1779: the success of the invasion hinged not only upon joining together fleets from several ports (Toulon, Cádiz, Brest . . .) but also upon picking up an army stationed in two different ports (St Malo and Le Havre): see Patterson, *The other Armada*.

28. In their defence, others besides Philip and his entourage at this stage favoured a junction between a fleet from Spain and troops from Flanders as the prelude to invading England, and saw no problem: see, for example, BAV *UL* 854/286–8v, 'Discorso sopra la guerra d'Inghilterra' (in Spanish), and *BMO*, II, 438–9, Juan del Águila to Philip II, 29 Nov. 1586.

29. *Reivindicación*, 308, two letters written by Hernando de Vega, president of the council of the Indies, to the king in March 1586; Library of Congress, Manuscript Division, *Sir Francis Drake Collection* #3, Medina Sidonia to Philip II, 25 Oct. 1586, minute, point 13. See also the similarly bellicose views of the merchants of Seville quoted in Lapèyre, *Une famille de marchands*, 422–3; and of Jean Richardot in the Netherlands, *CCG*, XII, 161, letter to Granvelle, 30 Mar. 1586.

30. On the concentration of the fleet in Lisbon, see *BMO*, II, xxxivff. On the troops sent to Flanders, see O'Donnell, *La fuerza de desembarco*; on those sent to Lisbon, see Gracia Rivas, *Los tercios de la Gran Armada*.

31. See *BMO*, II, 414, Philip II to the viceroys of Naples and Sicily, 12 Nov. 1587.

32. Heredía Herrera, *Catálogo*, I, 597, royal apostil on a consulta of the council of the Indies dated 3 Sept. 1586;

APO, III, 130–1, Philip II to Viceroy Dom Duarte de Meneses, 23 Feb. and 14 Mar. 1588; Headley, 'Spain's Asian presence', 638–45.

33. *BMO*, II, 135–6, royal cédula of 5 May 1586 (see also a copy in the archives of the English government: PRO *SP* 94/2/142), and 273–4 and 282–4, provisão of 30 July 1586. Interestingly, at this stage the king did not prohibit trade from Spain *to* England, and (for example) ordered the release of a ship arrested for carrying goods from Marseilles to England: KML *MSP: CR* 4/313, Philip to Medina Sidonia, 11 Aug. 1587.

34. KML *MSP: CR* 4/51 and 325, Philip II to Medina Sidonia, 10 Mar. and 25 Aug. 1587. In fact the Dutch States-General forbade all trade with Spain between 4 Apr. 1586 and 26 Jan. 1587: see Kernkamp, *De handel op den vijand*, I, 187, 204 and 221–9.

35. *BMO*, II, 305–7, Mendoza to Philip II, 13 Aug. 1586 (with copious royal apostils) and 338–9, Philip's reply, 5 Sept. 1586. Note that the English précis in *CSPSp.*, III, 603–8 and 614–16, contain some significant misreadings. The conspirators also received orders to capture Dom Antonio and kill him: *CSPSp*, III, 617, Idiáquez to Mendoza, 6 Sept. 1586.

36. For details see Hanselmann, *L'Alliance Hispano-Suisse*, and the more positive assessment of Bolzern, *Spanien, Mailand und die katholische Eidgenossenschaft*, 20–1, 25, 29 and 141.

37. *BMO*, II, 420–3, Philip II to Olivares, 18–19 Nov. 1586; ibid., 487–8, Olivares to Philip II, 22 Dec. 1586; and AGS *Estado*, 949/86, declaration of two Rome bankers, 29 July 1587, that 1 million ducats for the Armada had been deposited by papal agents. It seems ironic that Philip insisted that the money should become payable 'as soon as the army had landed in England' rather than when the Armada had put to sea: *BMO*, II, 420, Philip II to Olivares, 18 Nov. 1586. He evidently believed it more likely that Parma would get to England somehow than that Santa Cruz would ever get his ships to sea – a miscalculation that cost him 1 million ducats!

38. *BMO*, II, 28–9, Olivares to Philip II, 24 Feb. 1586.

39. See AMAE *MDFD* 237/94–5, Olivares to Philip II, 27 June 1588, 'en la materia secreta'. This fascinating document reviewed in turn the chances of securing a papal dispensation for Isabella to marry her cousins Rudolf, Ernest, Matthias, Maximilan and Albert. Presumably Philip intended this to form a prelude to investing Isabella and her new husband with the kingdoms of England and Ireland (as, ten years later, he invested her and Albert with the Netherlands: see p. 279 above).

40. AGS *Estado* 165/176–7, Philip II to Parma, 5 Apr. 1588, duplicate, about Allen's role; Meyer, *England and the Catholic church*, 520–3, prints the 29 July 1587 agreement. On the vexed question of 'investiture', see Rodríguez-Salgado, *Armada 1588–1988*, 21; for an examination of Philip's 'Lancastrian' claim, see idem, 'The Anglo-Spanish war'.

41. See the reports of the English envoys in Paris, Stafford and Waad, in *CSPF*, XXI.1, 236, 239, 242, 276; and Deyon, 'Sur certaines formes de la propagande religieuse', 20.

42. See Jensen, 'The phantom will of Mary queen of Scots'; AHN *OM* 3411/14, Mary Stuart to Sixtus V, 23 Nov. 1586, Spanish copy annotated by Philip II; and *BMO*, II, 402–3, Mendoza to Philip II, 8 Nov. 1586 (announcing that Elizabeth had sent copies of both the will and Mary's letter disinheriting her son to Henry III of France). For the 'affinity' see ASV *NS* 33/279, Philip II to Sixtus V, 20 June 1587, holograph; for payment of her legacies, see *BMO*, III, 1777, Philip II to Mendoza, 25 Jan. 1588, minute; for the friendship of Mary and Isabella, see Lynch, *Mary Stewart*, 75.

43. On the 'enterprise of Scotland', for which the king sent 10,000 ducats to

Scots conspirators, see *BMO*, II, 436–7 and 492–4, Mendoza to Philip II, 28 Nov. and 24 Dec. 1586, and 555–6, Philip II to Mendoza, 28 Jan. 1587; AGS *Estado* 592/49 and 73, Parma to Philip II, 22 Mar. and 27 Apr. 1587; AGS *Estado K* 1566/128, Mendoza to Philip, 20 May 1587, and 1565/60, Robert Bruce to Mendoza, 2 Oct. 1587; Masson, *Register of the Privy Council of Scotland*, IV, 316 n.; and *CSPScot*, IX, 589, 593.

44. Hunt *HA* 30881/120, Lord Huntingdon to Walsingham, 11 Aug. 1588 OS. On the rebellion of Lord Maxwell, who had actively sought foreign aid for his designs since 1583, see Brown, 'The making of a *politique*'.

45. *HMC Bath*, V, 84–5, Elizabeth to Shrewsbury, 3 Nov. 1587; and Hunt *HA* 30881/87v–8, Huntingdon to Privy Council, 23 June 1588.

46. For repatriating the Turks, see Dasent, *Acts of the Privy Council of England*, XIV, 205, order of 4 Aug. 1586. For the rumours, see OÖLA *KB* 4/269v, Khevenhüller to Rudolf II, 21 Sept. 1587, Madrid; ASP *CF* 154, unfol., Juan de Cernosa to Parma, 2 and 9 Jan. 1588, Venice; and AGS *Estado* 1089/289, Grand Master of the Order of Malta to Philip II, 16 June 1588, Valletta. On the diplomatic struggle in Istanbul, see Pears, 'The Spanish Armada and the Ottoman Porte'; Rawlinson, 'The embassy of William Harborne'; Skilliter, 'The Hispano-Ottoman armistice of 1581'; and Skilliter, *William Harborne*.

47. On these developments, see Dickerman, 'A neglected aspect of the Spanish Armada'; Jensen, 'Franco-Spanish diplomacy and the Armada'; and Constant, *Les Guise*, 164ff.

48. For the subsidies, see AGS *Estado K* 1573/42, receipt signed by Guise, 30 Dec. 1586, and AGS *CMC* 2a/23, unfol., 'Cuentas de Gabriel de Alegría'; for the 'leak', see Cimber and Danjou, *Archives curieuses*, 1ère série XI, 296, report of Nicholas Poulain.

49. Details from the excellent article of Pollitt, 'Bureaucracy and the Armada'.

50. Nolan, 'The muster of 1588'; Gerson, 'The English recusants and the Spanish Armada'.

51. On the 1587 operations in eastern France, see Jensen, *Diplomacy and dogmatism*, 89–92; on the troops from the Army of Flanders in Lorraine, see AGS *Estado* 592/127, marquis of Havré to Parma, 10 Sept. 1587, copy; *Estado* 2852, unfol., Parma's Instructions to Juan Bautista de Tassis, 22–23 Sept. 1587; and AGRB *Audience*, 1832/3 folder 2, letters of the duke of Lorraine to Parma, 1587, on the need for troops from the Army of Flanders in Lorraine.

52. No copy of Drake's Instructions seems to have survived, but their contents can be deduced from the queen's later attempt – on 9 Apr. 1587 OS – to countermand them: see Hopper, *Sir Francis Drake's memorable service*, 28–9. Drake's original commission to command the fleet being sent to the seas 'for the honor and safetie of our realmes', dated 15 Mar. OS, is at West Devon County Record Office, Plymouth, PCM 1963 37/15. His attempt to raise Dutch capital appears in *RSG*, V, 247 and 388–90 (Resolutions of 13–14 Nov. and 23 Dec. 1586); for other documents see Corbett, *Papers relating to the navy*, 97–206. The best description and evaluation of the whole episode is currently to be found in *BMO*, III, xxix–xlvi.

53. See full details in Leimon and Parker, 'Treason and plot', 1150–1. See also pp. 221–3 above. In fact Philip II received other intelligence about Drake's raid, but it also arrived too late to be of use: see *BMO*, III, xxix–xxx.

54. Drake's success in paralysing sea communication between the Mediterranean and the Atlantic has not always been appreciated, but see KML *MSP: CR* 4/149, Idiáquez to Medina Sidonia, 20 May 1587, and 167–8, Philip II to Medina Sidonia, 27 May 1587, about detaining the troopships sent from Italy at Gibraltar, and not letting them sail on to San Lúcar until Drake had gone.

55. *BMO*, III, 479, 692–4, 721–2, 773, 774–5, 816–17 and 862; and of course each letter had to be copied to other participants in the plan (see, for example, KML *MSP: CR* 4/273, 281 and 284, Philip II to Medina Sidonia, 10, 14 and 23 July 1587). Even this oversimplifies the story: besides the letters listed above, the king bombarded his various commanders with several others over these weeks.

56. *BMO*, III, 380 and 411, consulta of the council of War on 19 May 1587, royal resolution on the 23rd.

57. Maura, 167, Idiáquez to Medina Sidonia, 28 Feb. 1587.

58. ASV *NS* 19/256, Novara to Rusticucci, 6 May 1587, quoting Don Hernando de Toledo. For similar expressions see AGS *Estado* 2855, unfol., 'Lo que resolvió el consejo en materia de Inglaterra', 20 Jan. 1588; and Herrera Oria, 262–3, Don Juan Manrique to Idiáquez, 11 Aug. 1588.

59. For details see Martin and Parker, *Spanish Armada*, 136–7. When the transatlantic convoy escorts sailed to Lisbon in spring 1588, receiving the name 'the squadron of Castile', the total strength of the Grand Fleet reached some 130 vessels.

60. *BMO*, II, 621–2, Philip II to Parma, 28 Feb. 1587, in reply to Parma's letter of 24 Dec. 1586 (apparently now lost) and 17 Jan. 1587 (*BMO*, II, 535–6). In fact Philip had recognized the need for a deep-water port in his first letter to Parma about the 'enterprise', on 29 Dec. 1585: *BMO*, I, 550.

61. *BMO*, III, 479–80 and 770–2, Philip II to Parma, 5 June 1587, minute; Parma to Philip II, 20 July 1587.

62. *BMO*, III, 1006–7 and 1067–8, Instructions for Parma on 4 Sept., minute, and for Santa Cruz, 14 Sept. 1587, draft (although dated ten days later, internal evidence indicates that the two instructions were finalized on the same day: the king probably introduced a ten-day difference in order to allow Parma's letter to reach Brussels). Parma brought the oversights in the masterplan to Philip's attention on

numerous occasions but never received an answer: cf. AGS *Estado* 592/147–9, Parma to Philip II, Dec. 21, 1587; and *Estado* 594/6–7, 79 and 197, same to same, 31 Jan., 22 June and 21 July 1588.

63. Perhaps one should not be too critical, since similar defects have characterized other ventures. For example, in planning 'Operation Overlord' (the invasion of Normandy) in 1944 Allied strategists concentrated on only two objectives: (i) how to get the invasion forces ashore in sufficient strength to secure a bridgehead; and (ii) how to pursue the defeated German forces after breaking out of the bridgehead. No consideration seems to have been given to how precisely the 'breakout' would occur, and this oversight led to seven gruelling weeks of indecisive fighting. (I owe this point to Russell Hart.) Philip II's 'oversight' was of much the same order.

64. *BMO*, III, 1322–3, Philip II to Parma 30 Sept. 1587.

65. *BMO*, III, 1363, and 1458–59, Philip II to Parma, 25 Oct., 4 Nov. and 27 Nov. 1587; and 1225 and 1274, Philip II to Santa Cruz, 10 and 21 Oct. 1587. ASVe *Senato: dispacci Spagna* 20/374–89, Lippomano to Venice, 14 Nov. 1587, enclosing a copy of Santa Cruz's letter of the 4th (see a partial précis in *CSPV*, VIII, 320–3, 'undated').

66. *BMO*, III, 1398–1401, Parma to the king, 14 Nov. 1587. Parma received a number of reports from his friends and agents in Spain concerning the state of the Armada – see, for example, ASP *CF* 129, unfol., letters from Contador Alonso Carnero to Parma – so he must have known that it was far from ready by then. For evidence that Parma could not have 'put to sea' in November 1587 either, see p. 238 above.

67. *BMO*, III, 1391–2, 1536, 1579, 1616–17 and 1662–3 (Philip II to Santa Cruz, 9 Nov., 10, 21 and 29 Dec. 1587 and 4 Jan. 1588), and 1538 (Philip II to Parma, 11 Dec. 1587). In December Parma also reported for the

first time the presence of a Dutch blockade squadron off the Flemish coast, preventing any sortie: p. 241 above.

68. For the Instructions to Parma and Medina Sidonia on 1 Apr., see FD, II, 5–18; for Escalante's objections, see Casado Soto, *Discursos*, 157–64. Escalante had witnessed the power of the English fleet when they sacked Cadiz in 1587, which no doubt sharpened his appreciation of the dangers (see ibid., 191).

69. See AGS *Estado* 594/192, 'Relación' of the Army of Flanders, 29 Apr. 1588 (monthly cost = 454,315 crowns); and *Actas de las Cortes*, X (Madrid, 1886), 118 (Philip II claimed on 9 June 1588 that the Armada absorbed 900,000 ducats per month).

70. IVdeDJ 55/XI/62–3, Mateo Vázquez to Philip II and reply, 31 Mar. 1588; AGS *CJH* 249, carpetas 16–17 contain the 'Relaciones de sábado' for 1588; *CJH* 249 carpeta 21, unfol., Don Martín de Idiáquez to Rodrigo Vázquez, 16 Apr. 1588; BZ 141/160, Philip II to the count of Barajas, 18 June 1588, copy.

71. *BMO*, III, 1069–70, Philip II to Parma, 14 Sept. 1587, minute. See the papal nuncio's perceptive analysis of Spain's strategic dilemma should the enterprise not take place in 1587: ASV *NS* 19/283–4, Novara to Rusticucci, 10 Aug. 1587.

72. Jouanna, *Le Devoir de révolte*, 190–1.

73. Longlée, 380, letter to Henry III, 5 June 1588; BL *Addl* 35,841/88–9v, Sir Edward Stafford to Walsingham, 7 July 1588 OS. The forces of the Catholic League tried to take Boulogne again in spring 1588, but once more they failed: see Constant, *Les Guise*, 164–5 and BL *Addl* 35,841/69, Stafford to Walsingham, 18 June 1588 OS. For the other events in France at this time see Jensen, *Diplomacy and dogmatism*, chap. 6; Forneron, *Les ducs de Guise*, chaps 25–26; Jouanna, *Le Devoir de révolte*, 192–3; and Chevallier, *Henri III*, 625–45.

74. AMAE *Correspondance politique:*

Hollande 4/177–9v, 'Maladies de l'estat de Hollande' (Aug. 1587).

75. AGS *Estado* 2218/52, Philip II to Parma, 18 July 1586, minute; *CSPF*, XXI.2, 320–1, Wilkes to Elizabeth, 19 Jan. 1587 OS; *RSG*, V, 541–4 (Lord Buckhurst's explanation to the States-General, 14 Apr.) and 580–4 (on the Danish peace plan, 26 May 1587); *CSPF*, XXI.3, 83, letter of Buckhurst to the towns of the United Provinces, May 1587; Brugmans, *Correspondentie*, II, 236–41, Buckhurst to Elizabeth, 10 May 1587; and AGS *Estado* 592/105–6, Parma to Frederick of Denmark, 14 May 1587.

76. See Hibben, *Gouda in revolt*, chap. 7; ARA *Raad van State* 6/19v–20, debate of 16 June 1587; *RSG*, V, 559–72, and VI, 56–81, Resolutions of the States-General about the peace talks, Dec. 1587–Jan. 1588; and Groen van Prinsterer, *Archives*, 2nd series I, 83–4, William Louis to Maurice of Nassau, 20 June 1588 OS.

77. For Parma's relief over the death of the Danish king, see AGS *Estado* 594/62, Parma to Philip II, 13 May 1588; for his orders to keep negotiating with Elizabeth in spite of the deception involved, see AGS *Estado* 165/178, Philip II to Parma, 5 Apr. 1588. Croft had pocketed a Spanish pension since at least 1570: see *CSPSp*, II, 227, Guerau de Spes to Zayas, 9 Jan. 1570, and 674, Mendoza to Zayas, 14 May 1579.

78. For a convenient summary of the Bourbourg talks, see *CSPF*, XXII, 71–4; and MacCaffrey, *Queen Elizabeth*, 392–9. For further detail see van der Essen, *Alexandre Farnèse*, IV, 209ff.; and (using just the Spanish sources) Fernández Segado, 'Alejandro Farnesio'. The conference lacks a definitive study, although sources abound: see the list in Martin and Parker, *Spanish Armada*, 284.

79. OÖLA *KB* 4/311–12, Khevenhüller to Rudolf II, 13 July 1588. Even as he wrote, Daniel Rogers went to Denmark in order to craft an alliance of northern princes against Spain: he

failed (Slavin, 'Daniel Rogers in Copenhagen, 1588').

80. Ribadeneira's *Exhortación* quoted, with many other fascinating illustrations of the Jesuit's attempt to 'sacralize' the enterprise, by Gómez-Centurión, *La Invencible*, 67–70. See also p. 96 above.

81. Whitehead, *Brags and boasts*, 58–78, on the published items; on the processions and on the royal family at prayer, see BAV *UL* 1115/199–206, 'Avisos' of 28 May and 25 June 1588; ASMo *Ambasciatori Spagna* 15 unfol., Bishop Ripa to Ferrara, 25 June 1588; BAV *UL* 1115/205–6, 'Aviso' from Madrid, 25 June 1588); ASV *LP* 46/121, 'Breve instrucción para todos los que huvieren de ganar el Santíssimo Iubileo'.

82. AGS *Estado* 595/32, Idiáquez to Philip II and reply, Aug. 1588. On the king's anxiety to 'do his part' to perfection at this time, see p. 105 above; see also similar 'Providential' attitudes during the 1779 'descent upon England' recorded by Patterson, *The other Armada*, 14, 168–9, 214 and 222.

7   The Worst-kept Secret in Europe?

1. PRO *SP* 77/4/231–3, Dale to Elizabeth, 12 July 1588 OS: for further quotations from this letter, see p. 212 above.

2. Raleigh, *History of the World*, part I, book v, 305–6.

3. Von Clausewitz, *On war*, 119 and 86.

4. Machiavelli, *The Prince*, *passim* and above all chap. 25; Koninklijk Huisarchief, The Hague, Inv. 22.IX.E, unfol., William Louis to Maurice of Nassau, 4 Aug. 1614 NS: 'L'issue de la guerre dépend de la fortune, comme le jeu au dé'. I thank Alison Anderson for bringing this interesting quotation to my attention.

5. Murray, Knox and Bernstein, *The making of strategy*, 2–3.

6. Molyneux, *Conjunct expeditions*, part II, 21. I thank Adam Siegel for bringing this volume to my attention. The title of this chapter is inspired by the excellent article of de Lamar Jensen, 'The Spanish Armada: the worst-kept secret in Europe'. I wish to thank Alison Anderson for invaluable research assistance; and also Christopher Andrew, David Coleman, Nicholas Davidson, Rudolf de Smet, Miguel Angel Echevarría Bacigalupe, Friedrich Edelmayer, Robert Evans, Michael Handel, Georg Heilingsetzner, Richard Lundell, Jane Ohlmeyer, Robert Oresko, Ronald Pollitt and Christiane Thomas for providing references and illuminating sundry problems for me.

7. PRO *SP* 94/2/124, 'Copia en suma de una relación que el marqués de Santa Cruz y el contador Bernabé de Pedrossa an ymbiado a su Magestad, la qual relación se a despachado oy sávado a 22 de março 1586'. A second copy is at fo. 126, and an English translation at fo. 128. The original, from Simancas, may be found in *BMO*, II, 45–74, 'El Armada y exército que pareció que se havía de juntar para la conquista de Inglaterra . . . hiciéronla el marqués de Santa Cruz y el Contador Bernabé de Pedrosa'. An abridged copy may also be found in BNL *Fundo geral* 637/80–1.

8. ASV *NS* 32/220–2, Novara to Rusticucci, 23 July 1586, sent a copy first; followed by ASVe *Senato: dispacci Spagna* 19, from Lippomano on 6 Aug. 1586 (English précis in *CSPV*, VIII, 193–5), BNP *Fonds français*, 16,110/130–6, from Longlée on 23 Aug. 1586, and BAV *UL* 829/IV/621–35v. Philip II later lamented that this plan had become known all over Italy: BZ 143/77, Mateo Vázquez to Philip and reply, 3 June 1588. Little did he suspect that it had also become known in Paris and London!

9. *BMO*, II, 108–11, Parma to Philip II, 20 Apr. 1586. Parma bitterly

regretted this breach of security: see O'Donnell, 'El secreto'. For another important leaked document, see Bod. *Tanner* Ms 78/50–4, 'A discourse written by the marques of Sainctye Cruxe', 26 Oct. 1585 (original printed in *BMO*, I, 529–31, and discussed on p. 180 above).

10. ASF *MP* 4919/340, Alamanni to Florence, 25 Mar. 1588 – four whole months before the Armada reached the Channel; ASV *NS* 34/368, Novara to Montalto, 4 June 1588; *CSPV*, 367–8, Lippomano to Venice, 12 July 1588. Curiously, the 'original' seems not to have survived in the archives of the Spanish government. However, the data on which it was based were published in FD, II, 33 – a list of ships allocated to the right and left 'horns' of the formation – and a more detailed version may be found among the Medina Sidonia papers: see KML *MSP: CR* 5/142–6, 'La forma con que se avía de pelear con los galeones'. A description of the Armada's formation, no doubt based on these documents, was published by the popular historian Pigafetti, *Discorso*. See also the brilliant modern reconstruction in Pierson, *Commander of the Armada*, 134 and 235–43.

11. AGS *Estado* 2855, unfol., 'Lo que Su Magestad es servido que se responda a los cuatro papeles principales que le dio el Presidente Richardot' [Nov. 1589], answer to paper 2 (on England). Medina Sidonia's Instructions only specified where he was to join forces with Parma ('el cabo de Margat'), not where the troops would land: see FD, II, 6. The English who captured the galleass *San Lorenzo* on 8 Aug. thus discovered the former but not the latter: see Laughton, I, 344–50, Richard Tomson to Walsingham, 9 Aug. 1588 NS.

12. ASMa *AG* 600a, unfol., Cavriano to Mantua, 24 Oct. 1587 (similar sentiments in ASV *NS* 19/301, Novara to Rusticucci, 5 Oct. 1587); ASF *MP* 4919/89, Alemanni to Florence, 6 Feb. 1588; Longlée, 373–4, letter to

Henry III, 6 May 1588. For other expressions of frustration at the 'secrecy' of Philip and his ministers at this time, see Longlée, 294, letter to Henry III, 23 Aug. 1586; and ASG *AS* 2418/275, Spinola and Doria to Genoa, 10 Jan. 1587.

13. ASMa *AG* 601, unfol., Aqui to Mantua, 19 Feb, 1588; ASMo *CD* 15, unfol., Ripa to Ferrara, 6 Feb. 1588; HHStA *Staatenabteilung Spanien: Diplomatische Korrespondenz* 11 Konvolut 7/345, Khevenhüller to Rudolf II, 21 Feb. 1588.

14. Laughton, I, 213–14, Winter to Walsingham, 30 June 1588 NS; Brugmans, *Correspondentie*, III, 74, Leicester to the Privy Council, 27 Aug. 1587 NS.

15. PRO *SP* 77/4/231–3, Dale to Elizabeth, 12 July 1588 OS (see a précis of other parts of this letter in *CSPF*, XXII, 32–4); and *CSPF*, XXII, 51–2, Elizabeth to the commissioners, 27 July 1588 OS.

16. KML *Dr Valentine Dale: letters on talks with the duke of Parma*, #1, Dale to Leicester, 25 July 1588 OS, and #2, to (probably) Robert Beale, same date. Dale also sent similar letters to Walsingham, Burghley and Hatton. On Dale's unusual familiarity with history, see Jardine and Grafton, '"Studied for action"', 63–5.

17. See Handel, 'The politics of intelligence', 26. The division also works well for the seventeenth century: see Echevarría Bacigalupe, *La diplomacia secreta*, chap. 1; and Bély, *Espions*, part 1.

18. AGS *Estado* 949/6 and 22, Olivares to Philip II, 30 Dec. 1586 and 16 Mar. 1587.

19. Odo Colonna's confession, forwarded to Elizabeth by the Dutch on 9 Dec. 1587, is at PRO *SP* 84/19/151–2v. According to the well-informed van Reyd, *Historie*, 258, Colonna 'werdt niet gheloooft' (was not believed); and, indeed, the English only ordered a further interrogation some months later: BL *Cott. Vesp.* Cviii/95, Walsingham to Leicester, 5 May 1588. Young Odo

had joined an Italian regiment marching to Flanders after killing a knight
of Malta and earning the enmity of the
pope. He had kept his identity a secret
in the Army of Flanders because the
Colonna were traditional rivals of the
Farnese, whose clan chief was the duke
of Parma. For another similar intelligence coup, see PRO *SP* 101/90/38–
9, 'Certaine Spanishe occurrences',
being the interrogation of Ambassador Khevenhüller's secretary, intercepted and arrested in Nov. 1585 as
he sailed home to Germany after fourteen years in Spain.

20. For a suggestion that this information
might have contributed to England's
naval victory in the Armada campaign, see Martin and Parker, *Spanish
Armada*, 212–13.

21. PRO *SP* 12/214/16–19 and 47–65.
An excellent account of the questions
and the answers is provided by
Martin, *Spanish Armada prisoners*, 65–9
and 80–1.

22. See Martin and Parker, *Spanish
Armada*, 235.

23. The town of Plymouth, as well as the
queen, sent spy ships out to seek
news of Spanish naval preparations:
see Brayshay, 'Plymouth's coastal
defences', 189. Later, however,
English spies resided in at least some
Spanish ports: the journal of one of the
ships on the 1596 Cadiz expedition
recorded that the day before the attack
on the town 'two [men] swomme from
the towne to us and informed the
lords generalls of the state of Cales'
(Hammer, 'New light', 188).

24. *BMO*, III, 1750, Licenciado Guevara
to Philip II, 22 Jan. 1588 (although
the significance of the information
seems to have been overlooked: see p.
389 n. 68); *CSPSp*, IV, 219–22, 263–
6 and 326, depositions by Francisco
de Valverde and Pedro de Santa Cruz,
1588; and AGS *Estado K* 1448/77,
'Lo que refiere Manuel Blanco'.

25. See, for example, *CSPF*, XXI.4, 171–
2, R. Spencer to Lord Burghley, 5
Mar. 1588 OS.

26. PRO *SP* 77/4/204, Lord Derby to

Walsingham, 13 July 1588; and fos
114, 116, 'A report of the preparations at Dunkirk' (by Richard
Hogesone). See also fos 69 'A note of
the ships of war . . . at Dunkirk' (23
June 1588), 169 'View of the ships
at Dunkirk' (8 July 1588), and 303
'The state of the shipping in Dunkirk'
(Sept. 1588). Another very detailed
and accurate account of Parma's
preparations was forwarded in Mar.
1588 by Lord Cobham, a member of
the delegation at Bourbourg: BL *Harl.*
287/86, 'Advertisements decyphered'
(all dates 'new style'). See also Chapter
8 above.

27. See, for example, the dossiers of
information passed on by a German
prince in Apr. 1588 in *CSPF*, XXI.1,
556–64; or a Danish visitor to Spain
in autumn 1587 (ibid., 372–3).

28. Details are revealed in *CSPSp.*, IV,
326, deposition of Pedro de Santa
Cruz. Further information is available
in the excellent article of Morán
Torres, 'Los espías de la Invencible'.

29. PRO *SP* 77/4/185–6, S. de Grimaldi
to Fernando López de Vilanova, Brussels, 30 June 1588. See another piece
of excellent intelligence from a man
captured off the Flemish coast –
including the probable destination of
Parma's invasion force – in *CSPF*,
XXI.4, 511, 'Advertisements on ship-
board, taken the 22 of June, 1588, in
the road of Graveline'.

30. Details from Álava, 125 and 131–40,
and Devos, *Les Chiffres de Philippe II*.
See also Álava, 349–52, Zayas to
Álava, 27 June 1569, on the need to
change the 'cifra general' every five
years; and *BMO*, III, 1067, Philip II to
Santa Cruz, 14 Sept. 1587, enclosing a
unique cipher to use with Parma.

31. BMB Ms *Granvelle* 13/185, Philip II
to Granvelle, 3 Aug. 1564, on the
compromised general cipher; and
Bély, *Espions*, 156, on the dangers
of intercepting a ciphered copy of a
known text. See PRO *SP* 77/5/215,
245, 288–322, originals and deciphered versions of sundry letters
exchanged between Archduke Albert

and the Court of Spain about peace with France in 1597–98, for possible examples of this.

32. See the intercepted letters of 1576–77 in ARA *Staten Generaal* 11,915 and BL *Cott.* Caligula Cv/98, Juan de Escobedo to Philip II, 9 Apr. 1577. For details on Dutch success in decoding them, see Geurts, *De Nederlandse Opstand*, 59–60 and 64–5; AGS *Estado* 566/56, Balthasar López de la Cueva to Zayas, 7 Nov. 1576; Kervijn de Lettenhove, *Relations politiques*, IX, 411–12, Dr Rogers to Walsingham, 20 July 1577; and p. 347 n. 107 above. For details on other Spanish letters intercepted and deciphered at this time, see BPU *Favre* 61/44–5, Don John of Austria to Juan Andrea Doria, 16 Sept. 1578 and AGS *Estado* 579/118 and 124, Ottavio Gonzaga to Philip II, 13 Apr. and 21 May 1579. For further discussion of Juan del Castillo, see note 51 below.

33. BL *Addl* 28,360/1–2, Juan Bautista Gesio to Philip II, 18 Feb. 1578; Laubespine, 825, letter to Catherine de Medici, 10 Mar. 1561 ('I tried very hard to break the code but, although in my opinion it is not difficult, I could not'); Haynes, *Invisible power*, 7–8 and 18–19. See also the examples quoted by Strasser, 'Diplomatic cryptology', and the interesting data from later periods in Way, *Codes and cyphers*, and Bély, *Espions*, 153–7.

34. BL *Cott. Galba* Diii/95, Olivares to Philip II, 2 Mar. 1588, 'duplicate', apparently deciphered by an Italian ('io' instead of 'yo'). An incomplete English translation may be found at BL *Harl.* 295/207, and a better version – with amplifications and corrections presumably added as further codewords were 'cracked' – at PRO *SP* 94/3/3. The original, fully deciphered, is in AGS *Estado* 950/35–6 (English précis in *CSPSp*, IV, 225–7). In June Walsingham wrote to share his coup with the English ambassador in Paris, Sir Edward Stafford, who immediately told his Spanish paymaster, who in turn informed Philip II: *CSPSp.*, IV,

320–1, Mendoza to Philip II, 26 June 1588. Other intercepted and deciphered Spanish letters may be found at BL *Cott. Galba* D iii/60, Juan Andrea Doria to Philip II, 11 Mar. 1588; *HMC Salisbury*, III, 82–9, numerous letters from Parma, Olivares and Mendoza in spring 1589; PRO *SP* 94/3/131, 133 and 190, letters from the Court of Spain to Parma in 1590; *SP* 94/6/22, 29, 34–5 and 46, letters to the Archduke Albert in 1598; and the examples in note 32 above.

35. See Charrière, *Négociations*, II, 178 n.1, M. de Aramon to Henry II, 20 Jan. 1552; Lanz, *Korrespondenz*, III, 137, Instruction to M. de Rye, 22 Mar. 1552; and Kupke, *Nuntiaturberichte aus Deutschland*, XII, 246 and 269–70, Nuncio Camiani to secretary of state, 19 and 30 Mar. 1552. See, by contrast, *Epistolario*, I, 206, Alba to Don Francisco de Toledo, 21 June 1555, which cut short an interesting discussion of the strategic options to be followed in Italy with the words 'This is a matter that can be concluded orally, but not by letter'.

36. *BMO*, II, 338, Philip II to Mendoza, 5 Sept. 1586. On other occasions the king recommended sending orders by word of mouth only, without writing anything else down: to Parma on 4 Sept. 1587, on dispatching a messenger to Usshant to meet and liaise with the Armada; to Mendoza on 4 Jan. 1588 about plans for a rising in Scotland to coincide with the Armada's approach (*CSPSp.*, IV, 137, 188). Sometimes, however, operational plans simply had to be communicated in writing: see AA 5/69 Philip II to Alba, 7 Aug. 1567, partially ciphered by the king himself (see p. 122 above); and *Epistolario*, III, 136–8, Alba to Philip II, 18 July 1572, commenting on a detailed plan for an attack on Algiers which the king had sent for evaluation.

37. The location of the 'appointed place' remains somewhat mysterious even today. In his letter of 20 Apr. 1586, Parma had suggested 'the coast

between Dover and Margate, which is at the mouth of the Thames' (*BMO*, II, 110), but he never seems to have been more specific on paper. Apparently only two participants wrote it down for posterity: Juan Bautista de Tassis, inspector-general of the Army of Flanders, stated unequivocally in his manuscript history that the invasion forces were intended to sail into the anchorage of the Downs and storm ashore at Margate (Tassis, *Commentarii*, 491); and Paolo Rinaldi, Parma's chamberlain, made a similar assertion in his still unpublished 'Liber relationum': BRB Ms II.1155/216–v.

38. Standen described the system in a letter to Walsingham's secretary Manucci on 7 May 1587: see *CSPF*, XXI.1, 283–4. According to the envious nuncio in Spain, Philip II enjoyed Gianfigliazzi's company and spent 'much time' with him at the Escorial and his other country houses. Small wonder he provided Standen with such excellent information! (ASV *NS* 34/52v–3, Novara to Rusticucci, 6 Dec. 1587.)

39. BL *Harl.* 286/118, Standen to Walsingham, 30 July 1587); *HMC Salisbury*, III, 327–8, Standen to Walsingham, 7 June 1588. For further details, see Lea, 'Sir Anthony Standen'; Read, *Walsingham*, III, 288–90; Haynes, *Invisible power*, 87–8; and Hammer, 'An Elizabethan spy'. Standen's original letters from these years may be found in BL *Harl.* 285, 286, 295 and 296 (with copies of most in BL *Addl* 35,841). *CSPF*, XXI.1, 283–4, and *HMC Salisbury*, III, 262–3 and 327–8 provide some printed extracts.

40. PRO *SP* 12/202/55, 'A plotte'; *HMC Bath*, V, 86–7, Burghley to Lord Shrewsbury, 3 Mar. 1588. See also the cache of detailed letters from Lazaro Grimaldi in Genoa to Horatio Pallavicino, his relative, and to Burghley: PRO *SP* 81/4/52–6, 145, 150–1 and 160–4.

41. PRO *SP* 85/1/56, 'Capitano Jacopo da Pisa' to Walsingham, Milan, 31 Jan. 1587, noted nine letters written over the previous four months. He warned, however, that the Spanish ambassador in France was able to intercept all letters coming through Paris addressed to English destinations and therefore proposed to write in future via a friend in Lyon who would forward his letters through the English embassy in Paris. Since Ambassador Stafford was by then a Spanish spy, this procedure may explain why Jacopo da Pisa's letters – full of high-grade intelligence from the heart of Spanish Italy – suddenly disappear from the State Papers after May 1587: he was betrayed.

42. Bod. *Tanner* Ms 309/46v–7, Burghley to Powle, 25 Feb. 1588, copy. *CSPF*, XXI.1, 529, Powle to Walsingham, 10 Mar. 1588, stated that he had sent thirty-one letters since his arrival; several of them may be found in PRO *SP* 99/1 and in Bod. *Tanner* Mss 78 and 309. See also Stern, *Sir Stephen Powle*, chaps 4–5.

43. *CSPF*, XXI.1, 231–2, Richard Gibbes to Walsingham, Mar. 1587.

44. The states were Savoy, Genoa, Venice, Parma, Mantua, Ferrara, Urbino, Lucca, Tuscany and the Papacy. Almost all have left copious diplomatic archives for these years. For an interesting survey of what the nuncios of the 1590s discussed in their dispatches see Borromeo, 'Istruzioni generali'.

45. ASL *Offizio sulle differenze*, 268 unfol., Portico to Lucca, 23 Aug. 1585, copy (deciphered original in ASL *Anziani*, 644). The French envoy reported the same thing a month later: Longlée, 174, letter to Henry III, 20 Sept. 1585. The imperial ambassador had the story shortly afterwards and immediately interpreted Drake's raid as a *casus belli* (see p. 176 above; OÖLA *KB* 4/137, Khevenhüller to Rudolf II, 13 Oct. 1585, minute). The French ambassador reported the following day that the king had just written to his ambassador in Rome requesting papal support for his proposal to bring down

the Tudor state (Longlée, 184, letter to Henry III, 14 Oct. 1585).

46. ASMa *AG* 600a, unfol., Cavriani to Mantua, 2 Apr. 1586. Apparently, Philip II's letters went out shortly after 2 Apr. and not 'about ten days' before. See also Cavriani's well-informed dispatches of 4 and 9 Apr. in the same bundle. The imperial ambassador got the story a little later, but (as usual) in greater detail: OÖLA *KB* 4/152, Khevenhüller to Rudolf II, 26 Apr. 1586. For another extremely detailed account, see *CSPV*, VIII, 159, Gradinegro to Venice, 1 May 1586.

47. See, for example, ASV *NS* 34/404–5, Novara to Montalto, 29 June 1588, with details on the contents of letters from Medina Sidonia to the king that 'ho veduto', and on a letter from Parma that 'm'ha detto un amico mio che l'ha veduta'; while Longlée, 353, letter to Henry III, 5 Mar. 1588, claimed to have 'seen' several letters from Armada officers discussing their projected departure date.

48. BL *Addl* 28,528/26–7, Mateo Vázquez to Philip II and reply, 17 Feb. 1575, following the leak of a letter about Don John of Austria. During an earlier scare about poor security, the king asserted that he either kept sensitive letters under lock and key, or else burnt them: BMB *Granvelle* Ms 23/9–10, Philip II to Granvelle, 7 July 1566, holograph; and IVdeDJ 60/321, Philip II to Antonio Pérez, undated (but written at the same time). Admittedly, Philip always worked with his door open, which might have allowed someone to glimpse a state paper, but it seems unlikely; and in any case several ambassadors (including Fourquevaux and Donà) commented on the king's 'exquisite' ability to keep secrets: see pp. 20 and 33 above.

49. *CCG*, IV, 38–9, Granvelle to Sagantes, 10 Nov. 1570 (on indiscretion in general); and AGRB *Audience* 476/99, Viglius to Tisnacq, 5 Nov. 1564 (about Quiclet's sale of secrets in 1556). On Philip's valet Vandenesse see Juste, *Guillaume le Taciturne*, 56, n.; IVdeDJ 60/321, Antonio Pérez to Philip II and reply [undated but July 1566]; HHStA *Spanien Varia* 1b/s/45, 'Aviso' of 23 Sept. 1567; and AGS *Estado* 542/122, 'Requisitoria' against Vandenesse.

50. Fourquevaux, I, 177, letter to Charles IX, 13 Feb. 1567. See also ibid., 120, letter of 3 Sept. 1566, noting that Fourquevaux had followed the king to Segovia in order to monitor his reactions to the Netherlands crisis, but could find out little because most other ambassadors and his 'secret friends' had remained in Madrid; and *CSPV*, VIII, 193, Lippomano to Venice, 6 Aug. 1586, reporting the same lack of leaks when 'the Court is absent from Madrid'.

51. Details from Bor, *Geschiedenis*, book 16, fos 44–v (published in 1621), who added that Castillo had been betraying the ciphers for ten years, that his information enabled Marnix to decipher intercepted Spanish letters (see p. 216 above), and that Castillo was executed for his treason in October 1581. 'I have not been able to ascertain how these matters were discovered', Bor informed his readers. But how did the Dutch historian 'ascertain' the rest of his facts? In 1581 Granvelle reported Castillo's arrest in a letter, adding that some undelivered state papers had been found in his possession: *CCG*, VIII, 410–11, Granvelle to Margaret of Parma, 13 Sept. 1581. Cabrera de Córdoba, writing at much the same time as Bor, expressly refuted the charge of treason which (as he said) circulated 'not only in Spain but also in the Netherlands and Italy'. According to Cabrera, Castillo had been denounced by a personal enemy but, after a period in prison while the matter was investigated, he was vindicated, freed and allowed to hold responsible positions in Naples and the Netherlands (*Historia*, II, 685–6). Much of this is confirmed by a letter of Jan. 1583, in which Philip II informed the viceroy

of Naples that Castillo had been imprisoned 'for some days' (actually over a year!) 'because he was accused of espionage and of corresponding with, and having corresponded with, the prince of Orange about Netherlands affairs'. Nevertheless, the king added, a close investigation of the charges uncovered 'no offence concerning the loyalty of the said Castillo, although in some conversations – moved by drink and contentiousness – he was indiscreet in his speech'. Castillo therefore received a posting to Naples, a gift of 200 crowns for the journey and a monthly stipend of 10 crowns, while the viceroy received orders to provide a salaried position in which Castillo could use his 'talents' (BCR Ms 2174/225, Philip II to viceroy of Naples, 24 Jan. 1583, copy). All that, of course, does not necessarily mean that he was innocent; only that the charge could not be proved.

52. AGRB *MD* 5479/182, Granvelle to Idiáquez and reply, 8 Aug. 1584 (with an imperfect transcript in *CCG*, XI, 78–9). The culprit was Zayas.

53. OÖLA *KB* 4/152, Khevenhüller to Rudolf II, 26 Apr. 1586, minute (for Medina Sidonia's indiscretion); Vargas Hidalgo, 'Documentos inéditos', 414, 423 and 424. For examples of an ambassador purchasing information, see Edelmayer, 'Honor y dinero', 112–13.

54. Fourquevaux, I, 120, 183 and II, 388–9, letters to Charles IX, 3 Sept. 1566, 23 Feb. 1567 and 12 Nov. 1571; ASMa *AG* 623, unfol., Sixtus V to Philip II, 7 Aug. 1585, copy; *CSPV*, 186–7, Gradinegro to Venice, 4 Aug. 1586 (actually Gradinegro had heard some months before, from the nuncio, about Parma's involvement: see ibid., 159–60, letter of 1 May 1586).

55. See Buongiovanni's letters in ASV *NS* 36/404–69. For Parma's indiscretion, see p. 212 above; for Mendoza's, see p. 227; for Allen's, see BL *Harl.* 286/124, Cobham to Walsingham, 24 Mar. 1588 (details from an intercepted letter); for Medina Sidonia's, see (for example) AGS *CS* 2a/286/166

(patent to Captain John Gordon – sic! – of the galleon *San Felipe*, 6 Apr. 1588, stating that the Armada 'will put to sea in search of the fleet of the queen of England') .

56. On the ambassador's career see Khevenhüller-Metsch and Probst-Ohstorff, *Hans Khevenhüller*; and Edelmayer, 'Habsburgische Gesandte'. Thanks in part to his fluency in Spanish, Khevenhüller had already been sent to Madrid on special missions in 1560, 1566, 1568–69 and 1571–72. The ambassador of Ferrara, by contrast, was reduced to purchasing a 'vocabulario spagnuolo' in January 1588, after seven months in Madrid (the quality of his reports thereafter improved notably): ASMo *CD* 16, unfol., 'In questo libro si scriverano le spese strordinarie'.

57. María sometimes accompanied the king to his country houses (for example they went together to Aranjuez in spring 1587: BAV *UL* 1115/142, 147, 'Avvisi' of 30 May and 27 June 1587) and at other times she might spend an afternoon with him while he worked: see, for example, IVdeDJ 55/XI/155, Vázquez to Philip II and reply, 8 Nov. 1586; and Sánchez, 'Empress María'.

58. HHStA *Statenabteilung Spanien, Diplomatische Korrespondenz* 11, Konvolut 7/398, Khevenhüller to Rudolf II, 14 Sept. 1588. The size of the Mantuan embassy is given in ASMa *AG* 601, unfol., Aqui to Mantua, 7 Jan. 1588, noting proudly that this was somewhat larger than the other diplomatic establishments in Madrid.

59. Times from Edelmayer, 'Habsburgische Gesandte', 68, and Stone, *An Elizabethan*, 121.

60. See Mousset, *Un Résident de France*, 23–5. Longlée was only a 'resident' because the French court disapproved of Philip II's annexation of Portugal. Walsingham's 'Plot for intelligence' (see p. 217 above) also envisaged using the information relayed from Spain by Longlée, but clearly Mr Secretary did

not know the poor value of the product he wanted to buy.

61. Longlée, 233, letter to Henry III, 6 Mar. 1586. In 1584–85 Longlée had also failed to find out in advance Philip II's plan to marry his daughter to the duke of Savoy, Henry III's nephew and neighbour, and was smartly rebuked: see Mousset, *Un Résident de France*, 23.

62. ASV NS 19/80–1 and 124, Novara to Rusticucci, 4 Jan. and 6 Mar. 1587, decipherments.

63. Longlée, 342, letter to Henry III of 10 Jan. 1588. And beyond his powers it remained, for even one month later Longlée still 'had only conjectures to report' on the matter: see his letter of 6 Feb. 1588 (ibid., 344).

64. See, for example, *BMO*, III, 1963, 'Avisos de Londres' by Antonio de Vega (one of Mendoza's best agents in England), 15 Feb. 1588, with details of a letter written by Santa Cruz the previous October, sent by Longlée to Paris, and forwarded to the French ambassador in London, who unwisely showed it to Vega. Vega persuaded the ambassador that it was false and should not be shown to anyone else . . .

65. For a full discussion see Leimon and Parker, 'Treason and plot'.

66. AGS *Estado K* 1567/53, Mendoza to Philip II, 5 Apr. 1588, enclosing two lists (fos 62a and b). It is possible that by this time at least some of Elizabeth's ministers had realized that Stafford had become a traitor and were turning the fact to their advantage by sending him false information that they wanted to pass on (for example, relating to the superior power of the Royal Navy) surrounded by a bodyguard of truth that was either trivial or outdated: see Leimon and Parker, 'Treason and plot', 1150–1.

67. See, for example, the well-informed dispatches of the Florentine ambassadors in Paris: Canestrini and Desjardins, *Négociations diplomatiques* 679–817. Other English agents in the French capital also managed to find

out a great deal: see the anonymous report dated 20 Oct. 1587 sent from Paris to Lord Burghley, printed in *HMC Salisbury*, III, 288–90, bulging with accurate news of Spanish military preparations in Flanders, Burgundy and Lisbon.

68. All quotations from Leimon and Parker, 'Treason and plot', 1153–4 (all dates 'new style'); details on Stafford's payments from Philip at p. 1156.

69. De Bueil, *Le Jouvencal* (written in 1466), II, 34–5 (I thank Clifford Rogers for this reference); and the conflicting figures available for Elizabeth's espionage budget in Haynes, *Invisible power*, 48. On the other hand £11,000 was not negligible – it would have sufficed to build four new battleships each year: see p. 260 above.

70. See the excellent remarks of Stone, *An Elizabethan*, 234–8; Read, *Walsingham*, II, 415–33; and Morán Torres, 'Los espías'. Even Standen, a Catholic, had been a servant of Mary Stuart for twenty years and in the 1580s was certainly a double-agent, receiving pensions from both Spain and England: see Hammer, 'An Elizabethan spy', 280–4.

71. Of course the reverse was also true. The king knew a good deal about some English Catholics (or their parents) from his time as king of England (see *BMO*, II, 305–7, Mendoza to Philip II, 13 Aug. 1586, with copious royal annotations; and ibid., 338, Philip II to Mendoza, 5 Sept. 1586, draft). He was also able to emend 'avisos' received from England in which the place-names had been incorrectly deciphered because he knew what they should be. Parma, Olivares and several other royal ministers and advisers also possessed first-hand recollections from the 1550s of the geography of at least south-east England, and Mendoza had resided there (and built up a first-class espionage network) between 1577 and 1584.

72. Wohlstetter, *Pearl Harbor*, 382–4.

73. Ibid., 387–93 and 397. The same

'intractability' has been observed in other examples of strategic surprise: Germany's attack on the Soviet Union in 1941, Egypt and Syria's on Israel in 1973, Iraq's on Kuwait in 1990. I am very grateful to Barry Watts for bringing these parallels to my attention.

74. For example Sir Anthony Standen, who was extremely well informed about every aspect of the Armada preparations, nevertheless told the English government in June 1587 that 'the most and soundest opinion ys that this voyage ys about the fortification of La Raccia [Larache] in Barberia, although they gyve owte for England' (BL *Harl.* 295/183, 'Pompeo Pellegrini' to Walsingham, 5 June 1587). However, at least one Armada prisoner in Aug. 1588 claimed that he too had been told the Armada's destination would be Larache; only when they got to sea was the real plan revealed: PRO *SP* 12/214/55, Alonso de la Sarna's answer to question 2.

75. On the 'predictability' of a landing in Kent, and the ease with which a fleet of even small ships might effect it, see Malfatti, *Cuatro documentos*, 12, 'Descrittione de porti . . . d'Inghilterra', 6 July 1588. See also the illuminating pages on 'The conscious use of paradox in war' in Luttwak, *Strategy*, 7–17.

76. KML *Queen Elizabeth's Instruction to Admiral Howard*, 20 Dec. 1587 OS. No copy of this remarkable document seems to exist among the State Papers in London.

77. See the perceptive remarks on this point by Rodríguez-Salgado, *Armada 1588–1988*, 24–30; and van der Essen, *Alexandre Farnèse*, chaps 4–5. Sometimes, it is true, Elizabeth's advisers came very close to the truth – see, for example, BL *Cott. Vesp.* CVIII/12, Burghley's holograph minute of a policy meeting on 25 Feb. 1588 OS, which predicted a simultaneous invasion by two Spanish fleets, one to Ireland and the other to the Channel to link up with Parma – but Philip's subsequent changes of plan seemed to cast doubt on each guess.

78. Figures taken from the convenient summary in Wernham, *After the Armada*, 14–15.

79. Hunt *HA* 30,881/85, Walsingham to Lord Huntingdon, 19 June 1588 OS. The published calendars of Elizabeth's State Papers Foreign, which cover a whole year and sometimes more per volume for the earlier 1580s, required five volumes for the thirty months June 1586–Dec. 1588.

80. Sir John Norris, in charge of defence in southern England, strongly advocated concentrating the main army inland (see, for example, BL *Addl.* 69,907A, 'The advise and answere of Sir John Norreys' on the defence of Dorset, 20–24 Apr. 1588 OS), but Sir Thomas Scott, in charge of Kent's defences, favoured fighting on the beaches (see PRO *SP* 12/212/40, Scott to Burghley, 23 July 1588 OS).

81. Barber, 'England: monarchs, ministers and maps', 88 n. 35; O'Neil, *Castles and cannon*, 65–79; and idem, 'The fortification of Weybourne Hope'. Several Spaniards noted with enthusiasm the lack of 'modern' fortifications in England: see, for example, the 'Discorsi' advocating conquest in BAV *UL* 854/244v–5, 269 and 857/259v–61; and *BMO*, II, 208, 'Discurso' of Bernardino de Escalante, June 1586.

82. Hunt *HA* 30,881/76, Huntingdon to Burghley and Walsingham, 15 May 1588 OS and 85v–6, to Walsingham, 20 June 1588 OS; Flower-Smith, '"The able and the willynge"', 56. For sample documents on England's mobilization in 1588, see Noble, *Huntingdonshire*, and Historical Manuscripts Commission, *Fifteenth report*, appendix, part V, 34–58 (the Foljambe 'Book of musters').

83. Whitehead, *Brags and boasts*, 73, 77–90 and 102–3. See also Valentine Dale's report on Parma's indiscretion on 18 July: p. 212 above. The Dutch were, if anything, even less prepared: on 10 Aug. the States-General, meet-

ing at the Hague, received a report that the Spanish fleet had been off Gravelines two days before 'with the intention of invading either the kingdom of England or these provinces' and decided that it should mobilize its resources. It seems rather late to have thought of this: *RSG*, VI, 206, resolution of 10 Aug. 1588.

84. Hunt *HA* 30,881/83v–4, Elizabeth to Huntingdon, 16 June 1588 OS; Scott Thomson, 'The Twysden lieutenancy papers', 70–1, Privy Council to Lord Cobham, 18 July 1588 OS.

85. PRO *SP* 77/4/271–3, Elizabeth to her peace commissioners at Bourbourg, 17 July 1588 OS; *HMC Rutland*, I, 253, Robert Cecil to Lord Manners, 25 July 1588 OS; Historical Manuscripts Commission, *Fifteenth report*, appendix, part V, 48; and McGurk, 'Armada preparations in Kent'.

86. Christy, 'Queen Elizabeth's visit to Tilbury', 45–6. For a more positive view of England's defensive preparations see Nolan, 'The muster of 1588'.

87. Gould, 'The crisis of the export trade'; Laughton, I, 284–5, Burghley to Walsingham, 19 July 1588 OS, holograph.

88. See the perceptive remarks on this point by Handel, 'Technological surprise in war'; and idem, 'Intelligence and the problem of strategic surprise'.

89. Molyneux, *Conjunct expeditions*, part II, 24–5 (discussing Santa Cruz's Tercera campaign).

90. Canestrini and Desjardins, *Négociations diplomatiques*, IV, 814–15, Cavriana to Florence, 23 Aug. 1588.

8 Was Parma Ready?

1. The idea for this chapter originated in a conversation many years ago with María José Rodríguez-Salgado. My thanks for valuable advice and assistance go to her, and also to Gustav Asaert, Roland Baetens, Jaap Bruijn, Ben Cox, J. I. González-Aller Hierro,

Joost Schokkenbroek and Rob Stradling.

2. Vázquez, *Sucesos*, II, 352. No date is given for this episode, nor is it recorded in any other contemporary account; however, Vázquez (at the time a sergeant in the tercio of Sicily aboard the Armada who was captured by the Dutch, ransomed and brought to the Army of Flanders later in the year) added immediately after this anecdote: 'I have written faithfully what I saw and what I could find out'. See Vázquez's service record (to 1595) in AGS *CS* 2a/275 (under 'A' for Alonso).

3. Belda y Pérez de Nueros, *Felipe II*, 64–6, Bobadilla to Don Juan de Idiáquez, 20 Aug. 1588. (This important document, formerly in the Cabra archive, is now at AGS *Estado* 455/602–3.)

4. *Breeder verclaringhe*, 9. This revealing pamphlet, consisting of Pimentel's interrogation by his Dutch captors, was reprinted verbatim in Bor, *Geschiedenis*, III part 2, book 25, fos 11–12. Abbreviated translations into English, Spanish and French were made (see copies in PRO *SP* 84/26/5–12; and, in an even more abridged English version, in Laughton, II, 75–6). See also the complaints about Parma by Armada prisoners interrogated at Dover and Flushing (Laughton, I, 342–3, and II, 32); and by Fray Bernardo de Góngora, aboard the flagship (Harvard University, Houghton Library, fMs *Span.* 54, letter to Fray Martín de los Angeles, 15 Aug. 1588).

5. AGS *Estado K* 1568/113, Mendoza to Philip II, 24 Sept. 1588; *Estado* 1261/115, Don Jusepe de Acuña to Philip II, 6 Sept. 1588; Malfatti, *Cuatro documentos*, 43, Giulio Savorgnano to Filippo Pigafetta, 23 Sept. 1588; and ASF *MP* 4919/484v, Alemanni to Florence, 4 Oct. 1588 (a letter full of detail on the criticisms of Parma circulating at the Court of Spain). For yet more outspoken criticisms, see AGS *Estado* 1263/117, Acuña to Philip II, 13 Sept. 1588.

6. Fea, *Alessandro Farnese*, 308–10: Parma to Cardinal Farnese (undated but presumably 12 Aug. 1588).

7. AGS *Estado* 950/227, the count of Olivares to Philip II, 29 Oct. 1588, and 950/229, to Parma, 15 Oct. 1588, copy. The background to Cesi's mission is given in *Estado* 594/163, Parma to Idiáquez, 30 Dec. 1588, and his career in 594/110, Parma to Philip II, 7 Aug. 1588 (the count had served with Parma at Lepanto and then in the Army of Flanders under Requeséns, Don John and Parma).

8. AGS *Estado* 594/124, Parma to Philip II, 8 Aug. 1588; AGS *Estado* 2219/82, Idiáquez to Parma, 31 Aug. 1588.

9. ASV *NS* 34/492, Novara to Montalto, 6 Sept. 1588 (see also fos 510 and 551, 26 Sept. and 13 Oct. 1588); AGS *Estado* 2219/101–2, Idiáquez to Parma, 9 Nov. 1588, minute, heavily emended. A copy, probably sent by Parma to Cardinal Farnese, is at ASP *CF* 129, folder 3, unfol.

10. AGS *Estado* 594/163, Parma to Idiáquez, 30 Dec. 1588. This was precisely what Parma had claimed at the time: see *Estado* 594/125, Parma to Philip II, 10 Aug. 1588. Meanwhile, the government also started investigating those in Spain who might have been responsible for the Armada's failure – see *Estado* 165/210 ('Para verificar lo cierto de la victualla desta Armada') and fos 255–6, Don Juan de Cardona to Philip II, 20 Nov. 1588. Eventually the king condemned Diego Flores de Valdés, Medina Sidonia's principal naval adviser, to prison: AGS *GA* 228/131, Licenciado Santillán to Philip II, 23 Dec. 1588.

11. ASP *CF* 109 folder 3, unfol., 'Memoria de los papeles que entrego oy 5 de junio 1589 al Señor Presidente Richardot'; AGS *Estado* 2855, unfol., 'Lo que Su Magestad es servido que se responda a los cuatro papeles principales que dio el Presidente Richardot' (Nov. 1589), second point. Ironically, at precisely this moment other servants of the crown began to question Parma's commitment to

executing Philip II's policies in another area: France (see AGS *Estado* 597/128, Juan Moreo to Philip II, 18 Nov. 1589, with interesting royal apostils).

12. In 1593 Philip II's agents in Brussels received fourteen bundles of the duke's official papers (AGS *Estado* 604/55, 'Relación de los despachos y papeles que Cosme Masi entrega'), followed in 1595 by two more boxes (*Estado* 1277/46–7, Esteban de Ibarra to Domingo de Orbea, 14 Apr. 1595, and Orbea to Philip II, 12 July 1595). None of these documents now seem to be in the Brussels archives, however. The four 'principal papers' and most of the supporting material sent to Philip II by Parma in 1589 (pp. 273–4 above) have not been found at Simancas. The duke's correspondence has also suffered significant loss (see p. 399 below).

13. Thus Don Jorge Manrique received a substantial reward from Parma shortly after writing a favourable report on Parma's conduct: AGRB *SEG* 11/26 (order to pay 2,000 escudos in cash to Manrique, 30 Aug. 1588). See also the exceedingly friendly letters of Don Jorge to both Parma and his secretary Cosme Masi, dated 26–27 July 1589, in ASP *CF* 129, folder '1589', unfol. Other well-placed Armada refugees who might report directly to the king received similarly generous payments when they left Flanders: see AGRB *SEG* 11 fos 8v (Proveedor Pedrosa), 25 (Secretary Arceo), and 26 (Captain Heredía).

14. AGS *Estado* 591/33, Moreo to Don Juan de Idiáquez, 26 Oct. 1586 (Philip II wrote '¡Ojo!' [attention!] beside this passage); *Estado* 593/11, Tassis to Idiáquez, 19 Jan. 1587 (almost all of fos 1–45 in this legajo concern Tassis's bitter clashes with Parma and other senior military administrators); and the criticisms of the Armada campaign in Tassis's *Commentarii*, 489–93. For details on Parma's fall in 1591–92, see van der Essen, *Alexandre Farnèse*, V, *passim*; on

15. the judicial review, see Lefèvre, 'Le Tribunal de la Visite'.

16. After the campaign, the Dutch learned from its prisoners that the Armada 'has no boats suitable for disembarking [troops] except for those it awaits from [Parma]': PRO *SP* 84/26/ 48–9, States of Zealand to Elizabeth, 16 Aug. 1588. On the siege-train, see Martin and Parker, *Spanish Armada*, 41–2.

16. FD, II, 5–13, Philip's Instructions of 1 Apr. 1588, minute; KML *MSP: CR* 5/129, Don Juan de Idiáquez to Medina Sidonia, 28 Mar. 1588.

17. AGS *Estado* 455/320–1, Medina to Parma, 10 June 1588, copy sent to (and annotated by) Philip II (see also KML *MSP: CR* 5/264–7, minute of the same letter); Herrera Oria, 202–3, Philip II to Medina, 21 June 1588, minute; KML *MSP: CR* 5/278–9 (original) and 289 (Philip's further message of 26 June); FD, II, 221–2, Medina Sidonia to Philip II, 30 July 1588. Needless to say, Parma also reacted strongly when he received Medina's letter of 10 June, but his protest did not reach the king until 7 Aug.

18. FD, II, 221–2, Medina Sidonia to Philip II, 30 July 1588, written off the Lizard. This letter accompanied a longer missive completed earlier that same day (ibid., 217–21), which was itself an updated version of one written and sent on 29 July (Herrera Oria, 252–5): clearly Medina had begun to entertain serious doubts about the viability of the strategy he had been told to carry out. The interrogation of Don Pedro de Valdés indicates that at least some fleet commanders realized that Parma could not fight his way out: the duke, Don Pedro told his captors, had 36,000 men, but only 'some small ships just to carry them across' (PRO *SP* 12/214/65, answer to question 19).

19. AGS *Estado* 594/115, Medina Sidonia to Parma, 31 July/1 Aug. 1588, copy. ASP *CF* 129, folder 1, unfol., Bobadilla to Parma, 1 Aug. 1588

(adding tantalizingly that he dared not explain his reasons in writing, but his messenger would provide details); AGS *Estado* 594/116–17, Medina Sidonia to Parma, 4 and 5 Aug. 1588, copies.

20. Herrera Oria, 241, 'Relación del viaje'. This document, although organized as a day-by-day narrative, was clearly revised before being sent to Philip II on 12 Aug. 1588. In his first letter to Parma from before Calais on 6 Aug., Medina claimed only that 'the weather [*el tiempo*]' had forced him to drop anchor: AGS *Estado* 594/118. Much controversy surrounds the point at which Medina Sidonia decided to depart from the king's instructions to sail to 'Cape Margate' and await Parma: see most recently Adams, 'The battle that never was'. Adams's conclusion – that Medina took the decision at the last moment, as a direct result of the close proximity of the entire English fleet and the absence of communication between the two dukes – is confirmed by the papers of Juan Martínez de Recalde who, in notes sent to Medina Sidonia on 29 July and again on 1 Aug., still wrote of 'las Dunas' (the Downs) as the fleet's destination (AHN *OM* 3511/41).

21. AGS *Estado* 594/120, Medina Sidonia to Parma, 6 Aug. 1588, copy (his second letter of the day). As pointed out by Adams, 'The battle that never was', 187, the duke can only have meant a port in England.

22. AGS *Estado* 594/113, Parma to Philip II, 7 Aug. 1588, enclosing copies of Medina's letters between 25 July and 6 Aug.; Malfatti, *Cuatro documentos*, 34–8, Parma to Giuseppe de Cernosa, 10 Aug. 1588; and *CSPV*, VIII, 382–3, Parma's similar letter to a Venetian correspondent, dated 12 Aug. 1588. This chronology is confirmed by other sources: the English delegates at Bourbourg and the Dutch in Zeeland only heard about the Channel battles on 5 Aug. (BL *Sloane* 262/62; *Notulen van de Staten van Zeeland 1588*, 144); the news only arrived at Antwerp one

day later (PRO *PRO* 31/10/3, newsletter dated 6 Aug. 1588); and Don Rodrigo Tello de Guzmán, who had carried Medina Sidonia's letter of 25 July, by his own confession took seven days to reach Parma (AGS *SP* 1795, unfol., consulta of the council of Italy on applicants for the post of castellan of Pavia, 27 Sept. 1589: credentials of Tello).

23. On 14 July Parma sent Moresin back to find out what had happened to the Armada and to provide Medina with information on his own state of readiness. However, a bizarre combination of shipwreck, storms and an encounter with the English fleet delayed the messenger in a French port until after the Armada had sailed by: he only reached Spain on 2 Aug. AGS *Estado* 594/107, Parma to Philip II, 21 July 1588; *Estado* 165/271, 'Lo que refiere Don Rodrigo de Avilés'.

24. AGRB *CC* 26,136 Compte de Michel Fourlaux, fos 88–91, records departures up to 30 July; PRO *SP* 101/9/ 85, 'Advertisement' sent to Burghley in Sept. 1588, reported subsequent departures.

25. AGS *Estado* 594/122, Medina Sidonia to Parma, 7 Aug. 1588, copy, acknowledging the arrival of his letter dated 3 Aug. (see also Herrera Oria, 241, 'Relación del viaje'). Five of the six letters written by Parma to Medina during the Armada campaign have apparently disappeared and only one – which never reached its destination – has been preserved: ASP *CF* 129, Parma to Medina Sidonia, 15 Aug. 1588. My deductions concerning the lost letter of 3 Aug. rest upon the following considerations: (a) Parma received Medina Sidonia's letter of 25 July on the 2nd, the previous day; (b) at that time this was the only recent letter he had received from Medina; and (c) Don Rodrigo Tello, the bearer of Medina's letter of 25 July, also carried Parma's reply.

26. BRB Ms II.1155/216–216v, 'Liber relationum' of Paolo Rinaldi. This manuscript account contains a number of errors, probably because the author composed it much later: see van der Essen, 'De auteur en de beteekenis'. However, Rinaldi certainly witnessed the events he described at first hand: see his signature on numerous purchase orders for Parma's household throughout 1588 in ASN *CF* 1804.I, 'Fiandra: giustificazzione di spese'. Parma himself sent copies of all Medina's letters to the king, with annotations and clarifications (for example reminding Philip yet again that Medina's suggestion that the Flanders flotilla should put to sea before the defeat of the English fleet was 'impossible'): AGS *Estado* 594/113–21, Parma to Philip II, 7 Aug. 1588, followed by copies of Medina's letters from 25 July to 6 Aug.

27. AGS *Estado* 594/113, Parma to Philip II, 7 Aug. 1588, received at Court on the 25th, listed the arrival times of each of Medina's messengers. A little later the imperial ambassador reported complaints at Court that Parma had not 'acted earnestly enough in the matter and in the embarkation of his troops after the duke of Medina's arrival', but (shrewd as always) added, 'I believe this happened because he [Parma] could himself have known nothing of the Armada'. HHStA *Statenabteilung Spanien, Diplomatische Korrespondenz* 11, Konvolut 7/398v, Khevenhüller to Rudolf II, 14 Sept. 1588. According to the Florentine envoy two weeks later, Medina Sidonia blamed Don Rodrigo Tello for taking too long to tell Parma of the Armada's approach; but, the diplomat perceptively speculated, it seemed more likely that the messenger had been sent too late (ASF *MP* 4919/477, Battaglino to Florence, 27 Sept. 1588).

28. These figures, from O'Donnell, *La fuerza de desembarco*, 402, are clearly more reliable than any others available in print. A staff officer with Parma at Bruges confirmed that all units were indeed ready by late June: ASMa *AG*

574, unfol., Hercole Gonzaga to Mantua, 8 July 1588.

29. The billets of the Spanish units designated for the invasion are shown in O'Donnell, *La fuerza de desembarco*, 87. An eyewitness, Coloma, *Las guerras*, 16, noted the two 'rehearsals'.

30. AGS *Estado* 594/113, Parma to Philip II, 8 Aug. 1588, and 594/163, Parma to Idiáquez, 30 Dec. 1588, with full details. By way of comparison, in 1779 experts predicted that it would take between five and six days to embark the 24,000 men and their equipment assembled in Le Havre and St Malo for the invasion of England: see Patterson, *The other Armada*, 166.

31. Details in Parker, *The Army of Flanders*, 278; and O'Donnell, *La fuerza de desembarco*, chaps 2–3.

32. AGRB *Audience* 189/153–7, Parma to Philip II, 3 Feb. 1588, minute ('ilz sont diminuez d'ung ters pour le moings de ce qu'ilz estoient auparavant, oultre ung million de malades'); *BMO*, III, 1398, same to same, 14 Nov. 1587. Losses recorded in Parker, *Spain and the Netherlands*, 138.

33. For the high food prices see AGRB *Audience* 189/105, Parma to Philip II, 26 Apr. 1587 ('estant le bled quasi trois fois plus cher qu'il n'a oncques esté de mémoire d'homme'). For a pessimistic source on the Armada's state of readiness, see the letters of Contador Alonso Carnero, in Madrid, to Parma: 17 Oct. 1587 (ASP *CF* 129, folder 2), and 5 Mar. and 2 Apr. 1588 (ibid., folder 3).

34. BL *Sloane* 262/81v–2, from 'An ephemeris or diarie' of the English delegation sent to negotiate with Parma in 1588 (almost certainly written by Valentine Dale). For some statistics on the devastation of Flanders in the 1580s, see Parker, *Spain and the Netherlands*, 180–4.

35. ASN *CF* 2125/I, 'Registro di contabilità, 1588' (both the nuns and the Jesuits lent at 7 per cent interest, just like the secular creditors). See also Parma's anguished correspondence with three Antwerp bankers on 17, 18 and 23 Aug. 1588, begging for money to keep his army together: ASN *CF* 1722/II, unfol., letters to and from Colimo de Mazini, Nicolo Sinori and Bernardo Bonvisi.

36. Vázquez, *Sucesos*, II, 347; Piot, *Chroniques*, 672 (from an anonymous 'Vlaemsche Kronyk' composed in Dunkirk).

37. The author of the 'Vlaemsche Kronyk', who was present, offers the best account: Piot, *Chroniques*, 672–3. See also Malo, *Les Corsaires*, 191. The triumphant report of the incident by David Cabreth to Walsingham, printed in Rodríguez-Salgado, *Armada 1588–1988*, 121, appears to be totally false. BL *Harl.* 287/86, 'Advertisements' by Lord Cobham to Walsingham, and *Addl* 35,841/156, 'An ephemeris or diarie', both record that the three Dutch bombers escaped to Ostend, where the English garrison spirited them away to safety.

38. Brugmans, *Correspondentie*, III, 284–6, Leicester to Burghley, 5 Nov. 1587 OS.

39. BL *Harl.* 287/86, 'Advertisements' of Mar./Apr. 1588; PRO *SP* 101/9/80 '1588 occurents' (undated but probably June); van Meteren, *Historie*, 178–9.

40. ASN *CF* 1722/II, unfol., Don Luis de Queralt to Parma, 17 July 1588, holograph. Queralt and his men, many of them former bandits from Catalonia pardoned in return for enlistment, had arrived in the Netherlands the previous December.

41. Laughton, I, 213, Winter to Walsingham, 20 June 1588 OS. Winter based his estimate on his recollections of the English expedition to Scotland in 1544, which had involved 260 vessels. Note that Winter used 'tons burthen': tons displacement would be approximately 50 per cent higher (see p. 383 n. 9 below).

42. *BMO*, II, 110, Parma to Philip II, 20 Apr. 1586; II, 195, 'Lo que dixo Juan Bautista Piata'; and III, 1399, Parma to Philip II, 14 Nov. 1587. Juan

Bautista de Tassis, who had served in the Army of Flanders for fifteen years, also considered the idea of using barges at sea 'wholly stupid': Tassis, *Commentarii*, 492. The contrast between Parma's meticulous planning for the movement of troops by land and his cursory attention to their transport by sea was noted by Riaño Lozano, *Los medios navales*, 105–7.

43. ASN *CF* 1690, unfol., 'Relación de los baxeles que se hallan oy lunes 2 de noviembre en este puerto de Dunckerque' (recording only nine boats of 150–200 tons' burthen). Contrast Parma's optimistic reports to the king on his fleet on 18 Sept. and 14 Nov. 1587: *BMO*, III, 1084 and 1399. See also Riaño Lozano, *Los medios navales*, 239.

44. PRO *SP* 77/4/69, 'A note of the ships of war and vitallers and municions' at Dunkirk, 13 June 1588 OS (another copy at fo. 81). This document also recorded twelve culverins and twelve sakers lying upon the quay, 'besides two hepe of shot pertayning to them, in estimacion about 2000 and upwards', but added that 'these ordinance are for land and not for the ships'. Interestingly, Parma intercepted this piece of espionage: see the Dutch summary in AGRB *Audience* 587bis, unfol., last item. Falcons, falconets and fowlers were all anti-personnel weapons incapable of inflicting serious damage on other ships. Compare the ship weights in ASN *CF* 1690, unfol., 'Relación de baxeles'. See also ibid., Cristóbal de Aguirre to Cosme Masi, 14 Apr. 1588, recording the arrival of two 'vlitbotes' from Hamburg, each of 160 tons, one with 15 guns and the other with 12. All tonnages here are 'tons burthen' and not 'tons displacement'.

45. See the fragmented accounts of the paymaster of the Flanders fleet, Thorivio Martinez, for 1587–88 in AGS *CMC* 2a/8, 12, 16, 885, 1077 and 3a/692 and 713. Many extracts are quoted (not always accurately) in

Riaño Lozano, *Los medios navales*, 168–78. See also the more detailed account of the man responsible for feeding the crews: AGRB *CC* 26,136, 'Compte de Michel Fourlaux', fos 54–60. An ingenious but abortive plan to hijack thirty Scottish merchantmen and their six armed escorts as they sailed from Danzig to Aberdeen in spring 1587 is recorded in Martin and Parker, *Spanish Armada*, 152. AGS *CJH* 219 carpeta 15, documents the attempt by Alonso Gutiérrez to send six confiscated Dutch hulks from Seville to Dunkirk in 1587: only one got through.

46. BAV *UL* 1056/304, 'Aviso' from Antwerp, 18 June 1588; *CSPF* XXI.4, 511, 'Advertisements' of 22 June 1588 OS; PRO *SP* 77/4/114 and 116, 'A report of the preparations at Dunkirk by one who came from thence' (17 June 1588 OS). According to the last account Dunkirk harbour by then contained 37 'men of war' and 60 transports with victuals, with a further 27 ships almost ready and 'very well appointed'. Yet another English report, filed eleven days later, counted 22 warships but added that some 30 of the other vessels were 'all unrigged and broken, not servisable withoute newe buildinge' (ibid., fo. 169, 'A trewe note or viewe of all the shipps servisable in Dunkirke', 28 June 1588 OS; second copy in BL *Cott. Vesp.* CVIII/75).

47. *Notulen van de Staten van Zeeland 1588*, 117–18 and 119–21, letters to Count Maurice of Nassau and Queen Elizabeth, 13 July 1588.

48. AGS *Estado* 594/122, Medina Sidonia to Parma, 7 Aug. 1588, notes the receipt of Parma's now lost letter of the 3rd – that is, written before news of the Armada's arrival reached Flanders.

49. Herrera Oria, 262–3, Don Juan Manrique de Lara to Don Juan de Idiáquez, 'agosto un día después de San Lorenzo' [=11 Aug. 1588]. He did not blame Parma personally, asserting that things remained unprepared 'not through the duke of

Parma's failure to work and plead for them, because it would be hard to find in the world a man who would work half as hard as he did, but on account of the sailors and those to whom these duties had been delegated'. Manrique could draw on thirty-five years' experience of military service in Germany, the Mediterranean and the Netherlands: see details in AGRB *SEG* 11/126, order of 30 Apr. 1587.

50. Herrera Oria, 241–2, Medina Sidonia's 'Diario', twice states that Parma was not ready, and quotes the estimate of his secretary, Hierónimo de Arceo, that 'it seemed impossible that everything could be done in less than fifteen days' (Herrera Oria, 242). The same statement appeared in Recalde's journal (AHN *OM* 3512/34); in AGS *Estado K* 1567/102, 'Aviso' from Rouen, 11 Aug. 1588; and in Vázquez, *Sucesos*, II, 348–9. According to the Florentine ambassador in Spain, Don Balthasar de Zúñiga (Medina Sidonia's special envoy) reported, when he eventually returned to Spain, that Parma would have required ten days more to put his forces in readiness (ASF *MP* 4919/477, Battaglino to Florence, 27 Sept. 1588). Another Florentine ambassador (ibid., fo. 484, Alemanni to Florence, 4 Oct. 1588) claimed that the 'Relation' sent by Inspector-General Don Jorge Manrique severely criticized Parma, while the chronicle of Fray Juan de Vitoria reported a heated exchange between Parma and Manrique concerning the readiness of the fleet (Tellechea Idígoras, *Otra cara*, 177). However, Manrique's actual 'Relation', printed by Herrera Oria, 255–8, contains no criticism of the duke; and Vitoria, who was not an eyewitness, composed his vitriolic account from reports received in Spain (see Tellechea's masterly critique in *Otra cara*, 133–47).

51. Vázquez, *Sucesos*, II, 347–9. As stated in note 2 above, Vázquez was not at this stage an eyewitness: he was aboard the Armada.

52. Coloma, *Las guerras*, 17–18.

53. Vázquez, *Sucesos*, II, 348; Carnero, *Historia*, 230.

54. AGS *CMC* 2a/885, Account of Thorivio Martínez, pliego 145, 400 florins paid to Artus Estamelart; and 2a/1077, 2,400 florins paid to Hans Smit for painting almost 200 flags (note, however, that these payments concerned the ships at Antwerp: on the significance of this, see p. 241 above); PRO *SP* 101/9/85, 'Advertisements' sent to Burghley in Sept. 1588; ASN *CF* 1804/I/64, payment to Giovanni Batista Cagnola, 1 May 1588.

55. Herrera Oria, 265–6, Don Jorge Manrique to Philip II, 12 Aug. 1588. However, note the reservations about Manrique's testimony raised in notes 13 and 50 above.

56. The ships defending Antwerp during the siege are described in Asaert, 'Een brug te veel'. They included a ship of 500 tons' burthen (p. 130), probably the same as the later *Sant Alessandro*. Details on the ships built in 1587–88, from the accounts of Thorivio Martinez, are given in Riaño Lozano, *Los medios navales*, 185–8, 293–4 and 313–18. The weight and armament of the principal Antwerp ships are given in *CSPF*, XXI.4, 14–15 and 208, Hercules Annys and Robert Cecil to Burghley, 22 Jan. and 29 Mar. 1588 NS. Strangely, Paymaster Martínez (AGS *CMC* 3a/692) recorded only seventeen warships in the Scheldt in 1588; no doubt another source paid for the rest.

57. On his reconnaissance of the coast, see AGS *Estado* 592/149, Parma to Philip II, 21 Dec. 1587. An English spy acquired details of Parma's plan the following month: *CSPF* XXI.4, 14, 'Advertisements from Hercules Annys'. AGS *CMC* 2a/11, account of Juan de Lastur, unfol., payments to Cristóbal Roncoli and the bailiff of the Land van Waes for canal work: 10,000 crowns in all.

58. *Notulen van de Staten van Zeeland 1588*, 14–15 and 16–17, letters to Count

Maurice and Pieter Willemsen, 17 and 22 Jan. 1588.

59. AGS *CMC* 2a/11, Account of Juan de Lastur, 7,000 crowns paid to Roncoli for the opening of waterways between Bruges and Nieuwpoort. On this engineering feat see the detailed accounts in Vázquez, *Sucesos*, II, 332–3 and 336; Carnero, *Historia*, 230; and Coloma, *Las guerras*, 14. Extracts of these and other sources are cited in Parente, *Los sucesos de Flandes*, 127; and Malo, *Les Corsaires*, 191–2. See also Faulconnier, *Description historique*, I, 95–6. The opening of the 'cutt' is described in BL *Harl.* 287/86, 'Advertisements' from Lord Cobham (Mar. 1588 OS). This may have been the new 'sluice' illustrated in Plate 31.

60. AGS *Estado* 594/113, Parma to Philip II, 7 Aug. 1588. Details on the Dunkirk and Nieuwpoort fleets in AGS *CMC* 2a/885 and 1077, 'Datta' of Thorivio Martínez; and in Riaño Lozano, *Los medios navales*, 149–53.

61. See the calculations in Riaño Lozano, *Los medios navales*, 233–4, with 'tons burthen' changed to 'tons displacement' according to Jan Glete's formula (see p. 383, n. 9 below). It should be noted that, in the seventeenth century, Spanish troopships normally reckoned to load between one and two men per ton of a ship's 'burthen': see Parker, *The Army of Flanders*, 78, n. 2.

62. See the excellent study of Cox, *Vanden tocht*, 32, 35, 146–57. (Cox gives all ship weights in 'lasts' of approximately two tons' burthen: I have converted these figures to a rough 'tons displacement'.) By contrast, in 1688 William III assembled a fleet of 463 vessels, including 53 warships, to convey his invasion army of 21,000 men to England; while in 1780 the French reckoned they would need 1,100 transports and 63 warships for their descent on England with 50,000 men and 7,000 horse (see Israel and Parker, 'Of Providence and Protestant winds', 337–8, and Patterson, *The other Armada*, 227–8).

63. Baetens, 'An essay on Dunkirk', 134. See also the details on the capacity of 'pleiten' (20–23 metres long and 5–7 wide, drawing no more than a metre of water, and capable of carrying 200 men) and 'heuden' ('somewhat smaller') given by Parma's personal emissary to the king: *BMO*, II, 195–6: 'Lo que dixo Juan Bautista Piata de palabra a 24 de junio 1586'.

64. Admittedly the main Dutch invasion fleet in 1600 did not enter the open sea; but some 200 vessels sailed to Ostend (see Cox, *Vanden tocht*, 22 and 151–2).

65. *BMO*, III, 1579–83 and 1617–19, Parma to Philip II, 21 and 29 Dec. 1587 (received on 24 Jan. 1588); *CSPSp*, IV, 261–2, and AGS *Estado* 594/79, same to same, 5 Apr. and 22 June 1588.

66. On Parma's 'deception', see Le Glay and Finot, *Inventaire sommaire... Nord*, V, 324; Bor, *Geschiedenis*, book 25 fo. 5v; and PRO *SP* 84/26/54–5, James Digges to Walsingham, 6 Aug. 1588. In addition, Parma only issued patents to his deputy and to others who would take over military commands in the Netherlands 'from those I am taking with me' at the last possible moment: see AGRB *SEG* 11/2v–3, orders issued to Mansfeld, Olivera and others, 1 Aug. 1588 (admittedly he had issued patents for his civilian deputies much earlier, on 7 May: see AGRB *Audience* 782/175–6 and 1792/1).

67. *Notulen van de Staten van Zeeland 1588*, 117–18, letter to Maurice 13 July 1588, including a report of the previous day from Cornelis Lonck – which claimed that his fleet had already frustrated two attempts by Parma to break out (were these perhaps the 'rehearsals': p. 235 above?) See also ibid., 119–21, letter to Queen Elizabeth, 14 July 1588. Squadron strengths from Schokkenbroek, '"Wherefore serveth Justinus?"', 106; and Bor, *Geschiedenis*, book 25, fos 6–7.

68. *RSG*, VI, 206, Resolution of 10 Aug. 1588. See also PRO *SP* 84/25/51–2,

Maurice to the English Privy Council, 20 July 1588, stating that twenty warships 'at least' would henceforth always be on guard off the Flemish coast.

69. Laughton, I, 331 and 341, Seymour to the council, 6 Aug., and Howard to Walsingham, 8 Aug. 1588 NS.

70. Vázquez, *Sucesos*, II, 336.

71. See Plate 32 on p. 246 above, from BNM Ms *Res* 237, 'Recueil et pourtraite d'aulcunes villes maritimes', no. 17. This fascinating volume is discussed by Schilder, 'A Dutch manuscript rutter'. A direct channel inside the sandbanks leading from Calais to Dunkirk, shown on later maps, only came into use after 1621: see Stradling, *The Armada of Flanders*, 35–6; and Messiaen, *La Connaissance des bancs de Dunkerque*.

72. *BMO*, I, 412–13, 'Descripción sumaria de los puertos de Dunquerque y Neoport' (based on information from mariners in the two ports).

73. The English sources concerning the need for a spring tide are admirably presented in Rose, 'Was the failure of the Spanish Armada due to storms?', 215 and 226. The Dutch, who knew the Flemish coast better, maintained a careful watch at all times, but did increase their vigilance just before the spring tide: see *Notulen van de Staten van Zeeland 1588*, 144 (5 Aug. 1588).

74. AGS *Estado* 594/122, Medina Sidonia to Parma, 7 Aug. 1588, with Parma's denial appended; and 594/124–5, Parma to Philip II, 8 and 10 Aug. 1588. See also *BMO*, I, 412–13, 'Descripción sumaria'. According to the municipal records, between 1585 and 1605 vessels displacing up to 300 tons did indeed enter the port of Dunkirk: see Cabantous, *Histoire de Dunkerque*, 71–2.

75. Carnero, *Historia*, 230–1.

76. Elias, *De vlootbouw in Nederland*, 3.

77. Haak, *Johan van Oldenbarnevelt*, I, 139–40, Joachim Ortel to Oldenbarnevelt, 1 July 1588 OS. The English ambassador in The Hague had requested the naval assistance prom-

ised under the treaty of Nonsuch (1585) on 1 Jan. 1588 (ARA *Staten Generaal* 11,108/1). See also *RSG*, VI, 29 and 71–3, for evidence that these vessels were the largest warships possessed by the Dutch.

78. Van Overeem, 'Justinus van Nassau'; Bor, *Geschiedenis*, book 25, fos 6–7; Brugmans, *Correspondentie*, II, 439, Thomas Wilkes's 'Discourse'; Schokkenbroek, '"Wherefore serveth Justinus"', 110.

79. See the detailed figures in Bor, *Geschiedenis*, book 25, fo. 8.

80. PRO *SP* 84/26/135, list of the fleet with Justinus of Nassau, 27 July 1588 NS. This list no doubt accompanied Justinus's letter to Walsingham of the same date: see Laughton, II, 125–6.

81. ARA *1e Afdeling: Regeringsarchief* I.196, 'Twee staten van lasts van oorloge wegen de Admiraliteit van Suijt en Noort Hollandt'. On the withdrawal of these ships from blockade duty off Dunkirk see ARA *Raad van State* 7, unfol., resolution of 9 Aug. 1588; *Notulen van de Staten van Zeeland 1588*, 145–6, letter to Count Maurice, 9 Aug. 1588; and RAZ *Register van akten en brieven*, portefeuille 1625/260v, letter to Count Maurice, 11 Aug. 1588.

82. AGRB *CC* 26,136 Compte de Michel Fourlaux, fos 88–91, records departures up to 30 July; subsequent departures were reported in PRO *SP* 101/9/85, 'Advertisement' sent to Burghley in Sept. 1588 (précis in *CSPF*, XXII, 171–2); and Piot, *Chroniques*, 682. ASV *LP* 46/240, 'Relatione d'un grumete', narrates the journey of a seaman who sailed on one of these vessels, returned to Dunkirk, and sailed thence back to Corunna and Lisbon, arriving 5 Oct. 1588. The safe arrival of two Armada vessels appears in AGS *CMC* 3a/2761 (the zabras Santa Ana and Magdalena arrived on 17 and 25 Aug. respectively).

83. Laughton, I, 314, Edward Burnham (in Flushing) to Walsingham, 25 July 1588 OS; and II, 45, Seymour to Walsingham, 6 Aug. 1588 OS (also

reporting that the storm had broken the main topmast of his vice-admiral, the *Vanguard*). See also ibid., I, 254, Seymour to Walsingham, 12 July 1588 OS, reporting that storms had repeatedly blown his ships as far south as Calais and as far west as the coast of England; and ibid., I, 333, Sir William Winter to Walsingham, 27 July 1588 OS, also mentioning the storms that drove the blockade ships off station. See also *RSG*, VI, 87–8, report compiled in Dec. 1588 concerning the Dutch contribution to the Armada's defeat, admitting that the blockade squadron had been forced back to its home ports just before the Spanish fleet arrived.

84. Laughton, I, 233, Seymour to Walsingham, 26 June 1588 OS; ibid., I, 312, Burnham to Walsingham, 25 July 1588 OS.

85. RAZ *Register van Akten en Brieven*, portefeuille 1625/256v–7, States of Zeeland to Count Maurice of Nassau, 9 Aug. 1588, passing on Justinus's report.

86. AGS *Estado* 615/99 and 179, Archduke Albert to Philip II, 20 Apr. and 27 Aug. 1598. On the significance of the failure to secure Boulogne, see pp. 193 and 363 n. 73 above.

87. Cabrera, III, 288. Cabrera claimed to have told the king this in person at the time.

88. *BMO*, I, 412–13, 'Descripción sumaria'.

89. See Loades, *The Tudor navy*, 174, for 1558. Casado Soto, *Los barcos*, 206–21, gives the 'puntal' (the height of the deck above the keel) for each ship – those of the galleons of Castile were around six metres – so the draught would have been considerably less. Perhaps this explains why Recalde and others advocated 'going on' rather than anchoring off Calais: p. 234 above.

90. This possibility may explain the otherwise perplexing decision of Admiral Howard on 8 Aug., after the fireship attack, to destroy the flag galleass as it lay beached near Calais before assaulting the rest of the Armada: it was too dangerous to leave behind, especially since Seymour's squadron had abandoned the Downs.

91. Only Dutch sources mention Parma's attempt to break the blockade: Bor, *Geschiedenis*, book 25, fo. 12v; van Reyd, *Historie*, 262; and the Resolutions of the States of Holland and Zealand and of the Admiralty (see the quotations in Schokkenbroek, 'Wherefore serveth Justinus', 109). RAZ *Register van Akten en Brieven*, portefeuille 1625/257v–8, States of Zeeland to Maurice of Nassau, 10 Aug. 1588, reported much noise from Dunkirk, suggesting that a sortie was being planned, but noted no action. Strada, *De bello belgico*, II, 558, based in part upon Parma's now lost archive, also mentioned this detail but carefully prefaced it: 'some have written that . . . ' The only archival source on the Spanish side that supports the story is AGRB *CC* 26,136/91v, which records the issue of rations to the officers and crews of ten warships for three days' service at sea, 11–13 Aug. 1588, for an unspecified purpose. The silence of all Spanish sources concerning the attempted breakout – Parma and Manrique; Vázquez, Coloma and Carnero – and of the 'Vlaemsche kroniek', suggests that it never took place.

92. Brugmans, *Correspondentie*, III, 284–6, Leicester to Burghley, 5 Nov. 1587 OS. For the risks of hazarding the 'precious veterans' of the army see Carnero, *Historia*, 230.

93. In a striking parallel, the Franco-Spanish invasion plan of 1779 also failed largely because it required the junction of a fleet from one area (Corunna) with an army mustered in another (St Malo and Le Havre) before the invasion could take place: see Patterson, *The other Armada, passim*.

94. Laughton, II, 45, Seymour, Winter and Palmer to the Privy Council, 6 Aug. 1588 OS. Parma discharged his hired transports on 31 Aug. (see AGS *CMC* 2a/1077, account of Thorivio

Martinez). Certain news of the Armada's return to Spain only reached Flanders five weeks later: see ASN *CF* 1676bis, unfol., Marolin de Juan to Parma, 7 Oct. 1588, Dunkirk.

9 *The Guns of August*

1. I am most grateful for references and suggestions to Thomas Arnold, Jan Glete, Holger Herwig, Paul Kennedy, Peter Pierson, Glyn Redworth, Kevin Sharpe, I. A. A. Thompson, Nancy van Deusen and, especially, Nicholas Rodger. Further detail on the Tudor navy may be found in Parker, 'The *Dreadnought* revolution'.

2. FD, II, 9–10, Philip II's Instructions to Medina Sidonia, 1 Apr. 1588. The origins of this advice are interesting: it also featured verbatim in the Instructions sent to the duke's predecessor, Santa Cruz, on 14 Sept. 1587: see *BMO*, III, 1067–8. Ironically, the king repeated something Medina already knew: see the duke's own Instructions to the fleet leaving for America, 31 Mar. 1587, in Maura, 175–7. The reports ('avisos') mentioned by the king have not been found, but they might have included the description of English naval superiority and the need to use different (smaller) ships in order to counter it, in *AGS SP* libro 1550/569, Cardinal Albert to Philip II, 25 Oct. 1586, as well as a report by a Spanish agent from London in 1574 about how the English fired low in order to damage their opponents' hulls (*CSPSp*, II, 480). The detailed confirmation later provided by Francisco de Guevara seems to have been ignored: see p. 389 n. 68 below.

3. Gracia Rivas, 'El motín de la "Diana"'.

4. For the munitions, see Laughton, I, 338, John Gilberte to the Privy Council, 8 Aug. 1588 NS; ibid., II, 156–7, inventory of the stores taken on the *San Salvador*; and AGS *Estado K*

1568/127, 'Avisos de Inglaterra', 5 Nov. 1588. The large quantity of heavy-calibre ammunition found aboard these two ships – which can scarcely have been unique (see p. 289, figure 5, above) – underscores the significance of the failure of other vessels to use their ammunition effectively against the English in battle.

5. For examples, see Martin and Parker, *Spanish Armada*, 227–50.

6. Oppenheim, *History*, 163. Even so, the accounts compiled by the owners seem to have been 'padded': thus Drake charged the government £1,000 for his 200-ton bark *Thomas* (Devon County Record Office, Exeter, Deposit 346/F588, 'Accompte of sondrye charges').

7. Laughton, I, 358–62, Hawkins to Walsingham, 10 Aug. 1588 NS. See also the testimony of Howard (ibid., II, 59–60) and of the Florentine ambassador in Paris in Nov. 1587, that the Armada 'is the largest that has ever been in these seas [i.e. outside the Mediterranean] since the creation of the world' (Canestrini and Desjardins, *Négociations diplomatiques*, 737).

8. Kenyon, 'Ordnance and the king's fleet in 1548', 63–5; and Caruana, *English sea ordnance*, I 18–21 (summary of the artillery listed in the inventory of the navy by Anthony Anthony in 1546).

9. All ship weights in this chapter, unless otherwise stated, are given in 'tons displacement', even though almost all English records of the period – and subsequently – give only the 'tons and tonnage' for each ship, a measurement that relates to their internal volume. Glete, *Navies and nations*, II, 527–30, shows how to calculate displacement by multiplying the length, beam and draught of each ship, and then adjusting the total to establish how much of the hull lay under water (the 'block coefficient'). Since not all ships in the navy possessed the same design features, the 'block coefficient' differs slightly in each case. However, Dr Glete has estimated the

probable displacement for each vessel, based on its exact dimensions, and very generously shared his calculations with me. I am very grateful to him. I also thank Nicholas Rodger for pointing out to me the advantage of using Glete's method. The same can be done with Spanish *toneles*, also a measurement of carrying capacity and not displacement: see the erudite discussion in Casado Soto, *Los barcos*, 57–94, and the weights and measurements for each ship in the Armada of 1588 given later. Dr Glete also generously shared with me his calculations of displacement, based on Casado Soto's figures, although naturally these figures remain approximate.

10. PRO *WO* 55/1672, 'A view and survey of all her Majesty's Ordinnance', listing all ships except the *Warspite* and the *Repulse*; the totals for these two ships have been added from *WO* 55/1627, 'The booke of the remaynes'. Parker, 'The *Dreadnought* revolution', Appendix I, gives details for each capital ship.

11. The *Swiftsure*, also launched in 1573, only displaced 550 tons according to a survey of 1590–91, but was 'new built' in 1592, increasing her displacement to 650 tons. In 1595 she carried 37 guns with a total weight of 43 tons – 6.61 per cent of her total displacement. Calculations of displacement kindly supplied by Jan Glete; weight of ordnance calculated from the totals aboard each ship in Sept. 1595 according to PRO *WO* 55/1672, 'A view and survey of all Her Majestie's Ordinnance'. Note that the ordnance weights include only the gun barrels: the mountings, equipment and ammunition were additional.

12. See the most interesting document on the rotation programme presented by Adams, 'New light'; and also Glasgow, 'The shape of the ships'.

13. Naval totals from Parker, 'The *Dreadnought* revolution', Appendix II. These figures do not include the naval outlay of the Ordnance Office, which added at least another £100,000 to the wartime cost of Elizabeth's navy.

14. See Parker, *Spain and the Netherlands*, 36. Jan Glete has informed me that Sweden and Denmark may sometimes have devoted 30 per cent of their defence budgets to their navies during the 1560s, when they were at war (though not for two entire decades).

15. See the detailed description of the armament aboard the flag galleass in AGS *Estado* 594/152, 'Relación de lo que queda de la galeaza' – she carried 18 pieces firing between 15- and 50-pound balls. An Englishman who examined this 'mightie huge ship' on the sands at Calais claimed she carried a total of 64 guns: BL *Sloane* 262/66v. See also BNP *Fonds français* 5045/155, 'Discours' on the Armada with much detail on the wrecked galleass by an eyewitness at Calais; the 1589 'Addicoune' to John Mountgomerie's *Treatise concerning the Navie of England* (Magdalene College, Cambridge, *Pepys Ms.* 1774); AGS *Estado* 431/135, 'Relación de los naos que ay' (which gives a total weight of 2,000 *toneladas* for the four galleasses).

16. Admittedly, two galleasses had sailed with the marquis of Santa Cruz in 1583 and taken part in his victory off Terceira, but those that sailed against England were different vessels and only reached Lisbon in August 1587; the transatlantic guardships did not arrive there until Feb. 1588. On the other hand, several of the ships in the 1583 campaign served again in 1588: compare the list of names in Fernández Duro, *La conquista*, 402–17.

17. Taylor, *Troublesome voyage*, 154, and Rodger, *Safeguard*, 219. On the advice of Jan Glete, I have applied a rough conversion factor of 1.5 to the 'tons and tonnage' of these two private vessels to suggest their displacement (see note 9 above). The speed of England's mobilization in 1588 was truly remarkable: within three months Elizabeth concentrated a fleet larger than the Armada, which had

taken Philip three years to assemble. Moreover, her fleet was entirely English whereas Philip's fleet was by no means all Spanish.

18. On the *Grifón,* see AGS CS 2a/280 fo. 1939, statement of Juan Gómez de Medina, 8 Oct. 1588 (copy): 'maltratada de la mucha artillería con que algunos navios de la armada inglesa la batió, y de la que ella asimismo jugó contra ellos'. The same could happen to purpose-built warships: AGS *GA* 226/8, Don Jorge Manrique to Philip II, 19 Aug. 1588, described the *San Mateo,* a Portuguese galleon built in the 1570s which sank off the Flemish coast, as being 'abierto de su mesma artillería'.

19. Laughton, II, 11, Winter to Walsingham, 11 Aug. 1588 NS. Earlier in the letter (p. 10), Winter claimed that the English fleet did not begin to fire until they were 120 paces away.

20. *HMC Salisbury,* III, 345, Deposition of two Dutch sailors from the Armada, 11 Aug. 1588; FD, II, 405, Account of Friar la Torre, aboard the flagship; Laughton, II, 60, Howard to Walsingham, 8 Aug. 1588 NS, reporting claims made by his Spanish captives. See also the 'Observations' subsequently written by Sir Arthur Gorgas, who had fought in the action, concerning the ability of the English to discharge 'our broadsides of ordnance double for their single, we carrying as good and great artillery as they do and to better proof, and having far better gunners': Glasgow, 'Gorgas' seafight', 180–1.

21. FD, II, 392, Account of Captain Vanegas; AHN *OM* 3512/34, 'Relación hecha por un soldado en la Almiranta' (entry for 8 Aug.); and Laughton, II, 81, 'Report of deserters'.

22. FD, II, 241 (Medina Sidonia), and 261 (a Jesuit aboard the flagship).

23. The records of the munitions issued to the squadron commanded by Sir Francis Drake at Plymouth (6 royal and 32 merchant ships) have survived.

They reveal the delivery of some 5,220 rounds and almost 39,000 pounds of powder between Oct. 1587 and Apr. 1588 for the whole squadron, and the distribution of these munitions in May 1588 among individual ships; however, they unfortunately provide no indication either of munitions already aboard or of the quantities expended in the 1588 campaign. See West Devon County Record Office, Plymouth, *PCM* 1971/4, 'Powder and munition delivered at Plymouth'.

24. Usherwood, *The Counter-Armada,* 77; Pierson, *Commander of the Armada,* 201; PRO *WO* 55/1627, 'The booke of the remaynes of Her Majesties shippes returninge from the seas', Dec. 1595–Aug. 1596. According to their journals, the *Mary Rose* fired 400 and the *Repulse* 350 roundshot on 21 June: Hammer, 'New light', 192. It should be recalled that the Ordnance Office 'hundredweight' contained only 100 lb for powder, but 112 lb for guns.

25. PRO *WO* 55/1627 for the individual ships; Andrews, *The last voyage of Drake and Hawkins,* 72–3 for the totals (taken from PRO *AO* 1/1688/30). Note that the English – at Cadiz and in the Caribbean – also fired off substantial quantities of 'crossbar shot', 'chain shot', 'jointed shot', stone shot and 'hail shot': see the impressive totals in Andrews, *The last voyage.*

26. All English sources lamented the lack of powder and especially shot on and after 8 Aug.: see Laughton, I, 359 (Hawkins to Walsingham, 10 Aug. 1588); II, 11 and 13 (Winter to Walsingham, 11 Aug.), 38 (Fenner to Walsingham, 14 Aug.), 54 (Howard to Walsingham, 17 Aug.), 64 (Whyte to Walsingham, 18 Aug.) and so on (all dates new style). Raleigh, 'Excellent observations and notes concerning the royall navy', written before 1612 and printed in his *Judicious and select essayes,* part III, p. 26, commented on the need to match the issue of powder and shot to the

number of guns aboard each ship, 'as was seen in the sea-battaile with the Spaniards in the yeare 88, when it so neerly concerned the defence and preservation of the kingdome. So as then many of those great guns, wanting powder and shot, stood but as cyphers and scarecrows.'

27. Manuel's Instructions of Feb. 1500 in Greenlee, *The voyage of Pedro Alvares Cabral*, 183.

28. Oliveira, *A arte da guerra do mar*, fo. lxxii; he also warned, 'Do not place heavy artillery on small ships, because the recoil will pull them apart' (fo. xlviii). Oliveira served as a galley pilot in 1535–43 and 1544–45, fighting against the Royal Navy (see fos xl–xli, with an interesting account of the battles between French galleys and English warships in 1544–45). He spent the next two years in England.

29. Chaves, *Espejo de navigantes*, 'De la guerra o batalla que se da en la mar', a manuscript of *c.* 1540 published by Fernández Duro, *Armada española,* I, 379–91, and in more detail in idem, *De algunas obras desconocidas*.

30. The crescent-shaped formation of the Armada is discussed in Martin and Parker, *Spanish Armada*, 285. See also Plate 28 above.

31. Freitas de Meneses, *Os Açores*, I, 150–1, II, 59–61 (Cristobal de Erasso and Rodrigo de Vargas to Antonio de Erasso, 1 Aug. 1582) and II, 83 (Don Lope de Figueroa to Philip II, 3 Oct. 1582).

32. For an example of the former, from which the quotation comes, see KML, *MSP Capitanía General, Cuentas*, 9/66 (fos 146–7v), Instruction to Juan de Escandón, *escrivano de raciones* aboard the *San Bartholomé*, 29 June 1587; for the latter see AGS *CMC* 2a/772, papers of *La Concepción Menor*, pliego 132, statement of Antonio del Castillo, 'persona señalada . . . para el apercivimiento de la pelea y distribuición de las municiones y armas', 24 Aug. 1588. Alas, very few of these detailed records seem to have survived.

33. Figure based on the data in Parker, 'The *Dreadnought* revolution', 278–9.

34. AHN *OM* 3512/34, 'Relación hecha por un soldado en la Almiranta'; FD, II, 377–8, 384–5 and 392. Vanegas also estimated that the rest of the Armada fired 600 rounds on 31 July (against 2,000 from the English), and that the two fleets together fired over 5,000 rounds on 2 Aug., the same again on 3 Aug., and some 3,000 rounds on the 4th. Unfortunately for historians, the galleons of Portugal do not appear to have left the same meticulous records as the hired ships and the squadron of Castile, but Dutch salvors recovered almost one ton of powder from two wrecked Portuguese warships: RAZ *Rekenkamer* C2983, Account of Pieter Willemszoon. Likewise the wreck of the 50-gun *San Lorenzo*, flagship of the galleasses, a squadron noted by both sides as in the forefront of all the fleet actions in the Channel, yielded no fewer than 2,650 cannon-balls, implying that relatively few had been fired: see AGS *CMC* 3a/1704, no. 45, Account of Vicenzo de Bune; and AGS *GA* 221/1, 'La felicíssima Armada', fo. A9 (claiming that the galleass carried 2,500 rounds when it left Lisbon).

35. HHStA *Statenabteilung Spanien: Diplomatische Korrespondenz* 11 Konvolut 7/413v, Count Khevenhüller to Rudolf II, 12 Oct. 1588 (quoting Zúñiga); Herrera Oria, 245, Medina Sidonia's 'Relación del viaje' for 8 Aug. Others aboard the fleet said the same: see, for example, Harvard Houghton Library, *FMs Span* 54, Bernardo de Góngora to Martín de los Angeles, 15 Aug. 1588.

36. AGS *Estado* 594/116, Medina Sidonia to Parma, 6 Aug. 1588; Herrera Oria, 240, Medina's 'Relación' for the same day. See also Martin and Parker, *Spanish Armada*, 199–200.

37. AGS *CMC* 2a/905, Papers of *San Juan Bautista de la Esperanza*, pliegos 39–43. This 450-ton ship only joined the Armada on 13 June 1588, serving thereafter with the Levant squadron

but somehow missing all the standard 'censuses' of the Armada's strength.

38. PRO *SP* 12/220, 'Survey' of the queen's ships carried out on 25 Sept. 1588 OS (see extracts in Laughton, II, 241–9). Although a number of masts and other items are reported as 'decayed', which may be a euphemism for battle damage, they are not numerous; the only specific references to enemy action concerned some sails of the *Elizabeth Bonaventure* 'shot full of hooles' (fo. 50). However, a survey carried out three days later reported rather more damage: most notably it described the mainmast of the *Revenge* as 'decayed and perished with shot' (Laughton, II, 250–4, at p. 252).

39. Details from the 1588 account of the treasurer of the navy: PRO *E* 351/2225 and (more legibly) *AO* 1/1686/23. BL *Sloane* 2450, 'Sea causes extraordinary, A.D. 1588', also includes accounts for numerous repairs carried out in spring 1588, as well as in September (see fo. 54). My thanks to Nicholas Rodger for helping me interpret these figures. For some idea of the work required before the queen's ships set forth, see PRO *SP* 12/204/34–5, 'The present state of Her Majesty's navy', 12 Oct. 1587.

40. In 1590, building the *Merhonor* cost £3,600, the *Garland* cost £3,200 and the *Defiance* cost £3,000 (PRO *E* 351/2227 and *AO* 1/1686/25, Account of Sir John Hawkins); in 1595, new-building the *Triumph* and building the *Repulse* and the *Warspite* absorbed £9,372 (PRO *E* 351/2232 and *AO* 1/1688/31, Account of Margaret Hawkins); and in 1598 alone new-building the *Elizabeth Jonas* consumed £4,449 and 101 trees, 80 loads of timber, 31 loads of 'knees' (the strengthener for decks) and 3,000 metres of planking (*E* 351/2236 and *AO* 1/1689/34, Account of Roger Langford).

41. Paul Kennedy has reminded me that, in the eighteenth century, damage to (and loss of) ships due to weather stood in a proportion of four, five or even six to one, compared with damage due to enemy action.

42. AGS *Estado K* 1448/77, 'Lo que refiere Manuel Blanco'.

43. Bor, *Geschiedenis*, III part 2, fos 10–12, interrogation of Pimentel; Martin and Parker, *Spanish Armada*, 37, quoting Pedro Coco Calderón's evaluation of the *San Juan Bautista* of the squadron of Castile.

44. Data on guns from AGS *GA* 347/218, 'Las naves que fueron en esta última armada'; and Thompson, *War and society*, essay VII, 82. Weights computed from Casado Soto, *Los barcos*, 382–4, multiplying the weight in *toneles* by the 'block coefficient' calculated by Jan Glete (see note 9 above). Unfortunately, information on the ships of the squadron of Portugal – reputedly the finest in the Armada – has proved hard to find. Nevertheless the *San Martín* (the flagship), which in 1588 had carried 48 guns, in January 1591 carried 45, of which the heaviest were two 29-pounder cannon periers; only one other gun fired more than 14-pound balls (AGS *GA* 347/206, 'Relación particular'). RAZ *Rekenkamer* C2983, Account of Pieter Willemszoon, recorded the calibre of 38 guns recovered from the wrecked Portuguese galleons *San Mateo* and *San Felipe* (which had originally carried 34 and 40 guns respectively). The heaviest were nine 14-pounders, plus one 11-, seven 9-, and five 8-pounders along with sundry other small pieces.

45. PRO *E* 36/13, Inventory of the navy (see 55–62 for the *Mary Rose*). 'Truckles', 'extrees' (axle trees) and other items to make sea-carriages feature in, for example, Bod. *Ms Rawl. A* 204/1, Ordnance Office accounts for 1578 (including carriages made for the *Revenge*); PRO *E* 351/2607, Account of William Winter as master of the ordnance, 1586–89; PRO *AO* 1/1846/70, Account of Henry Killigrew as treasurer of the ordnance, 1587–88; PRO *E* 351/2632, Account of George Carew as lieutenant of the ordnance, 1596; and especially *WO*

55/1626, Ordnance Office issues for 1596 – every new 'shippe carriage' required two 'extrees' and two pairs of 'truckes' (see fos 3, 14, 15, 66–7v, etc.). Field carriages, with 'strakes, spykes, nave hoopes' and so on, were clearly constructed in an entirely different way (see fo. 36).

46.	AGS *CMC* 2a/1210, Miscellaneous accounts, order of Valdés dated 22 Apr. 1588; a second copy at *CMC* 1a/1718 fo. 759, noting that the gun (a 9-pound culverin) was exchanged for a medio sacre of 18 quintals.

47.	Martin and Parker, *Spanish Armada*, 208, 210 and the plate on p. 223.

48.	KML *MSP Casa de la Contratación* 8/30–41 (fos 171–236), Accounts of ordnance and munitions supplied to embargoed ships by the duke of Medina Sidonia in July 1587. #32 (for the *Santa Catalina*) called for wheels '3.5 palms high', or 72 centimetres (the size of the gun it would carry is unstated). They were certainly not 'truckles'.

49.	For gunners aboard the queen's ships see Laughton, II, 324–5, and Rodger, *Safeguard*, 312–13. On the Spanish side, surviving data for the Andalusian squadron demonstrate two things: first, that when the ships of this squadron (all but one of them built in Cantabria) were embargoed in Andalusia, most had relatively few gunners, and a number of them were foreign (Ragusan, Flemish, French, German, Italian, Polish and Danish); second, that although Medina Sidonia greatly increased the complement of mariners before sending the ships to Lisbon, he did little to augment the number of gunners – and many of those now rated 'marinero y artillero' had formerly been merely 'marinero'.

50.	Raleigh, 'Excellent observations', 23–4.

51.	FD, II, 373 (Vanegas) and 46 (Medina).

52.	Ibid., II, 44–5; Martin, 'The equipment', 364–5.

53.	See the wealth of quotations on this point in Rodger, *Safeguard*, 302–3.

54.	AGS *Estado* 455/602–3, Don Francisco de Bobadilla to Don Juan de Idiáquez, 20 Aug. 1588: 'La fuerza de nuestra armada heran hasta veynte bajeles, y estos an peleado muy bien'; Laughton, II, 13, Winter to Walsingham, 11 Aug. 1588 NS: 'If you had seen that which I have seen, of the simple service that hath been done by the merchant and coast ships, you would have said that we had been little holpen by them, otherwise than that they did make a show'. Admittedly, the exact armament of the rest of the English fleet seems impossible to ascertain: PRO *AO* 1/1686/23 (a copy in better repair than *E* 351/2225), Accounts of the treasurer of the navy for 1588, section 'Extraordinary: sea wages', gives the tonnage and crews of most of the ships mobilized to repel the Armada, but no armament.

55.	On the galleasses, see p. 253 above; on the two captured ships, see the inventories made by the English: Laughton, II, 154–7 and 190–1.

56.	FD, II, 9, Instructions to Medina Sidonia, 1 Apr. 1588. This point also featured in the draft Instructions prepared for Santa Cruz in Jan. 1588, but never sent (AGS *Estado* 165/29 and 33). These documents, among others, receive close scrutiny in Adams, 'The battle that never was'.

57.	*BMO*, III, 608–9, Philip II to Santa Cruz, 25 June 1587.

58.	Pierson, *Commander of the Armada*, 266, n. 34, in a brilliant discussion of the surviving documents, demonstrates that the king personally appointed Diego Flores.

59.	Lyon, *The enterprise of Florida*, 73; and H. and P. Chaunu, *Séville et l'Atlantique, 1504–1650*, III (Paris, 1955), 98, 122, 128, 136, 140, 168, 194, 214, 276, 292.

60.	AGS *Estado* 165/217–18, anonymous letter from Seville, 21 Feb. 1588.

61.	On Flores's fall see Martin and Parker,

Spanish Armada, 268 and 290, n. 10; on Recalde, see Parker, 'El testamento político', 10–11.

62. Tellechea Idígoras, *Otra cara*, 341; Recalde to Idiáquez, 29 July 1588; AHN *OM* 3511/41, Recalde to Medina, 29 July and 1 Aug. 1588, with the ducal replies in the margin. Two sources independently reported that at the council meeting Don Alonso de Leiva argued most strongly for an immediate assault on Plymouth: see FD, II, 374, 'Relación' of Alonso Vanegas, and PRO *SP* 12/214/51, testimony of Dr Góngora, in English (from which the quotation comes), after his capture on 1 Aug. Recent research confirms the view of Leiva and others (reported by Vanegas) that the land defences of Plymouth could scarcely have kept the Armada out: see Brayshay, 'Plymouth's coastal defences'.

63. AHN *OM* 3512/34, 'Relación hecha por un soldado en la Almiranta' (but evidently dictated by Recalde), entries for 29 and 30 July and 4 and 6 Aug. 1588; *OM* 3511/41, Recalde to Medina Sidonia and to Bobadilla, both on 1 Aug. 1588.

64. AGS *Estado* 455/320–1, Medina to Parma, 10 June 1588, copy sent to (and annotated by) Philip II (see also KML *MSP: CR* 5/264–7, minute of the same letter). See also pp. 233 and 315 n. 106 above.

65. Herrera Oria, 202–3, Philip II to Medina, 21 June 1588, minute; KML *MSP: CR* 5/278–9 (original) and 289 (Philip's further message of 26 June); FD, II, 221–2, Medina Sidonia to Philip II, 30 July 1588. For more about Medina's misconceptions at this point, see pp. 232–4 above.

66. AHN *OM* 3512/34, 'Relación', entries for 7 and 9 Aug. 1588. Cf. Herrera Oria, 241, Medina's 'Relación del viaje' for 6 Aug.

67. See the evidence in Parker, 'The *Dreadnought* revolution'; and the interesting analysis in Adams, 'The battle that never was'.

68. Lilly Library, Bloomington (Indiana), *Bertendona Papers* 171, Record of service (describing events on 'la víspera de San Domingo'); AGS *Estado* 594/116, Medina Sidonia to Parma, 4 Aug. 1588, copy. See also AHN *OM* 3511/41, ducal apostil on Recalde to Medina Sidonia, 1 Aug. 1588, stating that he awaited an opportunity to board. *BMO*, III, 1750, Guevara to Philip II, 22 Jan. 1588, having described English naval tactics observed during his captivity in England, drew entirely the wrong conclusion from his extremely useful intelligence: 'so it would be good to board at once and come hand-to-hand', he advised the king.

69. Raleigh, *History of the World*, part I, book V, 297–8. See the excellent summary of the battle in Pierson, *Commander of the Armada*, 139.

70. Kemp, *Papers of Admiral Sir John Fisher*, I, 40, Fisher to the Committee of Seven, May 1904.

71. See details on ship construction in Casado Soto, *Los barcos*, 206–9, and idem, 'La construcción naval'. For the last-minute concern over shortage of guns, see KML *MSP: CR* 5/86, Philip II to Medina Sidonia, 14 Mar. 1588, with the duke's holograph draft reply on the dorse.

72. FD, II, 16–18, Instructions for Parma, 1 Apr. 1588. Interestingly enough, these were precisely the terms that Don Juan de Zúñiga had proposed in his position paper of autumn 1585: p. 181 above.

73. AGS *Estado* 2219/84, Philip II to Parma, 31 Aug. 1588, and fos 85–6 'Apuntamiento en materia de armada que Su Magestad mandó hazer para que se considere y resuelva entre el duque de Parma, su sobrino, y el duque de Medina Sidonia' (four foolscap sheets); and *Estado* 2219/91, Notes by Idiáquez on 15 Sept. 1588. On 7 and again on 14 Aug. the king signed more letters insisting that the success of the enterprise depended upon his commanders' adherence to the 'agreed plan': see p. 71 above.

10   *After the Armada*

1. Aubrey, *Brief lives*, 147; Bruce, *The Liber Famelicus*, 12–13 (my thanks to Richard Kagan for bringing this reference to my attention).
2. Percyvall, *Biblioteca hispanica*; Cockle, *A bibliography of military books*, 43–4, 55; Blaylock, 'The study of Spanish'.
3. Borman, 'Untying the knot?', 308.
4. For details see Thompson and Yun Casalilla, *The Castilian crisis of the seventeenth century*, especially chaps 1–2; and Vassberg, *Land and society*, chap. 7. Philip II gave the figure of 10 million ducats to the Cortes of Castile in Dec. 1588: *Actas de las Cortes*, X, 348. See also Lovett, 'The vote of the *Millones*'.
5. AGS *GA* 277/230, Dr Espinosa to Philip II, 2 Jan. 1589, describing the strange deaths of Armada survivors sent to recover in his hospital at Salamanca; Hamilton, *Calendar of State Papers relating to Ireland . . . 1588–92*, 121, examination of John Brown of Clontarf, escaped from Ribadeo, 6 Feb. 1589 (on the itinerant mourners); Sigüenza, 120; and Zarco Cuevas, *Documentos . . . Escorial*, IV, 59 (Fray Gerónimo de Sepúlveda on the Armada's impact).
6. See the criticisms of the Grand Strategy reported by the Spanish resident in Venice, AGS *Estado* 1342/142, Giuseppe de Cernosa to Philip II, 3 Sept. 1588, and in note 14 below; the criticisms to Philip in person by a court preacher, reported in *CSPV*, VIII, 396, H. Lippomano to Venice, 1 Oct. 1588; and the data on the fall of the 'plaza prophets' in Kagan, 'Politics, prophecy and the Inquisition'.
7. AGS *Estado* 2219/82, Don Juan de Idiáquez to Parma, 31 Aug. 1588; IVdeDJ 51/190, Mateo Vázquez to Philip II and reply, 4 Sept. 1588.
8. ASV *LP* 46/82, Philip II to all Spanish prelates, 13 Oct. 1588, copy (another copy in BAV *UL* 1115/246).
9. BZ 145/76, Mateo Vázquez to Philip II and reply, 10 Nov. 1588.

10. AGS *Estado* 2851, unfol., 'Lo que se platicó en el Consejo de Estado a 12 de noviembre 1588', and consulta of 26 Nov. 1588 with Philip II holograph response; *Actas de las Cortes*, X, 348 and 422–3.
11. See details in Thompson, 'Spanish Armada gun procurement', 79; idem, *War and government*, 191–2; Rodríguez Salgado and Adams, *England, Spain and the Gran Armada*, 112–13 (including a contemporary design for the new galleons, clearly showing the broadside); and Goodman, *Spanish naval power*, 7–9. Botero's *Dalla Ragion di Stato* (1589) and *Relationi universali* (1591) quoted by Gil, 'Visión europea', 79–80.
12. AGS *Estado* 2855, unfol., 'Lo que se platicó en Consejo de Estado a 10 de henero de 1589, entendido el sucesso del duque de Guisa'.
13. On Saluzzo see Altadonna, 'Cartas de Felipe II a Carlos Manuel', 168–71: Philip II to the duke of Savoy, 23 June, 1 Nov. and 23 Dec. 1588. The League leaders received almost 1.5 million ducats in cash from Spain in 1589 and 1590: AGS *CMC* 2a/23, unfol., Accounts of Gabriel de Alegría.
14. AGS *Estado* 2219/176, Philip II to Parma, 11 May 1589. For examples of criticism, see Casado Soto, *Discursos*, 157–71 (discourses of Apr. and Sept. 1588); Martin and Parker, *Spanish Armada*, 268, Don Francisco de Bobadilla to Philip II, 20 Aug. 1588 (written aboard the Armada flagship); ASV *NS* 34/551–3, Novara to Montalto, 13 Oct. 1588, quoting a councillor of war 'who said he had affirmed from the start that it was impossible for the Armada to join with the duke of Parma'; and AGS *Estado* 2851, unfol., 'Lo que se platicó sobre la prosecución de la guerra', 12 Nov. 1588, 'voto' of Don Hernando de Toledo (perhaps the councillor quoted by the nuncio). Juan Martínez de Recalde, the Armada's second-in-command, advised the king on his return to Spain that 'If the enterprise

of England is to happen, His Majesty should remember that it would not be wise to do it the same way as before, but only from Spain' (see Parker, 'El testamento político', 18).

15. On the Anglo-Dutch offensive, see the detailed account of Wernham, *After the Armada*, chaps 4–6 and 11; and idem, *The expedition of Sir John Norris*. For a prediction that had the English persevered in their march on Lisbon they would have taken it, see BCR Ms 2417/17, Don Juan de Silva to Esteban to Ibarra, Coimbra, 19 June 1589.

16. AGS *Estado* 2219/197, Philip II to Parma, 7 Sept. 1589. A week later, at Arques, Henry IV routed the army of the Catholic League, graphically confirming the need to place France first amid Spain's strategic priorities.

17. AGS *Estado* 2855, unfol., 'Sumario de los quatro papeles principales que dio el presidente Richardot' and 'Lo que Su Magestad es servido que se responda a los quatro papeles' (11 Nov. 1589: paper three dealt with the possibility of peace talks).

18. See the important policy discussion in AGS *Estado* 2855, unfol., 'Lo que sobre las cartas de Francia de Don Bernardino y Moreo hasta las 6 de hebrero se ofrece' and the consulta on it.

19. AGS *Estado* 2220/1, fo. 157, Philip II to Parma, 4 Apr. 1590; and fo. 165, confirmation dated 16 Apr. On the course of Parma's intervention in France, and on the peace talks at Cologne, see van der Essen, *Alexandre Farnèse*, V; on the first Brittany expedition, see Tenace, 'Spanish intervention in Brittany', 189–94.

20. KML *MSP: CR* 6/174, Philip II to Medina Sidonia, 15 Dec. 1590; and AGS *Estado* 2220/1, fos 4 and 6, Philip II to Parma and the count of Olivares, 12 Nov. 1590 (and the correspondence in *Estado* 956–8). The king specifically alluded to the 'peace-plan' proposed by Parma, via his representative Jean Richardot, one year before: p. 274 above.

21. The phrase used by Don Juan de Idiáquez in 1588 about the Low Countries' Wars: see p. 195 above.

22. See the detailed account of Gracía Rivas, *La 'invasión' de Aragón en 1591*. The 'fugitive' was none other than Antonio Pérez, who escaped from prison in Castile while undergoing rigorous questioning concerning his role in the murder of Juan de Escobedo.

23. BZ 141/203, Philip II to Mateo Vázquez, 29 Jan. 1591; IVdeDJ 51/1, Vázquez to Philip II, 8 Feb. 1591 and reply; Casado Soto, *Discursos*, 180–9, a 'discurso' of Sept. 1591 transcribed from Escalante's own register (see however BL *Addl.* 28456/123–7 for another copy among the papers of Don Cristóbal de Moura, which demonstrates that it reached the king's entourage). At least Philip resisted pressure in 1594 from a new pope, Clement VIII, to resume hostilities against the Turks: see Borromeo, 'Istruzioni generali', 132–3.

24. AGS *Estado* 176, unfol., Philip II to Santa Gadea, 3 Oct. 1596 (my thanks to Edward Tenace for providing a transcript of this interesting document). The venture proved another disaster: in August Philip determined to send it to Ireland, where it would occupy a town or two in the south; when the fleet had still not left by mid-October, the king suddenly changed his mind and ordered it to capture Brest in Brittany instead and spend the winter there; however, they set forth too late as usual, storms struck just after the new Armada left Spain and one-quarter of the ships and some 2,000 men never returned: see Tenace, 'Spanish intervention in Brittary', 518–25.

25. Lilly Library, Bloomington, Indiana, *Bertendona Papers*, nos 21 and 24, Philip II to Bertendona, 23 June and 15 Nov. 1589. 'Security' at Court remained just as lax: in 1589 the Venetian ambassador sent to his government plans of Corunna copied from 'the one which the council of War had

26. *Actas de las Cortes*, XVI, 169–73, Philip II to Juan Vázquez, 6 May 1593.
27. Ibid., 195–7, Philip II to Juan Vázquez, 23 July 1593 (and replies from the towns at pp. 230–48); and Jago, 'Taxation and political culture in Castile', 52–4.
28. See Vargas Hidalgo, 'Documentos inéditos', on Philip's debility; Bouza Álvarez, 'Guardar papeles, I', 11, on the transaction of business; and Feros, 'El viejo monarca', on Moura's power. For an early example of Prince Philip taking decisions, see ACA *CA* 36/325, consulta of the council of Aragon, 25 Mar. 1594, with the prince's holograph 'rúbrica' and decision. For his powers after Sept. 1597 see pp. 28 and 310 n. 65 above.
29. Complaints from Moura and others noted in Feros, 'El viejo monarca'. On expelling the Jews, see AGS *SP* libro 1160/185v and 1161/223v, Philip II to the governor of Lombardy, 30 Oct. 1596 (with holograph postscript) and 21 Jan. 1597. For more on this strange episode see Segre, *Gli ebrei lombardi*.
30. PRO *SP* 94/5/273 'Relación del viaje del Adelantado', Oct. 1597: the reluctant mariners had a point – having finally left Corunna on 19 Oct., a storm drove them back a week later. See a second copy of this document at BAV *UL* 1113/611.
31. Rijksarchief Arnhem, *Archief van het Huis Berg*, 530, unfol., Herman van den Berg to count of Fuentes, 24 June 1595, minute. For further details on the Spanish collapse in the Netherlands and northern France in the 1590s, see Parker, *Dutch Revolt*, 230–3; for their wasted opportunities in Brittany, see Tenace, 'Spanish intervention in Brittany', chaps 5–11; for the mutinies, see Parker, *The Army of Flanders*, 185–206 and 290–2.
32. On Spanish aid to the Irish, see Morgan, *Tyrone's rebellion*, 206–10. On the Cadiz raid, see Usherwood, *The Counter-Armada*, 78–9, 84, 93 (entries in the journal kept by Sir George Carew); Pierson, *Commander of the Armada*, 203, 210, 278; and Chapter 9 above. On the destruction of the Indies fleet (14 ships lost, 5 escaped), see Chaunu, *Séville et l'Atlantique*, IV, 12–15, and the eyewitness Spanish account of Abreu, *Historia del saqueo*.
33. On Vervins, see Tenace, 'Spanish intervention in Brittany', 568–72; and Imhoff, *Der Friede von Vervins*. On Henry IV's conversion – promised since 1589 but only effected in 1593 – see Dickerman, 'The conversion of Henry IV'.
34. Quotation from Alcocer, *Consultas del consejo de Estado*, 278, Philip III's response to a consulta of 26 Nov. 1602. On the reasons for Spain's retreat, see Allen, 'The strategy of peace'; the essays in *Después de la Gran Armada: la historia desconocida*; and, from the English point of view, Wernham, *The return of the Armadas*.

Conclusion: Agent and Structure

1. Nightingale, *Letters from Egypt*, 74. Many thanks to Carole Fink for reading and commenting on this chapter.
2. IVdeDJ 114/21, Don Martín de Padilla, count of Santa Gadea and adelantado of Castile, to Philip III, 27 Oct. 1599, copy. Padilla went on to analyse the various failures of Spain's assaults on England between 1588 and 1599, and to offer specific suggestions for why they had all failed. I thank Paul Allen for bringing this fascinating document to my attention. See the interesting late examples of 'technological determinism' in explaining the failure of 1588 quoted in Goodman, *Spanish naval power*, 6–7 (one from 1620, the other from 1639). See also Fray José de Sigüenza's bitter judgement on the Armada débâcle, concluding 'and the worst of it is that no lesson was learnt from it' (Sigüenza, 119–20).
3. Kamen, *Philip*, 308, Padilla memo-

randum of 1596; *CSPSp*, IV, 690, Padilla to Philip III, 10 Dec. 1601; IVdeDJ 82/419, duke of Sessa (Spanish ambassador in Rome) to Don Balthasar de Zúñiga (Spanish ambassador in Brussels), 9 Nov. 1602; and p. 124 above (Alba).

4. See the important collection of essays in Farnham, *Avoiding losses, taking risks,* especially the essays by Jack Levy and Robert Jervis. I am very grateful to Derek Croxton for bringing this volume to my attention. See also Levy, 'Loss aversion', 186–9.

5. The duke of Sessa in 1600, quoted p. 111 above; AGS *Estado* 2025/36, Spínola to Philip III, 25 June 1607 (I thank Paul Allen for sharing this document with me); AGRB *Audience* 643bis, Luis Verreycken to Archduke Albert, Valladolid, 10 Feb. 1606.

6. The account in Allen, 'The strategy of peace', chaps 8–10, supersedes all others, demonstrating how the different goals of Archduke Albert in Brussels and Philip III and Lerma in Spain opened the door to concessions that Madrid had tried to avoid for thirty years. See also pp. 157–63 above on the different agendas of Brussels and Madrid in the reign of Philip II.

7. Levin, 'A Spanish eye on Italy', 339, Requeséns to Gonzalo Pérez, 3 Mar. 1565 (the letter bears an annotation showing that the king also read it).

8. *Monumenta historica societatis Iesu,* LX, *Ribadeneira,* 22–9, Ribadeneira to Cardinal Quiroga, 16 Feb. 1580. Teresa of Ávila agreed: Fernández Álvarez, *Felipe II,* 533–5. A very similar dilemma faced Philip II's great-grandson, Louis XIV of France, when Charles II of Spain bequeathed his entire inheritance to Philip of Anjou: if Louis (on Anjou's behalf) accepted, it would probably provoke a major European war; if he declined, the entire Spanish Monarchy would pass to France's enemies, the Austrian Habsburgs (and, if they refused, to the duke of Savoy). After agonized debate, Louis accepted: see Lossky, *Louis XIV,* 260–2.

9. *Actas de las Cortes,* III, 18–20, 'proposition' read by Francisco de Erasso, 1570; Lebow and Stein, *We all lost the Cold War,* 42–8; Gaddis, *We now know,* 260–78.

10. On the Philippines, see Phelan, *The hispanization of the Philippines,* 14; and Headley, 'Spain's Asian presence', 635; on Ceylon, described as early as 1603 as a 'sumidouro' (a 'bottomless pit'), see Abeyasinghe, *Portuguese rule,* especially 38–41.

11. *BMO,* II, 420, Philip II to the count of Olivares, 18 Nov. 1586, minute.

12. AGS *Estado* 590/23, Parma to Philip II, 28 Feb. 1586; BL *Sloane* 262/67v, from the 'Ephemeris or diarie'. The full passage reads: 'The duke of Parma, sore offended with God, hath saide he verilie thinketh that God is sworne Englishe (he is and so will alwaies shewe himselfe to be!).'

13. AGRB *SEG* 195/64, Philip IV to Infanta Isabella (Philip's daughter, still governing the Netherlands), 9 Aug. 1626. See also the resigned phrase of historian Virgilio Malvezzi, writing in the 1630s: 'It is a particular misfortune of this Monarchy never to be at war with one [enemy] at a time' (Malvezzi, *Los primeros años del reinado de Felipe IV,* 125).

14. AGRB *SEG* 183/170v-171, Zúñiga to Juan de Ciriza, 7 Apr. 1619, copy; Elliott, *Spain and its world,* 241–2, Olivares to the count of Gondomar, 2 June 1625. (Compare Olivares's emphasis on the need for leaders to retain their self-confidence with the very similar remarks of Alfred Jodl quoted on pp. 291–2 above.)

15. See the perceptive remarks of Iklé, *Every war must end,* especially 1–2, 18, 38–9 and 59.

16. Kagan, *Lucrecia's dreams,* 80–5 (Philip showed considerable interest in Lucrecia's dreams, and personally approved the order for the Inquisition to imprison and interrogate her: ibid., 129, 132); BCR Ms 2417/19, Silva to Esteban de Ibarra, 22 June 1589; Soons, *Mariana,* 124, n. 19, quoting

De rege et regis instructione, libri III (Toledo, 1599).

17. Kamen, *Philip*, 320 (quoting Braudel, *The Mediterranean*, II, 1244); Gaddis, *We now know*, 292.

18. See Bayly, 'Knowing the country', 10–17 (I thank Ian Petrie for bringing this article to my attention); and Bayly, *Empire and information*, chap. 1.

19. Wernham, *The return of the Armadas*, 131, quoting Essex to Lord Henry Howard, 7 Oct. 1596; *HMC Downshire*, III, 128–9, Sir Thomas Edmondes to William Trumble, 29 Aug. 1611. See also Walsingham's 1588 lament that he had too much to do: p. 226 above.

20. Millar, *The emperor and the Roman world*, 5–7 and 203–72; Bartlett, *Monarchs and ministers*, 206–7.

21. Bartlett, *Monarchs and ministers*, 4–5, 44, 53; quotations from 59–60 and 10. I thank Derek Croxton for drawing my attention to this fascinating work.

22. Details from Potter, 'Jefferson Davis', 106–11 (quotation from R. G. H. Kean at p. 109, n.). Compare Davis's micromanagement – on occasion he would visit battlefields and change the disposition of regiments during action – with Lincoln's disclaimer to General Grant in 1864: 'The particulars of your plans, I neither know nor seek to know' (ibid., 107–8). I thank Mark Grimsley for drawing this article to my attention.

23. Gaddis, *We now know*, 293. He added: 'I find it increasingly difficult, given what we know now, to imagine the Soviet Union or the Cold War without Stalin'. See also the substantial examination of a twentieth-century without Hitler by Turner, 'Hitler's impact'.

24. International Military Tribunal, *The Nuremberg Trial*, XV, 295: testimony of Alfred Jodl on 3 June 1946; Warlimont, *Inside Hitler's headquarters*, 177. It must be remembered that both Warlimont and Jodl stood accused of war crimes, for which the former received a prison sentence and the latter was executed: both therefore had every incentive to show that they

played only ancillary roles in Hitler's system. The nature of this 'polycratic' system has been much debated: see Kershaw, *The Nazi dictatorship*, and Hildebrand, *The Third Reich*, 136–40. See also the illuminating analysis of Haffner, *The meaning of Hitler* – for example, pp. 43–4 (the polycratic state), 113 (reluctance to commit combined with programmatic stubbornness), and 121 (seclusion combined with absolutism) – which offers an uncanny parallel with the habits of Philip II.

25. *The Nuremberg Trial*, XV, 299.

26. Jodl's exchange with Hitler quoted by Persico, *Nuremberg*, 248; his conclusions by Warlimont, *Inside Hitler's headquarters*, 257. In the end Hitler relented and Jodl kept his job – leading him to trial and execution for war crimes at Nuremberg.

27. From the diary entry of Hitler's disgusted chief of staff: Burdick and Jacobsen, *The Halder War Diary*, 516. This change of heart did not prevent Guderian's dismissal on Christmas Day 1941 for allowing his forces to withdraw before the Russian counter-offensive; but it did secure him lavish compensation in estates in Poland and in cash.

28. General Otto Förster quoted by Bullock, *Hitler and Stalin*, 578; Halder's diary entry for 22 Aug. 1941 quoted by Warlimont, *Inside Hitler's headquarters*, 191.

29. Warlimont, *Inside Hitler's headquarters*, 641, quoting unpublished notes kept by Jodl. Much the same problem apparently persists: a 1997 Pentagon study of recent United States military operations in Bosnia noted a tendency to 'saturate the warrior with data while starving him of useful information' (*Washington Post*, 3 Apr. 1997, A22: my thanks to Matthew Waxman for this item).

30. Raleigh, *History of the world*, 407; Philip to Alba in 1571 quoted on p. 105 above.

31. 'Thoughts on the late transactions respecting Falkland's islands' (1771),

in Samuel Johnson, *Political writings*, X, 365–6 (I thank Jeremy Black for bringing this reference to my attention). Cf. John F. Kennedy's similar reference to the 'dark and tangled stretches in the decision-making process' quoted at p. xv above.

32. On counterfactual protocols, see Tetlock and Belkin, *Counterfactual thought experiments*.

33. F. Aguilar de Terrones, 'Sermón', quoted in *El Escorial*, 237.

34. Philip quoted on p. 105 above; Gaddis, *We now know*, 291.

Note on Sources

I. Documents

'As anyone working in the recent period knows,' a recent article reminded diplomatic historians, 'it would take a lifetime to consult all the sources that in theory one should.' The same might be said for anyone working on the history of Philip II because, as Pascual de Gayangos (a notable nineteenth-century scholar of early modern Spain) observed with only slight exaggeration: 'The history of Philip II is in a way the history of the world'.[1] William H. Prescott, author of the first modern biography of the king (to whom Gayangos wrote), employed foreign service personnel and research assistants to locate and transcribe documents: Gayangos himself employed four copyists in the British Library alone and Prescott continued 'Philippizing', as he called it, until shortly before his death in 1859. Even so his three fat volumes, the product of sixteen years' research, only cover the first two decades of the reign.

Prescott and his team never located the core source upon which the present study rests: the archive of Philip's private secretary, Mateo Vázquez de Leca, which contains the king's correspondence with his most intimate policy advisers, and also letters addressed 'to be placed in the king's hands' (see pp. 26–7 above) from about 1565 until Vázquez's death in 1591. The tens of thousands of Philip's surviving holograph memoranda reveal more about the king's strategic aims and priorities – as well as about the matters that crossed the royal mind as he wrote – than any other single source. These documents passed through many hands (including those of the count-duke of Olivares, chief minister of Philip IV) until in 1711 they reached the archive of the counts of Altamira. There disaster struck them: in the nineteenth century some disappeared and the rest became scattered – almost at random – between repositories in Geneva, London and Madrid, so that the various memoranda written by the king to a secretary on the same day may turn up in all four archives, while a message from a minister may be found today in Geneva, with Vázquez's cover note in London and Philip's reply in Madrid. Carlos Riba García published the majority of the 'billetes' contained in just one volume (now in the British Library), providing a precious example of the genre;

397

but the collection contains over a thousand times as many documents. A modern 'concordance' of the Altamira collection represents one of the most urgent needs facing those who want to 'Philippize' today.[2]

The copious records housed in the Archivo General de Simancas constitute a second indispensable source for the study of Spanish policy in the later sixteenth century. First and foremost come the *Negociación de Estado* (State Papers), organized by country (Aragón, Castilla, Flandes, Inglaterra, Francia, Alemania, Roma, Génova and so on). This series contains the papers received and reviewed by the council of State, whose members discussed incoming letters that affected government policy, whether from countries ruled by Philip II or not. The papers of the council of War (in the series *Guerra Antigua*) concern principally the defence of Spain, but sometimes include documents relating to the Americas and Italy; those of the councils of Italy, Portugal and Flanders (in the series *Secretarías Provinciales*) mainly relate to patronage and internal administration in each dominion but occasionally include material on international relations. The financial issues that so perplexed Philip II generated several major series of records in Simancas: the deliberations of, and letters and memorials addressed to, the council of Finance (*Consejo y Juntas de Hacienda*); the audited accounts of those who disbursed government funds or provided government loans (*Contaduría Mayor de Cuentas*); the fiscal records of the various armies and navies financed by Castile (*Contaduría del Sueldo*, with more in *Contaduría Mayor de Cuentas*).

Simancas does not contain all the archives of the central government, however. To begin with, the records of the council of the Indies are in Seville (Archivo General de Indias, series *Indiferente General*);[3] those of the councils of the Orders and Inquisition are mostly in Madrid (Archivo Histórico Nacional, *Órdenes militares* and *Inquisición*); those of the council of Aragon are in Barcelona (Archivo de la Corona de Aragón, *Consejo de Aragón*). And from every series several documents – including many of the most important – are missing. Some may be found in the various parts of the Altamira collection (especially rich in consultas from the councils of Finance and the Indies); others were looted or purchased by the French in the nineteenth century (although many of these returned to Simancas in 1941).[4] Others still the king ordered to be burnt – although sometimes his secretaries disobeyed.[5] Finally, although Philip sought to collect the papers of his ministers at their death, he did not always succeed. Don Juan de Zúñiga and his brother Don Luis de Requeséns amassed perhaps the largest collection of 'state papers' in private hands – some 800 bundles and books of documents – which now also form part of the Altamira collection, and may be found in the same four locations as Vázquez's papers.[6] Cardinal Granvelle left almost as many documents, most of them now scattered between the Bibliothèque Municipale in Besançon, the Bibliothèque Royale in Brussels, and the Library of the Royal Palace in Madrid.[7] Two noblemen who served the king in prominent positions also left major archives: the duke of Alba, whose extensive correspondence remains in the library of his descendant's Liria Palace in Madrid, and the duke of Medina Sidonia, most of whose letters and papers may be consulted in the ducal archive at San

Lúcar de Barrameda (although the majority of those from 1587–89 are now in the Karpeles Manuscript Library in Santa Barbara, California).[8] By contrast, the archive of Alexander Farnese, duke of Parma, suffered a double tragedy: the bulk of his papers ended up in the Archivio di Stato in Naples, where most were burnt by German soldiers in 1943; many of the rest, in Parma, have suffered severe damage from damp.[9] Nevertheless, as one nineteenth-century collector of Spanish documents observed, 'More manuscripts are destroyed by ignorant people than by civil wars'; and examples abound of aristocratic archives 'sold by weight to the grocers' that have, for the most part, never been seen again.[10]

Naturally, each of the states governed by Philip II possessed its own institutions and generated separate records, permitting historians to study the implementation of the king's policies on the periphery – although, here too, losses often thwart the best-laid plans. The archives of several key Spanish institutions in Naples and Milan – especially those of the viceroy's or governor's advisory councils – have disappeared. The Brussels archives contain only the records of organs run by Netherlanders until the 1590s: those of the Spanish institutions created in the wake of the arrival of the duke of Alba in 1567 scarcely survive before the early seventeenth century. Unfortunately, most strategic decisions in the Low Countries after 1567 were taken by Spaniards. In Mexico, by contrast, two series of documents offer an unusual view of the impact of royal power. In the Archivo General de la Nación, the first nine volumes of the series *Mercedes* (sometimes known as the *libros de gobierno*) contain registered copies of apparently all the orders issued by the viceroys, many of them rehearsing the royal command that precipitated them; while the first two volumes of the series *Cédulas reales duplicadas* list hundreds of Philip's orders received in Mexico City, sometimes with a note of the action taken. The Historical Archive at Goa, capital of Portuguese India, likewise contains virtually all the letters received from Philip in the 1580s and 1590s (filed in the *Livros das Monções*) but sheds little light on either the execution of his orders or the policy debates in Goa about how to govern outposts that stretched from Sofala to Nagasaki.[11]

As noted in the Preface (p. xvii) above, the reports of the various envoys at the Court of Spain fill some lacunae in the surviving government records and also provide some detail on the decision-makers. Twelve governments maintained ambassadors throughout the reign: the emperor, the pope, France, Savoy, Genoa, Venice, Mantua, Parma, Ferrara, Lucca, Florence and Urbino. In addition, England maintained a resident envoy until 1568, as did Portugal until 1580. The dispatches of a few ambassadors have been published *in extenso*: for France, those of Laubespine (1559–62), St Sulpice (1562–65), Fourquevaux (1565–72) and Longlée (1582–92); for Venice, those of Donà (1570–73).[12] In addition, the letters of English agents in Spain were summarized in the *Calendar of State Papers Foreign: Elizabeth* (18 volumes to 1585, when the outbreak of war virtually closed the peninsula to Elizabeth's diplomats); while those of all Venetian envoys abroad (as well as the deliberations of the Senate) that contained material relating to Elizabethan England fill volumes VI to IX of the *Calendars of State Papers Venetian*.

The closing 'Relations' made by each Venetian ambassador to the Senate after his tour abroad, some of them running to over a hundred printed pages, have been published twice, once in a somewhat haphazard and incomplete form by E. Alberì in the nineteenth century, and in their entirety by L. Firpo, in *Relazioni*: volume VIII, pp. 232–938, of his series covers the envoys to Philip's Court 1557–98. L. Serrano printed the entire diplomatic correspondence between Rome and Madrid between 1565 and 1572 – both between Pope Pius V and his nuncios and between Philip II and his ambassadors – in four volumes; while N. Mosconi included many dispatches in his study of the nunciature of Cesare Speciano, bishop of Novara, (1586–88). The dispatches of the long-serving imperial ambassador Khevenhüller (1574–1606) remain unpublished (although most of his originals survive in Vienna, as do his own registers of outgoing letters in the Oberösterreichisches Landesarchiv in Linz), but his 'secret journal' has been printed.[13] As for the rest, the diplomatic dispatches in the archives of Florence, Genoa, Lucca, Mantua, Modena (for Ferrara), Parma, Turin (for Savoy) and the Vatican (for the Papacy and also Urbino) remain in manuscript; as do those of French Ambassador St Gouard (1572–80: in the Bibliothèque Nationale, Paris, *Ms Fonds français* 16,104–16,108), and those of the other long-serving imperial ambassador of this period, Adam Dietrichstein (1564–73: in the Haus-, Hof-, und Staatsarchiv, Vienna, with more material in the Rodinný Archiv Ditrichšteinu in the Moravian State Archives at Brno).

The papers of Philip's principal declared enemies also present problems. Those of the Ottoman empire and its North African vassals require linguistic and palaeographic skills which few possess, although some publications by those few reveal just how much material exists to reconstruct the Grand Strategy of one of the principal early modern Islamic states.[14] England has been superbly served by her archivists, who have published an astonishing range of sources. The series of *Calendars* of the various documentary series preserved in the Public Record Office are unique. In the words of the lapidary statement that opens every volume: 'The entries should be so minute as to enable the reader to discover not only the general contents of the originals, but also what *they do not* contain.'[15] The archive of the Secretaries of State has been particularly well served: every document concerning Ireland and Scotland has been summarized in separate series; those received from agents and well-wishers all over the continent, as well as from foreign sources, are résumé́d (often with substantial verbatim extracts) in a single chronological sequence entitled *State Papers, Foreign Series*. *State Papers, Domestic Series* calendars (often very briefly) every document received by the Secretary of State from correspondents in England and Wales. In addition, the Public Record Office sent scholars to other major European archives and libraries to transcribe documents relevant to British history, and a translated précis of these documents from Venice, Spain and (in rather less detail) Rome and Milan has been published (unfortunately no calendars were ever prepared for France, Germany, the Netherlands or Scandinavia). The registers of decisions taken by the Privy Council have been published in their entirety (although unfortunately for the present project the original volume covering June 1582–February 1586 has been lost).[16] By contrast, the huge surviving records of the financial officers of the Tudor state (also in the Public Record Office) have been largely neglected: none of the 'Declared Accounts' of those who handled public funds, preserved in the series *Exchequer* and *Audit Office* (PRO E315 and AO1), has been published or calendared; yet the series provides a relatively complete picture of how Elizabeth paid for her struggle against Philip II (just as the *Contaduría* records in Simancas do for Castile); while the section mysteriously labelled *Ordnance Office Miscellanous* (WO55) provides vital evidence of how she managed to avoid defeat.

Naturally, as in Spain, not all government records ended up in public archives. William Cecil, Lord Burghley, Elizabeth's principal adviser until his death in 1598, left an extensive collection of state papers now divided between the archive of his descendants at Hatfield House and several manuscript collections in the British Library; Francis Walsingham, her Secretary of State and 'Spymaster' from 1572 until his death in 1589, also left a substantial private archive, most of it also now in the British Library; while the copious papers of Robert Dudley earl of Leicester, her 'favourite' until his death in 1588, lie scattered among a bewildering array of private collections. Here again, however, British archivists have created a magnificent research tool: the Historical Manuscripts Commission publishes meticulous calendars for most of the leading private archives, providing verbatim transcripts of many important documents and a précis of the rest.[17] Details on other collections may be obtained through the National Register of Archives. Finally, in contrast to the archives of Philip II and his ministers, most papers generated by Elizabeth and her councillors remain in England: one significant exception is the splendid 'Hastings Collection' at the Huntington Library in San Marino, California, which contains the archive of the earl of Huntingdon, charged with the defence of northern England during the Armada emergency.

The surviving records of France and of the Dutch Republic in the later sixteenth century present far more problems. In the former, the religious wars and the French Revolution caused the loss or dispersion of many of the central government archives, so that it is now extremely difficult to trace the stages by which the French crown framed its foreign policy. Pride of place, however, goes to the massive published collections of letters written by Catherine de Medici, the dominant figure in government from 1560 almost until her death in 1589, and of her son Henry III; then to the various 'Mémoires' written by military and political leaders.[18] The published correspondence of Ambassadors Laubespine and Fourquevaux in Spain (p. 399 above) includes the letters directed to them from Paris and thus offers important insights on French policy. For the rest, however, the documents in the Bibliothèque Nationale and Archives Nationales (especially the section *Archives privés*) in Paris contain most of the surviving material.[19]

The documentary situation in the Netherlands is somewhat better. The archives of the 'sovereign body' from 1576, the States-General, have been extensively published: all their resolutions, and a considerable amount of supporting documentation, have been printed in a series of chronological volumes in each of which the entries are arranged thematically ('War', 'Trade', etc.). The domestic and foreign correspondence handled by officials of the assembly, however, must still be consulted in the Algemeen Rijksarchief in the Hague. At first the letters were filed in four series: England, France, Germany and 'ordinary' (for all the rest), which simplifies consultation at least for the 1580s.[20] From 1581 the council of State (Raad van State) oversaw the day-to-day conduct of war, and its registers of deliberations – kept in French until 1587 (for the benefit first of the duke of Anjou and then of the earl of Leicester and their advisers) and thereafter in Dutch – provide a wealth of information both on the Republic's military operations and on what it heard about the enemy.[21] Many crucial decisions were taken by the institutions of the various provinces that made up the Republic, however: the States of Holland, also meeting in the Hague (whose resolutions have been published verbatim: *Resolutiën van de Staten van Holland*); the States of Zeeland, meeting in Middelburg (whose resolutions have also been fully published: *Notulen van de Staten van Zeeland*); and so on. Each province also possessed its own Audit Office (*Rekenkamer*), which supervised the raising and disbursement of local money; its own Admiralty (*Admiraliteit*), which handled the collection of tolls and escort taxes as well as coastal defence; and its own law courts. Each province also had a governor (*stadhouder*), a post that in Holland, Zealand and some other provinces was almost always held after 1572 by members of the house of Nassau, and their family archive in the Hague (the Koninklijke Huisarchief) contains many riches besides the correspondence published by Groen van Prinsterer (*Archives ou correspondance de la maison d'Orange-Nassau*) and Gachard (*Correspondance de Guillaume le Taciturne*). Another important officer of the Republic during the reign of Philip II left important private archives: Johan van Oldenbarnevelt (pensionary of the States of Holland from 1586 until 1619). Much of his early correspondence was published by Haak, *Oldenbarnevelt*. Inevitably, many crucial documents concerning the defence of the Dutch Republic are to be found abroad: in Belgium, in England, in France, and above all in Spain – for until 1592, at least, Philip II dominated international relations throughout western Europe.

II. Published work

Perhaps because of this, Philip II has generally had a bad press. Outside Spain, few of his contemporaries found a good word for him. In 1581 Prince William of Orange, leader of the Dutch Republic, published an *Apology* which accused Philip (*inter alia*) of incest, lechery, sodomy and the murder of his eldest son.[22] In 1598, one of the king's exiled ministers, Antonio Pérez, published a volume of documents and commentaries that portrayed Philip II as a petty, vindictive and rather obtuse tyrant. Dutch, Latin, French and English translations soon followed.[23] In the same year João Teixeira, a Portuguese exile in England, completed a treatise entitled 'The anatomy of Spain', which included a searing indictment of Spanish imperialism in general and of Philip II in particular.[24] By then criticisms had begun to circulate widely in Spain as well. Also in 1598 Balthasar Álamos de Barrientos, an imprisoned supporter of Antonio Pérez, completed a tract that excoriated the weak international position in which Philip II had left Spain and called for a new offensive spirit; and the following year Iñigo Ibañez de Santa Cruz, a royal secretary, circulated a manuscript that ridiculed and condemned the late king's personal habits as well as his policies.[25]

These sundry works became the staple of almost every subsequent account written outside Spain, their details and anecdotes repeated and embellished time after time until they achieved immortality in the vivid prose of the Romantic American historian John Lothrop Motley, whose *Rise of the Dutch Republic* of 1856 presented an unforgettable portrait of Philip as a perfidious hypocrite in private and a pedantic autocrat in public: 'the common enemy of Christendom', a man whose 'malignity and duplicity' were almost superhuman, a monster who 'lacked a single virtue' and was prevented from possessing every vice only because 'no human can obtain perfection, even in evil'. With his narrative organized into five 'acts', like a drama for the stage, Motley presented a seductively intimate picture of an obsessive, weak and stupid man endowed with supreme power.[26]

Needless to say, it is a picture to be discarded: even though supported by extensive use of contemporary sources, Motley's account bristled with distortions, mainly because his sources were themselves distorted. If we are to understand Philip II and his strategic goals aright we must forget almost everything published by Pérez, Orange, Teixeira, Ibañez and Álamos; but what can be set in their place? The king did not welcome biographies as his father had done: although at least two of his officials composed them in his early years, they remained unpublished. When in 1585 Secretary of State Don Juan de Idiáquez commissioned the young Antonio de Herrera y Tordesillas to write a history of Philip's reign, he expressly forbade him to deal with the king's 'life', recommending instead a 'History of the world' starting in 1559. Herrera complied, presenting the king as the principal actor in all the major events of his day but never revealing his personality.[27] Early in the seventeenth century two collections of anecdotes about Philip appeared – Lorenzo vander Hammen's *Don Felipe el Prudente* in 1625 and Balthasar Porreño's *Dichos y hechos del Rey Felipe II* three years later – but they stood alone. Although some other writers, such as Cabrera de Córdoba, wrote histories of the king's times, no new biography by a Spaniard appeared until the nineteenth century.

Even so, relatively little has ever been written about the foreign policy of Philip II, and still less about his strategic vision. The most substantial work on the former is the study of Fernández Álvarez, *Política mundial de Carlos V y Felipe II*, although it contains more material on Charles V than on his son; but see also Braudel, *The Mediterranean*, part III; Lapèyre, *Las etapas de la política exterior de Felipe II*; Doussinague, *La política exterior de España en el siglo XVI*; and Pagden, *Spanish imperialism and the political imagination*. Two excellent monographs cover the 1550s: Lutz, *Christianitas Afflicta*; and Rodríguez-Salgado, *The changing face of empire.* Also recommended for the 1580s and early 1590s is Jensen, *Diplomacy and dogmatism.* See also the annotated bibliography in Aguardo Bleye, *Manual de Historia de España*, II.

Beyond these studies, those interested more generally in the king and his world can consult the legion of modern biographies available in a bewildering range of languages. Those published before 1983 are conveniently listed (by century) in Palau y Dulcet, *Manual del librero hispano-americano*, III, 86–90, with further items in the bibliography to *El Escorial. Biblioteca de una época*, 310–46. The recent works by Checa, *Felipe II*, Parker, *Philip II*, and Kamen, *Philip of Spain* also cite many subsequent works. Much, of course, remains to be done and the fourth centenary of the king's death in 1998 will surely bring forth many other new studies (besides this one) so that, like William Hickling Prescott, 'Philippizing' by historians will no doubt go on well into the twenty-first century.

Notes

1. Immerman, 'The history of United States foreign policy', 578; Gardiner, 'Prescott's most indispensable aide: Pascual de Gayangos', 99. Prescott himself merely claimed that 'The history of Philip the Second is the history of Europe during the latter half of the sixteenth century' (Prescott, *History*, I, iv).

2. On the remarkable history of the Altamira archive, see the seminal article of Andrés, 'La dispersión de la valiosa colección'. The documents may be found today among the *envíos* of the Instituto de Valencia de Don Juan and the *cajas* of the Biblioteca de Zabálburu in Madrid, in the 'Collection manuscrite Édouard Favre' of the Bibliothèque Publique et Universitaire in Geneva, and among the Additional Manuscripts of the British Library in London. The 436 pages of Riba Garcia, *Correspondencia privada*, published most (but not all) of the contents of BL *Addl* 28,263.

3. Heredía Herrera, *Catálogo*, printed in full the royal apostil to each surviving consulta in the Archivo General de Indias. The first two volumes in the series cover the reign of Philip II.

4. The documents were listed, while still in France, by Daumet, 'Inventaire de la Collection Tirán'; and Paz, *Catálogo de documentos españoles*. These documents now fill AGS *Estado* 8334–43 – a remarkably rich and unjustly neglected collection.

5. BMB *Ms Granvelle* 23/10, Philip II to Granvelle, 7 July 1566, claiming that many of Granvelle's letters 'he quemado por mayor seguridad'; in his last will and testament, the king ordered his entire correspondence with Diego de Chaves, his confessor, to be burnt (p. 333 n. 90 above). But see also IVdeDJ 38/70, Cardinal Espinosa to Philip II and reply, undated (but 1569) giving vent to his frustrations and ending 'Burn this paper once you have seen it, because it serves no purpose' (see the text on p. 45 above). The cardinal's secretary, Mateo Vázquez, wrote on the dorse: 'Attention! This must be seen by no one except His Majesty.' For more examples, see Bouza Álvarez, 'Guardar papeles – y quemarlos – en tiempos de Felipe II. La documentación de Juan de Zúñiga, I'.

6. See Bouza Álvarez, 'Guardar papeles – y quemarlos – en tiempos de Felipe II. La documentación de Juan de Zúñiga, II'. See also Andrés, 'La dispersión', for the process by which the Zúñiga brothers' papers came to the Altamira archive.

7. *PEG* and *CCG* published most of Granvelle's letters from the first two repositories, but included virtually none from Madrid (nor from the Altamira collection which also includes numerous holograph letters from the cardinal to the king): for a good survey of surviving sources see van Durme, *Cardenal Granvela*, 3–25.

8. Alba's outgoing letters were almost all published in the *Epistolario*, but the Archivo de la Casa de Alba preserves hundreds of incoming letters, including many from Philip II. Maura, *El designio*, printed extracts from some of the Medina Sidonia letters now in the Karpeles Manuscript Library in Santa Barbara.

9. See details in Dierickx, 'Les "Carte Farnesiane"'. In fact more of the duke's papers survive in Naples than Dierickx feared; and, equally fortunately, Professor Léon van der Essen copied extracts of many documents into notebooks ('cahiers') before these disasters. He published a large number in his biography, *Alexandre Farnèse*, and I am grateful to his son Alfred, and to Professor Jan van Houtte, for making the 'cahiers' in their possession available to me. See also Parker, *Guide to the archives*.

10. Munby, *Phillipps studies*, V, 13–14, Obediah Rich (a Boston bibliophile) to Sir Thomas Phillipps, 20 Nov. 1843 (noting that he had just bought 120 manuscript volumes at 2 shillings each from a Madrid bookseller who was about to 'sell by weight to the grocers'. The batch included at least some Philip II manuscripts, one of which Phillipps bought.) For further sales by weight see Andrés, 'La dispersión', 608–9 and 617. For a chance survival see BCR Ms 2417, a volume of letters excoriating almost every aspect of Philip II's government sent by Don Juan de Silva to Esteban de Ibarra, both of them senior royal ministers, in the 1580s and 1590s. Yet one must not protest too much: countless documents – especially diplomatic correspondence – from both public and private Spanish archives were published in *Co.Do.In.*: see the checklist in Fernández Álvarez, *Felipe II*, 20. Gómez del Campillo, *Negociaciones*, and Rodriguez, *Álava*, printed a lot more.

11. Almost all Philip II's extant letters to the viceroys were published in *APO*.

12. L. Paris, *Négociations*; E. Cabié, *Ambassade*; Douais, *Dépêches*; Mousset, *Dépêches*; and Brunetti and Vitale, *La corrispondenza*. Many more unpublished letters of Laubespine were tracked down by Fernand Braudel: see *The Mediterranean*, II, 1250.

13. Khevenhüller-Metsch and Probst-Ohstorff, *Hans Khevenhüller*.

14. For three examples see Hess, *The forgotten frontier*; Imber, *Studies*, 85–102; and Kortepeter, *Ottoman imperialism*, 214–25.

15. On this unique development, see Levine, *The amateur and the professional*, chap. 5.

16. The original transcripts from foreign archives may be found in the eponymous series PRO.PRO. Details on the various series of Calendars for the age of Philip II will be found in the Bibliography. The *Acts of the Privy Council* were edited by J. R. Dasent.

17. For Burghley's papers at Hatfield House, see *HMC Salisbury*; for Walsingham's, see the *apparatus criticus* of Read, *Walsingham*; for Leicester's, see Adams, 'Papers of Robert Dudley', and Brugmans, *Correspondentie*.

18. Ferrière and Baguenault de Puchesse, eds, *Lettres de Catherine de Médicis*, and François, ed., *Lettres de Henri III*. Other useful publications are described in the vintage study of Hauser, *Sources*.

19. For more detailed references, see the *apparatus criticus* of Wood, *The king's army*, and Holt, *The duke of Anjou*.

20. See *RSG*. Of special interest is a small collection of important Spanish state papers from 1567 to 1574 seized in Brussels in 1576: ARA *Staten Generaal* 12,548, especially loketkas 14A and 14B

21. ARA *Raad van State* 5 covers Mar–Aug. 1586; 6 covers June 1587–Mar. 1588; 7 covers May–Dec 1588.

22. William of Nassau, prince of Orange, *Apologie ou défense* (Leiden, 1581), with numerous further editions in French, Dutch, English and other languages. See the modern reprint of the original English edition by H. Wansink (Leiden, 1969).

23. Antonio Pérez, *Relaciones*: see the recent edition (from the 1598 text, published eleven days after Philip II's death) by A. Alvar Ezquerra (Madrid, 1986). See also the erudite discussion of the work in Ungerer, *A Spaniard in Elizabethan England*, II, 280–321.

24. Cambridge University Library, Ms Gg–6–19 'La anatomía de España'. The work was translated into English for the earl of Essex in 1599: see Beinecke Library, Yale University, Osborne shelves, fa. 20, 'The anatomie of Spayne', and the discussion in Ungerer, *A Spaniard in Elizabethan England*, II, 275–6.

25. Álamos de Barrientos, *Discurso político*, discussed on pp. 108–9 above. Ibañez's intemperate 'Pasquín', and papers on his subsequent trial for treason, may be found in AMAE *MDFD Espagne* 239/417–67; RAH Ms 9–3507; and BNM Ms 11,044.

26. Motley, *The rise of the Dutch Republic*. See the fascinating discussion of this work in Levin, *History as Romantic art*, 186–209, and Kagan, 'Prescott's paradigm'.

27. The 'Oratio' of Viglius, written in the Netherlands, covered the king's reign only until 1566 (and broke off in mid-sentence); the 'Historia' of Juan de Verzosa, written in Rome, began in 1548 but only reached the 1570s: see, for the former, Wauters, *Mémoires de Viglius et d'Hopperus*, 7–157; and, for the latter, the introduction to López de Toro, *Epistolas*. For Herrera y Tordesillas, whose *Historia general del mundo* began to appear in 1600, see the brilliant anaysis of Kagan, 'Felipe II' – who notes that Herrera coined Philip's enduring epithet 'el Prudente' in 1599.

Bibliography

This book rests principally upon manuscript material, and these are discussed in the Note on Sources above. The following bibliography provides the full title of all primary and secondary printed works cited in the notes.

Primary sources

Abreu, P. de, *Historia del saqueo de Cádiz por los ingleses en 1596* (ed. M. Bustos Rodríguez, Cádiz, 1996)

Actas de las Cortes de Castilla (17 vols cover the reign of Philip II, Madrid, 1882–89)

Aguado Bleye, P., *Manual de historia de España* (3 vols, Madrid, 1958)

Álamos de Barrientos, B., *Discurso político al rey Felipe III al comienzo de su reinado* (ed. M. Sánchez, Madrid, 1990)

Alcocer, M., *Consultas del consejo de Estado, 1600–1603* (Valladolid, 1930: Archivo Histórico Español, III)

Aldana, F. de, *Obras completas* (1593; ed. M. Moragón Maestre, Madrid, 1953)

Altadonna, G., 'Cartas de Felipe II a Carlos Manuel II Duque de Saboya (1583–96)', *Cuadernos de investigación histórica*, IX (1986), 137–90

Andrés, G. de, 'Diurnal de Antonio Gracián', in *Documentos . . . El Escorial*, V, 19–127 (for 1572–73) and VIII, 11–63 (for 1571 and 1574)

Andrews, K. R., *The last voyage of Drake and Hawkins* (Cambridge, 1972: Hakluyt Society 2nd series, CXLII)

Anon., 'The chronicle of Queen Jane and of two years of Queen Mary' (London: 1850: Camden Society, 1st series XLVIII)

Anon., *The edict and decree of Phillip king of Spain* (London, 1597)

Bain, J., *The Hamilton papers*, II (Edinburgh, 1892)

Berwick y Alba, duchess of, *Documentos escogidos del Archivo de la Casa de Alba* (Madrid, 1891)

Berwick y Alba, duke of, *Epistolario del III duque de Alba* (3 vols, Madrid, 1952)

Birch, T., *Memoirs of the reign of Queen Elizabeth from the year 1581 till her death*, I (London, 1754)

Bor, P., *Geschiedenis der Nederlandsche Oorlogen* (first edn. 1595–1601) II (Leiden, 1621), III (Amsterdam, 1626)

Borrell, C., *De Regis Catholici Praestantia* (Milan, 1611)

Bouza Álvarez, F. J., *Cartas de Felipe II a sus hijas* (Madrid, 1988)

Breeder verclaringhe vande Vloote van Spaegnien. De Bekentenisse van Don Diego de Piementel (The Hague, 1588: Knuttel pamphlet 847)

Brown, H. F., *Calendar of State Papers . . . Venice*, VIII (London, 1894)

Bruce, J., ed., *The Liber Famelicus of Sir James Whitelocke* (London, 1858: Camden Society Publications, LXX)

Brugmans, H., *Correspondentie van Robert Dudley, graaf van Leycester* (3 vols, Utrecht, 1931)

Brunetti, M. and E. Vitale, *La corrispondenza da Madrid dell' ambasciatore Leonardo Donà (1570–1573)* (2 vols, Venice–Rome, 1963)

Burdick, C. and H.-A. Jacobsen, *The Halder War Diary, 1939–1942* (Novato, 1988)

Burnet, G., *Memoires of the dukes of Hamilton* (London, 1677)

Bustamente Callejo, M., 'Consejos del capitán laredano Don Lope de Ocina y de la Obra, al rey Felipe II para la conquista de Inglaterra', *Altamira*, I (1952), 75–82

Cabié, E., *Ambassade en Espagne de Jean Ebrard, seigneur de Saint-Sulpice* (Albi, 1903)

Cabrera de Córdoba, L., *Historia de Felipe II, rey de España* (4 vols, Madrid, 1876 edn; vols I–II originally published in 1619)

Calendar of State Papers, Domestic Series, Elizabeth, II (1581–91) (London, 1865)

Calendar of State Papers, Foreign Series, of the reign of Elizabeth (22 vols to 1588, London, 1863–1936)

Calendar of State Papers relating to Scotland and Mary Queen of Scots (9 vols to 1588, Edinburgh and Glasgow, 1899–1915)

Calvar Gross, J., J. I. González-Aller Hierro, M. de Dueñas Fontán and M. del C. Mérida Valverde, *La batalla del Mar Océano* (3 vols, Madrid, 1988–93)

Camden, W., *The historie of the most renowned and victorious Princesse Elizabeth* (Latin original of Part I, London, 1615; English translation, London 1630)

Campanella, T., *De monarchia hispanica discursus* (1600–1610; Amsterdam, 1640)

Canestrini, G. and A. Desjardins, *Négociations diplomatiques de la France avec la Toscane*, IV (Paris 1872)

Carnero, A., *Historia de las guerras civiles que ha avido en los estados de Flandes* (Brussels, 1625)

Casado Soto, J. L., *Discursos de Bernardino de Escalante al rey y sus ministros (1585–1605)* (Laredo, 1995)

Cauchie, A. and L. van der Essen, *Inventaire des archives farnésiennes de Naples au point de vue de l'histoire des Pays-Bas catholiques* (Brussels, 1911)

Cimber, M. and F. Danjou, *Archives curieuses de l'histoire de la France*, 1st series XI (Paris, 1836)

Cockle, M. J. D., *A bibliography of military books up to 1642* (London, 1900)

Colección de documentos inéditos para la historia de España (112 vols, Madrid, 1842–95)

Coloma, C., *Las guerras de los Estados Baxos* (Antwerp, 1625)

Corbett, J. S., *Papers relating to the navy during the Spanish War, 1585–1587* (London, 1898)

Correa, G., *Lendas da India*, vol. I, part i (Coimbra, 1922)

Correa Calderón, E., *Registro de arbitristas, economistas y reformadores españoles (1500–1936). Catálogo de impresos y manuscritos* (Madrid, 1981)

Couto, D. de, *Da Ásia, decada X* (Lisbon, 1788)

Cunha Rivara, J. de, *Archivo Portuguez-Oriental* (6 vols, Nova Goa, 1857–76)

Dasent, J. R., *Acts of the Privy Council of England*, XIV (London, 1897)

Daumet, G., 'Inventaire de la Collection Tirán', *Bulletin hispanique*, XIX (1917), 189–99, XX (1918), 36–42 and 233–48, and XXI (1919), 218–30 and 282–95

Didier, L., *Lettres et négociations de Claude de Mondoucet, résident de France aux Pays-Bas (1571–1574)* (2 vols, Paris, 1891–92)

Donno, E. S., *An Elizabethan in 1582. The diary of Richard Madox, Fellow of All Souls'* (London, 1976: Hakluyt Society, 2nd series CXLVII)

Douais, C., *Dépêches de M. de Fourquevaux, ambassadeur du roi Charles IX en Espagne, 1565–72* (3 vols, Paris, 1896–1904)

Encinas, D. de, *Cedulario Indiano recopilado por Diego de Encinas* (1596; ed. A. García Gallo, 4 vols, Madrid, 1945–46)

Enno van Gelder, H. A., *Correspondance française de Marguerite d'Autriche duchesse de Parme. Supplément* (2 vols, Utrecht, 1942)

Evans, J. X., *The works of Sir Roger Williams* (Oxford, 1972)

Feltham, O., *A brief character of the Low-Countries* (written *c.* 1628; London, 1652; revised edn 1662)

Fernández Álvarez, M., *Corpus documental Carlos V* (5 vols, Salamanca, 1974–81)

Fernández Duro, C., *La Armada invencible* (2 vols, Madrid, 1888)

Ferrière-Percy, H. de la and G. Baguenault de Puchesse, eds, *Lettres de Catherine de Médicis* (11 vols, Paris 1880–1909)

Firpo, L., *Relazioni di ambasciatori veneti al Senato. III. Germania 1557–1654* (Turin, 1970)

Firpo, L., *Relazioni di ambasciatori veneti al Senato, VIII Spagna 1497–1598* (Turin, 1981)

Fortescue, Sir John, *The correspondence of King George the Third*, IV (London, 1928)

François, M., *Lettres de Henry III, roy de France* (6 vols, Paris, 1959)

Furió Ceriol, F., *El concejo y consejeros del príncipe y otras obras* (1559; ed. D. Sevilla Andrés, Valencia, 1952)

Gachard, L. P., *La Bibliothèque Nationale à Paris*, II (Brussels, 1877)

Gachard, L. P., *Correspondance de Guillaume le Taciturne* (6 vols, Brussels, 1849–57)

Gachard, L. P., *Correspondance de Philippe II sur les affaires des Pays-Bas* (5 vols, Brussels 1848–79)

Gachard, L. P., 'Notice de la collection dite des *Archives de Simancas* qui est conservée aux archives de l'Empire, à Paris', *Bulletin de la Commission Royale d'Histoire*, 3rd series III (1862), 9–78

Gentil da Silva, J., *Stratégie des affaires à Lisbonne entre 1595 et 1607. Lettres marchandes des Rodrigues d'Evora et Veiga* (Paris, 1956)

Gerlo, A. and R. de Smet, *Marnixi epistulae. De briefwisseling van Marnix van Sint-Aldegonde. Een kritische uitgave I. 1558–76* (Brussels, 1990)

Gómez del Campillo, M., *Negociaciones con Francia* (11 vols, Madrid, 1950–60: Archivo Documental Español)

González, T., 'Apuntamientos para la historia del rey D. Felipe II', *Memorias de la Real Academia de la Historia*, VII (1832)

González Dávila, G., *Teatro de las grandezas de la villa de Madrid* (Madrid, 1623)

González de Cellorigo, M., *Memorial de la política necessaria y útil restauración a la República de España* (Valladolid, 1600; ed. J. Pérez de Ayala, Madrid, 1991)

González Olmedo, F., *Don Francisco Terrones del Caño: Instrucción de predicadores* (1617; Madrid, 1946)

González Palencia, A., *Gonzalo Pérez, secretario de Felipe II* (2 vols, Madrid, 1946)

Gravel, M., *The Pentagon papers. The Defense Department history of United States decision-making on Vietnam*, IV (Boston, 1971)

Greenlee, W. B., *The voyage of Pedro Alvares Cabral to Brazil and India* (London, 1938: Hakluyt Society 2nd series LXXXI)

Groen van Prinsterer, G., *Archives ou correspondance inédite de la maison d'Orange-Nassau, 1552–1789* (1st series, 8 vols and supplement, Leiden 1835–47; 2nd series, I, Utrecht, 1857)

Groenveld, S. and J. Vermaere, 'Zeeland en Holland en 1569. Een rapport voor de hertog van Alva', *Nederlandse historische bronnen*, II (1980), 103–74

Grotius, H., *De rebus belgicis; or, the annals and history of the Low-Countrey-Wars* (London, 1665)

Guevara, F. de, *Comentarios de la pintura* (*c.* 1564; Madrid, 1788)

Guillén Tato, J., *Museo Naval. Colección de documentos y manuscritos inéditos compilados por Fernández de Navarrete*, XVIII (Nendeln, 1971)

Haak, S. P., *Johan van Oldenbarnevelt. Bescheiden betreffende zijn staatkundig beleid en zijn familie. I: 1570–1601* (The Hague, 1934)

Hair, P. E. H., *To defend your empire and the faith: advice offered to Philip, king of Spain and Portugal, c. 1590* (Liverpool, 1990)

Halliwell, J. O., *Letters of the kings of England*, II (London, 1846)

Hamilton, H. C., *Calendar of State Papers relating to Ireland: Elizabeth, 1588–92* (London, 1885)

Hauser, H., *Les Sources de l'histoire de la France. XVIe siècle (1494–1610). III. Les guerres de religion, 1559–1589* (Paris, 1912)

Heredía Herrera, A., *Catálogo de las consultas del consejo de Indias*, I (Madrid, 1972)

Herrera Oria, E., *La Armada invencible. Documentos procedentes del Archivo General de Simancas* (Valladolid, 1929: Archivo Histórico Español, II)

Herrera y Tordesillas, A., *Historia general del mundo del tiempo del Rey Felipe II, el prudente* (2 vols, Madrid, 1600–6)

Hicks, L., *Letters and memorials of Father Robert Persons*, I (London, 1942: Catholic Record Society, XXXIX)

Historical Manuscripts Commission *Calendar of the manuscripts of the Most Honourable the Marquess of Bath*, V (London, 1980)

Historical Manuscripts Commission *Calendar of the manuscripts of the Most Honourable the Marquess of Downshire*, III (London, 1938)

Historical Manuscripts Commission *Calendar of the manuscripts of the Most Honourable the Marquess of Salisbury*, III (London, 1889)

Historical Manuscripts Commission *Twelfth Report* (London, 1888), appendix, part IV, 'Manuscripts of His Grace the duke of Rutland'

Historical Manuscripts Commission *Fifteenth Report* (London, 1897), appendix, part V, 'Manuscripts of the the Rt. Hon. F. J. Savile-Foljambe'

Hopper, C., *Sir Francis Drake's memorable service done against the Spaniards in 1587* (London, 1863: Camden Miscellany, V)

Horozco y Covarrubias, J., *Tratado de la verdadera y falsa profesía* (Segovia, 1588)

Hume, M. A. S., *Calendar of letters and state papers relating to English affairs preserved in, or originally belonging to, the archives of Simancas: Elizabeth* (4 vols, London, 1892–99)

International Military Tribunal, *The Nuremberg Trial*, XV (English version, London, 1948)

Japikse, N., *Correspondentie van Willem I, prins van Oranje*, I (Haarlem, 1933)

Japikse, N., *Resolutiëen der Staten-Generaal van 1576 tot 1609* (14 vols, The Hague, 1917–70)

Johnson, Samuel, *Political writings*, X (ed. D. J. Greene, New Haven and London, 1977)

Keeler, M. F., *Sir Francis Drake's West Indian voyage, 1585–6* (London, 1981: Hakluyt Society, 2nd series CLXLVIII)

Kemp, P., *The papers of Admiral Sir John Fisher*, I (London, 1960)

Kervijn de Lettenhove, B., *Relations politiques des Pays-Bas et de l'Angleterre sous le règne de Philippe II*, I (Brussels, 1882)

Khevenhüller-Metsch, G. and G. Probst-Ohstorff, *Hans Khevenhüller: kaiserliche Botschafter bei Philipp II. Geheimes Tagebuch, 1548–1605* (Graz, 1971)

Kupke, G., *Nuntiaturberichte aus Deutschland, nebst ergänzenden Aktenstücken. 1er Abteilung 1533–59*, XII (Berlin, 1901)

Lalanne, L., *Oeuvres complètes de Pierre de la Bourdeille, sieur de Brantôme*, IV (Paris, 1870)

Lanz, K., *Korrespondenz des Kaisers Karl V* (3 vols, Leipzig, 1846)

Laughton, J. K., *State papers concerning the defeat of the Spanish Armada* (2 vols, London, 1895–1900)

Le Glay, A. and J. Finot, *Inventaire sommaire des archives départementales antérieures à 1790. Nord, série B* (6 vols, Lille, 1863–88)

López de Toro, J., *Epístolas de Juan de Verzosa* (Madrid, 1965)

López de Velasco, J., *Demarcación y división de las Indias* (1575; Madrid, 1871: Colección de documentos inéditos relativos al descubrimiento . . . de América, XV)

López de Velasco, J., *Geografía y descripción universal de las Indias* (1574; ed. J. Zaragoza, Madrid, 1894)

López Madera, Gregorio, *Excelencias de la Monarchia y reyno de España* (Madrid, 1597)

Machiavelli, N., *The Prince* (written in 1513, published 1532; English edn, ed. Q. Skinner and R. Price, Cambridge, 1988)

Malfatti, C. V., *Cuatro documentos italianos en materia de la expedición de la Armada invencible* (Barcelona, 1972)

Malvezzi, V., *Los primeros años del reinado de Felipe IV* (London, 1968)

Mansfelt, C. de, *Castra dei* (Brussels, 1642)

Masson, D., *Register of the Privy Council of Scotland*, IV (Edinburgh, 1881)

Maura Gamazo, G., duke of Maura, *El designio de Felipe II y el episodio de la Armada invencible* (Madrid, 1957)

Memoriën en adviezen van Cornelis Pieterszoon Hooft, I (Utrecht, 1871)

Mendoza, Bernardino de, *Comentarios de lo sucedido en las guerras de los Países Bajos* (1590; Biblioteca di Autores españoles, Madrid, 1948)

Monumenta historica societatis Iesu, LX, *Ribadeneira* (Madrid, 1923)

Mosconi, N., *La nunziatura di Spagna di Cesare Speciano, 1586–1588* (Brescia, 1961)

Mousset, A., *Dépêches diplomatiques de M. de Longlée résident de France en Espagne 1582–1590* (Paris, 1912)

Mulder, L., *Het Journael van Antonis Duyck* (1591–1602; 3 vols, The Hague, 1862–66)

Notulen van de Staten van Zeeland 1588

Oliveira, F., *A arte da guerra do mar* (1555; Lisbon, 1983)

Orange, William of Nassau prince of, *Apologie ou défense* (Leiden, 1581; English edn, ed. H. Wansink, Leiden, 1969)

Palau y Dulcet, A., *Manual del librero hispano-americano*, III (Madrid, 1983)

Paris, L., *Négociations, lettres et pièces diverses relatives au règne de François II, tirées du portefeuille de Sébastien de L'aubespine* (Paris, 1841)

Paz, J., *Catálogo de documentos españoles existentes en el Archivo del Ministerio de Asuntos Extrangeros de París* (Madrid, 1932)

Percyvall, R., *Biblioteca hispanica, containing a grammar, with a dictionarie in Spanish* (London, 1591)

Pérez, Antonio, *Relaciones* (1598; ed. A. Alvar Ezquerra, Madrid, 1986)

Pérez de Herrera, L., *Elogio a las esclarecidas virtudes de . . . Felipe II* (Valladolid, 1604)

Pigafetti, F., *Discorso sopra l'ordinanza dell'armata catolica* (Rome, 1588)

Piot, C., *Chroniques de Brabant et Flandre* (Brussels, 1879)

Porreño, B., *Dichos y hechos del Rey Don Felipe II* (Madrid, 1628)

Porreño, B., *Historia del Sereníssimo Señor Don Juan de Austria* (ed. A. Rodríguez Villa, Madrid, 1899)

Poullet, E. and C. Piot, *Correspondance du Cardinal de Granvelle 1565–1586* (12 vols, Brussels, 1877–96)

Raleigh, W., 'Excellent observations and notes concerning the royall navy', in Raleigh, *Judicious and select essayes and observations* (London, 1650), part III

Raleigh, W., *History of the world* (London, 1614)

Renold, P., *Letters of William Allen and Richard Barrett, 1572–1598* (Oxford, 1967: Catholic Record Society)

Riba García, C., *Correspondencia privada de Felipe II con su secretario Mateo Vázquez 1567–91* (Madrid, 1959)

Ricotti, E., 'Degli scritti di Emanuele-Filiberto, duca di Savoia', *Memorie della Real Accademia delle scienze di Torino: scienze, morali, storiche*, 2nd series XVII (1858), 69–164

Rodríguez, P. and J., *Don Francés de Álava y Beamonte. Correspondencia inédita de Felipe II con su embajador en París (1564–1570)* (San Sebastián, 1991)

Ruiz Martín, F., *Lettres marchandes échangées entre Florence et Medina del Campo* (Paris, 1965)

Salazar, J. de, *Política española* (Logroño, 1619; Madrid, 1945)

Salazar de Mendoza, Pedro, *Monarchia de España* (Madrid, 1770)

Sande, D. de, *De missione legatorum iaponensium* (Macao, 1590)

Santullano, J., *Obras completas de Teresa de Jesús* (Madrid, 1930)

Scott, W., *The Somers collection of tracts* (London, 1809)

Scott Thomson, G., 'The Twysden lieutenancy papers, 1583–1668', *Kent Records Society*, X (1926)

Serrano, L., *Correspondencia diplomática entre España y la Santa Sede durante el pontificado de San Pio V* (4 vols, Madrid, 1914)

Shaw, W. A., *Report on the manuscripts of Lord De L'Isle and Dudley preserved at Penshurst Place* (HMC Report No. 77), III (London, 1936)

Sigüenza, J. de, *La fundación del Monasterio de El Escorial* (1605; Madrid, 1988)

Solórzano y Pereira, J., *Política indiana* (Latin edn, 1629; Castilian edn, 1647; Biblioteca de autores españoles edn, Madrid, 1972)

Strada, F., *De bello belgico, decas secunda* (Rome, 1648)

Tassis, J. B. de, *Commentarii de tumultibus belgicis sui temporis*, in C. P. Hoynck van Papendrecht, *Analecta Belgica*, Vol. II, part 2 (The Hague, 1743)

Taylor, E. G. R., *The troublesome voyage of Captain Edward Fenton 1582–3. Narratives and documents* (London, 1959: Hakluyt Society, 2nd series CXIII)

Tellechea Idígoras, J. I., *Fray Bartolomé Carranza. Documentos históricos*, III (Madrid, 1966)

Teulet, A., *Relations politiques de la France et de l'Espagne avec l'Écosse*, V (Paris, 1862)

Theissen, J. S., *Correspondance française de Marguerite d'Autriche, duchesse de Parme, 1565–1567* (Utrecht, 1925)

Valdés, D. de, *De dignitate regum regnorumque Hispaniae* (Granada, 1602)

van der Essen, L., *Les Archives Farnésiennes de Parme au point de vue de l'histoire des anciens Pays-Bas* (Brussels, 1913)

van der Hammen, L., *Don Felipe el Prudente . . . rey de las Españas y Nuevo Mundo* (Madrid, 1625)

van Eeghen, I. H., *Dagboek van Broeder Wouter Jacobszoon . . . Prior van Stein* (2 vols, Groningen, 1959)

van Meteren, E., *Historie van de oorlogen en geschiedenissen der Nederlanden* (1599; Gorinchem, 1752)

van Reyd, E., *Historie der Nederlandtscher Oorlogen, begin ende voortganck tot den Jaere 1601* (1626; Arnhem, 1633)

van Someren, J. F., *La Correspondance du Prince Guillaume d'Orange avec Jacques de Wesenbeke* (Utrecht, 1896)

Vargas Hidalgo, R., 'Documentos inéditos sobre la muerte de Felipe II y la literatura fúnebre de los siglos XVI y XVII', *Boletín de la Real Academia de la Historia*, CXCII (1995), 377–460

Vázquez, A., *Los sucesos de Flandes y Francia del tiempo de Alejandro Farnesio*, II (*Co. Do. In.*, LXXIII)

Vázquez de Prada, V., *Lettres marchandes d'Anvers* (3 vols, Paris, 1961)

Velázquez, I., *La entrada que en el reino de Portugal hizo la S. C. R. M. de Don Philippe* (Lisbon, 1583)

Voci, A. M., 'L'impresa d'Inghilterra nei dispacci del nunzio a Madrid, Nicolò Ormanetto (1572–1577)', *Annuario dell'Istituto Storico Italiano per l'Età Moderna e Contemporanea*, XXXV–XXXVI (1983–84), 337–425

Wauters, A., *Mémoires de Viglius et d'Hopperus sur le commencement des troubles des Pays-Bas* (Brussels, 1858)

Weiss, C., *Papiers d'État du Cardinal de Granvelle* (9 vols, Paris, 1841–52)

Zarco Cuevas, J., G. de Andrés and others, *Documentos para la historia del monasterio de San Lorenzo El Real de El Escorial* (8 vols, Madrid, 1917–62)

Secondary sources

Abeyasinghe, T., *Portuguese rule in Ceylon 1594–1612* (Colombo, 1966)

Adams, S., 'The battle that never was: the Downs and the Armada campaign', in Rodríguez-Salgado and Adams, *England, Spain and the Gran Armada*, 173–96

Adams, S., 'Favourites and factions at the Elizabethan Court', in Asch and Birke, *Princes, patronage and the nobility*, 265–88

Adams, S., 'New light on the "Reformation" of John Hawkins: the Ellesmere Naval Survey of January 1584', *English Historical Review*, CV (1990), 96–111

Adams, S., 'The outbreak of the Elizabethan naval war against the Spanish empire', in Rodríguez-Salgado and Adams, *England, Spain and the Gran Armada*, 45–69

Adams, S., 'The papers of Robert Dudley, earl of Leicester', *Archives*, XX (1990), 131–44

Alcázar Molina, C., 'La política postal española en el siglo XVI en tiempo de Carlos V', in *Carlos V (1500–1558). Homenaje de la Universidad de Granada* (Granada, 1958), 219–32

Allen, E. J. B., *Post and courier service in the diplomacy of early modern Europe* (The Hague, 1972)

Allen, P. C., 'The strategy of peace: Spanish foreign policy and the "Pax hispanica", 1598–1609' (Yale University Ph. D. thesis, 1995)

Alvar Ezquerra, A., *Felipe II, la corte y Madrid en 1561* (Madrid, 1985)

Alvar Ezquerra, A., 'Unas "reglas generales para remitir memoriales" del siglo XVI', *Cuadernos de historia moderna*, XVI (1995), 47–71

Andrés, G. de, 'La dispersión de la valiosa colección bibliográfica y documental de la Casa de Altamira', *Hispania*, XLVI (1986), 587–635

Angiolini, F., 'Diplomazie e politica dell'Italia non spagnola nell'età di Filippo II', *Rivista storica italiana*, XCII (1980), 432–69

Antolín, G., 'La librería de Felipe II (Datos para su reconstrucción)', *Ciudad de Dios*, CXVI (1919), 477–88

Armitage, D., 'The Cromwellian Protectorate and the language of empire', *Historical Journal*, XXXV (1992), 531–55

Arnold, T. F., 'Fortifications and the military revolution: the Gonzaga experience, 1530–1630', in C. J. Rogers, ed., *The Military Revolution Debate* (Boulder, 1995), 201–26

Arrieta Alberdi, J., *El consejo supremo de la corona de Aragón (1494–1707)* (Zaragoza, 1994)

Asaert, G., 'Een brug te veel. Antwerpens scheepsmacht tijdens het Parmabeleg, 1584–1585', in *Van blauwe stoep tot citadel. Varia historica brabantica Ludovico Pirenne dedicata* ('sHertogenbosch, 1988), 129–40

Asch, R. G. and A. M. Birke, eds, *Princes, patronage and the nobility. The Court at the beginning of the modern age* (Oxford, 1991)

Atti dei convegni internazionali sulla storia del Finale. La Spagna, Milano ed il Finale: il ruolo del Marchesato Finalese tra medioevo ed età moderna (2 vols, Finale Ligure, 1994)

Aubrey, J., *Brief lives* (ed. O. L. Dick, London, 1967)

Aubrey, P., *The defeat of James Stuart's Armada, 1692* (Leicester, 1979)

Baetens, R., 'An essay on Dunkirk merchants and capital growth during the Spanish period,' in *From Dunkirk to Danzig. Essays in honour of Prof. Dr J. A. Faber* (Hilversum, 1988), 117–43

Baguenault de Puchesse, G., 'La Politique de Philippe II dans les affaires de France, 1559–98', *Revue des questions historiques*, XXV (1879), 5–66

Balderstone, T., 'War finance and inflation in Britain and Germany, 1914–1918', *Economic History Review*, XLI (1989), 222–44

Barbeito, J. M., *El Alcázar de Madrid* (Madrid, 1992)

Barber, P., 'England: monarchs, ministers and maps, 1550–1625', in D. Buisseret, ed., *Monarchs, ministers and maps. The emergence of cartography as a tool of government in early modern Europe* (Chicago, 1992), 57–98

Barkman, S. H., 'Guipuzcoan shipping in 1571', in *Anglo-American contributions to Basque studies: essays in honor of Jon Bilbao* (Reno, 1977)

Barnard, C., *The function of the executive* (rev. edn, Cambridge, MA, 1968)

Bartlett, B. S., *Monarchs and ministers. The Grand Council in mid-Ch'ing China, 1723–1820* (Berkeley, 1991)

Bataillon, M., *Erasmo y España: Estudios sobre la historia espiritual del siglo XVI* (2nd edn, Mexico, 1950)

Bayly, C.A., *Empire and information. Intelligence gathering and social communication in India, 1780–1870* (Cambridge, 1996).

Bayly, C. A., 'Knowing the country: empire and information in India', *Modern Asian Studies*, XXVII (1993), 3–43

Beaumont, R., *War, chaos and history* (Westport, CT, 1994)

Beinert, B., 'El testamento político de Carlos V de 1548. Estudio crítico', in *Carlos V. Homenaje de la Universidad de Granada* (Granada, 1958), 401–38

Belda y Pérez de Nueros, F., marqués de Cabra, *Felipe II. Cuarto centenario de su nacimiento* (Madrid, 1927)

Bell, G. M., 'John Man: the last Elizabethan resident ambassador in Spain', *The Sixteenth-century Journal*, VII.2 (October 1976), 75–93

Bély, L., *Espions et ambassadeurs au temps de Louis XIV* (Paris, 1990)

Benedict, P., 'The St Bartholomew's massacres in the provinces', *The Historical Journal*, XXI (1978), 205–25

Bennassar, B., *Valladolid au Siècle d'Or* (Paris, 1967)

Benson, N. L., 'The ill-fated works of Francisco Hernández', *The Library Chronicle of the University of Texas*, V (1954), 17–27

Berwick y Alba, duke of, *Discurso: contribución al estudio de la persona de Don Fernando Álvarez de Toledo, III duque de Alba* (Madrid, 1919)

Beyerchen, A., 'Clausewitz, non-linearity and the unpredictability of war', *International Security*, XVII.3 (1992–93), 59–90

Binchy, D. A., 'An Irish ambassador at the Spanish Court 1569–74', *Studies*, X (1921), 353–74 and 573–84

Bireley, R., *The Counter-Reformation Prince. Anti-Machiavellism or Catholic statecraft in early modern Europe* (Chapel Hill, 1990)

Bitossi, C., *Il governo dei magnifici. Patriziato e politica a Genova tra 500 e 600* (Genoa, 1990)

Bitton, D. and Q. A. Mortensen, 'War or peace: a French pamphlet polemic, 1604–06', in Thorp and Slavin, *Politics, religion and diplomacy*, 127–41

Black, J., *Convergence or divergence? Britain and the continent* (New York, 1994)

Blaylock, C., 'The study of Spanish in Tudor and Stuart England', in *Selected proceedings: the seventh Louisiana conference on Hispanic languages and literatures* (Baton Rouge, 1987), 61–72

Bolzern, R., *Spanien, Mailand und die katholische Eidgenossenschaft. Militärische, wirtschaftliche und politische Beziehungen zur Zeit Alfonso Casati* (Luzern, 1982)

Boratynski, L., 'Estebán Batory, la Hansa y la sublevación de los Países Bajos', *Boletín de la Real Academia de la Historia*, CXXVIII (1951), 451–500

Bordejé y Morencos, F. F., *El escenario estratégico español en el siglo XVI (1492–1556)* (Madrid, 1990)

Borman, T., 'Untying the knot? The survival of the Anglo-Dutch alliance, 1587–97', *European history quarterly*, XXVII (1997), 307–37

Borromeo, A., 'España y el problema de la elección papal de 1592', *Cuadernos de investigación histórica*, II (1978), 175–200

Borromeo, A., 'Istruzioni generali e corrispondenza ordinaria dei nunzi: obiettivi prioritari e resultati concreti della politica spagnola di Clemente VIII', in G. Lutz, ed., *Das Papsttum, die Christenheit und die Staaten Europas, 1592–1605. Forschungen zu den Hauptinstruktionen Clemens' VIII* (Tübingen, 1994: Bibliothek des deutschen historischen Instituts in Rom, LXVI), 119–204

Bosbach, F., *Monarchia universalis. Ein politischer Leitbegriff der frühen Neuzeit* (Göttingen, 1988)

Bouza Álvarez, F. J., 'Corte es decepción. Don Juan de Silva, Conde de Portalegre', in Martínez Millán, *La corte de Felipe II*, 451–99

Bouza Álvarez, F. J., 'Cortes festejantes, fiesta y ocio en el cursus honorum cortesano', *Manuscrits*, XIII (1995), 185–203

Bouza Álvarez, F. J., *Del escribano a la biblioteca. La civilización escrita europea en la alta edad moderna (siglos XV–XVII)* (Madrid, 1992)

Bouza Álvarez, F. J., 'Guardar papeles – y quemarlos – en tiempos de Felipe II. La documentación de Juan de Zúñiga', *Reales Sitios*, XXXIII.3 (1996), 2–15 and XXXIV.1 (1997), 18–33

Bouza Álvarez, F. J., 'Leer en palacio. De aula gigantium a museo de reyes sabios', in *El libro antiguo español. III. El libro en palacio y otros estudios bibliográficos* (Salamanca, 1996), 29–42

Bouza Álvarez, F., *Locos, enanos y hombres de placer en la corte de los Austrias. Oficio de burlas* (Madrid, 1991)

Bouza Álvarez, F. J., 'La majestad del rey. Construcción del mito real', in Martínez Millán, *La corte de Felipe II*, 36–72

Bouza Álvarez, F. J., 'Monarchie en lettres d'imprimerie. Typographie et propagande au temps de Philippe II', *Revue d'histoire moderne et contemporaine*, XLI (1994), 206–20

Bouza Álvarez, F. J., 'Portugal en la Monarquía hispánica 1580–1640. Felipe II, las Cortes de Tomar y la génesis del Portugal Católico' (Universidad Complutense de Madrid Ph.D. thesis, 1987)

Bouza Álvarez, F. J., 'Retórica da imagem real. Portugal e la memória figurada de Filipe II', *Penélope*, IV (1989), 20–58

Bouza Álvarez, F. J., 'Servidumbres de la soberana grandeza. Criticar al rey en la Corte de Felipe II' (forthcoming)

Boxer, C. R., 'Portuguese and Spanish projects for the conquest of Southeast Asia, 1580–1600', in Boxer, *Portuguese conquest and commerce in southern Asia, 1500–1750* (London, 1985), chap. 3

Boyden, J. M., *The courtier and the king. Ruy Gómez de Silva, Philip II and the Court of Spain* (Berkeley, 1995)

Brand, H. and J., eds, *De Hollandse Waterlinie* (Utrecht, 1986)

Bratli, C., *Philippe II, roi d'Espagne* (Paris, 1912)

Braudel, F., *The Mediterranean and the Mediterranean world in the age of Philip II* (2 vols, London, 1972–73)

Braudel, P., 'Braudel antes de Braudel', in C. A. Aguirre Rojas, ed., *Primeras jornadas Braudelianas* (Mexico, 1993), 84–96

Brayshay, M., 'Plymouth's coastal defences in the year of the Spanish Armada', *Reports and transactions of the Devonshire Association for the Advancement of Science*, CXIX (1987), 169–96

Brayshay, M., 'Royal post-horse routes in England and Wales: the evolution of the network in the later sixteenth and early seventeenth centuries', *Journal of Historical Geography*, XVII (1991), 373–89.

Breakwell, Glynis and Keith Spacie, *Pressures facing commanders* (Camberwell, 1997: Strategic and Combat Studies Institute, Occasional Papers XXIX)

Brown, J. and J. H. Elliott, *A palace for a king. The Buen Retiro and the Court of Philip IV* (New Haven, 1980)

Brown, K. M., 'The making of a *politique*: the Counter-Reformation and the regional politics of John, eighth Lord Maxwell', *Scottish Historical Review*, LXVI (1987), 152–75

Brulez, W., 'Het gewicht van de oorlog in de nieuwe tijden, enkele aspecten', *Tijdschrift voor Geschiedenis*, XCI (1978), 386–406

Bullock, A., *Hitler and Stalin. Parallel lives* (New York, 1992)

Burkholder, M. A. and L. L. Johnson, *Colonial Latin America* (2nd edn, Oxford, 1994)

Cabantous, A., *Histoire de Dunkerque* (Toulouse, 1983)

Calabria, A., *The cost of empire. The finances of the kingdom of Naples in the time of Spanish rule* (Cambridge, 1991)

Campbell, J., *Grammatical man. Information, entropy, language and life* (New York, 1982)

Cano de Gardoquí, J. L., *La cuestión de Saluzzo en las comunicaciones del Imperio Español, 1588–1601* (Valladolid, 1962)

Cano de Gardoquí, J. L., 'España y los estados italianos independientes en 1600', *Hispania*, XXIII (1963), 524–55

Cano de Gardoquí, J. L., *La incorporación del marquesado de Finale (1602)* (Valladolid, 1955)

Carlos Morales, C. J. de, *El consejo de Hacienda de Castilla, 1523–1602. Patronazgo y clientelismo en el gobierno de las finanzas reales durante el siglo XVI* (Valladolid, 1996)

Carlos Morales, C. J. de, 'El poder de los secretarios reales: Francisco de Eraso', in Martínez Millán, *La corte de Felipe II*, 107–48

Carrafiello, M. L., 'English Catholicism and the Jesuit mission of 1580–1', *Historical Journal*, XXXVII (1994), 761–74

Carter, C. H., 'The ambassadors of early modern Europe: patterns of diplomatic representation', in Carter, ed., *From the Renaissance to the Counter-Reformation. Essays in honour of Garrett Mattingly* (London, 1965), 269–95

Carter, C. H., *The secret diplomacy of the Habsburgs, 1598–1625* (New York, 1964)

Caruana, A. B., *The history of English sea ordnance, 1523–1870*, I (Rotherfield, 1994)

Casado Soto, J. L., *Los barcos españoles del siglo XVI y la Gran Armada de 1588* (Madrid, 1988)

Casado Soto, J. L., 'La construcción naval atlántica española del siglo XVI y la Armada de 1588', in *La Gran Armada* (Madrid, 1989: Cuadernos monográficas del Instituto de Historia y Cultura Naval, III), 51–85

Castillo, A., 'Dette flottante et dette consolidée en Espagne, 1557–1600', *Annales: Economies, Sociétés, Civilisations*, XVIII (1963), 745–59

Cerezo Martínez, R., 'La conquista de la isla Tercera (1583)', *Revista de historia naval*, I.3 (1983), 5–45

Céspedes del Castillo, G., 'La visita como institución indiana', *Anuario de estudios americanos*, III (1946), 984–1025

Chabod, F., 'Contrasti interni e dibattiti sulla politica generale di Carlo V', in P. Rassow and F. Schalk, eds, *Karl V: der Kaiser und seine Zeit* (Cologne, 1960), 51–66

Chabod, F., 'Milán o los Países Bajos? Las discusiones sobre la Alternativa de 1544,' in *Carlos V (1500–1558). Homenaje de la Universidad de Granada* (Granada, 1958), 331–72

Chandler, A. D., *Strategy and structure. Chapters in the history of the industrial enterprise* (Cambridge, MA, 1962)

Charrière, E., *Négociations de la France dans le Levant*, II (Paris, 1850)

Chaunu, H. and P., *Séville et l'Atlantique, 1504–1650* (8 vols, Paris, 1955–60)

Checa, F., 'Felipe II en El Escorial: la representación del poder real', in *El Escorial: arte, poder y cultura en la corte de Felipe II* (Madrid, 1989), 7–26

Checa, F., *Felipe II: Mecenas de las Artes* (2nd edn, Madrid, 1993)

Checa, F., *Tiziano y la monarquía hispánica. Usos y funciones de la pintura veneciana en España (siglos XVI y XVII)* (Madrid, 1994)

Chevallier, P., *Henri III. Roi shakespearien* (Paris, 1985)

Christy, M., 'Queen Elizabeth's visit to Tilbury in 1588', *English Historical Review*, XXXIV (1919), 43–61

Clark, P., ed., *The European crisis of the 1590s: essays in comparative history* (London, 1985)

Cline, H. F., 'The *Relaciones geográficas* of the Spanish Indies, 1577–84', *Hispanic-American Historical Review*, XLIV (1964), 341–74

Collinson, P., 'The Elizabethan exclusion crisis and the Elizabethan polity', *Proceedings of the British Academy*, LXXXIV (1993), 51–92

Collinson, P., *The English captivity of Mary Queen of Scots* (Sheffield, 1987)

Constant, J. M., *Les Guise* (Paris, 1984)

Costantini, C., *La Repubblica di Genova* (Turin, 1986)

Cowley, R. and G. Parker, eds, *The reader's companion to military history* (Boston, MA, 1996)

Cox, B., *Vanden tocht in Vlaenderen. De logistiek van Nieuwpoort 1600* (Zutphen, 1986)

Craeybeckx, J., 'La Portée fiscale et politique du 100e denier du duc d'Albe', *Acta historica bruxellensia*, I (Brussels, 1967), 342–74

Cressy, D., 'Binding the nation: the Bonds of Association, 1584 and 1696', in D. J. Guth and J. W. McKenna, eds, *Tudor rule and revolution* (Cambridge, 1982), 217–34

Cressy, D., *Bonfires and bells. National memory and the Protestant calendar in Elizabethan and Stuart England* (Berkeley, 1989)

Croft, P., 'English commerce with Spain and the Armada war, 1558–1603', in Rodríguez-Salgado and Adams, *England, Spain and the Gran Armada*, 236–63

Croft, P., *The Spanish Company* (London, 1973)

Cueto, R., '1580 and all that . . . Philip II and the politics of the Portuguese succession', *Portuguese Studies*, VIII (1992), 150–60

Cumming, W. P., 'The Parreus map (1562) of French Florida', *Imago mundi*, XVII (1963), 27–40

Dandelet, T. J., 'Roma hispanica: the creation of Spanish Rome in the Golden Age' (University of California at Berkeley Ph.D. thesis, 1995)

Danvila y Burguero, A., *Don Cristóbal de Moura* (Madrid, 1900)

Davies, J. M., 'The duc de Montmorency, Philip II and the house of Savoy: a neglected aspect of the sixteenth-century French civil wars', *English Historical Review*, CV (1990), 870–92

Davies, J. M., 'Neither politique nor patriot? Henry, duc de Montmorency and Philip II, 1582–1589', *Historical Journal*, XXXIV (1991), 539–66

Dean, E. T., ' "We live under a government of men and morning newspapers." Image, expectation and the peninsula campaign of 1862', *Virginia Magazine of History and Biography*, CXIII (1995), 5–28

de Bueil, J. *Le Jouvencal* (written in 1466; ed. C. Favre and C. Lecestre, Paris, 1889)

Delumeau, J., *Vie économique et sociale de Rome dans la seconde moitié du 16e siècle*, I (Paris, 1957)

de Reiffenberg, B., *Histoire de l'Ordre de la Toison d'Or depuis son institution jusqu'à la cessation des chapitres généraux* (Brussels, 1830)

Después de la Gran Armada: la historia desconocida (Madrid, 1993: Cuadernos monográficos del Instituto de historia y cultura naval, XX)

Destler, L. M., *Presidents, bureaucrats and foreign policy. The politics of organizational reform* (2nd edn, Princeton, 1974)

Deswarte-Rosa, S., *Ideias e imagens em Portugal na época dos descobrimentos: Francisco de Holanda e a teoria da arte* (Lisbon, 1992)

de Törne, P. O., *Don Juan d'Autriche et les projets de conquête de l'Angleterre. Etude historique sur dix années du seizième siècle* (2 vols, Helsingfors, 1915–28)

de Törne, P. O., 'Philippe II et Henri de Guise: le début de leurs relations (1578)', *Revue historique*, CLXVII (1931), 323–35

Devos, J. C., *Les Chiffres de Philippe II (1555–1598) et du despacho universal durant le XVIIe siècle* (Brussels, 1950)

Devos, J. C., 'La Poste au service des diplomates espagnols accrédités auprès des cours d'Angleterre et de France (1555–1598)', *Bulletin de la Commission Royale d'Histoire*, CIII (1938), 205–67

Devos, J. C., 'Un Projet de cession d'Alger à la France en 1572', *Bulletin philologique et historique*, LXXVIII (1953–54), 339–48

Deyon, P., 'Sur certaines formes de la propagande religieuse au XVIe siècle', *Annales: Economies, Sociétés, Civilisations*, XXXVI (1981), 16–25

Díaz Jimeno, F., *Hado y fortuna en la España del siglo XVI* (Madrid, 1987)

Díaz-Plaja, F., *La historia de España en sus documentos. IV: el siglo XVI* (Madrid, 1958)

Díaz-Trechuelo, L., 'Consecuencias y problemas derivados del Tratado en la experiencia oriental', in Ribot García, *El Tratado de Tordesillas*, 1519–39

Dickerman, E. H., 'The conversion of Henry IV: "Paris is well worth a Mass" in psychological perspective', *Catholic Historical Review*, LXIII (1977), 1–13

Dickerman, E. H., 'A neglected aspect of the Spanish Armada: the Catholic League's Picard offensive', *Canadian Journal of History*, XI (1976), 19–23

Dierickx, M., 'Les "Carte Farnesiane" de Naples par rapport à l'histoire des anciens Pays-Bas, d'après l'incendie du 30 septembre 1943', *Bulletin de la Commission Royale d'Histoire*, CXII (1947), 111–26

Dietz, F. C., *English public finance, 1558–1641* (2nd edn, London, 1964)

Díez del Corral, L., *La Monarquía hispánica en el pensamiento político europeo* (Madrid, 1975)

Donagan, B., 'Understanding Providence: the difficulties of Sir William and Lady Waller', *Journal of Ecclesiastical History*, XXXIX (1988), 433–44

Doria, G., 'Un quadrennio critico, 1575–78. Contrasti e nuovi orientamenti nella società genovese nel quadro della crisi finanziaria spagnola', in E. Dini et al., eds, *Fatti e idee di storia economica nei secoli XII–XX. Studi dedicati a Franco Borlandi* (Bologna, 1977), 377–94

Doussinague, J. M., *La política exterior de España en el siglo XVI* (Madrid, 1949)

Doussinague, J. M., *La política internacional de Fernando el Católico* (Madrid, 1944)

Drucker, P. F., 'The coming of the new organization', *Harvard Business Review* (Jan.–Feb. 1988), 45–53

Drucker, P. F., *The effective executive* (New York, 1967)

Durand-Lapié, P., 'Un roi détroné réfugié en France: Dom Antoine 1er de Portugal (1580–95)', *Revue d'histoire diplomatique*, XVIII (1904), 133–345, 275–307, 612–40 and XIX (1905), 113–28 and 243–60

Duviols, P., *La lutte contre les religions autochtones dans le Pérou colonial. 'L'extirpation de l'idolâtrie' entre 1532 et 1660* (Lima, 1971)

Echevarría Bacigalupe, M. A., *La diplomacia secreta en Flandes, 1598–1643* (Leioa, 1984)

Edelmayer, F., 'Habsburgische Gesandte in Wien und Madrid in der Zeit Maximilians II.', in W. Krämer, ed., *Spanien und Österreich in der Renaissance* (Innsbruck, 1989), 57–70

Edelmayer, F., 'Honor y dinero. Adam de Dietrichstein al servicio de la Casa de Austria', *Revista studia histórica*, XI (1993), 89–116

Edelmayer, F., *Maximilian II., Philipp II., und Reichsitalien. Die Auseinandersetzungen um des Reichslehen Finale in Ligurien* (Stuttgart, 1988)

Edwards, C. R., 'Mapping by geographical positions', *Imago mundi*, XXIII (1969), 17–28

Edwards, F., *The marvellous chance. Thomas Howard, fourth duke of Norfolk and the Ridolphi plot, 1570–1572* (London, 1968)

Edwards, M. U., 'Catholic controversial literature, 1518–1555: some statistics', *Archiv für Reformationsgeschichte*, LXXIX (1988), 189–204

Eguiluz, M. de, *Milicia, discurso y regla militar* (Madrid, 1592)

Einaudi, G., ed., *Storia d'Italia*, II (Turin, 1974)

Eire, C. M. N., *From Madrid to purgatory: the art and craft of dying in sixteenth-century Spain* (Cambridge, 1995)

El Escorial. Biblioteca de una época. La historia (Madrid, 1986)

Elias, J. E., *De vlootbouw in Nederland in de eerste helft der 17e eeuw* (Amsterdam, 1937)

Elliott, J. H., *The count-duke of Olivares. The statesman in an age of decline* (New Haven, 1986)

Elliott, J. H., 'The court of the Spanish Habsburgs: a peculiar institution?', in Elliott, *Spain and its world*, 142–61

Elliott, J. H., 'A Europe of composite monarchies', *Past and Present*, CXXXVII (1992), 48–71

Elliott, J. H., 'Foreign policy and domestic crisis: Spain, 1598–1659,' in Elliott, *Spain and its world*, 114–41

Elliott, J. H., 'Managing decline: Olivares and the grand strategy of Imperial Spain', in Kennedy, ed., *Grand strategies in war and peace*, 87–104

Elliott, J. H., *Spain and its world 1500–1700, Selected Essays* (New Haven, 1989)

Emmanuelli, R., *Gênes et l'Espagne dans la Guerre de Corse, 1559–1569* (Paris 1964)

Estal, J. M. de, 'Felipe II y su archivo hagiográfico de El Escorial', *Hispania sacra*, XXIII (1970), 193–333

Estèbe, J., *Tocsin pour un massacre: la saison de St Barthélemy* (Paris, 1968)

Fagel, R., *De Hispano-Vlaamse Wereld. De contacten tussen Spanjaarden en Nederlanders 1496–1555* (Brussels, 1996)

Farnham, B., ed., *Avoiding losses, taking risks: prospect theory and international conflict* (Ann Arbor, MI, 1994)

Faulconnier, H., *Description historique de Dunkerque*, I (Bruges, 1730)

Fea, P., *Alessandro Farnese, duca di Parma. Narrazione storica e militare* (Rome, 1886)

Fernández Albaladejo, P., *Fragmentos de monarquía. Trabajos de historia política* (Madrid, 1992)

Fernández Albaladejo, P., ' "*De Regis Catholici Praestantia*": una propuesta de "Rey Católico" desde el reino napolitano en 1611', in Musi, ed., *Nel sistema imperiale*, 93–111

Fernández Albaladejo, P., ' "Rey Católico": gestación y metamorfosis de un título', in Ribot García, *El Tratado de Tordesillas*, 209–16

Fernández Álvarez, M., *Felipe II y su tiempo* (Madrid, 1998)

Fernández Álvarez, M., 'Las instrucciones políticas de los Austrias mayores. Problemas e interpretaciones', *Gesammelte Aufsätze zur Kulturgeschichte Spaniens*, XXIII (1967), 171–88

Fernández Álvarez, M., *Madrid bajo Felipe II* (Madrid, 1966)

Fernández Álvarez, M., *Política mundial de Carlos V y Felipe II* (Madrid, 1966)

Fernández Álvarez, M., *Tres embajadores de Felipe II en Inglaterra* (Madrid, 1951)

Fernández Armesto, F., 'Armada myths: the formative phase', in Gallagher and Cruickshank, *God's obvious design*, 19–39

Fernández Duro, C., *De algunas obras desconocidas de cosmografía y de navegación* (Madrid, 1894–95)

Fernández Duro, C., *Armada española desde la unión de los reinos de Castilla y Aragón*, I (Madrid, 1895)

Fernández Duro, C., *La conquista de los Azores en 1583* (Madrid, 1886)

Fernández Segado, F., 'Alejandro Farnesio en las negociaciones de paz entre España y Inglaterra (1586–88)', *Hispania*, XLV (1985), 513–78

Feros, A., 'Lerma y Olivares: la práctica del valimiento en la primera mitad del seiscientos', in J. H. Elliott and A. García Sanz, eds, *La España del Conde Duque de Olivares* (Valladolid, 1990), 195–224

Feros, A., 'Twin souls: monarchs and favourites in early seventeenth-century Spain', in Kagan and Parker, *Spain, Europe and the Atlantic world*, 27–47

Feros, A., ' "Vicedioses, pero humanos": el drama del rey', *Cuadernos de historia moderna*, XIV (1993), 103–31

Feros, A., 'El viejo monarca y los nuevos favoritos: los discursos sobre la privanza en el reinado de Felipe II', *Studia histórica*, XVII (1998), 11–36

Ferrill, A., 'The Grand Strategy of the Roman empire', in Kennedy, *Grand strategies in war and peace*, 71–85

Feuillerat, A., ed., *The prose works of Sir Philip Sidney*, III (Cambridge, 1962)

Fichtner, P. S., 'Dynastic marriage in sixteenth-century Habsburg diplomacy and statecraft: an interdisciplinary approach', *American Historical Review*, LXXXI (1976), 243–65

Fichtner, P. S., *Ferdinand I* (New York, 1982)

Firth, C. H., 'Thurloe and the Post Office', *English Historical Review*, XII (1898), 527–33

Fleischer, C., 'The lawgiver as Messiah: the making of the imperial image in the reign of Suleiman', in G. Veinstein, ed., *Soliman le magnifique et son temps* (Paris, 1992), 159–77

Flower-Smith, M. A., ' "The able and the willynge": the preparations of the English land forces to meet the Armada', *British Army Review*, XCV (1990), 54–61

Forneron, H., *Les ducs de Guise et leur époque*, II (Paris, 1877)

Freitas de Meneses, A. de, *Os Açores e o domínio filipino (1580–1590)* (2 vols, Angra do Heroismo, 1987)

Fruin, R., *The siege and relief of Leiden in 1574* (The Hague, 1927)

Fukuyama, F. and A. N. Shulsky, *The 'virtual corporation' and army organization* (Washington, D.C., 1997)

Gachard, L. P., *Retraite et mort de Charles-Quint* (2 vols, Brussels, 1855)

Gaddis, J. L., *We now know. Rethinking Cold War history* (Oxford, 1997)

Gallagher, P. and D. W. Cruickshank, 'The Armada of 1588 reflected in serious and popular literature of the period', in Gallagher and Cruickshank, *God's obvious design*, 167–83

Gallagher, P. and D. W. Cruickshank, eds, *God's obvious design. Papers of the Spanish Armada symposium, Sligo, 1588* (London, 1990)

García Hernán, E., *La Armada española en la Monarquía de Felipe II y la defensa del Mediterráneo* (Madrid, 1995)

García Hernán, E., 'La curia romana, Felipe II y Sixto V', *Hispania sacra*, XLVI (1994), 631–49

García Hernán, E., 'La iglesia de Santiago de los Españoles en Roma: trayectoria de una institución', *Anthologica annua*, XLII (1995), 297–363

García Hernán, E., 'Pio V y el mesianismo profético', *Hispania sacra*, XLV (1993), 83–102

García Vilar, J. A., 'El Maquiavelismo en las relaciones internacionales: la anexión de Portugal a España en 1580', *Revista de estudios internacionales*, II (1981), 599–643

Gardiner, C. H., 'Prescott's most indispensable aide: Pascual de Gayangos', *Hispanic-American Historical Review*, XXXIX (1959), 81–115

Gerson, A. J., 'The English recusants and the Spanish Armada', *American Historical Review*, XXII (1917), 589–94

Geurts, P. A. M., *De Nederlandse Opstand in de pamfletten, 1566–1584* (Nijmegen, 1956)

Gil, X., 'Aragonese constitutionalism and Habsburg rule: the varying meanings of liberty', in Kagan and Parker, *Spain, Europe and the Atlantic world*, 160–87

Gil, X., 'Visión europea de la monarquía española como monarquía compuesta', in C. Russell and J. Andrés Gallego, eds, *Las monarquías del antiguo regimen. ¿Monarquías compuestas?* (Madrid, 1996), 65–95.

Gilissen, J., 'Les phases de la codification et de l'homologation des coûtumes dans les XVII provinces des Pays-Bas', *Tijdschrift voor Rechtsgeschiedenis*, XVIII (1950), 36–67 and 239–90

Gillès de Pélichy, C., 'Contribution à l'histoire des troubles politico-religieux des Pays-Bas', *Annales de la Société d'Émulation de Bruges*, LXXXVI (1949), 90–144

Gillespie, R., 'Destabilizing Ulster 1641–2,' in B. MacCuarta, ed., *Ulster 1641: aspects of the Rising* (Belfast, 1993), 107–21

Ginzburg, C., 'Due note sul profetismo cinquecentesco', *Rivista storica italiana*, LXXVIII (1966), 184–227

Glasgow, T., 'Gorgas' seafight', *Mariner's Mirror*, LIX (1973), 179–85

Glasgow, T., 'The shape of the ships that defeated the Spanish Armada', *Mariner's Mirror*, L (1964), 177–87

Glete, J., *Navies and nations. Warships, navies and state-building in Europe and America, 1500–1860* (2 vols, Stockholm, 1993)

Gómez-Centurión, C., *La Invencible y la empresa de Inglaterra* (Madrid, 1988)

Gómez-Centurión, C., 'The new crusade: ideology and revolution in the Anglo-Spanish conflict', in Rodríguez-Salgado and Adams, *England, Spain and the Gran Armada*, 264–99

González de Amezúa y Mayo, A., *Isabella de Valois, reina de España, 1546–68* (3 vols, Madrid, 1949)

González de León, F., 'The road to Rocroi: the duke of Alba, the count-duke of Olivares and the high command of the Spanish Army of Flanders in the Eighty Years' War, 1567–1659' (Johns Hopkins Ph.D. thesis, 1991)

González García, P., *Archivo general de Indias* (Madrid, 1995)

González Novalín, J. L., *Historia de la Iglesia en España*, vol. III part 2 (Madrid, 1980)

Goodman, D., *Power and penury. Government, technology and science in Philip II's Spain* (Cambridge, 1988)

Goodman, D., *Spanish naval power, 1589–1665. Reconstruction and defeat* (Cambridge, 1996)

Gordon, C., ed., *Power/knowledge. Selected interviews and other writings, 1972–1977, by Michel Foucault* (New York, 1980)

Gould, J. D., 'The crisis of the export trade, 1586–87', *English Historical Review*, LXXI (1956), 212–22

Gracia Rivas, M., *La 'invasión' de Aragón en 1591. Una solución militar a las alteraciones del reino* (Zaragoza, 1992)

Gracia Rivas, M., 'El motín de la "Diana" y otras vicisitudes de las galeras participantes en la jornada de Inglaterra', *Revista de historia naval*, II. 4 (1984), 33–45

Gracia Rivas, M., *Los tercios de la Gran Armada, 1587–88* (Madrid, 1989)

Gray, R., 'Spinola's galleys in the Narrow Seas, 1599–1603', *Mariner's Mirror*, LXIV (1978), 71–83

Green, J. M., '"I my self": Queen Elizabeth I's oration at Tilbury Camp', *Sixteenth Century Journal*, XXVIII (1997), 421–45

Groenhuis, G., *De predikanten: de sociale positie van de Gereformeerde predikanten in de Republiek der Verenigde Nederlanden voor 1700* (Groningen, 1977)

Guilmartin, J. F., *A very short war. The SS 'Mayaguez' and the battle of Koh Tan* (College Station, TX, 1995)

Haffner, S., *The meaning of Hitler* (London, 1979)

Hall, D. D., *Worlds of wonder, days of judgment. Popular religious belief in early New England* (New York, 1989)

Halperin, M. with P. Clapp and A. Kanter, *Bureaucratic politics and foreign policy* (Washington, 1974)

Hammer, P. E. J., 'An Elizabethan spy who came in from the cold: the return of Anthony Standen to England in 1593', *Historical Research*, LXV (1992), 277–95

Hammer, P. E. J., 'New light on the Cadiz expedition of 1596', *Historical Research*, LXX (1997), 182–202

Handel, M. I., 'Intelligence and the problem of strategic surprise,' *Journal of Strategic Studies*, VII (1984), 229–81

Handel, M. I., 'The politics of intelligence', *Intelligence and National Security*, II.4 (October 1987), 5–46

Handel, M. I., 'Technological surprise in war', *Intelligence and National Security*, II.1 (1987), 1–53

Hanke, L., *The Spanish struggle for justice in the conquest of America* (Boston, MA, 1949)

Hanselmann, J.-L., *L'alliance Hispano-Suisse de 1587* (Bellinzona, 1971)

Hardach, A., *The First World War, 1914–1918* (Berkeley, 1977)

Hart, G. 't, 'Rijnlands bestuur en waterstaat rondom het beleg en ontzet van Leiden', *Leids Jaarboekje*, LXVI (1974), 13–33

Haynes, A., *Invisible power. The Elizabethan secret services, 1570–1603* (London, 1973)

Hays Park, W., 'Linebacker and the law of war', *Air University Review*, XXXIV.2 (January–February 1983), 2–30

Hays Park, W., 'Rolling Thunder and the law of war', *Air University Review*, XXXIII.2 (January–February 1982), 2–23

Headley, J. M., 'The Habsburg world empire and the revival of Ghibellinism', in S. Wenzel, ed., *Medieval and Renaissance Studies*, VII (Chapel Hill, 1978), 93–127

Headley, J. M., 'Rhetoric and reality: messianic humanism and civilian themes in the imperial ethos of Gattinara', in M. Reeves, ed., *Prophetic Rome in the High Renaissance period. Essays* (Oxford, 1992), 241–69

Headley, J. M., 'Spain's Asian presence 1565–90: structures and aspirations', *Hispanic-American Historical Review*, LXXV (1995), 623–46

Hergueta, N., 'Notas diplomáticas de Felipe II acerca del canto-llano', *Revista de archivos, bibliotecas y museos*, XIII (1904), 39–50

Hess, A., *The forgotten frontier. A history of the sixteenth-century Ibero-African frontier* (Chicago, 1978)

Hibben, C. C., *Gouda in revolt: particularism and pacifism in the revolt of the Netherlands* (Utrecht, 1983)

Hildebrand, K., *Johan III och Europas katolska makter, 1568–80: studier i 1500-talets politiska historia* (Uppsala, 1898)

Hildebrand, K., *The Third Reich* (London, 1984)

Holsti, O. R., *Crisis, escalation, war* (Montreal, 1972)

Holt, M. P., *The duke of Anjou and the politique struggle during the wars of religion* (Cambridge, 1986)

Hopf, T., *Peripheral visions. Deterrence theory and American foreign policy in the third world, 1965–90* (Ann Arbor, 1994)

Howard, M., *The lessons of history* (New Haven and London, 1991)

Hübner, J., *Sixte-Quint* (2 vols, Paris, 1870)

Huerga, A., 'La vida seudomística y el proceso inquisitorial de Sor María de la Visitación (La monja de Lisboa)', *Hispania sacra*, XII (1959), 35–130

Humphreys, R. A., *William Hickling Prescott: the man and the historian* (London, 1959)

Iklé, F. C., *Every war must end* (revised edn, New York, 1991)

Imber, C., *Studies in Ottoman history and law* (Istanbul, 1996: Analecta Isisiana, XX)

Imhoff, A., *Der Friede von Vervins 1598* (Aarau, 1966)

Immerman, R. H., 'The history of United States foreign policy: a plea for pluralism', *Diplomatic History*, XIV (1990), 574–83

Israel, J. I., ed., *The Anglo-Dutch moment. Essays on the Glorious Revolution and its world impact* (Cambridge, 1991)

Israel, J. I., *The Dutch Republic and the Hispanic world, 1606–1661* (Oxford, 1982)

Israel, J. I., *The Dutch Republic. Its rise, greatness, and fall 1477–1806* (Oxford, 1995)

Israel, J. I., *Empires and entrepôts. The Dutch, the Spanish Monarchy, and the Jews, 1585–1713* (London, 1990)

Israel, J. I., 'Olivares, the Cardinal-Infante and Spain's strategy in the Low Countries (1635–43): the road to Rocroi', in Kagan and Parker, *Spain, Europe and the Atlantic world*, 267–95

Israel, J. I. and G. Parker, 'Of Providence and Protestant winds: the Spanish Armada of 1588 and the Dutch Armada of 1688', in Israel, *The Anglo-Dutch moment*, 335–63

Jablonsky, B., *The owl of Minerva flies at twilight: doctrinal change and continuity in the revolution in military affairs* (Carlisle, PA, 1994)

Jago, C. J., 'Taxation and political culture in Castile 1590–1640', in Kagan and Parker, *Spain, Europe and the Atlantic world*, 48–72

Janssens, G., *Brabant in het verweer. Loyale oppositie tegen Spanje's bewind in de Nederlanden, van Alva tot Farnese, 1567–78* (Kortrijk, 1989: *Standen en Landen*, XXXIX)

Janssens, G., 'Juan de la Cerda, hertog van Medina Celi', *Spiegel Historiael*, IX (1974), 222–7

Jarausch, K. H., *The enigmatic chancellor: Bethmann Hollweg and the hubris of imperial Germany* (New Haven and London, 1973)

Jardine, L. and A. Grafton, '"Studied for action": how Gabriel Harvey read his Livy', *Past and Present*, CXXIX (1990), 30–78

Jedin, H., *Chiesa della storia* (Brescia, 1972), 703–22

Jenkins, M., *The state portrait. Its origins and evolution* (New York, 1947)

Jensen, J. de Lamar, *Diplomacy and dogmatism. Bernardino de Mendoza and the French Catholic League* (Cambridge, MA, 1964)

Jensen, J. de Lamar, 'Franco-Spanish diplomacy and the Armada', in C. H. Carter, ed., *From the Renaissance to the Counter-Reformation: essays in honor of Garret Mattingly* (London, 1965), 205–29

Jensen, J. de Lamar, 'The phantom will of Mary queen of Scots', *Scotia*, IV (1980), 1–15

Jensen, J. de Lamar, 'The Spanish Armada: the worst-kept secret in Europe', *Sixteenth-century Journal*, XIX (1988), 621–41

Jervis, R., *Perception and misperception in international politics* (Princeton, 1976)

Johnson, F. R., 'Thomas Hood's inaugural lecture as mathematical lecturer of the city of London, 1588', *Journal of the History of Ideas*, III (1942), 94–106

Johnson, R. T., *Managing the White House. An intimate study of the presidency* (New York, 1974)

Jouanna, A., *Le Devoir de révolte. La noblesse française et la gestation de l'État moderne (1559–1661)* (Paris, 1989)

Juste, T., *Guillaume le Taciturne d'après sa correspondance et ses papiers d'État* (Brussels, 1873)

Juste, T., *Les Valois et les Nassau (1572–1574)* (Brussels, n. d.)

Kagan, R. L., 'Felipe II: el hombre y la imagen', in, *Felipe II y el arte de su tiempo* (Madrid, 1998), 457–73.

Kagan, R. L., *Lucrecia's dreams. Politics and prophecy in sixteenth century Spain* (Berkeley, 1990)

Kagan, R. L., 'Politics, prophecy and the Inquisition in late sixteenth-century Spain,' in M. E. Perry and A. J. Cruz, eds, *Cultural encounters: the impact of the Inquisition in Spain and the New World* (Berkeley, 1991), 105–24

Kagan, R. L., 'Prescott's paradigm: American historical scholarship and the decline of Spain', *American Historical Review*, CI (1996), 423–46

Kagan, R. L., *Spanish cities of the Golden Age. The views of Anton van den Wyngaerde* (Berkeley, 1989)

Kagan, R. L., *Students and society in early modern Spain* (Baltimore, 1974)

Kagan, R. L. and G. Parker, eds, *Spain, Europe and the Atlantic world. Essays in honour of John H. Elliott* (Cambridge, 1995)

Kaiser, D. E., *Politics and war. Sources and consequences of European international conflict, 1559–1945* (Cambridge, MA, 1990)

Kamen, H., *Philip of Spain* (New Haven and London, 1997)

Kennedy, P. M., ed., *Grand strategies in war and peace* (New Haven and London, 1991)

Kennedy, P. M., *The rise and fall of the Great Powers: economic change and military conflict from 1500 to 2000* (New York, 1987)

Kenyon, J. R., 'Ordnance and the king's fleet in 1548', *International Journal of Nautical Archaeology*, XII (1983), 63–5

Kern, S., *The culture of time and space, 1880–1918* (Cambridge, MA, 1983)

Kernkamp, J. W., *De handel op den vijand 1572–1609* (2 vols, Utrecht, 1931)

Kershaw, I., *The Nazi dictatorship: problems and perspectives of interpretation* (3rd edn, London, 1993)

Koenigsberger, H. G., *Politicians and virtuosi. Essays in early modern history* (London, 1986)

Koenigsberger, H. G., *The practice of empire* (Ithaca, NY, 1969)

Kohler, A., *Das Reich im Kampf um die Hegemonie in Europa 1521–1648* (Munich, 1990: Enzyklopaedie deutscher Geschichte, VI)

Kortepeter, C. M., *Ottoman imperialism during the Reformation: Europe and the Caucasus* (New York, 1992)

Kouri, E. I., *England and the attempts to form a Protestant alliance in the later 1560s: a case study in European diplomacy* (Helsinki, 1981: Annales Academiae Scientiarum Fennicae, series B CCX)

Kretzschmar, J., *Die Invasionsprojekte der katholischen Mächte gegen England zur Zeits Elisabeths* (Leipzig, 1892)

Lademacher, H., *Die Stellung des Prinzen von Oranien als Statthalter in der Niederlanden von 1572 bis 1584. Ein Verfassungsgeschichte der Niederlande* (Bonn, 1958)

Lagomarsino, P. D., 'Court factions and the formation of Spanish policy towards the Netherlands 1559–1567' (Cambridge University Ph.D. thesis, 1973)

Lamb, U. S., 'The Spanish cosmographic juntas of the sixteenth century', *Terrae incognitae*, VI (1974), 56–62

Lanzinner, M., *Friedenssicherung und politische Einheit des Reiches unter Kaiser Maximilian II (1564–76)* (Göttingen, 1993)

Lapèyre, H., *Las etapas de la política exterior de Felipe II* (Valladolid, 1973)

Lapèyre, H., *Une Famille de marchands: les Ruiz* (Paris, 1955)

Las Heras, J. de, 'Indultos concedidos por la cámara de Castilla en tiempos de los Austrias', *Studia historica*, I (1983), 115–41

Lea, K. M., 'Sir Anthony Standen and some Anglo-Italian letters', *English Historical Review*, XLVII (1932), 461–77

Lebow, R. N., *Between peace and war. The nature of international crisis* (Baltimore, 1981)

Lebow, R. N. and J. G. Stein, *We all lost the Cold War* (Princeton, 1994)

Lefèvre, J., 'Le Tribunal de la Visite (1594–1602)', *Archives, bibliothèques et musées de la Belgique*, IX (1932), 65–85

Leimon, M. and G. Parker, 'Treason and plot in Elizabethan England: the fame of Sir Edward Stafford reconsidered', *English Historical Review*, CVI (1996), 1134–58

Levin, D., *History as Romantic art: Bancroft, Prescott, Motley and Parkman* (Stanford, 1959)

Levin, M. J., 'A Spanish eye on Italy. Spanish ambassadors in the sixteenth century' (Yale University Ph.D. thesis, 1997)

Levine, P. J., *The amateur and the professional. Antiquarians, historians and archaeologists in Victorian England, 1838–1886* (Cambridge, 1986)

Levy, J. S., 'Loss aversion, framing, and bargaining: the implications of prospect theory for international conflict', *International Political Science Review*, XVII (1996), 179–95

Lisón Tolosana, C., *La imagen del rey. Monarquía, realeza y poder ritual en la casa de los Austrias* (Madrid, 1991)

Loades, D. M., *The Tudor navy. An administrative, political and military history* (London, 1992)

Loomie, A. J., *The Spanish Elizabethans. The English exiles at the court of Philip II* (New York, 1963)

López de Toro, J., *Los poetas de Lepanto* (Madrid, 1950)

López Piñero, J. M., *Ciencias y técnica en la sociedad española de los siglos XVI y XVII* (Madrid, 1979)

Lorenzo Sanz, E., *Comercio de España con América en la época de Felipe II* (2 vols, Valladolid, 1979–80)

Losada, A., *Juan Ginés de Sepúlveda a través de su 'Epistolario' y nuevos documentos* (2nd edn, Madrid, 1973)

Lossky, A., *Louis XIV and the French Monarchy* (New Brunswick, 1994)

Lovett, A. W., 'The Castilian bankruptcy of 1575', *The Historical Journal*, XXIII (1980), 899–911

Lovett, A. W., 'The General Settlement of 1577: an aspect of Spanish finance in the early modern period', *The Historical Journal*, XXV (1982), 1–22

Lovett, A. W., 'The Golden Age of Spain. New work on an old theme', *The Historical Journal*, XXIV (1981), 739–49

Lovett, A. W., 'Juan de Ovando and the council of Finance, 1573–5', *The Historical Journal*, XV (1972), 1–21

Lovett, A. W., 'A new governor for the Netherlands: the appointment of Don Luis de Requeséns', *European Studies Review*, I (1971), 89–103

Lovett, A. W., *Philip II and Mateo Vázquez de Leca: the government of Habsburg Spain 1572–1592* (Geneva, 1977)

Lovett, A. W., 'The vote of the *Millones* (1590)', *The Historical Journal*, XXX (1987), 1–20

Lunitz, M., *Diplomatie und Diplomaten im 16. Jahrhundert. Studien zu den ständigen Gesandten Kaiser Karls V. in Frankreich* (Constance, 1988)

Luttenberger, A. P., *Kurfürsten, Kaiser und Reich. Politische Führung und Friedenssicherung unter Ferdinand I und Maximilian II* (Mainz, 1994)

Luttwak, E. N., *The Grand Strategy of the Roman Empire from the first century to the third* (Baltimore, 1976)

Luttwak, E. N., *Strategy. The logic of war and peace* (Cambridge, MA, 1987)

Lutz, H., *Christianitas Afflicta. Europa, das Reich, und die päpstliche Politik im Niedergang der Hegemonie Kaiser Karls V 1552–1556* (Göttingen, 1964)

Lutz, H. and E. Müller-Luckner, eds, *Das römisch-deutsche Reich im politischen System Karls V* (Munich, 1982: Schriften des historischen Kollegs, Kolloquien, I)

Lyell, J. P. R., 'A commentary on certain aspects of the Spanish Armada drawn from contemporary sources' (Oxford B.Litt. thesis, 1932; Houghton Library, Harvard, fMs Eng. 714)

Lynch, J., 'Philip II and the Papacy', *Transactions of the Royal Historical Society*, 4th series XI (1961), 23–42

Lynch, M., ed., *Mary Stewart: queen in three kingdoms* (Oxford, 1988)

Lyon, E., *The enterprise of Florida. Pedro Menéndez de Avilés and the Spanish conquest of 1565–1568* (Gainesville, 1976)

MacCaffrey, W. T., *Queen Elizabeth and the making of policy 1572–1588* (Princeton, 1981)

MacCaffrey, W. T., *The shaping of the Elizabethan regime. Elizabethan politics, 1558–1572* (Princeton, 1968)

MacKay, R. F., 'To obey and comply: the limits of royal authority in seventeenth-century Castile' (University of California at Berkeley Ph.D. thesis, 1995)

Malo, H., *Les Corsaires. Les corsaires dunkerquois et Jean Bart*, I (Paris, 1913)

Maltby, W. S., *Alba. A biography of Fernando Alvarez de Toledo, third duke of Alba, 1507–82* (Berkeley, 1982)

March, J. M., *El Comendador Mayor de Castilla, Don Luis de Requeséns, en el gobierno de Milán (1571–3)* (2nd edn, Madrid, 1946)

Martin, A. L., *Henry III and the Jesuit politicians* (Geneva, 1973)

Martin, C. J. M., 'The equipment and fighting potential of the Spanish Armada' (St Andrews University Ph.D. thesis, 1983)

Martin, C. J. M. and G. Parker, *The Spanish Armada* (London, 1988)

Martin, H., *Histoire de France*, IX (Paris, 1857)

Martin, P., *Spanish Armada prisoners. The story of the 'Nuestra Señora del Rosario' and her crew, and of other prisoners in England 1587–97* (Exeter, 1988: Exeter Maritime Studies, 1)

Martínez Millán, J. ed., *La corte de Felipe II* (Madrid, 1994)

Martínez Millán, J., 'Un curioso manuscrito: el libro de gobierno del Cardenal Diego de Espinosa (1512?–1572)', *Hispania*, LIII (1993), 299–344

Mattingly, G., *The defeat of the Spanish Armada* (Harmondsworth, 1962)

Mattingly, G., 'William Allen and Catholic propaganda in England', *Travaux d'humanisme et renaissance*, XXVIII (1957), 325–39

McGiffert, M., 'God's controversy with Jacobean England', *American Historical Review*, LXXXVIII (1983), 1151–74

McGurk, J. J. N., 'Armada preparations in Kent and arrangements made after the defeat (1587–9)', *Archaeologia Cantiana*, LXXXV (1970), 71–93

McKenna, J. W., 'How God became an Englishman', in D. J. Guth and J. W. McKenna, eds, *Tudor rule and revolution* (Cambridge, 1982), 25–43

McNamara, R. with B. VanDeMark, *In retrospect. The tragedy and lessons of Vietnam* (revised edn, New York, 1996)

Merriman, M. H., 'Mary, queen of France', in M. Lynch. ed., *Mary Stewart: queen in three kingdoms* (Oxford, 1988), 53–70

Merritt, J., 'Power and communication: Thomas Wentworth and government at a distance during the Personal Rule, 1629–1635', in Merritt, ed., *The political world of Thomas Wentworth earl of Strafford, 1621–1641* (Cambridge, 1996), 109–32

Messiaen, J., *La Connaissance des bancs de Dunkerque du 17e siècle jusqu'à nos jours* (Dunkirk, 1976)

Meyer, A. O., *England and the Catholic church under Queen Elizabeth* (London, 1916)

Mignet, F. A. M., *Antonio Pérez et Philippe II* (Paris, 1845)

Milhou, A., *Colón y su mentalidad mesiánica en el ambiente franciscanista Español* (Valladolid, 1983: Cuadernos Colombinos, XI)

Millar, F., *The emperor and the Roman world, 31 BC–AD 337* (London, 1977)

Miranda, J., *España y Nueva España en la época de Felipe II* (Mexico, 1962)

Molyneux, T. M., *Conjunct expeditions, or expeditions that have been carried on jointly by the fleet and army* (London, 1759)

Morán Torres, E., 'Los espías de la Invencible', *Historia-16*, CLII (1988), 31–7

Morgan, H., *Tyrone's rebellion. The outbreak of the Nine Years War in Tudor Ireland* (London, 1993)

Morrill, J. S., *Oliver Cromwell and the English Revolution* (London, 1990)

Motley, J. L., *The rise of the Dutch Republic* (Boston, 1856)

Mousset, A., *Un Résident de France en Espagne au temps de la Ligue (1583–1590). Pierre de Ségusson* (Paris, 1908)

Mulcahy, R., *The decoration of the royal basilica of El Escorial* (Cambridge, 1994)

Mulcahy, R., 'Two murders, a crucifix and the Grand Duke's Serene Highness: Francesco I de Medici's gift of Cellini's "Crucified Christ" to Philip II', in J. M. de Bernardo Ares, ed., *I Conferencia Internacional 'Hacia un nuevo humanismo'*, II (Cordoba, 1997), 149–75

Munby, A. N. L., *Phillipps studies*, V (Cambridge, 1960)

Mundy, B. E., *The mapping of New Spain. Indigenous cartography and the maps of the 'Relaciones Geográficas'* (Chicago, 1996)

Muro, G., *La vida de la princesa de Eboli* (Madrid, 1877)

Murray, W. A., A. Bernstein and M. Knox, eds, *The making of strategy. Rulers, states and war* (Cambridge, 1994)

Musi, A., ed., *Nel sistema imperiale: l'Italia spagnola* (Naples, 1994)

Muto, G., 'Modelli di organizzazione finanziaria nell'esperienza degli stati italiani della prima età moderna', *Annali dell' istituto storico italo-germanico*, XXXIX (1995), 287–302

Neal, L., ed., *War finance*, III (Aldershot, 1994)

Neustadt, R., *Presidential power and the modern presidents. The politics of leadership from Roosevelt to Reagan* (2nd edn, New York, 1990)

Niccoli, O., *Prophecy and people in Renaissance Italy* (Princeton, 1990)

Nightingale, F., *Letters from Egypt: a journey on the Nile, 1849–50* (ed. A. Sattin, New York, 1987)

Noble, W. M., *Huntingdonshire and the Spanish Armada* (London, 1896)

Nolan, J. S., 'The muster of 1588', *Albion*, XXIII (1991), 387–407

O'Donnell y Duque de Estrada, H., 'El secreto, requísito para la Empresa de Inglaterra de 1588', *Revista de historia naval*, II.7 (1984), 63–74

O'Donnell y Duque de Estrada, H., *La fuerza de desembarco de la Gran Armada contra Inglaterra (1588)* (Madrid, 1989)

Ohlmeyer, J. H., 'Ireland independent: confederate foreign policy and international relations during the mid-seventeenth century', in Ohlmeyer, ed., *Ireland from independence to occupation, 1641–1660* (Cambridge, 1995), 89–111

Ohlmeyer, J. H., *Civil war and Restoration in the three kingdoms. The career of Randal McDonnell marquis of Antrim, 1609–83* (Cambridge, 1993)

Oliveira e Costa, J. L. and V. L. Gaspar Rodrigues, *Portugal y Oriente: el proyecto indiano del Rey Juan* (Madrid, 1992)

Oliveros de Castro, M. T. and R. Subiza Martín, *Felipe II: estudio médico-histórico* (Madrid, 1956)

Olivieri, A., 'Il significato escatologico di Lepanto nella storia religiosa del mediterraneo del 500', in G. Benzoni, ed., *Il Mediterraneo nella seconda metà del '500 alla luce di Lepanto* (Florence, 1974: Civiltà veneziani, studi XXX), 257–77

O'Neil, B. H. S., *Castles and cannon: a study of early artillery fortification in England* (Oxford, 1960)

O'Neil, B. H. S., 'The fortification of Weybourne Hope in 1588', *Norfolk Archaeology*, XXVII (1940), 250–62

Oosterhoff, F. G., *Leicester and the Netherlands 1586–87* (Utrecht, 1988)

Oppenheim, M., *A history of the administration of the Royal Navy 1509–1660* (London, 1896)

O'Rahilly, A., *The massacre at Smerwick (1580)* (Cork, 1928)

Orso, S. N., *Philip IV and the decoration of the Alcázar of Madrid* (Princeton, 1985)

Ozment, S., *Protestants: the birth of a revolution* (New York, 1992)

Pagden, A. R., *Lords of all the world. Ideologies of empire in Spain, Britain and France, c. 1500–c. 1800* (New Haven and London, 1995)

Pagden, A. R., *Spanish imperialism and the political imagination. Studies in European and Spanish-American social and political theory, 1513–1830* (New Haven and London, 1990)

Pape, R. A., 'Coercive air power in the Vietnam War', *International Security*, XV.2 (Fall, 1990), 103–46

Parente, G. et al., *Los sucesos de Flandes de 1588 en relación con la empresa de Inglaterra* (Madrid, 1988)

Parker, G., *The Army of Flanders and the Spanish Road 1567–1659. The logistics of Spanish victory and defeat in the Low Countries' Wars* (revised edn, Cambridge, 1990)

Parker, G., 'David or Goliath? Philip II and his world in the 1580s', in Kagan and Parker, *Spain, Europe and the Atlantic world*, 245–66

Parker, G., 'The *Dreadnought* revolution of Tudor England', *Mariner's Mirror*, LXXXII (1996), 269–300

Parker, G., *The Dutch Revolt* (revised edn, Harmondsworth, 1985)

Parker, G., *Guide to the archives of the Spanish institutions in or concerned with the Netherlands, 1556–1706* (Brussels, 1971)

Parker, G., 'The laws of war in early modern Europe', in M. Howard, G. Andreopoulos and M. Shulman, eds, *The laws of war. Constraints on warfare in the western world* (New Haven and London, 1994), 40–58

Parker, G., 'Maps and ministers: the Spanish Habsburgs', in D. Buisseret, ed., *Monarchs, ministers and maps: the emergence of cartography as a tool of government in early modern Europe* (Chicago, 1992), 124–52

Parker, G., *The Military Revolution. Military innovation and the rise of the West 1500–1800* (2nd. edn, Cambridge, 1996)

Parker, G., *Philip II* (3rd edn, Chicago, 1995)

Parker, G., *Spain and the Netherlands, 1559–1659. Ten studies* (revised edn, London, 1990)

Parker, G., 'El testamento político de Juan Martínez de Recalde', *Revista de historia naval*, XVI.1 (1998), 7–44

Parry, J. H., *The Spanish theory of empire in the sixteenth century* (Cambridge, 1940)

Partner, P., 'Papal financial policy in the Renaissance and Counter-Reformation', *Past and Present*, LXXXVIII (1980), 17–62

Patterson, A. T., *The other Armada: the Franco-Spanish attempt to invade Britain in 1779* (Manchester, 1960)

Pears, E. A., 'The Spanish Armada and the Ottoman Porte', *English Historical Review*, VII (1893), 439–66

Peña Cámara, J. de la, *Nuevos datos sobre la visita de Juan de Ovando al consejo de Indias, 1567–68* (Madrid, 1935)

Pereña Vicente, L., *Teoría de la guerra en Francisco Suárez*, I (Madrid, 1954)

Pérez Minguez, F., ed., *Reivindicación histórica del siglo XVI* (Madrid, 1928)

Persico, J. E., *Nuremberg: infamy on trial* (Harmondsworth, 1994)

Peytavin, M., *La Visite comme moyen de gouvernement dans la Monarchie Espagnole. Le cas des visites générales du Royaume de Naples, XVIe–XVIIe siècles* (Paris, 1997)

Phelan, J. L., *The hispanization of the Philippines. Spanish aims and Filipino responses, 1565–1700* (Madison, 1967)

Phelan, J. L., *The kingdom of Quito in the seventeenth century. Bureaucratic politics in the Spanish empire* (Madison, 1967)

Phelan, J. L., *The millenarial kingdom of the Franciscans in the New World. A study of the writings of Gerónimo de Mendieta (1525–1604)* (Berkeley, 1956)

Philippson, M., *Ein Ministerium unter Philipp II. Kardinal Granvella am spanische Hofe 1579–86* (Berlin, 1895)

Pi Corrales, M., *España y las potencias nórdicas. 'La otra invencible' 1574* (Madrid, 1983)

Pi Corrales, M., *Felipe II y la lucha por el dominio del mar* (Madrid, 1989)

Pierson, P. O., *Commander of the Armada. The seventh duke of Medina Sidonia* (New Haven, 1989)

Pincus, S., 'Popery, trade and universal monarchy', *English Historical Review*, CVII (1992), 1–29

Pipes, R., ed., *The unknown Lenin: from the secret archive* (New Haven and London, 1996)

Pissavino, P. and G. Signorotto, eds, *Lombardia borromaica, Lombardia spagnola, 1554–1659* (Milan, 1995)

Plaisant, M. J., *Aspetti e problemi di politica spagnola (1556–1619)* (Padua, 1973)

Pollitt, R., *Arming the nation, 1569–1586* (Navy Records Society, forthcoming)

Pollitt, R., 'Bureaucracy and the Armada: the administrator's battle', *Mariner's Mirror*, LX (1974), 119–32

Pollitt, R., 'Contingency planning and the defeat of the Spanish Armada', *American Neptune*, XLV (1984), 25–34

Potter, D. M., 'Jefferson Davis and the political factors in Confederate defeat', in D. Donald, ed., *Why the North won the civil war* (Baton Rouge, 1960), 91–114

Potter, L., *Secret rites and secret writing. Royalist literature 1641–1660* (Cambridge, 1989)

Prescott, W. H., *History of Philip the Second, king of Spain* (3 vols, London, 1855–9)

Preto, P., *I servizi segreti di Venezia* (Milan, 1994)

Quirino, C., *Philippine cartography* (2nd edn, ed. R. A. Skelton, Amsterdam, 1964)

Ramos, D., 'La crisis indiana y la Junta Magna de 1568', *Jahrbuch für Geschichte von . . . Lateinamerikas*, XXIII (1986), 1–61

Ramsay, G. D., *The City of London in international politics at the accession of Elizabeth Tudor* (Manchester, 1975)

Ramsay, G. D., *The queen's merchants and the revolt of the Netherlands* (London, 1986)

Rassow, P., *Die Kaiser-Idee Karls V dargestellt an der Politik der Jahre 1528–1540* (Berlin, 1932)

Rawlinson, H. G., 'The embassy of William Harborne to Constantinople, 1583–88', *Transactions of the Royal Historical Society*, 4th series V (1922), 1–27

Read, C., *Mr Secretary Walsingham and the policy of Queen Elizabeth* (3 vols, Oxford, 1925)

Read, C., 'Queen Elizabeth's seizure of the duke of Alva's pay-ships,' *Journal of Modern History*, V (1933), 443–64

Redworth, G., 'Felipe II y las soberanas de Inglaterra', *Torre de los Lujanes*, XXXIII (1997), 103–12

Reinhardt, V., *Uberleben in der frühneuzeitlichen Stadt. Annona und Getreideversorgung in Rom 1563–1797* (Tübingen, 1991)

Repgen, K., *Die römische Kurie und der westfälische Friede. I. Papst, Kaiser und Reich, 1521–1644* (Tübingen, 1962)

Riaño Lozano, F., *Los medios navales de Alejandro Farnesio (1587–1588)* (Madrid, 1989)

Riba y García, C., *El consejo supremo de Aragón en el reinado de Felipe II* (Valencia, 1914)

Ribot García, L. A., 'Milán, plaza de armas de la Monarquía', *Investigaciones históricas*, X (1990), 205–38

Ribot García, L. A., 'Las provincias italianas y la defensa de la Monarquía', *Manuscrits*, XIII (1995), 97–122

Ribot García, L. A., ed., *El Tratado de Tordesillas y su época* (3 vols, Valladolid, 1995)

Riley, C. D. G., 'The State of Milan in the reign of Philip II of Spain' (Oxford University D. Phil. thesis, 1977)

Rill, G., 'Reichsvikar und Kommissar. Zur Geschichte der Verwaltung Reichsitalien im Spätmittelalter und in der frühen Neuzeit', *Annali della Fondazione Italiana per la Storia Amministrativa*, II (1965), 173–98

Ritter, R., *La Soeur d'Henri IV. Catherine de Bourbon 1559–1604* (2 vols, Paris, 1985)

Rivero Rodríguez, M., 'Felipe II y los "potentados de Italia"', *Bulletin de l'Institut Belge de Rome*, LXIII (1993), 337–70.

Rivero Rodríguez, M., 'El servicio a dos cortes: Marco Antonio Colonna', in Martínez Millán, *La corte de Felipe II*, 305–78

Rivers, E. L., ed., *Poesía lírica del Siglo de Oro* (Madrid, 1983)

Rizzo, M., 'Centro spagnolo e periferia lombarda nell'impero asburgico tra 500 e 600', *Rivista storica italiana*, CIV (1992), 315–48

Rizzo, M., 'Competizione politico-militare, geopolitica e mobilitazione delle risorse nell'Europa cinquecentesca. Lo Stato di Milano nell'età di Filippo II', in *La Lombarda spagnola. Nuovi indirizzi di ricerca* (forthcoming)

Rizzo, M., 'Finanza pubblica, impero e amministrazione nella Lombardia spagnola: le "visitas generales"', in P. Pissavino and G. Signorotto, eds, *Lombardia borromaica, Lombardia spagnola*, 303–61

Rizzo, M., 'Poteri, interessi e conflitti geopolitici nei territori della Lunigiana durante l'età di Filippo II', in *Studi lunigianesi in onore di Cesare Vasoli* (forthcoming)

Rocca, F. X., 'Court and cloister: Philip II and the Escorial' (Yale University Ph.D. thesis, 1998)

Rodger, N. A. M., *The safeguard of the sea. A naval history of Britain*, I (London, 1997)

Rodríguez de Diego, J. L. and F. J. Alvarez Pinedo, *Los Archivos de Simancas* (Madrid, 1993)

Rodríguez-Salgado, M. J., 'The Anglo-Spanish war: the final episode in the "Wars of the Roses"?', in Rodríguez-Salgado and Adams, *England, Spain and the Gran Armada*, 1–44

Rodríguez-Salgado, M. J., ed., *Armada 1588–1988* (London, 1988)

Rodríguez-Salgado, M. J., *The changing face of empire. Charles V, Philip II and Habsburg authority, 1551–1559* (Cambridge, 1988)

Rodríguez-Salgado, M. J., 'The Court of Philip II of Spain', in Asch and Birke, *Princes, patronage and the nobility*, 205–44

Rodríguez-Salgado, M. J. and S. Adams, eds, 'The count of Feria's dispatch to Philip II of 14 November 1558', *Camden Miscellany*, XXVIII (1984), 302–44

Rodríguez-Salgado, M. J. and S. Adams, eds, *England, Spain and the Gran Armada 1585–1604. Essays from the Anglo-Spanish conferences, London and Madrid, 1988* (Edinburgh, 1991)

Romani, M. A., 'Finanza pubblica e potere politico: il caso dei Farnese (1545–93)', in Romani, ed., *Le corti farnesiane di Parma e Piacenza*, I (Rome, 1978), 3–89, at pp. 27 and 38

Romano, R., 'La pace di Cateau-Cambrésis e l'equilibrio europeo a metà del secolo XVI', *Rivista storica italiana*, LXI (1949), 526–50

Romero García, E., *El imperialismo hispánico en la Toscana durante el siglo XVI* (Lérida, 1986)

Rose, J. H., 'Was the failure of the Spanish Armada due to storms?', *Proceedings of the British Academy*, XXII (1936), 207–44

Roth, R., 'Is history a process? Nonlinearity, revitalization theory and the central metaphor of social science history', *Social Science History*, XVI (1992), 197–243

Rowen, H. H., *The Low Countries in early modern times* (New York, 1972)

Ruiz Martín, F., 'El pan de los países bálticos durante las guerras de religión: andanzas y gestiones del historiador Pedro Cornejo', *Hispania*, XXI (1961), 549–79

Russell, J. G., *Peacemaking in the Renaissance* (London, 1986)

Sacchi, D., *Mappe dal nuovo mondo: cartografie locali e definizione della Nuova Spagna (secoli XVI–XVII)* (Turin, 1977)

Sánchez, M. S., 'Empress María and the making of policy in the early years of Philip III's reign', in A. Saint-Saëns, ed., *Religion, body and gender in early modern Spain* (San Francisco, 1991), 139–47

Sánchez Bella, I., *La organización financiera de las Indias (siglo XVI)* (Seville, 1968)

Sánchez Montes, J., *Franceses, protestantes, turcos. Los españoles ante la política internacional de Carlos V* (2nd edn, Granada, 1995)

Schäfer, E., *El consejo real y supremo de las Indias. Su historia, organización y labor administrativa hasta la terminación de la Casa de Austria* (2 vols, Seville, 1935–47)

Schelling, T., *Arms and influence* (New Haven, 1966)

Schilder, G., 'A Dutch manuscript rutter: a unique portrait of the European coasts in the late sixteenth century', *Imago mundi*, XLIII (1991), 59–71

Schöffer, I., ed., *Alkmaar ontzet, 1573–1973* (Alkmaar, 1973)

Schokkenbroek, J. C. S. A., '"Wherefore serveth Justinus with his shipping of Zeeland?" The Dutch and the Spanish Armada', in Gallagher and Cruickshank, *God's obvious design*, 101–11

Scholten, F. W. J., *Militaire topografische kaarten en stadsplattegronden van Nederland, 1579–1795* (Alphen-aan-de-Rijn, 1989)

Segre, R., *Gli ebrei lombardi nell'età spagnola: storia di un'espulsione* (Turin, 1973)

Setton, K. M., *The Papacy and the Levant, 1204–1571*, IV (Philadelphia, 1984)

Sharpe, K. M., *The personal rule of Charles I* (New Haven and London, 1992)

Skilliter, S. A., 'The Hispano-Ottoman armistice of 1581', in C. E. Bosworth, ed., *Iran and Islam* (Edinburgh, 1971), 491–515

Skilliter, S. A., *William Harborne and the trade with Turkey* (London, 1977)

Slavin, A. J., 'Daniel Rogers in Copenhagen, 1588. Mission and memory', in Thorp and Slavin, *Politics, religion and diplomacy*, 245–66

Slicher van Bath, B. H., *Een Fries landbouwbedrijf in de tweede helft van de 16 eeuw* (Wageningen, 1958)

Smith, A. G. R., 'The secretariats of the Cecils, *circa* 1580–1612', *English Historical Review*, LXXXIII (1983), 481–504

Snapper, F., *Oorlogsinvloeden op de overzeese handel van Holland 1551–1719* (Amsterdam, 1959)

Soons, A., *Juan de Mariana* (Boston, 1982)

Sorensen, T. C., *Decision-making in the White House: the olive branch or the arrows* (New York, 1963)

Spaans, J. W., *Haarlem na de Reformatie. Stedelijke cultuur en kerkelijk leven* (The Hague, 1989: Hollandse historische reeks, XI)

Sproxton, J., *Violence and religion. Attitudes towards militancy in the French civil wars and the English Revolution* (London, 1995)

Stern, V., *Sir Stephen Powle of court and country* (London, 1992)

Stone, L., *An Elizabethan: Sir Horatio Palavicino* (Oxford, 1956)

Storrs, C. 'The Army of Lombardy and the resilience of Spanish power in Italy in the reign of Carlos II (1665–1700)', *War in History*, IV (1997), 371–97, and V (1998), 1–22.

Stradling, R. A., *The Armada of Flanders. Spanish maritime policy and European war 1568–1668* (Cambridge, 1992)

Strasser, G., 'Diplomatic cryptology and universal languages in the sixteenth and seventeenth centuries', in K. Neilson and B. McKercher, eds, *Go spy the land. Military intelligence in history* (Westport, CT, 1992), 73–97

Suárez Fernández, L., 'La situación internacional en torno a 1492', in Ribot García, *El Tratado de Tordesillas*, II, 793–800

Sutherland, N. M., *The massacre of St Bartholomew and the European conflict 1559–1572* (London, 1973)

Sutherland, N. M., 'The origins of the Thirty Years War and the structure of European politics', *English Historical Review*, CVII (1992), 587–625

Sutherland, N. M., 'William of Orange and the revolt of the Netherlands: a missing dimension', *Archiv für Reformationsgeschichte*, LXXIV (1983), 201–31

Tanner, M., *The last descendant of Aeneas. The Hapsburgs and the mythic image of the Emperor* (New Haven and London, 1993)

Tazón, J. E., 'The menace of the wanderer: Thomas Stukeley and the Anglo-Spanish conflict in Ireland' (paper given at the Center for Renaissance Studies, Amherst, in November 1996)

Tellechea Idígoras, J. I., *Otra cara de la Invencible. La participación vasca* (San Sebastián, 1988)

Tenace, E. S., 'The Spanish intervention in Brittany and the failure of Philip II's bid for European hegemony, 1589–98' (University of Illinois Ph.D., 1997)

Terry, A., 'War and literature in sixteenth-century Spain', in J. R. Mulryne and M. Shewring, eds, *War, literature and the arts in sixteenth-century Europe* (London, 1989)

Tetlock, P. E. and A. Belkin, eds, *Counterfactual thought experiments in world politics. Logical, methodological and psychological perspectives* (Princeton, 1996)

Thatcher, M., *The Downing Street years, 1979–1990* (London, 1993)

Theibault, J., 'Jeremiah in the village: prophecy, preaching, pamphlets and penance in the Thirty Years' War', *Central European History*, XXVII (1994), 441–60

Thomas, L., 'To err is human', in J. Gross, ed., *The Oxford book of essays* (Oxford, 1992)

Thomaz, L. F. F. R., 'Factions, interests and messianism: the politics of Portuguese expansion in the East, 1500–21', *Indian Economic and Social History Review*, XXVIII (1991), 97–109

Thompson, I. A. A., 'Spanish Armada gun procurement and policy', in Gallagher and Cruickshank, *God's obvious design*, 69–84

Thompson, I. A. A., *War and government in Habsburg Spain, 1560–1620* (London, 1976)

Thompson, I. A. A., *War and society in Habsburg Spain. Selected essays* (London, 1992)

Thompson, I. A. A. and B. Yun Casalilla, eds, *The Castilian crisis of the seventeenth century* (Cambridge, 1994)

Thorp, M. R., 'Catholic conspiracy in early Elizabethan foreign policy', *The Sixteenth-century Journal*, XV (1984), 431–48

Thorp, M. R., 'William Cecil and the antichrist: a study in anti-Catholic ideology', in Thorp and Slavin, *Politics, religion and diplomacy*, 289–304

Thorp, M. R. and A. J. Slavin, eds, *Politics, religion and diplomacy in early modern Europe: essays in honor of De Lamar Jensen* (Kirksville, MO, 1994: Sixteenth Century Essays and Studies, XXVII)

Timmer, E. M. A., 'Een verweerschrift tegen Prins Willem's *Apologie*, en drie andere Spaanschgezinde pamfletten', *Bijdragen voor Geschiedenis en Oudheidkunde*, 6th series VI (1928), 61–94

Torres Lanzas, P. and F. Navas del Valle, eds, *Catálogo de los documentos relativos a las Islas Filipinas existentes en el Archivo General de Indias de Sevilla*, II (Barcelona, 1926)

Tosini, A., 'Cittadelle lombarde de fine '500: il castello di Milano nella prima età spagnola', in C. Cresti, A. Fara and D. Lamberini, eds, *Architettura militare nell'Europa del XVI secolo* (Siena, 1988), 207–17

Trachtenberg, M., *History and strategy* (Princeton, 1991)

Turner, H. A., 'Hitler's impact on history', in D. Wetzel, ed., *From the Berlin Museum to the Berlin Wall. Essays on the cultural and political history of modern Germany* (Westport, CT, 1996), 109–26

Ulloa, M., *La hacienda real de Castilla en el reinado de Felipe II* (revised edn, Madrid, 1977)

Ungerer, G., *A Spaniard in Elizabethan England: the correspondence of Antonio Pérez's exile*, II (London, 1976)

Usherwood, S. and E., *The Counter-Armada, 1596. The 'Journall' of the 'Mary Rose'* (London, 1983)

van Creveld, M., *Command in war* (Cambridge, MA, 1985)

van de Vrught, M., *De criminele ordonnantiën van 1570. Enkele beschouwingen over de eerste strafrechtscodificatie in de Nederlanden* (Zutfen, 1978)

van der Essen, L., *Alexandre Farnèse, prince de Parme et gouverneur-général des Pays-Bas* (5 vols, Brussels, 1932–37)

van der Essen, L., 'De auteur en de beteekenis van de *Liber relationum*', *Mededelingen van de koninklijke Vlaamse Academie. Letteren*, V part i (1943)

van der Woude, A., 'De crisis in de Opstand na de val van Antwerpen', *Bijdragen voor de Geschiedenis van Nederland*, XIV (1959–60), 38–57 and 81–104

van Deusen, N. E., '*Recogimiento* for women and girls in colonial Lima: an institutional and cultural practice' (University of Illinois at Urbana-Champaign Ph.D. thesis, 1995)

van Durme, M., *El Cardenal Granvela 1517–1586* (Barcelona, 1957)

van Herwerden, P. J., *Het verblijf van Lodewijk van Nassau in Frankrijk. Huguenoten en Geuzen, 1568–1572* (Assen, 1932)

van Hoof, J. P. C. M., 'Met een vijand als bondgenoot. De rol van het water bij de verdeding van het Nederlandse grondgebied tegen een aanval over land', *Bijdragen en Mededelingen betreffende de Geschiedenis der Nederlanden*, CIII (1988), 622–51

van Nierop, H., 'The Blood Council of North Holland: ordinary people, the war and the law during the revolt of the Netherlands' (Unpublished paper presented to the University of Minnesota Center for Early Modern History, October 1996)

van Oerle, H. A., *Leiden binnen en buiten de Stadsvesten. De geschiedenis van de stedebouwkundige ontwikkeling binnen het Leidse rechtsgebied tot het einde van de Gouden Eeuw* (2 vols, Leiden, 1975)

van Overeem, J., 'Justinus van Nassau en de Armada van 1588,' *Marineblad*, LIII (1938), 821–30

Vassberg, D. E., *Land and society in Golden Age Castile* (Cambridge, 1984)

432 *Bibliography*

Vázquez Maure, F., 'Cartografía de la península: siglos 16 a 18,' in *Historia de la cartografía española* (Madrid, 1982), 59–74

Vermaseren, B., *De katholieke Nederlandsche Geschiedschrijving in de XVIe en XVIIe eeuw over de Opstand* (Maastricht, 1941)

Vicente Maroto, M. I. and M. Esteban Piñero, *Aspectos de la ciencia aplicada en la España del Siglo de Oro* (Valladolid, 1991)

Vigo, G., *Uno stato nell'impero. La difficile transizione al moderno nella Milano di età spagnola* (Milan, 1994)

Vilar, J. B., *Mapas, planos y fortificaciones hispánicos de Tunez (siglos XVI–XIX)* (Madrid, 1991)

Villari, R., *La rivolta antispagnola a Napoli. Le origini (1585–1647)* (Bari, 1967)

Villari, R. and G. Parker, *La política de Felipe II. Dos estudios* (Valladolid, 1996)

von Aretin, K. O., 'Die Lehensordnungen in Italien im 16. und 17. Jahrhundert und ihre Auswirkungen auf die europäische Politik: ein Beitrag zur Geschichte des europäischen Spätfeudalismus', in H. Weber, ed., *Politische Ordnungen und soziale Kräfte im Alten Reich* (Wiesbaden, 1980), 53–84

von Clausewitz, C., *On war*, ed. and trans. M. Howard and P. Paret (Princeton, 1976)

von der Osten Sacken, C., *San Lorenzo el Real de El Escorial: Studien zur Baugeschichte und Ikonologie* (Munich, 1979)

von Greyerz, K., *Vorsehungsglaube und Kosmologie: Studien zu englischen Selbstzeugnissen des 17. Jahrhunderts* (Göttingen, 1990)

von Ranke, L., *Sämmtliche Werke*, XXXIV (Leipzig, 1884)

Warlimont, W., *Inside Hitler's headquarters, 1939–45* (London, 1964)

Watts, B., 'Friction in future war', in A. R. Millett and W. A. Murray, eds, *Brassey's Mershon American defense annual 1996–7* (Washington, DC, 1996), 58–94

Waxman, M. C., 'Strategic terror: Philip II and sixteenth-century warfare', *War in History*, IV (1997), 339–47

Way, P., *Codes and cyphers* (London, 1977)

Wells, G. E., 'Antwerp and the government of Philip II, 1555–67' (Cornell University Ph.D. thesis, 1982)

Wernham, R. B., *After the Armada. Elizabethan England and the struggle for western Europe, 1588–95* (Oxford, 1984)

Wernham, R. B., *Before the Armada. The growth of English foreign policy 1488–1588* (London, 1966)

Wernham, R. B., *The expedition of Sir John Norris and Sir Francis Drake to Spain and Portugal, 1589* (London, 1988: Navy Records Society, CXXVII)

Wernham, R. B., *The making of English foreign policy 1558–1603* (Berkeley, 1980)

Wernham, R. B., *The return of the Armadas. The last years of the Elizabethan war against Spain, 1595–1603* (Oxford, 1994)

Wheeler, E., 'Methodological limits and the mirage of Roman strategy', *Journal of Military History*, LVII (1993), 7–41 and 215–41

Wheeler-Bennett, J. W., ed., *Action this day: working with Churchill* (London, 1968)

Whitehead, B. T., *Of brags and boasts. Propaganda in the year of the Armada* (Stroud, 1994)

Wiener, C. Z., 'The beleaguered isle. A study of Elizabethan and early Jacobean anti-Catholicism', *Past and Present*, LI (1971), 27–62

Williamson, J. A., *Hawkins of Plymouth* (2nd edn, London, 1969)

Wohlstetter, R., *Pearl Harbor: warning and decision* (Stanford, 1962)

Woltjer, J. J., *Friesland in hervormingstijd* (Leiden, 1962)

Wood, J. B., *The king's army. Warfare, soldiers and society during the Wars of Religion in France, 1562–1576* (Cambridge, 1996)

Woolf, D. R., *The idea of History in early Stuart England. Erudition, ideology and 'the light of truth' from the accession of James I to the Civil War* (Toronto, 1991)

Worden, B., 'Oliver Cromwell and the Sin of Achan', in D. E. D. Beales and G. Best, eds, *History, society and churches: Essays in honour of Owen Chadwick* (Cambridge, 1985), 125–45

Worden, B., 'Providence and politics in Cromwellian England', *Past and Present*, CIX (1985), 55–99

Yates, F., *Astraea. The imperial theme in the sixteenth century* (London, 1975)

Zijp, A., 'Hoofdstukken uit de economische en sociale geschiedenis van de Polder Zijpe in de 17e en 18e eeuw', *Tijdschrift voor Geschiedenis*, LXX (1957), 29–48 and 176–88

Index

Pérez, Gonzalo, Spanish Secretary of State, 1556–65, 25, 59, 65, 91, 102, 338 n. 16

Perrenot de Granvelle, Nicholas, principal adviser of Charles V, 325 n. 2

Peru, viceroyalty of, 10, 50, 295, 303 nn. 30–31

Philip I, king of Castile 1504–06, 48, 283

Philip II, king of Spain, 1556–98:

Administrative practices

  assassination, 14, 83, 134–5, 175, 190; audiences, 19–20, 305 n. 17, 230–6 n. 24, 307 n. 28; communications, 12, 40, 48, 52, 55–6, 212–13, 319; corruption, 31–3; Court factions, 25, 59, 118–19, 130, 141, 308 n. 46; delays, 65–70; delegating authority, 26–8, 30, 68, 144, 263; diplomacy, 48, 56, 82; innovations, 22, 23, 25, 29, 37–8, 116; legislation, 9, 37, 323 n. 66; maps, 59–60, 321 n. 46; routine, 14, 17, 18, 21–3, 28, 31–6, 66, 277; secrecy, 32, 122, 173, 219, 312 nn. 82–3; *see also* conciliar system, juntas

Government policies

  defence, 4–6, 89–90, 171–2, 180–1, 189, 271–2

  finance, 108, 124, 170, 198–9, 353 nn 79–80; State bankruptcies, 88, 101, 279; failure to understand, 21, 41–2, 198–9, 305 n. 19

  foreign policy, *see below*, relations with foreign powers; information, 48–65, 71; Messianic Imperialism, 92–3, 96, 98–109, 113, 159–62, 198, 270–1, 276, 286, 334 n. 96, 336 n. 117; naval, 122, 131, 189, 194–5, 267, 271–2, 388; propaganda, 3–5, 94–8, 301

religious policies:

  in Spain, 34, 42, 91, 96, 101, 118, 286; towards other Catholics, 130, 156–8, 273; towards Jews, 91, 277; towards Protestants, 86, 92, 104, 113, 119, 154–8, 170; *see also* Papacy (below)

Personal

  absences from Spain, 36, 151, 348; accession of, xv; assassination attempts on, 14, 304 n. 11; 'cognitive rigidity', xix, 43, 114, 272; compared with David, 96, 286; compared with Moses, 73, 286–7; criticisms of, 40, 65–6, 101–2, 270, 332 n. 78, 335 n. 109; despair of, 42–3, 143, 271; education of, 42; health, 13, 43–4, 195, 277–8, 304 n. 4, 316 n. 128; histories, 402–4; insecurity, 42; irresolution, 130–1, 194–5, 225, 275–6, 347; isolation, 40, 79, 163, 305 n. 17; limitations, 28–9, 42–5, 72–4; memory, 20, 58, 320 n. 43; military experience, 72, 268; popularity, 14; relations with other family members, 77–80, 117, 119; religion of, 93–101, 105–6, 162, 203, 314 n. 96, 333 nn. 88–89; 'reputation,' 89–90, 134, 156, 195; 'rex et sacerdos,' 96, 286–7; self-image, 13, 270–1; stress, 42–4; succession, 13, 279, 310 n. 65; verbal diarrhoea, 36, 314 n. 96; will, 42, 97, 98, 283; wives, *see* Anna of Austria, Elisabeth de Valois, María Manuela, Mary Tudor; 'zero defects' mentality, 37, 42, 71

Relations with foreign rulers and states

Baltic Powers, 86–7

England, xv, 86, 88, 105–6, 130–1, 147–203, 212, 302 n. 15; Armada, 41, 71, 180, 186, 194–6, 200–1, 210; economic relations, 124,

156–7, 173–6, 189; religious policy, 105–6, 148–9, 154–5;

France, 6, 88, 153, 272–3, 330; Catholic League, 86, 172, 192, 199–200, 272; armed intervention in, 125, 274–6, 328 n. 42; succession ambitions, 170–2, 274, 285; treaties with, 85–6, 116, 149, 192, 278–9; relations with kings of, 85–6, 93, 119, 157, 172, 273

Holy Roman Empire, 78–80

Ireland

  and Armada, 184, 186–7

  Irish Catholics, 158, 160, 164

  Thomas Stukeley, 160–2

  Tyrone's rebellion, 54, 278–9

Italy (independent states), 49, 81–2, 89

Ottoman Empire, 6–7, 70–1, 88, 89, 92, 121, 145, 152, 192, 324 n. 71

Papacy, 7, 80–2, 96–7, 150, 155, 164, 179–84, 190, 213, 274, 322 nn. 80–2

Portugal (before 1580), 86–7, 166–7

Scotland

  James VI, 191, 280

  Mary Stuart, 153–5, 157–63, 164–5, 169, 186, 190–1, 313 n. 89, 349 nn. 20, 23, 360 n. 42

Swiss cantons, 190, 201

Relations with his own subjects and states

  and domestic opposition, 54, 113, 332, 336; Aragon, 92, 275; Castile, 36, 73, 80, 88, 91, 96, 102, 269–70; Milan, 8, 33, 83–4, 170, 277, 347 n. 108; Mexico (New Spain), 9–10, 58–9, 70, 71, 87, 329 n. 45; Naples, xv, 97, 321 n. 46; Netherlands, xv, xvii, 4, 23, 39–40, 54, 89, 115–46, 179–80, 200, 274, 279, 347 n. 107; Philippines, 8, 50, 69, 89, 280; Portugal (after 1580), xv, 102, 257, 280, 283

Relations with subordinates

  Don John of Austria, 38–9, 144–5, 315 n. 106; duke of Alba, 13, 38–9, 55, 59, 121–3, 132, 141, 149, 152, 157–63, 282, 314 n. 103; duke of Medina Sidonia, 20, 38, 40, 71, 232, 263–5, 330 n. 64; duke of Parma, 38, 54, 82, 107, 182, 196, 200–1, 232, 244, 272–4, 287; financial officials, 41, 198–9; other ministers, 37–9, 59, 65, 119, 136–7, 144, 165, 182, 185, 269, 277, 314

Strategic style 2–3, 7, 77, 89–101, 105–6, 120, 139, 162, 188, 189, 194–5, 197, 251, 267, 273, 277

Philip III, king of Spain 1598–1621, 13, 28, 100, 138, 277, 279–80, 284, 310 n. 65

Philip IV, king of Spain 1621–65, 287, 333 n. 90

Philippines, archipelago:

  discovery of, 62, 69, 322 n. 50; role in Spanish grand strategy, 8, 50, 89, 280; settlement of, 94–5

Piatti, Giovanni Battista, military engineer, 35, 185, 214, 315 n. 111, 358 n. 22

Piedrola, Miguel de, soldier and 'prophet,' 34, 104

Pimentel, Don Diego de, Armada commander, 176, 229, 235, 261

Pius IV, pope 1559–65, 150

Pius V, pope 1565–72, 83, 120, 151, 157–9, 161

Plymouth, England, 197, 264, 366

Pole, Reginald, Cardinal, 332 n. 78

'Pompeo Pellegrini,' *see* Standen, Anthony